The BYTE Book of
Pascal

Edited by
Blaise W. Liffick

Second Edition

BYTE/McGraw Hill
70 Main St
Peterborough, N.H. 03458

Library of Congress Cataloging in Publication Data

Main entry under title:

The BYTE Book of Pascal.

(Language series)
A collection of articles from BYTE Magazine.
1. Pascal (computer program language) I. Liffick, Blaise W. II. BYTE. III. Series: Language series (Peterborough, N. H.)
QA76.73.P2B18   001.6'424   79-22958
ISBN 0-07-037823-1

Printed in the United States of America

TABLE OF CONTENTS

INTRODUCTION

This book is part of the "Language Series" of BYTE Books. It is a collection of the best articles from past issues of BYTE magazine, the leading technical journal in the microcomputer field. The language under discussion is a relatively new computer programming language, Pascal. Until recently, Pascal has only enjoyed a large following in the academic community, and only more recently has it been practical to use this language with microcomputers. But the curious thing about Pascal is its ability to win nearly instant converts; so, while Pascal may be one of the newest computer languages, especially in the field of microcomputers, it is also one of the fastest growing in use and acceptance.

The purpose of this book is twofold. First, for those uninitiated, the articles contained in this book can serve as a general introduction to Pascal, providing the background information necessary for a potential user. The **Comments** section itself is a general discussion of the properties, merits, and applicability of Pascal. It includes reprints from the "Languages Forum" of BYTE magazine, an ongoing dialogue among the magazine's knowledgeable readers. The Forum is intended as an interactive dialogue about the design and implementation of languages for personal computing. In addition, an editorial by Carl Helmers, one of the industry's leading proponents of Pascal, rounds this section out as a beginning point for those unfamiliar with the language.

Second, for those requiring a more in depth study of the merits of the language and its possible implementation, there are two sections, **About the Language** and **Applications**.

About the Language provides insights into the usefulness of Pascal by comparing it to BASIC and COBOL. Also, a detailed look at some possible implementations of the language helps define the scope of the impact on the industry. This includes listings of a Pascal to p-code compiler written in both Pascal and BASIC, and two listings in the appendices: one a p-code to 8080 assembly language conversion program in BASIC; the second a "tiny" Pascal compiler and p-code interpreter written in 8080 assembly language.

The final section is **Applications** and, as the name implies, includes several application and system programs written in Pascal. For general applications there is an automatic metric conversion program, nontrivial implementation of a chess program, and an implementation of a print utility program. In the area of system software there is the choice of two language implementations: one is a minimum implementation of a language, written in less than 256 words (it has surprising usefulness); the other is an APL interpreter.

So, this book provides not only a general introduction to the Pascal language, but is also a tremendous resource for software: two versions of a Pascal compiler, one written in BASIC and the other in 8080 assembly language; a p-code interpreter written in both Pascal and 8080 asembly language; a chess playing program; and an APL interpreter.

Finally, a note about how the articles in this book were updated. We have been very careful to make corrections to articles where an error has been made in the original article. However, because many of these articles are reprinted from back issues of BYTE magazine, some of the information contained in them is out of date. This information is flagged in the form of footnotes within the article, and includes such items as page references and the availablity of UCSD Pascal. All footnotes throughout this book can be taken as current as of 1 July 1979.

Blaise W. Liffick
Editor

Consistency — or a Lack Thereof . . .

Notes by C Helmers

Readers will note a lack of consistency in the typography of various articles on Pascal.

One area of questionable typography is a bit nebulous and less subject to editorial fiat when "camera ready" type is received from authors: the style of representation of Pascal program listings. The ideal style is of course that used by Niklaus Wirth in his book Algorithms + Data Structures = Programs, *published by Prentice-Hall in 1976. This style uses* **bold face type** *in lowercase for representation of the Pascal language keywords. It uses italics for the representation of specific variable names, procedure names and literal values which are part of the program. In articles by authors Ken Bowles (page 51), Charles Forsyth and Randall Howard (page 33), and Allan Schwartz (page 41) this notation was used. But in two of these cases, the authors supplied camera ready typeset copy along with the articles involved, in order to minimize potential errors due to keystroking. Since two of these were typeset at BYTE, and the other two were typeset with different type specifications on different machines, there is naturally a different aesthetic flavor to the listings in these articles. A close variant of this form is seen in the listings of David Mundie's article (page 7) where bold fact type and normal type are mixed in the listing.*

There is yet another variation on the graphics used to represent Pascal programs, provided by the listings accompanying Stephen Alpert's article (page 27). Here, the camera ready listing was supplied by the author as printed on an uppercase line printer, so keywords are indistinguishable from program details on the basis of typography alone.

*What can we conclude about this inconsistency? Our goal at BYTE is to asymptotically approach the notation of Pascal programs in the bold face and italic form whenever we do the actual typesetting of a listing. The italic and the bold face typography provides an excellent contrast to normal type when elements of a program are mentioned within text. But when a manuscript comes with a usable camera ready listing of a Pascal program, such details of aesthetics must take second place to the goal of minimizing errors of transcription: it is far better to use a camera ready image derived from a machine produced listing than to key in a program manually in order to create a typeset form of the listing. . . .***CH**

Comments

Languages Forum

UCSD PASCAL:

A (Nearly) Machine Independent Software System (for Microcomputers and Minicomputers)

Kenneth L Bowles

Overview

This article describes a complete interactive software system which can operate virtually without change on many different microcomputers and minicomputers. Because the semiconductor industry is evolving new equipment very fast, it is becoming a practical necessity to have machine independent software to prevent rapid obsolescence of large application programs. The software described here has been developed at the University of California San Diego (UCSD), and is available to anyone for a $200 subscription fee. This article presents an appeal to readers of BYTE for help to bring about a true community-wide software system for business, educational and other professional users of small computer systems. Help is needed from the user community, since the manufacturers have so far avoided standardizing software except as regards some aspects of programming languages. For single user microcomputers, it appears to be far more practical to *standardize the entire software system* than the language processor alone!

The Software System

UCSD Pascal is a complete interactive software system for small computers, yet it offers many features normally found only on medium and large scale machines. It is designed to operate, with minimal adaptation, on most microcomputers or minicomputers based on 8 bit bytes or 16 bit words. Supported versions are now available for use on machines based on the Digital Equipment LSI-11 or other PDP-11 processors, and on the 8080 and Z-80 microprocessors. Having first been sent to users in August 1977, the system is in use on approximately 60 mainframes using these processors (as of mid February 1978), and the list of both users and processors has started to grow rapidly. Versions not yet supported by the Project are operating, or nearly operating, on four other processors (General Automation 440, Univac V75, Nanodata QM-1, National Semiconductor PACE). The UCSD Pascal Project is discussing arrangements with various manufacturers whereby supported versions can be released for most other popular microprocessors, and additional inquiries would be welcomed.

The system is written almost entirely in the Pascal programming language, extended for system programming and for disk based interactive applications. Far more than a simple *compiler* for Pascal, it should be viewed as a complete and fully integrated system which is self-maintaining, and generally independent of software from any other source. The system operates in a small pseudomachine (interpreter) which can be written in the native machine language of conventional processors, or can be microprogrammed on machines which provide that capability. The object code processed by the Pascal pseudomachine is compressed relative to conventional object code, and consumes roughly one third to one half as much space as the native object code of most present day processors. A feature to be implemented soon will allow mixing Pascal pseudocode routines, for efficient use of memory, with native code routines, for fast processing.

The system is the product of a growing project team, and is evolving rapidly in an upward compatible way. As of early 1978, the system represents the equivalent of about 15 full-time years of programming and design effort. Major components of the system currently being distributed include the following:

- *Single user operating system.*
- *Pascal Compiler.* Standard Pascal plus extensions for strings, disk files, graphics, system programming (business oriented extensions are planned).
- *Editors.* High performance screen oriented editor for program development and word processing, line oriented editor for hard copy devices.
- *File Manager.* General purpose utility for maintaining a library of disk files (usually floppy disks).
- *Debugger.* Single statement and breakpoint processing, access to program variables.
- *Utilities.* Programs for printing, communicating, accessing disks written under DEC's RT11 system, diagnosing disk faults, desk calculator, etc...
- *BASIC language compiler.* Implemented for those who insist on using BASIC, but may wish to write powerful subroutines in Pascal. (The compiler works, but subroutine binding is not yet ready.)

Major components now operating, but not quite ready for general distribution, include the following:

- *CAI Package.* Adaptation of the major Computer Assisted Instruction package developed at University of California Irvine; includes automated materials for an introductory Pascal programming course.
- *Assemblers.* For the PDP-11, 8080 and Z-80, these are written in Pascal for machine independence, but generate native code for those processors.
- *TREEMETA.* A metacompiler developed at UC Irvine.

The UCSD Pascal Project

The Project is one of the principal activities of the Institute for Information Systems, an embryonic "organized research unit" concerned with interdisciplinary studies, and with related instructional and public service activities. The main objectives of the Project include the following:

- *Machine Independence.* To foster the widespread use of machine indepen-

dent software systems, particularly for small computers, as a means to avoid software obsolescence. A major premise of the project is that applications software can best be made truly portable by making *the entire operating system and support software* portable to a new processor at the cost of only a small effort (eventually: one to three programmer months; currently: about six months).

- *Pascal.* To promote the widespread use of standard Pascal, and standardized extensions, as (the basis of) a general purpose programming language, both for writing system programs such as operating systems and compilers, and for applications software in education, research and business data processing.
- *Software Exchange.* To foster the development of a national or international marketplace within which authors of computer based course materials, and other applications software, may receive reasonable *royalties* to compensate them for their work. As an initial step, the Project will operate a Software/Courseware Exchange, using Tele-Mail techniques, for users of the UCSD Pascal Software System.
- *Mass Education.* To demonstrate that it is practical to improve the quality of mass education at the college level (and adult training in technical topics), while simultaneously reducing costs, through the use of microcomputer based course materials.
- *Research and Development.* To provide facilities, a team working environment above critical size, and salary support for students and faculty members who wish to conduct research or development projects in software engineering and many related fields of study.

Hardware Configuration

The UCSD Pascal system has been designed to run as a single user interactive system with superior response characteristics when one or more floppy disks are used for secondary storage. Wherever possible, single character commands are used, and prompting messages remind the user of the significance of the various commands that are available in different contexts. While the system has proven that machine independence of a complex software system is practical, there are of course practical limits to the range of characteristics that can be accommodated on the host machine. The major characteristics of a typical system needed to run UCSD

Pascal include the following:

- *Main memory.* 56 K bytes (48 K will do, but only for compiling small programs).
- *Word Size.* 8 bit bytes, 16 bit words (hardware or simulated).
- *Secondary Storage.* Standard 8 inch floppy disk (the major system program files occupy roughly 70 K bytes).
- *Console Display.* 9600 bps ASCII terminal with x-y cursor addressing works best (slower CRTs or hard copy terminals can be handled, but less effectively).
- *Keyboard.* Uses ASCII keys for CR, ESC, ETX, BS, DEL and four positioning arrows (up, down, left, right).

In addition, the system is being used to drive a variety of printers such as the Diablo HYTYPE and Printronix 300, and for communicating via standard asynchronous lines.

Compatibility with Other Software Systems

In Project discussions with manufacturers of computers, on which the UCSD Pascal System might potentially be run, the most frequently asked question is: "How much effort will it take to adapt Pascal to run under my software system?" This question is understandable in view of the approach generally taken by the computer industry when a new language is to be installed on a machine produced in quantity. Unfortunately, this question misses the main point the Project is trying to make regarding transportable software. The effort needed to convert the Pascal compiler to run under the operating system of manufacturer "X" will generally be far greater than the effort to make the entire UCSD Pascal system run on that manufacturer's hardware. In the interest of promoting software transportability, the Project will generally not agree to adapt just the compiler to run under another operating system.

Pascal Language Extensions

Like many others who use Pascal as the basis for writing large system programs, the Project has found it necessary to extend the language. The most notable extensions have to do with strings of characters, for natural reading and writing from and to interactive files, and for tools needed in writing the software. A concerted effort has been made to implement all of the "standard" Pascal language as defined in *Pascal User Manual and Report*, by Kathleen Jensen and Niklaus Wirth (Springer Verlag, New York and Heidelberg, 1975). (However,

UCSD Pascal still lacks the ability to allow procedure and function names to be passed as parameters.) The Project is making an effort to serve as coordinator among several large industrial firms which are preparing to use extended versions of Pascal for major programming projects. It is hoped that a consensus will emerge from this effort on extensions to the language for system programming. UCSD Pascal implements integers in two's complement form in 16 bit words, and real numbers in a 32 bit field. Since neither form is suitable for large integers or for business applications, it is planned to add the facility to handle fixed decimal numbers whose precision may be declared by the programmer.

Speed of Execution

Although the system is entirely interpretive, as currently implemented, execution speed is fast enough to permit highly interactive programs to be run on microcomputers. For example, compilation speed ranges from 600 to 700 lines per minute on the DEC LSI-11, or on an 8085 with a 3 MHz clock.

Availability

Copies of the system may be obtained by writing to UCSD Pascal Project, Maildrop C-021, La Jolla CA 92093. The system is available at a subscription fee of $200, made payable to "Regents of the University of California," which pays for materials, handling, and a limited amount of direct assistance to users. Those who wish to order the system should send details describing the system on which they wish it to run, or should request an order blank from the project. The system is copyrighted, but rights are granted to educational institutions and to bonafide computer clubs to make additional copies for their own noncommercial uses. A copy of the latest package of printed user manuals (about 250 pages) is available at a charge of $15, again made payable to the Regents of the University of California.

Though plans are in motion to convert the system to run on many different processors and configurations, the only systems currently supported use LSI-11, 8080 or Z-80 microprocessors with at least 48 K bytes of main memory, and IBM 3740 compatible standard floppy disk drive(s). For 8080 and Z-80 users, the method of adapting the system to run on new hardware is similar to that used by Digital Research Inc in distributing the CP/M operating system; and the Project will distribute a conversion package similar to theirs. Versions of the sys-

As of this writing (1 July 1979), SofTech Microsystems Inc (94 Black Mountain Rd, Building 3, San Diego CA 92126) is the sole licensee of the UCSD Pascal system. Questions about prices and availability of the system can be directed to the above address.

Also, note that UCSD Pascal is a trademark of the Regents of the University of California.

tem for other microprocessors are not likely to be ready for release until October 1978 at the earliest. Release on floppy disks other than those compatible with the 3740 format will depend upon availability of hardware to the Project.

In addition to the main software system, educational materials are available separately for an introductory course on problem solving and programming using Pascal. A textbook *(Microcomputer) Problem Solving Using Pascal* is available from Springer Verlag Publishers, 175 Fifth Av, New York NY 10010 ($9.80). The Project can supply a set of automated quizzes designed for use with the textbook in a self-paced course of study.

Help from the User Community

Readers can help by letting their favorite hardware vendors know that they want UCSD Pascal to be available in machine independent form. The Project has noted an increasing number of manufacturers who report that customers are requesting Pascal, and this has a real influence on their business decisions. Readers can also help by joining the international Pascal Users' Group (send $4 c/o Andy Mickel, 227 EX, 208 SE Union St, University of Minnesota, Minneapolis MN 55455) and pressing PUG to establish a technical board to oversee UCSD Pascal as a community project.■

Note on the Pascal User's Group

As of July 1, 1979 the Pascal User's Group (PUG) has over 3300 members in 47 countries. Those interested in joining can contact Andy Mickel at the University of Minnesota Computer Center, 227 Ex Engr, University of Minnesota, Minneapolis MN 55455, (612) 376-7290. The Pascal Newsletter *is published four times a year on a July to June schedule, with a subscription fee of $6 per year. All issues for the current year are sent with a new subscription, and back issues are available.*

Languages Forum

In Praise of Pascal

David A Mundie

As has been pointed out in these pages before, personal computing will never achieve its full potential as long as our state of the art machines are hobbled down with a language as far from state of the art as BASIC is. Some have argued for designing a special high level language for microprocessors, but I personally fail to see why we don't just implement Pascal and be done with it. I would like to look briefly at the language itself and try to explain why it seems the logical choice to me.

I am an applications programmer with no theoretical interest in computing whatsoever. What I like about Pascal is not the theory of its design, though that seems sound enough, but rather the fact that it lets me formulate my problems in my own terms. In Pascal more than in any other language I know, I can remain on the abstract, algorithmic level where, as a human being, I function best. Because of this pragmatic bias, much of what follows will be an informal discussion appealing to the reader's intuitions rather than a technical demonstration. I shall use BASIC for comparative purposes, since it is the tyrant in the field.

I find Pascal easy to use because it allows me to define new data types which express my data meaningfully. It provides control structures with which I can express what I want done to my data clearly and naturally. Pascal allows and encourages me to formulate my thinking in a structured way. Let us examine these three aspects of Pascal in reverse order.

Program Structure

Pascal is a resolutely structured language. A Pascal program is structured into blocks. Each block bears a heading which gives it a name and specifies its parameters. Roughly speaking, a block consists of a definition part, in which constants, types, variables, and subroutines are defined, and an action part, which contains the algorithm of the block. This rigorous separation of data definition and algorithm expression is partly responsible, it seems to me, for the greater legibility of Pascal compared to ALGOL.

Subroutines are themselves block structured and may thus be nested within one another. This allows the declaration of "local" variables and subprograms, meaning that storage may be allocated efficiently; yet it is easy to guard against unwanted side effects.

What does all this mean for the practicing programmer? The answer may perhaps best be seen in the light of a claim recently repeated by David Higgins in the October 1977 BYTE ("Structured Program Design," page 146). Higgins presents the now well established arguments in favor of structured programming, but goes on to contend that once a program is designed in a structured way, using for example Warnier-Orr diagrams, "it does not matter what programming language you code it in." This assertion seems pretty improbable on the face of it, and if true it would be a powerful argument against Pascal. I think that a rapid examination of two test cases will show it to be quite unjustified.

Let us take our test cases from the "bug" program which Higgins uses as his own example. Higgins would have us break the program down into three parts, as expressed in the following Warnier-Orr diagram:

bug program $\left\{ \begin{array}{l} \text{begin program} \\ \text{games (1,g)} \\ \text{end program} \end{array} \right.$

Nothing in the BASIC listing which accompanies the article even remotely suggests this overall algorithm. Look at what we might have in an equivalent Pascal program:

```
program bug;
    begin
        beginprogram;
        games;
        endprogram
    end.
```

Need I point out that to all intents and purposes the Pascal program *is* the Warnier-Orr diagram, with only a few notational differences such as the replacement of the

brace by the symbols **begin** and **end**? Are we really asked to believe that this one to one correspondence between the problem and the program does nothing to simplify the programming task? On the contrary, it simplifies matters enormously.

Considerations of space prevent me from giving the rival BASIC and Pascal versions in full. Another striking example is presented in figure 1 and listings 1 and 2, which show the Warnier-Orr diagram for the "turn" subprogram, Higgins' coding of the subprogram in BASIC, and the Pascal equivalent. Higgins calls his BASIC coding "simple and straightforward." Tastes differ but that is a phrase I would have reserved for the Pascal version. Higgins has had to fake truly structured programming in a language which fights his efforts every step of the way, and the results are tortured and confusing. In contrast, the Pascal coding is, once again, a nearly perfect reflection of the Warnier-Orr diagram, so much so, in fact, that most Pascal users will probably feel, as I do, that the diagrams are a useless intermediary step, less clear and bulkier than the program itself. The intent of the Pascal program segment is so transparent that in my opinion it could almost be understood by a complete programming novice.

Before leaving the topic of program structure, we should perhaps remark that Pascal subprograms (procedures and functions) bear names, not numbers, virtually eliminating the need for the comments which pepper any well documented BASIC listing. Furthermore, because Pascal subprograms can have parameters, the programmer is encouraged to use a single subprogram for a single task. Higgins has written separate subprograms for each body part, whereas for a Pascal user it is virtually impossible to resist the temptation of passing the arrays body, neck, head, etc, to a single procedure "give" as parameters.

Algorithm Expression

Program structure alone does not explain the relative clarity of the Pascal listing in listing 2. We may also use that listing to illustrate the tools which Pascal provides for expressing algorithms.

Logical operators: Pascal provides the logical operators (**and, or,** and **not**) which are so painfully lacking in BASIC and without which expressing an algorithm is so clumsy. The use of the operator **and** in the turn subprogram is a good example; or the reader may want to express "if (x=1) or ((y>2)and(z=3)) then. . ." in BASIC.

Conditional statements: Pascal's **if** structure groups statements with the condi-

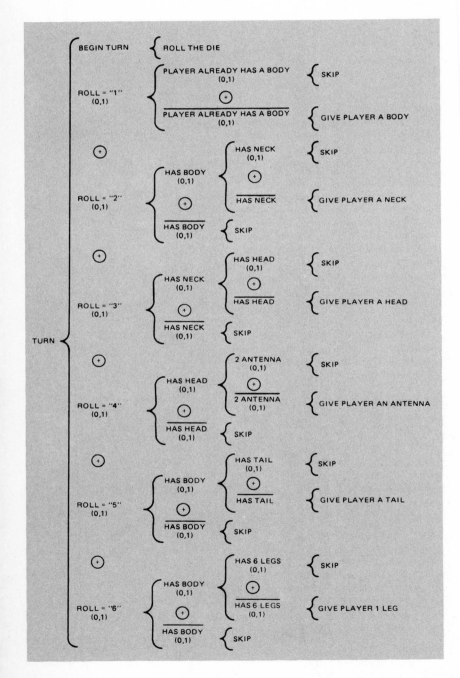

Figure 1: Warnier-Orr diagram for subprogram "turn" of the bug program. This is clear, but note how much bulkier it is than the Pascal program in listing 2. The Warnier-Orr diagram won't even run on a computer.

tions for their execution. The **if** statement is of the form:

```
if<expression>
    then<statement_1>
    else<statement_2>
```

The expression is evaluated as being either true or false. If it is true statement_1 is performed; otherwise statement_2 is performed. Suppose the expression is: X=1. In English the **if** statement translates to:

if X equals 1 then perform statement_1; else perform statement_2.

Pascal offers a very flexible **case** statement which is remotely related to the computed GOTO statement to be found in some BASICs. It is much more powerful because, among other things, selector values need not be contiguous, and actions are grouped with the conditions for their execution. A good example of the **case** statement's clarity is to be found in the procedure "turn," where the action taken depends on the value of roll.

Repetitive statements: BASIC provides only one repetitive control structure: the FOR statement. But there are innumerable situations where we do not know ahead of time how many times a given action is to be repeated. In such cases BASIC users have two choices. One is to set up a dummy FOR statement with a jump out of it when a certain condition is met: whence the ubiquitous "FOR I=1 TO 9999" statements in BASIC programming. This is bad because it seriously disguises the intention of the algorithm. One's natural expectation is for such a loop to be executed 9999 times, but that is not the case. The other solution is for the programmer to fake an appropriate control structure with GOTOs or conditional jumps. That is what Higgins has done in his program to express the fact that the computer and the human take turns until the game is over:

```
210 REM TURNS (1,T)
220 LET EGAM = 0
230 GOSUB 390
240 IF EGAM = 0 THEN 230
250 REM END GAME
260 GOSUB 1150
```

This is no doubt the best one can do in BASIC, but just consider how much more elegant the Pascal version is:

repeat turns **until** endofgame

This is typical of the way in which Pascal's control structures make algorithm expression a source of joy rather than a contortionist exercise. In addition to the **repeat** statement, Pascal offers a **while** statement for the case when an action is to be repeated as long as a condition is true.

Data Definition

Now that we have seen how much easier it is to express what one wants done to data in Pascal than in BASIC, let us turn to the wonderful data types which Pascal makes available for manipulation. Data types are the programmer's buffer between his abstract formulation of an algorithm and the messy realm of bit level details where that algorithm will eventually be executed. Pascal makes defining new types a trivial task. Once a new data type is defined, it is in effect indistinguishable from a predefined type and may be used in any way a predefined type may be. We leave BASIC behind at this point, since that language has no facilities for creating new types.

The bug program was too simple to provide examples of data structuring, so we shall have to turn elsewhere. Being a birdwatcher, I shall replace the traditional "Christmas card list" example by a bird data bank. I can do no more than skim the surface, so I ask the reader's indulgence if some of the listings are not fully explained. I am not trying to teach Pascal, but merely to spark intuitions.

Pascal distinguishes between simple

```
490  REM TURN SUBROUTINE
500  REM PLAY=1;PLAYERS TURN—PLAY=2;COMPUTERS TURN
510  REM ROLL DIE
520  LET ROLL = FIX@(((RND(0))*6.0))+1
530  PRINT:"ROLL IS A",ROLL
540  IF ROLL = 1 THEN IF BODY(PLAY)#1 THEN GOSUB 690 ELSE;ELSE;
550  IF ROLL = 1 THEN 650
560  IF ROLL = 2 THEN IF BODY(PLAY) = 1 THEN IF NECK(PLAY)#1 THEN GOSUB 760
570  IF ROLL=2 THEN 650
580  IF ROLL=3 THEN IF BODY(PLAY)=1 THEN IF NECK(PLAY)=1
     THEN IF HEAD(PLAY)#1 THEN GOSUB 820
590  IF ROLL=3 THEN 650
600  IF ROLL = 4 THEN IF HEAD(PLAY)=1 THEN IF ANTE(PLAY)#2
     THEN GOSUB 880
610  IF ROLL=4 THEN 650
620  IF ROLL = 5 THEN IF BODY(PLAY)=1 THEN IF TAIL(PLAY)#1 THEN GOSUB 940
630  IF ROLL=5 THEN 650
640  IF ROLL = 6 THEN IF BODY(PLAY)=1 THEN IF LEGS(PLAY)#6 THEN GOSUB 1000
650  LET A=3
660  RETURN
```

Listing 1: BASIC listing for Warnier-Orr diagram in figure 1. This is the best one can do in BASIC, but is still a far cry from the clarity of the Pascal listing.

```
procedure turn;
  begin roll:=trunc(random(1)*6)+1; writeln('roll is a',roll);
    case roll of
      1: if(body[player] ≠1)then give(body);
      2: if(body[player] =1)and(neck[player] ≠1) then give(neck);
      3: if(neck[player] =1)and(head[player] ≠1) then give(head);
      4: if(head[player] =1)and(ante[player] ≠2) then give(ante);
      5: if(body[player] =1)and(tail[player] ≠1) then give(tail);
      6: if(body[player] =1)and(legs[player] ≠6) then give(legs)
    end
  end;
```

Listing 2: The Pascal listing equivalent to listing 1. Note the clear affinity between the listing and the Warnier-Orr diagram. Notice that arrays are indexed using square brackets.

9

and structured types. Let us examine each in turn.

Simple types: These are the basic building blocks of which any structured type, no matter how complex, is ultimately composed. In addition to integer, real, and character types, Pascal offers two additional simple types which as far as I'm concerned come close to exhausting the simple types needed in a general purpose language. The first is the defined scalar type, and is defined by simply listing the values which a variable of the new type may take on. Suppose I need a data type for the various habitats in which a bird may appear. In Pascal I write:

> **type** h = (ocean,rivers,fields,suburbs,forests, mountains)

A variable of type h may take on any of the values listed. This means that while programming I may continue to think in terms of habitats, and am not forced to descend from that abstract level and think in integers, as I would have to do in BASIC. This also makes for virtually self-explanatory programs. Compare "IF HABITAT=3 THEN..." with the much more transparent "**if** habitat=fields **then**...."

The second simple data type is the Boolean, and is extremely useful in programming since one is constantly controlling program flow with Boolean expressions. Boolean variables take on the values true and false. Languages without such variables must make do with integers, which muddles things since one's natural expectation is for integers to count something. The Pascal user may simply write "**if** good **then**...", which is the way we think; the BASIC programmer must write "IF GOOD = 1 THEN...", which is alien to the way we think.

A large part of Pascal's elegance comes from the fact that in most contexts these simple or scalar types may be used indifferently. Thus for example the type h as defined above could be used as the index variable in a **for** statement:

> **for** habitat := ocean **to** mountains **do**

or in a case statement, or as the index type of an array:

> **if** foundin [fields] **then**

Furthermore, functions may return any scalar type: we have already seen the function "endofgame" which returns a Boolean value.

Structured types: In addition to the simple types, Pascal offers five different structuring methods: arrays, records, sets, files, and pointers. These different methods may be combined in virtually limitless ways. One may have files of arrays, pointers to records, arrays of sets, pointers to files of arrays of records, and so on. This extreme flexibility of data structuring methods is one of Pascal's most exciting features. The type array should be familiar, but let us look briefly at the other four structured types.

Sets: Each bird in my hypothetical data bank has associated with it a set of habitats in which the bird may be found. Having defined the type h as above, all I need to do to set up a variable habitats which will be a set of different habitats is to write:

> **var habitats: set of h**

When constructing the entry for the robin, I will write:

> habitats := [fields,suburbs]

thus assigning to the robin the set of habitats containing the two elements fields and suburbs. When going on a trip to the mountains, I can test whether mountains are in a given bird's set of habitats by the following simple test:

> **if** mountains in habitats **then**

Imagine trying to do this in BASIC. Pascal provides a variety of set operators which allow set manipulation in all its generality.

Records: Let us imagine that each entry in my data bank will contain the bird's name, its length, and a set of habitats where it may be found. The entry cannot be an array, since components of arrays must all be of the same type. The appropriate data type is the record, defined in Pascal as follows:

> **type** bird =   **record**
>   name: string;
>   length: real;
>   habitats: **set of** h
>   **end**

This is a simple and logical way of grouping data of different types into a meaningful whole. Given variables robin and redbreast of type bird, a simple assignment statement will set one equal to the other:

> robin := redbreast

To test whether a robin is more than 20 cm long, we would have:

> **if** robin.length>20 **then**

and so on. These are simple examples, but they suffice to illustrate the flexibility of the record type.

Files: Now let us suppose that I have 600 entries of type bird in my data bank, and want to make a list of all the birds whose length is greater than 20 cm. It is pointless and wasteful to keep all 600 records in memory for such a task; all I

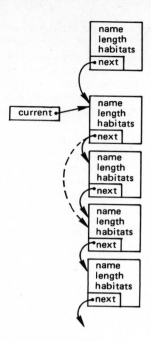

Figure 2: A linked list of records of type "bird" with addition of the pointer field "next." Deleting the third record is a simple matter of changing a pointer field, as shown by the dotted line.

really need is to store them in mass storage and read them in one at a time. In Pascal what I do is declare a file of records as follows:

```
var fb: file of bird
```

Now, supposing the file to have been written, all I need to perform the task is:

```
reset(fb) ;
repeat if fb↑.length>20
    then writeln(fb↑.name) ; get(fb)
until eof(fb)
```

Reset positions the file at its beginning; get advances it one record; fb↑ is the buffer variable containing the current record; and the writeln statement prints the bird's name. The Boolean function eof tests for the end of the file.

Pointers: Finally, let us suppose that I wish to update the data bank by deleting a bird. It is of course possible to do this by storing all the records in an array, but this is clumsy and inefficient, since all the records following the deleted record would have to be shifted one position. List processing provides a much better solution. The records are linked together into a list by inserting a pointer field "next" into each record. Each record will then "point" to

the record following it in the list. Deleting a record becomes the simple matter of changing a single pointer value as illustrated in figure 2. Given the pointer "current" pointing to the item just before the one to be deleted, the following simple statement will do the trick:

```
current↑.next := current↑.next↑.next
```

Adding a new record is only slightly more complicated.

Let me repeat that these simple examples are not meant to do more than provide a brief glimpse of the marvels of Pascal's structured types. For full explanations the reader is referred to the texts in the references.

Conclusion

Rapid though it has been, I hope that this survey of Pascal will have brought out some of the features which make it vastly superior to BASIC. BASIC offers an absolutely minimal set of features and expects you either to devise makeshift solutions or to design a new version of the language when they are inadequate. No wonder there are so many different versions of BASIC. Pascal offers a somewhat wider selection of features, but avoids the pitfall of trying to include every feature known to humanity. Pascal is a simple and streamlined language: the *Pascal Report* defining the language is a mere 32 pages long. Yet Pascal's designers seem to have chosen just those features which the user needs to expand the language when the need arises, so that it is a genuinely general-purpose language suited to a wide variety of problems. It is this combination of simplicity and power which seems to me to make Pascal the natural choice for a standard microprocessor language.■

REFERENCES

● Bowles, Ken, *Microprocessor Problem Solving Using Pascal*, Springer-Verlag, New York, 1977.

● Jensen, Kathleen and Wirth, Niklaus, *Pascal: User Manual and Report*, Springer Study Edition (2nd edition), Springer-Verlag, New York.

● Mickel, Andy, *Pascal News*, University Computer Center, 227 Experimental Eng, 208 SE Union St., University of Minnesota, Minneapolis, MN.

Comments on Pascal, Learning How to Program, and Small Systems

Gary A Ford

The editorial in the December 1977 BYTE[1] asked if Pascal is the next BASIC. Implicit in this question is the suggestion that personal computing needs a widely used programming language. Ostensibly, this will facilitate exchange of software, and thus help eliminate the existing software vacuum for personal computer systems. Should Pascal be the language used to begin to fill this void? To answer this question, we should look at the history of Pascal to see for what purposes it was developed.

Wirth states two principal goals for Pascal: "to make available a language suitable to teach programming as a systematic discipline based on certain fundamental concepts clearly and naturally reflected by the language," and "to develop implementations of this language which are both reliable and efficient on *presently available computers*" (emphasis added).

With regard to the first of these goals, Wirth contends that "the language in which the student is taught to express his ideas profoundly influences his habits of thought and invention." My experience shows that this is a remarkably accurate statement. I have taught computer science to university undergraduates for several years, and recently taught several intermediate level courses to students with a variety of programming backgrounds. The students had all had two or three quarters of formal computer science courses at the same university during the previous year, and all were familiar with the same computers. However, some had learned to program in BASIC, some in FORTRAN, and some in a structured variant of FORTRAN which included, among other features, two varieties of if-then-else, five varieties of iterative statements, two varieties

of multiple branch structures, and a simple but powerful procedure facility. The structured FORTRAN programmers proved to be significantly better performers in the intermediate level courses in all ways. They were much quicker to understand new algorithms, new data structures, and new applications. They were superior in applying this knowledge to new problems, which can, in part, be attributed to the fact that they were not thinking in the narrow terms required in BASIC and FORTRAN. They wrote better programs in assembly language, perhaps again because they could think in structured programming terms. They also, not unexpectedly, learned Pascal (which was taught in conjunction with a data structures course) much faster than the other students. In fact, some of the BASIC and FORTRAN programmers never did make the transition to Pascal; they wrote Pascal programs that looked like line by line translations of BASIC and FORTRAN programs. An informal follow-up of some of these students in more advanced courses showed that the BASIC and FORTRAN group continued to lag behind, especially in courses in analysis of algorithms and design of large systems.

Of course, this was not a controlled experiment, so the conclusions cannot be supported scientifically. However, I believe it is true that since so much of computer science involves abilities to analyze, to organize, and to plan, the thinking process taught in a first programming course, which in turn depends on the language used, has an enormous impact on the development of computer scientists.

Thus, Pascal sounds like a good language for beginners (ie: many of today's computer hobbyists). There are other reasons for supporting the spread of Pascal, including, for example, its out-

---

1. Page 17 of this edition.

standing data structuring facilities. Some problems are easily stated and solved in terms of such structures as sets, lists, sequences, trees, or groups of disparate items. Pascal allows the programmer to define and to deal directly with such structures, whereas BASIC and FORTRAN force the programmer to disguise these structures as arrays. Of course, obscuring the original ideas often leads to obscure program logic.

With regard to Wirth's second goal for Pascal, we suddenly have a problem. The personal computer systems of today are quite different from the "presently available computers" Wirth had in mind ten years ago. Therefore, some language features that are desirable for present personal computer systems are absent from Pascal. Perhaps the most important of these features are in the category of access to peripheral devices and processor hardware facilities.

Pascal has only two primitive IO operations: get and put. Each moves a single unit of data (character, integer, record, etc) from or to a sequential file. Files are not necessarily associated with or stored on secondary storage devices, although two special predefined files (named input and output) are available for those files associated with devices that will also be accessed by humans. There are in addition two predefined procedures (named read and write) that perform data transmission from or to files in particularly useful ways, but it is important to emphasize that these are procedures (subprograms) and not statements or operations in the language.

The peripheral devices of personal computer systems are extremely varied, and very few system configurations are exactly alike. Therefore, each user will need somewhat different IO capabilities in the language. Many users have an on line terminal, access to which requires the ability to access specific absolute addresses in memory or specific port addresses. Users with disks will need direct access file capabilities. Others may want the ability to process interrupts for real time applications. None of these capabilities exist in Pascal, and none can easily be implemented as a disguised sequential file.

The obvious conclusion is that if a push for Pascal as the language of personal computing is made, there will be a variety of nonstandard implementations. This is exactly what we have seen with BASIC. Implementors will add their own versions of their own favorite bells and whistles. We may expect numerous methods of specifying absolute memory addresses (peeks and pokes), direct access disk file

statements, and all kinds of facilities to handle the exotic peripherals being attached to personal systems. In addition, implementors will want to add their own favorite data type (for example, Pascal does not have a built-in string data type), and their own favorite operator (for example, Pascal does not have an exponentiation operator). Next, seeing the size of the resulting compiler, implementors will begin to delete their least favorite standard features (often meaning the ones they least understand), in order to come up with a 4 K version of "eensyweensy Pascal."

One approach to preventing some of the problems just mentioned is to get all of us hobbyists together to agree (is this possible?) on a standard set of additions and deletions, or perhaps a few standard sets in order to develop 8 K, 12 K, 16 K, etc, versions. The traumatization of the language could be minimized by requiring that all the new features be implemented as procedures, rather than as new statement types, thus maintaining the syntactic integrity of the language. Of course, this would require a capability to link external procedures to each Pascal program, and none of these procedures could be written in Pascal. This means either that all users will need to know another programming language, or that the implementors of the new varieties of Pascal will have to supply customized procedures for each customer.

There is a fundamental flaw in this approach, however. Pascal was not intended to be all things to all people. It was designed with specific, well thought out, predefined goals. All aspects of the language were designed to complement each other in attaining those goals. Any deletion from the language, however minor it seems, will upset this balance, and thus damage Pascal's ability to achieve its goals. Deletions and additions will also change the character of the language, and it is this overall character of Pascal that has brought it so many devotees.

A better approach, I believe, is for those of us in personal computing to get together to agree on *principles* for the next widely used language, rather than on the features to add to or delete from an existing language. This is not any kind of vote against Pascal; to the contrary, I hope Pascal will become available to all hobbyists with systems that can support *standard* Pascal, and that it be used for all *suitable* applications programming. I have used Pascal for at least 95% of my own programming over the last three years, and I cannot recommend it too strongly.

If a new personal computing language were developed from guiding principles,

I would hope that it would have much of the flavor of Pascal. I would hope it would be syntactically uncluttered like Pascal, not only because it makes the language easier to use, but also because it allows much simpler (smaller) language translators. I would hope it would have control structures at least as strong and as logical as those of Pascal, and data structuring facilities as simple and powerful as those of Pascal. It should be designed so that we can write almost all of our software in this one language, including both systems and applications programs. It should not try to provide every feature of every existing language, but rather, like Pascal, provide a small set of primitive constructs from which users can define their own powerful features. It should allow us to write truly portable programs and to maintain a library of procedures, since a good procedure facility, like that of Pascal, is perhaps the single most important tool for software developers. But whatever we choose to put in the language, let us design it from principles, and not evolve it from a set of independent features, as was the case with BASIC and FORTRAN. ∎

Editorial

Is Pascal the Next BASIC?

Carl Helmers

One of the most interesting phenomena in the academic world of computer science of late is the language Pascal. This language is the subject of much intense activity, and is rapidly gaining acceptance as the language of choice for training and illustration of computer concepts to new students of the field. Characteristic of this phenomenon is the existence of on the order of 100 different implementations of the language for various computers and a very active "Pascal User's Group."

Pascal began in the late 1960s as a tutorial experiment of Professor Niklaus Wirth: a method of teaching the concepts of programming in a systematic fashion using a consistent and highly structured program representation. Historically, Pascal has antecedents in the ALGOL language but with the addition of concepts such as record and file structures which were missing in ALGOL's definition. The following passage by Professor Wirth gives the essence of Pascal's purposes...

The development of the language Pascal is based on two principal aims. The first is to make available a language suitable to teach programming as a systematic discipline based on certain fundamental concepts clearly and naturally reflected by the language. The second is to develop implementations of this language which are both reliable and efficient on presently available computers.

The desire for a new language for the purpose of teaching programming is due to my dissatisfaction with the presently used major languages whose features and constructs too often cannot be explained logically and convincingly and which too often defy systematic reasoning. Along with this dissatisfaction goes my conviction that the language in which the student is taught to express his ideas profoundly influences his habits of thought and invention, and that the disorder governing these languages directly imposes itself onto the programming style of the students.

There is of course plenty of reason to be cautious with the introduction of yet another programming language, and the objection against teaching programming in a language which is not widely used and accepted has undoubtedly some justification, at least based on short term commercial reasoning. However, the choice of a language for teaching based on its widespread acceptance and availability, together with the fact that the language most widely taught is thereafter going to be the one most widely used, forms the safest recipe for stagnation in a subject of such profound pedagogical influence. I consider it therefore well worthwhile to make an effort to break this vicious circle. [Quoted from the second edition of the *Pascal User Manual and Report*, by Kathleen Jensen and Niklaus Wirth, Springer Verlag, New York, 1974, page 133.]

Since the time of Pascal's creation by Professor Wirth, the language has become widespread, primarily because his tutorial purposes also happen to coincide with what one might want in a systems and applications programming language used in software development. In fact acceptance has been sufficiently widespread that there now exist implementations for some of the more common microprocessors in the personal computing field (using the *Pascal*

User's Group Newsletter as a source for this information in a listing of implementations in issue #8 recently published). What are the ramifications of Pascal as it might affect personal computing users?

At the present time, outside of low level assemblers, the personal computing field is dominated by one language, BASIC. It is the high level language of choice for users of the equipment and for manufacturers who sell to the users of the equipment. Any attempted personal computing system design these days must come up to the standards of a reasonable BASIC (such as the Microsoft BASIC used by MITS, OSI, Commodore and others) or it will be at a relative disadvantage in the marketplace. This dominance of BASIC as a language is a fact of life in this field. A decade and a half of language design evolution has occurred since BASIC first came on the scene, yet it still dominates at the user level. Why?

In a casual enumeration mode, I can list several fairly obvious and interrelated reasons why this has become the case; out of these reasons will come a similar scenario for development of Pascal as a future option for personal computers.

- Everybody knows BASIC.
- BASIC has a manufacturer independent standard definition.
- Lots of implementations of BASIC are available.
- Much personal use applications software already exists in BASIC.
- BASIC is friendly.

At a superficial level, these reasons are part of a self-sustaining loop of circular reasoning: Since BASIC is friendly, everybody wants to know BASIC; since so many people learn BASIC, there tend to be lots of implementations. Much software for applications has been written in BASIC. Since a manufacturer independent standard for BASIC exists, conversion of programs from one machine to another is simplified, thus making widely available software useful to people, and so on . . . ad infinitum. . . This is Professor Wirth's "vicious circle."

Like many similar conventions, BASIC has been bootstrapped into the public awareness over time, and has acquired a certain inertia of its own that will keep it going for years in the same way that FORTRAN seems to live forever. Let's examine the reasons in this list, and in so doing compare BASIC to Pascal, a language which is quite possibly in an earlier stage of a similar bootstrap cycle and may indeed become a much demanded "language of choice" for the user community. Vicious circles can have positive aspects: it all depends on which circle one has established. A contention I make is that the same sort of "vicious circle" can be, and indeed is being established for the language Pascal.

Everybody Knows BASIC.

BASIC historically was introduced at a time when "big" computers dominated the field, and there was a need to partition the activities of such computers into small individually oriented packages for purposes of making the "big" computer available to many people. This partitioning succeeded admirably: when professor X (or Y or Z) wanted to make real exercises in programming available to students, BASIC was frequently employed, due to its availability and interactive simplicity. Like any technology, BASIC did not start out in an "everybody knows" state, but it got that way through its early availability and no small push from pedagogues of computer science.

Today, the teachers of programming are tending to push Pascal as the language of choice for teaching "good" programming concepts. The Pascal User's Group is evidence of the number of academic people who support the ideas of Professor Wirth to the extent of implementing their own local Pascal systems for educational purposes. (This is typically done using a number of techniques of machine independence conceived by early implementors of Pascal for purposes of spreading its implementations.) One result of this availability is that Pascal is becoming the tool of teaching programming concepts which Professor Wirth envisioned . . . and the beginnings of the "everybody knows" state for Pascal are already evident.

BASIC Has a Manufacturer Independent Standard Definition.

This comment is nominally true of BASIC. Work is indeed in progress on an ANSI standard for BASIC, and there is of course the original Dartmouth College definition of BASIC. The fact that people are trying to define a standard form of BASIC, however, is a result of the fact that the implementations of BASIC have been somewhat subject to variations. In the personal computing world, there are numerous differences at a detail level between language extensions of various BASIC interpreters, some as basic as the variations in string and array handling in various forms of minicomputer BASIC.

BASIC language implementors are no different from implementors of a number of languages, often succumbing to the "wouldn't it be neat if" syndrome and throwing in features not part of the original definitions of the language. The hitch with such featurism is that if anyone uses the features, the programs written with the feature may no longer be portable.

Of course Pascal would be no more immune to featurism on the part of implementors; at least that would be an obvious contention since there is no fundamental difference between people who implement BASIC and people who implement Pascal. But before making such a statement, an examination for the motives of implementation featurism should be made. BASIC in its original definition is a very limited and parochial language, one which represents a viewpoint of quick implementation of programs with limited IO formatting, standard floating point operations, and no intent to service large or complicated applications. Thus, many of the "feature" temptations presented to BASIC implementors are a result of attempts to correct the deficiencies of BASIC by adding omitted items (for example, strings, implemented differently in various BASIC interpreters).

Pascal, on the other hand, by having a definition which is more general in scope than BASIC (although by no means complicated to use in simple problems) helps cut down these "feature" temptations on the part of its implementors. One basic example of this slightly more general definition is in Pascal's inclusion of extensible data types which can be declared, as well as file and record structures missing from BASIC. Pascal is a block structured language allowing multiple character strings for procedure and data names, and is thus closer to the natural symbolic thought processes of designing a program than is BASIC.

A classical contrast between the two languages in this area of features is to pose the problem: How would I use the language to include complex numbers for use in engineering analysis or physics? In BASIC, I might not even want to consider the possiblity of using the language for complex numbers because of the kluge that would result. Using Pascal, I would simply use the type extensibility of data to declare a complex number type and code various procedures to implement complex number operations. An example of this concept, which involves no features not inherent in Pascal's definition, is given on pages 42ff of the *Pascal User Manual and Report* quoted earlier. Of course, perhaps not all possible or desirable features were included in Pascal's definition, so dialects may occur there as well as in BASIC. But the necessity of dialects generated through extensions is probably less in Pascal,

making the standard created by Professor Wirth a closer approximation to what actually gets implemented.

Lots of Implementations of BASIC Are Available.

Here is where BASIC no doubt has a considerable lead over Pascal at the present time. But Pascal is rapidly gaining in a catch up mode. As noted earlier, there are presently nearly 100 different implementations of Pascal, mostly for minicomputers and larger computers ranging in size and scope up to a CRAY-1 implementation of Pascal. At the low end, according to the *Pascal User's Group Newsletter*, number 8, page 64, there are presently compilers implemented for the Motorola 6800, Intel 8080 and Zilog Z-80 microprocessor architectures (although the listing did not mention whether the compilers were self-compilers or cross compilers). Implementations are coming, part of the history of the language and the active following it has among computer science people.

Much Personal Use Applications Software Already Exists in BASIC.

No argument here. The number of books and periodicals which publish programs in BASIC will probably exceed the number with Pascal representations of equivalent programs for a long time to come. But this is equivalent to saying that BASIC has been around longer in the public eye, for given time much of the same sort of software can and will be written in Pascal as more and more implementations become available.

BASIC is Friendly.

BASIC is fundamentally an interactive approach to programming in which programs are entered in source form and tested within the confines of one session with effectively instant change from editing to execution. If Pascal is to become an equivalent "friendly" language, it must be implemented in a way which allows a similar instant change from editing the design to trying out the design of an application.

Whether this friendliness requirement can be best met by an interpreter or a compiler is an open question, but it is a definite requirement. In BASIC the rule to date has been interpretive, or semicompiled code, where semicompiled means that symbols for language tokens are replaced by compact codes. In Pascal to date, compilation has been the rule rather than the exception. It is conceivable that a compiled Pascal coupled with an editing and object code maintenance facility oriented to the block level might give sufficiently quick response at the terminal with much faster execution times associated with compiled code.

Another open question concerning Pascal is that of how much memory is required for a Pascal self-compiler or resident interpreter in a typical personal computer's microprocessor based system. I suspect that a compiler or interpreter of Pascal can be built which will fit within 16 K to 32 K bytes of memory, but whether this is really possible or not is by no means clear to me.

To sum up the thesis, Pascal is well on its way to becoming the kind of widely known language which will be taught as a matter of course to new students of programming. This in turn will tend to boost the long term acceptance of Pascal and get it established as one of the major languages, a process which at an earlier date occurred for FORTRAN and BASIC. For our own part, we at BYTE are interested in giving Pascal a boost. We have a survey article about Pascal in preparation at the present time. We would also like to talk to implementors of the language who would be interested in marketing Pascal compilers or interpreters through software book publications which include source code and machine readable object code. For those who desire more background information on Pascal, we recommend the Pascal User's Group, run by Andy Mickel at the University of Minnesota Computer Center, 227 Exp Engr, University of Minnesota, Minneapolis MN 55455, (612) 376-7290. The *Pascal Newsletter* is published four times per year, and at the time of this writing costs $4 per year.∎

Note on the Pascal User's Group

As of July 1, 1979 the Pascal User's Group (PUG) has over 3300 members in 47 countries. Those interested in joining can contact Andy Mickel at the University of Minnesota Computer Center, 227 Ex Engr, University of Minnesota, Minneapolis MN 55455, (612) 376-7290. The Pascal Newsletter *is published four times a year on a July to June schedule, with a subscription fee of $6 per year. All issues for the current year are sent with a new subscription, and back issues are available.*

Concerning Pascal:

A Homebrew Compiler Project

Stephen P Smith

Your editorial in December 1977 BYTE[1] was commendable. It served to reinforce my conviction that Pascal is the next step up from BASIC for personal computing. As you and your readers know from the biographical sketch that preceded my article in November 1977 BYTE[2], a Pascal compiler is my pet microcomputer project. Because that sketch prompted a number of inquiries about the status of my work, I thought a letter to BYTE would be timely following your editorial.

My approach to the compiler is to start with a small subset of Pascal and add features as my resources and talents permit. I've begun by determining the minimum subset needed to describe its own compiler. Because statements written in the resulting language will still be valid Pascal, the initial version can be debugged and run as a cross compiler on any computer which supports the full language. When operational, my compiler will convert itself to machine code to be loaded on the target microcomputer. Further development will be done on that machine. Each subsequent revision will be written in the Pascal subset of the previous one.

At this writing, I have completed the parsing procedures and am testing them on a DECsystem 10 with the guidance of Dr Robert Mathis at Old Dominion University.

The production of machine code is still some way off, because I feel I need more experience with the instruction set of the target machine, MOS Technology's 6502. I expected to get this experience with a 6502 based Challenger I ordered from Ohio Scientific in August, but it has yet to be delivered. Perhaps this spring I will have an operating compiler to report.

As an alternative to my subset approach, there is another way to implement Pascal. It reflects upon your editorial discussion of the compiler/interpreter alternative. I am developing a pure compiler, but the standard Pascal implementation is a hybrid. A program is available to convert source programs into assembly code for a hypothetical stack computer (HSC code). The assembled hypothetical stack machine code is then interpreted by the target machine. This technique has speeded implementation of Pascal at several installations, and might be useful for personal computing since the hypothetical stack machine code is itself portable. A club, for example, might maintain the source to hypothetical stack machine compiler on one member's computer which had the necessary resources. Other members need only support the hypothetical stack machine assembler and interpreter for their machines. Although operationally more cumbersome than direct machine language compilation, this approach might speed up the availability of Pascal and reduce the hardware requirement for applications users. ∎

---

1. Page 17 of this edition.
2. "Simulation of Motion: An Improved Lunar Lander Algorithm."

Languages Forum

A Proposed Pascal Compiler

Kin-Man Chung
Herbert Yuen

A Note About the Tiny Pascal project . . .

The three part article "A 'Tiny' Pascal Compiler" plus the complete p-code to 8080 conversion program listing are included in this edition beginning on pages 59 and 203 respectively . . .BWL

In the Languages Forum of the April 1978 BYTE, page 150[1], we read Stephen Smith's report on his *homebrew* compiler project. Actually, he is developing the Pascal subset compiler on a mainframe computer at a university and planning to transfer it to a microcomputer. He said he had a minor problem with code generation (using 6502 machine code). We think his project might progress more smoothly if he uses another approach—that of generating assembly code for a hypothetical stack machine. This is the same method professionals use for implementing portable Pascal compilers on big computers.

Our own homebrew compiler project was developed in house on a microcomputer that uses an 8080 processor and has a North Star disk system. We began in mid December of 1977. Our motivation came from the fact that the North Star disk BASIC, although very good for general programming purposes, was not fast enough for system software development and some graphic games. For instance, our 8080 assembler, written in BASIC, takes 1 to 3 seconds to assemble one single assembly instruction. Assembling a 500 line program takes about one half hour. From various sources of information we know that Pascal is one of the easiest languages to implement. It also has many nice features that are desirable in a high level language.

The Pascal subset is small, otherwise it

would be very difficult to develop using a BASIC interpreter. All variables in the subset are 16 bit integers. Arrays are single dimensional. Character strings are declared as arrays and each character takes one array element; although wasting space, this is easy to implement. Procedures and functions may be recursive. Variables and constants, except arrays, can be passed as arguments to procedures and functions. Language statements include declaration, assignment, BEGIN-END, IF-THEN-ELSE, WHILE-DO, REPEAT-UNTIL, FOR-TO/DOWNTO-DO, CASE-OF-ELSE. The subset is big enough to provide useful features. The Pascal compiler can be written in the subset without much difficulty.

The actual coding of the compiler (in BASIC) began in January 1978. The compiler generates p-code for a hypothetical stack machine, the same one described in Wirth's book, *Algorithm + Data Structure = Programs.* (P-code is the intermediate code generated by the Pascal compiler. It is the machine language of a hypothetical Pascal oriented computer. Use of p-code makes the Pascal language portable since only a p-code interpreter needs to be written for a particular processor. This saves the user from writing the entire compiler for each individual machine.) Several instructions and input/output (IO) capabilities have been added. At the same time, an interpreter was also written (in BASIC) to execute and debug the p-code. It helps to verify the correctness of the codes generated by the compiler. In late January, after most parts

---

1. Page 21 of this edition.

of the two programs had been debugged, we began to design a run time support package in 8080 assembly language and also a translator that translates p-code to 8080 machine code. With the debug package and simulator in the system (see Kin-Man's article "An 8080 Simulator" in the October 1977 BYTE, page 70), we did not have much trouble debugging the run time routines. During March most of our time was spent in refining all the routines: revising some features and extensions in the compiler, adding local optimization capabilities in the translator and improving the efficiency of the run time routines. The run time routines, which perform all 16 bit integer arithmetic and logical operations and IO conversions, take only 1 K bytes of memory.

The first step in the bootstrapping process was to write the interpreter in Pascal since it is the slowest but shortest program.

It was coded by straightforward translation from the BASIC version. Debugging was smooth and the entire program was up and running within a week. Compared to the BASIC version, the Pascal version runs about 15 times faster; slightly better than we expected. Our next step will be writing the translator and compiler in the Pascal subset. After that, further development can be done in Pascal without the BASIC interpreter.

For three months, each of us have been spending about 10 to 15 hours a week on this project. The first version (in BASIC) of the compiler and supporting software were completed with an estimated effort of two working months. Considering such a short time period and a functioning compiler, we believe we are approaching the task from the right direction. We hope that our project will attract the attention of many readers so that we can share our interest and experience in Pascal with them.■

About The Language

Pascal

A Structurally Strong Language

People should be able to communicate their ideas to a computer in a language that people understand; not simply in a language they know. Additionally, if the computer can be made to understand the same language easily, all the more reason to consider its use. Such a language is Pascal. This language, perhaps more than any other common language, is the easiest to understand and more importantly, allows a straightforward presentation of most algorithms. Although many languages also make this claim, few have the overwhelming and energetic support from collegiate computer science departments. Let's consider some of the language features of Pascal.

This language is equipped with a precise syntactical description that defines both how programs may be constructed and how Pascal compilers should function. There is a required form for programs, statements within programs, and data operated upon by programs. At first glance, a naive user may rebel at this apparent lack of freedom (eg: BASIC allows a dimension statement virtually anywhere in a program). One soon learns that this structure admits very general programs and in no way limits the programmer in exercising his talents. On the contrary, it forces the user to think logically and plan out the program.

A program written in Pascal may utilize the free format form of programs that is conducive to structured programming. Unlike line oriented source languages, Pascal allows extra spaces, tabs and carriage controls to be inserted anywhere without significance except in the middle of identifiers or character strings. Comments may be inserted wherever spaces may be inserted and are delimited by "(* ... *)".

A program is made up of two parts, a heading and a block. The heading contains the name of the program and lists its parameters. The parameters are somewhat implementation dependent but normally specify the names of file pointers from which the default input is received and to which output is sent. A typical heading is

program parser (input, output)

A block consists of six separate segments or sections of a program. All but the last part are optional. These are:

- Label declaration section
- Constant declaration section
- Type declaration section
- Variable declaration section
- Procedure and function declaration section
- Statement section

Labels in Pascal identify statements to which control may be transferred. Labels are numeric; more specifically, unsigned integers. Not every statement requires a label. In fact, most Pascal users consider programs better if they have fewer labels. At first glance, these declarations might seem a nuisance, but they force the user to think about the entire program before sitting down at a terminal.

The constant declarations allow a user to create synonyms for constants used in the program. Thus

const pi=3.141592;
e=2.7182818;

defines the constants "pi" and "e" for use throughout the program. Clearly, it no longer is necessary to type 3.141592 in the several places required by a program. Addi-

> **PASCAL forces the user to think logically and plan out the program.**

> **Most PASCAL users consider programs better if they have fewer labels.**

tionally, one may name character strings as well

const title='matrix inversion program v01';

The type declaration section allows creation of user defined named data types. This will be discussed in some detail later. Pascal has four predefined data types: integer, real, Boolean, and character. Most versions of BASIC support the first three types and strings. Data of type character is very convenient in a microprocessor environment since a byte is the basic unit of memory.

The variable declaration section requires the naming of all identifiers that will be used as variables within this block. FORTRAN, BASIC, APL, and LISP do not adhere to this convention. Again Pascal forces the user to think about what he wants to say before he says it. A sample variable declaration section might be

```
var    x,y:integer;
       cost:real;
       flag:boolean;
```

Pascal's design allows the user to combine the utility of type declarations and variable declarations into data forms that would shame BASIC and FORTRAN. We have already seen Pascal's predefined scalar variable types above. These are actually known as simple types.

Another simple type is the subrange type. Often a variable in a program may be expected to take on values only from a subrange of a simple type, say integers. For example

var asiz:1..100;

meaning "asiz" will be an integer whose values should lie between 1 and 100. Note that the compiler might choose to store "asiz" as a byte rather than a word if it was efficient enough to do so. Alternatively, if several variables are of the same range, a type statement could have been used

```
type  lsiz=1..100;
var asiz, bsiz, f1:lsiz;
```

Another simple type is the symbolic scalar type. This feature permits identifiers to be used in place of a sequence of integers, greatly enhancing the readability of the program. Suppose a program needed to represent the months of the year as a variable associated with some billing information. The approach in BASIC would be to use the sequence 1, 2, . . . , 12. Pascal could use the subrange type 1 . . 12 or better

```
type
     months = (jan, feb, mar, apr, may, jun,
               jul, aug, sep, oct, nov, dec);
     var billmonth, duemonth: months
```

In the statement section of a program,

"billmonth" may be assigned one of the symbolic scalars from "months" or tested to see how its value compares with "duemonth." There are several functions available that operate on symbolic scalars, for example, ord(billmonth) would yield a number between 0 and 11 indicating the position of that month in the list "months."

Simple types are part of a more general data description called a type. Types include pointers which are used when dynamic data storage is referenced, file pointers which are used to reference secondary data storage, and arrays which are used with vector data storage. An example of an array declaration is

var cost: array [months] of real;

Notice that this array will be indexed, or subscripted, by "months." In general, arrays may be indexed by any simple types, may be multidimensional, and may be of any type, including arrays of arrays.

Two additional types set Pascal in a class by itself; these notions allow powerful algorithm descriptions. The set type allows user manipulation of sets. Consider

var special: set of months;

The union, intersection, and set difference operators as well as relational operators may be applied to sets. A variable of scalar type may be tested for membership in a set of the same scalar type, for example

if billmonth in special then. . .

The last type is the record type. Items of different types may be aggregated into a single entity that can be stored as one logical unit, for example as one element of an array.

```
type
     customer = record
                     name:array [1..20] of char;
                     bal,bal30:real;
                     datedue:daterec
                     end;
     daterec =   record
                     day:1..31;
                     mo:months;
                     year:integer
                     end;
     var
          database: array [1..100] of customer;
```

To reference fields of a record, the record name followed by a period, followed by the field name is used. Hence the over 30 day balance of customer 12 is "database[12]. bal30" and the day of the due date of the current bill of customer 27 is "database[27]. datedue.day." The full impact of record types cannot be explained in this short article; they must be used to be appreciated. One advantage of records is that items may

Arrays may be multi-dimensional and include arrays of arrays.

Items of different types may be aggregated into a single entity that can be stored as one logical unit.

be logically grouped together rather than stored in parallel arrays.

Procedure and function definitions would follow next in a program. They may be recursive and permit parameter passing in a style somewhat similar to ALGOL. Because of the position in a program of these declarations, procedures and functions may reference globally any variables or types defined in the main program. The body of a procedure or function is identical to the body of a program; hence, procedures may be defined within procedures, and so on. Any variables defined within procedures or functions are considered local to the procedure and are unique to each invocation of the procedure. The sample program in listing 1 has several examples.

The statement portion of a program is called a "compound." A compound is a sequence of the keyword **begin**, any number of statements separated by semicolons, and the keyword **end**. The program ends with a period. Each of the statements within a compound may be one of a variety of different kinds of statements. Assignments, like

```
database[i+k].bal:=total
```

are the most common statements. Pascal supports a large number of control statements which give the language its structure.

Pascal has a looping control similar to that of standard BASIC but the step or increment may be only +1 or −1. The **for** statement causes a single statement, which could be quite complex, to be executed some number, including zero, times. For example

```
for ind. =1 to 100 do
    begin
        due:=1.006*database[ind].bal;
        database[ind].bal:=0.0;
        sum:=sum+due;
        database[ind].bal30:=
            1.006* database[ind].bal30+due
    end
```

This segment shifts the balance 30 days, adds some interest charge and accumulates a sum of the recently aged balances. If in a **for** statement, the increment were to be −1, then the keyword **downto** would replace the keyword **to**.

Pascal supports both simple conditional and full conditional statements; that is

```
if <condition> then <statement>
            and
if <condition> then <statement>
            else <statement>
```

Any dangling **else**, an **else** which follows a sequence of "**if** . . . **then if** . . . **then** . . .," is paired with the innermost **if**.

When working with records, partial ad-

Listing 1: The Polish "compiler" listing. Notice that Pascal does not constrict the format of the program line. Indentation allows the program blocks to be easily separated from each other and makes the program easier to read.

```
PROGRAM PARSE(INPUT,OUTPUT);
(*PROGRAM PARSES SIMPLE ARITHMETIC EXPRESSIONS
  INTO THEIR RESPECTIVE POLISH CODE.  IT DOES
  THE PROPER TYPE CONVERSIONS NECESSARY FOR
  REAL AND INTEGER EXPRESSIONS ACCORDING TO
  THE FORTRAN CONVENTION:
        REAL: A-H, O-Z
        INTEGER: I-N
  VARIABLES ARE ONE LETTER LONG*)
LABEL 99; (*FOR ERROR RESTART*)
CONST
  DONTCARE='?'; (*MARKERS FOR CODE GENERATOR*)
  MAXPC=100;      (*MAXIMUM CODE SPACE*)
TYPE
  CODESPACE=1..MAXPC;  (*ADDRESS SPACE*)
  ATTR=(NONE,INT,REA); (*ATTRIBUTES OF OPCODES AND EXPRESSIONS*)
  LEXTY=(ADDOP,MULOP,LPAREN,RPAREN,IDENT,EOL);
            (*THESE LEXEMES FOR INPUT ASSUME A NON-HOSTILE USER*)
  INSTRUCTION=RECORD
                OPC:CHAR; (*OPCODE*)
                ITYPE:ATTR; (*OPCODE TYPE*)
                ADR:CHAR   (*NAME OF IDENT*)
              END;
VAR
  CODE:ARRAY[CODESPACE] OF INSTRUCTION; (*WHERE CODE GOES*)
  PC:CODESPACE; (*PC OF CURRENT INSTRUCTION*)
  GATTR:ATTR; (*GLOBAL TYPE OF EXPRESSIONS*)
  CH:CHAR;    (*CURRENT INPUT CHARACTER*)
  CHTYPE:ATTR; (*CURRENT CHARACTER ATTRIBUTE IF IDENT*)
  LEX:LEXTY;  (*LEXEME OF CURRENT INPUT*)
  BFR:PACKED ARRAY[1..80] OF CHAR; (*INPUT BUFFER*)
  BP:INTEGER; (*CHARACTER BUFFER POINTER*)
PROCEDURE SCAN; (*PROCESS NEXT INPUT CHARACTER*)
  BEGIN
    REPEAT
      BP:=BP+1;
      CH:=BFR[BP]
    UNTIL CH#' ';
    (*WORRY ABOUT END OF LINE*)
    IF ORD(CH)=0
      THEN LEX:=EOL
      ELSE
        IF CH IN ['A'..'Z']
          THEN
            BEGIN
              LEX:=IDENT;
              IF CH IN ['I'..'N']
                THEN CHTYPE:=INT
                ELSE CHTYPE:=REA
            END
          ELSE
            CASE CH OF
              '(': LEX:=LPAREN;
              ')': LEX:=RPAREN;
              '+','-': LEX:=ADDOP;
              '*','/': LEX:=MULOP
            END
  END (*OF SCAN*);
PROCEDURE ERROR;
  BEGIN
    WRITELN(' ':BP+1,'↑ ERROR'); (*COMPENSATE FOR USER PROMPT*)
    GOTO 99
  END (*OF ERROR*);
PROCEDURE GENCODE(F:CHAR; I:ATTR; A:CHAR);
  BEGIN PC:=PC+1;
    IF PC>MAXPC
      THEN BEGIN WRITELN('OVERFLOW');ERROR END;
    WITH CODE[PC] DO (*INDEX INSTRUCTION*)
      BEGIN OPC:=F;ITYPE:=I;ADR:=A END
  END (*OF GENCODE*);
PROCEDURE LISTCODE;
  VAR LPC:CODESPACE;
  BEGIN
    FOR LPC:=1 TO PC DO
      WITH CODE[LPC] DO BEGIN (*INDEX INSTRUCTION*)
        CASE OPC OF
          '+': WRITE('ADD');
          '-': WRITE('SUB');
          '@': WRITE('NEG');
          '*': WRITE('MUL');
          '/': WRITE('DIV');
          'F': WRITE('FLOAT');
          'P': WRITE('PUSH') END;
        IF OPC#'F'
          THEN
            BEGIN
              IF ITYPE=INT THEN WRITE('I') ELSE WRITE('R')
            END;
        IF OPC='P' THEN WRITELN(CHR(11B),ADR) ELSE WRITELN
      END (*OF WITH AND FOR*)
  END (*OF LISTCODE*);
```

```
PROCEDURE FIXUP(AX:CODESPACE;      (*PC OF FIX LOCATION OF OPERAND 1*)
               LOP:CHAR;           (*CURRENT OPERATOR*)
               LATTR:ATTR);        (*ATTRIBUTE OF OPERAND 2*)
  VAR TPC:CODESPACE;
  BEGIN
    IF GATTR#LATTR   (*TYPES DON'T AGREE*)
      THEN
        BEGIN
          IF GATTR=INT  (*FLOAT OPERAND 2*)
            THEN BEGIN GENCODE('F',NONE,DONTCARE);GATTR:=REA END
            ELSE  (*HAVE TO FLOAT OPERAND 1, MOVE CODE UP*)
              BEGIN
                IF PC=MAXPC THEN BEGIN WRITELN('OVERFLOW');ERROR END;
                FOR TPC:=PC DOWNTO AX DO CODE[TPC+1]:=CODE[TPC];
                PC:=PC+1;  (*TOOK ANOTHER WORD*)
                CODE[AX].OPC:='F'   (*FLOAT OPERAND 1*)
              END
        END;
    GENCODE(LOP,GATTR,DONTCARE)  (*GENERATE OPERATION*)
  END (*OF FIXUP*);
PROCEDURE EXPR;  (*HERE IS ALL THE WORK*)
  VAR
    LOP:CHAR;       (*CURRENT ADDOP*)
    LATTR:ATTR;     (*ATTRIBUTE OF OPERAND 2*)
    AXPC:CODESPACE; (*WHERE FLOAT OF OPERAND 1 GOES, IF NEEDED*)
  PROCEDURE TERM;
    VAR
      LOP:CHAR;       (*CURRENT MULOP*)
      LATTR:ATTR;     (*ATTRIBUTE OF OPERAND 2*)
      AXPC:CODESPACE; (*WHERE FLOAT OF OPERAND 1 GOES, IF NEEDED*)
    PROCEDURE FACTOR;
      BEGIN
        IF LEX=IDENT   (*IDENTIFIER*)
          THEN
            BEGIN
              GATTR:=CHTYPE;
              GENCODE('P',GATTR,CH);
              SCAN
            END
          ELSE
            IF LEX=LPAREN
              THEN
                BEGIN
                  SCAN;EXPR;
                  IF LEX=RPAREN THEN SCAN ELSE ERROR
                END
              ELSE ERROR   (*JUNK INPUT*)
      END (*OF FACTOR*);
    BEGIN (*OF TERM*)
      FACTOR;
      WHILE LEX=MULOP DO
        BEGIN
          LATTR:=GATTR; LOP:=CH;
          AXPC:=PC+1; (*SAVE ADDR OF NEXT INSTRUCTION*)
          SCAN;FACTOR;
          FIXUP(AXPC,LOP,LATTR)
        END
    END (*OF TERM*);
  BEGIN (*OF EXPR*)
    IF LEX=ADDOP   (*LEADING SIGN*)
      THEN
        BEGIN
          LOP:=CH;SCAN;TERM;
          IF LOP='-' THEN GENCODE('@',GATTR,DONTCARE)
        END
      ELSE TERM;
        WHILE LEX=ADDOP DO
          BEGIN
            LATTR:=GATTR;LOP:=CH;
            AXPC:=PC+1; (*SAVE ADDR OF NEXT INSTRUCTION*)
            SCAN;TERM;
            FIXUP(AXPC,LOP,LATTR)
          END
  END (*OF EXPR*);
BEGIN (*OF MAIN PROGRAM*)
  WHILE TRUE DO (*INFINITE LOOP*)
    BEGIN
99:   REPEAT
        WRITE('>>');  (*PROMPT USER*)
        BP:=0;  (*GET INPUT LINE*)
        WHILE NOT EOLN DO
          BEGIN
            BP:=BP+1;READ(BFR[BP])
          END;
        READLN (*RESET EOL INDICATOR*)
      UNTIL BP#1; (*GET A NON-EMPTY LINE*)
      BFR[BP]:=CHR(0); (* <NULL> FOR EOL*)
      PC:=0;BP:=0; (*SCAN FROM THE BEGINNING*)
      SCAN;
      EXPR; (*DOES ALL THE WORK*)
      IF LEX=EOL THEN LISTCODE ELSE ERROR
    END
END.
```

dressing can be done by using the "**with**" statement. This allows the fields of a record to be referenced as variables. The previous example then becomes

```
for ind:=1 to 100 do
  with database[ind] do
    begin
      due:=1.006*bal;
      bal:=0.0;
      sum:=sum+due;
      bal30:=1.006*bal30+due
    end
```

Three additional control statements are the **while**, **repeat**, and **case** statements. The **while** statement allows a given statement to be executed as long as some Boolean expression is true (the condition is tested first).

while <condition> **do** <statement>

The **repeat** statement allows one or more statements to be executed until a condition becomes true (the condition is tested last).

```
repeat <statement> { ;
  <statement> } until <condition>
```

The brackets denote a portion that may occur zero or more times; for example

```
ind:=0;
repeat;
  ind:=ind+1
until (database[ind].bal>100.0) or
  (ind=100)
```

This will find the first customer whose balance is greater than \$100, if one exists.

The **case** statement consists of an expression, known as the selector, and a list of statements, each labelled by one or more constants of the type of the selector. The statements whose constant is equal to the current value of the selector is executed. Some versions of Pascal admit subranges for labels and an **else** or **otherwise** clause within a **case** statement.

```
case database[ind].datedue.mo of
  jan,feb,may:   <statement 1>;
  mar,jun,jul:   <statement 2>;
  oct,dec:       <statement 3>
end
```

Statement 1 will be executed if the due month is January, February, or May, and so on. Notice that no statement is executed if the month is April, August, September, or November. Of course, the nesting of such control statements is permissible and allows much more complex control structures to be implemented.

The **reset** and **rewrite** statements initialize input and output channels, respectively. Some versions of Pascal do not require these for the default channels input and output. The IO commands are designed at two levels. To move primitive data to and from IO devices or files use the commands put or get respectively. To input or output an entire line or set of data we use **read**, **readln**, **write**, and **writeln** which are similar to FORTRAN IO commands. Formatting is done within the commands themselves. The **read** command will only input the necessary information (even if it must read several lines) while **readln** additionally discards the remainder of the current input line. The output commands, **write** and **writeln**, operate in an analogous fashion for output.

A significant example is now in order. Consider the problem of compiling an arithmetic expression. To greatly simplify the problem, assume all variables are one letter in length, no constants will appear, and the only operators will be +, −, *, and /. To make the problem interesting, assume that variables lettered a–h and o–z are of type **real** and the rest are of type **integer**. This is the same as the implicit types for FORTRAN. The program will produce code for a "stack machine." That is, the operators are applied only to operands already on the stack and the result will replace the operands on the stack. One task is the recognition of correct expressions. This may be done by several methods including precedence tables, LALR(1) parsers, and recursive descent. The latter will be used since it is the technique employed within most Pascal compilers. Recursive descent compilation utilizes a set of recursive procedures to recognize its input, with no backtracking. To understand the algorithm, consider the series of "syntax diagrams" in figure 1.

To generate a valid expression, for example, one enters the diagram from the left, selects an arbitrary path through the diagram, and exits to the right. Any box encountered is to be treated like a subroutine or procedure call. A circle or box with rounded edges is to be the current input item. An expression is thus an optional sign, a term, followed by any number (including zero) of addition or subtraction operators and terms. Similarly, one can define a term. These definitions build in the normal precedence of operators and correctly handle a unary minus. Notice that <expr> will call <term>, <term> will call <factor> and maybe <factor> will call <expr> again. This would occur whenever parentheses were encountered.

A second task to accomplish is to properly handle the necessary type conversion of intermediate results. Many textbooks refer to this problem when discussing syntax directed translation but few illustrate "real" solutions. As an example (using the above assumptions) consider

    J + K * X

It is not known that this expression must

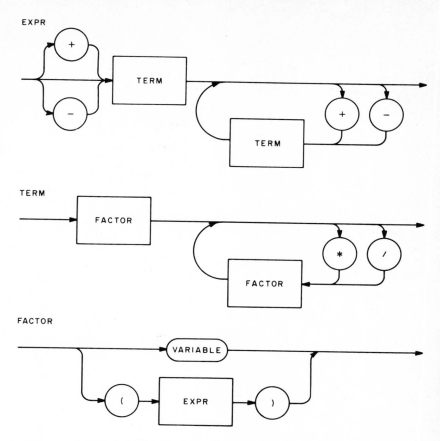

Figure 1: Syntax diagrams for generation of valid expressions. The diagram "expr" is entered from the left and calls term. Term calls "factor" which may call expr, etc. This model assumes that the only operations are addition, subtraction, multiplication and division.

have a real value until the X is seen. The recursive descent phase, independent of type conversion might translate this to

    PUSH J
    PUSH K
    PUSH X
    MUL
    ADD

for its equivalent Polish Notation: J K X * +. However, what is really required is

    PUSHI J
    FLOAT   (convert the top of the stack)
    PUSHI K
    FLOAT
    PUSHR X
    MULR
    ADDR

where the operators have either "R" or "I" suffixed to indicate a real or integer operator, respectively. The suffix for the PUSH instruction is known as soon as the variable name is seen. The types for the arithmetic operators and the insertion of the FLOAT instructions must be added somewhat after both operands have been seen; in other words, a fixup must be done. As one alternative, this may be accomplished by generating code in memory and keeping track of

An expression is an optional sign, a term, followed by any number of addition or subtraction operators and terms.

```
>>A+B
PUSHR    A
PUSHR    B
ADDR
>>A/I
PUSHR    A
PUSHI    I
FLOAT
DIVR
>>I/J
PUSHI    I
PUSHI    J
DIVI
>>J+K*X
PUSHI    J
FLOAT
PUSHI    K
FLOAT
PUSHR    X
MULR
ADDR
>>(I*J-(X+M))/(P+N)
PUSHI    I
PUSHI    J
MULI
FLOAT
PUSHR    X
PUSHI    M
FLOAT
ADDR
SUBR
PUSHR    P
PUSHI    N
FLOAT
ADDR
DIVR
>>A+B*
         ↑ ERROR
>>A*(B+I
           ↑ ERROR
>>I)*B
       ↑ ERROR
>>ZI
       ↑ ERROR
```

Listing 2: Sample program execution. After outputting a prompt the program waits for an expression to be input. It then lists all of the instructions that would be generated for a compiler code.

the type attribute of each operand and the addresses of where the last instruction for that operand was stored. If a type conversion is required on the first operand (of a binary operator), all code beyond the saved address is simply moved up one location and a FLOAT instruction is inserted. If a type conversion is required for the second operand, a FLOAT instruction is added as the last instruction in the evaluation of the second operand. *[In this paragraph and remaining text of the article, words in upper case refer to listing 1 . . . RGAC]*

The program in listing 1 is a solution to the expression evaluation problem. It is a direct implementation of the methods suggested. The main portion of the program is trivial; it asks for a line of input, calls procedure EXPR to parse the line, lists the output if there is no error, and repeats the process.

The type statements are important and quite varied. See that the constant MAXPC defines the maximum address space and is used in the declaration of the subrange type CODESPACE. The variables ATTR and LEXTY are symbolic scalar types and

INSTRUCTION is a record type.

The variable CODE is an array of instructions. This is where the "compiled" code will reside. The type attribute of the second operand of an operation is stored in GATTR which is global to all the program's procedures.

The procedure SCAN picks up the next character(s), ignoring spaces and determines the correct token and type if it is a variable. Note the use of the case statement and the sequential nested conditionals.

The procedure ERROR outputs a line with an upward pointing arrow to indicate where the error occurred.

The procedures GENCODE and LIST-CODE are responsible for encoding the instructions into the code array and decoding the code array for output respectively. The **with** statements simplify both the Pascal and compiled codes.

Any discrepancy in types of operands is resolved by FIXUP which inserts the code for the operator itself. In a full compiler, FIXUP would also worry about strings and other data types and issue the appropriate error messages when needed.

EXPR does most of the work, together with the procedures TERM and FACTOR. They function exactly as described above. They are quite simple in appearance but function correctly as the sample runs illustrate. The symbolic scalars ADDOP and MULOP are quite useful in this design.

When properly segmented, any program should be similarly constructed and as easy to read or modify. A lot may be gained from using a top down design. Given the time, anyone could stretch this program into a full compiler whose output was a similar Polish code, and alternatively encode this program into their favorite assembly language. All the hard work has really been done in expressing the algorithm to solve the problem.

I heartily recommend that anyone seriously interested in Pascal in particular and good programming style in general obtain the two books listed in the references. ∎

REFERENCES

● Jensen, Kathleen and Wirth, Niklaus, *Pascal: User Manual and Report*, Springer Study Edition (2nd Edition), Springer-Verlag, 175 Fifth Av, New York NY 10010, 1975.

● Wirth, Niklaus, *Algorithms + Data Structures = Programs*, Prentice-Hall, Englewood Cliffs NJ 07632, 1976.

Compilation and Pascal

on the New Microprocessors

Charles H Forsyth

Randall J Howard

We are concerned with the use of high level languages, and in particular Pascal, on microcomputer systems. We are most interested in the use of such languages for what is termed, on larger computer systems, *systems programming*. This includes writing code to drive floppy disks, interpreters for APL or BASIC, or all those bits of code that people have until now written in assembler, and which in some way make their microcomputer systems friendly.

Microcomputer users show a generally high level of sophistication, so it might be surprising at first that so much of their code is still written in assembler. The advantages of writing in a high level language have been often described in computing literature: programs can be made more portable; they exhibit better structure; and they are easier to write and debug. In addition, it is much easier to let a compiler worry about the efficiency of the object code; and deficiencies of the object machine are hidden. With the 8 bit microcomputers like the Intel 8080 and Motorola 6800, we feel that there is little choice but to write in assembler (or interpreter), since the facilities provided by their order codes are simply insufficient to support most high level languages.

Compilation may be inappropriate for 8 bit microcomputers, but it is the most attractive alternative for the hybrid 8 and 16 bit microcomputers (such as the Motorola 6809), especially with respect to eliminating most assembly code on these machines. We also feel that Pascal has facilities that enable a compiler to generate better code for such

machines than might be expected from compilers for other languages.

Jensen and Wirth provide the definition of and tutorial introduction to Pascal in the *Pascal User Manual and Report*. Aho and Ullman's book, *Principles of Compiler Construction*, provides an excellent description of the elements of a compiler.

Options

Tiny BASIC, Tiny C, APL, and FOCAL are implemented on microcomputers with interpretive code. Interpretation has a number of advantages. Since the interpretive language is highly specialized, it can be made compact. New *macro operations* can be added easily as time and experience dictate. Array and structure addressing and the block copying associated with array and structure assignment may be made particularly cheap. When interpreting array indexing, run time checks of the index values against the array bounds are possible (although often left out) at little extra cost. This is true of other kinds of debugging facilities as well, such as value traces or stack tracebacks. Both compiler and interpreter are easy to write, especially if the interpreted code implements a stack machine. Interpretation's main disadvantage is that it is slow.

An alternative to interpretation that alleviates this latter problem of speed somewhat is *threaded code*, which has been described as "interpretive code which needs no interpreter" (see references 2 and 3). Rather than having a sequence of codes and

The listings in this article were prepared by arrangement with Walter Banks of the University of Waterloo.

```
type
        index = 0..10;
        twiceIndex = 0..20;
        unsigned = 0..32767;
        short = −128..127;
        shortUnsigned = 0..255;
        thing = record
                        field1: 0..7;
                        field2: 0..31
                end;
        packedThing = packed record
                        field1: 0..7;
                        field2: 0..31;
                end;
var
        a, b: array [index] of integer;
        i, j: index;
        k: twiceIndex;

        s: set of (READY, BLOCKED, RUNNING, SWAPIN, SWAPOUT);
begin
        a[i] := b[j];           {the dreaded array-indexing example}

        k := i+j;               {subranges are useful}

        s := [READY, BLOCKED, RUNNING];{set operations}
        s := s − [READY, RUNNING];
        s := s + [SWAPIN];
        s := s * [SWAPIN, BLOCKED];

end
```

Listing 1: Pascal program fragment for array indexing.

```
tsx                     /Enable indexing off sp
lda     A, j(X)         /Fetch address of j relative..
lda     B, j+1(X)       /to sp into (A,B) register pair
asl     B               /Shift (AB) pair left by 1..
rol     A               /yielding integer offset
add     B, b+1(X)       /Add in 16-bit array
adc     A, b(X)         /pointer i to (A,B) pair
sta     A, temp         /Transfer (A,B) pair to X reg..
sta     B, temp+1       /..not re-entrant
ldx     temp
lda     A, 0(X)         /Finally, fetch b[j] into..
lda     B, 1(X)         /(A,B) pair..
psh     A               /and push onto stack
psh     B
tsx                     /Following code is repeat of..
lda     A, i(X)         /above for getting address of..
lda     B, i+1(X)       /array element a[i]
asl     B
rol     A
add     B, a+1(X)
adc     A, a(X)
sta     A, temp
sta     B, temp+1
ldx     temp            /X now points at a[i]
pul     B               /Pop b[j] from stack..
pul     A               /into (A,B) pair..
sta     A, 0(X)         /and store in a[i]
sta     B, 1(X)
```

Total code: 52 bytes

Listing 2: Motorola 6800 assembly code for the first line of the Pascal fragment shown in listing 1.

an interpreter which reads them, calling out to the routines implementing each operation, threaded code simply contains the sequence of machine addresses of the routines to process each operation. These routines, much like the code segments called by the interpreter to implement the pseudo-machine, provide the run time support for the threaded code. Rather than return to an interpreter after it has done its work, though, a routine simply jumps (indirectly) to the next such routine in the code flow. Arguments are passed to these routines in various ways — for example, by placing values or addresses between the code pointers.

The third approach to language implementation is that traditionally adopted on larger machines: real code generation. This approach provides the fastest program execution at the possible expense of space used by the object code. On almost any machine, the high level constructs of flow of control and logical expressions as well as calls to the intrinsic built-in functions can be directly implemented as branch or jump instructions with relatively little expenditure of speed or time. However, for many of the existing microcomputers, code generation for even the simplest of the fundamental high level language constructs proves effectively impossible. Such constructs include most common arithmetic operations, array and structure accessing, and automatic storage manipulation. Particularly difficult on some machines are multiply, divide, modulus and string operations. Therefore it is important to determine what properties of a particular machine make it suitable for real code generation.

8 Bit Microcomputers

A detailed study of the common 8 bit computers available today (eg: Motorola 6800, Intel 8080) quickly reveals that such machines are not conducive to real code generation by compilers for high level languages such as Pascal.

On such machines, compilations of even the simplest arithmetic or pointer expressions lead to a very high object to source code ratio, if such constructs can be compiled at all. Listing 2 gives an example of code which might be compiled for a Motorola 6800 to implement the Pascal assignment statement: a[i]:=b[j]; in listing 1. The assumption here is that automatic arrays are implemented as pointers on the stack to areas of storage residing elsewhere. In addition, we have assumed that the compiler keeps track of the stack offsets for its automatic variables relative to the moving stack pointer; we are using the notation j to represent the stack offset of variable j. In addition to this code segment, the procedure preamble must set up the pointers to the arrays a and b (stored at offsets *a* and *b* respectively), to point at the integer before the beginning of the array. Thus, for example, *a[1]* will then be identified with the beginning of the storage associated with the array a.

Beyond the actual code shown here, however, the most important insight to be gained from all of this is the sheer bulk of code that such a simple construct would generate (and it is not even reentrant at that). Imagine how large the object code size would be for even a reasonably short Pascal program.

Implementing threaded code is somewhat difficult on these machines because they require 16 bit memory pointers, an efficient mechanism for indirect addressing, and some method of incrementing such a pointer to the next 16 bit pointer. At least one of the above criteria is so troublesome on both the Motorola 6800 and the Intel 8080 that the threaded code becomes unwieldy. Thus, for these machines one has little choice but to interpret or write in assembler. This suggests that the interpreters themselves must be implemented in assembly language.

The above discussion is an attempt to analyze the reasons why programs written for 8 bit microcomputers have traditionally been interpreted or written in assembly or machine code, rather than being compiled into "true" code from a high level language.

16 Bit Microcomputers

Previously, the only alternative to the 8 bit architecture was that of the 16 bit microcomputer. Examples of such machines include the TI-990/4 and the DEC LSI-11. While the considerable costs of these processors tend to make them impractical for many computer experimenters, and for those applications in which many processors are required, it is instructive to consider what properties set these machines apart from their 8 bit counterparts with respect to code generation. In fact, it can be shown that, given a machine of sufficient sophistication, it should be possible for a compiler to do as good a job as an assembler programmer vis-à-vis machine resource utilization.

There are two main virtues of these 16 bit machines. In the first place, these machines have complete 16 bit instruction repertoires including hardware multiplication, division, and long shifts. As well, the 16 bit processors tend to have a good complement of addressing modes such as indexing, stack operations, automatic increment and decrement of pointers, and so on. (Here, as elsewhere in this article, the descriptive terms may seem fuzzy. *Good complement* does not admit of

Let

$$r := \{ X, Y, S, U \}$$
$$a := \{ A, B, D \}$$
$$x := \text{memory reference}$$
$$c := \text{constant value}$$

x	long relative, short relative, direct
$*x$	long & short relative indirect
$\$x$	immediate byte
$*\$x$	extended
$**\$x$	extended indirect
$c(r)$	±4, ±7, ±15 bit indexing
$*c(r)$	±7 and ±15 bit indirect indexing
$(r)+$	Auto Increment by 1 or 2
$-(r)$	Auto Decrement by 1 or 2
$*(r)+$	Indirect Auto Increment by 2
$*-(r)$	Indirect Auto Decrement by 2
$a(r)$	Accumulator Indexing
$*a(r)$	Indirect Accumulator Indexing

Table 1: A summary of the Motorola MC6809 addressing modes.

a precise meaning. With real machines, one usually loses clever addressing modes, for plenty of general purpose registers, and one must balance the benefits somehow. The final judgment will usually be that of the person writing the compiler.) With these attributes, it is a fairly straightforward task to construct a compiler for a high level language such as Pascal.

8 and 16 Bit Hybrids

The current trend in 8 bit microprocessor technology is towards a hybrid combination 8 and 16 bit machine. Essentially, these processors are capable of 16 bit operations while retaining 8 bit data paths throughout the processor architecture. A prime example of such a hybrid is the Motorola 6809, which is due for formal product release later this year. Table 1 gives a summary of the basic addressing capabilities of the Motorola 6809, expressed in a hypothetical assembler syntax which removes from the user the burden of understanding all of the details of the actual hardware addressing modes.

What advantages do these machines have over their pure 8 bit predecessors? In particular, these machines now have at least one accumulator for performing addition, subtraction, shifting and comparison operations on 16 bit data. A second feature of these machines is the 16 bit memory pointer, which, combined with the ability to automatically increment and decrement such pointers, provides a very general memory accessing capability. In addition, common high level language features such as stack frames and display pointers become quite easy with the general index and stack registers of the M6809. It is apparent that the Motorola 6809 is particularly well-endowed with addressing modes which tend to facilitate code generation for high level languages.

Consider again the array assignment which the 6800 handled so dismally. The Motorola 6809 code for the same construct is given in listing 3. (Note that the syntax of our assembler code is intended to be more or less consistent amongst the examples, and not necessarily that of the manufacturer's assembler. It is in fact the syntax used by our UNIX assemblers for these machines.) Code for the PDP-11/45, considered to be a good instruction set given in listing 4, is included for comparison.

It is rather precipitous to deduce much from this one example, although array indexing does exercise many of the addressing modes of a machine, and such assignment statements can provide a check on the register usage of a compiler. How a particular architecture fares with more general arithmetic expressions and function and procedure call, save, and return sequences would provide further basis of comparison. Indeed, other examples that we have tried suggest that the results of this comparison are typical.

```
/ 'X' points to top of stack (display)
lda     D, i(X)         / i
asl     B
rol     A               / *2
add     D, $a-2         / +offset of 'a'
lea     Y, D(X)         / +stack top
lda     D, j(X)         / j
asl     B
rol     A               / *2
add     D, $b-2         / +offset of 'b'
lda     D, D(X)         / +stack top
sta     D, (Y)          / a[i] := b[j]
```

Total code: 20 bytes

Listing 3: Motorola MC6809 assembly code for array indexing program fragment.

```
/ r5 points to the "top" of the
/ stack frame
mov     j(r5),r0        /j
asl     r0              / *2
add     r5,r0           /+ display pointer
mov     i(r5),r1        /i
asl     r1              / *2
add     r5,r1           /+ display pointer
mov     b-2(r0),a-2(r1)         / a[i] := b[j];
```

Total code: 22 bytes

Lisitng 4: DEC PDP-11 assembly code for array indexing example.

Special Advantages of Pascal

We feel that the use of Pascal and a competent compiler can lead to better code in many cases on hybrid 8 and 16 bit machines than can be achieved with many other languages. Obviously, the best results will require that Pascal be properly used — that subranges be used where possible, for example — and that these be declared to be as small as possible. A Pascal program can contain a great deal of information that allows even a straightforward compiler to generate code which makes good use of the available registers. The Pascal declarations of listing 1 provide illustration for the following discussion, and the code given is for the Motorola 6809. Remember that the intent is not to describe an implementation of Pascal.

The declaration of scalar and subrange types essentially allows the declaration of *small* integers and makes known the detailed characteristics of variables of such types to the compiler. Variables may thus be completely bounded, and the compiler can compute upper and lower bounds on the value of an expression.

In our example, variables of type *short* or *shortUnsigned* may be loaded into the 8 bit accumulators of the 6809, and both registers may be used simultaneously. A variable may be recognized as *unsigned* if there are no negative values in the subrange to which it belongs. In the assignment statement $k := i+j$; the variables i, and j, are both in the range 0 thru 10. The result is thus in the range 0 thru 20, and an 8 bit accumulator may again be used to compute this result. (All of this is particularly useful if array indexing is also involved.)

The Pascal *set* type may be regarded as providing a readable way to do "bit twiddling." A set is typically implemented as a sequence of bits, one for each element of the base type of the set. The variable s might then be a byte in which the low order bit corresponds to the element READY, the next to BLOCKED, and so on. The sequence of assignments might then be compiled as in listing 5.

Pascal, of course, provides pointers, **record** structures and arrays.

The use of pointers is strictly controlled: arbitrary arithmetic operations on pointers are not allowed. About the only things that may be done with a pointer variable are: indirect addressing, assigning another pointer to it, or passing it to a procedure or function. This structured use of pointers and indexing results in a very stylized use of pointers in the compiler's internal representation. This in turn allows the compiler to detect the places where double indexing may be used to advantage rather easily, on machines like the 6809 which have this feature.

Indexing of an array of records does require multiplication of the index by the width, in bytes, of the record. Often, this may be accomplished by a shift. Of course, this cannot always be done, since records need not be a power of 2 in length, though a compiler could arrange to round the size of a record up to an appropriate boundary if the difference were small. In any event, provided the size of the record is no more than eight bits (as an unsigned quantity), the code for the multiplication could reasonably be included in line.

We wondered how often division or multiplication is used in the UNIX system (an operating system developed at Bell Labs), and wrote a simple command file which would compile each of the source programs of the system and scan the resulting assembler for *mul* and *div* instructions. The number of multiplications was of interest in light of the above discussion; the number of divisions was collected as well, since these would have to be interpreted by subroutine on the 6809, and we wanted to know how many occurred in critical code. The results are shown in table 2.

Only one of the divide instructions occurs in a routine that might be regarded as significant, with respect to increasing system overhead, were a subroutine called to do the divide piecemeal; and that division was performed at a low priority level. 31 of the divide instructions in the device driver routines were in disk drivers, which had to compute track and cylinder offsets. The multiplications in all cases were of small amounts; it seems that (most likely by accident) record structures used in the kernel happened to be a power of 2 in length. It would have been more instructive, perhaps, to examine user programs, but in that case it would have been more difficult to separate multiplications written explicitly from those created implicitly by array indexing.

A Pascal programmer may declare particular record or array types as *packed*, which is a hint to the compiler that the programmer would prefer elements of the given type to occupy as little space as possible even if there is a cost in increased code to access them. This leaves the unit of packing to the compiler. For example, the types *thing* and *packedThing* (see listing 1) describe packed and unpacked records with similar fields (to Pascal, these record types are not compatible in any way). In a *thing*, both *field1* and *field2* will likely be bytes, but if a compiler implements the notion *packed* completely, then in a *packedThing*, *field1* will likely occupy three bits, and *field2* five bits, ie: they would share the same byte of storage. Packing of records on microcomputers is

```
/ X is display pointer
/ equates are in octal
READY = 01
BLOCKED = 02
RUNNING = 04
SWAPIN = 010
SWAPOUT = 020
lda      A, $READY+BLOCKED+RUNNING / immediate load
sta      A, s(X)
/
lda      A, s(X)
anda     A, $![READY+RUNNING]  / complement
sta      A, s(X)
/
lda      A, s(X)
ora      A, $SWAPIN
sta      A, s(X)
/
lda      A, s(X)
anda     A, $[SWAPIN+BLOCKED]
sta      A, s(X)
```

Listing 5: Set assignment code for the Motorola MC6809 processor.

often much easier than on the larger processors, because microprocessors do not have the alignment problems that plague compiler writers on those machines.

Finally, as in many other languages, the order of evaluation of expressions is left to the implementor, but since side effects are not allowed, no legal Pascal program can possibly be harmed by this. This has two related effects: in arithmetic expressions, the compiler may evaluate the operands in the order that leads to the least amount of code, and in Boolean expressions the left-hand side of the logical operators *and* and *or* need not be evaluated if the expressions on the right determines the truth value of the entire expression. Faster or smaller code will usually result if a compiler takes advantage of these properties.

Pascal: Problems?

We feel that there are a number of areas where Pascal is likely to require expensive mechanisms, and which would be inappropriate for a systems programming environment. One solution might be to implement a subset of the language, leaving these hard

Section	Lines of C Code	Number of Multiplications	Number of Divisions
UNIX Kernel	6,013	4	9
Device Drivers	8,640	62	41

Table 2: A search through a particular operating system to determine the number of multiplications and divisions used. This was done to determine how important the speed of a multiplication and division routine would be to a typical program.

features aside, but in most cases, since the expensive mechanisms are only invoked if the programmer asks for them, it should be sufficient to have the compiler avoid including the associated run time procedures when they are not requested. (This is worth mentioning, if only because this rule is often not followed.) We shall first mention those constructs which are expensive, but which appear only by programmer request.

The semantics of Pascal's *file* variables, and the input/output (IO) system in general tend to reflect characteristics of a batch environment, with a restricted character set. The basic IO procedures are badly designed for an interactive terminal. The *read* and *write* procedures are fairly expensive to implement, since they are extremely general and all encompassing.

On machines like the 6809 which lack a divide instruction of any sort (let alone a 16 bit one), division will be done by calling a run time support routine. Only if the programmer explicitly writes either a divide, or modulus operation, will the call be generated. Floating point numbers will be interpreted, as usual.

Pascal allows procedures and functions to be defined inside other procedures and functions. This requires either a display, which must be copied, or a system of pointers by which a routine may access the variables owned by routines in an outer scope. (The latter is the most likely choice.)

Strings, arrays, records and large sets (if implemented) may all be assigned or passed as parameters to routines. These operations require block copies, but only if the operations appear in the source program. Copying of actual parameters may be avoided, of course, by declaring the matching formal parameters as *var* parameters.

The remaining points concern some philosophical concerns about Pascal and its implementation. (Input and output might also be considered in this class.)

Philosophy

It has been observed that much of the checking done at run time in other languages may be done at compile time in Pascal. This is not always so, and run time checks are required on assignments of a variable from a larger subrange to a variable in a smaller subrange of a given type, or on similar use in array indexing, and pointers must always be checked to ensure that they are not *nil*. It might be argued that run time checks might not be done at all. It is better to arrange for them to be turned on and off, as required, in different sections of code.

The *Pascal Report* (see references) does not put boundaries on the number of ele-

ments in the base type of a *set* type, but it does say that an implementor will likely choose the word length of a given computer as that limit. Otherwise, routines are required to perform various Boolean operations on large bit strings. Unfortunately, a great many Pascal programs in existence, most notably those for the CDC 6600, assume that it is possible to delcare or use a *set of char*, as in:

> if *c* in [*'a'*..*'z'*] then
> { c is a letter }

where *c* is declared as a *char*. The CDC Pascal compiler restricts the number of elements in the base type of a set to about the number of bits in a word (58), but the CDC character set is small enough that it (nearly) fits within a **set**. On a microcomputer with the ASCII character set even 16 bits is clearly insufficient, and larger sets may need to be implemented.

There is no method provided to initialize variables in their declaration. This is of consequence when one wishes to create a table with values that remain constant throughout the life of the program (eg: a translation table). The only way to do this in standard Pascal is to write a sequence of assignment statements. This will typically result in several bytes of code for each assignment, as well as forcing two copies of each data value in the table. On a large machine like the CDC 6600, this may be of little consequence, but on a microcomputer with little core, this is a distinct disadvantage. Of course, various implementations of Pascal have provided a means to do this sort of thing efficiently, but this results in a portability problem because each implementor tends to have slightly different rules about where and how these initializations may be accomplished.

Conclusions

For languages like Pascal, compilation is the preferred method of implementation on hybrid 8 and 16 bit microprocessors. The object code size on these machines for common constructs in these languages seems to compare quite favorably with that for larger processors like the PDP-11 or the Honeywell 66/60. We illustrated this with a very simple array operation; the reader can try other operations.

When choosing a programming language, one typically considers not only the ease or difficulty of implementation and the efficiency of the compiled code, but stylistic qualities as well. For example, we have found the C language a pleasant and effective language for developing programs, but it does not, of course, follow that everyone else would. The same holds true for Pascal.

We merely note that the Pascal is interesting, in that Pascal programs may be so written as to allow a compiler to compile code which makes efficient use of 8 bit accumulators on machines that have them, and that amongst the other major high level languages this is an unusual property (PL/I is a likely exception). Whatever the language used, we hope to see the day when on microcomputer systems, as on UNIX, the use of assembly language for a program of any size is greeted with surprise, shock, despair, dismay, and outright hostility.■

REFERENCES

1. Jensen, K and Wirth, N, *Pascal User Manual and Report*, Springer-Verlag, New York 1975.
2. Bell, JR, "Threaded Code," *CACM*, volume 16, number 6, June 1973, pages 370 thru 372.
3. Dewer, RBK, "Indirect Threaded Code," *CACM,* volume 18, number 6, June 1975, pages 330 thru 331.
4. Aho, AV, and Ullman, JD, *Principles of Compiler Construction,* Addison-Wesley, Don Mills, Ontario 1977.
5. *990 Computer Family Systems Handbook*, manual number 945250-9701, Texas Instruments, Austin TX 1976.
6. *LSI11 PDP11/03 Processor Handbook*, Digital Equipment Corp, Maynard MA 1975.
7. *M6800 Microprocessor Programming Manual*, Motorola Semiconductor Products, Phoenix AZ 1975.
8. Kernighan, BW, and Ritchie, DM, *The C Programming Language,* Prentice-Hall, Englewood Cliffs NJ 1978.
9. Thompson, KL, and Ritchie, DM, "The UNIX Time-Sharing System," *CACM*, volume 17, number 7, July 1974, pages 365 thru 375.
10. *Honeywell 66/60 Macro Assembly Program*, Honeywell Information Systems, Phoenix AZ 1972.
11. Wiles, et al, "Compatibility Cures Growing Pains of Microcomputer Family," *Electronics*, 2 February 1978.
12. *M6809 Advanced Microprocessor,* Motorola, Austin TX.

Pascal versus BASIC:

An Exercise

Allan Schwartz

Introduction

Pascal is one of the newest high level languages on the personal computing scene. Pascal has been accepted at many universities for several years. It is being used more and more in industry outside of education, and has just recently been introduced in microcomputers. Why is there so much enthusiasm about Pascal?

Pascal is a general purpose language, the product of the long evolution of computer languages. It has a simple but elegant syntax and has been implemented in both large systems (CDC 6000, IBM 360 and 370, Burroughs 6700, etc) and microcomputers (LSI-11, 8080, 8085 and Z-80).

Historical Background

Just as computer hardware has been continuously evolving during the past 25 years, so too have computer software requirements. Originally, computers were employed to work on mathematical tasks such as solving ballistics problems, or generating tables of logarithms. Later it became economically feasible to use computers for data processing or working with voluminous amounts of data such as census data or bank statements. Recently we have seen computers participate in various customized, dedicated applications like the control of traffic lights, microwave ovens and automobile ignitions.

We have seen a variety of applications and language requirements lead to an evolution of computer languages. "Programming" originally entailed the translation of simple algorithms into machine code and bit by bit loading of the computer's memory via the front panel. Later, assembly languages were used, followed by equation or formula translators such as FORTRAN. When it was discovered that computing involved mostly computing decisions and repetition, the language ALGOL (*ALGO*rithmic *L*anguage) was designed to express algorithms more clearly and conveniently. The need for a language to structure and represent all of the data and files in business data processing applications was filled by COBOL. Today we have Pascal, which has flexible data representations, sufficient flow of control statements to represent algorithms, and a clear, simple syntax making it a favorite for a variety of applications. Pascal is the result of several evolutionary steps in the history of computer languages.

Why is Pascal so appealing? First, it is an expressive language. It has several control structures that make the coding of algorithms very natural. Second, Pascal has flexible data representation.

Expression of Algorithms in Pascal

Figure 1 presents an algorithm to compute the greatest common divisor (GCD) of X and Y. The greatest common divisor of the integers X and Y is the largest integer that will divide evenly into both X and Y. Note that three assertions are stated in the flowchart. The first, a necessary precondition, states that X and Y must be positive integers. The second is a loop invariant such that, when control passes through that path in the flowchart, the GCD(X, Y) is equal to the GCD(A, B). The third, a post condition, states that A is equal to B, which is equal to the result, the GCD(X, Y).

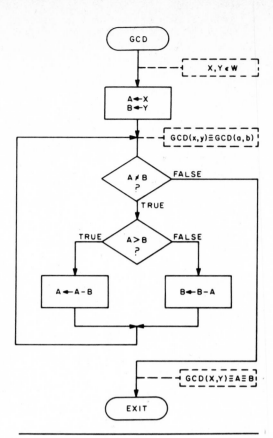

Figure 1: An algorithm to calculate the greatest common divisor (GCD) of two integers. (The greatest common divisor of two integers is the largest integer that will divide evenly into the two integers.)

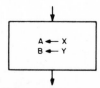

BYTE's use of flowcharts, a top to bottom flow of control is assumed with arrows used for exceptions; in this article we make a stylistic exception, using extra arrows to emphasize flow. . .CH]

The second flowchart element is selection. Selection is represented by:

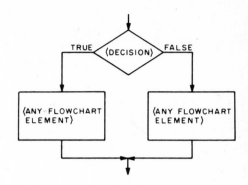

A selection flowchart element requires at least two or three boxes; however, it always has one entry and one exit.

The third flowchart element is repetition. It is represented by:

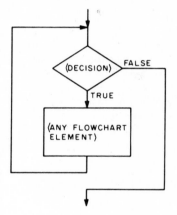

This form of repetition is called a "while loop," because while the decision is true, the element is repeated. Again, this element has one entry and one exit.

These flowchart elements have been translated directly into Pascal statements (see listing 1). Note that the sequence element

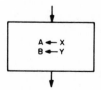

is translated into the two Pascal assignments:

$a := x;$ $b := y$

Now some of the syntax details of Pascal become evident. The assignment operator is $:=$, which is different from the FOR-

If we can prove these three points are true, then the algorithm is correct — that is, it will compute the greatest common divisor of X and Y. The loop invariance is easily proved, because if B is greater than A, the GCD(A,B) equals GCD(A, B−A) (a more rigorous proof is posed as an exercise in Wirth's book [see references]). The post condition is also easy to prove, because the path to this exit is taken only when A equals B, and then the GCD(A, A) certainly equals A.

We are now reassured that if the precondition is true, the algorithm will compute the desired result. Now, how do we code this algorithm into our favorite programming language? Before we answer that question, let's look at the elements of the flowchart. The flowchart in figure 1, and indeed any computable algorithm, is made up of three elements: *sequence, selection* and *repetition*. Sequences are represented in the flowchart by rectangular boxes such as:

Note that this flowchart element has one entry (the arrow going in) and one exit. [*In*

TRAN or BASIC "=" in that the := operator in Pascal is used for assignment only, while the = in BASIC and FORTRAN is used as both the assignment operator and the equals sign. Statements are separated by semicolons, and any number of statements may be typed on one line. If the above sequence were a subelement of a selection element, it would be bracketed by **begin** and **end** keywords. For example:

```
if (x>0) and (y>0) then
    begin  a  := x;  b  := y
    end
```

Any number of elements combined into one sequence element by **begin** and **end** brackets forms a *compound statement*.

The selection flowchart element is translated into the Pascal **if** statement:

```
if a>b then a  := a—b
       else  b  := b—a
```

And the repetition flowchart element is translated into the Pascal **while** statement:

```
while a <> b do <statement>
```

The expression *<statement>* is called a *metavariable*. For an explanation, see the accompanying text box. Notice, though, that the metavariable *< statement >* in the greatest common divisor **while** clause is an **if** statement.

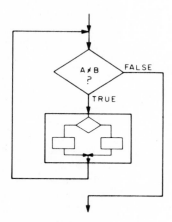

The real power in Pascal's algorithm descriptive capability lies in this sort of nesting. For example, any element can occur as a subelement of the **while** or **if** statement. These are called *structured* statements, and they can be nested to any depth.

Look again at the greatest common divisor (GCD) function in listing 1. Note that the routine consists of a heading and a variable declaration statement followed by one compound statement, bracketed by **begin** and **end**. Functions and procedures in Pascal can be thought of as named

statements with local variables. They always have one entry and one exit, and therefore, a call is flowcharted as a sequence element such as:

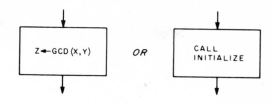

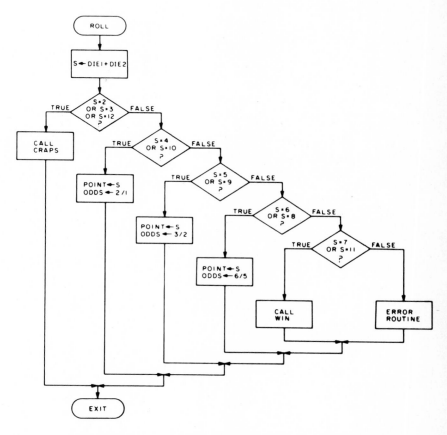

Figure 2: Flowchart for a portion of the dice game "craps." The five IF tests can be implemented in Pascal with one case statement.

Metavariables

Bracketed symbols such as ("< statement >") all call metalinguistic variables (or metavariables) or syntactic units. They represent a class of possible language elements. They are nonterminal symbols; that is, the symbol "< statement >" itself will not appear in a Pascal program. It represents a set of legal symbols that can appear in its place in the program. Nonterminal symbols are bracketed by "<" and ">" and are printed in italics to distinguish them from terminal symbols such as **for := if do**. *Terminal symbols are usually printed in heavy type if the symbol is a language key word, and appear exactly as they would in the Pascal program.*

Pascal has a second selection statement called the **case** statement. This statement is a concise representation of the special case of nested **if** statements. An example of this is the "craps first roll" algorithm used to implement the dice game called craps. A pair of dice can obviously have only one summed value from 2 to 12 on any given throw, making this an ideal use for the case statement (see figure 2). The five nested decisions can be represented with the following Pascal **case** statement:

```
s : = die 1 + die 2;
case s of
    2, 3, 12 :
        craps;
    4, 10 :
        begin point : = s; odds : = 2/1
        end;
    5, 9 :
        begin point : = s; odds : = 3/2
        end;
    6, 8 :
        begin point : = s; odds : = 6/5
        end;
    7, 11 : win
end    {of case statement}
```

Of course, this could be represented using **if** statements; however, the **case** statement is much more concise and clear. When the decisions in a group of nested **if** statements are mutually exclusive, that is, if any one being true implies that the rest are false, then a **case** statement is probably the appropriate representation.

Pascal allows two other forms of repetition: the **repeat** statement and the **for** statement. The **repeat** statement:

```
repeat
    <any statement>
until  <condition>
```

is represented by:

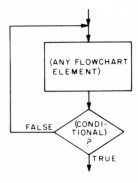

Repetitions can always be expressed as either **repeat** statements or **while** statements.

However, one form usually sounds better. For example:

> **repeat** *shoot craps*
> **until** *broke* **or** *out of time*

is equivalent to

> *shoot craps;*
> **while not** *broke*
> **and not** *out of time*
> **do** *shoot craps*

The **for** statement

> **for** *<var>:=*
> *<init val>* **to** *<final val>*
> *<any statement>*

is represented by:

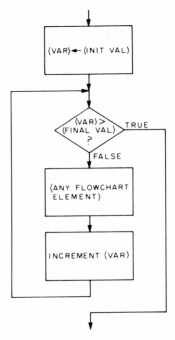

Notice that again there is one entry and one exit for this flowchart element.

Another element we might see in a flowchart is an arrow coming out of a subelement, perhaps to a different page of the flowchart. This exit from the normal flow of execution is the only use of the Pascal **goto** statement. Indeed, very few Pascal procedures need **goto** statements to express the algorithm. Goto statements can fog the otherwise clear logic of a routine.

A final element that might be found in flowcharts is an assertion and commentary such as:

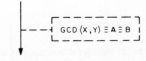

The Pascal greatest common divisor (GCD) function has all of these elements in an appropriate place in the source code. Pascal allows comments, delimited with braces, { and }, to be freely inserted anywhere a blank can be inserted.

We can conclude that for each Pascal language statement there is a corresponding flowchart element, and vice versa. Therefore, one could easily flowchart any algorithm just from its Pascal listing. Compare the Pascal program in listing 1 to the FORTRAN and BASIC programs in listings 2 and 3. They are fundamentally identical, but all of the statement numbers and GOTOs in the FORTRAN and BASIC versions obscure the logic. You might maintain that, for so simple an example, there is no advantage for Pascal. One could flowchart the greatest common divisor (GCD) algorithm just from the BASIC listing. Of course you could, but how about flowcharting that 1200 line FORTRAN headache you wrote a year ago that has returned to haunt you?

Data Representation in Pascal

Pascal has several flexible forms of data representation. A variable can be defined as a scalar (single value) or a structured type. The different scalar types are: real, integer, character, Boolean, and user defined or enumerated. The structured types include arrays, records, sets and files.

Users can define their own scalar types by enumeration. For example, in a traffic control program, there might be a variable called *signalcolor* which has a value of yellow, green or red. Or, in a microwave oven program, there might be a variable called *temp* which represents the cooking level specified. These concepts are represented by the following Pascal declarations:

```
type color = (red,yellow,green);
     cooking level = (warm,defrost,simmer,
                      roast,reheat,
                      maxpower);
var signalcolor: color;
    temp: cookinglevel;
```

In this example the **type** declaration describes the user defined types and the **var** declaration specifies variable names and their associated type.

Another innovation in Pascal is the ability to specify a subrange of a scalar type. For example, if the variable *count* is to be an integer between 1 and 10, the declaration would be:

```
var count: 1..10;
```

To further demonstrate these features, a

BASIC program that would benefit from Pascal data representation is next explored.

Mastermind Codebreaker Example

The Mastermind codebreaker algorithm I have chosen for this exercise was presented by WL Milligan in the October 1977 BYTE, pages 168 thru 171. His BASIC version is reproduced in listing 4. A Pascal translation is presented here in listing 5. Let us compare the two.

The first 15 lines of the Pascal version correspond to lines 10 to 45 in the BASIC version. These are the type declarations and the global variable declarations. These global variables can be referenced from within any

```
function gcd(x,y: integer): integer;
    var a,b: integer;          {x,y > 0}
begin
    a := x;  b := y;
    while a <> b do    { GCD(X,Y) = GCD(A,B) }
        if a>b then a :=a−b
               else b := b−a;
                           { GCD(X,Y) = A = B }
    gcd := a
end
```

Listing 1: Pascal function to calculate the greatest common divisor of two integers.

```
100    LET A=X
110    LET B=Y
120    IF A=B THEN 190
130        REM . . . GCD(X,Y) = GCD(A,B)
140        IF A>B THEN 170
150            LET B=B−A
160            GO TO 180
170            LET A=A−B
180    GO TO 120
190    REM . . . GCD(X,Y) = A = B
200    RETURN
```

Listing 2: BASIC subroutine to compute the greatest common divisor of two integers.

```
       INTEGER FUNCTION GCD(X,Y)
       INTEGER A,B,X,Y
       A=X
       B=Y
120    IF (A.EQ.B)  GO TO 190
C          . . . GCD(X,Y) = GCD(A,B)
           IF (A.GT.B)  GO TO 170
           B = B−A
           GO TO 180
170        A = A−B
180    CONTINUE
       GO TO 120
C
C          . . . GCD(X,Y) = A = B
190    RETURN
       END
```

Listing 3: FORTRAN function to compute the greatest common divisor of two integers.

procedure. The type declarations define new variable types such as:

type *colors* = (colorless, red, blue, brown, green, yellow, orange, space);

row = array [1..4] of *colors*;

eval = record
black, white: 0..4
end;

This means that a variable of type *colors* has a value equal to one of these enumerated items. A variable of type *row* is an array of four *colors*. The type *eval* represents a code-maker's response to a guessed row. What does this represent in the game? This response is the number of exact color and position matches (black key pegs) and the number of out of position color matches (white key pegs). The codemaker responds with between 0 and 4 black and white key pegs. The type *eval* in the Pascal version accurately models this: a record consisting of two components, *black* and *white*, each an integer between 0 and 4.

The variable *version* represents the version number, either 1 or 2. The 10 possible rows of code pegs in the game are recorded in the Pascal structure declared as:

var *rows*: array [1..10] of *row*;

Note that the careful selection of data representation makes the program much more clear and concise. The ability to deal with structures as a whole instead of just their elements tends to tighten up the logic of the program. For example, the BASIC lines:

820 REM ASSIGN NEXT ROW
830 FOR J=0 TO 3
840 LET R$(I+1,J)=D$(J)
845 NEXT J

are functionally equivalent to the Pascal assignment:

rows[i+1] := *hyp* {assign next row}

Also, the BASIC lines:

```
10 REM MASTER MIND "CODEBREAKER"
20 REM CODED IN RT-11 BASIC
30 RANDOMIZE
40 DIM R$(9,3),S(9,1)
45 DIM A$(6),B$(3),C$(3),D$(3)
50 REM INITIALIZATION
60 FOR J=0 TO 6
70 READ A$(J)
80 NEXT J
90 DATA "RED","BLUE","GREEN","YELLOW","BLACK","WHITE","SPACE"
100 LET L0=0
110 LET L1=0
120 LET L2=0
130 LET L3=0
140 PRINT "MASTER MIND CODEBREAKER"
145 PRINT "PLEASE BE PATIENT. SOMETIMES I TAKE A FEW MINUTES ON MY MOVE"
150 PRINT "WHICH VERSION (1 OR 2) ";
160 INPUT V
170 LET V=V+5
180 REM ASSIGN COLORS AT RANDOM FOR ROW 1
190 FOR J=0 TO 3
200 LET R$(0,J)=A$(INT(V*RND(J)))
210 NEXT J
220 REM START MAIN PLAY OF GAME HERE
230 REM I IS THE ROW COUNTER
240 FOR I=0 TO 9
245 PRINT
250 PRINT "MY MOVE FOR ROW"I+1" IS"
260 PRINT R$(I,0),R$(I,1),R$(I,2),R$(I,3)
270 PRINT "HOW MANY BLACK PEGS ";
280 INPUT S(I,0)
290 IF S(I,0)<>4 THEN 320
300 PRINT "THANKS FOR THE GAME"
305 PRINT
310 GO TO 870
320 IF S(I,0)<>3 THEN 360
330 LET S(I,1)=0\REM IF 3 BLACKS THEN 0 WHITES
340 GO TO 380
360 PRINT "HOW MANY WHITE PEGS ";
370 INPUT S(I,1)
380 REM GENERATE HYPOTHESIS
390 FOR I0=L0 TO V-1
400 FOR I1=L1 TO V-1
410 FOR I2=L2 TO V-1
420 FOR I3=L3 TO V-1
430 LET D$(0)=A$(I0)
440 LET D$(1)=A$(I1)
450 LET D$(2)=A$(I2)
460 LET D$(3)=A$(I3)
470 REM CHECK ALL ROWS FROM FIRST TO CURRENT FOR CONSISTENCY
490 FOR R=0 TO I
500 FOR J=0 TO 3
510 LET C$(J)=R$(R,J)
520 LET B$(J)=D$(J)
530 NEXT J
540 REM USE ROW EVALUATION SUBROUTINE TO CHECK CONSISTENCY OF
550 REM HYPOTHESIS AGAINST EACH ROW
555 LET N=0\LET M=0
560 GOSUB 910
570 REM CHECK FOR AGREEMENT OF BLACK & WHITE COUNT
580 IF N<>S(R,0) THEN 700
590 IF M<>S(R,1) THEN 700
600 NEXT R
610 REM MAKE SURE THAT HYPOTHESIS ROW DOESNT DUPLICATE ROW 1
```

```
620 LET Z=0
630 FOR J=0 TO 3
640 IF R$(0,J)<>D$(J) THEN 660
650 LET Z=Z+1
660 NEXT J
670 IF Z=4 THEN 700
690 GO TO 820
700 NEXT I3
710 NEXT I2
720 NEXT I1
730 NEXT I0
740 PRINT "I HAVE REACHED AN IMPASSE IN MY THINKING"
750 PRINT "COULD YOU HAVE MADE AN ERROR?"
760 GO TO 870
770 LET L0=I0
780 LET L1=I1
790 LET L2=I2
800 LET L3=I3+1
810 REM DO NOT RECHECK ELIMINATED POSSIBILITIES
820 REM ASSIGN NEXT ROW
830 FOR J=0 TO 3
840 LET R$(I+1,J)=D$(J)
845 NEXT J
850 NEXT I
860 PRINT "I AM STUMPED -- YOU WIN"
870 PRINT "ANOTHER GAME ";
880 INPUT R$
890 IF R$="Y" THEN 150
900 STOP
910 REM SUBROUTINE TO EVALUATE RESPONSE
920 REM COUNT BLACKS FIRST
930 FOR J1=0 TO 3
940 IF C$(J1)<>B$(J1) THEN 960
950 LET N=N+1
960 NEXT J1
970 REM NOW COUNT WHITES
980 FOR J1=0 TO 3
990 FOR J2=0 TO 3
1000 IF J1=J2 THEN 1080
1010 IF C$(J1)=B$(J1) THEN 1080
1020 IF C$(J2)=B$(J2) THEN 1080
1030 IF C$(J1)<>B$(J2) THEN 1080
1040 LET M=M+1
1050 LET B$(J2)="X"\REM DUMMY WRONG VALUE
1070 GO TO 1090
1080 NEXT J2
1090 NEXT J1
1100 RETURN
1110 STOP
2000 END
```

Listing 4: Codebreaker portion of W Lloyd Milligan's Mastermind game written in BASIC. The program appeared originally in the October 1977 BYTE, pages 169 and 170 (see page 49 of this edition for a description of Mastermind). Compare this with the Pascal version in listing 5.

```
610 REM MAKE SURE THAT
    HYPOTHESIS ROW DOESN'T
    DUPLICATE ROW 1
620 LET Z=0
630 FOR J=0 TO 3
640 IF R$(0,J)<>D$(J) THEN 660
650 LET Z=Z+1
660 NEXT J
670 IF Z=4 THEN 700
690 GO TO 820
```

are functionally equivalent to the Pascal statement:

if *hyp* <> *rows[1]* then goto 820

Mr Milligan's BASIC version is well written and well structured. It contains three key routines: initialization (lines 50 to 210); generate hypothesis (lines 380 to 845); and evaluate response (lines 910 to 1100). However, due to the inexpressiveness of BASIC, it takes careful study, even of this well-written BASIC program, to recognize its structure. On the other hand, looking at the Pascal version of the same algorithm, the expressiveness of the language shows the structure at a glance. Similarly, the use of meaningful variable names and Pascal record structures makes the data representation readable. Table 1 describes which variables in the Pascal version are used in the same context as variables in the BASIC version.

As careful as you are when coding BASIC, bugs are bound to creep in. For example, in the BASIC version (listing 4), lines 610 thru 690 are unnecessary. Additionally, there is no path through lines 770 to 810. Coding errors rarely creep into Pascal programs because the compiler enforces variable declarations and type agreement. For example, *evaluations[5] := rows[5]* is illegal because they are not type-compatible. Also *c := brown-red* is illegal because arithmetic is undefined for our user defined *colors* type. And, *version := 3* is illegal because the value 3 is outside the legal range for *version*.

Other Pascal Attributes

We have looked at some of the noteworthy features in Pascal. There are also the powerful features of block structured scope of names, recursion and dynamic allocation of storage. Pascal is known as a very "safe" language because it optionally has extensive compile and run time type checking including type compatability, subrange bounds and array index bounds. Pascal has many other data representations not illustrated here, such as sequential files, arrays, pointers and sets. I can't begin to explain all of these features here, but you don't have to under-

Listing 5: Pascal version of the Mastermind BASIC program in listing 4.

```
program mm2(input,output);

label   870;

type    colors = (colorless, red, blue, brown, green, yellow, orange, space);
        row    = array [1..4] of colors;
        eval   = record
                        black, white: 0..4
                 end;

var     evaluations: array [1..10] of eval;
        rows:        array [1..10] of row;
        name:        array [colors] of packed array [1..6] of char;
        color:       array [0..7] of colors;
        redrow: row;   { First hypothesis checked }
        last:   row;   { Last hypothesis formed   }
        version: 1..2;      maxcolor: orange..space;
        i: 1..9;  j: 1..4;  ch: char;

procedure initialization;
    var c: colors;  i: 1..4;
    begin
        name[red]    := 'RED    ';   name[green]  := 'GREEN ';
        name[blue]   := 'BLUE   ';   name[yellow] := 'YELLOW';
        name[brown]  := 'BROWN ';    name[space]  := 'SPACE ';
        for c := colorless to space do
            color[ord(c)] := c;
        for i := 1 to 4 do
            redrow[i] := red;
        last := redrow;
        writeln(' MASTERMIND CODEBREAKER');
        writeln(' PLEASE BE PATIENT. SOMETIMES I TAKE A FEW');
        writeln(' MINUTES ON MY MOVE.  WHICH VERSION (1 or 2)?');
        read (version);
        maxcolor := color[version+5];
        { Assign colors at random for row 1 }

        for i := 1 to 4 do
            rows[1,i] := color[ trunc((version+5)*random(0.0)+1.0) ]
    end   { Of Initialization Routine   } ;


procedure checkconsistancy (hypothesis,previousrow: row;
                               var e: eval);
    label 1090;
    var j1,j2: 1..4;
    begin
        { Count blacks first }
        e.black := 0;
        for j1 := 1 to 4 do
            if hypothesis[j1] = previousrow[j1] then
                e.black := e.black + 1;
        { Now count whites }
        e.white := 0;
        for j1 := 1 to 4 do
            begin
                for j2 := 1 to 4 do
                    if (j1≠j2) and
                       (hypothesis[j1] ≠ previousrow[j1]) and
                       (hypothesis[j2] ≠ previousrow[j2]) and
                       (hypothesis[j1] = previousrow[j2]) then
                       begin
                            e.white := e.white + 1;
                            { Dummy wrong value }
                            previousrow[j2] := colorless;
                            goto 1090    { Exit J2 loop }
                       end;
                1090:
            end
    end   { Of Check Consistancy Procedure }
```

47

```
function formhypothesis: Boolean;
    label 820;
    var i1,i2,i3,i4: colors;
        r: 0..9;
        hyp: row;
        eval1: eval;
        riable: Boolean;

    begin    { forming Hypothesis }
        riable := true;
        for i1 := last[1] to maxcolor do
        for i2 := last[2] to maxcolor do
        for i3 := last[3] to maxcolor do
        for i4 := last[4] to maxcolor do

            begin
                last := redrow;
                hyp[1] := i1; hyp[2] := i2; hyp[3] := i3; hyp[4] := i4;
                { Check all rows so far for consistancy }
                r := 0;
                repeat
                    r := r + 1;
                    checkconsistancy(hyp,rows[r],eval1);
                until (eval1 ≠ evaluations[r]) or (r = i);
                if eval1 = evaluations[r] then
                    { Make sure that hypothesis doesn't duplicate row 1;
                      if it hasn't then we have a viable hypothesis     }
                    if hyp ≠ rows[1] then goto 820;
                    { Otherwise, keep searching....NEXT i4,i3,i2,i1 }
            end;
        riable = false;    { No viable hypothesis left }
820:    if riable then
            begin    { Do not recheck eliminated possibilities }
                last := hyp;
                rows[i+1] := hyp    { Assign next row }
            end
        else begin
                writeln (' I HAVE REACHED AN IMPASSE. ');
                writeln (' COULD YOU HAVE MADE AN ERROR?')
            end;
        formhypothesis := riable    { Return with function value }
    end    { Of Form Hypothesis Procedure    } ;



    begin    { Mastermind Codebreaker }


    repeat
        initialize;
        { Start main play of game here }
        for i := 1 to 9 do
            begin
                writeln;    write ('MY MOVE FOR ROW',i: 2,' is');
                for j := 1 to 4 do
                    write (name[rows[i,j]]: 8); writeln;
                writeln ('HOW MANY BLACK PEGS?');
                read (evaluations[i].black);
                if evaluations[i].black = 4 then
                    begin
                        writeln ('THANKS FOR THE GAME'); goto 870
                    end;
                if evaluations[i].black = 3 then
                    evaluations[i].white := 0
                else begin
                        writeln (' HOW MANY WHITE PEGS?');
                        read (evaluations[i].white)
                    end;
                if not formhypothesis then goto 870
            end;
        writeln (' I AM STUMPED —— YOU WIN!');
870:    repeat
            writeln (' ANOTHER GAME?'); read (ch)
        until (ch = 'Y') or (ch = 'N')
    until ch = 'N'
end    {    Of Main Program }
```

stand all of them before you write your first Pascal program.

The main selling feature of Pascal is that properly developed programs are extremely easy to debug. Once you get a clean compile, the program usually runs! Why? Because the algorithms are expressed *clearly and naturally*. The range of all control variables are well specified and can be enforced at run time. The data types all agree and are appropriate to the problem. The program is readable — data types mean what they say — and it is therefore maintainable. Pascal encourages the methodical and systematic development of algorithms, an important structured programming method.

I hope this survey of Pascal has whet your appetite for the language. If so, read more about Pascal in this issue, then pick up any of the books in the references and dive in!

Pascal is a rich and fertile language that emphasizes the expression of algorithms and data representation naturally and clearly. When will your microcomputer speak Pascal?■

REFERENCES

Introductory books on Pascal:

Bowles, K L, *Microcomputer Problem Solving With Pascal,* Springer-Verlag, New York, 1977.

Grogono, P, *Programming in Pascal,* Addison-Wesley, Reading MA, 1978.

Schneider, G et al, *An Introduction to Programming and Problem Solving With Pascal,* Wiley, New York, 1973.

Wirth, N, *Systematic Programming — An Introduction,* Prentice-Hall, Englewood Cliffs NJ, 1973.

Other books:

Dahl, O J, Dijkstra, E W and Hoare, C A R, *Structured Programming,* Academic Press, New York, 1972.

Jensen, K and Wirth, N, *Pascal User Manual and Report* (second edition), Springer-Verlag, New York, 1976.

Wirth, N, *Algorithms + Data Structures = Programs,* Prentice-Hall, Englewood Cliffs NJ, 1976.

BASIC Version	Pascal Version
Lines 220 to 270 **and 850 to 900** I DIM R$(9,3) R$ DIM S(9,1)	**program** *mm2* *i: 1 . . 9; j: 1 . . 4* *rows:* **array** *[1 . . 10]* **of** *row* *ch: char* *evaluations:* **array** *[1 . . 10]* **of** *eval*
Lines 50 to 210 J DIM A$(6) V	**procedure** *initialization* *i: 1 . . 4; c: colors* *name:* **array** *[colors]* **of** *string* *color:* **array** *[0 . . 7]* **of** *colors* *version: 1 . . 2*
Lines 380 to 845 I0,I1,I2,I3 L0,L1,L2,L3 V DIM A$(6) DIM D$(3) R J N,M	**procedure** *formhypothesis* *i1,i2,i3,i4: colors* *redrow, last: row* *maxcolor: orange. . space* *hyp: row* *r: 0 . . 9* *eval1: eval*
Lines 910 to 1100 J1,J2 DIM C$(3) DIM B$(3) N,M	**procedure** *Checkconsistency* *j1,j2: 1 . . 4* *hypothesis: row* *previousrow: row* *e: eval*

Table 1: A comparison of the variables used in the two versions of the Mastermind game (see listings 4 and 5).

What Is Mastermind?

One of the most interesting conventional (ie: noncomputer) games on the market is "Mastermind," distributed by Invicta Plastics, Suite 940, 200 5th Av, New York NY 10010, and available in many local stores. Mastermind involves deductive logic, hypothesis testing and probabilistic inference. In Mastermind, the players take turns as "codemaker" and "codebreaker." The codemaker sets up a concealed row of four colored pegs from a set of **R**ed, **BL**ue, **BR**own, **G**reen, **Y**ellow and **O**range pegs. It is acceptable to use the same color or colors more than once. In version 2, a more advanced game, empty **S**paces are also permitted.

To challenge the computer program you are the codemaker. Write down a code. A row of four colors invokes the codebreaker computer program. It will take up to ten tries (rows) to discover the secret arrangement of colors in the concealed row. After printing each guess, the program will prompt you for the number of black and white key pegs.

The number of black pegs corresponds to the number of correct colors in correct positions. An important rule is that no position in the try is counted more than once.

When evaluating the program's try it is necessary to count black and white pegs carefully. If you make a mistake counting the number of exact or inexact correspondences, the program may exhaust all possible arrangements without finding a possible valid try. In this event the message:

I HAVE REACHED AN IMPASSE.
COULD YOU HAVE MADE AN ERROR?

is printed.

(Adapted from W Lloyd Milligan's article, "Mastermind," October 1977 BYTE, page 168.)

Pascal versus BASIC: Round 2 Includes FORTRAN

Lawrence C Andrews
2634 Wycliffe Rd
Baltimore MD 21234

The article "Pascal versus BASIC: An Exercise," by Allan M Schwartz (page 41) is a typical example of a language chauvinist using a language ineptly and then pointing to the faults in the code he has written as inherent properties of the language.

The function GCD (page 45) that he has written (leaving aside the BASIC version) has several faults, to wit:

1) X and Y are not declared in the Pascal version.
2) The FORTRAN version will develop an infinite loop if X or Y equals zero (no comment there excludes X, Y greater than zero).
3) The FORTRAN version *never* defines the functional value of GCD and so will not even compile in a good compiler.
4) There sure are a lot of GOTOs and statement numbers in his program; in particular, statement 180 is totally useless. GOTO 180 should be GOTO 120.
5) There is no reason to have any GOTOs. It could be written as in listing 1.
6) If you don't mind downward branching GOTOs (generally considered to be harmless) function GCD can be written as shown in listing 2.

As in Pascal the flow is clear and flowcharting is simple (Warnier-Orr diagrams are still better). I don't run down Pascal but I fail to see why Schwartz runs down FORTRAN just because he writes a pidgin dialect inexpertly. In FORTRAN, as in Pascal, "Go to statements can fog the otherwise clear logic of a routine," as Schwartz states in his article. FORTRAN 77 with IF. . . THEN . . . ELSE statements, and zero trip counts on DO loops, removes most of Schwartz's FORTRAN objection. Anyone can write a bad program in any language. Pascal is no exception to that statement. ■

```
INTEGER FUNCTION GCD (X,Y)
INTEGER X,Y, A,B, LIM

C . . .  X,Y .GT. 0
       A = X
       B = Y
       LIM = MAX0 (A,P)
       DO 1000 I = 1, LIM
       IF (A .GT. B) A = A−B
       IF (B .GT. A) B = B−A
       GCD = A
       IF (A. EQ. B) RETURN
1000   CONTINUE
       END
```

Listing 1: The GCD function written in FORTRAN with no GOTO statements.

```
       DO 1000 I = 1, LIM
       IF (A .GT. B) A = A−B
       IF (B .GT. A) B = B−A
       IF (A. EQ. B) GO TO 2000
1000   CONTINUE
2000   GCD = A
       RETURN
       END
```

Listing 2: A much shorter version of the GCD function using one downward branching GOTO statement.

Originally appeared in April 1979 BYTE magazine.

Pascal versus COBOL :

Where Pascal Gets Down to Business

Kenneth L Bowles

With a few important extensions, Pascal can be an extremely powerful tool for writing interactive business application programs on microcomputers and minicomputers. Pascal provides data structuring facilities generally superior to those of COBOL, and its control constructs allow a systematic and modular approach to program design that reduces development effort and improves reliability compared with BASIC or FORTRAN. The extensions needed make it easy to write interactive programs, use random access (floppy) disk files, handle business arithmetic, and recover from error situations.

A Case Study

In this article we will illustrate the use of Pascal for a program application one might find, with variations, in many small businesses. More general descriptions of the language are contained elsewhere in BYTE and in many published introductory textbooks.

The business we have in mind keeps records of information about transactions with its customers, and also records containing descriptive information about the people with whom it deals. The descriptive records might apply to clients of a law firm, patients of a medical or dental clinic, suppliers of a hardware store with a large and diverse stock, houses currently listed by a real estate firm, users of hardware and software products handled by a computer store, and so on. The transaction records would describe orders for goods to be sold, deliveries, invoices sent, payments, requests for information, promotional literature sent, customer property sent out for repairs,

medical tests ordered, etc. Typically each record in the file of descriptive records would correspond to many transaction records. Depending upon circumstances, the transaction records might be stored intermingled with the descriptive records (just as in the shoe boxes that some small businesses now use) or in a separate disk file. They might be stored on the same floppy disk if the files are small, or they might be stored on different disks. In any event, we assume that the number of items in the descriptive file is so large that manual processing of the transactions information represents a significant cost to the business for record keeping. We also assume that the business is small enough that it cannot afford to have its own full time data processing department.

We now consider how Pascal programs written for a small computer might help in the operations of a hypothetical small business, the Zyx Gizmo Store. With many competing manufacturers producing gizmos, it is necessary for Zyx to keep track of many different sizes, shapes, qualities and specialized forms of gizmos. Moreover, the buyer can start with a basic model, later adding modules to obtain a larger and more sophisticated gizmo. Gizmos require periodic maintenance and corrective repairs. Zyx stocks some replacement parts which are installed in customers' gizmos by the Zyx repair department or sold to users who do their own repair work. Some replacement parts are too expensive to stock locally, and Zyx must order them from regional distributors when needed. Gizmos are complicated enough to use that many users require textbooks or short training courses to understand how to use them. Zyx sells the textbooks and runs periodic training seminars for which users pay a small fee. Both the training and repair problems are made complex by the rate at which the technology of manufacturing gizmos is advancing, as new models are introduced by the manufacturers each year. While the similarity of the gizmo to the microcomputer is easily recognized by many readers, the gizmo model could apply equally well to technology based devices being sold in many fields today.

We can assume that Zyx is large enough to employ several salespeople, repair people, and at least one full time administrative assistant in addition to the owner of the company. In general, when a situation arises requiring communication with a customer, any one of these people may have occasion to refer to the filed records on previous transactions involving that customer. If the customer telephones to request advice about an apparently malfunctioning gizmo, the responding Zyx employee usually needs information about the make, model, size and other details describing the customer's gizmo. If a customer asks Zyx to order an additional module from a national distributor, he or she may call Zyx to inquire about the fate of the order before delivery is actually completed. If a manufacturer of modules for gizmos introduces a new line of devices, Zyx may wish to save on promotion costs by contacting only customers known to be using gizmos compatible with that manufacturer's devices. For these and many other reasons, designated employees of Zyx should have ready access to records on the customer's dealings with the firm. These records make it possible for Zyx to render a personalized service that probably is the main reason why customers come to the Zyx store for their gizmos rather than to a national or regional distribution company.

Of course now that low cost microcomputers have become moderately powerful, it is possible, in principle, for Zyx to maintain its descriptive and transaction records on customers in a floppy disk or small hard disk system. Ideally, the cost of adding a microcomputer to a small business operation is only a fraction of the value received, both in labor costs and in improved customer relations. Moreover, the company could use the microcomputer for maintaining its accounting records, sending bills, keeping track of inventory and so on. We say *ideally* because the effort to write a suite of programs to access and maintain the necessary files can be quite substantial if the programming is done in BASIC or FORTRAN (or assembly language). Using Pascal the effort should be very much less than the equivalent effort using BASIC or FORTRAN.

Since COBOL is becoming available on microcomputers, some comments on COBOL versus Pascal are appropriate. Here the principal issue has more to do with the operating system, within which business programs written in the language will run, than with the language comparison. Given reasonable operating system support of the language, no one versed in Pascal would consider backing up to COBOL. COBOL's principal attraction in the business computing community has been that it is the most standardized of all the widely used languages. COBOL provides facilities for storing dissimilar types of information mingled together in transaction records intended to be stored in off line media like disks and magnetic tape. Pascal too has very powerful facilities for storing complex data records, and its facilities for building complex programs are far superior to those of COBOL.

Regarding the operating system support, we'll assume in the rest of this article that the user's Pascal program is developed under, and runs within, the UCSD (University of California at San Diego) Pascal Software System (see "UCSD Pascal: A Machine Independent System," page 3). This system provides what amount to language extensions to Pascal which facilitate the use of Pascal in writing interactive business programs. Some of these extensions will be mentioned at points in the discussion where they are used in our example. The accepted informal standard for the Pascal language, as described by Niklaus Wirth in his revised report on Pascal (*Pascal User Manual and Report*, K Jensen and N Wirth, Springer Verlag, New York/Heidelberg, 1975), lacks definition of several facilities that are really essential if the language is to be convenient for writing business programs. On the other hand, Pascal provides an extremely high level from which these facilities can be added.

Transaction Records

In Pascal, the programmer is required to declare what type of information will be stored under the identifier of each variable. Readers of BYTE should be familiar with the concept of type as it refers to an integer (whole number), real (floating point number), or string (of characters) item stored in the program's memory. Readers may also be familiar with the concept of an array containing a collection of items all of the same type. In effect, an array is a composite type associating one identifier with a collection of many similar data items, ie: all integers or all reals, etc. Pascal allows one to declare one's own composite type containing a collection of items of dissimilar types. Listing 1 gives a concrete example that might apply to the records of the Zyx company.

In Pascal, any type declarations one wishes to make must appear in the main program or in a block (subroutine) before any variable identifiers are declared following the reserved word **var**. In the example above, representing part of a block, the variable identifier *inrec* is to be used for temporary working storage of a customer record read in from an external device such as disk. *outrec* is to be used to collect several data items together before writing out to the external device. Both variables are declared to be laid out in memory according to the type declaration for *customer*. In other words, the declaration of *customer* describes the various fields of information that will be found in any record of that type, whether currently stored in main memory or on an external medium.

The first field within a record of type *customer* is a name consisting of up to 30 characters. The name is of type, *string*, which is a UCSD extension of the standard Pascal concept of a packed array of characters. The type *string* is really just a predeclared record type within standard Pascal. In addition to the packed array of characters, the record also contains a single byte field representing the number of characters currently containing useful string information. In UCSD Pascal, a variable of type *string* with no reference to the maximum length (like the *[30]* in the *name* field) will be given a default maximum length of 80 characters. Characters are ASCII and are synonymous with the concept of 8 bit bytes.

The identifier *chargesunpaid* is an extended precision integer represented internally as a 32 bit binary number and limited to storing numbers with up to eight decimal digits of precision. Associated with *chargesunpaid* is a scale factor of two decimal digits, designed to represent dollars and cents. Both the extended precision concept and the decimal scaling factor are UCSD extensions to standard Pascal intended particularly for business use. Where no precision or scaling factor is mentioned in the type portion of an integer declaration (as with the fields *areacode*, *prefix* and *extension*), the system assumes that the programmer wants the standard integer precision on the machine being used. On most microcomputers this will be 16 bits, equivalent to about 4.5 decimal digits.

telephone is the identifier of a field within the *customer* record layout, where *telephone* is itself a record containing three fields, each of which is an integer. Depending upon the purpose one might have in mind for the data on telephone numbers, it might be better to represent the telephone

```
type customer =
    record
        name: string[30];
        chargesunpaid: integer[8:2];
        telephone:
            record
                areacode: integer;
                prefix: integer;
                extension: integer
            end;
        address:
            record
                street: string[40];
                citystate: string [40];
                zip: integer[5]
            end
    end {customer};

var
    x,y: real;
    i: integer;
    inrec, outrec: customer;
```

Listing 1: User declared composite type declaration in Pascal. In Pascal, the programmer is required to declare what type of information will be stored under the identifier of each variable. Examples of standard predeclared types include integer and real. Pascal allows one to declare one's own composite type containing a collection of items of dissimilar types. In this example, the type "customer" has been created, consisting of a record of the variable's name, chargesunpaid, telephone and address. String is a predeclared composite type provided by UCSD's Pascal system.

number field as a string of ten characters. We have used this representation mostly as an illustration of the language facilities.

address is also the identifier of a field which is itself a record containing three fields. Both *telephone* and *address* are said to be "nested" inside the record of type *customer*. Pascal would allow us to nest record type fields within either *telephone* or *address* if we wished to do so, and those record fields could in turn contain other records. In this respect Pascal and COBOL are similar, though the Pascal facilities for record declarations are generally more flexible. As in COBOL, one can declare that a particular transaction record may be used with several distinct field layouts, allowing a file to contain records with several different formats.

In Pascal, one refers to a complete record by its identifier alone. We could transfer the entire content of *inrec* to *outrec* using the statement:

outrec := inrec

No concept similar to COBOL's MOVE CORRESPONDING statement is available to allow the transfer of similarly named fields between records declared to be laid out differently.

If we wish to refer to a single field of a Pascal record, it is necessary to name both the record identifier and the field identifier. Thus we might assign a value to the *name* field of *outrec* as follows:

outrec.name := 'John Q. Public'

In the situation of complex record types with many nested records, one can often simplify the extra writing needed to refer to all the nested record identifiers by using the Pascal *with* statement.

Interactive Input and Output

Input and output (IO) is the area of greatest importance in business applications where the standard Pascal definition lacks a few essential features. Standard Pascal input and output *do provide* an orientation similar to some implementations of COBOL in that a file (an IO device) has an associated buffer variable of the same type as that of the file itself. In the next section we'll consider files associated with record types.

Published discussions of input and output in Standard Pascal are generally limited to handling files of type *char*, meaning that input and output are assumed to consist of a stream of characters. The standard identifier *text* is a convenient way to declare a file identifier as in:

fid: text;

which is equivalent to:

fid: file of char;

The standard Pascal read and write statements provide automatic formatting of external character strings representing integer or floating point numbers into and from their corresponding internal integer and real representations.

While the concept of type *text* is useful when working with magnetic tape devices or with card input and line printer output, it has proven difficult to use with interactive devices. The UCSD Pascal system is extended for this purpose. The principal problem with type *text* for interactive files is the standard Pascal definition of the *read* statement. *read(fid,x)* is equivalent to:

x : fid ↑;
get (fid)

in which the content of the buffer variable is first assigned to the variable *x*, following which a new character is loaded into the file's buffer variable from the external device. This is inconvenient when one would like to place a prompting message on a video display screen, using a simple write statement, following which the program should

wait for input demanded by a read statement. The standard mechanism implies that the system looks ahead for a character to be loaded into the buffer variable. This is a great idea for tape files, but not at all convenient for interactive devices. UCSD Pascal extends this concept by associating type *interactive* with interactive devices. Type *interactive* is the same as type *text* except that the buffer variable is loaded from the external device *before* the value in the buffer variable is moved to the program variable. In more explicit terms:

var fid: interactive;
.
.
.
get(fid);
x : = fid ↑

where the last two lines represent *read(fid,x)*.

UCSD Pascal extends the idea of types *text* and *interactive* by allowing a string to be handled with minimum fuss. On *read(fid,strg)* (or just *read(strg)*, when referring to the standard system file *input*), one types characters at a video display keyboard with each character appearing immediately on the screen. If a character is mistyped it can be erased from the screen and the input buffer by pressing the backspace key. If one wants to erase the entire input buffer for a clean start (with all typed characters wiped off the screen), one presses the delete or rubout key. The read operation is terminated when return is pressed, whereupon one can determine the number of characters actually input into the variable *strg* by using the built-in *string* function *length(strg)*. On output, the *write* statement determines how many characters to send from a string variable using the length field associated with that variable. For example,

write('Hello There');

and

strg := 'Hello There';
.
.
.
write(strg);

would both produce the same 2 word message on the output device. As in Standard Pascal, the width of the field of characters sent from the *write* statement can be controlled as follows:

write(strg: width)

Disk Input and Output

One of the main reasons for using a disk file is to allow rapid *random* access to any selected record in the file. Access to a floppy disk record takes roughly 0.25 seconds, whereas access to a record on a tape cassette or cartridge can take many seconds or more than a minute. Interactive business processing usually requires files to be maintained on an external medium like disk or tape because the main memory of a microcomputer or minicomputer is usually not large enough to contain a complete file at one time. Random access is almost mandatory in most cases to avoid long waiting times for the people using the computer.

For example, the Zyx company might have a database of customer records in a file *fcust* declared as follows:

fcust: file of customer;

within the variable declarations of a Pascal program. When a customer arrives to ask for information, a Zyx staff member wants immediate access to the record associated with that customer in the disk file. Standard Pascal provides no way to reach the customer's record without sequentially reading many other records: usually starting at the beginning of the file. UCSD Pascal allows one to position the record number pointer of the file using the built-in seek statement, for example:

seek(fcust, recnumber)

Following execution of this statement, the standard procedure call *get(fcust)* would load the selected record numbered *recnumber* into the buffer variable of the *fcust* file. Contents of the buffer could then be altered directly or moved to other variables in the program. *get* causes the record number pointer associated with the file to be advanced to the next record in sequence. If you want to change the contents of the buffer variable and then return the changed contents to the disk record numbered *recnumber* using *put(fcust)*, you would first have to call *seek* again. The *get* and *put* procedures of Standard Pascal are designed with sequential tape files in mind, and they can also be used for sequential reading of disk files. Use of the *seek* procedure as described allows random access to disk files with minimum alteration of the standard language.

Several aspects of disk file handling are very important for simplifying the task of the business application programmer, though not specified as part of the Pascal language. For example, standard floppy disk media are usually partitioned into sectors of 128 bytes each. In some operating systems, such as the Digital Equipment RT11 operating system, a file is made to appear as partitioned into physical records of 512 bytes called blocks (UCSD Pascal system uses this convention). Typically, the record layout a programmer

wants to use (such as *customer* in our example) does not result in a neat fit with the sector or block size demanded by the operating system. This means that a logical record associated with a record type declaration in Pascal may occasionally be split between two physical records on the disk. The operating system should allow the Pascal programmer to *get* a record from the disk or *put* a record to the disk without concern for this complication. The system should maintain a directory of disk files so that the programmer need not be concerned with the actual location of a file on the disk, but only with the number of a logical record counting from the beginning of the file.

The programmer of a business applications program package needs to have a simple way to cause a program to call for changes in the library of disk files maintained by the program. For example, an obsolete copy of a master file might be removed from the directory, or its directory name changed. The UCSD Pascal system provides these and other facilities to make disk file handling as painless as possible on a small machine.

Keeping Track of Categories of Data

One of the common problems in business programming is identifying people or things with certain groupings or categories in order to simplify the handling of data on those people or things. For example, the Zyx company might want to characterize some cus-

```
type
    manuf = (able, baker, charlie, davis, edwards, jones, smith, none);
    customer =
        record
            name: string[30];
            chargesunpaid: integer[8:2];
            equipment: set of manuf;
            telephone:
                record
                    areacode: integer;
                    prefix: integer;
                    extension: integer
                end;
            address:
                record
                    street: string[40];
                    citystate: string[40];
                    zip: integer[5]
                end
        end {customer};
var
    x,y: real;
    i: integer;
    supplier: manuf;
    inrec, outrec: customer;
```

Listing 2: An expansion of the Pascal code in listing 1 illustrating the use of sets. The type manuf has been added, which can be associated with a variable allowed to assume only the values enumerated in the declaration. For example, the new variable supplier, of type manuf, may take on the value of any of the items in the manuf list such as able or davis, but no others outside the type.

tomers as primarily oriented to gizmos made by certain manufacturers, such as the Able, Baker, Charlie, Davis, Edwards, Jones and Smith companies. Within the product lines of these companies, Zyx might also want to have ready access to a record showing which selection of all the possible gizmo modules a customer might have. Thus, when a customer makes an inquiry or a manufacturer brings out a new type of module, Zyx staff members could reduce the effort in knowing how to deal with the customer. For example, a printed promotional brochure might be sent only to the customers associated with an appropriate combination of categories.

In virtually any programming language, this problem can generally be solved by storing descriptive strings as additional fields of the *customer* record. However, the strings can take up far more space than one would like (particularly on a minifloppy disk!), and they are awkward to use when you are simply searching through a file for records corresponding to a particular combination of categories. For example, we might want to search the file to identify all customers who own gizmos made by the Able, Jones and Smith companies who also have a particular type of add-on module. (If you are having trouble relating to gizmos, how about S-100 bus microcomputers with a minimum of 16 K bytes of memory?)

To solve the space problems in storing categories information, a standard technique in traditional programming languages involves deciding on a set of codes to represent the various categories. In our simple example enumerating the gizmo manufacturers, we might store a single letter representing each manufacturer, such as A for Able, B for Baker, and so on. But how do we store the information that a particular customer is associated with two or more of these codes? Without a complex indexing mechanism, a random access disk file virtually requires that all logical records be of the same size. Do we provide an array for storing these codes? How long does the array need to be to account for all possible combinations of codes for our customers? Are we willing to put up with inaccurate data on a few customers in order to save large amounts of file space for the great majority of customers? How do we write a search program to go through the file quickly to find all the customers associated with a specific combination of categories? The reader might well pause at this point to consider how to accomplish these tasks with his or her favorite programming language.

The Pascal facilities for handling sets are designed to make program solutions for problems like these as painless as possible.

For example, we might expand the declarations given earlier as shown in listing 2.

We have added the declaration of a new type *manuf* which can be associated with a variable allowed to assume only the values enumerated in the declaration. For example, the new variable *supplier* is allowed to be assigned the value *able*, or *jones*, from the list of enumerated identifiers.

Also declared as a new field of the *customer* record type is *equipment*, a set of members selected from the type *manuf*. If a customer of Zyx owned gizmos made by Baker, Edwards and Smith companies, the following assignment statement might appear in a simple program:

outrec.equip := [baker, edwards, smith]

where the quantity in brackets on the right side is a set constant stating that items are present from the three manufacturers noted. For an interactive business file maintenance program, the record of a new customer showing no association with a manufacturer would most likely be initialized using an empty set constant:

outrec.equip := [ ]

Then, when the customer acquired his or her first gizmo, we might find a statement such as:

outrec.equip := outrec.equip + [edwards]

which would form the union of the old value of the *equip* set with a new set constant value. In other words, *equip* would now have a notation indicating the presence of *edwards* in addition to what was previously noted in *equip*. We could continue adding notations of other gizmo acquisitions when appropriate. In fact this process is likely to assign a value to a simple variable of the set type associated with *manuf*; then that variable would be used elsewhere in the program to augment the noted membership of *equip*.

Pascal's facilities for handling sets are advantageous in many ways. A set is generally stored in memory as an array of binary bits which are made accessible in a special way. In UCSD Pascal, a set is stored as a string of bytes, each byte containing up to 8 bits to indicate whether a corresponding value is present in the set. Only the number of bytes needed to hold the declared number of set members need be stored. If, as is usual, one needs several dozen members in a set for a business application, the space occupied is very little more than the minimum needed. UCSD Pascal allows a set to have as many as 4080 members.

Once the value of a set field of a record has been assigned, it is readily possible to test whether a customer record is associated with a desired combination of members. For example, to determine whether a customer is noted as owning gizmos made by Baker, Edwards or Jones companies, we could use an *if* statement such as:

if (outrec.equip * [baker,edwards,jones]) <> [ ]
    then
        begin . . . end;

Here the expression within parentheses (on the left of "<>") isolates the members of *equip* falling in the group Baker, Edwards and Jones. The parenthesized expression is said to be the intersection of the value in the *equip* field in *outrec* and the set constant within square brackets. The comparison indicated by <> then asks whether the result of the intersection operation has left any members by asking whether the result is an empty set. If not, then at least one of the three members must be present, and the compound statement *(begin . . . end)* following *then* is executed.

The alternative to this test for set membership would usually be a complex sequence of IF tests in the traditional languages. The set combining and testing operations can be implemented efficiently by the Pascal system. Thus they allow a program to be written more simply and occupy less space. They also make the operations undertaken by the program more obvious to anyone versed in Pascal, thus making a complex program more easily maintainable and bug free.

There's a Lot More

It is not possible to present a comprehensive view of how one uses a language for complex business programming within a short article. For example, we have not described the use of Pascal *subrange* variables, which allow a programmer to state that a variable is permitted to contain only certain declared values. If an attempt is made to assign to the variable a value outside the declared range, the program either terminates abnormally or (if Pascal is extended in a simple way) the programmer may provide a *recovery block* in which corrective measures may be taken. Data validation is one of the most common problems in business data processing. At UCSD, we feel that the addition of a simple recovery block mechanism is essential to allow reduction in program complexity for handling the many exceptional circumstances that show up in business data, without unnecessary interruption of processing.

A Note on Pascal Extensions

Though Pascal does seem to require a few extensions to make business application pro-

gramming truly practical, the language provides an extremely powerful base from which to work. One of the strengths of Pascal, according to the intentions of its designer, is that it offers all this power in a remarkably simple and self-consistent form. The necessary extensions can be made in ways that generally retain this consistency so as to be relatively obvious to the programmer. We feel that Pascal is by far the best language available for adaptation to interactive business processing on small machines. We would be happy to send further information about how we use the language for business or real time applications to anyone who writes to us.

The questions of whether standard Pascal should be extended, and how, are currently being debated intensely in the international Pascal Users Group. Each special interest community of Pascal users has its own list of extensions considered essential to make the language a practical tool for developing software products in that community. Even the question of what extensions are essential is being debated, since it is possible to use the facilities of the standard Pascal language to create a library of routines to handle the user's special problems in most cases. In general, an implementor should consider extending the language only in cases where the result will be simpler and more reliable or efficient programs.

This article discusses extensions that the author feels are essential for business applications. Other communities with very strong interests in Pascal work with real time applications, development of system software such as operating systems and compilers, interactive systems such as computer assisted instruction, scientific computations, and so on. Of course these communities do overlap substantially. If the essential extensions needed by all these communities were added to the standard Pascal language, the simplicity and self-consistency that make the language so important would probably be destroyed. Therefore, it is very unlikely that an eventual formal standard for the Pascal language will include any but the most widely needed extensions currently under discussion.

This situation leaves many Pascal advocates very much worried that there will be no effective standards for the extended language features needed by the special interest communities. There has been discussion within the Pascal Users Group about the possibility of encouraging development of common interest supersets of the language for specialized uses. Ideally, language standardization is a process which should proceed slowly giving attention to the ideas of all experts who wish to be heard. In practice, the use of Pascal is growing so fast throughout the computer industry that close coordination of the extensions made by many implementors has become virtually impossible. We at UCSD have set ourselves the limited goal of seeking coordination and cooperation on Pascal extensions for system programming (including those for business and real time applications) among a number of industrial firms that seem most active in use of the language, particularly as regards small computers. For reasons associated with their own proprietary interests, these firms will generally be able to cooperate on only some of the most widely used language extensions within their special interest communities. A Pascal language extensions workshop was held at UCSD in July of this year primarily to help bring about this coordination. We intend to continue working as closely as possible with the international Pascal Users Group, and to take guidance from the PUG leadership on extension issues whenever practical. ■

A "Tiny" Pascal Compiler

Part 1: The P-Code Interpreter

Kin-Man Chung
Herbert Yuen

Roughly speaking, a compiler is a program that translates the statements of a high level language (such as Pascal or FORTRAN) into a semantically equivalent program in some machine recognizable form (such as machine or assembly code). The former is usually referred to as the source program while the latter is called the object program. An interpreter, on the other hand, reads in the source program and starts execution directly, without producing an object program.

There is little doubt that compilers and interpreters are a necessary part of any computer system. The reason most personal computer systems do not have high level language compilers is not that there is no need for them. Compilers, being inherently more complex than interpreters, require more effort to write and more computer memory to run. The main advantage of a compiler over an interpreter is the relative speed. A compiled program typically runs an order of magnitude faster than an equivalent program executed interpretively. In fairness, it must be also pointed out that interpreters are usually easier to use, and more suitable for an interactive environment.

This series of articles is an attempt to describe how a compiler for a subset of Pascal was implemented on an 8080 computer system. It is not our intention to go into details for the reasons for the choice of the language. Pascal is widely recognized as superior to many other languages. For an overview of the language, readers are referred to August 1978 BYTE.[1] The publication, *Pascal: User Manual and Report*, by Kathleen Jensen and Niklaus Wirth (Springer-Verlag, 1974) should also be consulted as the authoritative source book on the language in its original form.

This is not, of course, the first Pascal compiler ever written for microcomputers. However, instead of waiting for a Pascal compiler to be written for our particular processor, we decided to undertake the project ourselves. In this way, we can add or subtract features from the original Pascal to suit our needs and system capabilities, so that it can be easily integrated with other system software developed so far.

2 Stage Compiler

The compiler is divided into two stages: a p-compiler and a translator. Instead of having the compiler generate machine code directly, it generates code for a hypothetical machine, called the p-machine. These codes, called p-codes, are then converted into the target machine codes by the translator. Dividing the task of a compiler into two stages offers several advantages. The compiler can be written abstractly, without committing oneself to a particular machine and worrying about details of code generation and optimization. Such a compiler is said to be portable, meaning that it can be used on other computer systems with minimal start up effort. It is only at the last stage of code translation from the p-codes to actual machine codes that we have to commit ourselves to a particular machine.

Another advantage this method offers is greater flexibility when writing the compiler. The compiler and the translator can be coded and debugged separately. The flexibility of such a compiler was apparent to us as we started to introduce more and more Pascal features into our original minimal

---

1. All of the Pascal articles from this issue are included in this volume.

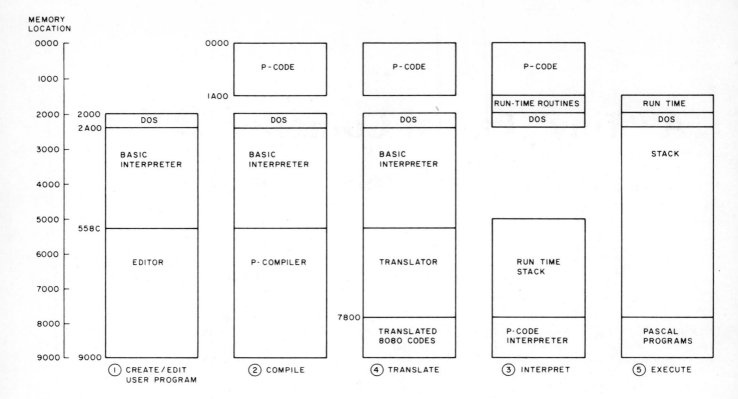

Figure 1: Memory overlay structure of the modules of the compiler. The North Star DOS and BASIC start at hexadecimal 2000 and take up approximately 14 K bytes of memory. The p-compiler is the largest BASIC program of the system; in its compressed form (void of all comments and blanks) it occupies 14 K bytes. It reads Pascal source programs created by the editor from disk files, and generates relocatable p-codes directly in memory. We use hexadecimal 0000 to 19FF for p-codes and find it adequate for Pascal source programs under about 300 lines in length. The smaller translator (9 K bytes) produces 8080 codes directly filled into memory. The origin of the codes can be specified. The run time routines (which total 1 K bytes of memory) are needed only when the translated 8080 codes are being executed. The interpreter is written in Pascal, compiled and translated. The BASIC interpreter is no longer needed when it or any other Pascal program is being run.

subset. Seldom was it necessary for us to introduce new p-codes other than those originally specified.

There is also one more reason for breaking the compiler into two stages: most small computers do not have enough memory space to store the complete compiler. After the p-codes are generated, the p-compiler is no longer needed, and can be overlaid with the translator. Therefore the compiler and the translator can share the same memory locations.

Actually we also use two other utility programs: a text editor and a p-code interpreter. The editor is used to prepare the Pascal source programs. The interpreter is used to interpret the p-codes produced by the p-compiler. This provides another alternative for running the Pascal programs. Because it is equipped with various debugging aids, such as setting up breakpoints in p-codes and outputting values for vari-

ables, debugging can be easily done. Only after a program is verified to be correct is the translator loaded, and 8080 code produced. This allows easy development of the Pascal programs without sacrificing efficiency at run time. Figure 1 shows the overlay structure for the various modules of the compiler. Figure 2 shows the logical flow during a program development.

In this part of the series on our project, we will describe the general plan. The Pascal subset is defined using syntax diagrams. A description of the p-machine and its codes are also given. We will discuss the p-compiler, translator and run time routines in the following parts.

Bootstrap Compiler

How does one introduce a new language into a computer system with limited computer resources? By computer resources we mean not only the computer hardware like memory and peripherals, but also software tools. We have learned from experience not to attempt programs with the complexity of a compiler in machine or assembly language. This left us with BASIC. Although it is not the most desirable language to write a compiler with, it turned out to be adequate. Some careful thought is needed, of course, to handle recursive subroutine calls from BASIC, a feature central to our compiler writing.

The alternative to BASIC is to go to a commercial computer and write the whole or part of the compiler in an appropriate language. The finished product (or part of it) can then be transferred to the smaller computer. This is, however, a luxury most of us cannot afford.

Of course, the compiler written in BASIC would be very inefficient and slow. But this actually would not matter, since it would only be used as a *bootstrap* compiler. The concept of bootstrapping should be familiar to most personal computer owners. We usually use it when initially starting up our computers. After turning on the power, a bootstrap loader is first loaded into the computer (either manually or through the use of read only memory). This bootstrap loader is then used to load the loader, which in turn loads the monitor into memory. The bootstrap loader is a smaller version of the loader; it is just big enough to load the main loader and not adequate to be a general purpose loader.

The same idea can be applied to compiler writing. A compiler for a small subset of a language is first written. This subset should be big enough so that a compiler for a bigger subset of the same language can be written in it. The larger compiler is then written and compiled, using the first compiler. Next, a compiler for a still bigger subset of the same language can then be written and compiled, using the second compiler, and so on until a compiler for the complete language is produced. In actual practice, no more than three stages are used. It does not matter if the first compiler is very inefficient. The idea is to get a working, albeit primitive and inefficient, compiler with minimum starting effort.

Pascal Subset Syntax

The syntax of Pascal can be described precisely by using a notation usually called Backus-Naur form (BNF). This is a collection of rules for the grammar of the language. Instead of dealing with Backus-Naur form directly, we use an equivalent but more understandable notation: the syntax diagrams. Figure 3 describes the syntax of the Pascal subset we are interested in.

In the syntax diagram, the square boxes are called nonterminal symbols, while the ovals are called terminal symbols. Terminal symbols are the basic building units of the language and require no further expansion. In our case, the names that represent the terminals are also their textual representations in the language. The nonterminal symbols in the syntax diagrams can be expanded using rules specified in another syntax diagram, and there is a syntax diagram for each nonterminal symbol in the syntax diagram. A branch in the diagram represents options allowable by the grammar. When all non-

terminal symbols are eliminated by expansion in this fashion, we would have a valid program. We start off a compilation with the nonterminal program. Looking at the syntax diagram we see that a program is a block followed by a period (.). Looking at the syntax diagram for block, we notice that it can have an optional declaration part followed by the main body which begins with the string **begin**, followed by any

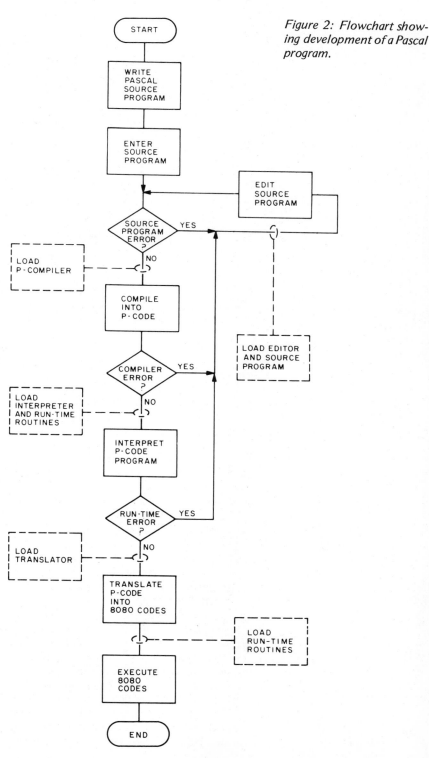

Figure 2: Flowchart showing development of a Pascal program.

PROGRAM

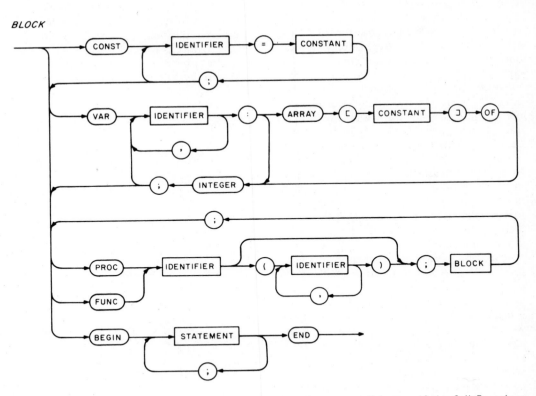

BLOCK

Figure 3: Syntax diagrams of the Pascal subset. For the syntax diagrams of the full Pascal set refer to the book by Kathleen Jensen and Niklaus Wirth, entitled Pascal: User Manual and Report. *These diagrams totally define the subset of the language that we are using.*

number of the nonterminal symbols, statement, separated by semicolons (;), and then the string **end**. The statement block can be further expanded by the syntax diagram for statement, and so on.

The reason we go through the details here is because it is important to precisely describe the features we want to include in our language before starting to write the compiler. It is the first step towards writing the compiler. These syntax diagrams will later become flowcharts for the syntax analyzer of the compiler.

Readers familiar with Pascal will no doubt notice several important features missing from our subset. There is no GOTO statement. The only data type we have is integer and integer array of one dimension. Also missing from the subset is the structured data type, pointer type, user defined type, and file type. A less obvious omission is passing the parameter of a procedure by address; the parameters are passed by value only. Aside from the fact that these features are difficult to implement, they are not indispensable in our bootstrap process. Of course, features like user defined type and

structured type are some of the unique features of Pascal, and should not be omitted in the long run. But we feel that they can be added later.

We have also included some trivial but nevertheless useful enhancements to the language, which we hope do not deviate from the standard too much. One is the addition of the optional clause **else** to the **case** statement which provides an exit path if the value of the variable does not fall into any of the **case** labels. Another is the inclusion of format controls in the read and write statements. Following an expression in a *write* statement, a pound sign, #, indicates numeric form and a percent sign, %, indicates hexadecimal format. If there is no format control, a character whose ASCII code equals the expression is output. Also a hexadecimal constant is prefixed by %. This allows processing of hexadecimal numbers without conversion by the user.

To allow interfacing Pascal programs with assembly programs, a facility is provided to read or write a byte from or to absolute memory locations. The array *mem* is a reserved array name that is used to do this.

For instance:

 mem [i]:=mem[j];

reads the byte from the memory location *j* and writes it back to memory location *i*. Machine language subroutines can be called from Pascal programs. The statement:

 Call (i);

can be used to make a call to memory address *i*.

The P-Machine

The p-machine is a stack oriented machine consisting of four registers and two memory storage areas. Memory is separated into program storage and data storage areas. The program storage area contains the pro-

EXPRESSION

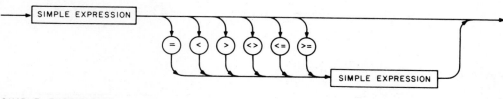

SIMPLE EXPRESSION

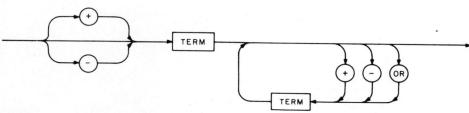

TERM

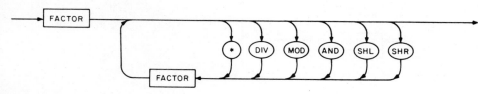

IDENTIFIER

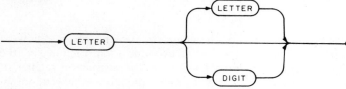

INTEGER

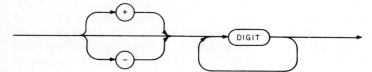

STRING

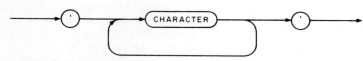

HEXINTEGER

Figure 3, continued: Elementary constructs for Pascal subset. Hexinteger is usually not defined in Pascal but is used here so that actual memory locations can be easily manipulated.

63

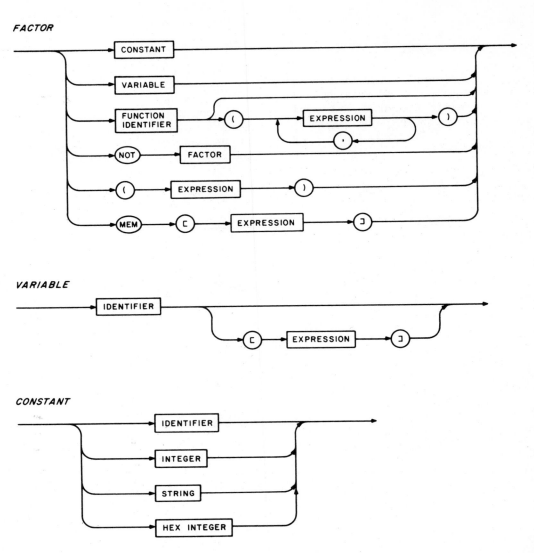

Figure 3, continued: Notice that some of the diagrams, for example FACTOR, contain themselves in their own definitions. This is known as a recursive definition.

gram codes (p-codes), and remains unchanged during program execution. The data storage area contains the values of variables. It is also used to store temporary values during arithmetical and logical operations.

Though the variables can be fetched and stored in a random fashion, the data storage area operates as a stack with respect to arithmetical and logical operations and runtime storage allocation. Arithmetical and logical operations are done on the top elements of the stack, and the results of the operations are pushed back on the stack. In this respect, one might call it a zero address machine, since operations (except store and load instructions, which must specify an address) are done without reference to any address. Later we will discuss the use of the stack during run time storage allocation.

The four registers in the p-machine are the program counter, P, which points to the next executable instruction in the program storage; the instruction register, I, which contains the current execution instruction; the stack pointer, T, which points to the top of the stack, and the base address register, B, which contains the current base address. The functions of the first three registers should be quite clear from the above discussion. The function of register B will become clear after we discuss storage allocation.

Each variable in a Pascal procedure has a scope and lifetime. The scope of a variable is the range within which it can be referenced. The scope of a Pascal variable is simply the procedure block to which it belongs. The lifetime of a variable is from the time storage is allocated for it to the time storage is disallocated. In Pascal, this is the time the procedure defining the variable is activated to the time a return is

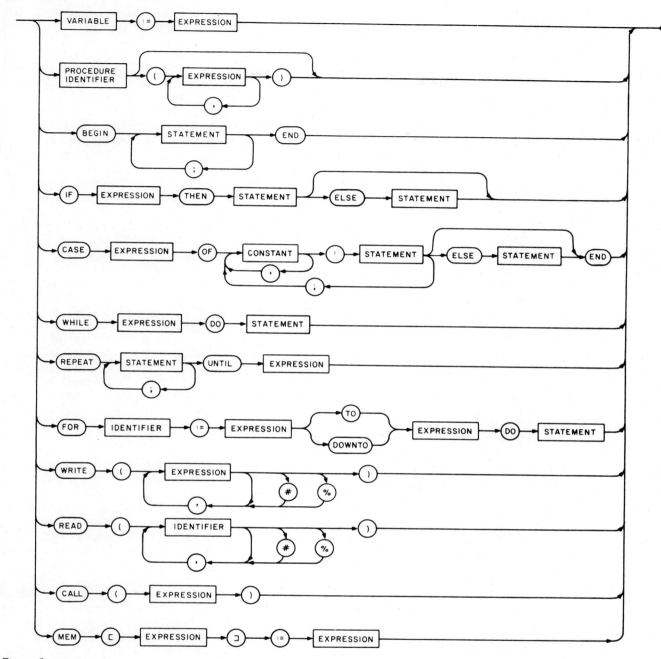

Figure 3, continued.

executed by the procedure. This is different from the way variables are treated in BASIC, where the scope of a variable is the entire program and its lifetime the entire execution time.

Since procedure activation is strictly a first in, last out process, the use of stack is an appropriate strategy. When a procedure is activated, storage for its local variables is allocated on the top of the stack, and is disallocated when the procedure is terminated. Thus the stack contains all the variables of the currently active procedures.

The variables of the last activated procedure are on the top of the stack, those of the second to last activated procedure next to it, and so on.

Since storage allocation is not static, addresses cannot be assigned at compile time, but must be calculated at run time. The base register, B, always points to the starting location of the segment of the data block in the stack. The addresses generated by the compiler are not absolute addresses, but displacements from some base addresses. If the variable is local, then its address is the

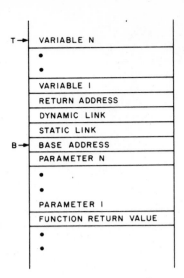

Figure 4: A typical activation record for a function. For a procedure, the function return value is omitted. Note that the procedure and function parameters, as well as the function return value, are below the base register B, and thus would have negative displacements.

displacement from the current base register B; but if the variable is from an outer procedure, then the base address for that procedure should be calculated, and added to the displacement.

To do this, and to ensure proper procedure or function linkage, extra storage is allocated on the stack when a procedure is activated. Figure 4 shows the various quantities present in each of the procedure blocks. The function return value is used only for function calls, and storage is allocated for any parameters needed by the procedure or function. The base address contains the value of the current base register B, and the return address contains the program return address at the place of the call. The functions of the dynamic linkage and the static linkage need further explanation.

The dynamic linkage forms a chain that reflects the procedure activation history. It points back to the base address of the procedure that was activated immediately before this one. For instance, if procedure A calls procedure B, which calls procedure C, then the dynamic link chain points from C to B, and then to A. It is used to ensure that the program returns to its previous state when exiting a procedure. In particular, the base register B must be loaded with the correct base address of the calling procedure. This would be easy to do if we follow a step through the dynamic link chain.

The static link, on the other hand, reflects the static hierarchical structure of the

procedures. Each active procedure has a link that points to the procedure (also active) that immediately contains it. The static links actually form a tree, with the main program block as the root. These links, which in general are different from the dynamic links, are used to let programs have access to the correct base address of the variables in an outer procedure, since at compiler time, only the static relationship among the procedures are known. The compiler therefore generates the pair (static level difference, relative displacement from the base address) as addresses for variables. The calculation of the addresses from these pairs would presumably slow down the process, but it is a small price to pay for nice features like recursive procedure calls.

The P-Codes

The p-machine has only 11 basic instructions, which are listed in table 1. For the sake of simplicity and easy handling in this version of the implementation, all instructions are four bytes long. The contents of the four bytes are as follows:

> byte 1: op — the operation code.
> byte 2: can be (i) v — static level difference.
>> or (ii) c — condition code in a jump instruction.
>> or (iii) 255 — denotes absolute addressing.
>> or (iv) not used for some instructions.
> bytes 3,4: can be (i) d — displacement from the base address.
>> or (ii) n — numeric constant.
>> or (iii) a — address in the p-code program.

The OPR (arithmetic and logical operations) and CSP (call standard procedure) are further subdivided into more instructions. The complete set of instruction mnemonics and operations is listed in table 2. The LODX and STOX instructions are used to load and store array elements with the value of the array subscript on top of the stack. The call standard procedure (CSP) instruction is primarily used for input and output (IO) operations. Besides the basic function of inputting and outputting single characters, additional procedures have been implemented to relieve the user from writing IO conversion routines in Pascal for numeric and hexadecimal numbers. In the future, more procedures can be added to handle the input and output of other data types such as floating point numbers and file records for tape or disk. Meanwhile these seven instructions are sufficient for convenient use in writing the bootstrap compiler and its related software.

Readers are urged to read the p-code interpreter listing which simulates the operations of the p-machine. The program statements are straightforward and self-explanatory. Familiarity with the p-machine instruction set is essential in understanding the code generation part of the p-compiler.

The P-Code Interpreter

Since the p-machine is a hypothetical computer, there has to be some method of executing the p-codes generated by the compiler. There are two simple solutions to this problem. One is to write an interpreter which can decode and execute the p-codes. The other solution is to write a translator which can decode the p-codes and output equivalent executable machine codes for an existing computer. Both methods have been used in our compiler system. The first method, although it runs slower, is good for developing programs because many debugging facilities can be implemented in the interpreter. The second method is good for production programs which may need faster execution speed. A p-code to 8080 machine code translator will be described in part 3 of this series.

The p-code interpreter is made up of two major modules:

- Main program.
- Procedure which simulates the p-machine.

Every call to the simulator will execute one p-machine instruction. Each p-machine

Op Code (Hexadecimal)	Mnemonic		Operation
00	LIT	0,n	load literal constant
01	OPR	0,n	arithmetic or logical operation
02	LOD	v,d	load variable
12	LODX	v,d	load indexed variable
03	STO	v,d	store variable
13	STOX	v,d	store indexed variable
04	CAL	v,a	call procedure or function
05	INT	0,n	increment stack pointer
06	JMP	0,a	jump unconditional
07	JPC	c,a	jump conditional
08	CSP	0,n	call standard procedure

Table 1: Basic p-codes. The v in call, load and store instructions is the difference in static level between the current procedure and the one being called or the one which contains the variable from the base address. An address in a p-code program is shown by a. The condition code, c, can either be 0 or 1.

instruction cycle can be divided into four stages:

- Fetch a p-code from memory.
- Increment the program counter.
- Decode the instruction.
- Execute the instruction.

Several global variables are used to hold the values of the p-machine registers such as program counter, stack pointer, current instruction, etc. A one-dimensional array represents the data stack. Functional operations of the various p-machine instructions are coded directly from the instruction set defined in table 2. The main program simply initializes the program counter to zero and then calls the simulator repeatedly to simulate machine execution. This sounds simple but not useful, because the user has

Mnemonic		Description		Mnemonic		Description
LIT	0, n	load literal constant		OPR	0,20	decrement (sp) by 1
OPR	0, 0	procedure return		OPR	0,21	copy (sp) to (sp+1)
OPR	0, 1	negate (sp)		LOD	v,d	load a word
OPR	0, 2	add (sp) to (sp—1)		LOD	255,0	load a byte from absolute address (sp)
OPR	0, 3	subtract (sp) from (sp—1)		LODX	v,d	load a word with index address (sp)
OPR	0, 4	multiply (sp—1) by (sp)		STO	v,d	store a word
OPR	0, 5	divide (sp—1) by (sp)		STO	255,0	store a byte to absolute address (sp—1)
OPR	0, 6	low order bit of (sp)		STOX	v,d	store a word with index address (sp)
OPR	0, 7	(sp—1) modulo (sp)		CAL	v,a	procedure call
OPR	0, 8	test for (sp—1)=(sp)		CAL	255,0	call procedure at absolute address (sp)
OPR	0, 9	test for (sp—1)<>(sp)		INT	0,n	increment sp by n
OPR	0,10	test for (sp—1)<(sp)		JMP	0,a	jump to location a
OPR	0,11	test for (sp—1)>=(sp)		JPC	0,a	jump to location a if low order bit (sp)=0
OPR	0,12	test for (sp—1)>(sp)		JPC	1,a	jump to location a if low order bit (sp)=1
OPR	0,13	test for (sp—1)<=(sp)		CSP	0,0	input 1 character
OPR	0,14	logical (sp—1) OR (sp)		CSP	0,1	output 1 character
OPR	0,15	logical (sp—1) and (sp)		CSP	0,2	input an integer
OPR	0,16	logical NOT of (sp)		CSP	0,3	output an integer
OPR	0,17	shift left (sp) logical		CSP	0,4	input a hexadecimal number
OPR	0,18	shift right (sp) logical		CSP	0,5	output a hexadecimal number
OPR	0,19	increment (sp) by 1		CSP	0,8	output a string

Table 2: The p-machine instruction set. The stack pointer, sp, points to the top element of the stack. The content of the stack element is represented by (sp). The operands of the OPR instructions are replaced by their results on the stack. The result of the six relational operations is 1 if the test is true and 0 if false. With the exception of single operand OPR instructions, all instructions adjust the stack pointer, sp, after execution.

G: *go* — Set program counter to zero; initialize other counters; start execution.

S: *single-step* — Execute one p-code; display the mnemonics of the next p-code pointed by the updated program counter.

R: *run/restart* — Start execution from current program counter until the program ends or a breakpoint is reached. This command is used to continue execution at a breakpoint.

B: *set breakpoint* — A p-code address is entered as a breakpoint after the interpreter prompts with a ?. Up to five breakpoints may be set.

C: *clear* — All breakpoints previously set are cleared.

Y: *display breakpoint* — Display the breakpoints already set.

X: *examine status* — Display the values of: current program counter, base address, stack pointer, the top two elements of the stack.

K: *stack content* — A value is entered as the stack pointer after the interpreter prompts with a ?. It will then display the values of six stack elements starting from this stack pointer.

T: *trace* — Display the address and mnemonics of the 16 p-codes last executed. This command is usually applied at a breakpoint. It is used for tracing the logic flow of the program.

E: *examine program* — A p-code address is entered as a display pointer (DP) after the interpreter prompts with a ?. It will then display the mnemonics of the p-code at this address. This command and the U and N commands are used for examining the p-codes anywhere in the program without altering the current program counter.

U: *up* — Decrement the display pointer by one and display the mnemonics of the p-code pointed by it.

N: *next* — Increment the display pointer by one and display the mnemonics of the p-code pointed by it.

Q: *quit* — Terminate the interpreter program and return to operating system.

Table 3: Interpreter commands. All commands for the p-code interpreter are single characters. A command is entered after the interpreter prompts the user with a > on the video display. Additional information is needed for some commands such as breakpoint and stack addresses. On entry to the interpreter it will ask for the starting memory address of p-codes and initialize the program counter to zero. On exit it will display the number of p-codes executed.

no control of the program during execution until it terminates.

In order to enable user control of an executing p-code program, the main program must accept commands from the user which instruct it to call the simulator a specified number of times or to display register and stack contents. This is the simple idea of a debugging interpreter. The debugging aids commonly known include single step execution, set and reset of breakpoints, and display of register and stack contents. A number of these debugging facilities have been incorporated in the p-code interpreter. Table 3 shows the 13 interpreter commands and their functions. Note that the trace command is particularly useful in analyzing mysterious logic flow of a program, such as discovering the path along which a breakpoint is reached. This command is more convenient to use and much faster than single step execution. The limits on the number of breakpoints and the number of instructions traced can be changed easily in the program.

The first version of the p-code interpreter was written in BASIC. While developing the p-compiler, different constructs of Pascal statements were tested one at a time using the interpreter to verify the correctness of the p-codes generated. After the compiler was debugged, the interpreter was rewritten in Pascal. The program logic is very similar to the BASIC version. Since the program structure of the Pascal version is neat and highly readable, the debugging time is minimal. The Pascal source program is shown in listing 1. The program design is rather straightforward. Readers with some programming experience in any high level language should be able to read and understand it without the help of a flowchart or further explanation on program logic. Note that in the main program and procedure *exec*, the **case...of** statement is put to good use. In the BASIC version the interpreter commands have to be tested within a FOR loop by comparing the input character with a string array, and then an ON...GOTO statement is used to branch to various parts of the program.

It must be emphasized again that the interpreter executes p-codes and not Pascal statements. Therefore the user is required to have some knowledge of the p-machine and p-codes. In addition to this, the p-compiler should be instructed to list p-codes together with Pascal program statements during compilation. They will be cross-referenced when running the interpreter. Obviously this procedure is not as convenient and easy to use as an ordinary BASIC interpreter, but still it provides the only way for debugging Pascal programs in our present version. A new debugging scheme is being planned for the future which will enable the user to debug programs at the **Pascal statement level**. This means the user may refer to variables and arrays and statements rather than stack contents and p-code addresses. Part 2 will go into details of the design and implementation of the p-compiler.■

Listing 1: Pascal source code for the p-code interpreter as output by the authors' system. This version implements all of the commands in table 3.

```
P-CODES STARTS AT 0000
WANT CODE PRINTED?N
   0 ?$P.INTS
   0 ( P-CODE INTERPRETER.  HY.1  3/31/78   BY  H.YUEN )
   0 ( LAST MOD 4/12/78 )
   0 CONST U=15;BPLIM=5;SIZE=500;SIZE1=480;
   1 VAR Z,P,B,T,BP,P0,TP,CMD,I,J,K,STOP:INTEGER;
   1     S:ARRAY[SIZE] OF INTEGER;
   1     TRACE:ARRAY[U] OF INTEGER;
   1     MN:ARRAY[26] OF INTEGER;
   1     BREAK:ARRAY[BPLIM] OF INTEGER;
   1
   1   ( IMPORTANT GLOBAL VARIABLES:
   1     P:PROGRAM COUNTER       B:BASE POINTER
   1     T:STACK POINTER         BP:BREAK POINT INDEX
   1     TP:TRACE STACK PTR      K:INSTRUCTION COUNTER
   1     S:DATA STACK            Z:STARTING ADDR OF P-CODE )
   1
   1 FUNC BASE(LEV);
   1   VAR B1:INTEGER;
   2   BEGIN B1:=B;
   5     WHILE LEV>0 DO BEGIN
   9       B1:=S[B1];LEV:=LEV-1 END;
  17     BASE:=B1
  18   END (BASE);
  20
  20 PROC INIT;
  20   VAR I:INTEGER;
  21   BEGIN T:=0;B:=1;P:=0;STOP:=0;
  30     S[1]:=0;S[2]:=0;S[3]:=-1;
  40     P0:=0;TP:=U;K:=0;
  46     FOR I:=0 TO U DO TRACE[I]:=-1
  55   END (INIT);
  63
  63 PROC CRLF;
  63   BEGIN WRITE(13,10) END;
  70
  70 PROC EXEC;
  70   VAR X,A,L,F,IDX:INTEGER;
  71   BEGIN X:=P SHL 2 + Z;
  78     A:=MEM[X+3] SHL 8 +MEM[X+2];
  90     TP:=TP+1;IF TP>U THEN TP:=0;
 100     TRACE[TP]:=P;
 103     P:=P+1;P0:=P;K:=K+1;
 113     F:=MEM[X];
 116     IF F<=8 THEN IDX:=0
 121     ELSE BEGIN IDX:=1;F:=F-16 END;
 129     CASE F OF
 130 0:BEGIN T:=T+1;S[T]:=A END;
 142 1: CASE A OF
 147   0 :BEGIN (RETURN)
 151       T:=B-1;B:=S[T+2];P:=S[T+3] END;
 166   1 :S[T]:=-S[T];
 176   2 :BEGIN T:=T-1;S[T]:=S[T]+S[T+1] END;
 194   3 :BEGIN T:=T-1;S[T]:=S[T]-S[T+1] END;
 212   4 :BEGIN T:=T-1;S[T]:=S[T]*S[T+1] END;
 230   5 :BEGIN T:=T-1;S[T]:=S[T] DIV S[T+1] END;
 248   6 :S[T]:=S[T] AND 1; (TEST FOR ODD)
 259   7 :BEGIN T:=T-1;S[T]:=S[T] MOD S[T+1] END;
 277   8 :BEGIN T:=T-1;S[T]:=S[T]=S[T+1] END;
 295   9 :BEGIN T:=T-1;S[T]:=S[T]<>S[T+1] END;
 313  10 :BEGIN T:=T-1;S[T]:=S[T]<S[T+1] END;
 331  11 :BEGIN T:=T-1;S[T]:=S[T]>=S[T+1] END;
 349  12 :BEGIN T:=T-1;S[T]:=S[T]>S[T+1] END;
 367  13 :BEGIN T:=T-1;S[T]:=S[T]<=S[T+1] END;
 385  14 :BEGIN T:=T-1;S[T]:=S[T] OR S[T+1] END;
 403  15 :BEGIN T:=T-1;S[T]:=S[T] AND S[T+1] END;
 421  16 :S[T]:=NOT S[T];
 431  17 :BEGIN T:=T-1;S[T]:=S[T] SHL S[T+1] END;
 449  18 :BEGIN T:=T-1;S[T]:=S[T] SHR S[T+1] END;
 467  19 :S[T]:=S[T]+1;
 478  20 :S[T]:=S[T]-1;
 489  21 :BEGIN (COPY)
 493       T:=T+1;S[T]:=S[T-1] END
 503     ELSE BEGIN WRITE(' ILLEGAL OPR');CRLF;STOP:=1 END
 521   END (CASE OF A);
 523 2:BEGIN (LOAD)
 527     L:=MEM[X+1];
 532     IF L=255 THEN S[T]:=MEM[S[T]]
 539     ELSE BEGIN IF IDX THEN A:=A+S[T];
 549           T:=T+1-IDX;S[T]:=S[BASE(L)+A] END
 564   END;
 565 3:BEGIN (STORE)
 569     L:=MEM[X+1];
 574     IF L=255 THEN BEGIN
 578       MEM[S[T-1]]:=S[T];T:=T-2 END
 589     ELSE BEGIN
 590       IF IDX THEN A:=S[T-1]+A;
 599       S[BASE(L)+A]:=S[T];T:=T-1-IDX END
 614   END;
 615 4:BEGIN (CALL)
 619     L:=MEM[X+1];
 624     IF L=255 THEN BEGIN CALL(S[T]);T:=T-1 END
 635     ELSE BEGIN
 636       S[T+1]:=BASE(L);S[T+2]:=B;
 649       S[T+3]:=P;B:=T+1;P:=A END
 660   END;
 661 5:IF T>(SIZE1-A) THEN BEGIN
 671     WRITE(' STACK OVFL');CRLF;STOP:=1 END
 687   ELSE T:=T+A;
 693 6:P:=A; (JMP)
 700 7:BEGIN IF S[T]=MEM[X+1] THEN P:=A;   (JPC)
 714     T:=T-1 END;
 719 8:CASE A OF (CSP)
 724   0:BEGIN T:=T+1;READ(S[T]) END;   (IN CHAR)
 736   1:BEGIN WRITE(S[T]);T:=T-1 END;  (OUT CHAR)
 748   2:BEGIN T:=T+1;READ(S[T]#) END;  (IN NUMBER)
 760   3:BEGIN WRITE(S[T]#);T:=T-1 END; (OUT NUMBER)
 772   4:BEGIN T:=T+1;READ(S[T]%) END;  (IN HEX)
 784   5:BEGIN WRITE(S[T]%);T:=T-1 END; (OUT HEX)
 796   8:BEGIN (OUT STRING)
 800       FOR IDX:=T-S[T] TO T-1 DO WRITE(S[IDX]);
 820       T:=T-S[T]-1 END
 827     ELSE BEGIN WRITE(' ILLEGAL CSP');CRLF;STOP:=1 END
 845   END (CASE OF A)
 846 ELSE BEGIN WRITE(' ILLEGAL OPCODE');CRLF;STOP:=1 END
 867   END (CASE OF F)
 868 END (EXEC);
 869
 869 PROC CODE(PC); (PRINT CODE)
 869   VAR X,N,IDX:INTEGER;
 870   BEGIN X:=PC SHL 2 +Z;N:=MEM[X]*3;
 882     IF N<=24 THEN IDX:=' '
 887     ELSE BEGIN N:=N-48;IDX:='X' END;
 895     WRITE(' ',PC#,' ',MN[N],MN[N+1],MN[N+2],IDX,'  ',
 924       MEM[X+1]#,',',MEM[X+3] SHL 8 +MEM[X+2]#);CRLF
 944   END (CODE);
 945
 945 PROC CKBP; (CHECK BREAK POINT)
 945   VAR I:INTEGER;
 946   BEGIN IF P<0 THEN STOP:=1
 952     ELSE BEGIN
 954     FOR I:=1 TO BP DO
 961       IF BREAK[I]=P THEN BEGIN
 966         WRITE(' BREAK ');CODE(P);
 978         STOP:=1 END END
 985   END (CKBP);
 986
 986 BEGIN (MAIN)
 986   FOR I:=0 TO 26 DO
 994     MN[I]:=MEM[I+%1E80]; (MNEMONICS ARE IN MEMORY)
1005   WRITE('ADDR?');READ(Z%);CRLF;
1015   INIT; CODE(P);BP:=0;
1021   REPEAT WRITE('>');READ(CMD);
1025   CASE CMD OF
1026 'R':BEGIN STOP:=0;REPEAT EXEC;CKBP UNTIL STOP END;
1037 'S':BEGIN EXEC; CODE(P) END;
1046 'X':BEGIN
1050     WRITE('  P=',P#,' B=',B#,' T=',T#,
1072       ' S[T]=',S[T]#,' S[T-1]=',S[T-1]#);CRLF
1099   END;
1100 'G':BEGIN INIT;REPEAT EXEC;CKBP UNTIL STOP END;
1110 'T':BEGIN WRITE(' *TRACE*');CRLF;
1125     FOR I:=0 TO U DO BEGIN
1132       TP:=TP+1;IF TP>U THEN TP:=0;
1142       IF TRACE[TP]>=0 THEN CODE(TRACE[TP]) END
1151   END;
1157 'K':BEGIN READ(I#);
1163     FOR J:=I TO I+6 DO
1172       WRITE('  ',S[J]#);CRLF
1185   END;
1186 'B':IF BP<BPLIM THEN BEGIN
1194     BP:=BP+1;WRITE(BP#,':');
1202     READ(BREAK[BP]#);CRLF END;
1207 'C':BEGIN (CLEAR BP)
1211     BP:=0;CRLF END;
1215 'Y':BEGIN FOR I:=1 TO BP DO
1226       WRITE('  ',BREAK[I]#);CRLF END;
1240 'E':BEGIN READ(P0#);CODE(P0) END;
1250 'U':IF P0>0 THEN BEGIN
1258     P0:=P0-1;CODE(P0) END;
1266 'N':BEGIN P0:=P0+1;CODE(P0) END;
1278 'Q':P:=-1
1283     ELSE BEGIN WRITE('??');CRLF END;
1291   END (CASE OF CMD)
1292   UNTIL P<0;
1296   CRLF; WRITE(K#,' INSTR. EXECUTED.');CRLF
1319 END (MAIN).
INTERPRET(I), OR TRANSLATE(T)?
```

69

A "Tiny" Pascal Compiler

Part 2: The P-Compiler

Kin-Man Chung

Herbert Yuen

When Niklaus Wirth introduced Pascal in 1971, one of the design objectives was to allow efficient program compilation. As far as we know, all existing Pascal compilers use the one pass compilation technique.

Newcomers to Pascal sometimes criticize features of the language such as declaring variables before use, and having constant and type declarations precede variable declarations. But such features are necessary to make a one pass compiler work (aside from the fact that it is also good programming practice to declare identifiers before use). Compared with multipass compilers, the job of writing a one pass compiler is relatively simple, since there is no need to store the program in its intermediate form.

Figure 1 shows the structure of our one pass Pascal compiler. The main portion is made up of the scanner, syntax analyzer, semantic analyzer and code generator. A brief overview of these functional portions of the compiler follows. Detailed descriptions will be given later.

The syntax analyzer is commonly called the *parser*. Its main function is to detect syntactical errors in the source program. The smallest unit of the source program that the parser looks at is called a *token*. For instance, the reserved word **while**, the symbol :=, or the identifier *idname* would be tokens. The main job of the scanner is to read the source program and output a token when needed by the parser. Irrelevant information such as blanks, comments and line boundaries are ignored.

To further simplify the work of the parser, the values of numeric constants are also evaluated by the scanner. The parser then parses the program according to the rules laid down by the syntax diagrams which were described in part 1 ("A Tiny Pascal Compiler," September 1978 BYTE, page 58[1]) and generates error messages if illegal constructs are found. Identifier names are entered into a symbol table as they are declared. The symbol table is consulted by

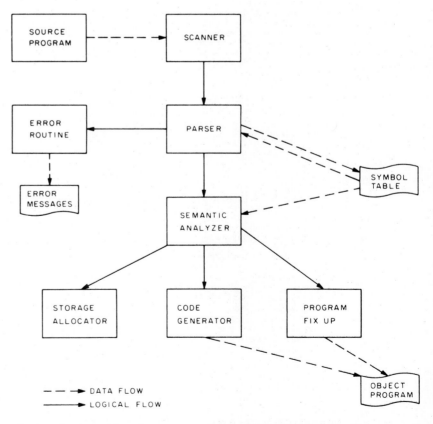

Figure 1: Logical arrangement and interconnections of the p-compiler modules.

1. Page 59 of this edition.

Listing 1: BASIC version of the p-compiler. This program takes the Pascal program and compiles it into p-code. The term p-code stands for pseudocode, an assembler language code for a hypothetical computer which can be converted into an existing assembler language. Listing continues thru page 78.

```
10REM PASCAL SUBSET COMPILER FOR P-MACHINE
20REM BY KIN-MAN CHUNG
30REM 1/78. LAST VERSION 4/78.
40 N0=32\REM # OF RESERVED WORDS
50 T0=50\REM SYM TABLE SIZE
60 N1=32767\REM LARGEST INT
70 N2=8\REM IDENT LEN
80 DIM W0$(5*N0)\REM RESERVED WORDS
90 DIM T$(T0*N2)\REM SYMBOL TABLE
100 DIM T0$(T0)\REM KIND OF IDENT IN SYM TAB\C,V,P
110 DIM L$(64)\REM LINE BUFFER
120 DIM A$(N2),B$(5)
130 DIM S(100),S$(100)\REM STACKS
140 DIM T1(T0)\REM LEVEL OF ID IN SYM TBL
150 DIM T2(T0)\REM VAL(FOR CONST) OR ADR(FOR INT)OF ID IN S.T.
160 DIM T3(T0)\REM ARRAY DIM OR# OF PROC PARAMETERS
170 W0$(1,40)="AND   ARRAYBEGINCALL CASE CONSTDIV  DO   "
180 W0$(41,80)="DOWNTELSE END  FOR  FUNC IF   INTEGMEM  "
190 W0$(81,120)="MOD  NOT  OF   PROC READ REPEASHL  "
200 W0$(121,160)="SHR  THEN TO   TYPE UNTILVAR  WHILEWRITE"
210 DIM M$(27),C$(80)
220 M$="LITOPRLODSTOCALINTJMPJPCCSP"\REM P-CODE MNEMONICS
230 P8=1
240 P7=0\P9=P7\REM START CODE=0000
250 !"P-CODES STARTS AT 0000"
260 Q9=4096*2\REM LAST USABLE MEM
270 F5=-1
280 INPUT "WANT CODE PRINTED?",Y$
290 IF Y$="Y" THEN Y9=0 ELSE Y9=1
300 X$=" "\GOSUB 1240\REM GET A TOKEN
310 GOSUB 5340\REM BLOCK
320 Z=FNE1(".",9)
330 FILL P9,255\FILL P9+1,255\REM FILL IN EOF MARK
340 INPUT"INTERPRET(I), OR TRANSLATE(T)?",Y$
350 IF Y$="" THEN END
360 IF Y$="I" THEN CHAIN "INTERP"
370 IF Y$="T" THEN CHAIN "TRANS"
380 END
390REM **********
400REM ERROR ROUTINES
410REM ***
420REM FNE1..IF CURRENT TOKEN<>K$ THEN ERROR #E
430 DEF FNE1(K$,E)
440 IF S0$<>K$ THEN Z=FNE(E)
450 RETURN 0
460 FNEND
470REM ***
480REM FNE2..IF NEXT TOKEN<>K$ THEN ERROR #E
490 DEF FNE2(K$,E)
500 GOSUB 1240
510 IF S0$<>K$ THEN Z=FNE(E)
520 RETURN 0
530 FNEND
540REM ***
550REM PRINT ERROR MSG
560 DEF FNE(E9)
570 !TAB(C0+4),"↑",E9
580 GOSUB 610
590 STOP
600 RETURN 0\FNEND
610REM ERROR MSGS
620 ON INT((E9-1)/5)+1 GOTO 630,640,650,660,670,680,690,700
630 ON E9 GOTO 710,720,730,740,750
640 ON E9-5 GOTO 990,990,990,760,770
650 ON E9-10 GOTO 780,790,800,990,990
660 ON E9-15 GOTO 810,820,830,840,850
670 ON E9-20 GOTO 860,870,880,990,890
680 ON E9-25 GOTO 900,910,920,990,930
690 ON E9-30 GOTO 940,990,950,960,970
700 ON E9-35 GOTO 980
710 !"MEM FULL"\RETURN
720 !"CONST EXPECTED"\RETURN
730 !"'=' EXPECTED"\RETURN
740 !"IDENTIFIER EXPECTED"\RETURN
750 !"';' OR ':' MISSING"\RETURN
760 !"'.' EXPECTED"\RETURN
770 !"';' MISSING"\RETURN
780 !"UNDECLARED IDENT"\RETURN
790 !"ILLEGAL IDENT"\RETURN
800 !"':=' EXPECTED"\RETURN
810 !"'THEN' EXPECTED"\RETURN
820 !"';' OR 'END' EXPECTED"\RETURN
830 !"'DO' EXPEXTED"\RETURN
840 !"INCORRECT SYMBOL"\RETURN
850 !"RELATIONAL OPERATOR EXPECTED"\RETURN
860 !"USE OF PROC IDENT IN EXPR"\RETURN
870 !"')' EXPECTED"\RETURN
880 !"ILLEGAL FACTOR"\RETURN
```

the parser as well as the semantic analyzer. After a Pascal construct is recognized, its meaning is analyzed by the semantic analyzer and appropriate p-codes are generated. Occasionally, there are forward references whose addresses cannot be determined at the time the codes are generated, but have to be resolved at a later time. Thus updates to the object program have to be done at the appropriate time.

This may sound complicated, but in fact a one pass compiler is actually the simplest compiler imaginable. The technique used by our parser is usually referred to as *top-down* parsing or goal oriented parsing. The top-down parsing algorithm assumes a general goal at the beginning. This goal is then broken down into one or more subgoals, depending on input strings and the rules in the syntax diagrams. The subgoals are realized by breaking them down into finer subgoals.

This is usually not a very efficient algorithm if backups are needed. The need for backups occurs if at some point we choose one subgoal from several others and find after some processing that we have made the wrong choice. We would then have to undo what had been done by the wrong choice and back up to the point where we could try other alternatives. This is usually a messy business and involves a lot of bookkeeping. Fortunately, in the parsing of Pascal, no backup is necessary. A keyword is present at each decision point, and it determines what subgoal we should choose. An example will make this clear.

Suppose our goal is to recognize a *statement*. A statement can be a number of basic constructs: it can be an assignment statement, an **if** statement, a **case** statement or any other construct defined by the syntax diagram. The Pascal grammar is so designed that we know which type of statement we should choose by just looking at the next token. If the token is **if**, then we know it is going to be an if statement; if the token is **case**, it is going to be a case statement, etc. There would seem to be a problem if the token is an identifier, since the statement can be the beginning of an assignment statement or a procedure call. But this can be easily resolved by consulting the symbol table, where we also keep the attributes (data types, addresses, etc) of the identifiers. This is one of the reasons why identifiers and procedures must be declared before use: it makes compiler writing easier.

A top-down parser without backup can be implemented by using a technique called *recursive descent*. Such a parser uses a recursive procedure for each nonterminal

Line Number	Remark
400	Error routines — FNE, FNE1, FNE2
1030	Get a character
1090	Input a line
1240	Get a token
1950	Enter entry into symbol table
2060	Search symbol table
2170	Constant declaration
2240	Get constant
2340	Variable declaration
2380	Simple expression
2610	Term
2850	Factor
3290	Expression
3490	Statement
5340	Block
6120	Push numeric
6150	Pop numeric
6180	Push string
6240	Pop string
6310	Code Generation — FNG
6520	Fixup forward references

Table 1: For easy reference the main subroutines of the p-compiler are listed here along with remarks regarding their uses.

in the syntax diagrams. A call is made to this procedure whenever a parse for such a nonterminal is required. It is easy to see why such a scheme would work. The stacking mechanism of the run time procedures ensures that we get back to the correct position in the syntax diagram after completing the parse of the nonterminal.

If you look at the syntax diagrams carefully, you will see that diagrams for certain nonterminals actually contain the nonterminal itself, either immediately or after several expansions. In terms of compiler writing this means that the procedures corresponding to these nonterminals would call themselves recursively.

One important part missing from our compiler is the ability to recover from errors. Of course all syntactical errors are caught by our compiler and somewhat meaningful messages are printed to indicate errors. However, if an error is found, the compiler is aborted prematurely and will not resume compiling. Such a compiler is, of course, not acceptable in practice. But with the understanding that this compiler will be used as a bootstrap compiler, as discussed in part 1, it is tolerable. A compiler with simple error recoveries would not be particularly difficult to implement but would involve a lot of programming codes and processing time. We hesitate to add things to an already big and slow program.

It is generally difficult to implement a compiler with sophisticated error recovery features. Such a compiler would not only detect errors, but would also try to repair the damages caused by such errors. The com-

```
890 !"'BEGIN' EXPECTED"\RETURN
900 !"'OF' EXPECTED"\RETURN
910 !"ILLEGAL HEX CONST"\RETURN
920 !"'TO' OR 'DOWNTO' EXPECTED"\RETURN
930 !"NUMBER OUT OF RANGE"\RETURN
940 !"'(' EXPECTED"\RETURN
950 !"'[' EXPECTED"\RETURN
960 !"']' EXPECTED"\RETURN
970 !"PARAMETERS MISMATCHED"\RETURN
980 !"DATA TYPE NOT RECOGNIZED"\RETURN
990 !"BUG"\RETURN
1000REM ******************
1010REM SCANNER
1020REM ******************
1030REM GETCHAR
1040 IF C0<L0 THEN 1060
1050 GOSUB 1090\GOTO 1040
1060 C0=C0+1\X$=L$(C0,C0)
1070 RETURN
1080REM *********
1090REM INPUT A LINE
1100 !%4I,C1," ",
1110 IF F5<0 THEN INPUT L$ ELSE 1160
1120 IF L$="" THEN 1100
1130 IF L$(1,1)="$" THEN 1210\REM MACRO FILE?
1140 L$=L$+" "\C0=0
1150 L0=LEN(L$)\RETURN
1160 IF TYP(F5)<>0 THEN 1190\REM EOF IF TYP=0
1170 CLOSE #F5\F5=F5-1\REM RETURN TO LAST ACTIVE FILE
1180 GOTO 1110
1190 READ #F5,L$\\!L$
1200 GOTO 1130
1210 F5=F5+1\OPEN #F5,L$(2,LEN(L$))
1220 GOTO 1090
1230REM *********
1240REM GET A TOKEN
1250REM RETURN S0$=TOKEN, A$=STRING, N3=NUMERIC
1260 IF X$<>" " THEN 1280
1270 GOSUB 1030\GOTO 1260\REM FLUSH BLANKS
1280 IF X$<"A" THEN1460\REM INDENTIFIER?
1290 IF X$>"Z" THEN1460
1300 K=0\A$="          "
1310 IF K>=N2 THEN 1330\REM ONLY 1ST N2 LETTERS ARE USED
1320 K=K+1\A$(K,K)=X$
1330 GOSUB 1030
1340 T=ASC(X$)
1350 IF T>47 AND T<58 OR T>64 AND T<91 THEN 1310\REM DGT OR LTTR
1360REM BIN SERACH FOR RES WORDS
1370 I=1\J=N0$*5-4
1380 B$=A$
1390 K=INT((I+J)/10)*5+1
1400 Z$=W0$(K,K+4)
1410 IF B$<=Z$ THEN J=K-5
1420 IF B$>=Z$ THEN I=K+5
1430 IF I<=J THEN 1390
1440 IF I-5>J THEN S0$=B$ ELSE S0$="IDENT"
1450 RETURN
1460 Z$=""
1470 IF X$<"0" THEN 1580\REM AN INTEGER?
1480 IF X$>"9" THEN 1580
1490 S0$="NUM"
1500 Z$=Z$+X$
1510 GOSUB 1030
1520 IF ASC(X$)>=48 AND ASC(X$)<=57 THEN 1500
1530 N3=VAL(Z$)
1540 IF N3<=N1 THEN RETURN
1550 E9=30\GOSUB 550
1560 N3=N1\RETURN
1570REM CHECK FOR SPECIAL SYMBOL
1580 IF X$<>":" THEN 1640
1590 GOSUB 1030
1600 IF X$="=" THEN 1620
1610 S0$=":"\RETURN
1620 S0$=":="
1630 GOSUB 1030\RETURN
1640 IF X$<>"<" THEN 1710
1650 GOSUB 1030
1660 IF X$=">" THEN 1690
1670 IF X$="=" THEN 1700
1680 S0$="<"\RETURN
1690 S0$="<>"\GOSUB 1030\RETURN
1700 S0$="<="\GOSUB 1030\RETURN
1710 IF X$<>">" THEN 1750
1720 GOSUB 1030\S0$=">"
1730 IF X$<>"=" THEN RETURN
1740 S0$=">="\GOSUB 1030\RETURN
1750 IF X$<>"'" THEN 1790
1760 S0$="STR"\C$=""
1770 GOSUB 1030\IF X$="'" THEN 1030
1780 C$=C$+X$\GOTO 1770
1790 IF X$<>"(" THEN 1820\REM IGNORE COMMENTS
1800 GOSUB 1030\IF X$<>")" THEN 1800
1810 GOSUB 1030\GOTO 1240
1820 IF X$<>"%" THEN 1930\REM HEX CONSTANT
1830 GOSUB 1030\S0$="NUM"\N3=0
1840 FOR I=1 TO 4
```

```
1850 T=ASC(X$)
1860 IF T>=48 AND T<=57 THEN 1880
1870 IF T>=65 AND T<=70 THEN T=T-7 ELSE 1910
1880 T=T-48
1890 N3=N3*16+T\GOSUB 1030\NEXT
1900 RETURN
1910 IF I>1 THEN Z=FNE(27)
1920 S0$="%"\RETURN
1930 S0$=X$\GOTO 1030
1940REM **********
1950REM ENTER SYMBOL INTO TABLE
1960 T1=T1+1
1970 T$((T1-1)*N2+1,T1*N2)=A$
1980 T0$(T1,T1)=K$\REM STORE TYPE
1990 IF K$<>"C" THEN 2010
2000 T2(T1)=N3\RETURN\REM STORE VALUE
2010 T1(T1)=L1\REM STORE LEVEL OF IDENT
2020 IF K$<>"V" THEN RETURN
2030 IF NOT F9 THEN RETURN\REM SP WAS ALLOCATED FOR PROC PARS
2040 T2(T1)=D0\D0=D0+1\RETURN\REM STORE OFFSET
2050REM **********
2060REM FIND IDENT A$ IN T$,STARTING FROM T1 AND UP
2070REM RETURN POINTER TO TABLE IF FOUND, ELSE RETURN 0
2080 J=(T1-1)*N2+1
2090 FOR I=T1 TO 1 STEP -1
2100 IF A$=T$(J,J+N2-1) THEN EXIT 2130
2110 J=J-N2\NEXT
2120 I=0
2130 RETURN
2140REM ******************
2150REM PARSER AND CODER
2160REM ******************
2170REM CONSTANT DECLARATION
2180 Z=FNE1("IDENT",4)
2190 Z=FNE2("=",3)
2200 GOSUB 1240\GOSUB 2240
2210 K$="C"\GOSUB 1950
2220 GOTO 1240
2230REM **********
2240REM CONSTANT
2250 IF S0$="NUM" THEN RETURN
2260 IF S0$="IDENT" THEN 2290\REM CONST?
2270 Z=FNE1("STR",2)
2280 N3=ASC(C$)\RETURN\REM TAKE 1ST CHAR
2290 GOSUB 2060\IF I=0 THEN FNE(2)
2300 IF T0$(I,I)<>"C" THEN FNE(2)
2310 N3=T2(I)\RETURN
2320 GOTO 1240
2330REM **********
2340REM VARIABLE DECLARATION
2350 Z=FNE1("IDENT",4)
2360 K$="V"\GOSUB 1950\GOTO 1240
2370REM **********
2380REM SIMPLE EXPRESSION
2390 IF S0$="+" THEN 2420
2400 IF S0$<>"-" THEN 2590
2410 Y$=S0$\GOSUB 6180
2420 GOSUB 1240
2430 GOSUB 2610
2440 GOSUB 6240
2450 IF Y$="-" THEN Z=FNG(1,0,1)
2460 IF S0$="+" THEN 2500
2470 IF S0$="-" THEN 2500
2480 IF S0$="OR  " THEN 2500
2490 RETURN
2500 Y$=S0$\GOSUB 6180
2510 GOSUB 1240
2520 GOSUB 2610
2530 GOSUB 6240
2540 IF Y$="-" THEN 2570
2550 IF Y$="+" THEN 2580
2560 Z=FNG(1,0,14)\GOTO 2460
2570 Z=FNG(1,0,3)\GOTO 2460
2580 Z=FNG(1,0,2)\GOTO 2460
2590 GOSUB 2610\GOTO 2460
2600REM **********
2610REM TERM
2620 GOSUB 2850
2630 IF S0$="*" THEN 2700
2640 IF S0$="DIV " THEN 2700
2650 IF S0$="AND " THEN 2700
2660 IF S0$="MOD " THEN 2700
2670 IF S0$="SHL " THEN 2700
2680 IF S0$="SHR " THEN 2700
2690 RETURN
2700 Y$=S0$\GOSUB 6180\REM PUSH
2710 GOSUB 1240\GOSUB 2850
2720 GOSUB 6240
2730 IF Y$="DIV " THEN 2790
2740 IF Y$="MOD " THEN 2800
2750 IF Y$="*" THEN 2810
2760 IF Y$="SHL " THEN 2820
2770 IF Y$="SHR " THEN 2830
2780 Z=FNG(1,0,15)\GOTO 2630\REM "AND"
2790 Z=FNG(1,0,5)\GOTO 2630
2800 Z=FNG(1,0,7)\GOTO 2630
```

piler has to make some assumptions about the nature of the errors and the intention of the author. This is usually difficult.

If our concern is solely that of locating all errors in a single parse of the source program, there are simple ways of doing it. Upon detecting an error, the compiler simply skips the input text until it can safely resume the compilation process. To do this the compiler looks for certain keywords or *stopping* symbols for hints to resume the parsing process. For instance, if we find an error while parsing a conditional expression, we skip the input tokens and search for

---

BASIC Recursive Subroutines

Most versions of BASIC do not adequately support recursive sub-routine calls. In North Star BASIC, the multiline function call can be invoked recursively, in a limited fashion. This is because the function parameters are local within the function definition and are pushed onto a stack when making a call.

The surprising fact is that most BASICs do not forbid a recursive call if one is made. For instance, the following BASIC subroutine, which is an inefficient way of printing the first N integers in descending order, is probably permitted in most BASICs:

```
100 PRINT N
200 IF N=0 THEN RETURN
300 N=N—1
400 GOSUB 100
500 RETURN
```

The problem of doing recursive calls in BASIC is that of preserving the values of the identifiers in the subroutines. This can be done by using a stack. The values of the identifiers are pushed onto the stack before a recursive call, and popped out of the stack in the reverse order when returning from the call. In BASIC, the stack can be simulated by an array:

```
10 DIM S(100)
11 P=0
12 REM INITIALIZE STACK POINTER
  .
  .
1000REM PUSH X INTO STACK
1010 S(P)=X
1020 P=P+1
1030 RETURN
2000REM POP X FROM STACK
2010 P=P—1
2020 X=S(P)
2030 RETURN
```

symbols, such as =, > =, etc, and keywords such as **then** and **do** or perhaps **begin**. If we do this for all the parts of the language constructs, we will at least have a compiler that would resume compilation after an error is encountered in the hope of finding all syntactic errors in one pass, and which would give meaningful diagnostics for most errors.

To reduce the size of the program shown in listing 1, comments are kept to a minimum. Each module or subroutine is clearly identified. To facilitate easy reference, the important subroutines and variables are shown in table 1 and table 2, respectively.

Scanner and Symbol Table Management

Each time the p-compiler calls the scanner (line 1260, listing 1), the input text is scanned and a new token is produced. This is done by calling a subroutine (line 1040) that returns a character from the input string. Since the input/output (IO) routines are line oriented instead of character oriented, a line buffer (L$) is used to hold a line, and a counter (C0) is used to indicate the character just read. When the end of a line is reached, the line input routine (line 1100) is called to read in a new line.

In our compiler we also provide the capability of invoking or recalling a file of Pascal text from disk. This is initiated by a command that starts with a dollar sign ($) in the first column followed immediately by the name of the disk file to be inserted and compiled. Since North Star BASIC allows four disk files to be open at the same time, there can be four levels of file nesting. The variable F5 is used to indicate this level. If it is equal to −1, then input is taken from the keyboard. The initial input is from the keyboard. This feature is quite useful, since we can store procedures that are commonly used in a disk library, and have them recalled when needed.

Usually, the token that the scanner returns is a number that represents the token class the symbol is in. To make the program more readable, we use string variable S0$. Possible values returned by the scanner are: ; , :=, BEGIN, IDENT, and NUM. The last two tokens, which are tokens for identifiers and numbers, require some further information. A$ and N3 are also used to store the textual representation of the identifier and the value of the number, respectively.

The recognition of a valid token is a straightforward process and will not be detailed here. Since : and := are both valid tokens, the scanner, after seeing the : , must also look at the next character to

```
2810 Z=FNG(1,0,4)\GOTO 2630
2820 Z=FNG(1,0,17)\GOTO 2630
2830 Z=FNG(1,0,18)\GOTO 2630
2840REM **********
2850REM FACTOR
2860 IF S0$="IDENT" THEN 2940
2870 IF S0$="NUM" THEN 3060
2880 IF S0$="STR" THEN 3080
2890 IF S0$="(" THEN 3100
2900 IF S0$="MEM  " THEN 3140
2910 IF S0$="NOT  " THEN 3260
2920 Z=FNE(23)
2930REM *** IDENTIFIER
2940 GOSUB 2060
2950 IF I=0 THEN Z=FNE(11)
2960 IF T0$(I,I)="P" THEN Z=FNE(21)\REM PROC NAME
2970 IF T0$(I,I)<>"Y" THEN 3000
2980 Z=FNG(5,0,1)\REM FUNC
2990 I=I-1\GOTO 4290\REM T2(I)=ADD OF FUNC
3000 IF T0$(I,I)="A" THEN 3190\REM ARRAY
3010 IF T0$(I,I)<>"C" THEN 3030
3020 Z=FNG(0,0,T2(I))\GOTO 1240\REM CONST
3030 Z=FNG(2,L1-T1(I),T2(I))\REM ID
3040 GOTO 1240
3050REM *** NUMERIC CONST
3060 Z=FNG(0,0,N3)\GOTO 1240
3070REM *** STRNG CONST
3080 Z=FNG(0,0,ASC(C$))\GOTO 1240
3090REM *** PAREN EXPR
3100 GOSUB 1240\GOSUB 3290
3110 IF S0$=")" THEN 1240
3120 Z=FNE(22)\RETURN
3130REM *** READ MEMORY
3140 Z=FNE2("[",33)
3150 GOSUB 1240\GOSUB 3290
3160 Z=FNE1("]",34)
3170 GOSUB 1240
3180 Z=FNG(2,255,0)\RETURN
3190 X=I\GOSUB 6120
3200 Z=FNE2("[",33)
3210 GOSUB 1240\GOSUB 3290
3220 Z=FNE1("]",34)
3230 GOSUB 6150\Z=FNG(18,L1-T1(X),T2(X))
3240 GOTO 1240
3250REM *** NEGATE
3260 GOSUB 1240\GOSUB 2850
3270 Z=FNG(1,0,16)\RETURN
3280REM **********
3290REM EXPRESSION
3300 GOSUB 2390\REM SIMPLE EXP
3310 IF S0$="=" THEN 3380
3320 IF S0$="<>" THEN 3380
3330 IF S0$="<" THEN 3380
3340 IF S0$="<=" THEN 3380
3350 IF S0$=">" THEN 3380
3360 IF S0$=">=" THEN 3380
3370 RETURN
3380 Y$=S0$\GOSUB 6180\REM PUSH
3390 GOSUB 1240\GOSUB 2390
3400 GOSUB 6240\REM POP
3410 IF Y$="=" THEN Z=FNG(1,0,8)
3420 IF Y$="<>" THEN Z=FNG(1,0,9)
3430 IF Y$="<" THEN Z=FNG(1,0,10)
3440 IF Y$=">=" THEN Z=FNG(1,0,11)
3450 IF Y$=">" THEN Z=FNG(1,0,12)
3460 IF Y$="<=" THEN Z=FNG(1,0,13)
3470 RETURN
3480REM **********
3490REM STATEMEMT
3500 IF S0$="IDENT" THEN 3630
3510 IF S0$="IF  " THEN 4440
3520 IF S0$="FOR  " THEN 5170
3530 IF S0$="WHILE" THEN 4800
3540 IF S0$="CASE " THEN 4890
3550 IF S0$="REPEA" THEN 4730
3560 IF S0$="BEGIN" THEN 4590
3570 IF S0$="READ " THEN 4040
3580 IF S0$="WRITE" THEN 3870
3590 IF S0$="MEM  " THEN 4650
3600 IF S0$="CALL " THEN 4240
3610 RETURN
3620REM *** ASSIGNMNT
3630 GOSUB 2060
3640 IF I=0 THEN Z=FNE(11)
3650 IF T0$(I,I)="A" THEN 3700\REM ARRAY
3660 IF T0$(I,I)="V" THEN 3760\REM INT VAR
3670 IF T0$(I,I)="Y" THEN 3760\REM FUNC RETURN VALUE
3680 IF T0$(I,I)="P" THEN 4290\REM PROC CALL
3690 Z=FNE(12)
3700 X=I\GOSUB 6120\REM PUSH TBL ADD
3710 X=16\GOSUB 6120\REM INDEX ADD MODE
3720 Z=FNE2("[",33)
3730 GOSUB 1240\GOSUB 3290
3740 Z=FNE1("]",34)
3750 GOTO 3780
3760 X=I\GOSUB 6120
```

```
3770 X=0\GOSUB 6120
3780 GOSUB 1240
3790 IF S0$=":=" THEN 3810
3800 Z=FNE(13)\GOTO 3820
3810 GOSUB 1240
3820 GOSUB 3290\GOSUB 6150
3830 K=X\GOSUB 6150
3840 Z=FNG(3+K,L1-T1(X),T2(X))
3850 RETURN
3860REM *** WRITE
3870 Z=FNE2("(",31)
3880 GOSUB 1240\IF S0$<>"STR" THEN 3950
3890 L=LEN(C$)\IF L>1 THEN 3910
3900 Z=FNG(0,0,ASC(C$))\Z=FNG(8,0,1)\GOTO 3940
3910 FOR I=1 TO L
3920 Z=FNG(0,0,ASC(C$(I,I)))\NEXT
3930 Z=FNG(0,0,L)\Z=FNG(8,0,8)
3940 GOSUB 1240\GOTO 4000
3950 GOSUB 3290\K=1
3960 IF S0$="#" THEN K=3\REM DEC
3970 IF S0$="%" THEN K=5\REM HEX
3980 IF K>1 THEN GOSUB 1240
3990 Z=FNG(8,0,K)
4000 IF S0$="," THEN 3880
4010 Z=FNE1(")",22)
4020 GOTO 1240
4030REM *** READ
4040 Z=FNE2("(",31)
4050 Z=FNE2("IDENT",4)
4060 GOSUB 2060\IF I=0 THEN Z=FNE(11)
4070 X=I\GOSUB 6120
4080 IF T0$(I,I)="A" THEN 4190
4090 IF T0$(I,I)="V" THEN L=0 ELSE Z=FNE(4)
4100 GOSUB 1240\K=0
4110 IF S0$="#" THEN K=2\REM DEC
4120 IF S0$="%" THEN K=4\REM HEX
4130 Z=FNG(8,0,K)
4140 IF K>0 THEN GOSUB 1240
4150 GOSUB 6150\Z=FNG(L+3,L1-T1(X),T2(X))
4160 IF S0$="," THEN 4050
4170 Z=FNE1(")",31)
4180 GOTO 1240
4190 Z=FNE2("[",33)
4200 GOSUB 1240\GOSUB 3290
4210 Z=FNE1("]",34)
4220 L=16\GOTO 4100
4230REM *** ABSOLUTE MEM CALL
4240 Z=FNE2("(",31)
4250 GOSUB 1240\GOSUB 3290
4260 Z=FNE1(")",22)
4270 Z=FNG(4,255,0)\GOTO 1240
4280REM *** PROC OR FUNC CALL
4290 K2=0\K3=I
4300 IF T3(I)=0 THEN 4400\REM NO PARAMETER
4310 Z=FNE2("(",31)
4320 X=K2\GOSUB 6120
4330 X=K3\GOSUB 6120
4340 GOSUB 1240\GOSUB 3290
4350 GOSUB 6150\K3=X
4360 GOSUB 6150\K2=X\K2=K2+1
4370 IF S0$="," THEN 4320
4380 IF K2<>T3(K3) THEN Z=FNE(35)
4390 Z=FNE1(")",22)
4400 Z=FNG(4,L1-T1(K3),T2(K3))
4410 IF K2<>0 THEN Z=FNG(5,0,-K2)
4420 GOTO 1240
4430REM *** IF
4440 GOSUB 1240
4450 GOSUB 3290
4460 Z=FNE1("THEN ",16)
4470 GOSUB 1240
4480 X=C1\GOSUB 6120\REM FORWARD REF POINT
4490 Z=FNG(7,0,0)\REM JPC
4500 GOSUB 3490
4510 IF S0$<>"ELSE " THEN 6520
4520 GOSUB 6150\K=X
4530 X=C1\GOSUB 6120
4540 Z=FNG(6,0,0)\REM JMP
4550 X=K\GOSUB 6540\REM FIXUP FORWD REF
4560 GOSUB 1240\GOSUB 3490
4570 GOTO 6520
4580REM *** COMPOUND STTMNT
4590 GOSUB 1240
4600 GOSUB 3490
4610 IF S0$=";" THEN 4590
4620 IF S0$="END  " THEN 1240
4630 Z=FNE(17)\RETURN
4640REM *** WRITE MEM
4650 Z=FNE2("[",33)
4660 GOSUB 1240\GOSUB 3290
4670 IF S0$<>"]" THEN Z=FNE(34)
4680 Z=FNE2(":=",13)
4690 GOSUB 1240\GOSUB 3290
4700 Z=FNG(3,255,0)
4710 RETURN
4720REM *** REPEAT .. UNTIL
```

determine the correct token. This can be done by using a one character look ahead. When the scanner is entered, a character is assumed to have been read, and upon exit from the scanner, a character beyond the current token is read.

Another problem that the scanner may have is that of recognizing reserved words. The reserved words are stored in a table in sorted order. When an identifier is found, it is compared with the entries in the table, by performing a binary search. If it is not in the table, it is assumed to be a user defined identifier.

In Pascal programs, identifiers are declared at the beginning of each procedure block. The scope of an identifier covers the entire block containing it (and any of the blocks inside that block). A simple symbol management scheme that reflects such scope rules makes use of a stack. When the compiler enters a procedure block, a segment of the stack is used to store identifiers for the block. If the procedure block contains another procedure block, then another segment of the stack on top of the existing segments is used for identifiers of this block. After successful compilation of a procedure, its segment of the stack can be discarded, since there is no further use for this part of the symbol table. In this way, we can also eliminate possible interference with identifiers in some other blocks. We also see that since the block delimiting mechanism is hierarchical, use of stack is also appropriate. Figure 2 illustrates two-level block nesting.

Readers may have noticed the similarities between this symbol table stacking scheme and the run time storage allocation scheme discussed in part 1. Since the symbol table deals with a static structure, it is much simpler.

Within the segment of the symbol table for a procedure block, further data structures can be set up for storing the identifiers. We chose to use what we feel is the simplest method: store the identifiers sequentially, in their order of appearance. This means that search also has to be done sequentially. Since most procedures have only a small number of identifiers, this should work well in most cases. Other more sophisticated structures such as a balanced binary tree or hashed table are commonly used in larger compilers.

The symbol table also contains some information about the identifiers. The identifier type has to be kept with the symbol table. Specific information is needed for each type of identifier. For constants, the information is the values of the constants; for program variables, the information is the address pair (level, offset from

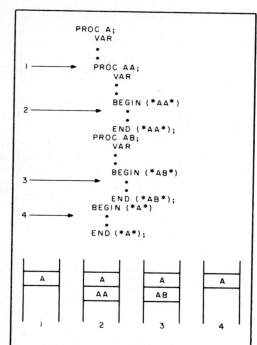

Figure 2: Example symbol table at various points of compilation.

Variable Name	Remark
A$	String of the token returned by the scanner
C0	Input buffer pointer
C1	P-code address pointer
D0	Run time storage counter
E9	Error code
F5	Active input file unit number; keyboard=−1
K1	Number of parameter in the previous block
L0	Length of the input line
L1	Static level of procedure
L$	Input line buffer
M$	P-code mnemonics
N0	Reserved word table size
N1	Largest integer
N2	Length of identifier name
N3	Numeric value of token (token = "NUM") or ASCII value of string (token = "STR")
P8	Stack pointer for S$
P9	P-code absolute memory address counter
S	Stack for numeric values
S9	Stack pointer for S
S$	Stack for strings
S0$	Next token
T0	Symbol table size
T1	Symbol table pointer
T$	Symbol table: identifier
T0$	Symbol table: type of identifier — V: variable A: array C: constant P: procedure F: function Y: parameter
T1( )	Symbol table: level
T2( )	Symbol table: value (constant) or displacement (variable) or address (proc or func)
T3( )	Symbol table: array size (array) or number of parameter (proc or func)
X	Value to be pushed or popped
X$	Next character to be read by the scanner
Y$	String to be pushed or popped
W0$	Table for reserved words

Table 2: Important variables used in the p-compiler.

base address); for procedures and functions, it is the address pairs and the number of parameters; and, lastly, for array variables, the information is the address pair as well as array sizes. See table 2 for actual variables that are used to store these quantities.

```
4730 X=C1\GOSUB 6120
4740 GOSUB 1240\GOSUB 3490
4750 IF S0$=";" THEN 4740
4760 Z=FNE1("UNTIL",10)
4770 GOSUB 1240\GOSUB 3290
4780 GOSUB 6150\Z=FNG(7,0,X)\RETURN
4790REM *** WHILE .. DO
4800 GOSUB 1240\X=C1\GOSUB 6120
4810 GOSUB 3290\X=C1\GOSUB 6120
4820 Z=FNG(7,0,0)
4830 Z=FNE1("DO    ",18)
4840 GOSUB 1240\GOSUB 3490
4850 GOSUB 6150\K=X\GOSUB 6150
4860 Z=FNG(6,0,X)
4870 X=K\GOTO 6540
4880REM *** CASE .. OF
4890 GOSUB 1240\GOSUB 3290
4900 Z=FNE1("OF    ",25)
4910 I2=1\REM # OF CASE STATMNTS
4920 I1=0\REM # OF CASE LABELS
4930 GOSUB 1240\GOSUB 2240
4940 Z=FNG(1,0,21)\Z=FNG(0,0,N3)\Z=FNG(1,0,8)
4950 GOSUB 1240\IF S0$=":" THEN 4990
4960 Z=FNE1(",",5)
4970 X=C1\GOSUB 6120\Z=FNG(7,1,0)\REM A MATCH FOUND?
4980 I1=I1+1\GOTO 4930
4990 K=C1\Z=FNG(7,0,0)\REM GOTO NEXT CASE STMNT IF NO MATCH
5000 FOR I=1 TO I1\GOSUB 6520\NEXT\REM FIXUP FORWD REFS
5010 X=K\GOSUB 6120
5020 GOSUB 1240\X=I2\GOSUB 6120
5030 GOSUB 3490\GOSUB 6150\I2=X
5040 IF S0$="ELSE " THEN 5090
5050 IF S0$<>";" THEN 5130
5060 K=C1\Z=FNG(6,0,0)\REM EXIT AFTER A CASE STMNT
5070 GOSUB 6520
5080 X=K\GOSUB 6120\I2=I2+1\GOTO 4920
5090 K=C1\Z=FNG(6,0,0)\GOSUB 6520
5100 X=K\GOSUB 6120
5110 GOSUB 1240\X=I2\GOSUB 6120
5120 GOSUB 3490\GOSUB 6150\I2=X
5130 Z=FNE1("END   ",17)
5140 FOR I=1 TO I2\GOSUB 6520\NEXT\REM FIXUP FORWD REFS
5150 Z=FNG(5,0,-1)\GOTO 1240\REM POP VAL OF CASE EXP
5160REM *** FOR
5170 Z=FNE2("IDENT",4)
5180 GOSUB 3630\GOSUB 6120
5190 F9=1\IF S0$="TO    " THEN 5210\REM REMEMBER UP OR DOWN
5200 Z=FNE1("DOWNT",28)\F9=0
5210 GOSUB 1240\GOSUB 3290
5220 GOSUB 6150\K=X\X=C1\GOSUB 6120
5230 Z=FNG(1,0,21)\Z=FNG(2,L1-T1(K),T2(K))
5240 Z=FNG(1,0,13-F9-F9)\X=C1\GOSUB 6120\Z=FNG(7,0,0)
5250 X=F9\GOSUB 6120\X=K\GOSUB 6120
5260 Z=FNE1("DO    ",18)\GOSUB 1240
5270 GOSUB 3490\GOSUB 6150\Z=FNG(2,L1-T1(X),T2(X))
5280 K=X\GOSUB 6150\Z=FNG(1,0,20-X)
5290 Z=FNG(3,L1-T1(K),T2(K))
5300 GOSUB 6150\K=X\GOSUB 6150\Z=FNG(6,0,X)
5310 X=K\GOSUB 6540
5320 Z=FNG(5,0,-1)\RETURN\REM POP OFF VAL OF LOOP CNTRL VAR
5330REM **********
5340REM BLOCK
5350 D0=3\REM RESERVED FOR STATIC LINK,DYNAMIC LINK & RETN ADD
5360 T2(T1-K1)=C1\REM INIT ADD OF THE PROC BLOCK
5370 Z=FNG(6,0,0)\REM JMP TO STARTING BLK ADD
5380 X=T1-K1\GOSUB 6120
5390 IF S0$="CONST" THEN 5460
5400 IF S0$="VAR  " THEN 5550
5410 IF S0$="PROC " THEN 5730
5420 IF S0$="FUNC " THEN 5770
5430 IF S0$="BEGIN" THEN 5980
5440 Z=FNE(25)
5450REM *** CONST DCL
5460 GOSUB 1240
5470 GOSUB 2170
5480 Z=FNE1(";",5)\GOSUB 1240
5490 IF S0$="VAR  " THEN 5550
5500 IF S0$="PROC " THEN 5730
5510 IF S0$="FUNC " THEN 5770
5520 IF S0$="BEGIN" THEN 5980
5530 GOTO 5470
5540REM *** VARIABLE DCL
5550 L=0\F9=1
5560 GOSUB 1240\GOSUB 2340
5570 L=L+1\IF S0$="," THEN 5560
5580 Z=FNE1(":",5)
5590 GOSUB 1240\IF S0$="ARRAY" THEN 5610
5600 Z=FNE1("INTEG",36)\GOTO 5670
5610 Z=FNE2("[",33)\GOSUB 1240\GOSUB 2240
5620 Z=FNE2("]",34)\Z=FNE2("OF   ",26)\Z=FNE2("INTEG",36)
5630 D0=D0-L
5640 FOR I=T1-L+1 TO T1
5650 T0$(I)="A"\T3(I)=N3+1
5660 T2(I)=D0\D0=D0+N3+1\NEXT
5670 Z=FNE2(";",5)
5680 GOSUB 1240\IF S0$="PROC " THEN 5730
```

```
5690 IF S0$="FUNC " THEN 5770
5700 IF S0$="BEGIN" THEN 5980
5710 L=0\F9=1\GOSUB 2340\GOTO 5570
5720REM *** PROC DCL
5730 Z=FNE2("IDENT",4)
5740 K1=0\K$="P"\GOSUB 1950
5750 L1=L1+1\GOTO 5810
5760REM *** FUNC DCL
5770 Z=FNE2("IDENT",4)
5780 K$="F"\GOSUB 1950\REM FUNC ADDRSS
5790 L1=L1+1\K1=1
5800 K$="Y"\GOSUB 1950\REM FUNC VALUE
5810 K2=K1\GOSUB 1240
5820 X=T1\GOSUB 6120
5830 X=D0\GOSUB 6120
5840 IF S0$<>"(" THEN 5890
5850 GOSUB 1240\F9=0\GOSUB 2340\K1=K1+1
5860 IF S0$="," THEN 5850
5870 Z=FNE1(")",22)
5880 GOSUB 1240\T3(T1-K1)=K1-K2
5890 Z=FNE1(";",5)
5900 FOR I=1 TO K1\REM FUNC VALUE & PARS HAVE - OFFSET
5910 T2(T1-I+1)=-I\NEXT
5920 GOSUB 1240\GOSUB 5340\L1=L1-1
5930 GOSUB 6150\D0=X
5940 GOSUB 6150\T1=X
5950 Z=FNE1(";",5)
5960 GOSUB 1240\GOTO 5410
5970REM *** START OF EXECUTIVE STTMNTS
5980 GOSUB 1240\GOSUB 6150\K=X
5990 X=T2(K)\GOSUB 6540
6000 T2(K)=C1\REM START BLOCK ADDR
6010 Z=FNG(5,0,D0)
6020 GOSUB 3490
6030 IF S0$<>";" THEN 6050
6040 GOSUB 1240\GOTO 6020
6050 IF S0$<>"END  " THEN Z=FNE(17)
6060 GOSUB 1240
6070 Z=FNG(1,0,0)
6080 RETURN
6090REM **********
6100REM END PARSER AND CODER
6110REM **********
6120REM PUSH X INTO STACK
6130 S(S9)=X\S9=S9+1\RETURN
6140REM *********
6150REM POP X FROM STACK
6160 S9=S9-1\X=S(S9)\RETURN
6170REM *********
6180REM PUSH Y$ INTO STACK
6190 L=LEN(Y$)
6200 S$(P8,P8+L-1)=Y$
6210 X=P8\GOSUB 6120\REM PUSH START & END STRNG POS
6220 X=P8+L-1\GOSUB 6120
6230 P8=P8+L\RETURN
6240REM POP Y$ FROM STACK
6250 GOSUB 6150
6260 L=X\GOSUB 6150
6270 Y$=S$(X,L)
6280 P8=P8-L+X-1
6290 RETURN
6300REM **********
6310REM GENERATE CODES
6320 DEF FNG(X1,X2,X3)
6330 B$="   "
6340 FILL P9,X1\FILL P9+1,X2
6350 FILL P9+2,FNA(X3)\FILL P9+3,FNB(X3)
6360 IF Y9 THEN 6400\REM IF INPUT FROM KEYBOARD THEN DONT ECHO
6370 IF X1<16 THEN 6390
6380 B$(1,1)="X"\X1=X1-16\REM INDEX
6390 !%4I,C1," ",M$(X1*3+1,X1*3+3),B$,%3I,X2,%6I,X3
6400 C1=C1+1\P9=P9+4
6410 IF P9>=Q9 THEN Z=FNE(1)
6420 RETURN 0
6430 FNEND
6440REM *********
6450 DEF FNB(Z)
6460 N=INT(Z/256)
6470 IF N<0 THEN N=256+N
6480 RETURN N
6490 FNEND
6500 DEF FNA(Z)=Z-INT(Z/256)*256
6510REM **********
6520REM FIXUP FORWORD REF
6530 GOSUB 6150
6540 N=P7+X*4
6550 FILL N+2,FNA(C1)\FILL N+3,FNB(C1)
6560 IF Y9 THEN RETURN
6570 !"ADD AT",X," CHANGED TO",C1
6580 RETURN
READY
```

The symbol table is used by both the parser and the semantic analyzer. The information in the symbol table is used in a number of ways. The type of identifier is used, for instance, to check the type consistency in an expression. When a variable is referenced or a procedure or function called, the symbol table is searched to obtain the level and relative address from the base address. The number of parameters in a procedure or function is used to check the correct matching of parameters in actual procedure or function calls.

An identifier is searched for by starting from the end of the symbol table and working towards the beginning. (Viewing the table as a stack, we say that we search from the *top* of the stack down to the *bottom*.) There are two reasons for this searching direction. First, identifiers in the current block are more likely to be referenced and should be searched first. Secondly, suppose that a variable X is declared in both an outer and an inner block: by searching for X from top to bottom of the stack, we can be sure that we will find X of the inner block first, in accordance with the scope rule.

Parser, Semantic Analyzer, and Coder

The parser, the semantic analyzer and the coder are not separate routines, but are intermixed in a large routine. In most cases, after the successful parsing of a statement, its meaning is also understood by the compiler. Thus the semantic analyzer either requires minimal extra processing or is implicit in the parser and disappears altogether.

The parser, as we have mentioned before, uses a top-down technique called recursive descent. Since there is a close correspondence between the parser and the syntax diagrams of the Pascal grammar, there should be no difficulties in understanding the parsing process. The parser adopts the convention of one token look ahead which is similar to the one character look ahead convention used by the scanner. The variable S0$ is used to hold the next token to be read by the parser.

There is a part of the Pascal grammar, commonly referred to as the dangling **else**, that is ambiguous. The statement:

if *cond1* **then if** *cond2* **then** *stat1* **else** *stat2;*

can be parsed in two ways. The **else** statement can be associated with the first **if** or with the second **if**, producing entirely different results.

We resolve this difficulty by always associating the **else** statement with the most recent **if**. If an **else** statement with the first **if** is desired, one of these two methods should be used:

```
if cond1 then
    if cond2 then stat1 else
else stat2;
```

or:

```
if cond1 then begin
    if cond2 then stat1
    end
else stat2;
```

The situation is similar to the **case** statement with the added feature of an optional **else** statement. If the statement for the last **case** label is an **if** statement, we then have the dangling **else** problem. This is resolved in the same manner.

There are three functions used to print messages when errors are detected. The function FNE(X) prints the error message corresponding to error code X. FNE1(A$,X) checks to see if the current token is equal to A$, and prints the error message corresponding to error code X if not. FNE2 is similar to FNE1 except that the scanner is first called to get a new token. As we mentioned earlier, the compiler aborts as soon as an error is found. Therefore these error routines do not return to the calling procedure.

The code generator requires more work: care must be taken to store important values in stacks due to the inability of BASIC to fully support recursive subroutine calls. Otherwise the coder is more or less straightforward, since the p-codes are so designed (see part 1) that there is a direct correspondence between simple Pascal statements and p-codes. Table 3 shows the almost direct translation of Pascal statements into p-codes.

The declarative statements (**const**, **var**, **proc**, and **func**) do not produce any executable statements; they merely provide information about declared identifiers. The first executable code encountered when entering a procedure or function block is a forward jump instruction to the main body of the block. This jump is necessary since in general there may be procedures and functions whose codes take up space. The second executable code of the block increments the stack pointer (INT). This allocates space for the triplet (static link, dynamic link and return address) plus any variables declared. The number of spaces for the variables is already known from the declaration portion of the procedure block. The variable D0 is used to keep track of the space to be allocated at the activation of the block.

Note that no space is allocated for con-

Pascal source		p-codes	
x+10*y[5]		LOD	X
		LIT	10
		LIT	5
		LODX	Y
		OPR	*
		OPR	+
a:=exp;		(exp)	
		STO	A
if exp then stm1 else stm2;		(exp)	
		JPC	0,1b1
		(stm1)	
		JMP	1b2
		(stm2)	
	1b1	...	
for i:=exp1 to exp2 do stm;	1b2	(exp1)	
		STO	I
		(exp2)	
	1b1	OPR	CPY
		LOD	I
		OPR	>=
		JPC	0,1b2
		(stm)	
		LOD	I
		OPR	INC
		STO	I
		JMP	1b1
while exp do stm;	1b2	INT	−1
	1b1	(exp)	
		JPC	0,1b2
		(stm)	
		JMP	1b1
case exp of	1b2	...	
c1b1,c1b2:stm1;		(exp)	
c1b3 :stm2;		OPR	CPY
else stm3		LIT	c1b1
end;		OPR	=
		JPC	1,1b1
		OPR	CPY
		LIT	c1b2
		OPR	=
		JPC	0,1b2
	1b1	(stm1)	
		JMP	1b4
	1b2	OPR	CPY
		LIT	c1b3
		OPR	=
		JPC	0,1b3
		(stm2)	
		JMP	1b4
	1b3	(stm3)	
repeat stm until exp;	1b4	INT	−1
	1b1	(stm)	
		(exp)	
i:=funca(exp1,exp2);		JPC	0,1b1
		INT	1
		(exp1)	
		(exp2)	
		CAL	funca
		INT	−2

Table 3: Code generation for various Pascal constructs. For readability, the p-codes are given in assembly form. The italic identifiers in the Pascal statements are nonterminals that can be substituted by any valid expansion. The codes for these quantities are represented by parenthesized identifiers.

stants. If a constant is referenced, a load literal (LIT) instruction is generated instead of a load (LOD) instruction. Also note that the procedure or function parameters and the function return value do not reserve any space in the procedure or function block called. Space is reserved before the call is made. Therefore, these values have negative displacement from the base address of the called procedure or function.

When a call is made to a function, the space for function return value is allocated by incrementing the stack pointer (line 2980 in listing 1) (this step is skipped for a procedure call). The parameter expression is then evaluated (line 4250), putting

```
P-CODES START AT 0000
WANT CODE PRINTED?N
   0 ?$LST2.2
   0 CONST CR=13;LF=10;
   1 VAR A,B,C,D:INTEGER;
   1 FUNC MAX4(X1,X2,X3,X4); {LARGEST OF 4 NUMBERS}
   1    FUNC MAX2(X1,X2); {LARGEST OF 2 NUMBERS}
   2       BEGIN
   3          IF X1>X2 THEN MAX2:=X1
   9          ELSE MAX2:=X2
  12          END;
  14    BEGIN
  14       MAX4:=MAX2(MAX2(X1,X2),MAX2(X3,X4))
  28       END;
  30 BEGIN
  30    REPEAT
  31       READ (A#,B#,C#,D#);
  39       WRITE ('THE LARGEST IS',MAX4(A,B,C,D)#,CR,LF)
  67    UNTIL A<0
  69 END.
INTERPRET(I), OR TRANSLATE(T)?N
READY
LOAD DECODE
READY
RUN
   0 JMP 0  30    JMP 0  14    JMP 0   3    INT 0   3
   4 LOD 0  -2    LOD 0  -1    OPR 0   >    JPC 0  11
   8 LOD 0  -2    STO 0  -3    JMP 0  13    LOD 0  -1
  12 STO 0  -3    OPR 0 RET    INT 0   3    INT 0   1
  16 INT 0   1    LOD 0  -4    LOD 0  -3    CAL 0   3
  20 INT 0  -2    INT 0   1    LOD 0  -2    LOD 0  -1
  24 CAL 0   3    INT 0  -2    CAL 0   3    INT 0  -2
  28 STO 0  -5    OPR 0 RET    INT 0   7    CSP 0 INNUM
  32 STO 0   3    CSP 0 INNUM  STO 0   4    CSP 0 INNUM
  36 STO 0   5    CSP 0 INNUM  STO 0   6    LIT 0  84
  40 LIT 0  72    LIT 0  69    LIT 0  32    LIT 0  76
  44 LIT 0  65    LIT 0  82    LIT 0  71    LIT 0  69
  48 LIT 0  83    LIT 0  84    LIT 0  32    LIT 0  73
  52 LIT 0  83    LIT 0  14    CSP 0 OUTST  INT 0   1
  56 LOD 0   3    LOD 0   4    LOD 0   5    LOD 0   6
  60 CAL 0  14    INT 0  -4    CSP 0 OUTNM  LIT 0  13
  64 CSP 0 OUTCH  LIT 0  10    CSP 0 OUTCH  LOD 0   3
  68 LIT 0   0    OPR 0   <    JPC 0  31    OPR 0 RET
```

Listing 2: Sample Pascal program with compiled p-code. The number at the beginning of each source line is the offset of the corresponding p-code from the base address.

the resultant value on the stack. Thus, space is allocated for each parameter and initialized with the value of the parameter expression. Upon return from a procedure, the stack pointer is decremented by an amount equal to the space allocated for the parameters, getting back to the state before the procedure call. Upon returning from a function call, the stack pointer is also decremented by the same amount, but since a space has been allocated before the function call, the function return value is now on top of the stack, ready for further processing. This simple scheme works very efficiently and should lower the overhead usually associated with procedure or subroutine calls.

Listing 2 gives an output from the compiler for a Pascal program that prints out the maximum of four numbers. There are of course better ways of writing the program, but it does illustrate some ideas of the compiler discussed so far.

There is no optimization of the p-codes produced. Limited optimization can be done on the local level, and some optimization is actually done in the p-code to machine code translator. The problem of producing efficient codes is a difficult one, and is not addressed properly in our project. Given the simplicity of the p-machine and p-code, the p-compiler is efficient. But whether the combination of p-compiler and translator produces efficient 8080 code is uncertain.

This completes our discussion of the p-compiler. In part 3 we give a detailed discussion of a translator for converting the p-code into executable 8080 machine code. ∎

REFERENCES

1. Jensen, K, and Wirth, N, *Pascal: User Manual and Report* (second edition) Springer Verlag, New York, 1974.

2. Wirth, N, "The Programming Language Pascal," *Acta Informatica,* 1, pages 35 thru 63, 1971.

3. Wirth, N, *Algorithms + Data Structures = Programs,* Chapter 5, "Language Structures and Compilers," Prentice-Hall, Englewood Cliffs NJ, 1976.

A "Tiny" Pascal Compiler

Part 3: P-Code to 8080 Conversion

Kin-Man Chung
Herbert Yuen

In part 1 of this series (September 1978 BYTE, page 58[1]) we defined a Pascal subset language in terms of syntax diagrams. The p-machine and its instruction set and a p-code interpreter were also described. In part 2 (October 1978 BYTE, page 34[2]) we presented the design and implementation of the p-compiler. The subject matter for this part is the translation of p-codes to executable 8080 machine codes. We will also discuss the implementation of run time support routines and code optimization.

Compiler-Interpreter Systems

To understand why we need a p-code to 8080 translator, we should first take a brief look at the different structures of compiler-interpreter systems. The most widely used structure for microcomputers is the *interpreter*. Since interpreters are written in the target computer's assembly language, their memory size is small. They are self-contained in the sense that they include an editor for creating source programs and run time routines to do all computations. Memory storage for source programs is also small. The only disadvantage is speed. Execution time for a typical BASIC program is estimated to be about 300 to 1000 times the execution time of the same program written in assembly language. Interpreters may spend more than 70 percent of their time scanning source symbols character by character, parsing the syntax and checking errors. No matter how many times a pro-

gram statement is executed, the parsing procedure is repeated every time.

This problem can be readily solved by separating the parsing and execution steps. Before execution, the source program is compiled and intermediate code is generated. Thus scanning and parsing are done only once for each program statement. This is the so-called *compiler-interpreter* scheme used in some BASIC compilers. Execution of the intermediate codes is by interpretation. The gain in speed over a pure interpreter is a factor of approximately 2 to 10. However, the gain in speed is paid for by extra memory storage needed for intermediate codes.

The *compile-go* and *compile-link-go* approaches are commonly used for many high level language compilers in mainframe computer systems. These compilers generate relocatable binary codes. The compile-link-go approach has the advantage of linking together different modules of programs that are compiled separately, such as those in a subroutine library. This is done by a linking loader. However, due to limited system resources like memory and peripheral devices in microcomputers, these two structures are rarely used. Further, since Pascal is designed for fast compilation, linkage of program modules may be done at the source language level.

Among those four structures just mentioned, the compiler-interpreter seems to be most appropriate for implementation on microcomputers. However, execution speed is still slow because intermediate codes are interpreted rather than executed directly by the computer. An obvious solution to this problem is to translate the intermediate codes into executable machine codes. Thus,

---

1. Page 59 of this edition.
2. Page 71 of this edition.

each intermediate code is decoded once by a program which we call a *translator*. The translated machine code can be expected to run about two to five times faster than interpreted intermediate codes. Therefore, the overall gain in speed, compared with a pure interpreter, is a factor of approximately 10 to 50. (Preliminary test runs in our system show that Pascal programs run about 15 times faster than the same program written in BASIC.) We call this structure *compile-translate-go*.

The five compiler-interpreter structures we discussed above are summarized in table 1. The compile-go and compile-translate-go are rather similar in structure. Compile-go actually combines the process of compiling and generating executable codes into one step. The binary codes are generated by straightforward algorithms without optimization, because code optimization would require more complex program logic and make the compiler even larger. Separating compilation and translation into two steps significantly reduces the size of the compiler. Local optimization techniques can also be applied during translation. Code optimization will be discussed later. Since p-codes are designed to be machine independent to make the compiler portable, the translator is responsible for producing efficient codes for a target computer.

Designing the Run Time Routines

Run time routines form an essential part of all compiler-interpreter systems in microcomputers. Large computers can do fixed point, floating point and decimal arithmetic with 32 bit or larger word sizes in single instructions. Many microcomputers, on the other hand, can do only basic integer arithmetic with 8 bit words (bytes). Therefore, multiple instructions are needed to implement 16 bit operations like multiply, divide, subtract, logical operations and multibit shifts. The run time routines, sometimes referred to as *run time support package*, are a collection of subroutines written in assembly language that can be called by an interpreter or any program to perform various arithmetic and logical operations. Usually they include subroutines for IO conversion between ASCII and binary data.

The design of run time routines for our compiler system is based on three principles:

- **Fast implementation and clarity:** A straightforward approach is followed so that the overall package can be debugged and tested quickly and modified easily.
- **Speed:** The best known algorithms are used for computer arithmetic to achieve fastest execution speed possible. However, tricks such as self-modifying code are not used.
- **Memory storage:** The package is expected to be fairly compact. Since p-codes are translated mostly into subroutine calls, the number of instructions to set up arguments to be passed to the subroutine should also be minimal.

As described in part 1, the p-machine has a data stack and four registers: stack pointer T, base register B, program counter P, instruction register I. Since the translator takes care of the program counter and p-code instructions are not needed after translation, all we need are the stack pointer and base register. In the current version of our run time routines, contiguous memory storage is used to represent the data stack. For the sake of program clarity and easy debugging, the 8080 machine stack is not used, although using it for dual purposes as a data

Table 1: Summary of different structures of compiler-interpreter systems.

Structure	Example	Step	Input	System software	Output	Remarks
interpreter	BASIC, APL interpreter	1	source program	interpreter (execution)		Most popular for microcomputers. Advantage: conserves memory space. Disadvantage: very slow execution speed.
compiler-interpreter	BASIC-E, Pascal compiler	1 2	source program intermediate code	compiler interpreter (execution)	intermediate code	The interpreter may overlay the compiler to save memory space. Advantage: faster execution speed.
compile-go	WATFIV, PL/C compiler	1	source program	compiler	executable code	Only used in large computers. Disadvantage: size is too big for microcomputers.
compile-link-go	FORTRAN IV, PL/I, COBOL compiler	1 2	source program binary code	compiler linking loader	binary code executable code	Widely used in large computers. Advantage: fast execution speed. Disadvantage: requires more system resources.
compile-translate-go	Pascal compiler (by authors)	1 2	source program p-code	compiler translator	p-code executable 8080 code	Advantage: size of compiler is reduced, fast execution speed, increased portability, easy implementation.

stack and temporary storage for normal program logic is possible and probably more efficient.

Figure 1 shows the structural differences between the p-machine stack which we implement and the 8080 machine stack. Since integer data is stored as pairs of 8 bit bytes (character strings are stored as single dimensional arrays, two bytes to each element and only the low order byte is used; see descriptions in part 1), each load instruction increments the stack pointer by 2. The order of the byte pair is arranged as high-low because it is more convenient to use than low-high. The stack pointer always points to the low order byte of the 16 bit integer, which is on top of the stack.

Register pair D,E is dedicated for use as the stack pointer, while registers H and L are mainly used for 16 bit operations such as DAD, LHLD, SHLD and PCHL. When needed, register pairs D,E and H,L can be easily exchanged using the XCHG instruction. Since the base address remains unchanged within a procedure block, a 2 byte fixed memory location (with symbolic name BB) is used to represent the base register. The LHLD and SHLD instructions are used to retrieve and update the base address value. A summary of register assignments for implementation of the p-machine is shown in table 2.

Coding the Run Time Routines

Most of the subroutines are easily understandable. The routines for load, store, call and load constant are coded by direct translation from the interpreter program to 8080 assembly language, keeping in mind that each stack element (one data item) occupies two bytes. The routines for arithmetic and logical operations and IO conversions require more programming effort. In general, single operand functions such as negate, logical not and increment are performed one byte at a time in register A. Double operand operations such as add, divide and logical or are performed with register pairs H,L and B,C. The entire runtime package occupies about 1 K bytes of memory. The following are remarks on coding some of the not-so-trivial subroutines.

PUSH and **POP**: for most double operand functions, subroutine POP is called first to get the two operands from the stack (memory) and put in register pairs H,L (first operand) and B,C (second operand). After the operations, subroutine PUSH is called to put the result from H,L back onto the stack.

Add and **subtract**: since DAD (double precision add) is the only 8080 instruction for double operand 16 bit operation, subtraction is done by adding the 2's comple-

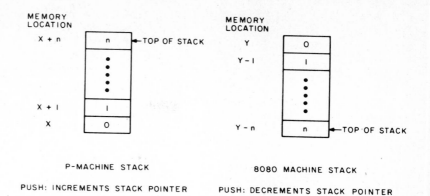

Figure 1. Differences between p-machine and 8080 stacks. This figure shows n+1 entries on each of the stacks.

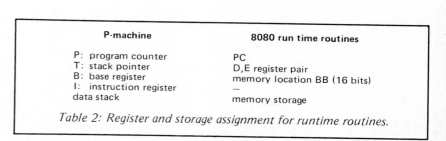

Table 2: Register and storage assignment for runtime routines.

ment of the second operand to the first. A message will be issued if overflow occurs and execution continues without any corrective action. The condition for overflow is detected by the rule:

if [sign(arg.1) ⊕ sign(arg.2) ⊕ carry ⊕ sign (result)] = 1, then overflow; otherwise nothing.

MULT16: 16 bit signed multiplication is done in two stages using an 8 bit multiplication routine. First, multiply the second operand by the high order byte of the first operand; the result is in register pair H,L. Second, continue the multiplication (left shift and double add) with the low order byte of the first operand; the result is in register pair H,L. This method is very efficient. In comparison, conventional 16 bit multiplication routines require more PUSH, POP and XCHG instructions because there are not enough registers to shift two 16 bit words and also update a loop counter. Overflows are ignored, as this is the usual practice for integer multiplication.

DIV16: 16 bit signed division is one of the most difficult routines to implement. First the signs of both operands are saved on a stack and are then converted to positive integers (actually the divisor is made negative in 2's complement because subtraction is done with a double add instruction). The divisor is also checked for zero value, and if so, a DIVIDE CHECK message is issued and the routine returns. Division is carried out as a sequence of subtraction and shifts. At the end, the signs of the quotient and remainder are corrected according to the original signs of the operands. The same routine is also used for calculation of the MOD function.

Relational operations: are done by comparing the high order and then the low order bytes of the operands. For testing less than, less than or equal, greater than, greater than or equal conditions, a common subroutine for testing less than is used. Register pair B,C is used as a flag to indicate whether the opposite of less than and equal to is wanted.

SHL and SHR: the logical left shift and right shift routines are symmetric in the sense that a negative argument (second operand) for the number of bits to be shifted will cause one routine to jump to the other, resulting in shifts in reverse direction.

INNUM: the conversion subroutine for input integers allows leading zeros and blanks and may optionally be preceded by a plus or minus sign (+ or −). It also checks for the absolute magnitude of the integer, which must be less than 32,768.

OUTNUM: conversion of binary integers to ASCII is done by repeated division by 10. The 16 bit divide routine is utilized.

P-code Translation

In general, p-codes are translated to subroutine call instructions which jump to the appropriate entry points in the run time routines. Output from the translator is an 8080 machine language program containing mostly subroutine call instructions. Some p-codes, such as load and store, require additional instructions to set up the arguments to be passed. Address offsets are always placed in register pair B,C and the static level difference is placed in register A. The jump instruction in p-code simply becomes a JMP instruction in 8080 with the correct address determined by the translator. The p-code addresses in CAL and JPC instruc-

Hexadecimal Op code	P-code	8080 Mnemonic	Commentary	Hexadecimal Op code	P-code	8080 Mnemonic	Commentary
00	LIT 0,n	LXI B,n CALL LIT		04	CAL v,a		
					a) v=0	CALL CAL JMP x	
01	OPR 0,0	JMP P00;	procedure return routine		b) v>0	MVI A,v CALL CAL1 JMP x	
	OPR 0,n	CALL Pn ;	one of the 21 arithmetic/logical routines		c) v=255	CALL CALA;	machine language subroutine interface
02	LOD v,d			05	INT 0,n	LXI H,2n CALL INT	
	a) v=0	LXI B,2d CALL LOD		06	JMP 0,a	JMP x	
	b) v>0	LXI B,2d MVI A,v CALL LOD1		07	JPC 0,a	LDAX D; DCX D	get conditional code
	c) v=255	CALL LODA;	load absolute address			DCX D; RAR ; JNC x	decrement stack pointer test conditional code
12	LODX v,d				JPC 1,a		(same as JPC 0,a except JC x)
	a) v=0	LXI B,2d CALL LODX		08	CSP 0,n (n=0...5)	CALL SYSn;	one of the 6 conversion routines
	b) v>0	LXI B,2d MVI A,v CALL LODX1			for n=8:		(output a string)
03	STO v,d				LIT 0,c_1 LIT 0,c_2	MVI C,n; CALL SYS8	# of char.
	a) v=0	LXI B,2d CALL STO			. .	DB c_1 DB c_2	
	b) v>0	LXI B,2d MVI A,v CALL STO1			. LIT 0,c_n	.	
	c) v=255	CALL STOA;	store absolute address		LIT 0,n CSP 0,8	. DB c_n	
13	STOX v,d						
	a) v=0	LXI B,2d CALL STOX					
	b) v>0	LXI B,2d MVI A,v CALL STOX1					

Table 3: P-code to 8080 translation. LIT, LOS, STOX1, INT, LODA, etc, are used as symbolic entry points in the run time routines. There are 22 routines for the OPR instructions: P00, P01, . . ., P21. There are seven standard routines for IO conversion: SYS0, SYS1, . . ., SYS5 and SYS8. The variable x is used as the memory address in the translated 8080 code corresponding to p-code address a in a call and jump instruction.

tions are similarly taken care of by the translator. The complete list of 8080 code corresponding to each p-code is shown in table 3.

The 2 Pass Translator

The structure of the translator is similar to that of the interpreter. Both programs

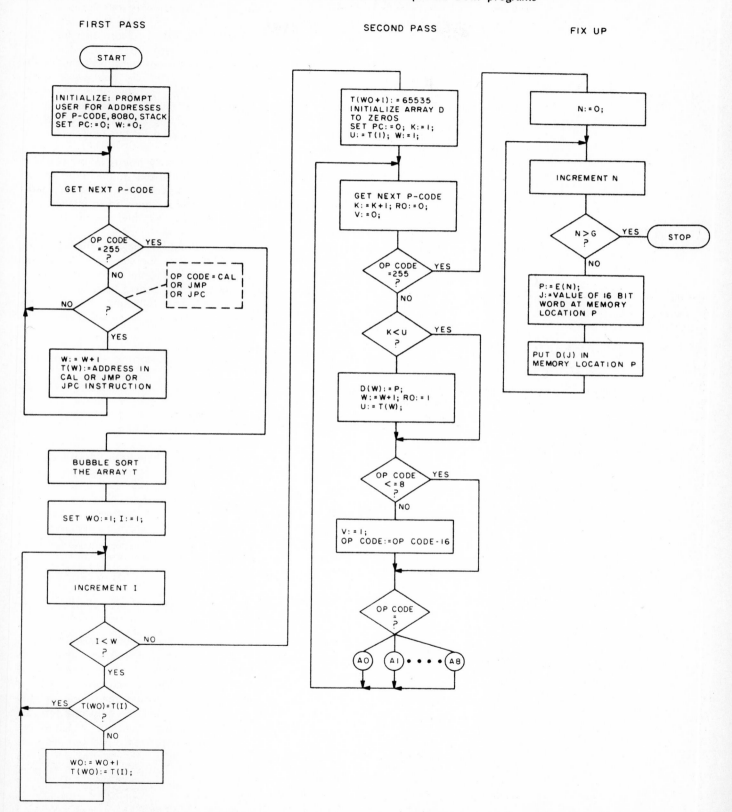

Figure 2: A simplified flowchart of the translator. A0, A1, . . .A8 are program segments for generating 8080 code for the p-code with peephole optimization as illustrated by the rules in table 4. Refer to table 5 for a description of the variables.

read p-codes from memory and decode them. The interpreter calls a simulator to execute the p-codes. The translator writes translated 8080 code in memory. The major difference between them is that the translator needs three additional tables to keep track of p-code and 8080 addresses. Since all p-code addresses are relative to the starting p-code of the program, the program is relocatable. The memory address corresponding to p-code address for any backward and forward referenced jumps can be calculated easily because all p-codes are four bytes long. The number of 8080 instructions generated per p-code is also not constant as shown in table 3. Therefore, it is necessary to build a table of 8080 addresses corresponding to p-code addresses to be used in jump and call instructions. However, it is not practical to build a table of 8080 addresses for every p-code because it will take too much memory storage for large programs. Only the addresses of those p-codes that are being referenced need be entered into the table.

P-code to 8080 machine code translation is done in two passes. During the first pass, p-code addresses in CAL, JMP and JPC instructions are entered into a table. The table is sorted after the completion of the first pass. Actual translation is carried out in the second pass. P-codes are fetched one by one from memory and decoded. The address of each p-code is checked with those in the address table. If it indicates that the current p-code is being referenced, the current 8080 address is entered to the corresponding 8080 address table. Then 8080 machine codes are produced according to the translation rules shown in table 3.

For CAL, JMP and JPC instructions, the p-code address in the instruction is looked up in the address table using a binary search. If the corresponding 8080 address has already been entered, it is output in the translated code; otherwise it is a forward referenced address. When the latter case occurs, it is necessary to record the current 8080 address in a *forward reference* table. Then, instead of the 8080 address (which is not yet known), its position in the table is output in the translated code. At the end of the second pass the forward referenced addresses are fixed up by the following procedure:

    a) Get the 8080 address from the forward reference table (call it P).

    b) Get the table entry (call it J) at address P in the translated program.

    c) Get the updated 8080 address (call it A) at table entry J.

    d) Write the correct address A back to memory location P.

Figure 2 is a simplified flowchart of the translator. The part for code generation is not shown, but it can be easily understood by referring to tables 3 and 4. Table lookup is done by binary search through the sorted table. The table elements are entered sequentially during the first pass. A simple bubble sort algorithm is used to sort the table. This method works fine for small Pascal programs. For larger programs, and thus more referenced addresses, the bubble sort algorithm is too slow because the number of comparisons is of order n^2 for n elements. A binary tree sorting algorithm with order $n\ log\ n$ will be used for our next version of the translator.

The various entry points in the runtime routines are initialized in the translator as a series of string constants. These hexadecimal addresses are converted to integers and placed in arrays so they can be accessed very easily later on.

When execution begins, the program prompts the user for starting addresses of the p-code program, the output 8080 code, and starting and ending addresses of the data stack. The following three instructions are generated to initialize the data stack and pointer:

LXI H,STK1	starting address of data stack.
LXI D,STK2	2's complement of stack ending address.
CALL #1A00	run time routine (initialization.

The program then begins its first pass. The number of address references and actual number of referenced addresses are displayed at the end of the first pass. During the second pass, cross references of p-code and 8080 addresses, which may be useful for future references, are listed in hexadecimal form. At the end of the translation, sizes of the p-code program and 8080 code are displayed.

Code Optimization

Code optimization is a technique employed by most compilers to improve the object code produced. Many sophisticated code optimization techniques are known today but are outside the scope of this article. We shall describe only one form of local optimization technique which is being used in our project. Local optimization is done within a straight line block of code with no jumps into or out of the middle of the block. *Peephole* optimization is one form of local optimization which examines only small pieces of object code.

Since most code optimization techniques are difficult to build in a syntax directed code generation algorithm, peephole optimization is particularly useful in improving the intermediate code. Each improvement may lead to opportunities for further improvements. The technique can be applied repeatedly to get maximum optimization. In our translator, peephole optimization is applied only once during the second pass.

The goal of optimization is to minimize the size of the translated 8080 code and to increase execution speed without sacrificing a lot of time during translation. The peephole technique is quite simple. It examines only a single code or two consecutive codes. Some redundant p-codes are obvious and can be easily recognized. For example, the JMP instruction generated at the beginning of a procedure block which does not contain inner blocks is redundant. Similarly, the p-code INT 0,0 (increment stack pointer) generated after a procedure call with no arguments can be eliminated. The biggest benefit comes from optimizing redundant load and store instructions, because they are relatively slow in the current implementation. For example, a LOD instruction immediately following a STO instruction of the same variable can be replaced by an increment stack pointer instruction, because the variable is still on the stack. How-

ever, if the LOD instruction has a label, ie: is being referenced somewhere in the program, we cannot be sure that the STO instruction is always executed immediately before the LOD instruction.

Other sources of peephole optimization are the replacement of specific operations by more efficient instructions. Addition and subtraction of small constants (less than 4) occur frequently in array subscripts and loop counters. They can be replaced by repeated increment or decrement instructions. Some p-codes are translated into in line 8080 code instead of a call to run time routines. Table 4 is a summary of peephole optimization used in the translator. Note that the optimized code always takes less memory space than the unoptimized code.

An Example

The various modules of the compiler system have been described. Now let us look at a complete program example. Listing 1 shows the compilation, translation and execution of a sample Pascal program. The program is stored in a disk file with file name T4. It is a sorting program that uses a binary tree algorithm. As mentioned before, it is more efficient than a bubble sort algorithm. The two subroutines in this program will

Table 4: Summary of peephole optimization. The goal is to reduce the size of the object program. The optimized code is more efficient than the unoptimized 8080 code. For the redundant store fix, the load instruction cannot be referenced elsewhere in the program.

Source of optimization	Example	P-code		8080 code		Optimized 8080 code
Redundant jump instructions	beginning of a procedure without inner procedure	n: JMP	0,n+1	JMP	x	no code generated
Redundant loads and stores	J:=J+5; A[J]:=X;	STO * LOD	v,d v,d	(as usual) (as usual)		(as usual) INX D; increment stack INX D; pointer
Repeated load of the same variable	A[J]:=A[J]+Y;	LOD LOD	v,d v,d	(as usual) (as usual)		(as usual) CALL P21; copy
INT instruction with small constant	procedure call without parameter	INT	0,0	LXI CALL	H,#0000 INT	no code generated
	procedure call	INT (−3 ≤ n ≤ 2)	0,n	LXI CALL	H,2n INT	INX D} (repeat n times INX D} (n > 0) DCX D} (repeat n times DCX D} (n < 0)
Load negative constants	B:= −20;	LIT OPR	0,n 0,1	LXI CALL CALL	B,n LIT P01	LXI B,−n CALL LIT
Add and subtract small constants (n ≤ 3)	array subscripts A[J+2] := B[K−1] := L:=L+1;	LIT OPR LIT OPR	0,n 0,2 0,n 0,3	LXI CALL CALL LXI CALL CALL	B,n LIT P02 B,n LIT P03	CALL P19; increment (repeat n times) CALL P20; decrement (repeat n times)
Load zeros	P:=0;	LIT	0,0	LXI CALL	B,#0000 LIT	XRA A INX D STAX D INX D STAX D

*Must be an unreferenced p-code

T$	—	table of p-code address labels
D$	—	table of 8080 address corresponding to address labels in array T$
E	—	table of forward references
W	—	count of address references
WO	—	count of actual labels
G	—	count of forward references
K	—	p-code instruction counter
X	—	memory location of current p-code
P	—	8080 program counter of the translated code
F	—	current op code
V	—	=1 means indexed load or store
RO	—	=1 means current p-code is being referenced
U	—	program counter of the next referenced p-code

Table 5: Table of important variables and arrays in the translator program shown in flowchart form in figure 2.

```
P-CODES STARTS AT 0000
WANT CODE PRINTED?N
   0  ?$T4
   0  ( PGM -- SORTING BY BINARY TREE )
   0  VAR I,J,K,N,NEW:INTEGER;
   1  T,L,R,S:ARRAY[110] OF INTEGER;
   1
   1  PROC ENTER(N);
   1  VAR J:INTEGER;
   2  BEGIN J:=0;
   5   REPEAT
   5    IF N<=T[J] THEN
   9     IF L[J]<>0 THEN J:=L[J]
  17     ELSE BEGIN L[J]:=NEW;J:=0 END
  24    ELSE IF R[J]<>0 THEN J:=R[J]
  32      ELSE BEGIN R[J]:=NEW;J:=0 END
  39   UNTIL J=0;
  43   T[NEW]:=N;NEW:=NEW+1
  48  END;
  51
  51 PROC TRAV(J);   ( TRAVERSE THE TREE )
  51  BEGIN IF L[J]<>0 THEN TRAV(L[J]);
  62   S[K]:=T[J];K:=K+1;
  70   IF R[J]<>0 THEN TRAV(R[J])
  79  END;
  80
  80 BEGIN (MAIN)
  80  T[0]:=255;NEW:=0;
  86  READ(K#);WRITE(13,10);
  92  FOR I:=0 TO K DO BEGIN
  99   L[I]:=0;R[I]:=0; ENTER(MEM[I+%1A00]) END;
 116  K:=0; TRAV(0);
 121  FOR I:=0 TO K-1 DO WRITE(' ',S[I]#);
 140  WRITE(13,10)
 144 END.
INTERPRET(I), OR TRANSLATE(T)?T

*** P-CODE TO 8080 TRANSLATION ***
ADDR (HEX) OF PAS.LIB:1A00

ADDR (HEX) OF P-CODE:0000
ADDR (HEX) OF OUTPUT 8080 PGM:0800
STACK START ADDR (HEX):5000
STACK END ADDR (HEX):7FFF
 20 REFERENCES
 15 ACTUAL LABELS

   0  0809 0C 0C 12 17 1D 23 29 31 34 3B 41 49 4E 51
  15  0858 5E 66 6C 6F 75 7D 85 8A 90 93 99 A1 A6 A9
  30  08B0 B6 BE C4 C7 CD D5 DD E2 E8 EE F3 F6 FD 05
  45  090B 13 1B 21 1E 26 29 29 2F 35 3D 42 45 4C 52
  60  095A 62 64 6C 72 7A 82 8A 90 8D 95 9B A3 A8 AB
  75  09B2 B8 C0 C8 CA CD D3 D8 DE E4 E9 EF F2 F8 FE
  90  0A01 09 0A 0F 15 1B 1E 24 27 2E 34 39 3F 45 4A
 105  0A50 56 5C 5F 62 68 6A 70 73 79 7C 7E 83 89 8E
 120  0A94 96 9B A1 A7 AD AA AD B3 B6 BD C3 C6 CC D2
 135  0AD5 DB DE E4 E7 E9 EF F2 F8 FB FE
  11 FORWARD REFERENCES
P-CODE.. 145 INSTRUCTIONS
8080.. 766 BYTES
P-CODE:8080 = 1.3206897
* END TRANSLATION *
BYE
*LF PAS.LIB 1A00
*JP0800
?7
  29 34 34 35 43 43 235 242
*JP0800
?20
  0 1 5 25 29 29 32 33 34 34 35 35 40 43 43 112 113 201 235 242 244
*JP2A04
READY
!CHR$(129)
```

Listing 1: Compilation and translation of a sample Pascal program. At the end of the translation, the ratio of p-code to 8080 code is determined for reference purposes.

be used in our next version of the translator (written in Pascal). The main program begins by asking the user to input an integer K (K must be less than 110) for the number of items to be sorted. It then reads the K+1 bytes of data starting from hexadecimal memory location 1A00 (the location where runtime routines are stored). The data items are read one at a time and procedure ENTER is called to build a binary tree with these items. Procedure TRAV is then called to traverse the tree recursively in the "left subtree..root..right subtree" fashion and the data with sorted order is placed in array S. Finally, array S is printed.

The p-compiler generates 145 p-codes (0 to 144) for this program. Afterwards, it uses a CHAIN statement (North Star BASIC) to load the translator program from disk, and overlays the compiler. The translator begins by asking the user to input memory addresses of run time routines, p-code program, output 8080 code and data stack. At the end of the first pass, 20 address references are recorded. After sorting, it is found that there are only 15 actual labels. Output from the second pass of the translator is a cross-reference of p-code program counter and memory addresses of the corresponding translated 8080 code. The leftmost column is the p-code program counter. Hexadecimal memory addresses are printed in groups of 15 per line. With the exception of the first one, only the two low order hexadecimal digits are printed. At the end of the second pass, 11 forward references are recorded. A total of 766 bytes of 8080 code are generated. Compared to the size of the p-code program, the translated code is 1.32 times larger. This ratio usually ranges between 1.05 and 1.35, depending on program structure and the types of statements used.

After translation is completed, control is transferred to the disk operation system (DOS). The run time routines are loaded from the disk file, PAS.LIB, to hexadecimal memory location 1A00. Then execution may begin by typing a JPxxxx command (jump to xxxx), where xxxx is the starting hexadecimal memory address of the translated code. In listing 1, two separate runs are shown: the first one sorts eight numbers (K+1 with K = 7) and the second sorts 21 numbers. The user may get back to BASIC by typing JP2A04, where 2A04 is the entry point of BASIC. (The command !CHR$(129) is an immediate BASIC statement used to turn off the printer.)

Summary

Compilers for high level languages are large, nontrivial programs. Their implementation usually requires a significant amount of computer system resources and human effort. Although our available system resources were limited, both in hardware and software, we managed to finish the bootstrap compiler within a relatively short time period. The reason is obvious: The Pascal subset we implemented is small. We followed the same approach professionals use for implementing portable Pascal compilers on mainframe computers. Syntax diagrams, which define the subset language, are used to construct the syntax directed, top-down parser of the compiler. The generation of p-code is also syntax directed. P-code is relocatable and portable, and its interpreter can be easily implemented on most microcomputers.

There are several features that are unique to our compiler project. First, the bootstrap compiler was written in BASIC (North Star disk BASIC). Although BASIC is not an appropriate language for compiler writing, it is the only high level language available in our system. Its ability to perform recursive function calls proved essential in simplifying the implementation of the compiler. Secondly, instead of writing a p-code interpreter in assembly language, a p-code to 8080 machine code translator was written in BASIC. The translated code can be expected to run more than twice as fast as interpreting p-codes. A p-code interpreter with debug facilities was also written (in Pascal). It can be used to debug p-code programs. Thirdly, minor extensions to the subset language were implemented. Absolute addressing of memory locations and machine language interface are desirable features for microcomputer systems. The availability of hexadecimal constants and IO conversions provides much user convenience.

Presently, the bootstrap compiler is very slow. It compiles at the rate of about eight lines per minute for a very dense Pascal program (using North Star BASIC with a 2 MHz 8080 processor). With some refinement in the compiler and run time routines, the Pascal version of the compiler can be expected to run 25 times faster, or approximately 200 lines per minute.

Completion of the bootstrap compiler is only a milestone in our compiler project. There are many tasks still to be done. Logically the next step is to write the translator and then the p-compiler in the Pascal subset and compile them using the BASIC version of the compiler. Since the compiler source and p-codes are big, there may be a minor problem in memory management. It may be necessary to write the p-codes onto disk to save memory. After these two programs have been debugged, any further development can be done in Pascal without the BASIC interpreter. It would be quite interesting to have the compiler (in object code) compile itself (in source code) and use the output object code to compile itself again. After each compilation, the object code could be compared with the previous one to provide a means of verification.

More Pascal features or extensions can be implemented one step at a time. They may include character type and pointer type variables, disk IO capabilities, floating point arithmetic, multidimensional arrays and built-in functions. It is also necessary to improve the error diagnosis and recovery scheme of the compiler. Further development should be aimed at user convenience. A dynamic debugging package that can display and alter the values of variables as specified by name at runtime would be desirable. Ultimately, we hope to see a Pascal system that is as convenient and easy to use as an interactive BASIC system.■

The Pascal run time routines and the p-code to 8080 conversion program are listed in Appendix A, beginning on page 203 . . . BWL

"Tiny" Pascal in 8080 Assembly Language

Dr. B. Gregory Louis

The p-code interpreter, Pascal to p-code compiler, and p-code to 8080 code translator described by Chung and Yuen in the September through November 1978 issues of BYTE magazine have been rewritten in 8080 assembly language. In addition to providing approximately two orders of magnitude increase in speed, the object versions run in far less memory. It is quite feasible to write and run "tiny" Pascal programs in a system havng 12 K bytes of programmable memory with these 8080 object code modules. The Pascal to p-code compiler occupies just under 8 K bytes of memory, while the p-code interpreter needs just under 4 K bytes including run time routines.

The articles by Chung and Yuen are required reading for potential users of this package. Not only do they describe in detail what the package does, they supply documentation without which these assembly listings will be difficult, if not impossible to understand or modify.

It should be noted that these three assembly language programs are essentially direct hand compilations of the high level programs written by Chung and Yuen. They could probably be reduced in length by 25 or 30 percent if rewritten with a view to such optimization. If this were done, a "tiny" Pascal development system including text editor could easily be fitted into a 12 K byte read only memory.

"Tiny" Pascal is a subset of the programming language Pascal. The book *Pascal User Manual and Report*, by Jensen and Wirth (Springer-Verlag, 1974) contains the full definition of standard Pascal. The present implementation is restricted in that there are no data types other than integer and array of integer, and parameters are passed by value only. However, there are several extensions which have been made.

In READ and WRITE statements, format control characters have been provided. If the variable name is followed by a numerical sign (#), the input or output string is taken as a decimal integer. If a percent sign (%) is used, the input or output string is taken as hexadecimal. If no format control character follows a variable name or constant, a single ASCII charcter is written or read. In write statements, quoted strings of up to 79 characters may be used.

In the body of a program, hexadecimal constants are specified by preceding them with a percent sign. ASCII constants may be specified, but only the first character of a quoted string is used. Source code lines may not exceed 63 characters exclusive of line number.

The compiler can accept input from the keyboard or from tape. If a line of input begins with the character $, the next five characters are taken as specifying the name of a file to be loaded from tape. (Such files may be prepared with an editor.) The rest of the input line is then ignored. If the file thus loaded does not contain either the end of the program or another line beginning with $, the compiler waits for further input from the keyboard. This is signalled by the appearance of a $ at the beginning of a new line. If the user wishes to continue input via the keyboard, the $ is erased with the rub out key; otherwise another file name is typed.

The words MEM and CALL are reserved and provide the user with access to memory. MEM is an array name that refers to memory space. For example, the statement MEM [0]: = MEM [1] would cause the contents of location 1 to be written into location 0. CALL is a way of transferring control to a machine language subroutine. The form is CALL(ADDRESS).

CASE statements may be concluded with ELSE. In any instance of possible ambiguity, ELSE is always taken as referring to the most recent CASE or IF statement encountered.

In this implementation of "tiny" Pascal, there are several changes with respect to Chung and Yuen's version.

Comments in "tiny" Pascal source code are begun and ended with right braces instead of left and right braces so it is teletypewriter compatible.

The single quote may be included in a quoted string by the usual trick of doubling, thus:

'This is how it''s done'.

Hexadecimal constants may be one to four characters long, and may be preceded by a minus sign if desired.

To increase flexibility, single character input is not echoed to the con-

sole. Although this necessitates an explicit WRITE statement in many applications, it allows for character mapping and for redefinition of control characters.

The assembly source code for the three modules is virtually devoid of comments, since the high level source already published is intended to act as documentation. Accordingly, the labels in the assembly language programs have been chosen to key to the previously published listings. However, reference is made to several I/O and utility routines external to the programs. These common utilities are already available in most systems. They must be provided by the user, and they perform the functions shown in table 1.

Addresses 5966 through 5A15 of the compiler implement a file input from mass storage. The contents of BOFP are used as the load address for the file, which is assumed to be in the form of a SYS/8 (or Processor Technology SP-1, or Poly 88) listing. That is, the file is broken into lines consisting of a length byte, a 4 digit line number, a space, and the text, ending with a carriage return.

Similarly, hexadecimal locations 6D7E and the following are used to implement the chain to the interpreter or translator.

One other thing to note in the compiler is that if a file has been input and the end of the file (length byte of 1) is encountered before the program ends, keyboard input resumes, but a $ keystroke is simulated. The code that does this is in locations 5921 to 5928. This code assumes a double buffered, interrupt driven keyboard input routine; for use with a polled keyboard, it would need modification.

These programs are relocatable in that all address calculations employ three byte instructions. For the interpreter, the move address space is hexadecimal 5000 to 5ECF, and the block of executable code to be scanned by the relocator runs from hexadecimal 5529 to 5ECF. The compiler move address space is hexadecimal 4F00 to 6DC5 and executable code runs from hexadecimal 57BA to 6DC5. The translator runs from hexadecimal 5A00 to 68FD with code starting at hexadecimal 6130. The run time routines occupy hexadecimal 6946 on. In addition, there are two jump instructions at the beginning of the interpreter, four at the beginning of the compiler, and one each at the start of the translator and run time routines that have to be changed on relocation.

A sample compilation in "tiny" Pascal

appears in listing 1 (Appendix B, page 221). The program is a simple p-code lister that displays p-codes a screenful at a time until control X is typed. An editor listing appears first, followed by the p-code compilation and translation. Then there is a dump of the resulting source code, and finally a disassembly listing.

Listings, 2, 3, 4, and 5 (pages 235 thru 286) are the run time routines, Pascal to p-code compiler, and the p-code interpreter. These programs are copyright 1979 by B Gregory Louis, Ph. D. They may be used or copied for noncommercial purposes only. The author accepts no liability for any damage resulting from the use or malfunction of these programs and no warranty express or implied applies to any of this material. ■

The program package "Tiny Pascal in 8080 Assembly Language" unfortunately contains a few minor errors. Although the package will function correctly as published in almost all cases, the errors do cause idiosyncratic behavior in some instances.

The corrections are:

Lines 1380 through 1440 following lable L1500 on page 245 should be replaced by:

```
PUSH H
LXI D, – 5
DAD D
POP H
JNC L1515
PUSH H
LXI D,6
DAD D
POP H
JNC L1530
```

Lines 2150 through 2200 following label L635 on page 248 should be omitted. This section of code contains an error and its function is unnecessary.

These errors are entirely my fault and I apologize to anyone who has run into difficulty because of them.

Finally, users should be aware that the stack-handling associated with procedure calls differs between the Chung-Yuen programs and my translation. As a result, P-code produced by their compiler will not be properly translated or interpreted by my translator or interpreter, and vice versa, even though the P-code from the assembly-language compiler works fine with the assembly-language translator and interpreter.

B. Gregory Louis, Ph.D.
OB/GYN Dept.
St. Michael's Hospital
30 Bond Street
Toronto, Canada M5B 1W8

Applications

WADUZITDO: How to Write

a Language in 256 Words or Less

Larry Kheriaty

Every computer owner likes to show his or her microcomputer to friends. The first question the friends usually ask is, "What does it do?" The software system presented here demonstrates what a computer can do in a manner simple enough for almost anyone to understand. Even if you have a larger, more capable system, it is often worthwhile to be able to demonstrate something that can be accomplished on a smaller scale. WADUZITDO is small enough to run on almost any microcomputer yet it allows even the novice user to make the computer "do something."

WADUZITDO is a complete high level language processor that fits in less than 256 bytes on either a 6800 or 8080 based system. The only other requirement is some kind of terminal. The system includes a text editor to allow a program to be entered and modified, and an interpreter to execute the program. The only external routines needed are single character input and single character output such as those provided by most system monitors.

The object of WADUZITDO is to run simple conversational programs. There are just five statement types, roughly derived from the PILOT language. To keep it small only the most essential capabilities are available. This also makes programming very easy. In fact, only a few minutes after my unsuspecting spouse had asked, "What does it do?", she had written the interactive dialogue program in listing 1 to help me make out a list of acceptable birthday gifts!

Programming in WADUZITDO is straightforward and uncomplicated. For example, to direct the computer to display a line of text on the terminal you use the *type* statement. The following example shows the format of the *type* statement.

T:WHAT COULD BE EASIER
THAN THIS?

The T is the operation code for *type*. A colon always follows the operation code. The text after the colon is displayed exactly as shown.

The *accept* statement allows the program to receive one input character from the terminal keyboard. Normally it is used after a *type* that asks for a response. For example:

T:CAN YOU TELL ME WHAT 2 + 3
EQUALS?

A:

The *accept* statement is just the A operation code followed by a colon. When it is encountered execution pauses until the user keys in any single character. Then the input character is saved internally for use in subsequent *match* statements.

The *match* statement is used to test the character entered by the user on the previous *accept. Match* is coded as an M (the operation code), followed by a colon and one character. The character in the statement is compared to the last character entered by the user. The result of the comparison is recorded internally in the match flag: Y if the match is equal, N if it is not equal.

Once set the match flag can be used to conditionally execute or skip any subsequent statement. This is done by placing either a Y (yes) or N (no) immediately before any operation code. If the Y or N is the same as the match flag the statement is executed, otherwise it is skipped. An elaboration of the previous example illustrates the use of *match*.

T:WHAT IS 2 + 3?

A:

M:5

YT:FIVE, RIGHT.

NT:NO, THE ANSWER IS 5.

Listing 1: WADUZITDO
program written by a non-
computer person. Notice
the last line of the pro-
gram, the J:0 command.
This instruction will make
the program execution
jump back to the accept
statement to try another
input.

```
T:IT IS BIRTHDAY LIST TIME.
T:THE PURPOSE OF THIS PROGRAM IS TO
T:DETERMINE WHAT GIFTS ARE ACCEPTABLE.
T:TYPE THE CODE LETTER ASSOCIATED WITH
T:THE POTENTIAL GIFT IDEA...
T:   A   HOME APPLIANCE
T:   B   SOMETHING BORING
T:   C   ITEM OF CLOTHING
T:   D   SOMETHING DECORATIVE FOR THE HOUSE
T:   G   GARBAGE DISPOSAL
T:   M   MY OWN COMPUTER
A:
M:A
YT:UNACCEPTABLE.
M:B
YT:NO WAY.
M:C
YT:ACCEPTABLE IF NOT UGLY.
M:D
YT:OKAY IF CHOSEN WITH GOOD TASTE
YT:SO AS NOT TO BE TACKY.
M:G
YT:YEAH !
M:M
YT:THE LAST THING IN THE WORLD
YT:I WOULD EVER WANT.
NM:A
NM:B
NM:C
NM:D
NM:G
NT:CANT YOU READ FOOL, THAT IS NOT
NT:ONE OF THE CHOICES.
NT:TRY A,B,C,D,G OR M
J:0
```

Listing 2: A NIM playing
program. This program
demonstrates the jumping
capability of the language.

```
T:LETS PLAY NIM WITH 7 PEBBLES.
T:WE TAKE TURNS TAKING 1,2 OR 3.
T:THE LAST ONE TO TAKE ONE LOSES.
T:THERE ARE 7, HOW MANY ?
A:
M:1
YJ:1
M:2
YJ:2
M:3
YJ:6
T:YOU CAN TAKE ONLY 1,2, OR 3.
J:0
*T:THAT LEAVES 6, I TAKE 1 LEAVING 5.
T:HOW MANY ?
A:
M:1
YJ:5
M:2
YJ:4
M:3
YJ:3
T:YOU MUST TAKE 1,2 OR 3.
J:0
*T:THAT LEAVES 5, I TAKE 1 LEAVING 4.
T:HOW MANY ?
A:
M:1
YJ:3
M:2
YJ:2
M:3
YJ:1
T:YOU MUST TAKE 1,2 OR 3 ONLY .
J:0
*T:THAT LEAVES THE LAST ONE.
T:I TAKE IT ... YOU WIN.
J:5
*T:THAT LEAVES 2, I TAKE 1 LEAVING 1.
J:3
*T:THAT LEAVES 3, I TAKE 2 LEAVING 1.
J:2
*T:THAT LEAVES 4, I TAKE 3 LEAVING 1.
*T:HOW MANY ?
A:
M:1
NT:YOU HAVE NO CHOICE BUT TO TAKE 1.
NT:HOW MANY ?
NJ:0
T:YOU JUST TOOK THE LAST ONE ... I WIN.
*T:TO PLAY AGAIN PUSH THE DOLLAR SIGN.
S:
```

Normally statements are executed sequentially. The *jump* statement is used to
alter the normal sequence. The format of the
jump statement is J, followed by a colon,
and a number from zero to nine. The statement J:0 causes a branch back to the last
accept statement executed. Execution
resumes from that statement. The J:0
statement can be used to allow the user to
reanswer a previous question. For example:

T:HOW MANY FEET IN A YARD?

A:

M:3

YT:RIGHT.

NT:WRONG STUPID, TRY AGAIN.

NJ:0

The second form of the jump makes use of
program markers. A program marker is an
asterisk, *, preceding any statement. The
statement J:n, where n is a number from
1 to 9, causes a branch to the nth program
marker forward from the *jump*. This form of
the *jump* is shown in the sample program in
listing 2 which plays NIM.

The last type of statement is *stop*. This
statement merely terminates execution of
the program and returns control to the program editor. The format of the *stop* statement is S:

To increase the versatility of the language
the S: statement can, at the user's option,
be made to call a user written machine
language subroutine from within the
WADUZITDO program. To do this requires
a one statement modification to the system
which is detailed below. If you choose to
make this modification you can consider
S: to be the operation code for *subroutine*
rather than *stop*. The format of the *subroutine* statement is S:x where x is any
single character which serves as a parameter
to the user written program. The value x will
be stored in register A in both the 6800 and
8080 version. It can be used to select different functions to be performed by the
program.

During execution any statement which
does not fit the syntax of one of the five
statement types is printed in its entirety,
then execution resumes normally with the
next statement. Table 1 summarizes the
WADUZITDO instruction set.

When WADUZITDO is first entered control is passed to the program editor which
is used to enter or alter source programs.
Also an internal program pointer, called
LOC, is automatically set to the beginning of

the source area. As each statement is entered on the keyboard the characters are stored and the internal pointer advances. Typing errors may be corrected by entering a backspace and the correct character. To reset the pointer to the start of the program enter a backslash, \. To display the next line of the program enter the mirror image of the reset slash, /. To replace a line, display each line up to but not including the one to be replaced, then enter the new line. The new line should be no longer than the line it replaces. If it is longer, the next line of text is also overwritten. End the replacement line with a percent key rather than a carriage return. The % causes null characters to be stored as filler up to the start of the next line. To begin execution of the program enter a dollar sign, $. (The editing commands are summarized in table 2.)

If you already have a good text editor in your system it may be used instead of the one included. Each statement is variable length, terminated by a carriage return character. All other control characters between statements are ignored.

Complete 6800 and 8080 assembly listings containing source and object code are included to simplify implementation on your system. The 6800 version in listing 3 uses the MIKBUG monitor; the 8080 version in listing 4 uses the SOLOS/CUTER monitor. If you have one of these two system monitors you need not modify the program at all.

The entry point to the system is at location zero. Upon entry the stack pointer is assumed set to address some scratchpad memory area large enough to accommodate a few levels of call. In MIKBUG or SOLOS/CUTER, as with most system monitors, this is handled automatically by the GO or EXEC command. The 2 byte value stored in LOC (hexadecimal 100) must point to the place where the user program is to be stored. In the assembly listings note that this value is shown as hexadecimal 0106, the first location not occupied by the system.

If you don't have one of the above monitors you must supply character input and character output routines and change the references to IN and OUT to address these routines. In the listings you will find one reference to IN and one to OUT which needs to be changed. If your terminal requires a delay after each carriage return you can set the number of null padding characters by a one byte modification to the statement labeled PLF.

Any of the special characters used by the text editor ($, %, \, /, bs) can be easily changed to another more convenient character on your keyboard.

As shown in the assembly listings the S:

STATEMENT	FORMAT	WHAT IT DOES
type	T:text	Display text on the terminal.
accept	A:	Input one character from the terminal keyboard.
match	M:x	Compare x to last input character and set match flag to Y if equal, N if not equal.
jump	J:n	If n=0 jump to last *accept*. If n=1 thru 9 jump to nth program marker forward from the J.
stop	S:	Terminate program and return to text editor.
subroutine	S:x	Call user machine language program (requires modification).
conditionals	Y N	May precede any operation code. Execute only if match flag is Y. Execute only if match flag is N.
program marker	*	May precede any statement, serves as a *jump* destination.

Table 1: Program instructions for the WADUZITDO language.

EDIT CHARACTER	HEX	MEANING
$	24	Start execution.
\	5C	Move edit pointer to program start.
/	2F	Display next line of program.
%	25	Pad inserted line with nulls.
bs or ←	08 or 5F	Backspace to correct typing error.
cr	0D	End of statement.
any other		Character stored in program and edit pointer advances.

Table 2: Editing characters used by the built-in text editor.

statement halts execution by branching to the text editor. If you don't modify this you can treat it as a *stop* statement. To use it as a subroutine call you must modify the JMP SUB instruction to be a JSR or CALL (depending on the system) to the appropriate address. Upon entry to the subroutine the index register (6800) or HL register pair (8080) contains the location of the next program statement and should be saved and restored before returning from the subroutine. In the 8080 version the DE register pair should also be saved. Register A will contain the one character parameter, x, of the S:x. Its use is totally up to the subroutine.

The system has been organized so that the six bytes of changeable data are isolated from the read only portion. This means the rest of the 256 byte system could be

Text continued after listings on page 103

```
0 0 0 0 0 0 0 0 0 0 0 0
0 0 0 0 0 0 0 0 0 0 0 1
0 1 2 3 4 5 6 7 8 9 0
─────────────────────
0 0 0 0 0 0 0 0 0 0
0 0 0 0 0 0 0 0 0 0
0 1 3 4 6 7 9 A C D
0 9 2 A 2 B 3 C 5 E
```

```
0 0 0 0 0 0 0 0 0 0 0 0
0 0 0 0 0 0 0 0 0 0 0 1
0 1 2 3 4 5 6 7 8 9 0
```

```
*                    WADUZITDO
*          6800 VERSION BY LARRY KHERIATY
*
*      MIKBUG SUBROUTINES USED
IN       EQU   $E1AC      INPUT FROM KEYBOARD TO ACCA
OUT      EQU   $E1D1      OUTPUT FROM ACCA TO TERMINAL
         ORG   $0000
SUB      EQU   $0000      USER SUBR START (CAN BE MODIFIED)
*   ENTER SYSTEM AT LOCATION 0 WITH STACK POINTER PRESET
*      TO SCRATCH PAD RAM ENOUGH FOR A FEW LEVELS OF CALL
0000 FE 0100  START  LDX   LOC       SOURCE PROGRAM AREA START
0003 8D 45    EGET   BSR   JIN       ACCEPT SOURCE CHAR
0005 81 5C           CMP A #$5C      \  ?
0007 27 F7           BEQ   START     YES, BACK UP TO PROGRAM START
*
0009 81 24           CMP A #$24      $  ?
000B 27 45           BEQ   EXEC      YES, GO EXECUTE THE PROGRAM
*
000D 81 08           CMP A #$08      BS  ?
000F 26 03           BNE   DIS       NO
0011 09              DEX             YES, BACK UP ONE IN SOURCE
0012 20 EF           BRA   EGET      LOOP BACK
*    PROCESS DISPLAY OF NEXT LINE
0014 81 2F    DIS    CMP A #$2F      /  ?
0016 26 07           BNE   PAD       NO
0018 BD 00D5         JSR   PRT       GO PRINT TO CR
001B 8D 21    EPLF   BSR   PLF       PRINT LINE FEED AND NULLS
001D 20 E4           BRA   EGET      LOOP
*     DO LINE REPLACEMENT- PAD TO END OF STMT WITH NULLS
001F 81 25    PAD    CMP A #$25      %  ?
0021 26 12           BNE   CHAR      NO
0023 86 0D           LDA A #$0D      CR
0025 8D 27           BSR   JOUT      PRINT IT
0027 86 0D           LDA A #$0D      CR
0029 C6 40           LDA B #$40      COUNT OF 64
002B A1 00    PADL   CMP A 0,X       AT CR YET ?
002D 27 06           BEQ   CHAR      YES QUIT PADDING
002F 6F 00           CLR   0,X       PAD WITH NULL
0031 08              INX             INCR LOC PTR
0032 5A              DEC B           DECREMENT SAFETY COUNTER
0033 26 F6           BNE   PADL      LOOP TILL CR OR 64 NULLS
*     STORE ENTERED SOURCE CHAR IN PROGRAM
0035 A7 00    CHAR   STA A 0,X       CHAR TO SOURCE LOC
0037 08              INX             MOVE LOC PTR UP ONE
0038 81 0D           CMP A #$0D      IS IT A CR ?
003A 27 DF           BEQ   EPLF      YES, ECHO A LINE FEED
003C 20 C5           BRA   EGET      NO, GET ANOTHER CHAR
*     SUBROUTINE TO PRINT LINE FEED TO TERMINAL
003E C6 00    PLF    LDA B #$00      NUMBER OF NULLS TO PRINT
0040 4F      PLFL   CLR A           NULL
0041 8D 0B           BSR   JOUT      WRITE A NULL
0043 5A              DEC B           DECREMENT COUNTER
0044 2A FA           BPL   PLFL      LOOP TILL ENOUGH NULLS
0046 86 0A           LDA A #$0A      LINEFFEED
0048 20 04           BRA   JOUT
*     NEXT FEW LINES MUST BE ALTERED IF YOU DONT USE MIKBUG
004A BD E1AC  JIN    JSR   IN        CALL CHAR INPUT ROUTINE
004D 39              RTS             RETURN TO CALLER
004E BD E1D1  JOUT   JSR   OUT       CALL CHARACTER OUTPUT ROUTINE
0051 39              RTS             RETURN TO CALLER
*
*     COME HERE TO BEGIN EXECUTION OF THE SOURCE PROGRAM
*
0052 FE 0100  EXEC   LDX   LOC       STARTING LOC OF PROGRAM
0055 09              DEX             LESS ONE
0056 08      LOOPI  INX             ADR OF NEXT PGM BYTE
0057 A6 00    LOOP   LDA A 0,X       NEXT PGM BYTE
0059 81 2A           CMP A #$2A      *  CHAR ?
005B 2F F9           BLE   LOOPI     YES(OR IGNOREABLE CONT CHAR)
*
*     PROCESS Y OR N FLAG TESTS
005D 81 59           CMP A #$59      Y  ?
005F 27 04           BEQ   TFLG      YES
0061 81 4E           CMP A #$4E      N  ?
0063 26 0F           BNE   XA        BRANCH IF NOT A FLAG TEST
*
0065 08      TFLG   INX             STEP LOC OVER Y OR N
0066 B1 0105         CMP A FLG       COMPARE TO CURRENT MATCH FLAG
0069 27 EC           BEQ   LOOP      ITS EQUAL SO EXECUTE THE STMT
*
*     ITS A FLAG FAILURE, SKIP OVER THE STMT
006B 08      SKIP   INX             STEP LOC PTR
006C A6 00           LDA A 0,X       NEXT CHAR IN PGM
```

Listing 3: 6800 version of the WADUZITDO language. A dump of the MIK-BUG format of WADUZITDO (shown in listing 3a, page 102) can be used for manual entry of the program. This version was run locally at BYTE using a SwTPC 6800.

```
006E 81 0D              CMP A #$0D        TO END OF STMT ?
0070 26 F9              BNE   SKIP        NOT YET, SO LOOP
0072 20 E2              BRA   LOOPI       AT NEXT STMT, GO DO IT
          *
          *     PROCESS ACCEPT STATEMENT
0074 81 41      XA      CMP A #$41        A  ?
0076 26 11              BNE   XM          NO
0078 FF 0102            STX   LST         YES, SAVE LOC OF LAST ACCEPT
007B 8D CD              BSR   JIN         ACCEPT ONE CHAR FROM KYBD
007D B7 0104            STA A CHR         SAVE IT
0080 08                 INX               MOVE OVER A
0081 86 0D      PCR     LDA A #$0D        CR
0083 8D C9              BSR   JOUT        PRINT IT
0085 8D B7              BSR   PLF         PRINT LINE FEED
0087 20 CD              BRA   LOOPI       STEP OVER : AND GO ON
          *
          *     PROCESS MATCH STMT
0089 81 4D      XM      CMP A #$4D        M  ?
008B 26 12              BNE   XJ          NO
008D 08                 INX               STEP OVER M
008E 08                 INX               STEP OVER :
008F A6 00              LDA A 0,X         GET MATCH CHAR
0091 C6 59              LDA B #$59        ASSUME Y
0093 B1 0104            CMP A CHR         COMP MATCH CHAR TO INPUT CHAR
0096 27 02              BEQ   MX          BRANCH IF IT MATCHES,FLG=Y
0098 C6 4E              LDA B #$4E        RESULT IS N
009A F7 0105    MX      STA B FLG         SET MATCH FLAG TO Y OR N
009D 20 B7              BRA   LOOPI       STEP OVER MATCH CHAR AND GO ON
          *
          *     PROCESS JUMP STATEMENT
009F 81 4A      XJ      CMP A #$4A        J  ?
00A1 26 17              BNE   XS          NO
00A3 E6 02              LDA B 2,X         DESTINATION


00A5 C4 0F              AND B #$0F        CLEAR ZONE
00A7 26 05              BNE   JF          ITS A JUMP FORWARD
00A9 FE 0102            LDX   LST         ZERO.. JUMP BACK TO LAST ACCEPT
00AC 20 A9              BRA   LOOP        CONTINUE FROM THERE
          *
          *   SKIP FORWARD UNTIL PASS N *-MARKERS ( N IS IN ACCB )
00AE 08         JF      INX               STEP PGM LOC
00AF A6 00              LDA A 0,X         NEXT CHAR
00B1 81 2A              CMP A #$2A        *-MARKER ?
00B3 26 F9              BNE   JF          NO, KEEP LOOPING
00B5 5A                 DEC B             FOUND ONE, COUNT IT
00B6 26 F6              BNE   JF          LOOP IF NEED TO FIND MORE
00B8 20 9C              BRA   LOOPI       DESTINATION FOUND, GO EXECUTE
          *
          *     PROCESS STOP OR SUBROUTINE STATEMENT
00BA 81 53      XS      CMP A #$53        S  ?
00BC 26 0A              BNE   XT          NO
00BE 08                 INX               STEP OVER S
00BF 08                 INX               STEP OVER :
00C0 A6 00              LDA A 0,X         PARAMETER TO REG A
00C2 08                 INX               STEP OVER PARAMETER
          *   NEXT STMT MAY BE MADE TO BE A  JSR TO USER SUBR
00C3 7E 0000            JMP   SUB         GO TO USER SUBR (OR TO EDITOR)
00C6 20 8F              BRA   LOOP        GO ON UPON RETURN FROM USER SUBR
          *
          *     PROCESS TYPE STATMENT AND SYNTAX ERRORS
00C8 81 54      XT      CMP A #$54        T  ?
00CA 26 02              BNE   TE          NO, ITS AN ERROR
00CC 08                 INX               YES, STEP OVER T
00CD 08                 INX               STEP OVER :
00CE 8D 05      TE      BSR   PRT         PRINT UP TO CR
00D0 BD 003E            JSR   PLF         PRINT LNE FEED
00D3 20 82              BRA   LOOP        DONE WITH T
          *
          *   SUBR TO PRINT UP TO NEXT CR
00D5 C6 40      PRT     LDA B #$40        COUNT OF 64
00D7 A6 00      PRTA    LDA A 0,X         NEXT CHAR
00D9 5A                 DEC B             DECREMENT SAFETY COUNTER
00DA 27 0A              BEQ   PRTB        EXIT IF OVER 64 TILL CR
00DC BD 004E            JSR   JOUT        PRINT IT
00DF A6 00              LDA A 0,X         RELOAD CHAR TO ACCA
00E1 08                 INX               STEP LOC PTR
00E2 81 0D              CMP A #$0D        CR ?
00E4 26 F1              BNE   PRTA        NOT CR, LOOP
00E6 39         PRTB    RTS               DONE, RETURN
          *
          *   ABOVE IS END OF READ ONLY PORTION OF THE PROGRAM
          *
          *   THE FOLLOWING IS CHANGEABLE DATA
          *
                        ORG   $100        MOVE TO START OF DATA AREA
0100   0106    LOC      FDB   $0106       ADDR OF SOURCE PROGRAM AREA
0102   0000    LST      FDB   0           PLACE TO SAVE LOC OF LAST A:
0104   00      CHR      FCB   0           PLACE TO SAVE LAST INPUT CHAR
0105   00      FLG      FCB   0           PLACE TO SAVE MATCH FLAG
          *
                        END
```

101

Listing 4: 8080 version of the WADUZITDO language. A hexadecimal dump (shown in listing 4a) is provided for manual entry. This version was run locally at BYTE using a SOL-20.

```
                    *           WADUZITDO
                    *      8080 VERSION BY LARRY KHERIATY
                    *
                    *    SOLOS/CUTER SUBROUTINES USED
              IN      EQU     0C01FH    INPUT FROM KEYBOARD TO A-REG
              OUT     EQU     0C019H    OUTPUT FROM B-REG TO TERMINAL
                    *
                      ORG     0000H
              SUB     EQU     0000H     USER SUBR START (CAN BE MODIFIED)
                    * ENTER SYSTEM AT LOCATION 0 WITH STACK POINTER PRESET
                    * TO SCRATCH PAD RAM ENOUGH FOR A FEW LEVELS OF CALL
                    *
0000 2A 0001  START   LHLD    LOC       SOURCE PROGRAM AREA START
0003 CD 4600  EGET    CALL    JIN       ACCEPT SOURCE CHAR
0006 FE 5C            CPI     5CH       \ ?
0008 CA 0000          JZ      START     YES, BACK UP TO PROGRAM START
                    *
000B FE 24            CPI     24H       $ ?
000D CA 5200          JZ      EXEC      YES, GO EXECUTE THE PROGRAM
                    *
0010 FE 5F            CPI     5FH       BS ?
0012 C2 1900          JNZ     DIS       NO
0015 2B               DCX     H         YES, BACK UP ONE IN SOURCE
0016 C3 0300          JMP     EGET      LOOP BACK
                    *
                    *   PROCESS DISPLAY OF NEXT LINE
0019 FE 2F    DIS     CPI     2FH       / ?
001B C2 2400          JNZ     PAD       NO
001E CD DF00          CALL    PRT       GO PRINT TO CR
0021 C3 0300          JMP     EGET      LOOP
                    *
                    *   DO LINE REPLACEMENT- PAD TO END OF STMT WITH NULLS
0024 FE 25    PAD     CPI     25H       % ?
0026 C2 3C00          JNZ     CHAR      NO
0029 06 0D            MVI     B,0DH     CR
002B 78               MOV     A,B       CR TO A ALSO
002C CD 4D00          CALL    JOUT      PRINT IT
002F 0E 40            MVI     C,40H     COUNT OF 64
0031 BE      PADL     CMP     M         AT CR YET ?
0032 CA 3C00          JZ      CHAR      YES QUIT PADDING
0035 36 00            MVI     M,00H     PAD WITH NULL
0037 23               INX     H         INCR LOC PTR
0038 0D               DCR     C         DECREMENT SAFETY COUNTER
0039 C2 3100          JNZ     PADL      LOOP TILL CR OR 64 NULLS
                    *
                    *   STORE ENTERED SOURCE CHAR IN PROGRAM
003C 77      CHAR     MOV     M,A       CHAR TO SOURCE LOC
003D 23               INX     H         MOVE LOC PTR UP ONE
003E FE 0D            CPI     0DH       IS IT A CR ?
0040 CC F000          CZ      PLF       YES, ECHO A LINE FEED
0043 C3 0300          JMP     EGET      NO, GET ANOTHER CHAR
                    *
                    *   CHANGE NEXT FEW LINES IF YOU DONT USE SOLOS/CUTER
0046 CD 1FC0  JIN     CALL    IN        CALL CHAR INPUT ROUTINE
0049 CA 4600          JZ      JIN       TRY AGAIN IF NO CHAR YET THERE
004C 47               MOV     B,A       PREPARE TO ECHO THE CHAR
004D CD 19C0  JOUT    CALL    OUT       CALL CHARACTER OUTPUT ROUTINE
0050 78               MOV     A,B       RESTORE JIN CHAR TO A
0051 C9               RET               RETURN TO CALLER
                    *
                    *   COME HERE TO BEGIN EXECUTION OF THE SOURCE PROGRAM
                    *
0052 2A 0001  EXEC    LHLD    LOC       STARTING LOC OF PROGRAM
0055 2B               DCX     H         LESS ONE
0056 23      LOOPI    INX     H         ADR OF NEXT PGM BYTE
0057 7E      LOOP     MOV     A,M       NEXT PGM BYTE
0058 FE 2B            CPI     2BH       * CHAR ? (NOTE 2BH IS '*'+1)
005A FA 5600          JM      LOOPI     YES(OR IGNOREABLE CONT CHAR)
                    *
                    *   PROCESS Y OR N FLAG TESTS
005D FE 59            CPI     59H       Y ?
005F CA 6700          JZ      TFLG      YES
0062 FE 4E            CPI     4EH       N ?
0064 C2 7600          JNZ     XA        BRANCH IF NOT A FLAG TEST
                    *
0067 23      TFLG     INX     H         STEP LOC OVER Y OR N
0068 BA               CMP     D         COMPARE TO CURRENT MATCH FLAG
0069 CA 5700          JZ      LOOP      ITS EQUAL SO EXECUTE THE STMT
                    *
                    *   ITS A FLAG FAILURE, SKIP OVER THE STMT
006C 23      SKIP     INX     H         STEP LOC PTR
006D 7E               MOV     A,M       NEXT CHAR IN PGM
006E FE 0D            CPI     0DH       TO END OF STMT ?
0070 C2 6C00          JNZ     SKIP      NOT YET, SO LOOP
0073 C3 5600          JMP     LOOPI     AT NEXT STMT, GO DO IT
                    *
                    *   PROCESS ACCEPT STATEMENT
0076 FE 41    XA      CPI     41H       A ?
0078 C2 8E00          JNZ     XM        NO
```

```
S1130000FE01008D45815C27F781242745810B2660
S1130010030920EFB12F2607BD00D59D2120E4811F
S11300202526128600BD27860DC640A10027066F52
S11300300085A26F6A70008810D27DF20C5C60050
S11300404F8D0B542AFA860A2004BDE1AC39BDE172
S11300500D139FE0100090BA600B12A2FF9B15927BR
S1130060004811E260F08B1010527EC08A620810D76
S11300702667920E28141261AFF0192BDCDB79104A4A
S1130080008860DBDC78DB720CDB14D2612080BA68E
S113009000C659B101042702C64EF7010520B781F5
S11300A004A2617E6002C40F2605FE010220A908A667
S11300B000812A26F95A26F6209C8153260A080B2C
S11300C00A600087E0000208F8154260208088D05B2
S11300D0BD003E20B2C640A6005A270ABD004EA697
S10A00E000008810D26F1392F
```

Listing 3a: MIKBUG format for the 6800 version of WADUZITDO.

```
00002A0001CD4600FE5CCA0000FE24CA5200
0010FE5FC219002BC30300FE2FC22400CDDF
002000C30300FE25C23C00060D7BCD4D000E
003040BECA3C003600023D0C231007723FE0D
0040CCF000C30300CD1FC0CA460047CD19C0
00507BC92A000012B237EFE2BFA5600FE59CA
006067000FE4EC2760023BACA5700237EFE0D
0070C26C00C35600FE41C28E00220201CD46
00800005F23060DCD4D00CDF000C35600FE4D
0090C2A10023237E1659BBCA9E00164EC356
00A000FE4AC2C30023237EE60F47C2B5002A
00B00201C35700237EFE2AC2B50005C2B500
00C0C35000FE53C2D20023237E23C30000C3
00D05700FE54C2D90023233CDDF00C357000E
00E040460DCAF000CD4D007E23FE0DC2E100
00F00E000600CD4D000DF2F20060AC34D00
01000601000000000
```

Listing 4a: Dump of the 8080 version of WADUZITDO. The format consists of 4 character hexadecimal address and 16 hexadecimally coded bytes of information. There is no checksum computed for any of the information.

PAPERBYTE® Bar Codes for WADUZITDO

In figure 1 and figure 2, we provide a PAPERBYTE® bar code representation for the WADUZITDO programs of listing 3 and listing 4. These bar code representations were created in the absolute loader format documented in detail in the PAPERBYTE book, *Bar Code Loader*, written by Ken Budnick of Micro-Scan Associates, and available for $2 at local computer stores or by mail (add $.60 postage and handling) from BYTE Books, 70 Main St, Peterborough, NH 03458.

placed in read only memory. It would fit in a single 1702A EROM chip.

It is easy to see how this language could be used to write a question and answer conversation using multiple choice or true, false answers. It may not be so obvious that more complex logic is possible. The example in listing 2 is a computer versus user NIM game which demonstrates a way this can be done.

Although WADUZITDO is not the ultimate answer to personal computing, it is something that almost anyone can have some fun with, and it definitely squeezes the most out of 256 bytes of memory.

A Pascal WADUZITDO

Notes by Ray Cote
Program by Larry Kheriaty

Along with the assembly language versions of WADUZITDO, Larry Kheriaty sent us the Pascal version shown in listing 5. The program is basically self-documenting and very easy to translate into assembly level programs for any particular processor. The program is indented to show logical relationships between related areas of text. This is sometimes known as prettyprinting.

The first four lines of the program are definition lines for the main program. In Pascal, all variables must be defined completely at the start of the section in which they are used. "Completely" means name and data type. This is a great help since all variables must be explicitly defined. You can easily check to see what type of variable is being used.

WADUZITDO uses two types of variables: integer and character. There is also a definition for constants (CONST). CONST informs the compiler that the value being assigned to this variable will not change. Integer variables will only take on whole number values.

The type character (CHAR) means that the variables will take on the values of ASCII characters, including all letters, numbers and special symbols.

The last line of the definition section defines a variable PROG as an array of characters. This definition also states that the relative base address of the array will be unity and the variable PZ will be used to specify locations within the array.

After defining our variables we are ready to start the first executable part of the program. In Pascal, the logical parts of the pro-

```
007B  22 0201        SHLD  LST      YES, SAVE LOC OF LAST ACCEPT
007E  CD 4600        CALL  JIN      ACCEPT ONE CHAR FROM KYBD
0081  5F             MOV   E,A      SAVE IT
0082  23             INX   H        MOVE OVER A
0083  06 0D          MVI   B,0DH    CR
0085  CD 4D00        CALL  JOUT     PRINT IT
0088  CD F000        CALL  PLF      PRINT LINE FEED
008B  C3 5600        JMP   LOOPI    STEP OVER : AND GO ON
      *
      *        PROCESS MATCH STMT
008E  FE 4D    XM    CPI   4DH      M  ?
0090  C2 A100        JNZ   XJ       NO
0093  23             INX   H        STEP OVER M
0094  23             INX   H        STEP OVER :
0095  7E             MOV   A,M      GET MATCH CHAR
0096  16 59          MVI   D,59H    ASSUME Y
0098  BB             CMP   E        COMP MATCH CHAR TO INPUT CHAR
0099  CA 9E00        JZ    MX       BRANCH IF IT MATCHES,FLG=Y
009C  16 4E          MVI   D,4EH    RESULT IS N
009E  C3 5600  MX    JMP   LOOPI    SET MATCH FLAG TO Y OR N
      *
      *        PROCESS JUMP STATEMENT
00A1  FE 4A    XJ    CPI   4AH      J  ?
00A3  C2 C300        JNZ   XS       NO
00A6  23             INX   H        STEP OVER J
00A7  23             INX   H        STEP OVER :
00A8  7E             MOV   A,M      DESTINATION
00A9  E6 0F          ANI   0FH      CLEAR ZONE
00AB  47             MOV   B,A      NUMBER OF *S TO SKIP
00AC  C2 B500        JNZ   JF       ITS A JUMP FORWARD
00AF  2A 0201        LHLD  LST      ZERO.. JUMP BACK TO LAST ACCEPT
00B2  C3 5700        JMP   LOOP     CONTINUE FROM THERE
      *
      *   SKIP FORWARD UNTIL PASS N *-MARKERS ( N IS IN BREG )
00B5  23       JF    INX   H        STEP PGM LOC
00B6  7E             MOV   A,M      NEXT CHAR
00B7  FE 2A          CPI   2AH      *-MARKER ?
00B9  C2 B500        JNZ   JF       NO, KEEP LOOPING
00BC  05             DCR   B        FOUND ONE, COUNT IT
00BD  C2 B500        JNZ   JF       LOOP IF NEED TO FIND MORE
00C0  C3 5600        JMP   LOOPI    DESTINATION FOUND, GO EXECUTE
      *
      *   PROCESS STOP OR SUBROUTINE STATEMENT
00C3  FE 53    XS    CPI   53H      S  ?
00C5  C2 D200        JNZ   XT       NO
00C8  23             INX   H        STEP OVER S
00C9  23             INX   H        STEP OVER :
00CA  7E             MOV   A,M      PARAMETER TO REG A
00CB  23             INX   H        STEP OVER PARAMETER
      *   NEXT STMT MAY BE MADE TO BE A CALL TO USER SUBR
00CC  C3 0000        JMP   SUB      GO TO USER SUBR (OR TO EDITOR)
00CF  C3 5700        JMP   LOOP     GO ON UPON RETURN FROM USER SUBR
      *
      *   PROCESS TYPE STATMENT AND SYNTAX ERRORS
00D2  FE 54    XT    CPI   54H      T  ?
00D4  C2 D700        JNZ   TE       NO, ITS AN ERROR
00D7  23             INX   H        YES, STEP OVER T
00D8  23             INX   H        STEP OVER :
00D9  CD DF00  TE    CALL  PRT      PRINT UP TO CR
00DC  C3 5700        JMP   LOOP     DONE WITH T
      *
      *   SUBR TO PRINT UP TO NEXT CR
00DF  0E 40    PRT   MVI   C,40H    COUNT OF 64
00E1  46       PRTA  MOV   B,M      NEXT CHAR
00E2  0D             DCR   C        DECREMENT SAFETY COUNTER
00E3  CA F000        JZ    PLF      EXIT IF OVER 64 BEFORE CR
00E6  CD 4D00        CALL  JOUT     PRINT IT
00E9  7E             MOV   A,M      RELOAD CHAR TO ACCA
00EA  23             INX   H        STEP LOC PTR
00EB  FE 0D          CPI   0DH      CR ?
00ED  C2 E100        JNZ   PRTA     NOT CR, LOOP
      *
      *   SUBROUTINE TO PRINT LINE FEED AND PAD
00F0  0E 00    PLF   MVI   C,00H    NUMBER OF NULLS TO PRINT
00F2  06 00    PLFL  MVI   B,00H    NULL
00F4  CD 4D00        CALL  JOUT     WRITE A NULL
00F7  0D             DCR   C        DECREMENT COUNTER
00F8  F2 F200        JP    PLFL     LOOP TILL ENOUGH NULLS
00FB  06 0A          MVI   B,0AH    LINE FEED
00FD  C3 4D00        JMP   JOUT     PRINT THEN RETURN
      *
      *   ABOVE IS END OF READ ONLY PORTION OF THE PROGRAM
      *
      *   THE FOLLOWING IS CHANGEABLE DATA
      *
               ORG   0100H    MOVE TO START OF DATA AREA
0100  0601     LOC   DW    0106H    ADDR OF SOURCE PROGRAM AREA
0102  0000     LST   DW    0000H    PLACE TO SAVE LOC OF LAST A:
      *   THE NEXT TWO BYTES ARE ONLY FOR 6800 COMPATIBILITY
0104  00       CHR   DB    00H      UNUSED, LAST INPUT CHAR IN EREG
0105  00       FLG   DB    00H      UNUSED,MATCH-FLAG IN DREG
      *
               END
```

gram are broken into procedures, equivalent to subroutines in languages such as FOR-TRAN. Every procedure is blocked off by BEGIN and END statements. The name of the first procedure is CHIN. After we have determined the name, we are told to begin executing procedure ACCEPT (which will return to us input values in variable CBUF). This is a subroutine which is not shown since it is specific to the processor being used. The next two procedures are also calls to subroutines used to DISPLAY the contents of the buffer and move the output to a new line. These two procedures are also machine dependent. Notice that Pascal allows you to use descriptive names. This is very important when writing a program that you want other people to read or that you want to understand at a later date.

Listing 5: Pascal listing of WADUZITDO. See notes by Ray Cote.

```
PASCAL VERSION OF WADUZITDO, LARRY KHERIATY
PROGRAM WADUZITDO;
  CONST PZ=5000; BS=127; EOL=10;
  VAR LOC,LST,I : INTEGER; LCHR,FLG,CBUF,CBS,CEOL : CHAR;
    PROG : ARRAY[1..PZ] OF CHAR;

  PROCEDURE CHIN; BEGIN ACCEPT (CBUF); END;
  PROCEDURE CHOUT; BEGIN DISPLAY (CBUF); END;
  PROCDURE NEWLINE; BEGIN DISPLAY (NL) ; END;

  PROCEDURE LIST; VAR I:INTEGER;
    BEGIN I:= 0;
      REPEAT
        CBUF := PROG [LOC]; LOC := LOC+1; I:=I+1;
        CHOUT
      UNTIL (I>64) OR (CBUF=CEOL); NEWLINE
    END;

  PROCEDURE EXECUTE; VAR DONE : BOOLEAN;
    BEGIN LOC := 1; DONE := FALSE;
      REPEAT
        CBUF := PROG[LOC] ; IF CBUF < '*' THEN CBUF := '*';
        IF NOT(CBUF IN ['*','Y','N','A','M','J','T','S'])THEN LIST ELSE
          CASE CBUF OF
            '*': LOC := LOC+1;
            'Y','N' : IF CBUF=FLG THEN LOC := LOC+1
                        ELSE REPEAT CBUF := PROG[LOC]; LOC:=LOC+1
                            UNTIL CBUF=CEOL;
            'A' : BEGIN LST := LOC; CHIN; LCHR :=CBUF;
                    NEWLINE; LOC :=LOC+2 END;
            'M' : BEGIN IF LCHR=PROG[LOC+2] THEN FLG :='Y'
                      ELSE FLG := 'N';
                    LOC := LOC+3 END;
            'J' : IF PROG[LOC+2] = '0' THEN LOC :=LST
                    ELSE BEGIN I:= ORD(PROG[LOC+2])-48;
                      REPEAT LOC:=LOC+1;
                          IF PROG[LOC] = '*' THEN I := I-1;
                      UNTIL I=0 END;
            'T' : BEGIN LOC := LOC+2; LIST END;
            'S' : BEGIN DONE := TRUE; LOC := 1 END
          END
      UNTIL DONE
    END;

BEGIN CBS := CHR(BS); CEOL := CHR(EOL); CBUF :='\';
  WHILE TRUE DO BEGIN
    IF CBUF ='\' THEN LOC :=1
    ELSE IF CBUF=CBS THEN LOC := LOC-1
    ELSE IF CBUF='/' THEN LIST
    ELSE IF CBUF='$' THEN EXECUTE
    ELSE IF CBUF='%' THEN
      BEGIN I:=0;
        WHILE (I<64) AND (PROG[LOC] <> CEOL) DO
          BEGIN PROG[LOC] := CHR(0); LOC := LOC+1 END;
        PROG[LOC] := CEOL; LOC := LOC +1; NEWLINE
      END
    ELSE BEGIN PROG[LOC] := CBUF; LOC := LOC+1;
      IF CBUF=CEOL THEN NEWLINE END;
    CHIN
  END
END.
```

The next procedure, LIST, first defines its own local variables, which it will use only within the LIST routine. As before, the procedure is delimited by BEGIN and END statements. This procedure introduces us to the concept of loops. Here we have a related pair of commands: REPEAT and UNTIL. These two commands cause the one line of three instructions and the call to procedure CHOUT to execute until either the value I is greater than 64 or the variable CBUF is equal to CEOL. Once either of these two conditions occurs, the program logic proceeds to call procedure NEWLINE. At this point the LIST procedure ends and returns to whatever procedure called it.

Procedure EXECUTE looks structurally the same as procedure LIST. There is a definition of variables, the BEGIN and END delimiters, and a REPEAT-UNTIL structure. This time the REPEAT-UNTIL statement is not waiting for a relation to be true, but is rather checking against one variable. Looking at how DONE was defined at the beginning of the procedure, we see that its designation is BOOLEAN. This means that the variable is being used as a logical variable and can take on the value true or false. The REPEAT-UNTIL instruction waits to see if the variable DONE is true. If so, we have finished this procedure and can stop it.

Procedure EXECUTE also contains an IF-THEN-ELSE statement. If the value of CBUF is not contained within the brackets, perform procedure LIST. If the value of CBUF is somewhere within the square brackets, we want to perform an operation related to that value. We now come to another Pascal instruction, the CASE statement.

We are given a set of cases to choose from. The CASE statement tells us that we will be using the value in variable CBUF to determine what is to be done. We scan down each of the cases and find the one labeled with the value in CBUF. Since CBUF is type character we are looking at ASCII characters. Once we find the value of CBUF we execute the statements associated with it that are blocked off by another set of BEGIN and END statements. After we have finished, we move to the end of the CASE statement and then the last line of REPEAT-UNTIL statement.

The next section of the program does not look like the preceding sections. It does not start with a PROCEDURE statement, but has a BEGIN statement. So far we have discussed procedures. Any of the procedures that needed to use variables have defined their own. So why did we define those variables at the very beginning of the program? The reason is not to use them in a procedure, but to use them in the main program. This BEGIN statement is nothing more than the start of the mainline logic for program WADUZITDO. The mainline logic inputs characters and either stores them in an array as program or executes them as commands. This routine will not jump out of the loop and will have to be interrupted to stop. Of course it is possible to create another command that will allow you to exit from this cycle.

Now that we have looked at the Pascal version of WADUZITDO, the reader should refer back to either of the assembly versions. The Pascal version performs the same function as the assembly versions.

The assembly language versions need to be heavily commented for the reader to understand what is happening. Even liberal comments will not help when converting from one assembly language to another. The Pascal version can be easily converted into any machine language. It is also self-documenting. Notice that even without a single comment, the Pascal listing is extremely easy to decipher. . . . RGAC■

Creating a Chess Player

Part 1: An Essay on Human and Computer Chess Skill

Peter W Frey
Larry R Atkin

In a recent *Time* essay (see references) Robert Jastrow, director of NASA's Goddard Institute for Space Studies, predicted that history is about to witness the birth of a new intelligence, a form superior to humanity's. The pitiful human brain has "a wiring defect" that causes it to "freeze up" when faced with "several streams of information simultaneously." Jastrow suggests that "the human form is not likely to be the standard form for intelligent life" in the cosmos. Even on our own small planet, a new day is near at hand: "In the 1990s, . . . the compactness and reasoning power of an intelligence built out of silicon will begin to match that of the human brain."

We have always been fascinated by the idea of a machine that is capable of rational thought. Jastrow is neither the first nor the last person who is betting on rapid improvements in machine intelligence. His expectation that computers will rival humanity within 15 years seems optimistic to anyone who has watched half-a-dozen excited technicians flutter about for several hours trying to bring a crashed system back to life. This prophecy seems even more fanciful to those who have attempted to program machines to cope with pattern recognition, language translation or a complex game such as chess.

The chess environment, in fact, provides a particularly good example of the difficult problems which still need to be solved before silicon intelligence can become a reality. More than 20 years ago, Herbert Simon, a recognized expert in the field of artificial intelligence, predicted that within a decade, the world's chess champion would be a computer. This prognostication has not come to pass. Why was an informed scientist like Simon so wrong in his assessment of computer capabilities? A major factor is that computer scientists have often failed to appreciate the level of knowledge which is required to play master-level chess. They have also commonly underestimated the tremendous information-processing capacity of the human brain. Even though chess is a game of logic in which all legal moves can be precisely specified and in which nothing is left to chance, several centuries of intensive analysis have not exhausted the perennial challenge and novelty of the game. Psychologists have been actively studying the human brain for several decades and have discovered a fascinating mystery wrapped within an enigma. The more we learn about the brain, the more we are aware of our lamentable state of ignorance.

The Mind of the Chess Player

At a general level of knowledge, we have several provocative insights on the nature and structure of human chess skill. We know, for example, that the skilled chess player does not examine hundreds of possible continuations before selecting a move. We also know that superior chess players are not formidable "thinking machines" but in fact display a normal range of intelligence scores. Strong chess players, as a group, do not even appear to have special retention abilities such as having "photographic" memories. In most

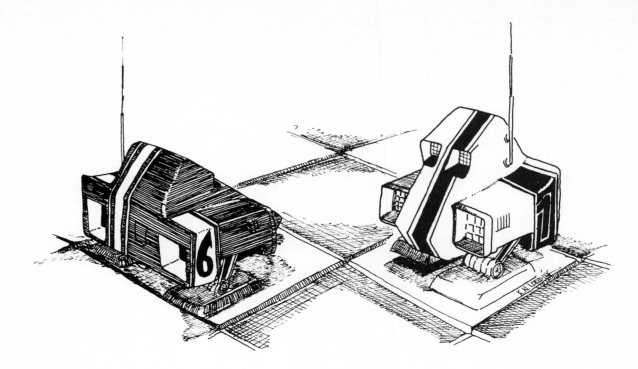

Artwork by K N Lodding.

De Groot's "law" of chess is that Grandmasters play better chess simply because they pick better moves.

respects, top-flight chess players have the same intellectual capacities as the rest of the population and, in the technical details of move selection, seem to engage in the same type of information processing that is observed in much weaker players.

Our knowledge in these matters is based on the early work of Binet in France and that of de Groot in Holland and on more recent investigations by other scientists in the USSR and the United States. In the late nineteenth century, Binet was surprised to discover that masters did not have a vivid image of the board when playing blindfolded chess. Instead, they seemed to remember positions in abstract terms such as by specific relations among pieces. Interviews with masters clearly indicated that a photographic memory was not a prerequisite for being able to play many simultaneous games of blindfolded chess. In the 1930s and 1940s, de Groot worked with a number of strong chess players (from Grandmasters to strong club players) and had them verbalize their thought processes while selecting a move in a complicated position. His research indicated that the Grandmasters' general approach was highly similar to that of weaker players. They analyzed a similar number of moves (about four) from the initial position, a similar number of total moves (about 35), made a similar number of fresh starts (about six), and calculated combinations to the same maximal depth (about seven plies or half-moves, where a move is defined as a play by one side and a response by the

other). The only clear measurable difference was that the Grandmasters invariably chose the strongest move while the weaker players did not. Thus de Groot concluded that Grandmasters play better chess because they pick better moves. Unfortunately, this conclusion is not very informative since it is obviously circular. The fact that de Groot's extensive study did not uncover any prominent differences in the move-selection strategies used by strong and average players implies that the analysis procedure itself is not the critical factor which determines chess skill.

An important clue to the difference between skilled and unskilled players was discovered by de Groot when he displayed an unfamiliar chess position to his subjects for a few seconds and then asked them to recall the position from memory. He found that masters recalled almost all the pieces while club players remembered only about half of them. Recent work in this country by Chase and Simon at Carnegie-Mellon University has indicated that novice players recall only about a third of the pieces. Chase and Simon also added an important control procedure. They demonstrated that the differences in recall ability completely disappear if the pieces are positioned randomly. This outcome indicates that the superior memory of the chess master is chess-specific and not a general trait.

Simon and Gilmartin have proposed that skilled chess players learn to recognize a large number of piece combinations as perceptual chunks and perform well in the recall task because they remember four or five chunks rather than four or five pieces like the novice. If the average chunk size is three to four, the skilled player will recall 16 to 18 pieces.

On the basis of this analysis, skill in chess depends on a learned perceptual ability which is highly similar to that acquired by every schoolchild as he or she slowly builds up a large repertoire of words. Initially the child learns to read each word character by character and often does not understand the meaning of the word. The novice chess player perceives the chessboard in a similar way, assessing a position piece by piece and failing to recognize the *meaning* of common piece configurations. The adult reader recognizes words and phrases as basic units (chunks) rather than individual characters and has a recognition vocabulary of approximately 50,000 words. The skilled chess player, in a similar vein, recognizes a very large number of piece configurations (chunks) and understands what they imply both individually and in combination.

The critical aspect of move selection occurs in the first few seconds of the task. Based on his assessment of the position, the skilled player immediately recognizes appropriate long-term and short-term goals and has a good feel for the specific moves which are compatible with these goals. For this reason, only two to four moves on the average are given serious consideration. The difference between the Grandmaster and the expert lies in the fine distinctions which are made in the first few seconds of their analysis. Skilled chess players can play a remarkably strong game when they are given only five seconds for each move. In this short time, it is not possible to make a careful analysis of many different continuations. The player must have an "instinctive" feel for the correct move and be able to recognize key features and to understand both their immediate and long-term implications.

Human chess skill, therefore, is based on two highly refined capacities, pattern recognition and rapid information retrieval. The latter ability depends on the fact that human memory is content-addressable rather than location-addressable like that of a computer. Computer systems often have to search for a specific item of information in memory by conducting an exhaustive, linear search of an entire file. Human memory however is organized in an amazingly complex fashion such that most of us can easily recall a specific fact on the basis of a completely novel retrieval cue. For example, name a flower that rhymes with

nose. In this case, your quick response demonstrates that words are grouped together on the basis of their phonetic similarity (ie: sound). Your ability to quickly recall words which are similar in meaning to the word *fat* (such as obese, chubby, rotund, flabby, plump and stout) demonstrates that human memory is also organized by semantic similarity (ie: meaning). When a person is given a retrieval cue which does not elicit an immediate response, he or she can usually find the correct information after a brief search of related ideas or concepts. This facility contrasts sharply with the extremely limited linear searches which are generally conducted with large computer based storage systems. Even sophisticated computer retrieval strategies which arrange the data base in multilinked lists with elaborate tree structures presently lack the large system efficiency displayed by their biological counterparts.

Pattern recognition and rapid information retrieval are not only key capacities for chess, but are also essential for a wide range of important human problem solving skills. Whether your field is medicine, engineering, plumbing or computer programming, you would be a complete failure at your job without these essential abilities. Jastrow's claim that machine intelligence will soon equal man's intelligence seems to overlook the important points made in BYTE by Ernest Kent (see references). Kent emphasizes the fact that biological information processors have a vastly different architecture than their silicon imitations. In fact, he suggests that our lack of success in building a thinking machine stems from our attempts "to make a wrench do a screwdriver's job." Our modern high-speed computers were designed to do important tasks which men are not very good at, such as complex mathematical calculations.

The human brain evolved, in contrast, on its ability to identify important environmental events and to quickly recognize their significance. Natural selection has never placed much emphasis on our ability to multiply or our ability to compute the inverse of a matrix. Kent also reminds us that organic evolution worked with a very different kind of hardware than that which is available to the modern computer engineer. Biological information processors have an incredibly slow cycle time, less than 100 operations per second. The basic unit, the neuron, operates in milliseconds rather than in nanoseconds. The brain, however, makes up in quantity and in structural complexity what it lacks in speed. Computers, on the other hand, have many fewer components and a much simpler

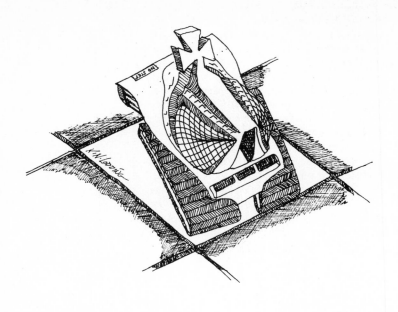

gating architecture, but are orders of magnitude faster.

It may be that present machine hardware configurations are simply inappropriate for efficient pattern recognition or semantic recall. An analysis of the history of computer chess is instructive. Although there have been numerous advocates for chess programs which imitate human playing methods, only a few have been attempted, and none of these have played reasonable chess. The earliest paper on machine chess, written by Claude Shannon in 1950 (see references), proposed a mechanical algorithm which was not modeled on human chess play. Shannon suggested a workable procedure for representing the board and piece locations, specified simple mathematical algorithms for generating the legal moves of each piece and gave an example of a straightforward technique for evaluating a position (see *Chess Skill in Man and Machine*, chapter 3). The key feature of Shannon's proposal was the adoption of the *minimax* technique as described by von Neuman and Morgenstern in 1944. The basic idea of the minimax technique is to assume that the player whose turn it is to play will always choose the move which minimizes his opponent's maximum potential gain. Hence, the name minimax.

The Type B Strategy

One of the difficulties of this approach is that a complete analysis of all possible continuations (type A strategy) very rapidly leads to an overwhelming number of potential positions. The look-ahead tree grows at an exponential rate and with an average,

according to de Groot, of 38 legal moves at each position, a search involving three moves (three half-moves for each player) produces over 3 billion (38^6) terminal positions. You may recall that de Groot's research indicated that human players regularly searched a tree to seven plies and sometimes much deeper. Because of this, Shannon concluded that it would not be possible for the machine to consider all possible legal continuations at each *node* of the game tree. Instead, he proposed a type B strategy in which only reasonable (ie: plausible) moves are pursued at each branching point. If the program considered only five continuations at each node instead of all 38, a 6 ply look-ahead would involve only 15,625 (5^6) terminal positions.

The attractiveness of the type B approach seems overwhelming when the number of terminal positions increases exponentially with depth. The fact that skilled human players explore only a limited number of continuations at each choice point is additional evidence which favors the adoption of this strategy. It is not surprising, therefore, that most programmers have used Shannon's type B strategy in designing a chess program.

Sometimes our understanding of the real world, however, is not always as accurate as we presume. In selecting a type B strategy in preference to a type A strategy, the programmer does not necessarily simplify the problem. This approach was competently implemented in 1967 by Greenblatt at MIT. His program played reasonable, and at that time, fairly impressive chess. The major design problem in a selective search is the possibility that the look-ahead process will exclude a key move at a low level in the game tree. The failure to consider an important move can lead to a very serious miscalculation. A chess game can be lost by a single weak move. For this reason, it is of critical importance that a necessary move not be missed. The type B programs place a critical dependence on the accuracy of their plausible move generator. Chess is an extremely complex game and in many situations a move which at a superficial level seems unlikely, is, in fact, the best one. Grandmasters find these moves while lesser players, including machines, fail to see them. For a decade, several dozen individuals have tried to create a plausible move generator that is superior to Greenblatt's. The evidence is fairly clear, however, that type B programs have improved very little since 1967.

As strange as it may seem, recent progress in computer chess has come by abandoning the type B strategy. Shannon's logical analysis was made in a "stone-age" hardware environment and without knowledge of several important algorithms. Today, the type A strategy is not as ridiculous as it seemed in 1950. In addition, very few individuals anticipated the immense difficulty involved in constructing a competent plausible move generator. To become a chess master, a man has to study chess intensively (20 hrs or more a week) for at least 5 years. During this time he acquires an immense amount of detailed knowledge about the game of chess. Subtle features of a particular position are recognized immediately and suggest both short-term and long-term goals as well as specific moves. This kind of knowledge is sufficiently abstract that most players find it impossible to verbalize the relevant thought processes. The one factor which stands out clearly, however, is that the chess master has acquired a tremendous library of factual information which can be retrieved quickly and applied in apparently novel situations. No chess program has been able to duplicate this facility and, without it, the creation of a workable plausible move generator is next to impossible.

When a type A strategy is employed, however, this problem can be bypassed. By making all the moves *plausible*, the program never overlooks a subtle but important one. In fact, by reverting to a brute force search of all possible continuations, the program often finds interesting combinations that are commonly missed even by strong human players. It seems ironic that the brute force approach (full width searching) produces many more brilliant moves than the smart approach (selective searching). This important discovery was made independently by Slate and Atkin at Northwestern (the authors of the current world champion chess program, Chess 4.6) and by the Russian KAISSA team.

Minimax and the Alpha-Beta Algorithm

Slate and Atkin's work has demonstrated that a full width search can be conducted considerably more efficiently than anyone had previously suspected (including Slate and Atkin; see references). There are a number of important developments which are responsible for this reassessment. The most important discovery was made in the late 1950s by Newell, Shaw and Simon as well as by Samuels. Because of the basic logic underlying a minimax search, it is not necessary to search the entire look-ahead tree before selecting the best move. Consider a simple 2 ply search (one move for you and one for your opponent). First you examine one of your possible moves and the 38 or so terminal positions which result from each

of your opponent's legal replies. You select the one reply which is best, according to your evaluation function, for your opponent (ie: the one which minimizes your own maximum potential gain). Next, you consider a second move for yourself and the 38 or so replies that your opponent can make to this move. In considering these moves, you discover that the third reply you examine would give your opponent a better outcome than his best reply to your first candidate. Immediately you realize that it is a complete waste of time for you to analyze any more of his replies to your second candidate. Since you are already guaranteed a worse position after the second move than after the first, it is reasonable to reject the second one and turn to your third candidate. This decision eliminates the need for evaluating 35 of the potential replies to your second candidate. A very tidy savings.

Historically, the score for the best move so far for White has been designated as α and the score for the best move so far for Black has been called β. Thus the name alpha-beta $(\alpha-\beta)$ algorithm. When the tree is both wide and deep, this algorithm can reduce the number of terminal nodes to a small fraction of the number which would be examined by a complete minimax search. The beauty of this procedure is that it always produces the same result as the full minimax search.

An important factor in determining the efficiency of the alpha-beta algorithm is the order in which the moves are examined. If White's best moves and Black's best replies

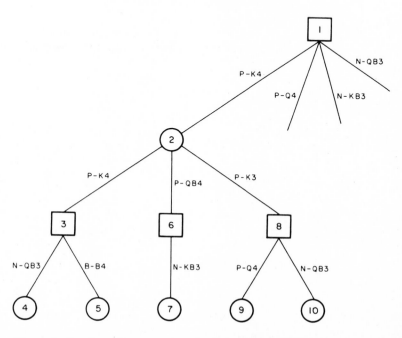

Figure 1: Portion of a game tree for the opening game in chess. Square nodes indicate that White is to play; round nodes that Black is to play. Techniques such as alpha-beta pruning and minimax strategy are used to optimize the use of trees like this.

are considered first at each choice point, the search of the uniform game tree of height h (number of plies deep) and width d (number of successors at each node) will involve approximately $2 \cdot d^{h/2}$ terminal positions instead of d^h (see references, Knuth and Moore). The potential magnitude of this saving can be appreciated by considering our previous example with a 6 ply search: 38^6 is more than 3 billion while 2×38^3 is about 110,000. Shannon might have given more consideration to the type A strategy if he had been aware of the alpha-beta algorithm and some of the other technical improvements which were to follow.

General Strategy

To maximize the benefit of the alpha-beta procedure, it is necessary to devise an efficient strategy for generating the moves at each node in an order which is likely to produce a cut-off, such that searching can be terminated at that node. There are several general heuristics which have proven their value time and time again. One is extremely simple and powerful: try capturing moves first. Because a full width search includes many ridiculous moves, a reply which involves a capture will often remove a piece which was "stupidly" placed *en prise* (ie: attacked and insufficiently defended). Captures also have the beneficial effect of reducing the number of potential offspring. An additional important characteristic of a capturing move is that it will generally have to be examined sooner or later in order to insure the quiescence of the terminal position. Because of this, every capture that is examined early generally reduces the amount of work which will have to be done later. In practice, investigators have reported a speed-up in search time of as much as 2 to 1 by simply putting all the captures at the beginning of the move list.

In addition to captures, there is another class of moves which is also effective for producing cut-offs. These are called *killers* because they are moves which have produced cut-offs in the immediate past and have been specifically remembered for that reason. A short list of killers is maintained by the program and whenever the legal capturing moves fail to produce a cut-off, each of the killers (if legal in the given position) is then examined. This *killer heuristic* is quite effective in producing a move order which enhances the probability of a quick cut-off.

The general features of the alpha-beta algorithm and its important servants, the capture and killer heuristics, were reasonably well-known late in the 1960s. In recent years, several important refinements have been added to this list. One of the most important is the staged or iterative alpha-beta search. For example, instead of conducting a 5 ply search all at once the search is done in stages, first a 2 ply search, then a 3 ply search, then a 4 ply search, and finally a 5 ply search. Superficially this might appear to be wasteful since the staged search requires the full 5 ply search eventually anyway. This is not at all the case. As each search is completed, the principal variation (best moves for each side at each depth) is used as the base for the next (1 ply deeper) search. The 3 ply search therefore starts with a move at ply 1 and a reply at ply 2 which has already been proven to be reasonable (from the machine's limited perspective). The 4 ply search starts with reasonable moves at its first three plies. The 5 ply search has the benefit of reasonable moves at its first four plies. Because the efficiency of the alpha-beta algorithm is tremendously sensitive to move ordering, the spill-over in information from one iteration to the next has a surprisingly powerful effect. A single 1 stage 5 ply search might require 120 seconds of processor time. The last segment of the staged 5 ply search might require only half as much time (ie: 60). Since each iteration requires about five times as much processor time as its predecessor (the exponential character of the look-ahead tree is diminished somewhat by the alpha-beta algorithm), the staged 4 ply search would take about 12 seconds, the staged 3 ply search about 3 seconds, and the 2 ply search about 1 second. The total time for the iterative search would be approximately 76 seconds (1 + 3 + 12 + 60) rather than 120 seconds.

An added benefit of the iterative search, and, incidentally, the reason for its discovery in the first place, is that it provides a useful mechanism for time control. In tournaments, a move must be calculated within a fixed time limit such as 90 to 120 seconds. If one decides to do a 5 ply search in a single stage, it is possible to find oneself tied up in calculation after 120 seconds with no idea of how much more time will be needed to complete the search, and without a move to make until the search is completed. In some complex situations the search might take as long as 10 minutes — a disaster for time control. An iterative search allows one to predict the probable duration of the next iteration and to make a decision whether it is cost effective to initiate the next one. If this decision is a go and the search, for some reason, fails to terminate in the anticipated time, the machine can abort and play the move selected by the last iteration. This provides relatively neat and tidy time control. The iterative search was first mentioned by Scott in 1969 and was apparently discovered independently several years later by Jim Gillogly at Carnegie-Mellon, by Slate and Atkin at Northwestern and by the Russian KAISSA team.

Refinements to the Type A Strategy

Several other refinements have also made the type A strategy more manageable. One of the time intensive activities involved in tree searching is move generation. This can be minimized by generating only one move at a time and seeing if it produces a cut-off before generating the next move. If a cut-off occurs and the node is abandoned, one can avoid generating a large number of potential moves. With the n-best approach, it is customary to generate all moves at each node and then invest time attempting to decide which ones are worthy of further consideration. Thus the smaller tree, obtained by selective searching, has to be partially paid for by an additional time investment in plausibility analysis.

Another time-intensive activity in the tree search is the repeated use of the evaluation function. Since many thousands of terminal nodes have to be evaluated in each move selection, any refinement that reduces the work of the evaluation function will pay rich dividends. There are three important techniques which fall in this category. One of these is called *incremental updating*. In order to make an evaluation of a node, it is necessary to have certain key facts available, such as which squares are attacked by each piece, which pieces are present, etc. This information can be newly calculated at each terminal node or can be incrementally maintained by updating the appropriate tables as the tree is generated during the search. This latter procedure is more complex to program but tremendously more efficient in terms of computing time because neighboring terminal positions are highly similar. They usually differ in respect to only a single piece, and therefore the updating procedure requires about 10 percent of the computations that would be expended if the evaluation data base were recalculated from scratch for each evaluation.

A second refinement in this category is the use of serial organization in the evaluation function. In order to assess the relative merit of a chess position, most programs place heavy emphasis on the material balance (ie: the relative number of pieces for each side). This tradition is founded on the idea that winning or losing is strongly correlated with being ahead or behind in material. An additional rationale is that this information is readily available and easily updated.

In most programs material factors are so dominant that the other evaluation terms, such as mobility, pawn structure, King safety, area control, etc, taken together almost never account for more than two pawns. Because of this, it makes sense to compute the material balance factor first and then determine if the result is within two pawns of the target value. If not, there is no need to assess the other factors, because the final decision will be independent of their value.

This simple idea encourages one to organize the evaluation function in strict serial order such that influential (heavily weighted) terms are analyzed first and the result examined to see if a decision is possible based on this initial information. If not, the next most influential term(s) are examined and another determination is made. This process is repeated until an escape condition occurs or until all terms have been examined. In most cases, the evaluation will be terminated long before the list of potential terms has been exhausted. This technical refinement can save a significant amount of time.

A third procedure for speeding the evaluation process is to remember past evaluations. For instance, one should avoid reassessing the same position two or more times. In chess, there are many pathways by which one can reach identical positions. In a 3 ply sequence in which the middle move remains constant, for example, the first and third moves can be interchanged and the resulting position will be the same. Transpositions such as this occur frequently in the end game where the King may have literally hundreds of 4 move pathways that end on the same square. Rooks, Bishops and Queens also have a special facility for reaching a particular destination square in multiple moves rather than in one or two.

A full width search (ie: type A strategy) greatly accentuates this foolishness. By creating a large table of past positions which have been already evaluated, and using a hashing procedure to check if the present position is in the table, the programmer can completely eliminate a portion of the evaluation effort. In most middle game positions, this technique will produce a 10 to 50 percent saving. In certain end game positions, however, the transposition table can eliminate more than 80 percent of the evaluation effort. This idea seems to have been implemented first by Greenblatt in 1967.

An extension of this idea is to use the table to store likely moves as well as evaluations. By remembering a move which previously produced a cut-off, the table can facilitate move ordering decisions. In addition, the use of the same reply at a familiar position may have the added benefit of increasing the number of transpositions which will be encountered at later nodes. Additional details on the use of a transposition table are discussed in chapter 4 of *Chess Skill in Man and Machine*.

One of the most difficult challenges for a chess program is the end game. A machine which calculates a move for each position has difficulty competing with humans who "know" the correct move on the basis of their own or someone else's past experience. There are a huge number of end game situations in which a specific and highly technical strategy is required. Strong chess players study these intricacies at great length and use this knowledge at the chessboard to avoid unnecessary calculations. For example, a

King and a pawn against a lone King is a win in some positions, and a draw otherwise. The same is true for a King and two pawns against a King and a pawn. If a Rook or minor piece is added to each side, the situation changes dramatically. Unfortunately our present day programs are oblivious to these subtleties. For this reason they can find the correct move only by engaging in prodigious calculations. Their human counterpart, on the other hand, "knows" the correct move after a cursory glance at the position.

Newborn (see references) has introduced a useful technique for reducing this knowledge gap. The main idea is to categorize familiar end game positions as wins or draws. Many games end with a King and a pawn fighting a lone King. Skilled players usually terminate the contest before it runs its inevitable course because the outcome is not in doubt. Newborn has shown that it is feasible, taking advantage of the symmetries of the chessboard, to make a bit map that indicates either a win (1) or a draw (0) for each potential square on which the lone King might reside for each of the potential locations of the opposing King and pawn. This knowledge can be encoded in approximately 300 bit boards of 64 bits each (see chapter 5 of *Chess Skill in Man and Machine*).

Although a tremendous amount of work and chess knowledge is required to complete this task, the end result is well worth the effort. When a position involving two Kings and a pawn is encountered anywhere in the look-ahead tree, it can be immediately scored with 100 percent accuracy as a win or a draw. This extends the look-ahead horizon of the program by as much as 12 to 15 plies for these specific situations, and eliminates all the tree searching effort which would normally be required. Furthermore, it permits accurate evaluations at the end points of a deep search, which allows the program to select a continuation which leads to a favorable end game. If this approach were extended to a wider range of situations, the machine's present knowledge deficit with respect to the end game would be greatly reduced.

These programming refinements, together with rapid hardware advances, have made the Shannon type A strategy feasible if not particularly elegant. For this reason it is possible to program a machine to play a game of chess which is free of gross blunders and which sometimes even contains an innovative move or two. Although this approach is clearly not a final solution, it does provide a solid base which can be used as a reliable starting point for future developments.■

REFERENCES

Charness, N, "Human Chess Skill," *Chess Skill in Man and Machine,* Frey, P W (editor), New York, Springer-Verlag, 1977.

Frey, P W, "An Introduction to Computer Chess," *Chess Skill in Man and Machine,* Frey, P W (editor), New York, Springer-Verlag, 1977.

Jastrow, R, "Toward an Intelligence Beyond Man's," *Time,* February 20 1978, page 59.

Kent, Ernest W, "The Brains of Men and Machines" (4 part series): January 1978 BYTE, page 11; February 1978 BYTE, page 84; May 1978 BYTE, page 74; and April 1978 BYTE, page 66.

Knuth, D E and Moore, R, "An Analysis of Alpha-Beta Pruning," *Artificial Intelligence,* volume 6, 1975, pages 293 thru 326.

Newborn, M, "PEASANT: An Endgame Program for Kings and Pawns," *Chess Skill and Man and Machine,* Frey, P W (editor), New York, Springer-Verlag, 1977.

Shannon, C E, "Programming a Computer For Playing Chess," *Philosophical Magazine,* volume 41, 1950, pages 256 thru 275.

Slate, D J and Atkin, L R, "CHESS 4.5 — The Northwestern University Chess Program," *Chess Skill in Man and Machine,* Frey, P W (editor), New York, Springer-Verlag, 1977.

Creating Chess Player

Part 2: Chess 0.5

Peter Frey
Larry Atkin

Part 1 of this series ("Creating a Chess Player," October 1978 BYTE, page 182[1]) was an essay on human and computer skill. In Parts 2 and 3 we present Chess 0.5, a program written in Pascal by Larry Atkin, who is coauthor with David Slate of the world championship computer chess program Chess 4.6. The program is readily adaptable to personal computers having Pascal systems such as the UCSD Pascal project software. Part 4 of the series will conclude with some thoughts about computer chess strategy.

We have attempted to incorporate several features which make the search process more efficient and others which increase the user's options. Both of these enhancements are important. The first set of features (incremental updating, iterative searching, staged move generation, etc) were described in general terms in part 1. These features reduce computation to the point where a move can be selected in a reasonable amount of time even with a full-width search. The second set of features (special control and print commands, accepting chess moves in standard notation) not only add to the pleasure of using the program, but also make the debugging process much easier. The price for these enhancements is a longer, more complicated program. We hope the length of our listing will not discourage the reader from becoming actively involved.

Pascal was developed to provide a logical and systematic higher level language which could produce reasonably efficient machine code for existing hardware. Computer programs can be conceptualized in terms of two essential parts, descriptions of data and descriptions of actions which are to be performed on the data. Pascal requires that

every variable occurring in the program be introduced by a declaration statement which associates an identifier and a data type with that variable. The data type defines the set of values which may be assumed by the variable. Since a chess program involves a large number of variables, our program begins with a long list of declaration statements.

A constant definition introduces an identifier as a synonym for a constant. This is very useful since the value of the constant as stated in the declaration list can be changed at some later date, and this change will then be reflected throughout the program in every place where the constant is used. In the chess program, the values of some of the constants depend on the characteristics of the user's hardware. For example, the values of ZK (maximum search depth) and ZW (move stack limit) will reflect the amount of memory which is available on your system. On personal computers, ZX will generally be set at 7 if you have an 8 bit processor and at 15 if you have a 16 bit processor. Note also that the value of PZX8 depends on the value of ZX. To implement this program on a given computer, it is necessary to insert at the beginning of the program the appropriate values for these constants.

For the sake of clarity, specific data types

Note: *The Pascal subset described in "A 'Tiny' Pascal Compiler" (page 182[2]) is not compatible with the more sophisticated Pascal used here . . . CM*

1. **Page 107 of this edition.**
2. **Page 81 of this edition.**

are declared for a number of different chess concepts and for certain useful indices. The program also takes advantage of the different properties represented in Pascal's data structures: the set, array and record. It is unlikely that anyone will immediately memorize the names of all the variables. Therefore it is useful to have them listed at the beginning where they can easily be found for later reference.

There is a comment statement accompanying almost every instruction in the program. Although these brief statements may not initially be very meaningful, we expect them to be helpful when the user becomes familiar with the program. Because Pascal requires that all procedures and functions be defined in the serial listing before they are called by another portion of the program, the procedures and functions which are first defined tend to be primitives. The main part of the program is concentrated at the end of the listing.

The most important part of the variable declaration list in terms of understanding the program is the portion which specifies the global data base. This includes the current board (BOARD, a record) and a number of important arrays. The look-ahead board (NBORD) is an array listing the piece occupying each square. The attacks emanating from each square are represented by ATKFR, an array which lists an 8 by 8 bit board for each of the 64 squares. The attacks to each square are represented by a similar array, ATKTO. The combined attacks for each side are represented by a 2 item array of 8 by 8 bit boards called ALATK.

The location of all pieces by type is represented by an array of 12 8 by 8 bit boards, TPLOC. The location of all pieces by color is represented by an array of two 8 by 8 bit boards, TMLOC. The moves are stored in an array (MOVES) of records. Each record (RM) contains information about the from square, to square; whether a capture is involved and the type of piece captured, whether the move affects castle status, involves check or mate, involves a piece promotion, and whether the move has been searched yet. Additional arrays provide information on castling squares, en passant squares, the location of all pieces, the location of pawns, etc. To be successful, a chess program must organize the data base in a logical manner and be able to manipulate it efficiently.

For reasons of efficiency, the program often stores the same information in two or more different ways. Because of this, it is necessary to be able to translate from one form to the other. These activities are handled by special arrays. For example, the

XTPC array allows one to use a piece designator (LP, LQ, LK, DQ, etc) as an index and returns the corresponding character (1 thru 6 for Black pieces and A thru F for White pieces) which is used when a board representation is printed on the terminal.

There are several general purpose routines which are needed by the program. Two functions, MIN and MAX, provide the smaller or larger of two numbers upon request. A third function, SIGN, applies the sign of one number to the absolute value of another number. A general purpose sort routine, SORTIT, is also provided.

Manipulating the Bit Boards

There are a number of primitive operations which involve the manipulation of information represented in bit board form. A bit board is one or more computer words which have a bit set in specific locations to represent the occurrence or nonoccurrence of a particular event. For example eight 8 bit words can be used to represent the eight rows of a chessboard. Each bit corresponds to one square. To represent the location of all White pawns, a bit is set (ie: 1) in the proper locations and all other locations remain clear (ie: 0). This method for representing and manipulating information is very useful in chess programming. For this reason, the first actions defined by our chess program are a set of procedures and functions for manipulating bit boards.

The actions represented are:

(1) the intersection of two bit boards (ANDRS);
(2) the union of two bit boards (IORRS);
(3) the complement of a bit board (NOTRS);
(4) setting a bit in a bit board (SETRS);
(5) removing a bit from a bit board (CLRRS);
(6) counting the number of bits that are set on a bit board (CNTRS);
(7) making a copy of a bit board (CPYRS);
(8) setting all bits to 0 (NEWRS);
(9) shifting all bits in a particular direction (SFTRS);
(10) determining whether a particular bit is set (INRSTB);
(11) determining whether a bit board is empty, ie: has no bits set (NULRS); and
(12) finding and reporting integer value for a location where a bit is set (NXTTS).

Since these routines are used repeatedly by the program, you can decrease the move calculation time quite a bit by implementing these primitives in assembly language. You will note that the function NXTTS is written in two ways: machine independent code, and code which is compatible only with the Control Data 6000 series machines. There are a number of places in the program where execution time can be enhanced by substituting machine dependent code which takes advantage of one or more special features of the hardware you are using. It would be helpful, also, if functions in Pascal could return an array or record instead of just a single value. There are many places in the program where this type of function would be more logical and more efficient than using a procedure (ie: subroutine). If one were to consider the best of all possible worlds, it would be especially nice if the bit map manipulations could be compiled in line. With the Pascal arrangement, many of the procedure calls take as much time as the execution of the procedure.

Initial Steps

It is also necessary at the beginning of the program to provide values for the variables which define the chess environment, such as piece characteristics. For example, a White pawn is represented as LP for some purposes and as the letter A for other purposes. It has the color LITE, is not a sweep piece, and moves only in certain directions. It is necessary to initialize the translation tables, the constant and variable 8 by 8 bit boards, and a number of other tables. The three routines which are called to do this when the program is first activated are INISYN, INIXTP and INICON. A fourth procedure (INITAL) is called by the main program to get ready for a new game. It will be called more than once if the user wishes to play more than one game.

During the development of the program, it is necessary to determine whether the individual procedures are functioning properly. To do this, it is helpful to have a few primitive print routines which can provide information about the internal workings in a form which is understandable to the programmer. These same routines are also called by the main input/output (IO) routine (READER) which appears later in the program.

One of these routines (PRIMOV) prints an internal representation of the machine's move. Another prints an 8 by 8 array representing the board (PRINTB). This consists of numbers for Black's pieces (Black pawn = 1; Black King = 6) and letters for White's pieces (White pawn = A; White King = F) with empty squares represented by a —. The PRINBB routine prints an 8 by 8 array representing a bit board. In this case an asterisk (*) stands for a square where a bit is set and a minus sign (—) stands for a square where a bit has not been set. An attack map is printed by PRINAM and this consists of 64 (one for each square) 8 by 8 bit maps in which an * stands for a bit which is set and a — stands for a clear bit.

Other useful print routines include one which permits a user controlled pause during printing (PAUSER) and one which informs the programmer of the status of particular control switches (PRISWI). Because of Pascal's serial requirement (ie: every procedure must be defined before it can be called by another procedure), these routines appear early in the program so that they can be used to test the procedures and functions which follow.

In part 1 we mentioned incremental updating as an important feature of an efficient chess program. It is necessary to apply an evaluation function to the terminal nodes of the look-ahead tree. These evaluations, if they are at all sophisticated, require a substantial amount of detailed information about the position. Although it is possible to calculate this information separately for each evaluation, this is not a very efficient procedure, because adjacent nodes are almost identical. Most of the information which would be calculated each time would be redundant. A more efficient alternative is to "update" and "downdate" the relevant data base incrementally as the program moves about in the look-ahead tree. This capability requires quite a bit of special programming.

Several primitive routines are very useful for this. If the move involves a capture, it is necessary to change the material balance function. The actual scoring itself is handled by MBEVAL. This routine is called either by MBCAPT or MBTPAC when a piece is lost (update) or gained (downdate); or by MBPROM or MBMORP when a pawn is promoted (update); or when a newly promoted pawn is demoted (downdate). There are other changes which are required in the data base for both capture and noncapture moves. The new squares which are attacked by the piece need to be added to the attack maps (ATKFR, ATKTO, ALATK). This is done by ADDATK. The new square for the piece is added to the data base by ADDLOC. The attacks of sliding pieces which are blocked by the newly moved piece are recomputed by CUTATK. The attacks of sliding pieces which are unblocked by vacating the former square are recomputed by PRPATK. The attacks which emanated from the piece on its former square are deleted by DELATK. These primitive routines are called by LOSEIT when a capture is involved or by MOVEIT otherwise. If the move affects castling status, the necessary data base changes are made by PROACA and PROACS. If a pawn promotion is involved, PROMOT makes the necessary adjustments.

Move Generation

A major part of any chess program is the move generation module. Because of the complexity of the game, many programs simply ignore some of the more unusual moves, such as Queenside castling, en passant pawn captures, or promotion of a pawn to a piece other than a Queen (ie: underpromotion). This arrangement will suffice to play legal chess, but it may be costly if one of the omitted move types is highly desirable in a specific game situation. In addition, an incomplete move generation facility prevents the machine from checking the legality of its opponent's moves.

Rather than being satisfied with an approximate solution, we have heeded the old maxim, "If a job is worth doing, it is worth doing well," and have implemented a move generator which permits the program to play a complete game of legal chess. As you can see from the listing, this requires extensive programming.

The first step in move generation is to create the data base for the important features of the existing board configuration. This is done by CREATE. Once a move has been selected, it is necessary to change the data base. This is done by UPDATE which makes use of the routines which were just described (eg: ADDATK, CUTATK, ADDLOC, CLSTAT, PRPATK, DELATK, MOVEIT, LOSEIT). The move is placed on the move stack by GENONE. Special routines exist for generating moves which involve the promotion of a pawn (PWNPRO) and for generating the standard pawn moves (GENPWN). When a move is tried and produces an α-β cutoff, the program backs down the look-ahead tree and begins to explore moves at a different node. Several procedures are employed to downdate the data base. These include the main routines RTRKIT and DNDATE, which are essentially the complement of MOVEIT and UPDATE. Two other procedures are also needed, one to unpromote a pawn (PAWNIT) and one to resurrect a captured piece (GAINIT). This set of routines permits the program to move about the look-ahead tree and incrementally update or downdate the data base.

The executive routines which are responsible for move generation are GENFSL, which generates all legal moves from a set of squares, and GENTSL, which generates all legal moves to a set of squares. The rationale for having two routines is that we wish to generate the moves in stages. For example, captures should be searched first at each node (ie: the capture heuristic). To do this, we identify the square locations of the opponent's pieces, and then call GENTSL to generate all capturing moves. These moves are searched before any other moves are generated. If one of these produces a cut-off the rest of the moves need not be generated at all. A third executive routine (GENCAS) generates all castling moves. These moves are generated after the captures if castling is still legal.

A fourth executive routine for move generation is GENALL. This procedure generates all legal moves and is used by the program to check the legality of the opponent's move. It is called by LSTMOV which makes a list of all the legal moves and each of these are compared with the opponent's move by YRMOVE (presented later). If the opponent's move is not on the list, the machine prints "illegal move." If the opponent's move is compatible with more than one of the moves on the list (eg: P-R3 could be either P-QR3 or P-KR3), the machine prints the message, "ambiguous move." When the machine has completed its own move selection or has determined that the opponent's move is legal and not ambiguous, the move is actually made by THEMOV.∎

Listing 1 (opposite): The first half of Chess 0.5, written in Pascal. The second half of the program will be presented in part 3 (December 1978 BYTE)[3] of this series. The portion of the program presented here covers initialization of the program, variable declaration, manipulation of the "bit boards" (used to represent positions on the chessboard), user print routines and move generation. The second half of the listing will include procedures for evaluation of terminal positions, the look-ahead procedure, and user commands.

---

3. Page 131 of this edition.

```
PROGRAM CHESS(INPUT,OUTPUT);
LABEL

    1,                              (* INITIALIZE FOR A NEW GAME *)
    2,                              (* EXECUTE MACHINES MOVE *)
    9;                              (* END OF PROGRAM *)


CONST

    AA = 1; ZA = 10;                (* CHARACTERS IS A WORD *)
    AC = "A"; ZC = ",";             (* CHARACTER LIMITS *)
    AD = -21; ZD = +21;             (* DIRECTION LIMITS *)
    AJ = 0; ZJ = 73;                (* CHARACTERS IN A STRING *)
    AK = 0; ZK = 16;                (* SEARCH DEPTH LIMITS *)
    AKM2 = -2;                      (* AK-2 *)
    ZKP1 = 17;                      (* ZK+1 *)
    AL = 0; ZL = 119;               (* LARGE BOARD VECTOR LIMITS *)
    AZL = -119; ZAL = 119;          (* LARGE BOARD DIFFERENCES
                                       LIMITS *)
    AN = 1; ZN = 30;                (* MESSAGE LIMITS *)
    AS = 0; ZS = 63;                (* BOARD VECTOR LIMITS *)
    AT = -1; ZT = 63;               (* BOARD VECTOR LIMITS AND
                                       ANOTHER VALUE *)
    AV = -32767; ZV = +32767;       (* EVALUATION LIMITS *)
    AW = 1; ZW = 500;               (* MOVE STACK LIMITS *)
    AX = 0; ZX = 31;                (* SUBSETS OF SQUARES *)
    AY = 0; ZY = 1;                 (* ARRAY OF SUBSETS TO FORM A SET
                                       OF ALL SQUARES ON BOARD *)

    LPP = 20;                       (* LINES PER PAGE *)
    PZX8 = 16777216;                (* 2^(ZX-7) *)

    SYNCF = 1;                      (* FIRST CAPTURE SYNTAX *)
    SYNCL = 36;                     (* LAST CAPTURE SYNTAX *)
    SYNMF = 37;                     (* FIRST MOVE SYNTAX *)
    SYNML = 47;                     (* LAST MOVE SYNTAX *)


TYPE

    (* SIMPLE TYPES *)

    TA = AA..ZA;                    (* INDEX TO WORDS OF CHAR *)
    TB = BOOLEAN;                   (* TRUE OR FALSE *)
    TC = CHAR;                      (* SINGLE CHARACTERS *)
    TD = AD..ZD;                    (* DIRECTIONS *)
    TE = (B1,B2,B3,B4,S1,S2,S3,S4,N1,N2,N3,N4,N5,N6,N7,N8);
                                    (* NUMBER OF DIRECTIONS *)
    TF = (F1,F2,F3,F4,F5,F6,F7,F8); (* FILES *)
    TG = (PQ,PP,PN,PB);             (* PROMOTION PIECES *)
    TH = (H0,H1,H2,H3,H4,H5,H6,H7); (* TREE SEARCH MODES *)
    TI = INTEGER;                   (* NUMBERS *)
    TJ = AJ..ZJ;                    (* INDEX TO STRINGS *)
    TK = AK..ZK;                    (* PLY INDEX *)
    TL = AL..ZL;                    (* LARGE (10X12) BOARD *)
    TM = (LITE,DARK,NONE);          (* SIDES *)
    TN = AN..ZN;                    (* INDEX TO MESSAGES *)
    TP = (LP,LR,LN,LB,LO,LK,DP,DR,DN,DB,DQ,DK,MT);
                                    (* PIECES: LIGHT PAWN, LIGHT
                                       ROOK, ... , DARK KING, EMPTY
                                       SQUARE *)
    TQ = (LS,LL,DS,DL);             (* QUADRANTS *)
    TR = (R1,R2,R3,R4,R5,R6,R7,R8); (* RANKS *)
    TS = AS..ZS;                    (* SQUARES *)
    TT = AT..ZT;                    (* SQUARES, AND ANOTHER VALUE *)
    TU = (EP,ER,EN,EB,EQ,EK);       (* TYPES: PAWN, ROOK, ... ,
                                       KING *)
    TV = AV..ZV;                    (* EVALUATIONS *)
    TW = AW..ZW;                    (* MOVES INDEX *)
    TX = AX..ZX;                    (* SOME SQUARES *)
    TY = AY..ZY;                    (* NUMBER OF TX'S IN A BOARD *)
    TZ = REAL;                      (* FLOATING POINT NUMBERS *)

    (* SETS *)

    SC = SET OF AC..ZC;             (* SET OF CHARACTERS *)
    SF = SET OF TF;                 (* SET OF FILES *)
    SQ = SET OF TQ;                 (* SET OF CASTLING TYPES *)
    SR = SET OF TR;                 (* SET OF RANKS *)
    SX = SET OF TX;                 (* SET OF SOME SQUARES *)

    (* RECORDS *)

    RB = RECORD                     (* BOARDS *)
      RBTM : TM;                    (* SIDE TO MOVE *)
      RBTS : TT;                    (* ENPASSANT SQUARE *)
      RBTI : TI;                    (* MOVE NUMBER *)
      RBSQ : SQ;                    (* CASTLE FLAGS *)
      CASE INTEGER OF
        0: ( RBIS: ARRAY [TS] OF TP);    (* INDEXED BY SQUARE *)
        1: ( RBIRF: ARRAY [TR,TF] OF TP); (* INDEXED BY RANK AND FILE *)
      END;

    RA = PACKED ARRAY [TA] OF TC;   (* WORDS OF CHARACTERS *)
    RC = ARRAY [TS] OF TP;          (* BOARD VECTORS *)
    RN = PACKED ARRAY [TN] OF TC;   (* MESSAGES *)
    RJ = PACKED ARRAY [TJ] OF TC;   (* STRINGS *)

    RD = PACKED RECORD              (* SYNTAX DESCRIPTOR FOR
                                       SINGLE SQUARE *)
      RDPC : TB;                    (* PIECE *)
      RDSL : TB;                    (* / *)
      RDKQ : TB;                    (* K OR Q *)
      RDNB : TB;                    (* R, N, OR B *)
      RDRK : TB;                    (* RANK *)
    END;

    RK = RECORD                     (* KLUDGE TO FIND NEXT BIT *)
      CASE INTEGER OF
        0: (RKTB: SET OF 0..47);    (* BITS *)
        1: (RKTZ: TZ);              (* FLOATING POINT NUMBER *)
    END;

    RM = PACKED RECORD              (* MOVES *)
      RMFR : TS;                    (* FROM SQUARE *)
      RMTO : TS;                    (* TO SQUARE *)
      RMCP : TP;                    (* CAPTURED PIECE *)
      RMCA : TB;                    (* CAPTURE *)
      RMAC : TB;                    (* AFFECTS CASTLE STATUS *)
      RMCH : TB;                    (* CHECK *)
      RMMT : TB;                    (* MATE *)
      RMIL : TB;                    (* ILLEGAL *)
      RMSU : TB;                    (* SEARCHED *)
      CASE RMPR : TB OF             (* PROMOTION *)
        FALSE: (
          CASE RMOO : TB OF
            FALSE: (RMEP : TB);     (* CASTLE *)
            TRUE: (RMQS : TB);      (* ENPASSANT *)
          );                        (* QUEEN SIDE *)
        TRUE: (RMPP : TG);          (* PROMOTION TYPE *)
    END;

    RS = RECORD                     (* BIT BOARDS *)
      CASE INTEGER OF
        0: (RSSS: ARRAY [TY] OF SX);  (* ARRAY OF SETS *)
        1: (RSTI: ARRAY [TY] OF TI);  (* ARRAY OF INTEGERS *)
    END;

    RX = ARRAY [TS] OF RS;          (* ATTACK MAPS *)

    RY = PACKED RECORD              (* MOVE SYNTAX DESCRIPTOR *)
      RYLS : RD;                    (* LEFT SIDE DESCRIPTOR *)
      RYCH : TC;                    (* MOVE OR CAPTURE *)
      RYRS : RD;                    (* RIGHT SIDE DESCRIPTOR *)
    END;

    RE = ARRAY [TW] OF TV;          (* ARRAY OF VALUES *)
    RF = ARRAY [TW] OF RM;          (* ARRAY OF MOVES *)


VAR

    (* DATA BASE *)

    BOARD : RB;                     (* THE BOARD *)
    NBORD : ARRAY [TS] OF TP;       (* LOOK-AHEAD BOARD *)
    ATKFR : ARRAY [TS] OF RS;       (* ATTACKS FROM A SQUARE *)
    ATKTO : ARRAY [TS] OF RS;       (* ATTACKS TO A SQUARE *)
    ALATK : ARRAY [TM] OF RS;       (* ATTACKS BY EACH COLOR *)
    TPLOC : ARRAY [TP] OF RS;       (* LOCATIONS OF PIECE BY TYPE *)
    TMLOC : ARRAY [TM] OF RS;       (* LOCATIONS OF PIECE BY COLOR *)
    MOVES : ARRAY [TW] OF RM;       (* MOVES *)
    VALUE : ARRAY [TW] OF TV;       (* VALUES *)
    ALLOC : ARRAY [TK] OF RS;       (* ALL PIECES *)
    BSTMV : ARRAY [TK] OF TW;       (* BEST MOVE SO FAR *)
    BSTVL : ARRAY [AKM2..ZKP1] OF TV; (* VALUE OF BEST MOVE *)
    CSTAT : ARRAY [TK] OF RS;       (* CASTLING SQUARES *)
    ENPAS : ARRAY [TK] OF RS;       (* ENPASSANT SQUARES *)
    GENPN : ARRAY [TK] OF RS;       (* PAWN ORIGINATION SQUARES *)
    GENTO : ARRAY [TK] OF RS;       (* MOVE DESTINATION SQUARES *)
    GENFR : ARRAY [TK] OF RS;       (* MOVE ORIGINATION SQUARES *)
    MBVAL : ARRAY [TK] OF TV;       (* MATERIAL BALANCE VALUES *)
    MVSEL : ARRAY [TK] OF TI;       (* COUNT MOVES SELECTED BY PLY *)
    INDEX : ARRAY [AK..ZKP1] OF TW; (* CURRENT MOVE BY PLY *)
    KILLR : ARRAY [TK] OF RM;       (* KILLER MOVES BY PLY *)
    LINOX : ARRAY [TK] OF TW;       (* LAST MOVE FOR PLY *)
    SRCHM : ARRAY [TK] OF TH;       (* SEARCH MODES *)
    GOING : TI;                     (* NUMBER OF MOVES TO EXECUTE *)
    LSTMV : RM;                     (* PREVIOUS MOVE *)
    MAXPS : TV;                     (* MAXIMUM POSITIONAL SCORE *)
    MBLTE : TV;                     (* MATERIAL BALANCE LITE EDGE *)
    MBPWN : ARRAY [TM] OF TI;       (* NUMBER OF PAWNS BY SIDE *)
    MBTOT : TV;                     (* TOTAL MATERIAL ON NBORD *)
    NODES : TI;                     (* NUMBER OF NODES SEARCHED *)

    JNTK : TK;                      (* PLY INDEX *)
    JMTK : TK;                      (* ITERATION *)
    JNTM : TM;                      (* SIDE TO MOVE *)
    JNTW : TW;                      (* MOVES STACK POINTER *)

    (* LETS *)

    FKPSHD : TI;                    (* KING PAWN SHIELD CREDIT *)
    FKSANQ : TI;                    (* KING IN SANCTUARY CREDIT *)
    FMAXMT : TI;                    (* MAXIMUM MATERIAL SCORE *)
    FNODEL : TI;                    (* NODE LIMIT FOR SEARCH *)
    FPADCR : ARRAY [TF] OF TI;      (* PAWN ADVANCE CREDIT BY FILE *)
    FPBLOK : TI;                    (* PAWN BLOCKED PENALTY *)
    FPCONN : TI;                    (* PAWN CONNECTED CREDIT *)
    FPFLNX : TI;                    (* PAWN PHALANX CREDIT *)
    FRDUBL : TI;                    (* DOUBLED ROOK CREDIT *)
    FRK7TH : TI;                    (* ROOK ON SEVENTH CREDIT *)
    FTRADE : TI;                    (* TRADE-DOWN BONUS FACTOR *)
    FTRDSL : TI;                    (* TRADE-DOWN TUNING FACTOR *)
    FTRPOK : TI;                    (* PAWN TRADE-DOWN RELAXATION *)
    FTRPWN : TI;                    (* PAWN TRADE-DOWN FACTOR *)
    FWKING : TI;                    (* KING EVALUATION WEIGHT *)
    FWMAJM : TI;                    (* MAJOR PIECE MOBILITY WEIGHT *)
    FWMINM : TI;                    (* MINOR PIECE MOBILITY WEIGHT *)
    FWPAWN : TI;                    (* PAWN EVALUATION WEIGHT *)
    FWROOK : TI;                    (* ROOK EVALUATION WEIGHT *)
    WINDOW : TI;                    (* SIZE OF ALPHA-BETA WINDOW *)


    (* SWITCHES *)

    SWEC : TB;                      (* ECHO INPUT *)
    SWPA : TB;                      (* PAGING *)
    SWPS : TB;                      (* PRINT PRELIMINARY SCORES *)
    SWRE : TB;                      (* REPLY WITH MOVE *)
    SWSU : TB;                      (* PRINT STATISTICS SUMMARY *)
    SWTR : TB;                      (* TRACE TREE SEARCH *)

    (* COMMAND PROCESSING DATA *)

    ICARD : RJ;                     (* INPUT CARD IMAGE *)
    ILINE : RJ;                     (* CURRENT COMMAND *)
    JNTJ : TJ;                      (* CURRENT INPUT LINE POSITION *)
    JMTJ : TJ;                      (* CURRENT COMMAND POSITION *)
```

```
    MOVMS : RN;                         (* MOVE MESSAGE *)

    (* TRANSLATION TABLES *)

    XSPB : ARRAY (TP) OF TB;            (* TRUE FOR SWEEP PIECES *)
    XFPE : ARRAY (TP) OF TE;            (* FIRST DIRECTION *)
    XLLD : ARRAY (AZL..ZAL) OF TD;      (* DIRECTION FOR LARGE BOARD
                                           SQUARE DIFFERENCES *)
    XLPE : ARRAY (TP) OF TE;            (* LAST DIRECTION *)
    XRFS : ARRAY (TF) OF RS;            (* BIT BOARD FOR FILES *)
    XRRS : ARRAY (TR) OF RS;            (* BIT BOARD FOR RANKS *)
    XNFS : ARRAY (TF) OF RS;            (* COMP BIT BOARD FOR FILES *)
    XNRS : ARRAY (TR) OF RS;            (* COMP BIT BOARD FOR RANKS *)
    XRSS : ARRAY (TS) OF RS;            (* BIT BOARD FOR 8X8 INDEX *)
    XRQM : ARRAY (TQ) OF RM;            (* MOVES FOR CASTLE TYPES *)
    XSQS : ARRAY (TQ) OF RS;            (* BIT BOARD FOR CASTLE TYPES *)
    XSSX : ARRAY (TS) OF SX;            (* SET ELEMENT FOR 8X8 INDEX *)
    XTBC : ARRAY (TB) OF TC;            (* CHARACTERS FOR BOOLEANS *)
    XTED : ARRAY (TE) OF TD;            (* DIRECTION NUMBER TO 10X12
                                           SQUARE DIFFERENCE *)
    XTGC : ARRAY (TG) OF TC;            (* CHARACTERS FOR PROMOTION *)
    XTGMP: ARRAY (TG,TM) OF TP;         (* PIECE FOR PROMOTION TYPE
                                           AND COLOR *)
    XTLS : ARRAY (TL) OF TT;            (* 8X8 INDEX FOR 10X12 INDEX *)
    XTMA : ARRAY (TM) OF RA;            (* WORDS FOR COLORS *)
    XTMQ : ARRAY (TM) OF TQ;            (* CASTLE TYPES FOR SIDE *)
    XTMV : ARRAY (TM) OF TV;            (* SCORE FACTOR FOR SIDE *)
    XTPC : ARRAY (TP) OF TC;            (* CHARACTERS FOR PIECES *)
    XTPM : ARRAY (TP) OF TM;            (* SIDES FOR PIECES *)
    XTPU : ARRAY (TP) OF TU;            (* TYPE FOR PIECE *)
    XTPV : ARRAY (TP) OF TV;            (* VALUES OF PIECES *)
    XTQA : ARRAY (TQ) OF RA;            (* WORDS FOR CASTLES *)
    XTQS : ARRAY (TQ) OF TS;            (* TO SQUARES FOR CASTLE TYPES *)
    XTRFS: ARRAY (TR,TF) OF TS;         (* 8X8 INDEX FOR RANK AND FILE *)
    XTSF : ARRAY (TS) OF TF;            (* FILES FOR SQUARES *)
    XTSL : ARRAY (TS) OF TL;            (* 10X12 INDEX FOR 8X8 INDEX *)
    XTSR : ARRAY (TS) OF TR;            (* RANKS FOR SQUARES *)
    XTSX : ARRAY (TS) OF TX;            (* ELEMENT NUMBER FOR 8X8
                                           INDEX *)
    XTSY : ARRAY (TS) OF TY;            (* ARRAY SUBSCRIPT INTO BIT BOARD
                                           FOR 8X8 INDEX *)
    XTUC : ARRAY (TU) OF TC;            (* CHARACTER FOR TYPE *)
    XTUMP: ARRAY (TU,TM) OF TP;         (* PIECE FOR TYPE AND SIDE *)

    XRQSO: ARRAY (TQ) OF RS;            (* UNOCCUPIED SQUARES FOR
                                           CASTLING *)
    XRQSA: ARRAY (TQ) OF RS;            (* UNATTACKED SQUARES FOR
                                           CASTLING *)

    EDGE : ARRAY (TE) OF RS;            (* EDGES IN VARIOUS DIRECTIONS *)
    CORNR: RS;                          (* KING SANCTUARY *)
    NULMV: RM;                          (* NULL MOVE *)
    OTHER: ARRAY (TM) OF TM;            (* OTHER COLOR *)
    SYNTX: ARRAY(SYNCF..SYNML) OF RY;   (* MOVE SYNTAX TABLE *)


FUNCTION MAX(A,B:TI):TI;                (* LARGER OF TWO NUMBERS *)

BEGIN
  IF A > B THEN
    MAX := A
  ELSE
    MAX := B;
END;  (* MAX *)


FUNCTION MIN(A,B:TI):TI;                (* SMALLER OF TWO NUMBERS *)

BEGIN
  IF A < B THEN
    MIN := A
  ELSE
    MIN := B;
END;  (* MIN *)


FUNCTION SIGN(A,B:TI):TI;               (* SIGN OF B APPLIED TO
                                           ABSOLUTE VALUE OF A *)

BEGIN
  SIGN := TRUNC(B/ABS(B)) * ABS(A);
END;  (* SIGN *)


PROCEDURE SORTIT                        (* SORT PRELIMINARY SCORES *)
  (VAR A:RE;                            (* ARRAY OF SCORES *)
   VAR B:RF;                            (* ARRAY OF MOVES *)
   C:TM);                               (* NUMBER OF ENTRIES *)

VAR
  INTB : JB;                            (* LOOP EXIT FLAG *)
  INTW : TM;                            (* OUTER LOOP INDEX *)
  INTI : TI;                            (* INNER LOOP INDEX *)
  INTV : TV;                            (* HOLD SCORE *)
  INRM : RM;                            (* HOLD MOVE *)

BEGIN
  FOR INTW := AW+2 TO C DO
  BEGIN
    INTI := INTW - 1;
    INTV := A[INTW];
    INRM := B[INTW];
    INTB := TRUE;
    WHILE (INTI > AW) AND INTB DO
      IF INTV < A[INTI] THEN
        BEGIN
          A[INTI+1] := A[INTI];
          B[INTI+1] := B[INTI];
          INTI := INTI - 1;
        END
      ELSE
```

```
          INTB := FALSE;               (* EXIT *)
          A[INTI+1] := INTV;
          B[INTI+1] := INRM;
      END;
END;  (* SORTIT *)


PROCEDURE ANDRS                         (* INTERSECTION OF TWO BIT
                                           BOARDS *)
  (VAR C:RS;                            (* RESULT *)
   A, B:RS);                            (* OPERANDS *)

VAR
  INTY : TY;                            (* BIT BOARD WORD INDEX *)

BEGIN
  FOR INTY := AY TO ZY DO
    C.RSSS[INTY] := A.RSSS[INTY] * B.RSSS[INTY];
END;  (* ANDRS *)


PROCEDURE CLRRS                         (* REMOVE SQUARE FROM BIT
                                           BOARD *)
  (VAR C:RS;                            (* BIT BOARD *)
   A:TS);                               (* SQUARE TO REMOVE *)

BEGIN
  C.RSSS[XTSY[A]] := C.RSSS[XTSY[A]] - XSSX[A];
END;  (* CLRRS *)


PROCEDURE CPYRS                         (* COPY OF A BIT BOARD *)
  (VAR C:RS;                            (* RESULT *)
   A:RS);                               (* OPERAND *)

VAR
  INTY : TY;                            (* BIT BOARD WORD INDEX *)

BEGIN
  FOR INTY := AY TO ZY DO
    C.RSSS[INTY] := A.RSSS[INTY];
END;  (* CPYRS *)


PROCEDURE IORRS                         (* UNION OF TWO BIT BOARDS *)
  (VAR C:RS;                            (* RESULT *)
   A, B:RS);                            (* OPERANDS *)

VAR
  INTY : TY;                            (* BIT BOARD WORD INDEX *)

BEGIN
  FOR INTY := AY TO ZY DO
    C.RSSS[INTY] := A.RSSS[INTY] + B.RSSS[INTY];
END;  (* IORRS *)


PROCEDURE NEWRS                         (* CLEAR BIT BOARD *)
  (VAR A:RS);                           (* BIT BOARD TO CLEAR *)

VAR
  INTY : TY;                            (* BIT BOARD WORD INDEX *)

BEGIN
  FOR INTY := AY TO ZY DO
    A.RSSS[INTY] := [];
END;  (* NEWRS *)


PROCEDURE NOTRS                         (* COMPLEMENT OF A BIT BOARD *)
  (VAR C:RS;                            (* RESULT *)
   A:RS);                               (* OPERAND *)

VAR
  INTY : TY;                            (* BIT BOARD WORD INDEX *)

BEGIN
  FOR INTY := AY TO ZY DO
    C.RSSS[INTY] := [AX..ZX]-A.RSSS[INTY];
END;  (* NOTRS *)


FUNCTION NXTTS                          (* NEXT ELEMENT IN BIT BOARD *)
  (VAR A:RS;                            (* BIT BOARD TO LOCATE FIRST
                                           SQUARE, AND THEN REMOVE *)
   VAR B:TS                             (* SQUARE NUMBER OF FIRST SQUARE
                                           IN BIT BOARD *)
  ):TB;                                 (* TRUE IFF ANY SQUARES WERE SET
                                           INITIALLY *)

LABEL
  11;                                   (* RETURN *)

VAR
  INTX : TX;                            (* BIT BOARD BIT INDEX *)
  INTY : TY;                            (* BIT BOARD WORD INDEX *)
  X : RK;                               (* KLUDGE WORD *)

BEGIN
  FOR INTY := ZY DOWNTO AY DO           (* LOOP THRU BIT BOARD WORDS *)
    IF A.RSTI[INTY] <> 0 THEN
    BEGIN

(*** BEGIN CDC 6000 DEPENDANT CODE *)
(*** FOLLOWING CODE REQUIRES THE "EXPO" FUNCTION TO RETURN
(*** THE EXPONENT FROM A FLOATING POINT NUMBER.  IT ALSO ASSUMES
(*** THAT FLOATING POINT NUMBERS HAVE 48 BIT COEFFICIENTS RIGHT-
(*** JUSTIFIED IN A WORD, AND THAT SETS ARE RIGHT-JUSTIFIED IN
(*** A WORD. *)
(*    X.RKTZ := A.RSTI[INTY];          (* FLOAT WORD *)
(*    B := EXPO(X.RKTZ) + INTY * (ZX+1);
(*                                      (* CONVERT TO SQUARE NUMBER *)
```

```
(*        X.RKTB := X.RKTB - [47];          (* REMOVE MOST SIGNIFICANT BIT *)
(*        A.RSTI[INTY] := TRUNC(X.RKTZ);    (* INTEGERIZE *)
(*        NXTTS := TRUE;                     (* RETURN A BIT SET *)
(*        GOTO 11;                           (* RETURN *)
(*** END CDC 6000 DEPENDANT CODE *)

(*** BEGIN MACHINE INDEPENDENT CODE *)
        FOR INTX := ZX DOWNTO AX DO          (* LOOP THROUGH BITS IN WORD OF
                                                SET *)
            IF INTX IN A.RSSS[INTY] THEN
            BEGIN
                B := INTX+INTY*(ZX+1)         (* RETURN SQUARE NUMBER *)
                A.RSSS[INTY] := A.RSSS[INTY] - [INTX];
                                              (* REMOVE BIT FROM WORD *)
                NXTTS := TRUE;                (* RETURN A BIT SET *)
                GOTO 11;                      (* RETURN *)
            END;
(*** END MACHINE INDEPENDENT CODE *)

        END;
    NXTTS := FALSE;                           (* ELSE RETURN NO BITS SET *)
11: (* RETURN *)
END; (* NXTTS *)


FUNCTION CNTRS                                (* COUNT MEMBERS OF A BIT
                                                BOARD *)
    (A:RS):TS;                                (* BIT BOARD TO COUNT *)

VAR
    INTY : TY;                                (* BIT BOARD WORD INDEX *)
    INTS : TS;                                (* TEMPORARY *)
    IMRS : RS;                                (* SCRATCH *)
    IMTS : TS;                                (* SCRATCH *)

BEGIN
    INTS := 0;

(*** BEGIN MACHINE INDEPENDENT CODE *)
    CPYRS(IMRS,A);
    WHILE NXTTS(IMRS,INTS) DO
        INTS := INTS+1;                       (* COUNT SQUARES *)
(*** END MACHINE INDEPENDENT CODE *)

(*** BEGIN CDC 6000 DEPENDENT CODE *)
(*** FOLLOWING CODE REQUIRES THE 'CARD' FUNCTION TO
(*** COUNT THE MEMBERS IN A SET. *)
(*FOR INTY := AY TO ZY DO
(*    INTS := INTS + CARD(A.RSSS[INTY]);
(*** END CDC DEPENDENT CODE *)

    CNTRS := INTS;                            (* RETURN SUM *)
END; (* CNTRS *)


PROCEDURE SETRS                               (* INSERT SQUARE INTO BIT
                                                BOARD *)
    (VAR C:RS;                                (* BIT BOARD *)
    A:TS);                                    (* SQUARE TO INSERT *)

BEGIN
    C.RSSS[XTSY[A]] := C.RSSS[XTSY[A]] + XSSX[A];
END; (* SETRS *)


PROCEDURE SFTRS                               (* SHIFT BIT BOARD *)
    (VAR A:RS;                                (* RESULT *)
    B:RS;                                     (* SOURCE *)
    C:TE);                                    (* DIRECTION *)

VAR
    INRS : RS;                                (* SCRATCH *)
    INTS : TS;                                (* SCRATCH *)
    INTY : TY;                                (* BIT BOARD WORD INDEX *)

BEGIN

(*** BEGIN MACHINE INDEPENDENT CODE *)
    NEWRS(A);                                 (* CLEAR NEW BIT BOARD *)
    WHILE NXTTS(B,INTS) DO
        IF XTLS[XTSL[INTS]+XTED[C]] > 0 THEN
                                              (* SHIFT EACH BIT *)
            SETRS(A,XTLS[XTSL[INTS]+XTED[C]]);
(*** END MACHINE INDEPENDENT CODE *)
(*** BEGIN CDC 6000 DEPENDENT CODE *)
(*** FOLLOWING CODE ASSUMES THAT MULTIPLICATION OR DIVISION
(*** BY A CONSTANT POWER OF 2 IS DONE WITH A SHIFT INSTRUCTION. *)
(*CASE C OF
(*S1: FOR INTY := AY TO ZY DO               (* SHIFT ONE PLACE *)
(*        BEGIN
(*            B.RSSS[INTY] := B.RSSS[INTY] - EDGE[S1].RSSS[INTY];
(*            A.RSTI[INTY] := B.RSTI[INTY] DIV 2;
(*        END;
(*    END;
(*S2: BEGIN
(*        FOR INTY := AY TO ZY DO           (* SHIFT WORDS *)
(*        BEGIN
(*            B.RSSS[INTY] := B.RSSS[INTY] - EDGE[S2].RSSS[INTY];
(*            INRS.RSSS[INTY] := B.RSSS[INTY] * [ZX-7..ZX];
(*            A.RSSS[INTY] := B.RSSS[INTY] - [ZX-7..ZX];
(*            A.RSTI[INTY] := A.RSTI[INTY] * 256;
(*        END;
(*        FOR INTY := AY+1 TO ZY DO         (* CARRY BETWEEN WORDS *)
(*            A.RSTI[INTY] := A.RSTI[INTY] + INRS.RSTI[INTY-1] DIV PZX8;
(*    END;
(*S3: BEGIN
(*        FOR INTY := AY TO ZY DO           (* SHIFT ONE PLACE *)
(*        BEGIN
(*            A.RSSS[INTY] := B.RSSS[INTY] - EDGE[S3].RSSS[INTY];
(*            A.RSTI[INTY] := A.RSTI[INTY] * 2;
(*        END;
```

```
(*        END;
(*S4: BEGIN
(*        FOR INTY := AY TO ZY DO           (* SHIFT WORDS *)
(*        BEGIN
(*            B.RSSS[INTY] := B.RSSS[INTY] - EDGE[S4].RSSS[INTY];
(*            INRS.RSSS[INTY] := B.RSSS[INTY] * [AX..AX+7];
(*            A.RSTI[INTY] := B.RSTI[INTY] DIV 256;
(*        END;
(*        FOR INTY := AY TO ZY-1 DO         (* CARRY BETWEEN WORDS *)
(*            A.RSTI[INTY] := A.RSTI[INTY] + INRS.RSTI[INTY+1] * PZX8;
(*    END;
(*B1: BEGIN
(*        SFTRS(INRS,B,S1);
(*        SFTRS(A,INRS,S2);
(*    END;
(*B2: BEGIN
(*        SFTRS(INRS,B,S2);
(*        SFTRS(A,INRS,S3);
(*    END;
(*B3: BEGIN
(*        SFTRS(INRS,B,S3);
(*        SFTRS(A,INRS,S4);
(*    END;
(*B4: BEGIN
(*        SFTRS(INRS,B,S4);
(*        SFTRS(A,INRS,S1);
(*    END;
(*N1: BEGIN
(*        SFTRS(INRS,B,B1);
(*        SFTRS(A,INRS,S2);
(*    END;
(*N2: BEGIN
(*        SFTRS(INRS,B,B2);
(*        SFTRS(A,INRS,S2);
(*    END;
(*N3: BEGIN
(*        SFTRS(INRS,B,B2);
(*        SFTRS(A,INRS,S3);
(*    END;
(*N4: BEGIN
(*        SFTRS(INRS,B,B3);
(*        SFTRS(A,INRS,S3);
(*    END;
(*N5: BEGIN
(*        SFTRS(INRS,B,B3);
(*        SFTRS(A,INRS,S4);
(*    END;
(*N6: BEGIN
(*        SFTRS(INRS,B,B4);
(*        SFTRS(A,INRS,S4);
(*    END;
(*N7: BEGIN
(*        SFTRS(INRS,B,B4);
(*        SFTRS(A,INRS,S1);
(*    END;
(*N8: BEGIN
(*        SFTRS(INRS,B,B1);
(*        SFTRS(A,INRS,S1);
(*    END;
(*END;
(*** END CDC 6000 DEPENDENT CODE *)

END; (* SFTRS *)


FUNCTION INRSTB                               (* SQUARE IN BIT BOARD BOOLEAN *)
    (A:RS;                                    (* BIT BOARD *)
    B:TS):TB;                                 (* SQUARE IN QUESTION *)

BEGIN
    INRSTB := XSSX[B] <= A.RSSS[XTSY[B]];
END; (* INRSTB *)


FUNCTION NULRS                                (* NULL BIT BOARD *)
    (A:RS)                                    (* BIT BOARD TO CHECK *)
    :TB;                                      (* TRUE IF BIT BOARD EMPTY *)

VAR
    INTY : TY;                                (* BIT BOARD WORD INDEX *)
    INTB : TB;                                (* TEMPORARY VALUE *)

BEGIN
    INTB := TRUE;
    FOR INTY := AY TO ZY DO
        INTB := INTB AND (A.RSTI[INTY] = 0);
    NULRS := INTB;
END; (* NULRS *)


FUNCTION NULMVB                               (* NULL MOVE BOOLEAN *)
    (A:RM)                                    (* MOVE TO TEST *)
    :TB;                                      (* TRUE IF NULL MOVE *)
BEGIN
    WITH A DO
        NULMVB := RMAC AND RMPR AND (NOT RMCA);
END; (* NULMVB *)


PROCEDURE INICON;                             (* INITIALIZE GLOBAL CONSTANTS *)
VAR
    INTD : TD;                                (* DIRECTION INDEX *)
    INTE : TE;                                (* DIRECTION *)
    INTF : TF;                                (* FILE INDEX *)
    INTI : TI;                                (* SCRATCH *)
    INTL : TL;                                (* LARGE BOARD INDEX *)
    INTQ : TQ;                                (* CASTLE TYPE INDEX *)
    INTR : TR;                                (* RANK INDEX *)
    INTT : TT;                                (* SQUARE INDEX *)
    INTX : TX;                                (* SET ELEMENT INDEX *)
    INTY : TY;                                (* BIT BOARD WORD INDEX *)
    IMTI : TI;                                (* SCRATCH *)
    INRS : RS;                                (* SCRATCH *)
```

```
PROCEDURE INISYN                    (* INITIALIZE MOVE SYNTAX
                                       TABLE ENTRY *)

  (A:RA);                           (* MOVE SYNTAX *)

BEGIN
  WITH SYNTX[INTI] DO
  BEGIN
    WITH RYLS DO
    BEGIN
      RDPC := TRUE;
      RDSL := A[AA+0] <> " ";
      RDKQ := A[AA+1] <> " ";
      RDNB := A[AA+2] <> " ";
      RDRK := A[AA+3] <> " ";
    END;
    RYCH := A[AA+4];
    WITH RYRS DO
    BEGIN
      RDPC := A[AA+5] <> " ";
      RDSL := A[AA+6] <> " ";
      RDKQ := A[AA+7] <> " ";
      RDNB := A[AA+8] <> " ";
      RDRK := A[AA+9] <> " ";
    END;
  END;
  INTI := INTI+1;
END; (* INISYN *)


PROCEDURE INIXTP                    (* INITIALIZE PIECE TRANSLATION
                                       TABLES *)

  (A : TP;                          (* PIECE TO BE TRANSLATED *)
   B : TC;                          (* DISPLAY EQUIVALENT *)
   C : TM;                          (* COLOR OF PIECE *)
   D : TU;                          (* TYPE OF PIECE *)
   E : TB;                          (* TRUE IF SWEEP PIECE *)
   F : TE;                          (* FIRST DIRECTION OF MOVEMENT *)
   G : TE;                          (* LAST DIRECTION OF MOVEMENT *)
   H : TV);                         (* VALUE OF PIECE *)

BEGIN
  XTPC[A] := B;
  XTPM[A] := C;
  XSPB[A] := E;
  XFPE[A] := F;
  XLPE[A] := G;
  XTPU[A] := D;
  XTPV[A] := H;
  IF A <> MT THEN
    XTUMP[D,C] := A;
END; (* INIXTP *)


BEGIN  (* INICON *)

  (** INITIALIZE PIECE CHARACTERISTICS *)

  INIXTP(LP,"A",LITE,EP,FALSE,B1,B2,1*64);
  INIXTP(LR,"B",LITE,ER,TRUE ,S1,S4,5*64);
  INIXTP(LN,"C",LITE,EN,FALSE,N1,N8,3*64);
  INIXTP(LB,"D",LITE,EB,TRUE ,B1,B4,3*64);
  INIXTP(LQ,"E",LITE,EQ,TRUE ,B1,S4,9*64);
  INIXTP(LK,"F",LITE,EK,FALSE,B1,S4,0);
  INIXTP(DP,"1",DARK,EP,FALSE,B3,B4,-1*64);
  INIXTP(DR,"2",DARK,ER,TRUE ,S1,S4,-5*64);
  INIXTP(DN,"3",DARK,EN,FALSE,N1,N8,-3*64);
  INIXTP(DB,"4",DARK,EB,TRUE ,B1,B4,-3*64);
  INIXTP(DQ,"5",DARK,EQ,TRUE ,B1,S4,-9*64);
  INIXTP(DK,"6",DARK,EK,FALSE,B1,S4,0);
  INIXTP(MT,"-",NONE,EP,FALSE,B2,B1,0);

  XTGMP[PQ,LITE] := LQ;  XTGMP[PQ,DARK] := DQ;  XTGC[PQ] := "Q";
  XTGMP[PR,LITE] := LR;  XTGMP[PR,DARK] := DR;  XTGC[PR] := "R";
  XTGMP[PN,LITE] := LN;  XTGMP[PN,DARK] := DN;  XTGC[PN] := "N";
  XTGMP[PB,LITE] := LB;  XTGMP[PB,DARK] := DB;  XTGC[PB] := "B";

  XTUC[EK] := "K";
  XTUC[EQ] := "Q";
  XTUC[ER] := "R";
  XTUC[EN] := "N";
  XTUC[EB] := "B";
  XTUC[EP] := "P";

  (** INITIALIZE OTHER CONSTANTS *)

  XTBC[FALSE] := "-";
  XTBC[TRUE ] := "*";

  OTHER[LITE] := DARK;   XTMV[LITE] :=  1;
  OTHER[DARK] := LITE;   XTMV[DARK] := -1;
  OTHER[NONE] := NONE;

  XTMA[LITE] := "  WHITE ";
  XTMA[DARK] := "  BLACK ";
  XTMA[NONE] := "  NO ONE ";

  XTQA[LS] := "WHITE KING";
  XTQA[LL] := "WHITE LONG";
  XTQA[DS] := "BLACK KING";
  XTQA[DL] := "BLACK LONG";

  (** INITIALIZE 10X12 TO 8X8 AND 8X8 TO 10X12 TRANSLATION TABLES *)

  FOR INTL := AL TO ZL DO           (* LOOP THROUGH LARGE BOARD *)
    XTLS[INTL] := -1;               (* PRESET ARRAY TO OFF BOARD *)

  INTL := 21;                       (* INDEX OF FIRST SQUARE ON LARGE
                                       BOARD *)
  INTT := -1;                       (* INDEX OF FIRST SQUARE ON SMALL
                                       BOARD *)
  FOR INTR := R1 TO R8 DO           (* LOOP THROUGH RANKS *)
  BEGIN
    FOR INTF := F1 TO F8 DO         (* LOOP THROUGH FILES *)
    BEGIN
      INTT := INTT+1;               (* ADVANCE SMALL BOARD INDEX *)
```

```
      XTRFS[INTR,INTF] := INTT;     (* SET MATRIX TO VECTOR
                                       TRANSLATION *)
      XTLS[INTL] := INTT;           (* SET LARGE BOARD TRANSLATION
                                       TABLE WITH SMALL BOARD
                                       INDEX *)
      XTSL[INTT] := INTL;           (* SET SMALL BOARD TRANSLATION
                                       TABLE WITH LARGE BOARD
                                       INDEX *)
      XTSR[INTT] := INTR;           (* SET RANK OF SQUARE *)
      XTSF[INTT] := INTF;           (* SET FILE OF SQUARE *)
      INTL := INTL+1;               (* ADVANCE LARGE BOARD INDEX *)
    END;
    INTL := INTL+2;                 (* ADVANCE LARGE BOARD INDEX TO
                                       SKIP BORDER *)
  END;

  (** INITIALIZE 8X8 TO BIT BOARD TABLES *)

  INTT := -1;
  FOR INTY := AY TO ZY DO
  BEGIN
    FOR INTX := AX TO ZX DO
    BEGIN
      INTT := INTT+1;
      XTSX[INTT] := INTX;
      XTSY[INTT] := INTY;
      XSSX[INTT] := [INTX];
      NEWRS(XRSS[INTT]);
      XRSS[INTT].RSSS[INTY] := [INTX];
    END;
  END;

  (** INITIALIZE CONSTANT BIT BOARDS *)

  FOR INTR := R1 TO R8 DO
    NEWRS(XRRS[INTR]);

  FOR INTF := F1 TO F8 DO
    NEWRS(XRFS[INTF]);

  FOR INTR := R1 TO R8 DO
    FOR INTF := F1 TO F8 DO
    BEGIN
      SETRS(XRRS[INTR],XTRFS[INTR,INTF]);
      SETRS(XRFS[INTF],XTRFS[INTR,INTF]);
    END;

  FOR INTF := F1 TO F8 DO
    NOTRS(XNFS[INTF],XRFS[INTF]);

  FOR INTR := R1 TO R8 DO
    NOTRS(XNRS[INTR],XRRS[INTR]);

  (** INITIALIZE EDGES *)

  CPYRS(EDGE[S1],XRFS[F1]);
  CPYRS(EDGE[S2],XRRS[R8]);
  CPYRS(EDGE[S3],XRFS[F8]);
  CPYRS(EDGE[S4],XRRS[R1]);
  IORRS(EDGE[B1],EDGE[S1],EDGE[S2]);
  IORRS(EDGE[B2],EDGE[S2],EDGE[S3]);
  IORRS(EDGE[B3],EDGE[S3],EDGE[S4]);
  IORRS(EDGE[B4],EDGE[S4],EDGE[S1]);
  IORRS(EDGE[N1],EDGE[B1],XRRS[R7]);
  IORRS(EDGE[N2],EDGE[B2],XRRS[R7]);
  IORRS(EDGE[N3],EDGE[B2],XRFS[F7]);
  IORRS(EDGE[N4],EDGE[B3],XRFS[F7]);
  IORRS(EDGE[N5],EDGE[B3],XRRS[R2]);
  IORRS(EDGE[N6],EDGE[B4],XRRS[R2]);
  IORRS(EDGE[N7],EDGE[B4],XRFS[F2]);
  IORRS(EDGE[N8],EDGE[B1],XRFS[F2]);

  (** INITIALIZE CORNER MASK *)

  IORRS(INRS,XRRS[R1],XRRS[R2]);
  IORRS(INRS,INRS,XRRS[R7]);
  IORRS(INRS,INRS,XRRS[R8]);
  IORRS(CORNR,XRFS[F1],XRFS[F2]);
  IORRS(CORNR,CORNR,XRFS[F7]);
  IORRS(CORNR,CORNR,XRFS[F8]);
  ANDRS(CORNR,CORNR,INRS);

  (** INITIALIZE DIRECTION TABLE *)

                   XTED[N1]:= 19;               XTED[N2]:= 21;
  XTED[N8]:=  8;XTED[B1]:=  9;XTED[S2]:= 10;XTED[B2]:= 11;XTED[N3]:= 12;
                   XTED[S1]:= -1;               XTED[S3]:= -1;
  XTED[N7]:=-12;XTED[B4]:=-11;XTED[S4]:=-10;XTED[B3]:= -9;XTED[N4]:= -8;
                   XTED[N6]:=-21;               XTED[N5]:=-19;

  (** INITIALIZE SQUARE DIFFERENCE TO DIRECTION TABLE *)

  FOR INTI := AZL TO ZAL DO
    XLLD[INTI] := 0;
  FOR INTE := B1 TO S4 DO
  BEGIN
    INTD := XTED[INTE];
    FOR INTI := 1 TO 7 DO
      XLLD[INTI*INTD] := INTD;
  END;
  FOR INTE := N1 TO N8 DO
    XLLD[XTED[INTE]] := XTED[INTE];

  (** INITIALIZE CASTLING TRANSLATION TABLES *)

  IORRS(XSQS[LS],XRSS[XTRFS[R1,F8]],XRSS[XTRFS[R1,F5]]);
  IORRS(XSQS[LL],XRSS[XTRFS[R1,F1]],XRSS[XTRFS[R1,F5]]);
  IORRS(XSQS[DS],XRSS[XTRFS[R8,F8]],XRSS[XTRFS[R8,F5]]);
  IORRS(XSQS[DL],XRSS[XTRFS[R8,F1]],XRSS[XTRFS[R8,F5]]);

  IORRS(XRQSO[LS],XRSS[XTRFS[R1,F6]],XRSS[XTRFS[R1,F7]]);
  IORRS(XRQSO[LL],XRSS[XTRFS[R1,F4]],XRSS[XTRFS[R1,F3]]);
  IORRS(XRQSA[LS],XRSS[XTRFS[R1,F5]],XRQSO[LS]);
  IORRS(XRQSA[LL],XRSS[XTRFS[R1,F5]],XRQSO[LL]);
  IORRS(XRQSO[LL],XRSS[XTRFS[R1,F2]],XRQSO[LL]);

  IORRS(XRQSO[DS],XRSS[XTRFS[R8,F6]],XRSS[XTRFS[R8,F7]]);
  IORRS(XRQSO[DL],XRSS[XTRFS[R8,F4]],XRSS[XTRFS[R8,F3]]);
```

```
      IORRS(XRQSA[DS],XRSS[XTRFS[R8,F5]],XRQSO[DS]);
      IORRS(XRQSA[DL],XRSS[XTRFS[R8,F5]],XRQSO[DL]);
      IORRS(XRQSO[DL],XRSS[XTRFS[R8,F2]],XRQSO[DL]);

      FOR INTQ := LS TO DL DO
        WITH XRQM[INTQ] DO
        BEGIN
          RMCP := MT;
          RMCA := FALSE;
          RMAC := TRUE;
          RMCH := FALSE;
          RMMT := FALSE;
          RMIL := FALSE;
          RMSU := FALSE;
          RMPR := FALSE;
          RMOO := TRUE;
        END;

      XRQM[LS].RMFR := XTRFS[R1,F5]; XRQM[LS].RMTO := XTRFS[R1,F7];
      XRQM[LL].RMFR := XTRFS[R1,F5]; XRQM[LL].RMTO := XTRFS[R1,F3];
      XRQM[DS].RMFR := XTRFS[R8,F5]; XRQM[DS].RMTO := XTRFS[R8,F7];
      XRQM[DL].RMFR := XTRFS[R8,F5]; XRQM[DL].RMTO := XTRFS[R8,F3];

      XRQM[LS].RMQS := FALSE;
      XRQM[LL].RMQS := TRUE;
      XRQM[DS].RMQS := FALSE;
      XRQM[DL].RMQS := TRUE;

      XTMQ[LITE] := LS;
      XTMQ[DARK] := DS;

      XTQS[LS] := XTRFS[R1,F8];
      XTQS[LL] := XTRFS[R1,F1];
      XTQS[DS] := XTRFS[R8,F8];
      XTQS[DL] := XTRFS[R8,F1];

      (** INITIALIZE NULL MOVE *)

      WITH NULMV DO
      BEGIN
        RMFR := AS;
        RMTO := AS;
        RMCP := MT;
        RMCA := FALSE;
        RMAC := TRUE;
        RMCH := FALSE;
        RMMT := FALSE;
        RMIL := FALSE;
        RMSU := FALSE;
        RMPR := TRUE;
        RMPP := PB;
      END;

      (** INITIALIZE COMMAND PROCESSING VARIABLES *)

      JMTJ := ZJ;
      ICARD[ZJ] := ";";
      ILINE[ZJ] := ";";

      (** INITIALIZE MOVES SYNTAX TABLE *)

      INTI := SYNCF;
      INISYN("   *P    ");
      INISYN("   *P/  1");
      INISYN("/  1*P   ");
      INISYN("   *P/ R ");
      INISYN("/ R *P   ");
      INISYN("   *P/ R1");
      INISYN("/ R1*P   ");
      INISYN("   *P/KR ");
      INISYN("/KR *P   ");
      INISYN("   *P/KR1");
      INISYN("/KR1*P   ");
      INISYN("/  1*P/  1");
      INISYN("/ R *P/ R ");
      INISYN("/  1*P/ R ");
      INISYN("/ R *P/  1");
      INISYN("/ R1*P/  1");
      INISYN("/  1*P/ R1");
      INISYN("/ R1*P/ R ");
      INISYN("/ R *P/ R1");
      INISYN("/  1*P/KR ");
      INISYN("/KR *P/  1");
      INISYN("/  1*P/KR ");
      INISYN("/ R *P/KR ");
      INISYN("/KR *P/ R ");
      INISYN("/  1*P/KR1");
      INISYN("/KR1*P/  1");
      INISYN("/ R *P/KR1");
      INISYN("/KR1*P/ R ");
      INISYN("/ R1*P/KR ");
      INISYN("/KR *P/ R1");
      INISYN("/ R1*P/KR ");
      INISYN("/KR *P/KR ");
      INISYN("/KR1*P/ R1");
      INISYN("/ R1*P/KR1");
      INISYN("/KR1*P/KR ");
      INISYN("/KR *P/KR1");
      INISYN("/KR1*P/KR1");

      INISYN("   -   R1");
      INISYN("   -  KR1");
      INISYN("/  1-   R1");
      INISYN("/ R -   R1");
      INISYN("/  1-  KR1");
      INISYN("/ R -  KR1");
      INISYN("/ R1-   R1");
      INISYN("/KR -   R1");
      INISYN("/ R1-  KR1");
      INISYN("/KR -  KR1");
      INISYN("/KR1-  KR1");

      (** INITIALIZE LETS *)

      FKPSHQ := 10;
      FKSANQ := 150;
```

```
      FMAXHT := 256;
      FMODEL := 10;
      FPADCR[F1] := 8;
      FPADCR[F2] := 8;
      FPADCR[F3] := 5;
      FPADCR[F4] := 10;
      FPADCR[F5] := 15;
      FPADCR[F6] := 5;
      FPADCR[F7] := 8;
      FPADCR[F8] := 8;
      FPBLOK := 28;
      FPCOMM := 5;
      FPFLNX := 12;
      FRDUBL := 68;
      FRK7TH := 120;
      FTRADE := 36;
      FTRDSL := 5156;
      FTRPOK := 2;
      FTRPWN := 8;
      FWKING := 50;
      FWMAJM := 1;
      FWMINM := 200;
      FWPAWN := 100;
      FWROOK := 2;
      WINDOW := 30;

      (** INITIALIZE SWITCHES *)

      SWEC := TRUE;
      SWPA := TRUE;
      SWPS := FALSE;
      SWRE := TRUE;
      SWSU := FALSE;
      SWTR := FALSE;

      (** INITIALIZE MAIN LOOP CONTROL VARIABLES *)

      GOING := 0;

END;  (* INICON *)


PROCEDURE INITAL(VAR A:RB);              (* INITIALIZE FOR A NEW GAME *)
VAR
    INTF : TF;                           (* FILE INDEX *)
    INTR : TR;                           (* RANK INDEX *)
BEGIN
    WITH A DO
    BEGIN
      RBTM := LITE;                      (* SIDE TO MOVE *)
      RBTS := -1;                        (* NO ENPASSANT SQUARE *)
      RBTI := 0;                         (* GAME HAS NOT STARTED *)
      RBSQ := [LS,LL,DS,DL];             (* ALL CASTLING MOVES LEGAL *)
      FOR INTF := F1 TO F8 DO            (* LOOP THROUGH ALL FILES *)
      BEGIN
        RBIRF[R2,INTF] := LP;            (* SET LIGHT PAWNS ON BOARD *)
        FOR INTR := R3 TO R6 DO          (* LOOP THRU MIDDLE OF BOARD *)
          RBIRF[INTR,INTF] := MT;        (* SET MIDDLE OF BOARD EMPTY *)
        RBIRF[R7,INTF] := DP;            (* SET DARK PAWNS ON BOARD *)
      END;
      RBIRF[R1,F1] := LR;                (* SET REMAINDER OF PIECES ON
                                             BOARD *)
      RBIRF[R1,F2] := LN;
      RBIRF[R1,F3] := LB;
      RBIRF[R1,F4] := LQ;
      RBIRF[R1,F5] := LK;
      RBIRF[R1,F6] := LB;
      RBIRF[R1,F7] := LN;
      RBIRF[R1,F8] := LR;
      RBIRF[R8,F1] := DR;
      RBIRF[R8,F2] := DN;
      RBIRF[R8,F3] := DB;
      RBIRF[R8,F4] := DQ;
      RBIRF[R8,F5] := DK;
      RBIRF[R8,F6] := DB;
      RBIRF[R8,F7] := DN;
      RBIRF[R8,F8] := DR;

      MOVMS := " ENTER MOVE CR TYPE GO.        ";
      WRITELN(MOVMS);
      LSTMV := NULMV;                    (* INITIALIZE PREVIOUS MOVE *)
    END;
END;  (* INITAL *)


PROCEDURE PAUSER;                        (* PAUSE FOR CARRIAGE RETURN *)

BEGIN
    IF SWPA THEN
    BEGIN
      WRITELN(" PAUSING ");
      READLN;
    END;
END;  (* PAUSER *)


PROCEDURE PRIMOV(A:RM);                  (* PRINT A MOVE *)

BEGIN
    WITH A DO
    BEGIN
      WRITE(" FROM ",RMFR:2," TO ",RMTO:2);
      IF NULMVB(A) THEN
        WRITE(", NULL MOVE")
      ELSE
      BEGIN
        IF RMCA THEN
          WRITE(", CAPTURE ",XTPC(RMCP),",")
        ELSE
          WRITE(", SIMPLE,");
        IF NOT RMAC THEN
          WRITE(" NO");
        WRITE(" ACS");
        IF RMCH THEN
```

125

```
        WRITE(", CHECK");
      IF RMMT THEN
        WRITE(", MATE");
      IF RMIL THEN
        WRITE(", ILLEGAL");
      IF RMSU THEN
        WRITE(", SEARCHED");
      CASE RMPR OF
      FALSE:  (* NOT PROMOTION *)
        CASE RMOO OF
        FALSE:  (* NOT CASTLE *)
          IF RMEP THEN
            WRITE(", ENPASSANT");
        TRUE:   (* CASTLE *)
          BEGIN
            WRITE(", CASTLE ");
            IF RMQS THEN
              WRITE("LONG")
            ELSE
              WRITE("SHORT");
          END;
        END;
      TRUE:    (* PROMOTION *)
        BEGIN
          WRITE(", PROMOTE TO ");
          CASE RMPP OF
          PQ:  WRITE("QUEEN");
          PR:  WRITE("ROOK");
          PB:  WRITE("BISHOP");
          PN:  WRITE("KNIGHT");
          END;
        END;
      END;
    END;
    WRITELN(".");
END;  (* PRIMOV *)


PROCEDURE PRINTB(A:RC);                (* PRINT A BOARD *)

VAR
  INTR : TR;                           (* RANK INDEX *)
  INTF : TF;                           (* FILE INDEX *)

BEGIN
  WRITELN;                             (* WRITE A BLANK LINE *)
  FOR INTR := R8 DOWNTO R1 DO          (* LOOP DOWN THROUGH RANKS *)
  BEGIN
    WRITE (" ",ORD(INTR)+1:1," ");     (* OUTPUT RANK LABEL *)
    FOR INTF := F1 TO F8 DO            (* LOOP ACROSS THROUGH FILES *)
      WRITE (XTPC(A[XTRFS[INTR,INTF]]));
                                       (* OUTPUT CONTENTS OF SQUARE *)
    WRITELN;                           (* WRITE OUT A RANK *)
  END;
  WRITELN (" W RNBQKBNR");             (* WRITE OUT BOTTOM LABEL *)
END;  (* PRINTB *)


PROCEDURE PRINBB(A:FS);                (* PRINT A BIT BOARD *)

VAR
  INTR : TR;                           (* RANK INDEX *)
  INTF : TF;                           (* FILE INDEX *)

BEGIN
  WRITELN;                             (* WRITE OUT A BLANK LINE *)
  FOR INTR := R8 DOWNTO R1 DO          (* LOOP DOWN THROUGH RANKS *)
  BEGIN
    WRITE (" ",ORD(INTR)+1:1," ");     (* OUTPUT RANK LABEL *)
    FOR INTF := F1 TO F8 DO            (* LOOP ACROSS THROUGH FILES *)
      WRITE (XTBC(INRSTB(A,XTRFS[INTR,INTF])));
                                       (* OUTPUT CONTENTS OF SQUARE *)
    WRITELN;                           (* WRITE OUT A RANK *)
  END;
  WRITELN (" W RNBQKBNR");             (* WRITE OUT BOTTOM LABEL *)
END;  (* PRINBB *)


PROCEDURE PRINAM(A:FX);                (* PRINT ATTACK MAP *)

VAR
  INTR, JNTR : TR;                     (* RANK INDICES *)
  INTF, JNTF : TF;                     (* FILE INDICES *)

BEGIN
  WRITELN;
  FOR INTR := R8 DOWNTO R1 DO
  BEGIN
    FOR JNTR := R8 DOWNTO R1 DO
    BEGIN
      FOR INTF := F1 TO F8 DO
      BEGIN
        WRITE(" ");
        FOR JNTF := F1 TO F8 DO
        BEGIN
          WRITE(XTBC(INRSTB(A[XTRFS[INTR,INTF]],XTRFS[JNTR,JNTF])));
        END;
        WRITE(" ");
      END;
      WRITELN;
    END;
    WRITELN;
    IF INTR IN [R1,F3,R5,R7] THEN PAUSER;
  END;
END;  (* PRINAM *)


PROCEDURE PRISWI(A:FA;B:TB);           (* PRINT A SWITCH *)

BEGIN
```

```
    WRITE(" ",A[AA],A[AA+1]);
    IF B THEN
      WRITELN(" ON")
    ELSE
      WRITELN(" OFF");
END;  (* PRISWI *)


PROCEDURE MBEVAL;                      (* EVALUATE MATERIAL BALANCE *)

VAR
  INTI : TI;                           (* COUNT PAWNS OF WINNING SIDE *)

BEGIN
  IF MBLTE <> 0 THEN
    IF MBLTE > 0 THEN
      INTI := MBPWN[LITE]
    ELSE
      INTI := MBPWN[DARK]
  ELSE
    INTI := 0;

  MBVAL[JNTK] := SIGN(MIN(MIN(FMAXMT,ABS(MBLTE))
    +FTRADE*ABS(MBLTE)*(FTRDSL-MBTOT)*(4*INTI+FTRPOK)
    DIV (4*INTI+FTRPWN) DIV 262144,16320),MBLTE);

END;  (* MBEVAL *)


PROCEDURE MBCAPT                       (* EVALUATE MATERIAL AFTER
                                          CAPTURE *)

  (A:TP);                              (* PIECE CAPTURED *)

BEGIN
  MBTOT := MBTOT - ABS(XTPV[A]);       (* TOTAL MATERIAL ON BOARD *)
  IF XTPU[A] = EP THEN
    MBPWN[XTPM[A]] := MBPWN[XTPM[A]] - 1;
                                       (* REMOVE PAWN IF NECESSARY *)
  MBLTE := MBLTE - XTPV[A];            (* LITE ADVANTAGE *)
  MBEVAL;                              (* EVALUATE MATERIAL *)
END;  (* MBCAPT *)


PROCEDURE MBTPAC                       (* REMOVE CAPTURE FROM
                                          MATERIAL BALANCE DATA.  THIS
                                          IS THE INVERSE OF MBCAPT *)

  (A:TP);                              (* PIECE UNCAPTURED *)

BEGIN
  MBTOT := MBTOT + ABS(XTPV[A]);
  IF XTPU[A] = EP THEN
    MBPWN[XTPM[A]] := MBPWN[XTPM[A]] + 1;
  MBLTE := MBLTE + XTPV[A];
END;  (* MBTPAC *)


PROCEDURE MBPROM                       (* EVALUATE MATERIAL BALANCE
                                          CHANGE DUE TO PAWN
                                          PROMOTION *)

  (A:TP);                              (* PIECE TO PROMOTE TO *)

BEGIN
  MBTOT := MBTOT + ABS(XTPV[A]-XTPV[XTUMP[EP,XTPM[A]]]);
                                       (* TOTAL MATERIAL ON BOARD *)
  MBPWN[XTPM[A]] := MBPWN[XTPM[A]] - 1;(* COUNT PAWNS *)
  MBLTE := MBLTE + XTPV[A]-XTPV[XTUMP[EP,XTPM[A]]];
  MBEVAL;                              (* EVALUATE RESULT *)
END;  (* MBPROM *)


PROCEDURE MBMORP                       (* REMOVE PAWN PROMOTION
                                          FROM MATERIAL BALANCE DATA.
                                          THIS IS THE INVERSE
                                          OF MBPROM *)

  (A:TP);                              (* PIECE PROMOTED TO *)

BEGIN
  MBTOT := MBTOT - ABS(XTPV[A]-XTPV[XTUMP[EP,XTPM[A]]]);
  MBPWN[XTPM[A]] := MBPWN[XTPM[A]] + 1;
  MBLTE := MBLTE - (XTPV[A]-XTPV[XTUMP[EP,XTPM[A]]]);
END;  (* MBMORP *)


PROCEDURE ADDATK                       (* ADD ATTACKS OF PIECE TO DATA
                                          BASE *)

  (A:TS);                              (* SQUARE OF PIECE TO ADD
                                          ATTACK *)

VAR
  INTB : TB;                           (* LOOP CONTROL BOOLEAN *)
  INTD : TO;                           (* CURRENT DIRECTION OFFSET *)
  INTE : TE;                           (* CURRENT DIRECTION INDEX *)
  INTM : TM;                           (* COLOR OF CURRENT PIECE *)
  INTP : TP;                           (* CURRENT PIECE *)
  INTT : TT;                           (* RUNNING SQUARE *)

BEGIN
  INTP := NBORD[A];                    (* PIECE OF INTEREST *)
  INTM := XTPM[INTP];                  (* COLOR *)
  FOR INTE := XFPE[INTP] TO XLPE[INTP] DO
  BEGIN
    INTT := A;                         (* INITIALIZE RUNNING SQUARE *)
    INTB := XSPB[INTP];                (* TRUE IF SWEEP PIECE *)
    INTD := XTED[INTE];                (* OFFSET *)
    REPEAT
      INTT := XTLS[XTSL[INTT] + INTD]; (* STEP IN PROPER DIRECTION *)
      IF INTT >= 0 THEN
      BEGIN
        SETRS(ATKFR[A],INTT);
        SETRS(ATKTO[INTT], );
        SETRS(ALATK[INTM], NTT);
        IF NBORD[INTT] <> MT THEN
          INTB := FALSE;
```

```
            END
         ELSE
            INTB := FALSE;
      UNTIL NOT INTB;
   END;
END;  (* ADDATK *)


PROCEDURE ADDLOC                        (* ADD PIECE TO DATA BASE *)
   (A:TS;                               (* SQUARE WITH NEW PIECE ON IT *)
    B:TP);                              (* NEW PIECE TO ADD *)


BEGIN
   CLRRS(TPLOC[MT],A);                  (* BIT BOARD OF EMPTY SQUARES *)
   SETRS(TPLOC[B],A);                   (* BIT BOARD OF ALL SAME PIECE *)
   SETRS(TMLOC[XTPM[B]],A);             (* BIT BOARD OF ALL SAME COLOR *)
   SETRS(ALLOC[JNTK],A);                (* BIT BOARD OF ALL PIECES *)
   NBORD[A] := B;                       (* SET NEW PIECE ON BOARD *)
END;  (* ADDLOC *)


PROCEDURE CLSTAT;                       (* CLEAR POSITION STATUS *)

BEGIN
   WITH BOARD DO
      BEGIN
         RBTM := LITE;                  (* WHITE TO MOVE *)
         RBTS := -1;                    (* NO ENPASSANT *)
         RBSQ := [];                    (* NO CASTLING LEGAL *)
      END;
END;  (* CLSTAT *)


PROCEDURE CUTATK                        (* CUT ATTACKS THROUGH SQUARE *)
   (A:TS);                              (* SQUARE *)

VAR
   INRS : RS;                           (* ATTACKING PIECES *)
   INTS : TS;                           (* ATTACKING PIECE SQUARE *)
   IMRS : RS;                           (* SCRATCH *)
   INTD : TD;                           (* STEP SIZE *)
   INTM : TM;                           (* ATTACKING PIECE SIDE *)
   INTL : TL;                           (* NO LONGER ATTACKED SQUARE *)
   INTT : TT;                           (* NO LONGER ATTACKED SQUARE *)

BEGIN
   CPYRS(INRS,ATKTO[A]);                (* ALL PIECES ATTACKING SQUARE *)
   WHILE NXTTS(INRS,INTS) DO
      IF XSPB(NBORD[INTS]) THEN         (* IF SWEEP PIECE *)
         BEGIN
            INTD := XLLD[XTSL[A]-XTSL[INTS]];
                                        (* STEP SIZE ON 10 X 12 BOARD *)
            INTM := XTPM[NBORD[INTS]];  (* SIDE OF ATTACKING PIECE *)
            INTL := XTSL[A]+INTD;       (* FIRST SQUARE BEYOND PIECE *)
            INTT := XTLS[INTL];         (* FIRST SQUARE BEYOND PIECE ON
                                           8X8 BOARD *)
            WHILE INTT > AT DO          (* WHILE ON BOARD *)
               BEGIN
                  CLRRS(ATKFR[INTS],INTT);  (* CLEAR ATTACK MAP *)
                  CLRRS(ATKTO[INTT],INTS);
                  ANDRS(IMRS,ATKTO[INTT],TMLOC[INTM]);
                                        (* OTHER ATTACKS ON SQUARE BY
                                           SAME SIDE *)
                  IF NULRS(IMRS) THEN   (* IF NO ATTACKS BY THAT SIDE *)
                     CLRRS(ALATK[INTM],INTT);  (* CLEAR ATTACKS BY SIDE *)
                  IF NBORD[INTT] = MT THEN
                     BEGIN
                        INTL := INTL+INTD;  (* STEP BEYOND SQUARE *)
                        INTT := XTLS[INTL];
                     END
                  ELSE
                     INTT := AT;        (* STOP SCAN *)
               END;
         END;
END;  (* CUTATK *)


PROCEDURE DELATK                        (* DELETE ATTACKS FROM SQUARE *)
   (A:TS);                              (* SQUARE TO REMOVE PIECE *)
VAR
   INRS : RS;                           (* SQUARES ATTACKED BY PIECE ON
                                           SQUARE *)
   IMRS : RS;                           (* SCRATCH *)
   INTS : TS;                           (* SQUARE ATTACKED BY PIECE ON
                                           SQUARE *)
   INTM : TM;                           (* SIDE OF PIECE ON SQUARE *)

BEGIN
   CPYRS(INRS,ATKFR[A]);                (* SQUARES ATTACKED BY PIECE
                                           ON SQUARE *)
   NEWRS(ATKFR[A]);                     (* CLEAR ATTACKS FROM SQUARE *)
   INTM := XTPM[NBORD[A]];              (* SIDE OF PIECE ON SQUARE *)
   WHILE NXTTS(INRS,INTS) DO            (* LOOP THROUGH ALL ATTACKS BY
                                           PIECE *)
      BEGIN
         CLRRS(ATKTO[INTS],A);          (* CLEAR ATTACK TO OTHER
                                           SQUARE *)
         ANDRS(IMRS,ATKTO[INTS],TMLOC[INTM]);
                                        (* OTHER ATTACKS BY SAME SIDE *)
         IF NULRS(IMRS) THEN
            CLRRS(ALATK[INTM],INTS);    (* CLEAR ATTACKS BY SIDE *)
      CLRRS(TPLOC[NBORD[A]],A);         (* CLEAR PIECE *)
      CLRRS(TMLOC[INTM],A);             (* CLEAR PIECE FROM SIDE *)
      CLRRS(ALLOC[JNTK],A);             (* CLEAR PIECE FROM ALL PIECES *)
      SETRS(TPLOC[MT],A);               (* SET EMPTY *)
      NBORD[A] := MT;
      END;
END;  (* DELATK *)
```

```
PROCEDURE PRPATK                        (* PROPAGATE ATTACKS THROUGH
                                           SQUARE *)
   (A:TS);                              (* SQUARE *)

VAR
   INRS : RS;                           (* ATTACKING PIECES *)
   INTS : TS;                           (* ATTACKING PIECE SQUARE *)
   INTD : TD;                           (* STEP SIZE *)
   INTM : TM;                           (* ATTACKING PIECE SIDE *)
   INTL : TL;                           (* NEW ATTACKED SQUARE *)
   INTT : TT;                           (* NEW ATTACKED SQUARE *)

BEGIN
   CPYRS(INRS,ATKTO[A]);                (* ALL PIECES ATTACKING SQUARE *)
   WHILE NXTTS(INRS,INTS) DO
      IF XSPB(NBORD[INTS]) THEN         (* IF SWEEP PIECE *)
         BEGIN
            INTD := XLLD[XTSL[A]-XTSL[INTS]];
                                        (* STEP SIZE ON 10 X 12 BOARD *)
            INTM := XTPM[NBORD[INTS]];  (* SIDE OF ATTACKING PIECE *)
            INTL := XTSL[A]+INTD;       (* FIRST SQUARE BEYOND PIECE *)
            INTT := XTLS[INTL];         (* FIRST SQUARE BEYOND PIECE ON
                                           8X8 BOARD *)
            WHILE INTT >= 0 DO          (* WHILE ON BOARD *)
               BEGIN
                  SETRS(ATKFR[INTS],INTT);  (* SET ATTACK MAP *)
                  SETRS(ATKTO[INTT],INTS);
                  SETRS(ALATK[INTM],INTT);  (* SET ATTACKS BY SIDE *)
                  IF NBORD[INTT] = MT THEN
                     BEGIN
                        INTL := INTL+INTD;  (* STEP BEYOND SQUARE *)
                        INTT := XTLS[INTL];
                     END
                  ELSE
                     INTT := -1;        (* STOP SCAN *)
               END;
         END;
END;  (* PRPATK *)


PROCEDURE GAINIT                        (* UNPROCESS CAPTURE MOVE *)
   (A:RM);                              (* CAPTURE MOVE *)

BEGIN
   WITH A DO
      BEGIN
         ADDLOC(RMFR,NBORD[RMTO]);      (* PUT PIECE ON ORIGINAL
                                           SQUARE *)
         ADDATK(RMFR);
         CUTATK(RMFR);                  (* STOP ATTACKS AT THIS SQUARE *)
         DELATK(RMTO);                  (* REMOVE THEM FROM
                                           DESTINATION SQUARE *)
         ADDLOC(RMTO,RMCF);             (* REPLACE CAPTURED PIECE *)
         ADDATK(RMTO);
         MBTPAC(NBORD[RMTO]);           (* UPDATE SCORE *)
      END;
END;  (* GAINIT *)


PROCEDURE LOSEIT                        (* PROCESS CAPTURE MOVE *)
   (A:RM);                              (* CAPTURE MOVE *)

BEGIN
   WITH A DO
      BEGIN
         MBCAPT(NBORD[RMTO]);           (* UPDATE SCORE *)
         DELATK(RMTO);                  (* DELETE ATTACKS OF CAPTURED
                                           PIECE *)
         ADDLOC(RMTO,NBORD[RMFR]);      (* ADD PIECE TO DESTINATION
                                           SQUARE *)
         DELATK(RMFR);                  (* DELETE ATTACKS OF MOVING
                                           PIECE *)
         PRPATK(RMFR);                  (* PROPAGATE ATTACKS THROUGH
                                           FROM SQUARE *)
         ADDATK(RMTO);                  (* ADD ATTACKS OF MOVING PIECE *)
      END;
END;  (* LOSEIT *)


PROCEDURE MOVEIT                        (* PROCESS ORDINARY MOVE *)
   (A:RM);                              (* ORDINARY MOVE *)

BEGIN
   WITH A DO
      BEGIN
         ADDLOC(RMTO,NBORD[RMFR]);      (* ADD PIECE TO NEW SQUARE *)
         CUTATK(RMTO);                  (* CUT ATTACKS THROUGH NEW
                                           SQUARE *)
         DELATK(RMFR);                  (* DELETE ATTACKS FROM OLD
                                           SQUARE *)
         PRPATK(RMFR);                  (* PROPAGATE ATTACKS THROUGH OLD
                                           SQUARE *)
         ADDATK(RMTO);                  (* ADD ATTACKS FROM NEW SQUARE *)
      END;
END;  (* MOVEIT *)


PROCEDURE RTRKIT                        (* UNPROCESS ORDINARY MOVE *)
   (A:RM);                              (* THE MOVE TO RETRACT *)

BEGIN
   WITH A DO
      BEGIN
         ADDLOC(RMFR,NBORD[RMTO]);      (* PUT PIECE ON ORIGINAL
                                           SQUARE *)
         CUTATK(RMFR);                  (* CUT ATTACKS THROUGH ORIGINAL
                                           SQUARE *)
         DELATK(RMTO);                  (* DELETE ATTACKS FROM
                                           DESTINATION SQUARE *)
         PRPATK(RMTO);                  (* PROPAGATE ATTACKS THROUGH
                                           DESTINATION SQUARE *)
         ADDATK(RMFR);                  (* ADD ATTACKS FROM ORIGINAL
                                           SQUARE *)
      END;
END;  (* RTRKIT *)
```

```
PROCEDURE PAWNIT                          (* UNPROMOTE A PAWN *)
   (A:RM);                                (* PROMOTION MOVE *)

BEGIN
   WITH A DO
   BEGIN
      MBMORP(NBORD[RMTO]);                 (* UPDATE SCORE *)
      NBORD[RMTO] := XTUMP[EP,XTPM[NBORD[RMTO]]];
   END;
END;  (* PAWNIT *)


PROCEDURE PROACA                          (* PROCESS CASTLE STATUS
                                             CHANGES *)
   (A:TS);                                (* SQUARE *)

VAR
   INRS : RS;                             (* SCRATCH *)
   IMRS : RS;                             (* SCRATCH *)

BEGIN
   CLRRS(CSTAT[JNTK],A);                  (* CLEAR THIS SQUARE *)
   ANDRS(INRS,CSTAT[JNTK],XRRS[XTSR[A]]);
                                          (* CASTLE BITS FOR THIS SIDE *)
   IF NOT INRSTB(INRS,XTRFS[XTSR[A],F5]) THEN
                                          (* IF KING MOVE *)
      ANDRS(CSTAT[JNTK],CSTAT[JNTK],XNRRS[XTSR[A]]);
                                          (* CLEAR ALL CASTLE MOVES FOR
                                             SIDE *)
   ANDRS(IMRS,INRS,XRFS[F8]);             (* KING ROOK SQUARE *)
   ANDRS(INRS,INRS,XRFS[F1]);             (* QUEEN ROOK SQUARE *)
   IORRS(INRS,INRS,IMRS);                 (* BOTH ROOK SQUARES *)
   IF NULRS(INRS) THEN                    (* IF BOTH ROOKS GONE *)
      ANDRS(CSTAT[JNTK],CSTAT[JNTK],XNRRS[XTSR[A]]);
END;  (* PROACA *)


PROCEDURE PROACS                          (* PROCESS MOVES AFFECTING CASTLE
                                             STATUS *)
   (A:RM);                                (* MOVE WITH RMAC *)

BEGIN
   WITH A DO
   BEGIN
      IF INRSTB(CSTAT[JNTK],RMFR) THEN    (* FROM SQUARE *)
         PROACA(RMFR);
      IF INRSTB(CSTAT[JNTK],RMTO) THEN    (* TO SQUARE *)
         PROACA(RMTO);
   END;
END;  (* PROACS *)


PROCEDURE PROMOT                          (* PROCESS PROMOTION *)
   (A:RM);                                (* PROMOTION MOVE *)
BEGIN
   WITH A DO
   BEGIN
      MBPROM(XTGMP[RMPP,JNTM]);           (* UPDATE SCORE *)
      NBORD[RMFR] := XTGMP[RMPP,JNTM];
   END;
END;  (* PROMOT *)


PROCEDURE CREATE;                         (* CREATE GLOBAL DATA BASE *)

VAR
   INRS : RS;                             (* SCRATCH BIT BOARD *)
   INTM : TM;                             (* COLOR INDEX *)
   INTP : TP;                             (* PIECE INDEX *)
   INTQ : TQ;                             (* CASTLE TYPE INDEX *)
   INTS : TS;                             (* SQUARE INDEX *)

BEGIN
   WITH BOARD DO
   BEGIN

      JNTM := AW+1;                       (* INITIALIZE MOVES STACK
                                             POINTER *)

      JNTK := AK;                         (* PLY INDEX *)
      JNTM := RBTM;                       (* SIDE TO MOVE *)

      NODES := 0;                         (* INITIALIZE TOTAL NODES *)

      LINDX[JNTK] := JNTM;                (* MOVES ARRAY LIMIT *)
      SRCHM[JNTK] := HQ;                  (* SEARCH MODE *)

      FOR INTS := AS TO ZS DO
      BEGIN
         NEWRS(ATKFR[INTS]);              (* CLEAR ATTACKS FROM *)
         NEWRS(ATKTO[INTS]);              (* CLEAR ATTACKS TO *)
         NBORD[INTS] := MT;               (* CLEAR LOOKAHEAD BOARD *)
      END;

      NEWRS(ALLOC[JNTK]);                 (* CLEAR ALL PIECE LOCATIONS *)

      FOR INTP := LP TO MT DO
         NEWRS(TPLOC[INTP]);              (* CLEAR PIECE LOCATIONS *)

      FOR INTM := LITE TO NONE DO
      BEGIN
         NEWRS(TMLOC[INTM]);              (* CLEAR COLOR LOCATIONS *)
         NEWRS(ALATK[INTM]);              (* CLEAR COLOR ATTACKS *)
      END;

      MBTOT := 0;
      MBPWN[LITE] := C;
      MBPWN[DARK] := 0;
      MBLTE := 0;
```

```
      FOR INTS := AS TO ZS DO
         IF RBIS[INTS] <> MT THEN
            BEGIN
               ADDLOC(INTS,RBIS[INTS]);
               MBTPAC(RBIS[INTS]);
            END
         ELSE
            SETRS(TPLOC[MT],INTS);

      MBEVAL;                             (* EVALUATE MATERIAL *)

      CPYRS(INRS,ALLOC[JNTK]);            (* COPY BIT BOARD OF ALL
                                             PIECES *)

      WHILE NXTTS(INRS,INTS) DO
         ADDATK(INTS);                    (* ADD ATTACKS OF ALL PIECES *)

      NEWRS(CSTAT[JNTK]);                 (* INITIALIZE CASTLING SQUARES *)
      FOR INTQ := LS TO DL DO
         IF INTQ IN RBSQ THEN
            IORRS(CSTAT[JNTK],CSTAT[JNTK],XSQS[INTQ]);

      NEWRS(ENPAS[JNTK]);                 (* INITIALIZE ENPASSANT SQUARE *)
      IF RBTS >= 0 THEN
         SETRS(ENPAS[JNTK],RBTS);

      CPYRS(GENPN[JNTK],TPLOC[XTUMP[EP,JNTM]]);
      NOTRS(GENTO[JNTK],TMLOC[JNTM]);
      NOTRS(INRS,GENPN[JNTK]);
      ANDRS(GENFR[JNTK],TMLOC[JNTM],INRS);
   END;
END;  (* CREATE *)


PROCEDURE DNDATE                          (* DOWNDATE DATA BASE TO BACK
                                             OUT A MOVE *)
   (A:RM);                                (* THE MOVE TO RETRACT *)
VAR
   INTS : TS;                             (* SCRATCH *)
   INTR : TR;                             (* ROOK RANK FOR CASTLING *)
   INTF : TF;                             (* ROOK FILE FOR CASTLING *)

   RKFR : TS;                             (* ROOK FROM SQUARE *)
   RKTO : TS;                             (* ROOK TO SQUARE *)

BEGIN
   WITH A DO
   BEGIN
      CASE ORD(RMCA)*4 + ORD(RMAC)*2 + ORD(RMPR) OF
         0:  (* ORDINARY MOVE *)
            RTRKIT(A);
         1:  (* PAWN MOVE AND PROMOTE *)
            BEGIN
               PAWNIT(A);
               RTRKIT(A);
            END;
         2:  (* MISCELLANEOUS ACS *)
            IF RMOO THEN
            BEGIN  (* CASTLE *)
               IF RMQS THEN
                  INTF := F1            (* ROOK ON QUEEN ROOK FILE *)
               ELSE
                  INTF := F8;           (* ROOK ON KING ROOK FILE *)
               INTR := XTSR[RMFR];      (* ROOK FILE *)
               RKFR := XTRFS[INTR,INTF];  (* ROOK FROM SQUARE *)
               RKTO := (RMFR+RMTO) DIV 2;  (* ROOK TO SQUARE *)
               ADDLOC(RKFR,NBORD[RKTO]);  (* REPLACE ROOK *)
               DELATK(RKTO);
               PRPATK(RKTO);
               ADDATK(RKFR);
               RTRKIT(A);               (* RETRACT KING MOVE *)
            END
            ELSE  (* NOT CASTLE *)
               RTRKIT(A);
         3:; (* NULL MOVE *)
         4:  (* CAPTURE *)
            IF RMEP THEN
            BEGIN  (* CAPTURE ENPASSANT *)
               INTS := XTRFS[XTSR[RMFR],XTSF[RMTO]];
               ADDLOC(INTS,RMCP);
               CUTATK(INTS);
               ADDATK(INTS);
               RTRKIT(A);               (* RETRACT PAWN MOVE *)
               MBTPAC(NBORD[INTS]);     (* ADD PIECE TO SCORE *)
            END
            ELSE  (* CAPTURE NOT ENPASSANT *)
               GAINIT(A);
         5:  (* CAPTURE AND PROMOTE *)
            BEGIN
               PAWNIT(A);               (* UNPROMOTE *)
               GAINIT(A);               (* UNCAPTURE *)
            END;
         6:  (* CAPTURE ACS *)
            GAINIT(A);                   (* UNCAPTURE *)
         7:  (* CAPTURE ROOK ACS, PROMOTE *)
            BEGIN
               PAWNIT(A);
               GAINIT(A);
            END;
      END;
      JNTM := LINDX[JNTK];                (* RESET MOVE GENERATION
                                             POINTER *)
      JNTK := JNTK-1;                     (* BACK UP PLY INDEX *)
      JNTM := OTHER[JNTM];                (* SWITCH SIDE TO MOVE *)
   END;
END;  (* DNDATE *)


FUNCTION UPDATE                           (* UPDATE DATA BASE FOR A MOVE *)
   (VAR A:RM)                             (* THE MOVE *)
   :TB;                                   (* RETURNS TRUE IF MOVE IS
                                             LEGAL *)

VAR
   INRS : RS;                             (* SCRATCH *)
   IMRS : RS;                             (* SCRATCH *)
   INTS : TS;                             (* SCRATCH *)
   INTF : TF;                             (* ROOK FILE FOR CASTLING *)
```

```
        INTR : TR;                          (* ROOK RANK FOR CASTLING *)
        RKTO : TS;                          (* ROOK DESTINATION SQUARE *)
        RKFR : TS;                          (* ROOK ORIGIN SQUARE *)
BEGIN
  WITH A DO
  BEGIN
    JNTK := JNTK+1;                         (* ADVANCE PLY INDEX *)
    NEWRS(ENPAS[JNTK]);                     (* CLEAR ENPASSANT BIT BOARD *)
    CPYRS(CSTAT[JNTK],CSTAT[JNTK-1]);       (* INITIALIZE CASTLE STATUS *)
    CPYRS(ALLOC[JNTK],ALLOC[JNTK-1]);       (* INITIALIZE ALL LOCATIONS *)
    MBVAL[JNTK] := MBVAL[JNTK-1];           (* INITIALIZE MATERIAL SCORE *)
    LINDX[JNTK] := JNTW;                    (* MOVES ARRAY LIMIT *)
    CASE ORD(RMCA)*4 + ORD(RMAC)*2 + ORD(RMPR) OF
      0:  (* ORDINARY MOVE *)
          IF RMEP THEN
            BEGIN                           (* PAWN MOVE 2 SPACES *)
              SFTRS(INRS,XRSS(RMTO),S1);
              SFTRS(INRS,XRSS(RMTO),S3);
              IORRS(INRS,INRS,IMRS);        (* SQUARES NEXT TO DESTINATION *)
              ANDRS(INRS,INRS,TPLOC[XTUMP[EP,OTHER[JNTK]]]);
                                            (* INTERSECT WITH ENEMY PAWNS *)
              IF NOT NULRS(INRS) THEN
                SETRS(ENPAS[JNTK],(RMTO+RMFR) DIV 2);
                                            (* SET ENPASSANT SQUARE *)
              MOVEIT(A);                     (* MOVE PAWN *)
            END
          ELSE
            MOVEIT(A);                       (* MOVE PIECE *)
      1:  (* MOVE AND PROMOTE *)
          BEGIN
            PROMOT(A);                      (* PROMOTE PAWN *)
            MOVEIT(A);                       (* MOVE PROMOTED PIECE *)
          END;
      2:  (* MISCELLANEOUS ACS *)
          BEGIN
            IF RMOO THEN
              BEGIN  (* CASTLE *)
                IF RMQS THEN
                  INTF := F1                (* ROOK ON QUEEN ROOK FILE *)
                ELSE
                  INTF := F8;               (* ROOK ON KING ROOK FILE *)
                INTR := XTSR(RMFR);         (* ROOK ON KINGS RANK *)
                RKFR := XTRFS(INTR,INTF);   (* ROOK ORIGIN SQUARE *)
                RKTO := (RMFR+RMTO) DIV 2;  (* ROOK DESTINATION SQUARE *)
                ANDRS(CSTAT[JNTK],CSTAT[JNTK],XNRS[INTR]);
                                            (* DISALLOW FURTHER CASTLING
                                               BY THIS SIDE *)
                ADDLOC(RKTO,NBORD[RKFR]);   (* PUT ROOK ON NEW SQUARE *)
                ADDATK(RKTO);               (* ADD ITS ATTACKS *)
                DELATK(RKFR);               (* DELETE FROM ORIGINAL SQUARE *)
                MOVEIT(A);                   (* MOVE KING *)
              END
            ELSE   (* NOT CASTLE *)
              BEGIN
                PROACS(A);                  (* PROCESS CASTLE STATUS MODS *)
                MOVEIT(A);                   (* MOVE TO OR FROM KING OR ROOK
                                               SQUARE *)
              END;
          END;
      3:  (* NULL MOVE *)
      4:  (* CAPTURE *)
          IF RMEP THEN
            BEGIN  (* CAPTURE ENPASSANT *)
              INTS := XTRFS[XTSR(RMFR),XTSF(RMTO)];
                                            (* CAPTURED PAWN SQUARE *)
              MBCAPT(NBORD[INTS]);          (* UPDATE SCORE *)
              DELATK(INTS);                 (* DELETE CAPTURED PAWN
                                               ATTACKS *)
              PRPATK(INTS);                 (* PROPAGATE ATTACKS THROUGH
                                               PAWN *)
              MOVEIT(A);                     (* MOVE CAPTURING PAWN *)
            END
          ELSE   (* CAPTURE NOT ENPASSANT *)
            LOSEIT(A);                       (* PROCESS CAPTURE *)
      5:  (* CAPTURE AND PROMOTE *)
          BEGIN
            PROMOT(A);                      (* PROMOTE PAWN *)
            LOSEIT(A);                       (* PROCESS CAPTURE WITH PROMOTED
                                               PIECE *)
          END;
      6:  (* CAPTURE ACS *)
          BEGIN
            PROACS(A);                      (* PROCESS CASTLE STATUS MODS *)
            LOSEIT(A);                       (* PROCESS ROOK CAPTURE *)
          END;
      7:  (* CAPTURE ROOK ACS, PROMOTE *)
          BEGIN
            PROMOT(A);                      (* PROMOTE PAWN *)
            PROACS(A);                      (* CHANGE CASTLE STATUS *)
            LOSEIT(A);                       (* PROCESS ROOK CAPTURE *)
          END;
    END;

    (* INITIALIZE MOVE GENERATION *)

    JNTM := OTHER[JNTM];                     (* SWITCH SIDE TO MOVE *)
    CPYRS(GENPN[JNTK],TPLOC[XTUMP[EP,JNTM]]);
    NOTRS(GENTO[JNTK],TMLOC[JNTM]);
    NOTRS(INRS,GENPN[JNTK]);
    ANDRS(GENFR[JNTK],TMLOC[JNTM],INRS);

    (* DETERMINE IF MOVE LEAVES KING IN CHECK, OR MOVES
       KING INTO CHECK *)

    ANDRS(INRS,TPLOC[XTUMP[EK,JNTM]],ALATK[OTHER[JNTM]]);
    RMCH := NOT NULRS(INRS);
    ANDRS(INRS,TPLOC[XTUMP[EK,OTHER[JNTM]]],ALATK[JNTM]);
    RMIL := NOT NULRS(INRS);
    UPDATE := NOT RMIL;
    IF NOT RMIL THEN                         (* COUNT LEGAL MOVES *)
      MVSEL[JNTK-1] := MVSEL[JNTK-1] + 1;

    (* INITIALIZE MOVE SEARCHING *)

    SRCHM[JNTK] := H1;
```

```
        NODES := NODES+1;                   (* COUNT NODES SEARCHED *)
      END;
END;  (* UPDATE *)


PROCEDURE GENONE                            (* STACK ONE GENERATED MOVE *)
    (A:TT;                                  (* FROM SQUARE *)
     B:TS);                                 (* TO SQUARE *)
VAR
  INRS : RS;                                (* SCRATCH *)
BEGIN
  WITH MOVES[JNTW] DO
  BEGIN
    RMFR := A;                              (* FROM SQUARE *)
    RMTO := B;                              (* TO SQUARE *)
    RMCP := NBORD[B];                       (* CAPTURED PIECE *)
    RMCA := (NBORD[B] <> MT);               (* CAPTURE *)
    IORRS(INRS,XRSS[A],XRSS[B]);
    ANDRS(INRS,INRS,CSTAT[JNTK]);
    RMAC := NOT NULRS(INRS);                (* AFFECTS CASTLE STATUS *)
    RMCH := FALSE;                          (* CHECK *)
    RMMT := FALSE;                          (* MATE *)
    RMIL := FALSE;                          (* ILLEGAL *)
    RMSU := FALSE;                          (* SEARCHED *)
    RMPR := FALSE;                          (* PROMOTION *)
    RMOO := FALSE;                          (* CASTLE *)
    RMEP := FALSE;                          (* ENPASSANT *)
  END;
  VALUE[JNTW] := 0;                         (* CLEAR VALUE *)
  IF JNTW < ZW THEN
    JNTW := JNTW+1;                         (* ADVANCE MOVES STACK POINTER *)
END;  (* GENONE *)


PROCEDURE PWNPRO;                           (* GENERATE ALL PROMOTION
                                               MOVES *)
VAR
  INTG : TG;                                (* PROMOTION TYPE *)
BEGIN
  MOVES[JNTW-1].RMPR := TRUE;               (* SET PROMOTION *)
  MOVES[JNTW-1].RMPP := PQ;                 (* PROMOTE TO QUEEN FIRST *)
  FOR INTG := PR TO PB DO                   (* PROMOTE OTHER PROMOTIONS *)
  BEGIN
    MOVES[JNTW] := MOVES[JNTW-1];           (* COPY LAST MOVE *)
    MOVES[JNTW].RMPP := INTG;               (* CHANGE PROMOTE TO PIECE *)
    JNTW := JNTW+1;                         (* ADVANCE MOVE INDEX *)
  END;
END;  (* PWNPRO *)


PROCEDURE GENPWN                            (* GENERATE PAWN MOVES *)
    (A:RS;                                  (* PAWNS TO MOVE *)
     B:RS);                                 (* VALID DESTINATION SQUARES *)
VAR
  INRS, IMRS : RS;                          (* SCRATCH *)
  INTS : TS;                                (* DESTINATION SQUARE *)
BEGIN
  IF JNTM = LITE THEN
    BEGIN                                   (* WHITE PAWNS *)
      SFTRS(INRS,A,S2);                     (* ADVANCE ONE RANK *)
      ANDRS(INRS,TPLOC[MT],INRS);           (* ONLY TO EMPTY SQUARES *)
      CPYRS(IMRS,INRS);                     (* SAVE FOR 2 SQUARE MOVES *)
      ANDRS(INRS,B,INRS);                   (* ONLY VALID DESTINATION
                                               SQUARES *)
      WHILE NXTTS(INRS,INTS) DO
      BEGIN
        GENONE(XTLS[XTSL[INTS]-XTED[S2]],INTS);
                                            (* GENERATE SIMPLE PAWN MOVES *)
        IF INTS >= XTRFS[R8,F1] THEN
          PWNPRO;                           (* PROCESS PROMOTION *)
      END;
      ANDRS(INRS,IMRS,XRRS[R3]);            (* TAKE ONLY PAWNS ON THIRD *)
      SFTRS(INRS,INRS,S2);                  (* ADVANCE ONE MORE RANK *)
      ANDRS(INRS,INRS,TPLOC[MT]);           (* ONLY TO EMPTY SQUARES *)
      ANDRS(INRS,INRS,B);                   (* ONLY VALID DESTINATION
                                               SQUARES *)
      WHILE NXTTS(INRS,INTS) DO
      BEGIN
        GENONE(XTLS[XTSL[INTS]-2*XTED[S2]],INTS);
                                            (* GENERATE DOUBLE PAWN MOVES *)
        MOVES[JNTW-1].RMEP := TRUE;         (* FLAG AS TWO SQUARES *)
      END;

      SFTRS(INRS,A,B1);                     (* TRY CAPTURES TO THE LEFT *)
      IORRS(IMRS,TMLOC[OTHER[JNTM]],ENPAS[JNTK]);
                                            (* OPPONENT PIECES + EP SQUARE *)
      ANDRS(INRS,INRS,B);                   (* VALID DESTINATION SQUARES *)
      ANDRS(INRS,INRS,IMRS);               (* CAPTURE MOVES TO LEFT *)
      WHILE NXTTS(INRS,INTS) DO
      BEGIN
        GENONE(XTLS[XTSL[INTS]-XTED[B1]],INTS);
                                            (* GENERATE CAPTURE MOVE *)
        MOVES[JNTW-1].RMCA := TRUE;         (* FLAG CAPTURE *)
        MOVES[JNTW-1].RMEP := INRSTB(ENPAS[JNTK],INTS);
                                            (* FLAG ENPASSANT CAPTURE *)
        IF MOVES[JNTW-1].RMEP THEN
          MOVES[JNTW-1].RMCP := DP;         (* SET CAPTURED PIECE TYPE *)
        IF INTS >= XTRFS[R8,F1] THEN
          PWNPRO;                           (* PROCESS PROMOTION *)
      END;

      SFTRS(INRS,A,B2);                     (* TRY CAPTURES TO THE RIGHT *)
      IORRS(IMRS,TMLOC[OTHER[JNTM]],ENPAS[JNTK]);
                                            (* OPPONENT PIECES + EP SQUARE *)
      ANDRS(INRS,INRS,B);                   (* VALID DESTINATION SQUARES *)
      ANDRS(INRS,INRS,IMRS);               (* CAPTURE MOVES TO LEFT *)
      WHILE NXTTS(INRS,INTS) DO
      BEGIN
        GENONE(XTLS[XTSL[INTS]-XTED[B2]],INTS);
                                            (* GENERATE CAPTURE MOVE *)
```

```
      MOVES[JNTW-1].RMCA := TRUE;        (* FLAG CAPTURE *)
      MOVES[JNTW-1].RMEP := INRSTB(ENPAS[JNTK],INTS);
                                         (* FLAG ENPASSANT CAPTURE *)
      IF MOVES[JNTW-1].RMEP THEN
        MOVES[JNTW-1].RMCP := DP;        (* SET CAPTURED PIECE TYPE *)
      IF INTS >= XTRFS[R8,F1] THEN
        PWNPRO;                          (* PROCESS PROMOTION *)
    END;
  END
  ELSE
  BEGIN                                  (* BLACK PAWNS *)
    SFTRS(INRS,A,S4);                    (* ADVANCE ONE RANK *)
    ANDRS(INRS,TPLOC[MT],INRS);          (* ONLY TO EMPTY SQUARES *)
    CPYRS(IMRS,INRS);                    (* SAVE FOR 2 SQUARE MOVES *)
    ANDRS(INRS,B,INRS);                  (* ONLY VALID DESTINATION
                                            SQUARES *)
    WHILE NXTTS(INRS,INTS) DO
    BEGIN
      GENONE(XTLS[XTSL[INTS]-XTED[S4]],INTS);
                                         (* GENERATE SIMPLE PAWN MOVES *)
      IF INTS <= XTRFS[R1,F8] THEN
        PWNPRO;                          (* PROCESS PROMOTION *)
    END;
    ANDRS(IMRS,IMRS,XRRS[R6]);           (* TAKE ONLY PAWNS ON THIRD *)
    SFTRS(INRS,IMRS,S4);                 (* ADVANCE ONE MORE RANK *)
    ANDRS(INRS,INRS,TPLOC[MT]);          (* ONLY TO EMPTY SQUARES *)
    ANDRS(INRS,INRS,B);                  (* ONLY VALID DESTINATION
                                            SQUARES *)
    WHILE NXTTS(INRS,INTS) DO
    BEGIN
      GENONE(XTLS[XTSL[INTS]-2*XTED[S4]],INTS);
                                         (* GENERATE DOUBLE PAWN MOVES *)
      MOVES[JNTW-1].RMEP := TRUE;        (* FLAG AS TWO SQUARES *)
    END;

    SFTRS(INRS,A,B3);                    (* TRY CAPTURES TO THE LEFT *)
    IORRS(IMRS,TMLOC[OTHER[JNTM]],ENPAS[JNTK]);
                                         (* OPPONENT PIECES + EP SQUARE *)
    ANDRS(INRS,IMRS,B);                  (* VALID DESTINATION SQUARES *)
    ANDRS(INRS,INRS,IMRS);               (* CAPTURE MOVES TO LEFT *)
    WHILE NXTTS(INRS,INTS) DO
    BEGIN
      GENONE(XTLS[XTSL[INTS]-XTED[B3]],INTS);
                                         (* GENERATE PAWN CAPTURE MOVE *)
      MOVES[JNTW-1].RMCA := TRUE;        (* FLAG CAPTURE *)
      MOVES[JNTW-1].RMEP := INRSTB(ENPAS[JNTK],INTS);
                                         (* FLAG ENPASSANT CAPTURE *)
      IF MOVES[JNTW-1].RMEP THEN
        MOVES[JNTW-1].RMCP := LP;        (* SET CAPTURED PIECE TYPE *)
      IF INTS <= XTRFS[R1,F8] THEN
        PWNPRO;                          (* PROCESS PROMOTION *)
    END;

    SFTRS(INRS,A,B4);                    (* TRY CAPTURES TO THE RIGHT *)
    IORRS(IMRS,TMLOC[OTHER[JNTM]],ENPAS[JNTK]);
                                         (* OPPONENT PIECES + EP SQUARE *)
    ANDRS(INRS,IMRS,B);                  (* VALID DESTINATION SQUARES *)
    ANDRS(INRS,INRS,IMRS);               (* CAPTURE MOVES TO LEFT *)
    WHILE NXTTS(INRS,INTS) DO
    BEGIN
      GENONE(XTLS[XTSL[INTS]-XTED[B4]],INTS);
                                         (* GENERATE PAWN CAPTURE MOVE *)
      MOVES[JNTW-1].RMCA := TRUE;        (* FLAG CAPTURE *)
      MOVES[JNTW-1].RMEP := INRSTB(ENPAS[JNTK],INTS);
                                         (* FLAG ENPASSANT CAPTURE *)
      IF MOVES[JNTW-1].RMEP THEN
        MOVES[JNTW-1].RMCP := LP;        (* SET CAPTURED PIECE TYPE *)
      IF INTS <= XTRFS[R1,F8] THEN
        PWNPRO;                          (* PROCESS PROMOTION *)
    END;
  END;
END;  (* GENPWN *)


PROCEDURE GENFSL                         (* GENERATE ALL MOVES FROM
                                            A SET OF SQUARES *)
  (A:RS);                                (* ORIGIN SET OF SQUARES *)

VAR
  INRS : RS;                             (* OUTER LOOP BIT BOARD *)
  IMRS : RS;                             (* INNER LOOP BIT BOARD *)
  IPRS : RS;                             (* PAWN ORIGIN BIT BOARD *)
  INTS : TS;                             (* OUTER LOOP SQUARE NUMBER *)
  IMTS : TS;                             (* INNER LOOP SQUARE NUMBER *)

BEGIN
  ANDRS(INRS,A,GENFR[JNTK]);             (* ONLY VALID FROM SQUARES *)
  NOTRS(INRS,A);
  ANDRS(GENFR[JNTK],GENFR[JNTK],IMRS);   (* REMOVE ORIGIN SQUARES *)
  ANDRS(IPRS,A,GENPN[JNTK]);             (* VALID PAWN FROM SQUARES *)
  ANDRS(GENPN[JNTK],GENPN[JNTK],IMRS);   (* REMOVE PAWNS *)

  WHILE NXTTS(INRS,INTS) DO              (* LOOP THROUGH ORIGINS *)
  BEGIN
    ANDRS(IMRS,ATKFR[INTS],GENTO[JNTK]);
                                         (* GET UNPROCESSED DESTINATION
                                            SQUARES *)
    WHILE NXTTS(IMRS,IMTS) DO            (* LOOP THROUGH DESTINATIONS *)
    GENONE(INTS,IMTS);                   (* GENERATE MOVE *)
  END;
  GENPWN(IPRS,GENTO[JNTK]);              (* GENERATE PAWN MOVES *)
END;  (* GETFSL *)


PROCEDURE GENTSL                         (* GENERATE ALL MOVES TO A
                                            SET OF SQUARES *)
  (A:RS);                                (* TARGET SET OF SQUARES *)

VAR
  INRS : RS;                             (* OUTER LOOP BIT BOARD *)
  IMRS : RS;                             (* INNER LOOP BIT BOARD *)
  IPRS : RS;                             (* PAWN BIT BOARD *)
  INTS : TS;                             (* OUTER LOOP SQUARE NUMBER *)
```

```
  IMTS : TS;                             (* INNER LOOP SQUARE NUMBER *)
BEGIN
  ANDRS(INRS,A,GENTO[JNTK]);             (* ONLY VALID TO SQUARES *)
  NOTRS(IMRS,A);
  ANDRS(GENTO[JNTK],GENTO[JNTK],IMRS);   (* REMOVE DESTINATION SQUARES *)
  CPYRS(IPRS,INRS);                      (* SAVE FOR PAWN MOVES *)

  WHILE NXTTS(INRS,INTS) DO              (* LOOP THROUGH DESTINATIONS *)
  BEGIN
    ANDRS(IMRS,ATKTO[INTS],GENFR[JNTK]);
                                         (* GET PIECES OF SIDE TO MOVE *)
    WHILE NXTTS(IMRS,IMTS) DO            (* LOOP THROUGH ORIGINS *)
    GENONE(IMTS,INTS);                   (* GENERATE MOVE *)
  END;
  GENPWN(GENPN[JNTK],IPRS);              (* GENERATE PAWN MOVES *)
END;  (* GENTSL *)


PROCEDURE GENCAP;                        (* GENERATE CAPTURE MOVES *)

VAR
  INRS : RS;                             (* DESTINATION SQUARES *)

BEGIN
  IORRS(INRS,ENPAS[JNTK],TMLOC[OTHER[JNTM]]);
  GENTSL(INRS);                          (* GENERATE MOVES TO
                                            ENEMY SQUARES *)
END;  (* GENCAP *)


PROCEDURE GENCAS;                        (* GENERATE CASTLE MOVES *)

VAR
  INTQ : TQ;                             (* CASTLE TYPE INDEX *)
  IMRS : RS;                             (* OCCUPIED SQUARES TEST *)
  IMRS : RS;                             (* ATTACKED SQUARES TEST *)

BEGIN
  FOR INTQ := XTMQ[JNTM] TO SUCC(XTMQ[JNTM]) DO
  IF INRSTB(CSTAT[JNTK],XTQS[INTQ]) THEN
                                         (* IF CASTLING IS LEGAL *)
  BEGIN
    ANDRS(INRS,XRQSO[INTQ],ALLOC[JNTK]); (* CHECK OCCUPIED SQUARES *)
    ANDRS(IMRS,XRQSA[INTQ],ALATK[OTHER[JNTM]]);
                                         (* CHECK ATTACKED SQUARES *)
    IF NULRS(INRS) AND NULRS(IMRS) THEN
                                         (* IF CASTLING IS LEGAL AND
                                            POSSIBLE *)
    BEGIN
      MOVES[JNTW] := XRQM[INTQ];         (* GENERATE CASTLING MOVE *)
      VALUE[JNTW] := G;
      JNTW := JNTW+1;
    END;
  END;
END;  (* GENCAS *)


PROCEDURE GENALL;                        (* GENERATE ALL LEGAL MOVES *)

BEGIN
  GENFSL(ALLOC[JNTK]);                   (* GENERATE SIMPLE MOVES *)
  GENCAS;                                (* GENERATE CASTLE MOVES *)
END;  (* GENALL *)


PROCEDURE LSTMOV;                        (* LIST LEGAL PLAYERS MOVES *)

VAR
  INTW : TW;                             (* MOVES INDEX *)

BEGIN
  CREATE;                                (* CREATE DATA BASE *)
  GENALL;                                (* GENERATE ALL MOVES *)
  FOR INTW := AW+1 TO JNTW-1 DO
  BEGIN
    IF UPDATE(MOVES[INTW]) THEN;         (* SET ILLEGAL FLAG *)
    ONDATE(MOVES[INTW]);
  END;
END;  (* LSTMOV *)


PROCEDURE THEMOV;                        (* MAKE THE MOVE FOR REAL *)
  (A:RM);                                (* THE MOVE TO MAKE *)

VAR
  INTB : TB;                             (* SCRATCH *)
  INRS : RS;                             (* SCRATCH *)
  INTQ : TQ;                             (* CASTLE TYPE INDEX *)
  INTS : TS;                             (* SCRATCH *)

BEGIN
  LSTMV := A;                            (* SAVE AS PREVIOUS MOVE *)
  INTB := UPDATE(A);                     (* UPDATE THE DATA BASE *)
  WITH BOARD DO                          (* AND COPY ALL THE RELEVANT DATA
                                            BACK DOWN *)
  BEGIN
    RBTM := JNTM;                        (* SIDE TO MOVE *)
    CPYRS(INRS,ENPAS[JNTK]);
    IF NXTTS(INRS,INTS) THEN             (* FIND ENPASSANT SQUARE *)
      RBTS := INTS
    ELSE
      RBTS := AT;
    IF JNTM = DARK THEN
      RBTI := RBTI+1;                    (* ADVANCE MOVE NUMBER *)
    FOR INTQ := LS TO DL DO
      IF INRSTB(CSTAT[JNTK],XTQS[INTQ]) THEN
        RBSQ := RBSQ+[INTQ]              (* CASTLE LEGAL *)
      ELSE
        RBSQ := RBSQ-[INTQ];             (* CASTLE NOT LEGAL *)
    FOR INTS := AS TO ZS DO
      RBIS[INTS] := NBORD[INTS];         (* COPY POSITION *)
  END;
END;  (* THEMOV *)
```

Creating Chess Player

Part 3: Chess 0.5 (continued)

Peter Frey

Larry Atkin

In Part 3 we conclude the listing and commentary of Chess 0.5 begun in Part 2. The program was written by Larry Atkin, who is coauthor with David Slate of the world championship chess program, Chess 4.6. The program is readily adaptable to personal computers having Pascal systems such as the UCSD Pascal project software. Part 4 concludes the series with a discussion of chess strategy and tactics.

Evaluating Terminal Positions

Another important aspect of any chess program is the function which provides a static evaluation of terminal positions in the look-ahead tree. In the present program, this routine also doubles as a preliminary scoring function for sorting moves at the first ply, at the beginning of the look-ahead search. Since the evaluation function is used repetitively in the search, efficiency demands that it be carefully engineered. We have left this task as an exercise for the reader. Our function presently includes only a few basic essentials.

The most important feature is material. We employ essentially the same function for this that is used by Chess 4.5. A trade-down bonus is also incorporated, ie: trade pieces but not pawns when ahead in material. A second feature which is considered is piece mobility. The mobility of Knights and Bishops is weighted more heavily than that for Rooks and Queens. Special credit is given to a King which is located in one of the four corner squares in each corner of the board, ie: 16 squares total. This encour-

ages early castling. Pawn structure is considered by providing a bonus for advancing the pawns in the four center files, for having a pawn near the King, and for having a pawn adjacent to or defended by another pawn. This indirectly penalizes isolated or backward pawns. There is a direct penalty if the square in front of a pawn is occupied. The position of the Rooks is considered by providing a bonus for placing a Rook on the seventh rank and for attacking another Rook of the same color (ie: doubled Rooks). The executive routine for these assessments is EVALU8.

The Look-Ahead Procedure

The look-ahead procedure is controlled by an executive routine called SEARCH. Several subprocedures are also defined which handle specific tasks. NEWBST keeps track of the move which is currently thought to be best, and dynamically reorders the moves at the first ply level each time a new best-move is selected. MINMAX determines whether the move under consideration will produce an α-β cutoff. SCOREM is called into action when the program can find no legal moves at a node. It determines whether the position should be scored as a checkmate or as a stalemate. SELECT is responsible for move ordering at each node. It determines whether there are any more moves to be searched and if so, makes sure that they are generated in the correct order (ie: captures, killers, castling moves, and then the remaining moves).

SEARCH incorporates a number of important features which make the look-ahead search more efficient. These include staged move generation, preliminary ordering scores, setting a narrow α-β window at the beginning of the search, conducting the search in an iterative fashion, and dynamically recording moves at the first ply as the search proceeds. Because of these features, the full-width search takes a long time instead of taking forever.

User Commands

For the user's convenience, the program should be able to respond to a few simple commands. Inputs to the program are processed by a lengthy routine, READER, which has many component subprocedures. The translation of the input string is handled by a group of routines: RDRERR, RDRGNT, RDRSFT, RDRCMP, RDLINE, RDRMOV and RDRNUM. Each of the commands is executed by a separate routine.

When the human player wishes to terminate the game before it has reached its conclusion (eg: when he is hopelessly lost and does not want to stay around to be crushed), he can simply type an END command and the ENDCMD routine will terminate the program. If the user simply wishes to start a new game, he can type INIT and the INICMD routine will set up for a new game. If the user would like to set up a specific position from the previous game or some other game, he can call the BOACMD routine, which will set up any position he desires. To use this instruction, the pieces are designated in the standard way (eg: K, Q, R, B, N and P) and the colors are designated by L for light and D for dark. The board is described by starting at the lower lefthand corner and listing, row by row, the 64 squares. Numbers are used to represent consecutive empty squares. The command to set up the position after 1. P-K4, P-K4, 2. N-KB3, N-QB3 is: BOARD, LRNBQKB1 RPPPP1PPP5N24P34DP33N4PPPP1PPPR1B QKBNR.

If the human player is lazy or simply wishes to test the program, he or she can type GO and the machine will select a move. By repeatedly typing GO the user can sit back and watch the machine play against itself. The routine that handles this is GONCMD. To specify a value for selected program parameter variables, the player can use LETCMD. For example, the amount of time the machine spends calculating a move can be controlled by specifying a limit for the number of nodes to be searched. The command LET FNODEL = 1000 will cause the machine to set a target value of 1000 for the number of nodes to be searched. In this case it will not start another iteration if it has already searched 1000 nodes. If the user is confused about the current board configuration, the command PRINT will activate PRICMD which calls PRINTB for a representation (8 by 8 array) of the board. For diagnostic purposes the user can also ask for other information. The routine PAMCMD is activated by PB and provides an 8 by 8 attack map for each of the 64 squares. The routine POPCMD is activated by PO and gives information concerning the side to move (White or Black), the en passant status after the last move, the present castle status and the move number. If the user types PM, the routine PMVCMD will provide a list of all moves which are legal for the side to move in the current position. The command PL activates PLECMD which prints the value of a designated variable; for example, the user can determine the present limit for the number of nodes to be searched by typing PL FNODEL.

The user also has control over several switches. He can ask the machine to repeat (echo) each entry, to pause after 20 lines of output, and to reply automatically each time the opponent enters a move. These switches are set by the switch commands (eg: SW EC OFF), and are processed by SWICMD. If the user wishes to manually alter one or more of the status conditions (eg: side to move, move number, en passant, castling), this can be done by activating STACMD.

Notes on Notation

The program also processes standard chess notation. This is not strictly necessary. Many programs use their own convention for entering and reporting moves. A common procedure is to denote the squares using a number (1 through 8) for each row and a letter (A through H) for each column. A move is defined by listing the present square of the piece and then the destination square. For example, the common opening move, P-K4, would be E2E4. Moving the White Knight on the kingside from its original square to KB3 would be G1F3. This convention works nicely but it forces an experienced chess player to learn a new system. Most would prefer standard chess notation.

Because there are multiple ways to express the same move in standard notation, the translation routine needs to be fairly sophisticated. Consider a position in which the White Queen's Rook is on its original square and the neighboring Knight and Bishop have been moved. A move which places the Rook on the Queen Bishop file can be designated as R-B1, R-QB1, R/1-B1, R/1-QB1, R/R1-B1, or R/R1-QB1. It is important that the program recognize that each of these character strings represents the same move. How is this done?

One way is to have the machine generate a list of all legal moves and then compare each of these with the move entered by the player. If his move matches one on the list, that move is noted. The rest of the list is then checked and if no more matches are found, the noted move is assumed to be the correct one. If no match is found, the machine prints "illegal move." If a second match is found (eg: P-B3 matches both P-KB3 and P-QB3), the machine prints "ambiguous move." The process of translating the opponent's move into machine compatible form and checking its legality or ambiguity is done by YRMOVE. The process of translating the machine's move into standard notation is handled by MYMOVE. Both of these procedures call MINENG, which is responsible for constructing the appropriating character strings.

Final Thoughts

This completes our listing of our demonstration chess program. Despite the program's length, there are many desirable features which have been omitted. The reader with an interest in chess and programming should use this listing as a starting point for developing a program. The time required for move calculation can be reduced by writing machine dependent code for some of the frequently used routines. There are also features which can be added to improve the level of play.

One useful addition would be an opening library. An effective technique for this is described by Slate and Atkin in their chapter in *Chess Skill in Man and Machine* (P W Frey, editor, Springer-Verlag, New York, 1977). An opening library provides the user with a challenging set of opening moves and directs the game into situations which are familiar to the experienced chess player. By including various options at the early choice points and using a random selection procedure, the programmer can insure that the machine will not always select the same move sequence. The programmer can also give the user the option of specifying a particular opening against which he would like to practice. For important matches, the programmer can prepare surprise openings for the machine in order to gain a psychological edge on the opponent.

A second and somewhat more challenging project would be to develop a transposition table for the program. This requires the availability of unused memory (at least 8 K bytes and preferably 16 K or 32 K bytes), an efficient hashing scheme, and a set of decision rules to select among positions when a collision occurs (ie: two positions hash to the same address in the table). Another problem is that the use of a staged evaluation process and the α-β algorithm often provides an imprecise evaluation score (ie: the machine has determined that a position was not optimal but has not invested the time to find out exactly how bad it was). If the programmer succeeds with the transposition table, however, move calculation will take 30 to 50 per cent less time in most middle game positions and 60 to 90 per cent less time in many end game positions.

A third area for improvement is the evaluation function. Our program presently has only a rudimentary function. The reader should compare it with the one used by Chess 4.5 which is described in detail by Slate and Atkin. Their evaluation function provides an excellent starting point for revising our present function. In part 4 we will discuss the advantages of using a conditional evaluation function, ie: one that changes depending on the stage of the game and on the presence of special features. One implementation of this strategy is the special end game program described by Monroe Newborn in *Chess Skill in Man and Machine*.

It is appropriate for us to add two important disclaimers at this juncture. Although we have carefully tested each of the routines in the program and played several chess games, it is still possible that there are a few minor bugs in the program. If you find one, a letter to one of us or to BYTE would be appreciated. Secondly, our chess program was written primarily for pedagogical purposes. For this reason it is not a production program and does not run very efficiently. If you are the competitive type, our program should provide many useful ideas, but you should not expect it to compete successfully in tournament play unless you make extensive modifications and additions.

A chess program has a tendency to grow and change its personality as the programmer becomes more familiar with each of its many limitations. It provides a constant challenge for those of us who are too compulsive to tolerate obvious weaknesses. In fact one must be careful not to become totally obsessed with this project. We do not wish any of you to lose your job or your spouse because of a chess program.∎

```
PROCEDURE EVALU8;                        (* EVALUATE CURRENT POSITION *)

VAR
  INTV : TV;                             (* SCORE *)


  FUNCTION EVKING                        (* EVALUATE KING *)
    (A:RS;                               (* KING BIT BOARD *)
     B:RS):TV;                           (* FRIENDLY PAWN BIT BOARD *)

    VAR
      INTS : TS;                         (* SCRATCH *)
      INRS : RS;                         (* SCRATCH *)
      INTV : TV;                         (* SCRATCH *)

    BEGIN
      ANDRS(INRS,A,CORNR);
      IF NULRS(INRS) THEN                (* KING NOT IN CORNER *)
        INTV := 0
      ELSE
        INTV := FKSANQ;                  (* KING SAFELY IN CORNER *)

      INRS := A;
      IF NXTTS(INRS,INTS) THEN
      BEGIN
        ANDRS(INRS,ATKFR[INTS],B);       (* FIND PAWNS NEXT TO KING *)
        INTV := INTV + CNTRS(INRS)*FKPSHD;
                                         (* CREDIT EACH CLOSE PAWN *)
      END;

      EVKING := INTV;                    (* RETURN KING SCORE *)
    END; (* EVKING *)


  FUNCTION EVMOBL                        (* EVALUATE MOBILITY *)
    (A,B:TP):TV;                         (* PIECE TYPES TO EVALUATE *)

    VAR
      INRS : RS;                         (* SCRATCH *)
      INTS : TS;                         (* SCRATCH *)
      INTV : TV;                         (* SCRATCH *)

    BEGIN
      IORRS(INRS,TPLOC[A],TPLOC[B]);     (* MERGE PIECE TYPES *)
      INTV := 0;                         (* INITIALIZE COUNT *)
      WHILE NXTTS(INRS,INTS) DO          (* COUNT ATTACKS *)
        INTV := INTV + CNTRS(ATKFR[INTS]);
      EVMOBL := INTV;                    (* RETURN TOTAL ATTACKS *)
    END; (* EVMOBL *)


  FUNCTION EVPAWN                        (* EVALUATE PAWNS *)
    (A:RS;                               (* LOCATION OF PAWNS *)
     B:TE;                               (* PAWN FORWARD DIRECTION *)
     C:TR):TV;                           (* PAWN HOME RANK *)

    VAR
      INRS : RS;                         (* SCRATCH *)
      IMRS : RS;                         (* SCRATCH *)
      INTS : TS;                         (* SCRATCH *)
      INTV : TV;                         (* SCRATCH *)

    BEGIN
      SFTRS(INRS,A,S1);
      ANDRS(INRS,INRS,A);                (* BIT SET FOR SIDE BY SIDE *)
      INTV := CNTRS(INRS)*FPFLNX;        (* SCORE PHALANX *)

      SFTRS(INRS,A,B1);
      ANDRS(INRS,INRS,A);                (* BIT SET FOR PAWN DEFENSE *)
      INTV := INTV + CNTRS(INRS)*FPCONN; (* CREDIT CONNECTED PAWNS *)

      SFTRS(INRS,A,B2);
      ANDRS(INRS,INRS,A);
      INTV := INTV + CNTRS(INRS)*FPCONN; (* AND OTHER CONNECTED PAWNS *)

      SFTRS(INRS,A,B);                   (* MOVE FORWARD *)
      NOTRS(IMRS,TPLOC[MT]);             (* OCCUPIED SQUARES *)
      ANDRS(INRS,INRS,IMRS);             (* BLOCKED PAWNS *)
      INTV := INTV - CNTRS(INRS)*FPBLOK; (* PENALIZE BLOCKED PAWNS *)

      CPYRS(INRS,A);
      WHILE NXTTS(INRS,INTS) DO          (* FOR EACH PAWN *)
        INTV := INTV +(ABS(ORD(C)-ORD(XTSR[INTS])))*FPADCR[XTSF[INTS]];
                                         (* CREDIT PAWN ADVANCEMENT *)

      EVPAWN := INTV;                    (* RETURN PAWN SCORE *)
    END; (* EVPAWN *)


  FUNCTION EVROOK                        (* EVALUATE ROOKS *)
    (A:RS;                               (* ROOK LOCATIONS *)
     B:RS):TV;                           (* SEVENTH RANK *)

    VAR
      INTV : TV;                         (* SCRATCH *)
      INTI : TI;                         (* SCRATCH *)
      INTS : TS;                         (* SCRATCH *)
      INRS : RS;                         (* SCRATCH *)

    BEGIN
      INTV := 0;                         (* INITIALIZE *)
      INRS := A;
      IF NXTTS(INRS,INTS) THEN           (* LOCATE FIRST ROOK *)
      BEGIN
        ANDRS(INRS,A,ATKFR[INTS]);
```

```
        IF NOT NULRS(INRS) THEN          (* ROOK ATTACKS FRIENDLY ROOK *)
          INTV := INTV + FRDUBL;         (* GIVE DOUBLED ROOK CREDIT *)
      END;

      ANDRS(INRS,A,B);                   (* ROOKS ON SEVENTH *)
      INTI := CNTRS(INRS);
      EVROOK := INTV + INTI*INTI*FRK7TH; (* CREDIT ROOKS ON SEVENTH *)
    END; (* EVROOK *)


BEGIN
  IF XTMV[JNTM]*MBVAL[JNTK] + MAXPS <= BSTVL[JNTK-2] THEN
                                         (* MOVE WILL PRUNE ANYWAY *)
    INTV := XTMV[JNTM] * MBVAL[JNTK]
  ELSE
  BEGIN
    INTV :=( FWPAWN*(EVPAWN(TPLOC[LP],S2,R2)-EVPAWN(TPLOC[DP],S4,R7))
           + FWMINM*(EVMOBL(LB,LN)            -EVMOBL(DB,DN)
           + FWMAJM*(EVMOBL(LR,LQ)            -EVMOBL(DR,DQ)        )
           + FWROOK*(EVROOK(TPLOC[LR],XRRS[R7])
                      -EVROOK(TPLOC[DR],XRRS[R2])                   )
           + FWKING*(EVKING(TPLOC[LK],TPLOC[LP])
                      -EVKING(TPLOC[DK],TPLOC[DP])                  )
           ) DIV 64;
    MAXPS := MAX(MAXPS,ABS(INTV));
    INTV := XTMV[JNTM]*(MBVAL[JNTK]+INTV);
  END;
  IF SWTR THEN
  BEGIN
    WRITE(" EVALU8",JNTK,JNTW,INDEX[JNTK],INTV);
    PRIMOV(MOVES[INDEX[JNTK]]);
  END;
  VALUE[INDEX[JNTK]] := INTV;            (* RETURN SCORE *)
END; (* EVALU8 *)


FUNCTION SEARCH                          (* SEARCH LOOK-AHEAD TREE *)
  :TW;                                   (* RETURNS THE BEST MOVE *)

LABEL
  L1,                                    (* START NEW PLY *)
  L2,                                    (* TRY DIFFERENT FIRST MOVE *)
  L3,                                    (* FLOAT VALUE BACK UP *)
  L4,                                    (* FIND ANOTHER MOVE *)
  L5,                                    (* BACK UP A PLY *)
  L6;                                    (* EXIT SEARCH *)


  PROCEDURE NEWBST                       (* SAVE BEST MOVE INFORMATION *)
    (A:TK);                              (* PLY OF BEST MOVE *)

    VAR
      INTW : TW;                         (* MOVES INDEX *)
      INRM : RM;                         (* SCRATCH *)

    BEGIN
      BSTMV[A] := INDEX[A+1];            (* SAVE BEST MOVE *)
      IF A = AK THEN                     (* AT FIRST PLY *)
      BEGIN
        INRM := MOVES[BSTMV[A]];         (* SAVE BEST MOVE *)
        FOR INTW := BSTMV[A]-1 DOWNTO AW+1 DO
          MOVES[INTW+1] := MOVES[INTW];  (* MOVE OTHER MOVES DOWN *)
        MOVES[AW+1] := INRM;             (* PUT BEST AT BEGINNING *)
        BSTMV[AK] := AW+1;               (* POINTS TO BEST MOVE *)
      END
      ELSE
        IF NOT MOVES[BSTMV[A]].RMCA THEN
          KILLR[JNTK] := MOVES[BSTMV[A]];(* SAVE KILLER MOVE *)
    END; (* NEWBST *)


  FUNCTION MINMAX                        (* PERFORM MINIMAX OPERATION *)
    (A:TK)                               (* PLY TO MINIMAX AT *)
    :TB;                                 (* TRUE IF REFUTATION *)

    BEGIN
      MINMAX := FALSE;                   (* DEFAULT IS NO PRUNING *)
      IF SWTR THEN
        WRITE(" MINMAX",A,-BSTVL[A-1],BSTVL[A],-BSTVL[A+1]);
      IF -BSTVL[A+1] > BSTVL[A] THEN
      BEGIN
        BSTVL[A] := -BSTVL[A+1];
        NEWBST(A);                       (* SAVE BEST MOVE *)
        MINMAX := BSTVL[A+1] <= BSTVL[A-1];
                                         (* RETURN TRUE IF REFUTATION *)
        IF SWTR THEN
          WRITE(" NEW BEST. PRUNE: ",BSTVL[A+1] <= BSTVL[A-1]);
      END;
      IF SWTR THEN
        WRITELN;                         (* PRINT TRACE LINE *)
    END; (* MINMAX *)


  PROCEDURE SCOREM;                      (* SCORE MATE *)

  BEGIN
    MOVES[INDEX[JNTK]].RMMT := TRUE;     (* INDICATE MATE *)
    IF MOVES[INDEX[JNTK]].RMCH THEN      (* CHECKMATE *)
      VALUE[INDEX[JNTK]] :=  64*JNTK - ZV
    ELSE                                 (* STALEMATE *)
```

134

```
        VALUE[INDEX[JNTK]] := 0;
     IF SWTR THEN
        WRITELN(" SCOREM",JNTK,JNTW,INDEX[JNTK],VALUE[INDEX[JNTK]]);
END; (* SCOREM *)


FUNCTION SELECT                        (* SELECT NEXT MOVE TO SEARCH *)
   :TB;                                (* TRUE IF MOVE RETURNED *)

LABEL
   21,                                 (* NEW SEARCH MODE *)
   22;                                 (* EXIT SELECT *)

VAR
   INTB : TB;                          (* RETURN VALUE *)
   INTK : TK;                          (* SCRATCH *)
   INTW : TW;                          (* MOVE INDEX *)
   INTM : TM;                          (* SCRATCH *)
   INTV : TV;                          (* SCRATCH *)


   PROCEDURE SELDON;                   (* SELECT EXIT - DONE.
                                          CALLED WHEN NO FURTHER
                                          MOVES ARE TO BE SEARCHED
                                          FROM THIS POSITION.
                                          THE CURRENT POSITION MUST
                                          HAVE BEEN EVALUATED. *)

   BEGIN
     INTB := FALSE;                    (* RETURN NO MOVE SELECTED *)
     IF SWTR THEN
        WRITELN(" SELECT",JNTK," END.");
     GOTO 22;                          (* EXIT SELECT *)
   END; (* SELDON *)


   PROCEDURE SELMOV                    (* SELECT EXIT - SEARCH.
                                          CALLED WHEN A MOVE TO
                                          BE SEARCHED HAS BEEN
                                          FOUND. *)
      (A:TM);                          (* INDEX TO SELECTED MOVE *)

   BEGIN
     INTB := TRUE;                     (* RETURN MOVE SELECTED *)
     INDEX[JNTK+1] := A;               (* POINT TO SELECTED MOVE *)
     MOVES[A].RMSU := TRUE;            (* FLAG MOVE AS SEARCHED *)
     IF SWTR THEN
     BEGIN
        WRITE(" SELECT",JNTK,ORD(SRCHM[JNTK]),A);
        PRIMOV(MOVES[A]);
     END;
     GOTO 22;                          (* EXIT SELECT *)
   END; (* SELMOV *)


   PROCEDURE SELNXT                    (* SELECT EXIT - NEW MODE.
                                          CALLED WHEN A NEW SEARCH
                                          MODE IS TO BE SELECTED *)
      (A:TH);                          (* NEW SEARCH MODE *)

   BEGIN
     INDEX[JNTK+1] := LINDX[JNTK]-1;   (* RESET MOVES POINTER *)
     SRCHM[JNTK] := A;                 (* CHANGE SEARCH MODE *)
     GOTO 21;                          (* EXECUTE NEXT MODE *)
   END; (* SELNXT *)


   PROCEDURE SELANY;                   (* SEARCH ALREADY GENERATED
                                          AND NOT ALREADY SEARCHED *)

   VAR
     INTW : TW;                        (* MOVES INDEX *)

   BEGIN
     FOR INTW := INDEX[JNTK+1]+1 TO JNTW-1 DO
        IF NOT MOVES[INTW].RMSU THEN
           SELMOV(INTW);
   END; (* SELANY *)


BEGIN
21: (* NEW SEARCH MODE *)
   CASE SRCHM[JNTK] OF

      H0: (* INITIALIZE FOR NEW MOVE *)
         BEGIN
           MVSEL[JNTK] := 0;          (* CLEAR MOVES SEARCHED *)
           INTV := BSTVL[JNTK-2];     (* SAVE ALPHA *)
           BSTVL[JNTK-2] := -ZV;      (* INHIBIT PRUNING IN EVALU8 *)
           MAXPS := 0;                (* INITIALIZE MAXIMUM POSITIONAL
                                          SCORE *)
           GENALL;                    (* GENERATE ALL MOVES *)
           FOR INTW := AW+1 TO JNTW-1 DO
           BEGIN
             IF UPDATE(MOVES[INTW]) THEN
             BEGIN
               INDEX[JNTK] := INTW;   (* POINT TO CURRENT MOVE *)
               EVALU8;                (* SCORE POSITION *)
             END;
             DNDATE(MOVES[INTW]);
           END;
           BSTVL[JNTK-2] := INTV;     (* RESTORE ALPHA *)
           SORTIT(VALUE,MOVES,JNTW-1);  (* SORT PRELIMINARY SCORES *)
           FOR INTK := AK TO ZK DO
             KILLR[INTK] := NULMV;    (* CLEAR KILLER TABLE *)

           IF SWTR OR SWPS THEN
           FOR INTW := AW+1 TO JNTW-1 DO
           BEGIN
             WRITE(" PRELIM",INTW,VALUE[INTW]);
             PRIMOV(MOVES[INTW]);     (* PRINT PRELIMINARY SCORES *)
             IF INTW/LPP = INTW DIV LPP THEN
               PAUSER;
              END;
              SELNXT(H6);             (* SEARCH ALL MOVES *)
           END;

      H1: (* INITIALIZE AT NEW DEPTH *)
         BEGIN
           MVSEL[JNTK] := 0;          (* CLEAR MOVES SEARCHED *)
           IF JNTK > JMTK THEN
           BEGIN
             EVALU8;                  (* EVALUATE CURRENT POSITION *)
             INDEX[JNTK+1] := AW;
             BSTVL[JNTK+1] := -VALUE[INDEX[JNTK]];
             IF MINMAX(JNTK) OR (JNTK = ZK) THEN
               SELDON;                (* THIS MOVE PRUNES *)
             SRCHM[JNTK] := H2;       (* CAPTURE SEARCH *)
           END
           ELSE
             SRCHM[JNTK] := H3;       (* CAPTURES IN FULL SEARCH *)
           GENCAP;                    (* GENERATE CAPTURES *)
           SELNXT(SRCHM[JNTK]);       (* CHANGE SEARCH MODE *)
         END;

      H2: (* CAPTURE SEARCH *)
         BEGIN
           INTM := AW;                (* BEST MOVE POINTER *)
           INTV := AV;                (* BEST VALUE *)
           FOR INTW := LINDX[JNTK] TO JNTW-1 DO
             WITH MOVES[INTW] DO
               IF NOT RMSU THEN
                 IF ABS(XTPV[RMCP]) > INTV THEN
                 BEGIN
                   INTV := ABS(XTPV[RMCP]);

                   INTM := INTW;
                 END;
           IF INTM <> AW THEN         (* MOVE FOUND *)
             SELMOV(INTM)             (* SELECT BIGGEST CAPTURE *)
           ELSE
             SELDON;                  (* QUIT *)
         END;

      H3: (* FULL WIDTH SEARCH - CAPTURES *)
         BEGIN
           INTM := AW;                (* BEST MOVE POINTER *)
           INTV := AV;                (* BEST VALUE *)
           FOR INTW := LINDX[JNTK] TO JNTW-1 DO
             WITH MOVES[INTW] DO
               IF NOT RMSU THEN
                 IF ABS(XTPV[RMCP]) > INTV THEN
                 BEGIN
                   INTV := ABS(XTPV[RMCP]);

                   INTM := INTW;
                 END;
           IF INTM <> AW THEN         (* MOVE FOUND *)
             SELMOV(INTM)             (* SELECT BIGGEST CAPTURE *)
           ELSE
             IF NOT NULMVB(KILLR[JNTK]) THEN
             BEGIN
               INTW := JNTW;          (* SAVE CURRENT MOVES INDEX *)
               GENFSL(XRSS[KILLR[JNTK].RMFR]);  (* GENERATE MOVE BY KILLER *)
               SRCHM[JNTK] := H4;     (* SET NEXT SEARCH MODE *)
               FOR INTW := INTW TO JNTW-1 DO
                                      (* LOOK AT MOVES BY KILLER *)
                 IF KILLR[JNTK].RMTO = MOVES[INTW].RMTO THEN
                   SELMOV(INTW);      (* SELECT KILLER MOVE *)
             END;
           SELNXT(H4);                (* GO TO NEXT STATE *)
         END;

      H4: (* INITIALIZE SCAN OF CASTLE MOVES AND OTHER MOVES
             BY KILLER PIECE *)
         BEGIN
           GENCAS;                    (* GENERATE CASTLE MOVES *)
           SELNXT(H5);                (* GO TO NEXT STATE *)
         END;

      H5: (* FULL WIDTH SEARCH - CASTLES AND OTHER MOVES BY KILLER
             PIECE *)
         BEGIN
           SELANY;                    (* SELECT ANY MOVE *)
           GENFSL(ALLOC[JNTK]);       (* GENERATE REMAINING MOVES *)
           SELNXT(H6);                (* NEXT SEARCH MODE *)
         END;

      H6: (* FULL WIDTH SEARCH - REMAINING MOVES *)
         BEGIN
           SELANY;                    (* SELECT ANYTHING ON LIST *)
           IF MVSEL[JNTK] = 0 THEN
             SCOREM;                  (* SCORE MATE *)
           SELDON;                    (* EXIT SELECT *)
         END;

      H7: (* RESEARCH FIRST PLY *)
         BEGIN
           JNTW := LINDX[AK+1];       (* POINT TO ALREADY GENERATED
                                          MOVES *)
           MVSEL[AK] := 0;            (* RESET MOVES SEARCHED *)
           FOR INTW := AW+1 TO JNTW-1 DO
             MOVES[INTW].RMSU := FALSE;
                                      (* CLEAR SEARCHED BIT *)
           IF SWTR THEN
             WRITELN(" REDO ",JMTK,BSTVL[AK-2],BSTVL[AK-1]);
           SELNXT(H6);                (* SEARCH ALL MOVES *)
         END;
   END;


   22: (* SELECT EXIT *)
     SELECT := INTB;                  (* RETURN VALUE *)
   END; (* SELECT *)

BEGIN (* SEARCH *)
   BSTMV[AK] := AW;                   (* INITIALIZE MOVE *)
   INDEX[JNTK] := AW;                 (* INITIALIZE TREE *)
```

```
        MOVES[AW] := LSTMV;                  (* INITIALIZE MOVE *)
        EVALU8;                              (* INITIAL GUESS AT SCORE *)
        BSTVL[AK-2] := VALUE[AW] - WINDOW;   (* INITIALIZE ALPHA-BETA
                                                WINDOW *)
        BSTVL[AK-1] := - VALUE[AW] - WINDOW;
        JNTK := AK+1;                        (* INITIALIZE ITERATION NUMBER *)
        WHILE (NODES < FNODE) AND (JNTK < MAX(ZK DIV 2, ZK-8)) DO
        BEGIN
11:       (* START NEW PLY *)
          BSTVL[JNTK] := BSTVL[JNTK-2];      (* INITIALIZE ALPHA *)

12:       (* DIFFERENT FIRST MOVE *)
          IF NOT SELECT THEN
          BEGIN
            BSTVL[JNTK] := VALUE[INDEX[JNTK]];
            NEWBST(JNTK);
          END
          ELSE
          BEGIN
            IF UPDATE(MOVES[INDEX[JNTK+1]]) THEN
              GOTO 11                         (* START NEW PLY *)
            ELSE
            BEGIN
              DNDATE(MOVES[INDEX[JNTK]]);
              GOTO 12;                        (* FIND ANOTHER MOVE *)
            END;
          END;

13:       (* FLOAT VALUE BACK *)
          IF MINMAX(JNTK) THEN
            GOTO 15;                          (* PRUNE *)

14:       (* FIND ANOTHER MOVE AT THIS PLY *)
          IF SELECT THEN
            IF UPDATE(MOVES[INDEX[JNTK+1]]) THEN
              GOTO 11                         (* START NEW PLY *)
            ELSE
            BEGIN
              DNDATE(MOVES[INDEX[JNTK]]);
              GOTO 14;                        (* FIND ANOTHER MOVE *)
            END;
          END;

15:       (* BACK UP A PLY *)
          IF JNTK > AK THEN
          BEGIN (* NOT DONE WITH ITERATION *)
            DNDATE(MOVES[INDEX[JNTK]]);       (* RETRACT MOVE *)
            GOTO 13;
          END;

          (* DONE WITH ITERATION *)
          IF (BSTVL[AK] <= BSTVL[AK-2]) OR (BSTVL[AK] >= -BSTVL[AK-1]) THEN
          BEGIN (* NO MOVE FOUND *)
            IF MVSEL[AK] = 8 THEN
            BEGIN (* NO LEGAL MOVES *)
              GOTO 16;                        (* GIVE UP *)
            END;
            BSTVL[AK-2] := -ZV;               (* SET ALPHA-BETA WINDOW LARGE *)
            BSTVL[AK-1] := -ZV;
            SRCHM[AK] := H7;
            JNTW := AK+1;
            GOTO 11;                          (* TRY AGAIN *)
          END;
          BSTVL[AK-2] := BSTVL[AK] - WINDOW;  (* SET ALPHA BETA WINDOW *)
          BSTVL[AK-1] := - BSTVL[AK] - WINDOW;
          JNTK := JNTK+1;                     (* ADVANCE ITERATION NUMBER *)
          SRCHM[AK] := H7;
        END;
16:     (* EXIT SEARCH *)
        SEARCH := BSTMV[AK];                  (* RETURN BEST MOVE *)
END; (* SEARCH *)


PROCEDURE READER;                            (* READ INPUT FROM USER *)

LABEL
  11;                                        (* COMMAND FINISHED EXIT *)

VAR
  INRA : RA;                                 (* SCRATCH TOKEN *)
  INTJ : TJ;                                 (* ECHO COMMAND INDEX *)


  PROCEDURE RDRERR(A:RN);                    (* PRINT DIAGNOSTIC AND EXIT *)

  VAR
    INTJ : TJ;                               (* STRING INDEX *)
    INTN : TN;                               (* MESSAGE INDEX *)

  BEGIN
    IF NOT SWEC THEN                         (* ECHO LINE IF NOT ALREADY
                                                DONE *)
    BEGIN
      WRITE(" ");
      FOR INTJ := AJ TO ZJ-1 DO
        WRITE(ILINE[INTJ]);                  (* WRITE INPUT LINE *)
      WRITELN;
    END;
    FOR INTJ := AJ TO JNTJ DO
      WRITE(" ");                            (* LEADING BLANKS BEFORE ARROW *)
    WRITELN("^");                            (* POINTER TO ERROR *)
    FOR INTN := AN TO ZN DO
      WRITE(A[INTN]);                        (* WRITE DIAGNOSTIC *)
    WRITELN;
    GOTO 11;                                 (* COMMAND EXIT *)
  END; (* RDRERR *)
```

```
FUNCTION RDRGNT(VAR A:RA):TB;                (* GET NEXT TOKEN FROM COMMAND
                                                RETURNS TOKEN IN A.
                                                RETURNS TRUE IF NON-EMPTY
                                                TOKEN.
                                                A TOKEN IS ANY CONSECUTIVE
                                                COLLECTION OF ALPHANUMERIC
                                                CHARACTERS.
                                                LEADING SPECIAL CHARACTERS
                                                IGNORED. *)
VAR
  INTJ : TJ;                                 (* STRING INDEX *)

BEGIN
  WHILE (JNTJ < ZJ) AND (ORD(ILINE[JNTJ]) >= ORD("+")) DO
    JNTJ := JNTJ+1;
  A := "            ";
  INTJ := AA;
  WHILE (JNTJ < ZJ) AND (INTJ < ZA) AND (ILINE[JNTJ] IN ["A".."9"]) DO
  BEGIN
    A[INTJ] := ILINE[JNTJ];                  (* COPY CHARACTER TO TOKEN *)
    INTJ := INTJ+1;                          (* ADVANCE POINTERS *)
    JNTJ := JNTJ+1;
  END;
  RDRGNT := INTJ <> AA;                      (* RETURN TRUE IF ANYTHING
                                                MOVED *)
  WHILE (INTJ < ZJ) AND (ILINE[JNTJ] IN ["A".."9"]) DO
    JNTJ := JNTJ+1;                          (* SKIP REST OF TOKEN *)
END; (* RDRGNT *)


PROCEDURE RDRSFT;                            (* SKIP FIRST TOKEN IN COMMAND
                                                LINE *)

VAR
  INRA : RA;                                 (* SCRATCH *)
  INTB : TB;                                 (* SCRATCH *)

BEGIN
  JNTJ := AJ;                                (* INITIALIZE SCAN *)
  INTB := RDRGNT(INRA);                      (* THROW AWAY FIRST TOKEN *)
END; (* RDRSFT *)


PROCEDURE RDRCMD                             (* TEST FOR AND EXECUTE COMMAND
                                                EXITS TO COMMAND EXIT IF
                                                COMMAND IS PROCESSED. *)

  (A:RA;                                     (* POTENTIAL COMMAND KEYWORD *)
   PROCEDURE XXXCMD);                        (* PROCEDURE TO EXECUTE
                                                COMMAND *)

BEGIN
  IF INRA = A THEN
  BEGIN
    XXXCMD;                                  (* EXECUTE COMMAND *)
    GOTO 11;                                 (* EXIT *)
  END;
END; (* RDRCMD *)


PROCEDURE RDLINE;                            (* GET NEXT INPUT LINE FROM
                                                USER *)

VAR
  INTC : TC;                                 (* SCRATCH *)
  INTJ : TJ;                                 (* STRING INDEX *)

BEGIN
  READLN;                                    (* ADVANCE TO NEXT LINE *)
  INTJ := AJ;
  WHILE NOT EOLN AND (INTJ < ZJ) DO
  BEGIN
    READ(ICARD[INTJ]);                       (* COPY INPUT LINE *)
    INTJ := INTJ+1;
  END;
  WHILE NOT EOLN DO
    READ(INTC);                              (* SKIP REST OF INPUT LINE *)
  WHILE INTJ < ZJ DO
  BEGIN
    ICARD[INTJ] := " ";                      (* BLANK REST OF LINE *)
    INTJ := INTJ+1;
  END;
  ICARD[ZJ] := ";";                          (* SET END OF COMMAND *)
  JNTJ := AJ;                                (* RESET INPUT LINE POINTER *)
END; (* RDLINE *)


FUNCTION RDPMOV:TB;                          (* EXTRACT NEXT COMMAND
                                                FROM INPUT LINE.
                                                RETURNS TRUE IF NON-EMPTY
                                                COMMAND. *)
VAR
  INTJ : TJ;                                 (* STORING POINTER *)

BEGIN
  WHILE (JNTJ < ZJ) AND (ICARD[JNTJ] = " ") DO
    JNTJ := JNTJ+1;                          (* SKIP LEADING BLANKS *)
  INTJ := AJ;
  WHILE (JNTJ < ZJ) AND (ICARD[JNTJ] <> ";") DO
  BEGIN
    ILINE[INTJ] := ICARD[JNTJ];
    INTJ := INTJ+1;
    JNTJ := JNTJ+1;
  END;
  IF (ICARD[JNTJ] = ";") AND (JNTJ < ZJ) THEN
    JNTJ := JNTJ+1;                          (* SKIP SEMI-COLON *)
  RDRMOV := INTJ <> AJ;                      (* RETURN TRUE IF NON-EMPTY *)
  WHILE INTJ < ZJ DO
  BEGIN
    ILINE[INTJ] := " ";                      (* BLANK FILL LINE *)
```

```
            IMTJ := IMTJ+1;
    END;
    ILINE(ZJ) := ":";                          (* STORE COMMAND TERMINATOR *)
    JNTJ := AJ;                                 (* PRESET COMMAND SCAN *)
END; (* RDRMOV *)


FUNCTION RDRNUM:TI;                             (* CRACK NUMBER FROM COMMAND
                                                   LINE.  RETURNS NUMBER IF NO
                                                   ERROR.  EXITS TO COMMAND EXIT
                                                   IF ERROR. *)

VAR
    INTB : TB;                                  (* SIGN *)
    INTI : TI;                                  (* VALUE *)

BEGIN
    WHILE (JNTJ < ZJ) AND (ILINE(JNTJ) = " ") DO
        JNTJ := JNTJ+1;                         (* SKIP LEADING BLANKS *)
    IF ILINE(JNTJ) = "-" THEN
    BEGIN
        INTB := TRUE;                           (* NUMBER IS NEGATIVE *)
        JNTJ := JNTJ+1;                         (* ADVANCE CHARACTER POINTER *)
    END
    ELSE
    BEGIN
        INTB := FALSE;                          (* NUMBER IS POSITIVE *)
        IF ILINE(JNTJ) = "+" THEN
            JNTJ := JNTJ+1;                     (* SKIP LEADING + *)
    END;
    INTI := 0;
    WHILE ILINE(JNTJ) IN ("0".."9") DO
    BEGIN
        IF INTI < MAXINT/10 THEN
            INTI := 10*INTI+ORD(ILINE(JNTJ))-ORD("0")
        ELSE
            RDRERR(" NUMBER TOO LARGE        ");
        JNTJ := JNTJ+1;                         (* ADVANCE *)
    END;
    IF ILINE(JNTJ) IN ("A".."Z") THEN
        RDRERR(" DIGIT EXPECTED         ");
    IF INTB THEN
        INTI := -INTI;                          (* COMPLEMENT IF NEGATIVE *)
    RDRNUM := INTI;                             (* RETURN NUMBER *)
END; (* RDRNUM *)


PROCEDURE BOACMD;                               (* COMMAND - SET UP POSITION *)

VAR
    INTM : TM;                                  (* COLOR *)
    INTS : TS;                                  (* POSITION ON BOARD *)

    PROCEDURE BOAADV(A:TI);                     (* ADVANCE N FILES *)

    BEGIN
        IF INTS+A < ZS THEN
            INTS := INTS+A
        ELSE
            INTS := ZS;
    END; (* BOAADV *)


    PROCEDURE BOASTO(A:TP);                     (* STORE PIECE ON BOARD *)

    BEGIN
        BOARD.RBIS(INTS) := A;
        IF INTS < ZS THEN
            INTS := INTS+1;
    END; (* BOASTO *)


BEGIN (* BOACMD *)
    CLSTAT;                                     (* CLEAR STATUS FLAGS *)
    LSTMV := NULMV;                             (* CLEAR PREVIOUS MOVE *)
    FOR INTS := AS TO ZS DO
        BOARD.RBIS(INTS) := MT;                 (* CLEAR BOARD *)
    INTM := LITE;
    INTS := 0;
    REPEAT
        IF ILINE(JNTJ) IN ("P","R","N","B","Q","K","L","D","1".."8") THEN
        CASE ILINE(JNTJ) OF
            "P": BOASTO(XTUMP(EP,INTM));
            "R": BOASTO(XTUMP(ER,INTM));
            "N": BOASTO(XTUMP(EN,INTM));
            "B": BOASTO(XTUMP(EB,INTM));
            "Q": BOASTO(XTUMP(EQ,INTM));
            "K": BOASTO(XTUMP(EK,INTM));
            "L": INTM := LITE;
            "D": INTM := DARK;
            "1","2","3","4","5","6","7","8":
                BOAADV(ORD(ILINE(JNTJ))-ORD("0"));
        END
        ELSE
            IF ILINE(JNTJ) IN ("A".."9") THEN
            BEGIN
                FOR INTS := AS TO ZS DO
                    BOARD.RBIS(INTS) := MT;
                CLSTAT;                          (* CLEAR STATUS *)
                RDRERR(" ILLEGAL BOARD OPTION      ");
            END;
        JNTJ := JNTJ+1;
    UNTIL JNTJ = ZJ;
END; (* BOACMD *)


PROCEDURE ENDCMD;                               (* COMMAND - END PROGRAM *)

BEGIN
    GOTO 9;                                     (* END PROGRAM *)
END; (* ENDCMD *)


PROCEDURE GONCMD;                               (* COMMAND - GO N MOVES *)
```

```
    BEGIN
        GOING := RDRNUM;                        (* CRACK NUMBER *)
        IF GOING <= 0 THEN
            GOING := 1;
        GOTO 2;                                 (* EXECUTE MACHINES MOVE *)
    END; (* GONCMD *)


PROCEDURE INICMD;                               (* COMMAND - INITIALIZE FOR A NEW
                                                   GAME *)

BEGIN
    GOTO 1;                                     (* INITIALIZE FOR A NEW GAME *)
END; (* INICMD *)


PROCEDURE LETCMD;                               (* COMMAND - CHANGE VARIABLE *)

LABEL
    21;                                         (* LET COMMAND EXIT *)

PROCEDURE LETONE                                (* TEST FOR AND SET ONE
                                                   VARIABLE *)
    (A:RA;                                      (* VARIABLE NAME *)
     VAR B:TI);                                 (* VARIABLE *)

BEGIN
    IF A = INRA THEN
    BEGIN
        B := RDRNUM;                            (* GET VALUE *)
        GOTO 21;                                (* EXIT *)
    END;
END; (* LETONE *)


BEGIN
    IF RORGNT(INRA) THEN
    BEGIN
        LETONE("FKPSHD     ",FKPSHD);
        LETONE("FKSANQ     ",FKSANQ);
        LETONE("FMAXMT     ",FMAXMT);
        LETONE("FNODEL     ",FNODEL);
        LETONE("FPADQR     ",FPADCR(F1));
        LETONE("FPADQN     ",FPADCR(F2));
        LETONE("FPADQB     ",FPADCR(F3));
        LETONE("FPADQF     ",FPADCR(F4));
        LETONE("FPADKF     ",FPADCR(F5));
        LETONE("FPADKB     ",FPADCR(F6));
        LETONE("FPADKN     ",FPADCR(F7));
        LETONE("FPADKR     ",FPADCR(F8));
        LETONE("FPBLOK     ",FPBLOK);
        LETONE("FPCONN     ",FPCONN);
        LETONE("FPFLNX     ",FPFLNX);
        LETONE("FRDUBL     ",FRDUBL);
        LETONE("FRK7TH     ",FRK7TH);
        LETONE("FTRADE     ",FTRADE);
        LETONE("FTRDSL     ",FTRDSL);
        LETONE("FTRPOK     ",FTRPOK);
        LETONE("FTRPWN     ",FTRPWN);
        LETONE("FWKING     ",FWKING);
        LETONE("FWMAJM     ",FWMAJM);
        LETONE("FWMINM     ",FWMINM);
        LETONE("FWPAWN     ",FWPAWN);
        LETONE("FWROOK     ",FWROOK);
        LETONE("WINDOW     ",WINDOW);
        RORERR(" ILLEGAL LET VARIABLE NAME     ");
    END;
21: (* LET COMMAND EXIT *)
END; (* LETCMD *)


PROCEDURE PLECMD;                               (* COMMAND - PRINT VARIABLE *)

LABEL
    21;                                         (* PRINT LET COMMAND EXIT *)

PROCEDURE PRIONE                                (* TEST FOR AND PRINT VARIABLE *)
    (A:RA;                                      (* TEST VARIABLE NAME *)
     B:TI);                                     (* VARIABLE *)

BEGIN
    IF INRA = A THEN
    BEGIN
        WRITELN(A,B);
        GOTO 21;                                (* EXIT *)
    END;
END; (* PRIONE *)


BEGIN (* PLECMD *)
    WHILE RORGNT(INRA) DO
    BEGIN
        PRIONE("FKPSHD     ",FKPSHD);
        PRIONE("FKSANQ     ",FKSANQ);
        PRIONE("FMAXMT     ",FMAXMT);
        PRIONE("FNODEL     ",FNODEL);
        PRIONE("FPADQR     ",FPADCR(F1));
        PRIONE("FPADQN     ",FPADCR(F2));
        PRIONE("FPADQB     ",FPADCR(F3));
        PRIONE("FPADQF     ",FPADCR(F4));
        PRIONE("FPADKF     ",FPADCR(F5));
        PRIONE("FPADKB     ",FPADCR(F6));
        PRIONE("FPADKN     ",FPADCR(F7));
        PRIONE("FPADKR     ",FPADCR(F8));
        PRIONE("FPBLOK     ",FPBLOK);
        PRIONE("FPCONN     ",FPCONN);
        PRIONE("FPFLNX     ",FPFLNX);
        PRIONE("FRDUBL     ",FRDUBL);
        PRIONE("FRK7TH     ",FRK7TH);
        PRIONE("FTRADE     ",FTRADE);
        PRIONE("FTRDSL     ",FTRDSL);
        PRIONE("FTRPOK     ",FTRPOK);
        PRIONE("FTRPWN     ",FTRPWN);
        PRIONE("FWKING     ",FWKING);
```

```
        PRIONE("FWMAJM    ",FWMAJM);
        PRIONE("FWMINM    ",FWMINM);
        PRIONE("FWPAWN    ",FWPAWN);
        PRIONE("FWROOK    ",FWROOK);
        PRIONE("WINDOW    ",WINDOW);
        RORERR(" ILLEGAL VARIABLE NAME      ");

21:    (* PRINT LET COMMAND EXIT *)
   END;
END;  (* PLECMD *)


PROCEDURE PRICMD;                         (* COMMAND - PRINT BOARD *)

BEGIN
   IF RORGNT(INRA) THEN
      PRINTB(NBORD)
   ELSE
      PRINTB(BOARD.RBIS);
END;  (* PRICMD *)


PROCEDURE PAMCMD;                         (* COMMAND - PRINT ATTACK MAP *)

BEGIN
   WHILE RORGNT(INRA) DO
      IF INRA(AA) = "T" THEN
         PRINAM(ATKTO)
      ELSE
         IF INRA(AA) = "F" THEN
            PRINAM(ATKFR)
         ELSE
            RORERR(" ATTACK MAP NOT 'TO' OR 'FROM'");
END;  (* PAMCMD *)


PROCEDURE POPCMD;                         (* COMMAND - PRINT OTHER STUFF *)

VAR
   INTQ : TQ;                             (* CASTLE TYPE INDEX *)

BEGIN
   WITH BOARD DO
   BEGIN
      WRITELN(XTMA(RBTM)," TO MOVE.");
      WRITELN(RBTS," ENPASSANT.");
      WRITELN("MOVE NUMBER",RBTI);
      FOR INTQ := LS TO DL DO
         IF INTQ IN RBSQ THEN
            WRITELN(XTQA(INTQ)," SIDE CASTLE LEGAL.");
   END;
END;  (* POPCMD *)


PROCEDURE PMVCMD;                         (* COMMAND - PRINT MOVE LIST *)

VAR
   INTM : TM;                             (* MOVES LIST INDEX *)

BEGIN
   LSTMOV;
   FOR INTM := AM TO JNTM-1 DO
   BEGIN
      WRITE(INTM:4," ");
      PRIMOV(MOVES[INTM]);
      IF INTM/LPP = INTM DIV LPP THEN
         PAUSER;
   END;
END;  (* PMVCMD *)


PROCEDURE SWICMD;                         (* COMMAND - FLIP SWITCH *)

LABEL
   21;                                    (* SWITCH OPTION EXIT *)


   PROCEDURE SWIONE                       (* PROCESS ONE SWITCH *)
      (A:RA;                              (* SWITCH NAME *)
       VAR B:TB);                         (* SWITCH *)

   VAR
      INTJ : TJ;                          (* SAVE COMMAND INDEX *)

   BEGIN
      IF INRA = A THEN
      BEGIN
         INTJ := JNTJ;                    (* SAVE CURRENT POSITION *)
         IF RORGNT(INRA) THEN
         BEGIN
            IF INRA = "ON       " THEN
               B := TRUE                  (* TURN SWITCH ON *)
            ELSE
               IF INRA = "OFF      " THEN
                  B := FALSE              (* TURN SWITCH OFF *)
               ELSE
                  JNTJ := INTJ;           (* RESTORE CURRENT POSITION *)
                  PRISWI(A,B);            (* PRINT SWITCH VALUE *)
         END
         ELSE
            PRISWI(A,B);
         GOTO 21;                         (* SWITCH OPTION EXIT *)
      END;
   END;  (* SWIONE *)
```

```
BEGIN (* SWICMD *)
21:   (* SWITCH OPTION EXIT *)
   WHILE RORGNT(INRA) DO
   BEGIN
      SWIONE("EC        ",SWEC);
      SWIONE("PA        ",SWPA);
      SWIONE("PS        ",SWPS);
      SWIONE("RE        ",SWRE);
      SWIONE("SU        ",SWSU);
      SWIONE("TR        ",SWTR);
      RORERR(" INVALID SWITCH OPTION      ");
   END;
END;  (* SWICMD *)


PROCEDURE STACMD;                         (* COMMAND - STATUS CHANGES *)

LABEL
   21;                                    (* STATUS COMMAND OPTION EXIT *)
VAR
   INRA : RA;                             (* CURRENT TOKEN *)
   INTM : TM;                             (* SIDE BEING PROCESSED *)


   PROCEDURE STAEPF                       (* PROCESS EP FILE *)
      (A:RA;                              (* TEST TOKEN *)
       B:TF);                             (* EQUIVALENT FILE *)

   BEGIN
      IF A = INRA THEN
      BEGIN
         IF INTM = LITE THEN
            BOARD.RBTS := XTRFS[R6,B]
         ELSE
            BOARD.RBTS := XTRFS[R3,B];
         GOTO 21;                         (* EXIT STATUS OPTION *)
      END;
   END;  (* STAEPF *)


   PROCEDURE STACAK;                      (* ALLOW CASTLE KING SIDE *)

   BEGIN
      IF INTM = LITE THEN
         BOARD.RBSQ := BOARD.RBSQ + (LS)
      ELSE
         BOARD.RBSQ := BOARD.RBSQ + (DS);
   END;  (* STACAK *)


   PROCEDURE STACAQ;                      (* ALLOW CASTLE QUEEN SIDE *)

   BEGIN
      IF INTM = LITE THEN
         BOARD.RBSQ := BOARD.RBSQ + (LL)
      ELSE
         BOARD.RBSQ := BOARD.RBSQ + (DL);
   END;  (* STACAQ *)


   PROCEDURE STADRK;                      (* SET BLACK OPTIONS *)

   BEGIN
      INTM := DARK;
   END;  (* STADRK *)


   PROCEDURE STAENP;                      (* SET ENPASSANT FILE *)

   BEGIN
      IF NOT RORGNT(INRA) THEN
      BEGIN
         CLSTAT;                          (* CLEAR STATUS *)
         RORERR(" ENPASSANT FILE OMITTED     ");
      END;

      STAEPF("QR        ",F1);
      STAEPF("QN        ",F2);
      STAEPF("QB        ",F3);
      STAEPF("Q         ",F4);
      STAEPF("K         ",F5);
      STAEPF("KB        ",F6);
      STAEPF("KN        ",F7);
      STAEPF("KR        ",F8);
      CLSTAT;                             (* CLEAR STATUS *)
      RORERR(" ILLEGAL ENPASSANT FILE     ");
   END;  (* STAENP *)


   PROCEDURE STAGOS;                      (* SET SIDE TO MOVE *)

   BEGIN
      BOARD.RBTM := INTM;
      JNTM := INTM;
   END;  (* STAGOS *)


   PROCEDURE STALIT;                      (* SET WHITE OPTIONS *)

   BEGIN
      INTM := LITE;
   END;  (* STALIT *)


   PROCEDURE STANUM;                      (* SET MOVE NUMBER *)

   BEGIN
      BOARD.RBTI := RORNUM;
   END;  (* STANUM *)
```

```
PROCEDURE STAOPT                    (* TEST STATUS OPTION *)
    (A:RA;                          (* TEST OPTION *)
     PROCEDURE STAXXX);             (* PROCEDURE TO EXECUTE IF
                                        EQUAL *)

    BEGIN
    IF INRA = A THEN
      BEGIN
        STAXXX;                     (* EXECUTE PROCEDURE *)
        GOTO 21;                    (* EXIT STATUS OPTION *)
      END;
    END;  (* STAOPT *)


BEGIN  (* STACMD *)
    CLSTAT;                         (* CLEAR STATUS *)
    INTM := LITE;                   (* DEFAULT SIDE WHITE *)
21:  (* STATUS OPTION EXIT *)
    WHILE RDRGNT(INRA) DO
      BEGIN
        STAOPT("D        ",STADRK);
        STAOPT("EP       ",STAENP);
        STAOPT("G        ",STAGOS);
        STAOPT("L        ",STALIT);
        STAOPT("N        ",STANUM);
        STAOPT("OO       ",STACAK);
        STAOPT("OOO      ",STACAQ);
        CLSTAT;
        RDRERR(" INVALID STATUS OPTION        ");
      END;
END;  (* STACMD *)


PROCEDURE WHACMD;                   (* COMMAND - WHAT? *)

    BEGIN
    WRITELN(MOVMS);                 (* PRINT LAST MESSAGE *)
    END;  (* WHACMD *)


BEGIN  (* READER *)
11:  (* COMMAND EXIT *)
    WHILE NOT RDRMOV DO
      RDLINE;
    IF SWEC THEN
      BEGIN                         (* ECHO LINE *)
        WRITE(" ");
        FOR INTJ := AJ TO ZJ-1 DO
          WRITE(ILINE[INTJ]);
        WRITELN;
      END;
    IF ILINE[AJ+1] IN ["A".."W","Y","Z"] THEN
      BEGIN
        INRA := "        ";
        INRA(AA) := ILINE[AJ];      (* EXTRACT KEYWORD *)
        INRA(AA+1) := ILINE[AJ+1];
        RDRSFT;                     (* SKIP FIRST TOKEN *)
        RDRCMD("BO       ",BOACMD);
        RDRCMD("EN       ",ENDCMD);
        RDRCMD("GO       ",GONCMD);
        RDRCMD("IN       ",INICMD);
        RDRCMD("LE       ",LETCMD);
        RDRCMD("PB       ",PAWCMD);
        RDRCMD("PO       ",POPCMD);
        RDRCMD("PL       ",PLECMD);
        RDRCMD("PM       ",PMVCMD);
        RDRCMD("PR       ",PRICMD);
        RDRCMD("ST       ",STACMD);
        RDRCMD("SW       ",SWICMD);
        RDRCMD("WH       ",WHACMD);
        RDRERR(" INVALID COMMAND           ");
      END;
END;  (* READER *)


PROCEDURE MINENG                    (* GENERATE MINIMUM
                                       ENGLISH NOTATION *)
    (A:RM;                          (* MOVE TO NOTATE *)
     B:RA);                         (* LEADING COMMENT *)

VAR
    INTN : TM;                      (* MESSAGE INDEX *)

    PROCEDURE ADDCHR                (* ADD CHARACTER TO MESSAGE *)
        (A:TC);                     (* CHARACTER *)

    BEGIN
    MOVMS[INTN] := A;               (* ADD CHARACTER *)
    IF INTN < ZN THEN
      INTN := INTN+1;               (* ADVANCE POINTER *)
    END;  (* ADDCHR *)


    PROCEDURE ADDSQR                (* ADD SQUARE TO MESSAGE *)
        (A:TS;                      (* SQUARE TO ADD *)
         B:RD);                     (* SQUARE SYNTAX *)

    BEGIN
    WITH B DO
      BEGIN
        IF RDPC THEN
          ADDCHR(XTUC(XTPU[NBORD[A]]));
        IF RDSL THEN
          ADDCHR("/");
        IF RDKQ THEN
          IF XTSF(A) IN [F1..F4] THEN
            ADDCHR("Q")
          ELSE
            ADDCHR("K");
        IF RDNB THEN
          CASE XTSF(A) OF
            F1,F8: ADDCHR("R");
            F2,F7: ADDCHR("N");
            F3,F6: ADDCHR("B");
            F4   : ADDCHR("Q");
            F5   : ADDCHR("K");
          END;
        IF RDRK THEN
          IF JNTM = LITE THEN
            CASE XTSR(A) OF
              R1: ADDCHR("1");
              R2: ADDCHR("2");
              R3: ADDCHR("3");
              R4: ADDCHR("4");
              R5: ADDCHR("5");
              R6: ADDCHR("6");
              R7: ADDCHR("7");
              R8: ADDCHR("8");
            END
          ELSE
            CASE XTSR(A) OF
              R1: ADDCHR("8");
              R2: ADDCHR("7");
              R3: ADDCHR("6");
              R4: ADDCHR("5");
              R5: ADDCHR("4");
              R6: ADDCHR("3");
              R7: ADDCHR("2");
              R8: ADDCHR("1");
            END;
      END;
    END;  (* ADDSQR *)


    PROCEDURE ADDWRD                (* ADD WORD TO MESSAGE *)
        (A:RA;                      (* TEXT OF WORD *)
         B:TA);                     (* LENGTH OF WORD *)

    VAR
        INTA : TA;                  (* CHARACTER INDEX *)

    BEGIN
    FOR INTA := AA TO B DO
      ADDCHR(A[INTA]);
    END;  (* ADDWRD *)


FUNCTION DIFFER                     (* COMPARE MOVES *)
    (A,B:RM)                        (* MOVES TO COMPARE *)
     :TB;                           (* TRUE IF MOVES ARE DIFFERENT *)

VAR
    INTB : TB;                      (* SCRATCH *)

BEGIN
    INTB := (A.RMFR <> B.RMFR) OR
            (A.RMTO <> B.RMTO) OR
            (A.RMCP <> B.RMCP);
    IF A.RMPR = B.RMPR THEN
      IF A.RMPR THEN
        DIFFER := INTB OR (A.RMPP <> B.RMPP)
      ELSE
        IF A.RMOQ = B.RMOO THEN
          IF A.RMOO THEN
            DIFFER := INTB OR (A.RMQS <> B.RMQS)
          ELSE
            DIFFER := INTB
        ELSE
          DIFFER := TRUE
      ELSE
        DIFFER := TRUE;
END;  (* DIFFER *)


PROCEDURE SETSQD                    (* DEFINE SPECIFIC SQUARE
                                       DESCRIPTOR *)
    (A:TS;                          (* SQUARE TO DESCRIBE *)
     B:RD;                          (* SYNTAX TO USE *)
     VAR C:SR;                      (* SET OF POSSIBLE RANKS *)
     VAR D:SF);                     (* SET OF POSSIBLE FILES *)
BEGIN
    C := [R1..R8];
    D := [F1..F8];                  (* INITIALIZE TO DEFAULTS *)
    WITH B DO
      BEGIN
        IF RDKQ AND RDNB THEN
          D := [XTSF(A)];
        IF (NOT RDKQ) AND RDNB THEN
          CASE XTSF(A) OF
            F1,F8: D := [F1,F8];
            F2,F7: D := [F2,F7];
            F3,F6: D := [F3,F6];
            F4   : D := [F4];
            F5   : D := [F5];
          END;
        IF RDRK THEN
          C := [XTSR(A)];
      END;
END;  (* SETSQD *)


PROCEDURE MINGEN                    (* PRODUCE MINIMUM
                                       ENGLISH NOTATION FOR
                                       MOVES AND CAPTURES *)
    (A:RM;                          (* MOVE OR CAPTURE *)
     B:TI;                          (* FIRST SYNTAX TABLE ENTRY *)
     C:TI);                         (* LAST SYNTAX TABLE ENTRY *)

LABEL
    21,                             (* EXIT AMBIGUOUS MOVE SCAN *)
    22;                             (* EXIT MINGEN *)

VAR
    INTG : TG;                      (* PROMOTION PIECE *)
    INTI : TI;                      (* SYNTAX TABLE INDEX *)
```

```
      INTW : TW;                       (* MOVES INDEX *)
      INLR : SR;                       (* RANKS DEFINED ON LEFT *)
      INRR : SR;                       (* RANKS DEFINED ON RIGHT *)
      INLF : SF;                       (* FILES DEFINED ON LEFT *)
      INRF : SF;                       (* FILES DEFINED ON RIGHT *)

   BEGIN
      FOR INTI := B TO C DO            (* FOR EACH SYNTAX ENTRY *)
         WITH SYNTX[INTI] DO
            BEGIN
               IF A.RMPR THEN
                  INTG := A.RMPP
               ELSE
                  INTG := PB;
               SETSQD(A.RMFR,RYLS,INLR,INLF); (* SET SQUARE SETS *)
               SETSQD(A.RMTO,RYRS,INRR,INRF);
               FOR INTW := AW+1 TO JNTW-1 DO
                  IF DIFFER(MOVES[INTW],A) THEN
                     IF (NBORD(A.RMFR) = NBORD(MOVES[INTW].RMFR)) AND
                        (A.RMCP = MOVES[INTW].RMCP) THEN
                        WITH MOVES[INTW] DO
                           IF (XTSR[RMFR] IN INLR) AND
                              (XTSR[RMTO] IN INRR) AND
                              (XTSF[RMFR] IN INLF) AND
                              (XTSF[RMTO] IN INRF) AND
                              ((RMPR AND (INTG = RMPP)) OR (NOT RMPR)) THEN
                                 GOTO 21;                 (* ANOTHER MOVE LOOKS THE SAME *)

               (* NO OTHER MOVE LOOKS THE SAME *)
               ADDSQR(A.RMFR,RYLS);     (* ADD FROM SQUARE *)
               ADDCHR(RYCH);            (* ADD MOVE OR CAPTURE *)
               ADDSQR(A.RMTO,RYRS);     (* ADD TO SQUARE *)
               GOTO 22;                 (* EXIT MINGEN *)
21:            (* TRY NEXT SYNTAX *)
            END;
22:   (* EXIT MINGEN *)
   END;  (* MINGEN *)


BEGIN  (* MINENG *)
   MOVMS := "                    ";    (* CLEAR MESSAGE *)
   INTN := AW+1;                       (* INITIALIZE MESSAGE INDEX *)
   ADDWRD(B,ZA);                       (* ADD INITIAL COMMENT *)
   ADDWRD("-          ",2);
   WITH A DO
   BEGIN
      IF RMOO THEN                     (* CASTLE *)
      BEGIN
         ADDWRD("O-O     ",3);
         IF RMQS THEN
            ADDWRD("-O      ",2);
      END
      ELSE
         IF RMCA THEN                  (* CAPTURE *)
            MINGEN(A,SYNCF,SYNCL)
         ELSE                          (* SIMPLE MOVE *)
            MINGEN(A,SYNMF,SYNML);
      IF RMPR THEN                     (* PROMOTION *)
      BEGIN
         ADDCHR("=");
         ADDCHR(XTGC[RMPP]);
      END;
      ADDWRD(".        ",3);
      IF RMCH THEN                     (* CHECK *)
      BEGIN
         ADDWRD("CHECK    ",5);
         IF RMMT THEN                  (* CHECKMATE *)
            ADDWRD("MATE     ",4);
         ADDCHR(".");
      END
      ELSE
         IF RMMT THEN                  (* STALEMATE *)
            ADDWRD("STALEMATE.",10);
   END;
END;  (* MINENG *)


PROCEDURE MYMOVE;                      (* MAKE MACHINES MOVE *)

VAR
   INRM : RM;                          (* THE MOVE *)

BEGIN
   CREATE;                             (* INITIALIZE DATA BASE *)
   INRM := MOVES[SEARCH];              (* FIND THE BEST MOVE *)
   IF INRM.RMIL THEN
   BEGIN                               (* NO MOVE FOUND *)
      GOING := 0;
      IF LSTMV.RMCH THEN               (* CHECKMATE *)
         WRITELN(" CONGRATULATIONS.")
      ELSE                             (* STALEMATE *)
         WRITELN(" DRAWN. ")
   END
   ELSE
   BEGIN
      MINENG(INRM," MY MOVE ");        (* TRANSLATE MOVE TO ENGLISH *)
      WRITELN(MOVMS);                  (* TELL THE PLAYER *)
      THEMOV(INRM);                    (* MAKE THE MOVE *)
      IF SWSU THEN
         WRITELN(BOARD.RBTI,".",NODES," NODES.",BSTVL[AK]);
   END;
END;  (* MYMOVE *)


PROCEDURE YRMOVE;                      (* MAKE PLAYERS MOVE *)

LABEL
   11, 12, 13, 14, 15,                 (* SYNTAX NODES *)
```

```
   16,                                 (* SYNTAX ERROR *)
   17,                                 (* AMBIGUOUS MOVE *)
   18;                                 (* NORMAL EXIT *)

VAR
   INTB : TB;                          (* VALID MOVE FOUND *)
   INTC : TC;                          (* CURRENT CHARACTER *)
   INTW : TJ;                          (* MOVES INDEX *)

   INTP : TP;                          (* MOVING PIECE *)
   INCP : TP;                          (* CAPTURED PIECE *)
   IFCA : TB;                          (* CAPTURE *)
   IFPR : TB;                          (* PROMOTION *)
   IFOO : TB;                          (* CASTLE *)
   IFQS : TB;                          (* QUEEN SIDE CASTLE *)
   INTG : TG;                          (* PROMOTION TYPE *)
   IFMV : TB;                          (* MOVE FOUND *)

   IFLD : TB;                          (* R, N, OR B ON LEFT *)
   IFLF : TB;                          (* K OR Q ON LEFT *)
   IFRD : TB;                          (* R, N, OR B ON RIGHT *)
   IFRF : TB;                          (* K OR Q ON RIGHT *)

   INLF : SF;                          (* FILES ON LEFT *)
   INLR : SR;                          (* RANKS ON LEFT *)
   INRF : SF;                          (* FILES ON RIGHT *)
   INRR : SR;                          (* RANKS ON RIGHT *)

   INRM : RM;                          (* THE MOVE *)

   FUNCTION NCHIN                      (* DETERMINE IF NEXT INPUT
                                          CHARACTER IS NOT IN A GIVEN
                                          SET *)
      (A:SC;                           (* SET OF CHARACTERS TO CHECK *)
       PROCEDURE YRMXXX)               (* SEMANTICS ROUTINE TO CALL
                                          IF NEXT CHARACTER IS IN SET *)
      :TB;                             (* TRUE IF CHARACTER IS NOT IN
                                          SET *)

   VAR
      INTB : TB;                       (* SCRATCH *)

   BEGIN
      INTB := NOT (INTC IN A);
      IF NOT INTB THEN
      BEGIN
         YRMXXX;                       (* EXECUTE SEMANTICS ROUTINE *)
         JNTJ := JNTJ+1;               (* ADVANCE PAST CHARACTER *)
         WHILE (JNTJ < ZJ)
            AND ((ILINE[JNTJ] = " ") OR (ORD(ILINE[JNTJ]) > ORD(ZC))) DO

            JNTJ := JNTJ+1;            (* SKIP BLANKS *)
         INTC := ILINE[JNTJ];          (* NEXT CHARACTER *)
         IF (INTC = ".") OR (INTC = "!") THEN
            GOTO 15;                   (* EXIT SCAN *)
      END;
      NCHIN := INTB;                   (* RETURN TRUE IF CHARACTER IS
                                          NOT IN STRING *)
   END;  (* NCHIN *)


   PROCEDURE YRMHIT;                   (* FOUND A MOVE.  EXITS
                                          TO AMBIGUOUS MOVE IF THIS
                                          IS THE SECOND POSSIBLE MOVE.
                                          SAVES THE MOVE IN INRM
                                          OTHERWISE. *)

   BEGIN
      IF IFMV THEN GOTO 17;            (* SECOND POSSIBLE MOVE *)
      IFMV := TRUE;                    (* FIRT POSSIBLE MOVE *)
      INRM := MOVES[INTW];             (* SAVE MOVE *)
   END;  (* YRMHIT *)


   PROCEDURE YRMCOM;                   (* COMPARE SQUARES.  CALLS YRMHIT
                                          IF MOVES[INTW] MOVES THE
                                          RIGHT TYPE OF PIECE, CAPTURES
                                          THE RIGHT TYPE OF PIECE, AND
                                          MOVES TO AND FROM POSSIBLE
                                          SQUARES *)

   BEGIN
      WITH MOVES[INTW] DO
         IF (XTSR[RMFR] IN INLR) AND
            (XTSF[RMFR] IN INLF) AND
            (XTSR[RMTO] IN INRR) AND
            (XTSF[RMTO] IN INRF) AND
            (NOT RMIL) AND
            (BOARD.RBIS[RMFR] = INTP) THEN
            IF RMCA = IFCA THEN
               IF RMCA THEN
                  IF RMCP = INCP THEN
                     YRMHIT
                  ELSE
               ELSE
                  YRMHIT;
   END;  (* YRMCOM *)


   PROCEDURE YRMCAP;                   (* SEMANTICS - CAPTURE *)

   BEGIN
      IFCA := TRUE;
   END;  (* YRMCAP *)


   PROCEDURE YRMCAS;                   (* SEMANTICS - CASTLE *)

   BEGIN
      IFOO := TRUE;
   END;  (* YRMCAS *)


   PROCEDURE YRMCPC;                   (* SEMANTICS - CAPTURED PIECE *)
```

```
BEGIN
  CASE INTC OF
    "P": INCP := XTUMP(EP,OTHER[JNTM]);
    "R": INCP := XTUMP(ER,OTHER[JNTM]);
    "N": INCP := XTUMP(EN,OTHER[JNTM]);
    "B": INCP := XTUMP(EB,OTHER[JNTM]);
    "Q": INCP := XTUMP(EQ,OTHER[JNTM]);
  END;
END; (* YRMCPC *)


PROCEDURE YRMCQS;                    (* SEMANTICS - CASTLE LONG *)

BEGIN
  IFQS := TRUE;
END; (* YRMCQS *)


PROCEDURE YRMLKQ;                    (* SEMANTICS - K OR Q ON LEFT *)

BEGIN
  CASE INTC OF
    "K": INLF := [F5..F8] * INLF;    (* KING SIDE *)
    "Q": INLF := [F1..F4] * INLF;    (* QUEEN SIDE *)
  END;
  IFLF := TRUE;
END; (* YRMLKQ *)


PROCEDURE YRMLRB;                    (* SEMANTICS - R, N, OR B ON
                                        LEFT *)

BEGIN
  CASE INTC OF
    "R": INLF := [F1,F8] * INLF;     (* ROOK FILE *)
    "N": INLF := [F2,F7] * INLF;     (* KNIGHT FILE *)
    "B": INLF := [F3,F6] * INLF;     (* BISHOP FILE *)
  END;
  IFLD := TRUE;
END; (* YRMLRB *)


PROCEDURE YRMLRK;                    (* SEMANTICS - RANK ON LEFT *)

BEGIN
  IF JNTM = LITE THEN

    CASE INTC OF
      "1": INLR := [R1];
      "2": INLR := [R2];
      "3": INLR := [R3];
      "4": INLR := [R4];
      "5": INLR := [R5];
      "6": INLR := [R6];
      "7": INLR := [R7];
      "8": INLR := [R8];
    END
  ELSE
    CASE INTC OF
      "1": INLR := [R8];
      "2": INLR := [R7];
      "3": INLR := [R6];
      "4": INLR := [R5];
      "5": INLR := [R4];
      "6": INLR := [R3];
      "7": INLR := [R2];
      "8": INLR := [R1];
    END;
END; (* YRMLRK *)


PROCEDURE YRMNUL;                    (* SEMANTICS - NULL *)

BEGIN
END; (* YRMNUL *)


PROCEDURE YRMPCM;                    (* SEMANTICS - PIECE MOVED *)

BEGIN
  CASE INTC OF
    "P": INTP := XTUMP(EP,JNTM);     (* PAWN *)
    "R": INTP := XTUMP(ER,JNTM);     (* ROOK *)
    "N": INTP := XTUMP(EN,JNTM);     (* KNIGHT *)
    "B": INTP := XTUMP(EB,JNTM);     (* BISHOP *)
    "Q": INTP := XTUMP(EQ,JNTM);     (* QUEEN *)
    "K": INTP := XTUMP(EK,JNTM);     (* KING *)
  END;
END; (* YRMPCM *)


PROCEDURE YRMPRO;                    (* SEMANTICS - PROMOTION *)

BEGIN
  CASE INTC OF
    "R": INTG := PR;                 (* ROOK *)
    "N": INTG := PN;                 (* KNIGHT *)
    "B": INTG := PB;                 (* BISHOP *)
    "Q": INTG := PQ;                 (* QUEEN *)
  END;
  IFPR := TRUE;
END; (* YRMPRO *)


PROCEDURE YRMRKQ;                    (* SEMANTICS - K OR Q ON RIGHT *)

BEGIN
  CASE INTC OF
    "K": INRF := [F5..F8] * INRF;    (* KING SIDE *)
    "Q": INRF := [F1..F4] * INRF;    (* QUEEN SIDE *)
  END;
        IFRF := TRUE;
      END; (* YRMLKQ *)



PROCEDURE YRMRRB;                    (* SEMANTICS - R, N, OR B ON
                                        RIGHT *)

BEGIN
  CASE INTC OF
    "R": INRF := [F1,F8] * INRF;     (* ROOK FILE *)
    "N": INRF := [F2,F7] * INRF;     (* KNIGHT FILE *)
    "B": INRF := [F3,F6] * INRF;     (* BISHOP FILE *)
  END;
  IFRD := TRUE;
END; (* YRMLRB *)


PROCEDURE YRMRRK;                    (* SEMANTICS - RANK ON RIGHT *)

BEGIN
  IF JNTM = LITE THEN
    CASE INTC OF
      "1": INRR := [R1];
      "2": INRR := [R2];
      "3": INRR := [R3];
      "4": INRR := [R4];
      "5": INRR := [R5];
      "6": INRR := [R6];
      "7": INRR := [R7];
      "8": INRR := [R8];
    END
  ELSE
    CASE INTC OF
      "1": INRR := [R8];
      "2": INRR := [R7];
      "3": INRR := [R6];
      "4": INRR := [R5];
      "5": INRR := [R4];
      "6": INRR := [R3];
      "7": INRR := [R2];
      "8": INRR := [R1];
    END;
END; (* YRMLRK *)



BEGIN (* YRMOVE *).
  INTB := FALSE;
  WHILE NOT INTB DO
  BEGIN
    READER;                          (* READ NEXT MOVE *)
    LSTMOV;                          (* LIST LEGAL MOVES *)
    IFCA := FALSE;
    IFPR := FALSE;
    IFOO := FALSE;
    IFQS := FALSE;
    IFLD := FALSE;
    IFLF := FALSE;
    IFRD := FALSE;
    IFRF := FALSE;
    INTP := MT;
    INCP := MT;
    INLF := [F1..F8];
    INRF := [F1..F8];
    INLR := [R1..R8];
    INRR := [R1..R8];

    INTC := ILIME[JNTJ];

    IF     NCHIN((["P","R","N","B","Q","K"],YRMPCM) THEN GOTO 14;
    IF     NCHIN((["/"]                    ,YRMNUL) THEN GOTO 11;
    IF     NCHIN((["K","Q"]                ,YRMLKQ) THEN;
    IF     NCHIN((["R","N","B"]            ,YRMLRB) THEN;
    IF     NCHIN((["1".."8"]               ,YRMLRK) THEN;
11: (* LEFT SIDE DONE *)
    IF NOT NCHIN((["-"]                            ) THEN GOTO 12;
    IF     NCHIN((["*","X"]                ,YRMCAP) THEN GOTO 16;
    IF     NCHIN((["P","R","N","B","Q"]    ,YRMCPC) THEN GOTO 16;
    IF     NCHIN((["/"]                    ,YRMNUL) THEN GOTO 13;
12: (* RIGHT SIDE SQUARE *)
    IF     NCHIN((["K","Q"]                ,YRMRKQ) THEN;
    IF     NCHIN((["R","N","B"]            ,YRMRRB) THEN;
    IF     NCHIN((["1".."8"]               ,YRMRRK) THEN;
13: (* PROMOTION *)
    IF     NCHIN((["="]                    ,YRMNUL) THEN GOTO 15;
    IF     NCHIN((["R","N","B","Q"]        ,YRMPRO) THEN GOTO 16;
    GOTO 15;

14: (* CASTLING *)
    IF     NCHIN((["O","8"]                ,YRMNUL) THEN GOTO 16;
    IF     NCHIN((["-"]                    ,YRMNUL) THEN GOTO 16;
    IF     NCHIN((["O","0"]                ,YRMCAS) THEN GOTO 16;
    IF     NCHIN((["-"]                    ,YRMCQS) THEN GOTO 15;
    IF     NCHIN((["O","8"]                ,YRMNUL) THEN GOTO 16;
15: (* SYNTAX CORRECT *)

    IF IFRF AND NOT IFRD THEN
      INRF := INRF * [F4,F5];         (* SELECT K OR Q FILE *)
    IF IFLF AND NOT IFLD THEN
      INLF := INLF * [F4,F5];         (* SELECT K OR Q FILE *)
    IFMV := FALSE;                    (* NO MOVE FOUND YET *)
    INTW := AM;                       (* INITIALIZE INDEX *)
    WHILE INTW < JNTW DO
      WITH MOVES[INTW] DO
      BEGIN
        IF RMPR = IFPR THEN
          IF RMPR THEN
            IF RMPP = INTG THEN       (* CORRECT PROMOTION TYPE *)
              YRMCOM                  (* COMPARE SQUARES AND PIECES *)
            ELSE
          ELSE
            IF RMOO = IFOO THEN       (* NOT PROMOTION *)
              IF RMOO THEN            (* CASTLING *)
                IF RMQS = IFQS THEN   (* CASTLING SAME WAY *)
                  YRMHIT
```

141

```
              ELSE
            ELSE                      (* NOT CASTLING *)
              YRMCOM;                 (* COMPARE SQUARES AND PIECES *)
        INTW := INTW+1;               (* ADVANCE MOVES INDEX *)
      END;
    IF IFMV THEN                      (* ONE MOVE FOUND *)
    BEGIN
      MINENG(INRM,"YOUR MOVE ");      (* CONVERT TO OUR STYLE *)
      WRITELN(MOVMS);                 (* PRINT MOVE *)
      THEMOV(INRM);                   (* MAKE THE MOVE *)
      IMTB := TRUE;                   (* EXIT YRMOVE *)
    END
    ELSE                              (* NO MOVES FOUND *)
      WRITELN(" ILLEGAL MOVE.");
    GOTO 18;                          (* EXIT *)

16: (* SYNTAX ERROR *)
    WRITELN(" SYNTAX ERROR.");
    GOTO 18;                          (* EXIT *)

17: (* AMBIGUOUS MOVE *)
    WRITELN(" AMBIGUOUS MOVE.");
18: (* EXIT *)
  END;
END; (* YRMOVE *)



BEGIN (* THE PROGRAM *)
  WRITELN(" HI.   THIS IS CHESS .5");
  INICON;                            (* INITIALIZE CONSTANTS *)

1: (* INITIALIZE FOR A NEW GAME *)
  INITAL (BOARD);                    (* INITIALIZE FOR A NEW GAME *)
  REPEAT
    REPEAT
      YRMOVE;                        (* EXECUTE PLAYERS MOVE *)
    UNTIL SWRE;

2: (* EXECUTE MACHINES MOVE *)
    REPEAT
      MYMOVE;
      IF GOING > 0 THEN
        GOING := GOING-1;
    UNTIL GOING = 0;
  UNTIL FALSE;

9: (* END OF PROGRAM *)
END.
```

Creating a Chess Player

Part 4: Thoughts on Strategy

Peter W Frey

Larry R Atkin

The chess program that we have presented in parts 2 and 3 of this series (November 1978 and December l978 BYTE, pages 162[1] and 140[2], respectively) represents a modern implementation of the basic type A strategy described by Shannon in 1950 (see references). If run on a powerful computer, this type of program can play a reasonably good game of chess. Its major weakness lies in its inability to engage in long-range planning. In many middle and end game positions, it will make seemingly aimless moves. Once it attains a position which optimizes the general heuristic goals of its evaluation function, it is faced with the prospect of finding a move which alters the position as little as possible. If the opponent is skillful in developing a long-range attack while not providing any immediate targets, the machine may simply shuffle its pieces back and forth until its position becomes hopeless. The absence of reasonable goal directed behavior is a common limitation of problem solving techniques which are based solely on forward search. The solution of this problem would have important implications for a wide variety of artificial intelligence tasks.

To play a strong game of chess, it is necessary to have a plan. To have a plan, however, the program must recognize specific patterns and relate them to appropriate goals. This, in turn, requires that the program have access to the detailed kind of chess knowledge which is characteristic of

the skilled human player. Thus, we seem to have come round in a circle. In order to avoid selective searching, we have adopted a strategy which does not require very much chess knowledge. In examining the weaknesses of this approach, we discover that the forward search can only be truly successful if we have a clear idea of what we are looking for. To know what we are looking for, however, we must have more knowledge about chess.

So where do we go from here? The highly skilled players who are familiar with the chess programming literature (notably, Berliner, Botvinnik and Levy) are unanimous in their enthusiasm for a selective search strategy. Berliner (see references), for example, advocates a procedure in which very small (for a computer) look-ahead trees are generated, eg: 200 to 500 nodes. His idea is that the program should make an intensive analysis at each node "in order to ascertain the truth about each issue dealt with." Chess knowledge should play a primary role in directing the tree search. The search itself would discover additional relevant information and this would provide an even more knowledgeable focus for the search. This procedure is analogous to the progressive deepening technique which de Groot discovered in the human grandmaster and is the exact antithesis of the brute force (type A) strategy (see October 1978 BYTE, "Creating a Chess Player, An Essay on Human and Computer Chess Skill," page 182[3]).

The efforts of the last decade have demonstrated that the selective search strat-

---

1. Page 117 of this edition.
2. Page 131 of this edition.
3. Page 107 of this edition.

egy is harder to implement than the full-width approach. In addition, full-width searching has consistently produced superior chess. Despite this, there is hardly anyone familiar with chess programming who does not believe that further progress depends on increasing the amount of chess knowledge in the program. The key question is not whether this should be done but how to do it. Since the selective search approach has not led to notable progress, perhaps it is time to consider a different approach.

We believe that a viable alternative exists which combines the proven virtues of the full-width procedure with the potential advantage of a goal-directed search. The central idea is the development of a unique evaluation function for each position. In addition to the general heuristics which are presently employed, evaluations should consider features which are germane to appropriate goals.

According to this plan, move selection would involve two separate stages. In the first phase, a static analysis of the position would be made in an attempt to discover key patterns. This process would involve a hierarchical analysis in which the features of the position would be compared with a general set of library patterns. Highly specific features would be identified and relevant chess-specific knowledge would be accessed. This information, including appropriate short term and long term goals, would be used to construct a conditional evaluation function which would assess the usual general features (eg: material, mobility, King safety, etc) and also other features which are meaningful only in specific situations. Once the conditional evaluation function has been constructed, the second phase of analysis would begin, a conventional full-width tree search employing the special evaluation function.

The first phase of this process would rely heavily on domain specific knowledge (ie: information about chess). It would require a pattern recognition facility and an organizational plan for storing a vast amount of chess knowledge in a manner conducive to rapid retrieval. When this first phase was successful in identifying appropriate goals and producing relevant modifications in the evaluation function, the full-width search which followed would select a move which was thematic with the appropriate goal. If the first phase were unable to identify a key feature, the evaluation function would employ the same general heuristics which it presently uses. For this reason, the pattern recognition and information retrieval modules can be gradually implemented without a lengthy period in which serious blunders are frequent occurrences. This is a

major advantage that the conditional evaluation function has in comparison to a selective search strategy.

Chess Structure

To implement a conditional evaluation function, it is necessary to develop a hierarchical descriptive structure for chess. At the top level, one can make the conventional distinctions between the opening, the middle game, and the end game. Within each of these three major divisions, there would be many specific subdivisions. Within each subdivision, there would be many specific variations.

The opening has three major themes: to develop a pawn structure which is favorable for you but unfavorable for your opponent; to increase the mobility of your minor pieces and limit the mobility of your opponent's minor pieces; and to castle as soon as possible and delay your opponent's opportunity to castle. These general goals provide a framework for evaluating specific variations. They do not provide a specific prescription for selecting a move because a sequence of moves which is thematic with these goals may have a tactical refutation. An apparently good move may not work because it loses material. For this reason, general principles are best applied at the terminal points of a look-ahead search rather than being used as a checklist for selecting the most thematic move as advocated by Church and Church in *Chess Skill in Man and Machine* (see references).

The tournament player who knows opening theory as well as many specific move variations will have a clear advantage over an opponent who knows the general principles but is not familiar with the specific variations. For this reason, tournament players and good chess programs rely on a library of memorized opening variations. The contestant who has carefully planned his opening variations can often gain an important advantage early in the game. To maximize the benefit of a well-prepared opening library, it is also necessary to continue the general theme of the opening once the predigested move sequences have been exhausted. At this stage it is necessary to have a conditional evaluation function. When the machine leaves the library and starts to use a look-ahead procedure to calculate its move, it should use an evaluation function that augments general opening principles with special goals which are thematic with that type of opening.

A portion of the work required to implement this proposal has already been started. Chess specialists have prepared highly detailed analyses of specific opening variations and have developed well-defined rules for categorizing different move sequences into specific subdivisions. For example, a game which starts (1) P-K4, P-K3 is labeled as the French defense. If the game continues (2) P-Q4, P-Q4; (3) N-QB3, B-N5, it is called the Nimzovich (or Winawer) variation of the French defense. If it continues (2) P-Q4, P-Q4; (3) N-QB3, N-KB3, the game is labeled as the classical variation. A continuation of (2) P-Q4, P-Q4; (3) N-QB3, PxP is called either the Rubinstein variation or the Burn variation depending upon subsequent moves. A different approach develops from (2) P-Q4, P-Q4; (3) N-Q2, which is labeled as the Tarrasch variation. And there are many more. The important point, however, is that each of these variations can be objectively identified, and that for each there are well-developed strategical ideas and specific immediate goals. These ideas can be stored in the opening library and can be retrieved when the machine leaves the library. In addition to general opening heuristics, the evaluation function would reflect the specific theoretical ideas which are appropriate to the particular opening at hand. In principle, this idea can be implemented without difficulty. In practice, however, a tremendous amount of chess knowledge is needed and hours and hours of effort are required. To our knowledge no serious attempt has yet been made to implement this strategy. The information on opening theory is needed only once during a game and thus could be stored on disk, since rapid access is not critical.

Pattern Recognition and the Middle Game

From a conceptual point of view, the application of chess knowledge to the evaluation function in the middle game is much more challenging. In this case, pattern recognition becomes an important ingredient. In implementing a goal oriented move selection strategy, Church and Church limited their middle game strategy to either a Kingside attack, a Queenside attack, or concentration on a weak point (ie: a target). The Kingside or Queenside attack is triggered when the machine determines that it has superior forces on one side or the other. This determination can be based on who controls key squares. In calculating the power relationship of different pieces over given squares, it is important to note that less valuable pieces exert more control than valuable pieces. A pawn has greater control over territory than a Queen because it is harder to dislodge. If an attack on one side or the other is deemed appropriate, the evaluation function can be modified to give an extra bonus for moves which augment the attack on that side and for moves which increase the pressure on critical squares.

Pattern analysis is also important in detecting an appropriate target. There are several well-known chess relations which provide obvious targets for attack. One is the *backward pawn* which is prevented from advancing by a pawn or a minor piece. Another natural target is the minor piece which is pinned to the King or Queen. The third is the overworked piece, a key element in the defense against two or more different attacks. If the latter is removed in an exchange, the pieces it is defending will be open for attack. A fourth natural target is a square which would permit a Knight to fork two major pieces (ie: Rook, Queen, King) or a Bishop to skewer two major pieces. If the machine threatens to control that square and to locate an appropriate piece there, the opponent will be forced to devise a defense. Once one of these targets has been detected, the evaluation function can be modified to give a bonus for moves directed at the target. In addition, a plan might be devised to encourage the use of a decoy (a pawn or minor piece which is sacrificed to bring an important piece to a particular square) or to capture a piece which is serving an important defensive function.

A Chess "Snapshot"

In the past, programmers have attempted to implement such plans by using a selective search (eg: Berliner, Zobrist and Carlson) or by using no search at all (eg: Church and Church). Zobrist and Carlson (see references) have developed an innovative technique in which "computer snapshots" are devised which summarize important piece relationships such as attacks, pins, skewers, forks, etc, which presently exist in the given position, or which could occur after one or two moves. Each snapshot is given a weight based on the relative values of the pieces involved and the location of the pieces in respect to the opposing King and the center of the board. The weighted snapshots are then used to select moves for inclusion in a Shannon type B tree search. This procedure provides considerable goal direction to the move selection process.

Although the Zobrist-Carlson snapshot procedure has much to offer (including a highly efficient bit map implementation strategy), it incorporates a common problem shared by all selective search techniques. Occasionally an important continuation is overlooked and this results in the selection of an inappropriate move which may be a gross blunder. By implementing the plans derived from the computer snapshots in the form of a conditional evaluation function, instead, the program can benefit from goal directedness without risking the oversights which are characteristic of selective searching. In this way, the machine can retain the benefits of the full-width search and at the same time engage in strategic planning.

There is a special class of positions for which this approach is especially appropriate. In his thesis at Carnegie-Mellon University Berliner described a special problem, the horizon effect, which plagues the conventional look-ahead approach (see *Chess Skill in Man and Machine*, pages 73 thru 77). One version of this problem involves a piece which is trapped and cannot be saved. Forward searching programs often engage in a bit of foolishness by making forcing but poor moves (such as attacking pieces with pawns or sacrificing pawns for no advantage) which delay the capture of the trapped piece and push its eventual loss beyond the horizon of the tree search. By doing this, the program erroneously concludes that the piece is safe, when in reality the planned move sequence weakens a reasonable position and is still insufficient to save the piece. In this type of situation, the trapped piece should be given up for lost and the program should do its best to take advantage of the tempo required by the opponent to capture the piece. A piece whose time has come is sometimes referred to as a desperado. The only option available is to make the opponent pay as dearly as possible for the capture. If the desperado can be traded for a pawn or a piece of lesser value, this is preferable to being given up for nothing.

This strategy can be implemented with a conditional evaluation function by simply assuming that the trapped piece has a material value of zero. This change would cause the search process to trade the piece for the highest valued candidate that can be found. This is obviously better than having the program engage in useless sacrifices of position and material in a hopeless attempt to resurrect a lost piece. The key element to this implementation is the ability to determine when a piece is truly lost and can be labeled as a desperado. This is a very difficult problem even for a very sophisticated pattern analysis facility.

End Game Considerations

The most interesting application of the conditional evaluation function is in the end game. Because end game strategy is highly dependent on the specific characteristics of the position, a general purpose evaluation function is not very effective. It is necessary to understand what is required in a given position and then select moves which are clearly directed at an appropriate goal. Church and Church list three common goals in the end game: to mate the opponent's King, capture a weak pawn, or promote a pawn. In this case, pattern analysis is important. First the machine must be able to identify the position as one belonging to the end game. Then it has to determine whether a mate attempt is reasonable or whether a pawn can be captured or promoted. Church and Church (see *Chess Skill in Man and Machine*, pages 151 thru 154) describe a general strategy for identifying and capturing a weak pawn. Although their approach does not involve a forward tree search, the specific techniques which they describe can be adapted to the full-width search strategy. Let us consider several specific end game positions involving either a mate, a pawn capture, or a pawn promotion.

For a number of mating situations, a specific algorithm (step-by-step instructions) or a complete lookup table can be developed to produce mate in a minimum number of moves. Typical applications would be King and Queen versus King; King and Rook versus King; and King, Bishop, and Knight versus King. The mating algorithm for each case would include rules for assigning the potential piece relationships into a few general categories, and a prescription for an appropriate type of move for each category. This approach requires no search. A second approach involving a lookup table is even more explicit. An appropriate move is stored in a table for every possible piece configuration. To play the mate perfectly, the machine uses the position to determine an address in the table and then simply reads the correct move.

Both of these procedures are perfectly feasible and avoid many problems which can be encountered in the end game. The limitation of this approach is that there are a very large number of mating situations and a tremendous amount of work would be required to make a detailed analysis of each one. In addition, this strategy requires the storage of a great deal of information which would be used only infrequently.

A third approach, and one which is thematic with the idea of conditional evaluations, is to make a small modification in the evaluation function for each specific mating situation. The notion is that a shallow search combined with a few key ideas should suffice to produce a mate in a reasonable number of moves. With King and Queen or King and Rook versus King, it is sufficient for the program to "know" that the defending King must be forced to the edge. To do this, the program simply needs to add bonus points to the evaluation function when the defending King is near the edge. The size of the bonus should be a linear function of closeness to the edge. This modification of the evaluation function causes the minimax search to select a pathway in the look-ahead tree which forces the defending King to the edge.

With King, Bishop, and Knight against King, the job is slightly more complicated. In this case it is important to know that the defending King must be forced to one of the two corners having the same color as the Bishop's squares. The trick is to add a large bonus when the defending King is on the appropriate corner squares and a smaller credit when it is near these corners. This modification will cause the minimax procedure to find a sequence of moves which forces the defending King into one of the appropriate corners. The general theme is that the full-width search is a powerful device by itself and that the addition of a small amount of chess knowledge is sufficient to produce the desired outcome.

Kings and Pawns in the End Game

Some of the most challenging positions in the end game involve only Kings and pawns. Many of these require an approach which is more sophisticated than those described previously. Consider, for example, the position diagrammed in figure 1. This is a modification of a position presented in Berliner's thesis which demonstrates one of the major weaknesses of a full-width forward search. White has a pawn on f6 which could advance and be promoted if the Black King were out of the way. *[Algebraic notation is used throughout this article to designate chessboard squares. The horizontal rows (ranks) are numbered from 1 to 8, starting at the bottom (White). The files are labeled a through h from left to right . . . . CM]* To win, White must do an end run with his King and bring it to the aid of the pawn. Since Black cannot attack White's pawns on c3 or g5 without leaving the passed pawn, he is helpless to stop White's maneuver. Although this analysis is obvious at a glance to an experienced player, a program that discovers truth by doing a full-width search is faced with a difficult problem. In order to determine that the King can force promotion of the pawn, White must complete a look-ahead search of approximately 35 plies. This is beyond the scope of even the most powerful computer. If the machine employs a general purpose algorithm which encourages the King to centralize its position during the end game, it will search for a pathway which eventually places it on its present square (f4) or one of the neighboring squares (e3 or f3).

Because of this, the correct sequence of moves would never be discovered.

In order for a full-width search to make progress in this type of position, the evaluation function must produce goal direction. One way to do this is to provide a bonus for moves which reduce the distance between the White King and the passed pawn. A secondary goal is to reduce the distance between the White King and any Black pawns which are not defended by another pawn. A tertiary goal is to centralize the White King. The first step in developing a specific implementation of this plan is to identify the territory which is denied to the White King. For this purpose, we wish to determine which squares are controlled by the pawns. The White King cannot move to a square occupied by one of its own pawns, nor can it move to a square attacked by an opposing pawn. Figure 2 presents a map of the position with each of the forbidden squares darkened. The location of these "taboo" squares provides the defining boundaries for potential access routes to the desired goals. The second step in implementing this plan is to use a technique described by Church and Church. Starting at each goal object, work backward toward the attacking piece(s). In our case, we are interested in creating a reward gradient which encourages the White King to approach its own passed pawn and the target pawns. To do this, we consider one goal object at a time. All passed pawns are identified. In our example, only the White pawn at f6 qualifies. The two squares diagonally in front of it (e7 and g7) are each credited with 8 "points" each. All squares immediately adjacent to these squares (but not including squares inaccessible to the White King) are credited with 7 points. Next all squares adjacent to these squares (excluding inaccessible squares) are credited with 6 points. This process is continued until we run out of squares or until we have assigned all credits down to and including 1.

The next step in the process is to identify Black pawns which are not defended by other pawns (ie: targets). In this case, the pawns at e6 and g6 qualify. Credit these two squares and the adjacent ones with 5 points each, excluding darkened squares. Next, credit squares adjacent to these with 4 points. Continue this process until all available squares have been exhausted or until the value of 1 has been assigned. This process is executed independently for each target pawn. The last step involves credit for centralization. The four most central squares (d4, d5, e4, e5) are credited with 3 points. The squares which surround these squares are credited with 2 points. The squares which surround those squares are credited

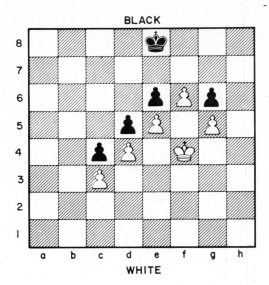

BLACK

WHITE

Figure 1: Chess position which demonstrates a weakness of the full-width forward search. In this example, White has a pawn on square f6 which could advance and be promoted if the Black King were out of the way. To win, the White King must come to the aid of the pawn. Since Black cannot attack White's pawns on c3 or g5 without leaving the passed pawn, he is helpless to stop White's maneuver. Although this analysis is obvious to an experienced player, a program using a full-width search would have to search its decision tree to a depth of 35 plies (ie: 35 half moves; a ply is defined as a move by one side) in order to come to the same conclusion.

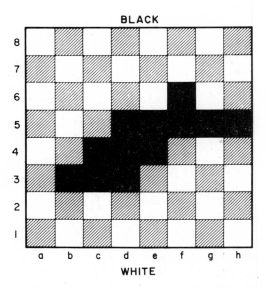

BLACK

WHITE

Figure 2: Forbidden squares in the figure 1 position used to help White (the computer) evaluate the position more efficiently. The White King cannot move to a square occupied by one of its own pawns, nor can it move to a square attacked by an opposing

pawn. All of these squares are darkened in the figure. This diagram is used in implementing the goal directed technique described by Church and Church (see figure 3).

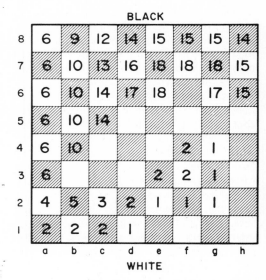

BLACK

WHITE

Figure 3: Bonus map for the White King in the position of figure 1, based on a technique described by Church and Church (see references). A goal is established for a particular attacking piece, in this case the White King, and an iterative numerical technique is used to implement it. The goal is to encourage the White King to approach its own passed pawn and the target pawns. (A target pawn is an enemy pawn not defended by other pawns.) Numerical figures of merit are assigned to strategic squares close to White's passed pawn and Black's undefended pawns. Points are also awarded or subtracted for positional characteristics such as centralization of squares, etc. A type of flow algorithm assigns lower and lower values to squares in direct proportion to their distances from the strategic squares, avoiding any forbidden squares. The resulting map of numbered squares enables the King to find the right pathway by constantly searching for ascending values of squares whenever possible.

with 1 point. Points are then removed from any square which is inaccessible to the White King. When this process has been completed, the credits are totaled for each square to provide a bonus map for the White King. This map is presented in figure 3. By applying this bonus map to the terminal positions of the look-ahead search, the evaluation process will select a move sequence which causes the White King to gravitate in the proper direction. In fact, the correct sequence of moves will be selected even if White is restricted to a 5 ply search each time a move is selected. The bonus map, though simple in concept, has a tremendously beneficial effect.

There is an additional point which needs consideration. In our exposition, we have assumed that the pawns remained stationary. If a pawn were to move, the bonus map would have to be changed. This is not a major problem, however, since there are only a small number of positions that can result from pawn moves, and once the bonus map has been computed for a given configuration, it can be stored and used each time that configuration is encountered in the look-ahead tree. For this reason, the calculations which are required will not be particularly time consuming.

Another example of this strategy is based on the position presented in figure 4. This is a slight modification of figure 6.7 from the chapter of *Chess Skill in Man and Machine* by Church and Church. To apply our technique with respect to the bonus map for the White King it is necessary to determine which squares are not accessible to the White King by virtue of pawn control. As before, these include squares occupied by White pawns and squares attacked by Black pawns. The relevant squares are darkened in figure 5.

The next step is to locate passed pawns for White. There is only one and it is located at c6. The two squares diagonally in front of this pawn (b7 and d7) are credited with 8 points. Squares adjacent to these squares which are not among the darkened squares in figure 5 are credited with 7 points. Squares adjacent to these receive 6 points. This process is continued until there are no more available squares or until the credit value of 1 has been assigned. The next step is to determine whether any Black pawns are potential targets. As before, a target pawn is defined as one which is not defended by a friendly pawn. In the present example, there are three candidates: the pawns at a6, d6 and h7. For each pawn, the value of 5 is credited to the pawn's square and the adjacent squares. Then the value of 4 is credited to each adjacent square. This process of establishing a gradient of decreasing values from 5 down to 1 as distance increases from the target is continued until the last values have been assigned. This is done for each target pawn and in each case, squares darkened in figure 5 are always excluded from the process. The last assignment process is conducted for centralization, with center squares (d4, d5, e4 and e5) receiving 3 credits each and neighboring squares receiving 2 credits. The squares one move in from the edge are assigned the value of 1 and

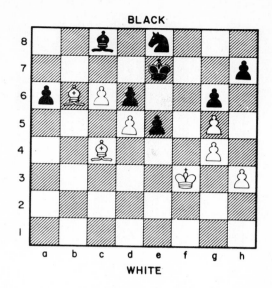

Figure 4: Another end game position, analyzed by the method of Church and Church in figures 5 and 6.

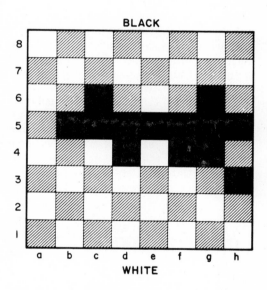

Figure 5: Forbidden squares for the position in figure 4.

then credits are removed from any square which has been darkened. The final step in developing a bonus map for the White King is to total the credits for each square.

The composite map is presented in figure 6. This set of bonus points will encourage the White King to move in the appropriate direction. Without this strategy an 11 ply search would be required for White to discover that the pawn at a6 can be captured. With the implementation of these attack gradients for the White King, however, the correct move can be selected with only a 3 ply search. As was the case in the previous example, the establishment of a

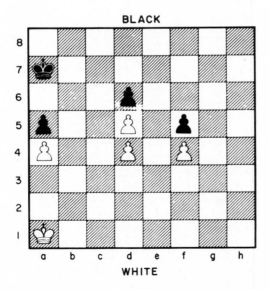

BLACK

	a	b	c	d	e	f	g	h
8	14	15	16	16	16	15	13	11
7	15	18	18	19	18	16	14	11
6	15	17		19	19	17		11
5	14							
4	11	12	10		6			
3	8	9	10	7	5	3	1	
2	5	6	6	6	4	2	1	
1	3	3	3	3	3	1		

WHITE

Figure 6: Bonus map for the position of figure 4. Without this map, an 11 ply search would be required for the computer (White) to discover that the pawn at a6 can be captured. Using the map, only a 3 ply search is required.

plan within the evaluation function produces a goal directed search without requiring an enormous look-ahead tree. This increase in efficiency is highly desirable.

Because the process is directed by the location of the pawns, changes in the map will occur infrequently and therefore only a relatively small number of bonus maps will be required for any one search. Once a map has been calculated for a particular pawn configuration, it can be stored and used later whenever it is needed. Although this strategy seems to work well in the examples we have presented, it is reasonable to ask whether this procedure will work in all end game situations. Unfortunately, the answer is no.

Consider the position presented in

figure 7. This is a famous end game problem which appears as diagram 70 in Reuben Fine's classic chess book, *Basic Chess Endings* (see references). It was analyzed in 1975 by Monroe Newborn to determine if his special end game program, Peasant, could solve it. After several unsuccessful efforts, Newborn concluded that the problem would require about 25,000 hours of processor time before a solution could be found (see *Chess Skill in Man and Machine*, page 129). The problem is difficult, but not as impossible as Newborn suggests. Because Peasant does not have a transposition table, the program did not take advantage of the tremendous number of identical terminal positions which are encountered when an exhaustive search is made of this position. Because the pawns are locked, the only moves which are possible are King moves, and this greatly increases the potential number of transpositions.

The position was submitted to Northwestern's chess program Chess 4.5 running on the CYBER 176 system at Control Data headquarters in Minneapolis. David Cahlander discovered that Chess 4.5 could solve the problem after a 26 ply search! This required ten minutes of processor time on the powerful CYBER 176. Although it is interesting to know that the problem can be solved by a brute force search, this type of solution is not particularly elegant and it requires a level of hardware sophistication that is not likely to be available in the small system for a few years yet.

The Coordinate Squares Approach

What can be done to make this problem more manageable? Interestingly enough, there is a rather neat approach to problems of this type which has been examined in some detail by Ken Church in his undergraduate thesis at MIT. Working with Richard Greenblatt as his advisor, Church applied the chess concept of coordinate squares to this position. The basic notion is that the Black King must coordinate precisely with the moves of the White King in order to successfully defend its pawns. For any particular square which the White King occupies, there are only a limited number of squares which the Black King can occupy and still hold his act together.

In his thesis, Ken Church presents a fairly extensive analysis of King and pawn end games. For our present purpose, we will limit our analysis to King and pawn end games in which the pawns are locked and we will modify Church's approach to suit our conditional evaluation strategy. The major difference is that Church attempts to dis-

Figure 7: A chess position which can be analyzed efficiently by means of the coordinate square concept proposed by Ken Church (see references). In this approach, the Black King must coordinate precisely with the White King in order to successfully defend its pawns. The technique is illustrated in table 1.

cover a complete solution to the problem using the coordinate squares idea. We propose, instead, to use the coordinate squares approach to provide the evaluation function with additional chess knowledge. With this modification, a full-width search of reasonable depth can find the correct move.

Using figure 7 as an example, the first step in this process is to determine which squares are denied to each of the Kings by the existing pawn configuration. By noting that each King cannot move to a square that is occupied by its own pawn or that is attacked by an opponent's pawn, one can easily determine that squares a4, b4, c5, d4, d5, e4, e5, f4 and g4 are denied to the White King. Likewise, squares a5, b5, c5, c6, d6, e5, e6, f6 and g6 are denied to the Black King. Neither side has a passed pawn, but there are multiple targets, since none of the pawns are defended by friendly pawns.

By applying the strategy described earlier, it is possible to calculate a composite attack map for the White King on the basis of the target pawns at a5, d6, and f5 and taking into account the centralization subgoal. The resulting map for Fine's position is presented in figure 8. The squares without a number are the squares which are denied to the White King because of the pawn structure. Given the position of the White King (a1), a shallow search using this attack map as part of the evaluation function would encourage the White King to approach the target pawn at a5 (eg: b2, c3, c4, b5, a5). If the Black King were more than five moves from a5, this sequence of moves would lead to suc-

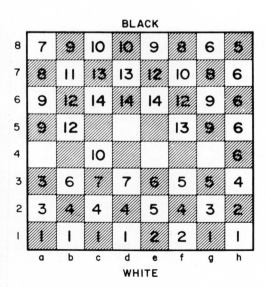

Figure 8: Bonus map for the position of figure 7, a composite attack map for White based on the target pawns at a5, d6 and f5, and taking into account the centralization subgoal.

Figure 9: The square control concept applied to the position of figure 7. Each of the squares is assigned to one of three categories: under the influence of the Black King, under the influence of the White King, or contested. To do this, the distance from each King to each square is computed, given the constraints imposed by the existing pawn structure. Each square closer in moves to the Black King and not denied to the Black King is assigned to Black, and vice-versa. The remaining squares are labelled as contested. Through a complex series of manipulations and the use of so-called frontier squares (see text), White is actively directed to attack Black's pawns using the strategy of trying to prevent Black from moving onto strategic coordinate squares which are vital to Black's defense.

cess. Given that the Black King is at a7, however, this plan is doomed to failure. In fact, the first move in the sequence, b2, is fatal and transforms a winning position into a draw. There are two important conclusions that follow from this discovery. The first is that our simple goal-gradient approach does not always work. The second is that chess end games are much more difficult than a novice player might suppose.

Let us extend Ken Church's ideas and apply the concept of coordinate squares to this position. First, we wish to assign each of the squares to one of three categories: under the influence of the Black King, under the influence of the White King, or contested. To do this we compute the distance from each King to each square, given the constraints imposed by the existing pawn structure. This creates two distance maps, one for the White King and one for the Black King. For squares which are not accessible to one or both of the Kings, we assign a distance score based on the number of King moves required to reach that square by traveling across accessible squares. Next, each square which is closer in moves to the Black King than to the White King and is not denied to the Black King is assigned to Black. Each square which is closer to the White King than to the Black King and is not denied to the White King is assigned to White. The remaining squares are assigned to the contested category. The results of this procedure are summarized in figure 9. The squares assigned to Black are indicated by the letter B and the squares assigned to White are indicated by a W. The blank squares belong in the contested category.

If the territory under the influence of either King is adjacent to an opponent's pawn, the contest is essentially settled since that pawn would be open for capture. Since this is not the case for the present position, we wish to define a special category of squares called *frontier squares*. A frontier square is any square under your influence that is adjacent to an accessible contested square or is adjacent to an accessible square under the influence of the opponent.

For the position diagramed in figure 7, the frontier squares for White are c4 and h4. The next step is to determine, for each of these frontier squares, the set of squares under Black's influence which, if the Black King were located on that square, would prevent the White King from moving from the frontier square to any of the contested squares or to any of Black's squares. For the frontier square at c4, the Black King would have to be at either a6 or b6 to prevent the White King from penetrating to b5. For the frontier square at h4, the Black King would have to be at g6 or h6 to prevent penetration by the White King. (Note that the Black King could not legally be at h5 if the White King were at h4.) These defense squares for Black can be determined by the machine by placing the White King on the frontier square and conducting a shallow tree search with White to move first and determining empirically which locations for the Black King successfully repel the invader.

The next step in this process is to determine the shortest distance between each pair of frontier squares. For the present position, there are only two frontier squares and thus one minimal distance. Five King moves are required to travel between the two frontier squares. If Black is to be successful in defending, the Black King must be able to move from a defense square for h4 to a defense square for c4 in the same number or in fewer moves than it takes the White King to travel between the two frontier squares.

For this reason, each square in Black's defense set for c4 must be five or fewer moves from one of the defense squares for h4. Also, each square in the defense set for h4 must be five or fewer moves from one of the defense squares for c4. This requirement places a further restriction on those squares which satisfy the necessary defense conditions. One will note that a6 is six moves from the nearest square in the defense set

for h4. Also, h6 is six moves from the nearest square in the defense set for c4. Therefore, the true defense set for c4 contains only b6 (a6 will not suffice). The true defense set for h4 contains only g6 (h6 will not suffice). Thus, we have determined that when the White King is on c4 and has the move, there is one, and only one, coordinate square for the Black King (b6). If the White King is on h4 and has the move, there is one, and only one, coordinate square for the Black King (g6).

The next step is to generalize this analysis to squares in White's territory which are immediately adjacent to the frontier squares. In this case, squares b3, c3, d3, g3 and h3. The square at b3 is one King move from the frontier square at c4 and six moves from the frontier square at h4. If the White King is at b3, therefore, the Black King must be on a square which is simultaneously one move from b6 and six or fewer moves from g6. The squares which satisfy this condition (ie: the coordinate squares for b3) are a6, a7, b7, and c7. This same set of calculations can be made for the other adjacent squares. The coordinate squares for c3 are b7 and c7. For d3, there is only one coordinate square, namely c7. Since the White King can move directly from c3 to d3 and Black must move to c7, and only c7, to maintain his defense, it is not possible for him to be on c7 when the White King is on c3. If he were, he would not be able to move when White moved from c3 to d3 and still satisfy the defense requirements. For this reason, only square b7 is sufficient for Black when White is on c3. In addition, since b3 is adjacent to c3, the coordinate square for c3 is not available for b3. Thus the set for b3 is further restricted to a6, a7 and c7.

If we examine g3, we will discover that it is one move from the frontier square at h4 and four moves from the frontier square at c4. This implies that the Black King must be on a square which is one move from b6 and four or fewer moves from g6. There are only two squares which satisfy this requirement, namely, f6 and f7. Therefore we can conclude that no square other than f6 or f7 will serve as a coordinate for g3. When we examine h3, we will find that there are three potential coordinate squares: f6, f7 and g7. Since this set shares f6 and f7 with the defense squares for g3, further restrictions are implied. It is not possible for the same square to serve as a coordinate square for two adjacent squares since it is not possible for Black to pass when it is his turn to move. Therefore if f6 is assigned to h3, then f7 *must* be assigned to g3. If f7 is assigned to h3, then f6 *must* be assigned to g3.

The next step in this process is to determine the set of coordinate squares for each

Square of the White King	Coordinate Squares for the Black King
b3	a6, a7, c7
c3	b7
c4	b6
d3	c7
e2	d7, d8
e3	d7, d8
f2	e7, e8
f3	e7, e8
g3	f6, f7
h3	f6, f7, g7
h4	g6

Table 1: Results of the coordinate square analysis for the position of figure 7. Shown are the potential squares for the Black King which defend against the White King's threats when it is White's turn to move.

square on the minimum pathway(s) between the two frontier squares for which the coordinate squares have not yet been determined. The new squares are e2, e3, f2 and f3. By following the same analysis as before, we can determine that the coordinate squares for e2 and e3 are d7 and d8. The coordinate squares for f2 and f3 are e7 and e8. Because of the adjacency restrictions, the assignment of one of these values automatically restricts the other square to the remaining value.

The results of our coordinate square analysis are summarized in table 1. When it is Black's turn to move and White has moved to one of the squares listed in the table, Black must be able to move to a coordinate square. For this reason, the evaluation function for the machine can be modified to give a bonus of 20 points to White for any terminal position in the look-ahead tree where it is Black's turn to move and the Black King is more than one move from a necessary coordinate square. If it is White's turn to move, a 20 point bonus will be awarded to any terminal position in the look-ahead tree where Black is not located on a necessary coordinate square.

Let us consider how this in combination with the White King attack map (figure 8) will affect the outcome of the look-ahead search. The machine will try to find a pathway to squares c3 or d3 because their attack value of 7 is higher than any of the surrounding squares. Even better would be a pathway to c4, since its attack value of 10 is larger than 7. In each of these cases, the machine will also try to satisfy the condition that Black cannot be on a proper coordinate square when the White King reaches c3, d3, or c4 so that the additional 20 point bonus is also earned. In attempting to do this, it will find that if the White King moves from a1 to either a2 or b2 on his first move, the 20 point bonus will be lost forever. The reason is that either of these moves allows the

Black King to coordinate and, because of the minimax strategy, the tree search will always assume replies for Black which maintain this coordination. If the White King's first move is to square b1, the Black King cannot coordinate and the 20 point bonus will still be available at some of the terminal positions in the tree. It is not surprising, therefore, to find Reuben Fine advising that K-N1 is the only move for White which preserves the win.

In order for the machine to find this move, assuming that both the attack map and the coordinate squares information are incorporated in the evaluation function, a search of nine plies is required. This is a tremendous improvement over the 26 ply search required by the unmodified program. In order to actually win a Black pawn, the White King must move to c3 or c4 with Black not in coordination and make a 13 ply look-ahead search. If the White King moves to d3 with Black not in coordination, an 11 ply search will suffice. In order to prevent a draw, White will avoid repeating identical positions and thus will eventually travel to e3. From this vantage point, the win of a pawn can be visualized with a 9 ply search. Therefore, the problem could be solved by the machine if it searched to a depth of nine plies for each move calculation. With a program such as Chess 4.5, a 9 ply search for this position can be conducted in less than two minutes on even a medium power computer.

The procedures which we have described are applicable to a wide range of end game positions. The coordinate squares analysis demonstrates that even highly complex end game positions are manageable when the full-width search employs a sufficiently knowledgeable evaluation function. Although the examples we have discussed encompass only a few types of chess positions, we hope that the reader will envision the power which is potentially available when the evaluation function is modified to incorporate relevant chess knowledge. The implementation of this approach on a broad scale should eventually produce chess programs which can be run on medium power machines and still compete on equal terms with strong human players.

Quiescence

Another important area for the application of chess knowledge is the problem of *quiescence*. It is essential that the static evaluation function not be applied to a turbulent position. If the next move has the potential to produce a major perturbation of the situation, the evaluation which is rendered will not be accurate. For example, it makes little sense to apply a static evaluation function in the middle of a piece exchange or when one of the Kings is in check. In each case, the judgment which is rendered will not be reliable. For this reason Chess 4.5 presently goes beyond the predetermined search depth at "terminal" positions where a capture might be profitable for the side whose turn it is to move, where certain types of checking moves are possible, or where a pawn is on the seventh rank. This extended search facility is called the quiescence search, and its major objective is to produce reasonably static positions for which the evaluation function can provide accurate assessments.

A weakness of this present implementation is that the definition of a turbulent position is much too narrow. There are many situations in addition to capture threats, checks on the King, and pawn promotion threats which are clearly turbulent. Larry Harris has characterized some of these in chapter 7 of *Chess Skill in Man and Machine*. Harris includes in this category positions which involve a pawn lever, a back rank mate threat, or sacrifice potential. The interested reader can consult Harris' chapter for operational definitions of these patterns. It is essential to note that these and other important patterns are not easily detected. In each case, a fairly sophisticated pattern analysis capability is required. A reasonable goal for improving the present forward search chess programs would be the development of an efficient procedure for detecting potential sources of turbulence. The central objective would be to use this information as one of the decision criteria for terminating search at a node. If the position is not quiescence in respect to a potential perturbation which has been detected, the look-ahead process should be continued.

For example, during the opening when the machine leaves its library with information that the control of a particular square is an important objective, the decisions about search termination can consider whether the position is quiescent in respect to perturbations which might influence control of the key square. Another example of this idea involves the end game. If the preliminary analysis indicates that a particular pawn should be an attack target, the decision for search termination should consider whether each position is quiescent with respect to this goal. Positions at the predetermined depth level will be evaluated only if all potential attackers are more than two moves away from the target. When one or more attackers are close to the goal, the search process will be continued to determine if capture is feasible. This modification of the search process introduces a goal directed

selective search at the terminal positions of the full-width tree. The addition of several extra plies of search at relevant nodes in the tree can mean the difference between finding and just missing an important continuation. This type of facility is difficult to implement and difficult to control properly, but the potential gains are such that the effort is worthwhile.

Establishing Appropriate Goals

In order to implement this goal direction feature in the evaluation function and quiescence search, it is necessary to recognize that a goal which may be of paramount importance at the base node of the look-ahead tree may no longer be relevant at some of the terminal nodes. Intervening moves may accomplish the necessary goal or may alter the situation such that it is no longer possible. In these cases, the conditional evaluation function would be directed at an inappropriate goal. One way to deal with this problem would be to select goals which were both general and long range. In this case, they should continue to be relevant at the terminal nodes of the look-ahead tree. Unfortunately, this is a fairly severe limitation on the goal directed search and is therefore not desirable. A second approach would be to apply pattern analysis at each terminal node instead of at the base node only. In this case, the goals which were selected would always be relevant to the position. This procedure would be very time-consuming, since feature analysis is a complex process. The essential aspect of the problem is a time relevance trade-off in which a guarantee that relevant goals are being pursued requires a heavy investment in additional computing time. The third and most reasonable approach would be to designate which features of the position are crucial to each particular goal and to incrementally update our goals (and thus the evaluation function and the decision rules for the quiescence search) whenever these features change. This is a highly sophisticated approach which would be difficult to implement.

Conclusion

Let us summarize our conclusions and relate them to the world of personal computing. We have attempted to argue that a full-width search strategy is feasible with a small computer, and that ultimately this approach will produce better chess than a selective search strategy. For this plan to be successful, it is necessary to employ software and hardware suited to the task. The software must incorporate recent improvements in tree searching strategy (ie: α-β pruning, the capture and killer heuristics, iterative searching, staged move generation, incremental updating, serial evaluation and transposition analysis) as well as other refinements such as conditional evaluations which provide goal direction to the search process.

On the hardware side, it is necessary to have a reasonably powerful system. Although there have been a number of recent efforts to program microprocessor systems to play chess, the games which have resulted have not been comparable to those played by established large system programs. Although it is quite an accomplishment to produce even rudimentary chess from a microprocessor system, the level of play to date is not very encouraging. An example of this type of game appeared in March 1978 BYTE, "Microchess 115 versus Dark Horse," page 166.

The type of chess program described in this article requires reasonably powerful hardware in order to provide an interesting game. Because of the many operations requiring bit map manipulation, a 16 bit processor is much more desirable than an 8 bit processor. It is more efficient to represent a set of 64 squares with four 16 bit words than with eight 8 bit words. With a need for computing power in mind, one might select a microprocessor system based on one of the new high-speed 16 bit processors such as the Zilog Z-8000 or the Intel 8086. In addition, this type of program will require quite a bit of memory. The program itself will require about 20 K bytes and the transposition table, if implemented, will need at least another 20 K bytes. If the programmer plans to add chess knowledge for conditional evaluations, a total of 64 K bytes is desirable. An opening library which is sufficient to keep a skilled opponent on his toes requires disk storage.

These considerations may dampen the enthusiasm of many would-be chess programmers. On the other hand, a realistic orientation at the start could save a great deal of grief along the way. When implemented on fairly sophisticated hardware, our demonstration chess program will usually provide a reasonable chess move after two or three minutes of computation. If more time is available (eg: selecting a move for a postal chess game by letting the machine "think" for several hours), a fairly respectable level of play can be anticipated. With future hardware improvements, this type of program may soon become reasonably competitive at tournament time limits, even on a personal computing system.■

REFERENCES

1. Berliner, H, *Chess as Problem Solving: The Development of a Tactics Analyzer,* unpublished doctoral thesis, Carnegie-Mellon University, Pittsburgh, 1974.
2. Church, K W, "Coordinate Squares: A Solution to Many Chess Pawn Endgames," undergraduate thesis, Massachusetts Institute of Technology, June 1978.
3. Church, R M, and Church, K W, "Plans, Goals, and Search Strategies for the Selection of a Move in Chess," Frey, P W (ed), *Chess Skill in Man and Machine*, Springer-Verlag, New York, 1977.
4. Fine, Reuben, *Basic Chess Endings*, David McKay Company Inc, New York, 1941.
5. Harris, L R, "The Heuristic Search: An Alternative to the Alpha-Beta Minimax Procedure," Frey, P W (ed), *Chess Skill in Man and Machine*, Springer-Verlag, New York, 1977.
6. Newborn, M, "PEASANT: An Endgame Program for Kings and Pawns," *Chess Skill in Man and Machine,* Frey, P W (ed), Springer-Verlag, New York, 1977.
7. Shannon, C E, "Programming a Computer for Playing Chess," *Philosophical Magazine,* volume 41, 1950, pages 256 thru 275.
8. Zobrist, A L, and Carlson, F R Jr, "An Advice-Taking Chess Computer," *Scientific American*, volume 228, number 12, June 1973, pages 92 thru 105.

An APL Interpreter in Pascal

Alan Kaniss

Vincent DiChristofaro

John Santini

For our APL interpreter we used Michael Wimble's flowcharts (see "An APL Interpreter for Microcomputers," BYTE, Aug, Sept and Oct 1977) as generalized guidelines rather than coding directly from them. We used most of his ideas on function implementation, table storage, input scanning, and statement parsing. There were a few minor errors in logic, but for the most part the flowcharts were clear and easy to work with. We expanded the interpreter to include functions that Wimble made reference to but did not flowchart — inner product, outer product, catenate, and index-of. We made the interpreter extremely portable by making the character set machine (as well as keyboard) independent. We accomplished this by having the program read in the installation's character set from a file at the start-up of the program.

Values

We store all values as real numbers. We decided to do this based on the fact that although APL's data structures are weak (eg, reals and integers can be stored in the same array), Pascal's data structures are very strongly typed. Numbers are checked to be whole numbers (nonfractional) for certain operations such as index generation (monadic iota) and reshaping (dyadic rho). Numbers are checked to be Boolean for such operations as logical negation (tilde), ANDs, and ORs.

Tables

Rather than using Wimble's method of storing tables in arrays (variable table, function table, token table), we took advantage of one of Pascal's data structures, the *linked list*. This offers two big advantages to the design of the interpreter:

- Array sizes do not have to be declared anywhere in the program. There is no way of telling which tables will grow very large and which ones will stay small; this is dependent on the calculations being performed with the interpreter and will vary from one terminal session to another. With linked lists, storage allocation is dynamic and can be used for each table as needed (storage is taken from a common pool of storage reserved for linked lists).
- It is a simple procedure to deallocate storage (using the standard procedure "dispose" in Pascal) so that it can be re-used by the program as needed. This helps to keep the size of the running program to a minimum.

Character Sets

In keeping with the goal by easy transportability, the character set is installation (as well as keyboard) independent. This is accomplished by storing the character set on a file (created at installation time) and reading it into storage each time the interpreter is activated. Due to the development in a CDC environment some special considerations had to be made:

- The normal CDC character set consists of 64 characters — letters, digits, and special characters. These characters are represented by 6 bit bytes (octal display codes 00 thru 77) stored 10 to a computer word (60 bits).
- The APL interpreter requires 89 distinct characters excluding overstrikes (over-strikes are considered APL characters, but are not implemented in this version of APL). CDC's ASCII mode fulfills this requirement in that in ASCII mode, upper and lowercase letters are differentiated (in "normal" mode, they are not), thus yielding the extra 26 characters needed.
- In ASCII mode, characters are

represented in one of two ways — a 6 bit display code (uppercase A: octal 01, uppercase Z: octal 32, etc.), b) a 6 bit prefix (octal 74 to 76) and a 6 bit root (lowercase a: octal 7601, lowercase z: octal 7632, etc.).

- CDC's version of Pascal (obtained from University of Minnesota with local modifications made at NADC) does not recognize the special ASCII mode (i.e., octal 7601, the lowercase a, would be picked up as two distinct characters — the circumflex (^) and capital A).
- To compensate for this, the program does two things:

A test is made for the special prefix when characters are read in (the "ORDs" of these prefixes are 60 and 62 respectively).

Rather than the characters being stored, their "ORDs" are. If a character has a prefix, it is stored as (100 times the "ORD" of the prefix plus the "ORD" of the character root) — thus lowercase a, (octal 7601 display code) would be stored as $100 \times ORD$ (^) + ORD (A). Characters without prefixes will be stored by their ORDs.

- Characters will be packed five to a word. Characters with prefixes will have a value greater than 6000, thus flagging them for special input/output (I/O) consideration.

Due to the fact that DCD's interactive system responds to the user in uppercase letters only, (and in APL, the uppercase are special symbols, [↑,↓,ᵒ,~,Γ,L,°, □, etc], the lowercase are capital letters A...Z), the messages to be returned to the user (diagnostics, etc.) are also typed in lowercase into the character set file at installation time.

These local considerations and adjustments will be removed or will be transparent (in input routines, two sections of code will be removed; in output routines, the code will be transparent) for another system.

This implementation of APL will use *all of the correct APL symbols* (← for assign, ρ for reshape, ° for null, etc.) with the exception of log-to-a-base [O overstruck with *] — it will be O (large circle) only.

Procedures and Functions

INITIALIZE CHARACTER SET — Reads installation character set from a file, stores "orders" of characters in character set array (APLCHARSET) which is indexed by the name of the characters.

READINERROR MESSAGES — Reads user-feedback and error messages in from a file and stores them in a two dimensional array (ERRORMSGS).

FILLUP TABLES — Initializes tables of monadic, dyadic, and reduction operators and special characters with the orders of characters from the character set.

PRINTAPLSTATEMENT — Echoes an input statement back to the user.

SERROR — Scanner error-handling routine. Invokes echo of statement causing the error and prints a pointer to the item causing the error.

GETAPLSTATEMENT — Reads in and stores (in APLSTATEMENT) an input line from the terminal. Checks input line for being null (carriage return only) and being too long (greater than MAXINPUTLINE).

SKIPSPACES — Self-explanatory.

ITSADIGIT — (Boolean function) — Determines whether a character passed to it is a digit (0..9).

ITSALETTER — (Boolean function) — Determines whether a character passed to it is a letter (A..Z).

CHARTONUM — (integer function) — Returns the integer representation of a number in character representation.

NAMESMATCH — (Boolean function) — Determines whether the two names passed to it are identical.

TABLELOOKUP — Determines whether the character passed to it is contained in the table passed to it (MOPTAB, DOPTAB, REDTAB, CHARTAB, SPECTAB). If contained, the index (array position) of the character is returned; 0 otherwise (TABLEINDEX).

IDENTIFIER — Determines if the next token of the APL statement is an identifier (variable name). If so, the identifier is returned (NAME). The length of the name is checked for length error (greater than MAXVARNAMELENGTH).

MAKENUMBER — Determines if the next token of the APL statement is a number. If so, the number is returned (REALNUMBER). The number is checked for validity (digit must follow a minus sign; digit must follow a decimal point).

MONADICREFERENCE — (Boolean function) — Determines whether an operator passed to it is monadic in tl e context of line (operator cannot be preceded by a FORMAL ARGU-

Number of Arguments	0 (NILADIC)	1 (MONADIC)	2 (DYADIC)
No explicit result	NAME	NAME B	A NAME B
explicit result	Z←NAME	Z←NAME B	Z←A NAME B

MENT, FORMAL RESULT, GLOBAL VARIABLE, CONSTANT, PERIOD, LEFT PAREN, or LEFT BRACKET to be considered monadic in context).

DYADICOPCHECK — Checks to see if next character in input line is a dyadic operator, special character, comment delimeter (rest of statement is ignored), or invalid character. If valid, the operator/special character is stored in TOKENTABLE.

CHECKOTHERTABLES — Checks to see if next charcter in input line is a valid reduction operator or a valid monadic operator. If so, it is stored in TOKENTABLE.

TRYTOGETANUMBER — If next token in input line is a number (scalar or vector), it is assembled and stored in VALTAB (value table). It is also stored in TOKENTABLE.

NAMEINVARTABLE — (Boolean function) — Checks to see if the identifier (name) passed to it is in VARTAB (variable table). If so, the address (pointer) to the name is returned.

ADDNAMETOVARTABLE —. Adds the name (identifier) passed to it to the variable table (VARTAB).

FUNCTIONALREADYDEFINED — (Boolean function) — Checks to see if the function name passed to it is in the function table (FUNCTAB). If so, the pointer to its address in FUNCTAB is returned.

MAKETOKENLINK — Sets up a new link of storage in TOKENTABLE and ties it to the rest of the table.

PROCESSFUNCTION HEADER — Scans function header to check for characteristics of function and the validity of the header. There are six legitimate types of function headers as shown in table 1.

The procedure checks the validity of the result (if present), arguments (if present), the function, extraneous characters following function header, the function being previously defined. If the header is valid, it is stored in the function table (FUNCTAB).

DESTROYSTATEMENT — Returns (disposes) links of TOKENTABLE after the statement is scanned and parsed (if in immediate mode). This releases unneeded storage for further use. Also, returns links of subroutine call information from the parser.

SCANNER — (main program) — Drives above routines until /* (slash asterisk) appears as the first two characters on an input line.

Parser Routines

The parsing and execution of a string of tokens is accomplished utilizing the following routines:

ERROR
PARSER
RELEASE
EXPRESSION
RETURNTOCALLINGSUBR
SPECSYMBOL
CALLSUBR
FUNCALL
NUMWRITE
OUTPUTVAL
INPUTVAL
GETARRAYPOSITION
LINKRESULTS
STACKPOINTERS
SIMPLEVARIABLE
INDEX
VARIABLE
PRIMARY
VECTOR
ASSIGNMENT
MOP
DOP
FUNCTCALL

ERROR — Given control upon detection of improper syntax within either the SCANNER or PARSER. An error code is printed accompanied by an appropriate diagnostic message. (See table 2 for error messages.)

PARSER — Controls all parsing; calls RELEASE, EXPRESSION, RETURNTOCALLINGSUBR, OUTPUTVAL to print last resultant (OPERTABPTR′). Whenever an assignment has not been detected in current statement, detects function completion and returns control to calling token via RETURNTOCALLINGSUBR's action upon current subroutine table pointer (SUBRTABPTS′); SPECSYMBOL detects branching directive "→";

prior to exiting parser RELEASE clears unneeded memroy allocations to the resultant table (OPERTAB).

RELEASE — Calls upon PRIMARY, FUNCALL, EXPRESSION (recursive), ASSIGNMENT, MOP, MONADIC, DOP and DYADIC to interpret a valid expression. The parsing of all expressions and their components proceeds from the right most token to the left. PRIMARY is first called to process the right most token which is required to be in primary component; FUNCALL then detects and executes a monadic or dyadic function with a recursive call to EX-PRESSION, else; an assignment, if found, is processed by ASSIGNMENT else; MOP detects a monadic operator and PRIMARY is called to distinguish the preceding primary else; the previously found primary

returns the call from EXPRESSION with a valid indication.

RETURNTOCALLINGSUBR — Called from PARSER; returns control from the current function to the calling function or, if none, to the current subroutine table pointer (destroys old pointers; utilizes NAMEINVAR-TABLE to check result name).

SPECSYMBOL — Called from various parser modules, detects various special symbols (:/→/←/°/./()/[/]/;/□) yielding a true if the passed symbol is found in the current token.

CALLSUBR — Called from PRIMARY or FUNCTCALL to provide necessary subroutine table (SUBRTAB') pointers, pass function parameters, and ex-ecute branch to called function's first token. (Utilizes NAMEINVARTAB to check argument names.)

FUNCALL — Called from EXPRESSION,

Table 2: Error messages displayed by APL interpreter.

Code	Message
00002	DIGIT MUST FOLLOW A DECIMAL POINT
00003	EXTRANEOUS CHARACTERS FOLLOW FUNCTION HEADER
00004	INVALID CHARACTER ENCOUNTERED
00005	FUNCTION ALREADY DEFINED
00006	ILLEGAL NAME TO RIGHT OF EXPLICIT RESULT
00007	INVALID FUNCTION/ARGUMENT NAME
00008	RESULT OF ASSIGNMENT NOT VALID VARIABLE
00009	INVALID FUNCTION RIGHT ARGUMENT NAME
00010	INVALID EXPRESSION
00011	SYMBOL NOT FOUND
00012	STATEMENT NUMBER TO BRANCH TO NOT INTEGER
00013	DYADIC OPERATOR NOT PRECEDED BY PRIMARY
00014	INVALID EXPRESSION WITHIN PARENTHESES
00015	MISMATCHED PARENTHESES
00016	NOT USED
00017	LEFT ARGUMENT OF DYADIC FUNCTION NOT A PRIMARY
00018	NOT USED
00019	VALUE NOT BOOLEAN
00020	ATTEMPTED DIVISION BY ZERO
00021	ARGUMENT NOT A SCALAR
00022	ARGUMENT IS NEGATIVE
00023	ARGUMENT IS NOT AN INTEGER
00024	ARGUMENT IS A SCALAR OR EMPTY VECTOR
00025	NOT USED
00026	INVALID OUTER PRODUCT EXPRESSION
00027	INVALID INNER PRODUCT EXPRESSION
00028	NOT USED
00029	LEFT ARGUMENT IS NOT A VECTOR
00030	NOT USED
00031	NOT USED
00032	ERROR IN FUNCTION ARGUMENT
00033	ERROR IN FUNCTION ARGUMENT
00034	INVALID INDEX EXPRESSION
00035	NON-SCALAR INDICES
00036	ASSIGNED EXPRESSION NOT A SCALAR
00037	NON-INTEGER INDICES
00038	INDEX OUT OF RANGE
00039	INVALID INDEX EXPRESSION
00040	NOT USED
00041	NOT USED
00042	NOT USED
00043	NOT USED
00044	NOT USED
00045	NOT USED
00046	NOT USED
00047	NOT USED
00048	NOT USED
00049	NOT USED
00050	NUMBER AND BASE OF DIFFERENT SIGN
00051	ARGUMENT IS A VECTOR OF LENGTH ONE
00052	ARGUMENTS NOT COMPATIBLE FOR INNER PRODUCT
00053	ARGUMENT(S) WITH RANK GREATER THAN ONE
00054	ATTEMPTED INVERSE OF ZERO
00055	ARGUMENTS INCOMPATIBLE FOR DYADIC OPERATION
00056	LEFT ARGUMENT NOT A VECTOR
00057	NOT USED
00058	NOT USED
00059	NOT USED
00060	GREATER THAN THREE DIMENSIONS
00061	NIL
00062	RE-ENTER LAST LINE
00063	INPUT
00064	NOT USED
00065	NOT USED
00066	NOT USED
00067	NOT USED
00068	NOT USED
00069	NOT USED
00070	IDENTIFIER TOO LONG
00071	INPUT LINE TOO LONG
00072	INVALID REDUCTION OPERATOR
00073	DYADIC REDUCTION REFERENCE
00074	MONADIC REFERENCE TO DYADIC OPERATOR
00075	FUNCTION DEFINED WITH NO STATEMENTS
00076	NOT USED
00077	NOT USED
00078	NOT USED
00079	NOT USED
00080	NOT USED
00081	NOT USED
00082	NOT USED
00083	NOT USED
00084	NOT USED
00085	NOT USED
00086	NOT USED
00087	NOT USED
00088	NOT USED
00089	NOT USED
00090	NOT USED
00091	NOT USED
00092	NOT USED
00093	NOT USED
00094	NOT USED
00095	NOT USED
00096	NOT USED
00097	NOT USED
00098	NOT USED
00099	VARIABLE NOT ASSIGNED A VALUE

calls FUNCTCALL, PRIMARY, and CALLSUBR; if FUNCTCALL finds a function name, PRIMARY is called to get a primary component if function is dyadic; CALLSUBR is used to establish function pointers in SUBRTAB'. Having transferred control to the called function a valid function indication is returned to EXPRESSION.

NUMWRITE — Prints a signed numeric value, yielding the APLFILE define negative symbol.

OUTPUTVAL — Prints the vector indicated by the last stacked resultant (OPERTABPTR'); greater than three dimensions are not printed, nil vectors are not printed; calls NUMWRITE to ensure correct printing of sign. Called by PARSER and VARIABLE.

INPUTVAL — Called from VARIABLE; inputs vectors of one dimension or SCALARS via keyboard. Input is requested with the prompt "input," a carriage return, and a line feed.

GETARRAYPOSITION — Called from LINKRESULTS and STACKPOINTERS; produces a pointer to an array value given the indices of the value and a pointer to the array.

LINKRESULTS — Called from VARIABLE; places results (OPERTAB') into its assigned position, utilizes GETARRAYPOINTER if result is to be positioned within an indexed array.

STACKPOINTERS — Called from VARIABLE; places a result on the stack (OPERTAB'), utilizes GETARRAYPOINTER if result comes from an indexed array.

SIMPLEVARIABLE — Called from VARIABLE; detects a variable's name and type and assembles a pointer to the variable's values; returns a valid indication if variable found.

INDEX — Called from VARIABLE; determines indices utilizing EXPRESSION and stacks the indices in the resultant table (OPERTAB'); SPECSYMBOL insures that the indices are delimited by semicolons.

VARIABLE — Called from PRIMARY and ASSIGNMENT; calls SPECSYMBOL, INDEX, INPUTVAL, OUTPUTVAL, SIMPLEVARIABLE, LINKRESULTS, STACKPOINTERS in order to parse a valid variable, which is comprised of: a simple variable, a quad indicating I/O or an indexed variable.

PRIMARY — Called from EXPRESSION and FUNCALL; calls VECTOR, VARIABLE, SPECSYMBOL, EXPRESSION, FUNCTCALL, and CALLSUBR;

The primary may be a vector, a variable, an expression enclosed in parens, or a niladic function call; if any are found a valid indication is returned to the calling procedure.

VECTOR — Called from PRIMARY; yields a valid indication if SPECSYMBOL detects a left arrow (←) and VARIABLE finds a valid variable after the arrow.

ASSIGNMENT — Called from EXPRESSION; yields a valid indication if SPECSYMBOL detects a left arrow (←) and VARIABLE finds a valid variable after the arrow.

MOP — Called EXPRESSION; determines if the current token points to a reduction operator; if found, a valid indication is returned to EXPRESSION.

DOP — Called by EXPRESSION; determines if the next grouping of tokens indicate a dyadic operator, an inner product or an outer product; if one of these are found, a valid indication is returned to EXPRESSION.

FUNCTCALL — Called by PRIMARY and FUNCALL; calls FUNCTIONALREADYDEFINED to determine if current token is a function name, if true a new subroutine table (SUBTAB') is created and a valid indication is returned to the calling procedure.

Implemented Operators and Functions

DYADCOMP — Routine that performs mathematical and logical operations for reduction and dyadic computations

INDEXGENERATOR — Routine that performs the index generator function (also referred to as the monadic iota operator). Produces a vector of the first ARG integers.

RAVEL — Routine that performs the ravel function (also referred to as monadic comma operator). The result is a vector containing all elements of ARG in odometer order.

SHAPEOF — Routine that performs the shape of or size function (also referred to as the monadic rho operator). The result is a vector containing the dimensions of ARG.

REDUCTION — Routine that performs the interpretation of the reduction monadic argument and calls DYADCOMP to perform the indicated mathematical or logical operation

MONADIC — Routine that performs the interpretation of valid monadic operators or calls the necessary routines for reduction or mixed monadic operations.

CATENATE — Routine that performs the concatenate function of joining two arguments (also referred to as dyadic comma operator).

INDEXOF — Routine that performs the index-function which returns for each element of vector RIGHTARG the least index I in the vector LEFTARG for which RIGHTARG [I] equals the element. If no value in LEFTARG is equal, the result element is 1 plus THE SIZE OF LEFTARG (also referred to as dyadic iota operator).

RESHAPE — Routine that performs the reshape function which forms a result having the dimension specified by LEFTARG and having elements taken from RIGHTARG in odometer order (also referred to as dyadic rho operator).

INNERPRODUCT — Routine that performs the inner product function which applied a scalar dyadic function (associated with RIGHTARG) between each vector along the last coordinate of LEFTARG, and each vector along the first coordinate of RIGHTARG, then performs a reduction using the scalar dyadic function (associated with LEFTARG) to that result.

OUTERPRODUCT — Routine that performs the outer product function which applies a scalar dyadic function using all elements of LEFTARG and all elements of RIGHTARG where the rank of the result is the number of coordinates of LEFTARG plus the number of coordinates of RIGHTARG and the dimensions of the result are size of LEFTARG, size of RIGHTARG.

DYADIC — Routine that performs the interpretation of valid dyadic operators and calls DYADCOMP to perform the operations for simple dyadic operators or calls the necessary routines to perform inner and outer products, index-of, reshape, or concatenate.

REVERSELINKLIST — Routine that performs the reversing of the order of the elements in the value table (VALUES).

The entire interpreter, written in Pascal for the CDC 6600 is given in Appendix C, page 291. Since Pascal is a portable language, it should be possible to run this program on other Pascal systems. ∎

A Pascal Print Utility

by Carl Helmers

A personal computer system is only useful when it is programmed to personal tasks, whether by purchasing canned software or by using one's ingenuity to write original software. Since I am the type of person who tends to like to program as a recreation as much as for getting the final job done, I prefer to write my own applications. One of the first such applications for my UCSD Pascal oriented machine was a file printing utility, begun with its earliest versions within a month of delivery of the computer.

In my occupation, I do a lot of writing. Whether the subject is an editorial for BYTE magazine, a memo for circulation within our company, or a letter to an author, I tend to write the text using the excellent large file (L2) editor of the UCSD Pascal system. But being able to edit texts does not complete what I need to get done with the computer. I also have to be able to print out the files in a formatted manner, so that annoying creases in the fanfold paper do not come in the middle of lines and so that I keep track of page counts. The program described here, called PRINT, is what I have contrived. It represents several months of evolution of its functions toward what I actually do.

The PRINT program is written with a *menu* list orientation for all main functions and their selection. In the notes which follow, we cover the main functional aspects of the print program, but not the details of the Pascal code of the

program. Within the program (see listing 1), verbal comments are made at the beginning of most procedures to document purpose and point out any machine dependencies or subtleties of the code (yes, such can exist even in Pascal). When going through the menu lists, references to procedures in the program are made by name enclosed in quotation marks.

The main functional menu of the program is shown in figure 1 as it would appear on computer. This menu contains the highest level functions of the program. For aesthetic purposes, the list of functions has two parts. The upper list of functions are single letter commands which change options and standard data for the program. The lower list of functions are executable actions the program may take. The menu is printed out by the procedure print—menu, found on page 20 of listing 1.

The actual main routine of the PRINT program consists of a WHILE loop. This loop starts out by performing print menu. Then it reads a single character from the keyboard. This character is checked to see if it is an ASCII <ESC> character (decimal equivalent "27"). If it is not an escape character, then a CASE statement is used to decode which active key was pressed.

If a "D" is pressed, then the program executes a procedure called diablo which sets up the printer spacing constants for my Diablo printer. In using this program with another system, a customized version of this setup may be re-

163

quired if the printer is not a Diablo HYTYPE II. This diablo procedure provides facilities for either 10 or 12 pitch horizontal spacing, and either single or double spacing vertically on the paper. The setup here applies to all the print functions.

The "#" option is used to preset a page number different from the one currently listed. On entering the program for the first time, a starting page count of 1 is guaranteed by initialization to 0. Typing "#" followed by a carriage return will cause the page number to be cleared to 0 again. The procedure pagenumber, which sets the page number, is found on page 19 of listing 1. It contains its own menu of three options: clearing (<return>), initializing (!), or keeping the previous value (<ESC>).

Printing always assumes we will have a file specified. The "N" option is used to specify a file name for the program to use. When the program is first activated, a default value of the system work file SYSTEM.WRK.TEXT is initialized. Then, when actually using the program, this is usually changed. When "N" is pressed, the routine namefile is executed, which asks for the new file name. The program always assumes a ".TEXT" file name extension. Thus when it was set up to print its own listing, after pressing "N", I simply entered the word "PRINT," resulting in the name "PRINT.TEXT" as seen in the menu of figure 1 and in listing 1.

Now since I am involved in a publishing occupation, one of the options I put into the program is that of specifying copyrights. For my own version of the program, I use either no copyright (rarely), BYTE Publications Inc. for business applications of the printer, or (most often) a personal tag of Carl T Helmers Jr. The menu list of figure 1 was made using my personal version of the program to produce listing 1. It thus

shows my own personal option as the copyright option. (In the actual listing and in the version to create the samples of figures 2 and 4, I recompiled the program using generic forms of strings such as "< < < your name > > >".) This copyright option is invoked by use of the command character "C" in response to the main menu. The procedure getcopyspec performs these actions.

The option "Q" in the main menu is one which controls whether or not the print program should search for the keyword "procedure" in lines which happen in the last fourth of the page. Each time the "Q" command is given, the option toggles between "YES" and "NO." The "YES" form of the option is used to implement a very crude form of Pascal pretty printing. A heuristic rule is used, that if a procedure begins in the last quarter of a page, the printing program will go to the next page and start the procedure at the top of that page. This option is implemented by execution of the procedure proccheck.

The final options-oriented choice in the main menu list is "W," used to specify the date field for printouts. In the best of all possible worlds this would not be needed at all, since the operating system's data routines would be accessed to get the current system date. But at this writing I have not figured out how to do that with UCSD Pascal, so I put in an explicit date definition routine and date field. The routine get_the_date is used to define this field and is found on page 5 of listing 1.

The remaining choices of the main menu are executable actions. The most often used such action is the first choice, "P," which invokes the procedure called any_file_print. This routine performs printing with a standard header that includes the file name, copyright specification, date field, running page count, and the current page header. This is the original print routine which has been running essentially unchanged for about six months at this writing.

In operation the any_file_print routine (as well as the two letter printing routines) treats the first line read from the file as a beginning page header string. This string is, for example, the comments string printed above the dashed line on every page of listing 1. After the initial header definition which is a default action of the program, explicit new header strings can be set up during the printing operation by a two line sequence within the file: the first line con-

Figure 1: This is a printed image of the display of the main menu for the print program, as compiled from the author's custom version. The options have all been set up to refer to the file PRINT.TEXT which contains listing 1, as printed on July 20 1979.

```
Carl's Printing Program... 7/18/79

Pick an option from the following list...

        D --> printer spacing = normal text
        # --> set starting page number =    0
        N --> file name = PRINT.TEXT
        C --> copyright = Carl T Helmers, Jr.
        Q --> toggle PROCEDURE search option = YES
        W --> date = July 20 1979

        P --> print routine
        L --> print as personal letter
        B --> print as business letter
        T --> enter typewriter routine
        R --> prepare return addresses on envelopes

Type <esc> to leave the program
```

Second Line of Salutation
Third Line of Salutation
* dummy end of salutation line
Dear Recipient   a

    This is a letter which signifies absolutely nothing
to you, but tells us whether the letter writing routines work.
It starts out with a first page, then following the end of
the first page, skips to the next page...

    We are about to skip to the next page using the special
code of "#" in the second column of the input text...

                    <<< your name here >>>
                    <<< your street here >>>
                    <<< your town here >>>
                    <<< your state, zip here >>>

                        July 20 1979

To:
Letter Test Text...
Second Line of Salutation
Third Line of Salutation   b

Dear Recipient

    This is a letter which signifies absolutely nothing
to you, but tells us whether the letter writing routines work.
It starts out with a first page, then following the end of
the first page, skips to the next page...

    We are about to skip to the next page using the special
code of "#" in the second column of the input text...

Figure 2: When printing a letter form of a file, the first few lines are assumed to contain the address of the correspondent. Here are three pages taken from listings of a dummy letter file made by the compiled form of the program shown in listing 1. At (a) we see a printout of the first few lines of the file made with the "P" format; line 1 of the file becomes the heading line, and the rest is an image of the lines of the file, in particular showing the line with a single "*" character in column 1 which terminates the correspondent address if it is less than 5 lines long.

At (b) we see the same file, but this time printed in the personal letter format, showing how the personally oriented strings of a return address are included, as well as appropriate spacings down the listing.

And finally, at (c) we see a continuation page in the letter format, where an abbreviated header format is used rather than the first page form. The first line of the correspondent address appears in the header of each continuation page, as well as a page number.

    There now, if all worked properly, we are now on the
second page of the letter, illustrating the form used for headings
on successive pages...

                                                                   c

That's all we have to test...

                    Yours truly,

                        Somebody...

```
Typing routine...
   <return>      = print the current line input
   <back space>  = delete one character
   <ctrl> "I"    = skip to new page
   <ctrl> "J"    = delete line
   <ctrl> "G"    = confirm line buffer
   <esc> to leave typewriter

----------------------------------------------

This is a test of the typewriter...
This is a test of the typewriter...
```

Figure 3: The "T" option of the main menu invokes this typing routine. The display is shown as copied to the printer using a feature of my computer system called "print screen." The menu of possible options is refreshed whenever a carriage return causes a line to be printed on the printer.

tains the arbitrarily chosen character "$" in the second character position of the line; the second line contains the new value of the header string to be used on all subsequent headings. The reason for checking the second column is to allow the first column to be used for the opening comment brace of a Pascal comment, so that the first line of the new heading sequence will be "{$}" in a Pascal program.

A similar technique of embedding command codes in the text is used to force page headings for reasons related to the logic of the text other than filling up a page or beginning a new procedure. This explicit *page eject* feature is accessed by embedding a "#" character in column 2 of a line. Again, in a Pascal program, a single line with "{#}" acts as a comment and does not affect the compilation of a program.

Both the heading redefinition and the page eject codes also work when using either the personal letter or business letter printing routines. These routines are invoked by the "L" and "B" command choices of the main menu, respectively. In each case, similar actions and formats are used. The example provided in figure 2b shows the letter format applied to a test file.

In preparing a letter, we assume that the file begins with up to 5 lines of correspondent address. If less than 5 lines are used, the last line of the address is followed by a line containing an asterisk (*) character in its first character position. In figure 2a, we see a printout of the first page of the letter test file, interpreted with the "P" option, so that the asterisk which terminates a 3 line correspondent address can be seen.

In printing a letter file, this assumed correspondent address is used in the heading for the first page, following the printing of the word "To:". Also, on the first page, a formally centered version of the appropriate return address will be printed. Again, in the example of figure 2b, as printed by the compiled form of

listing 1, generic strings identify where a reader might substitute personal information in using this program. On second and succeeding pages of a letter (see figure 2c), an abbreviated page break is used rather than a repetition of the complete return address.

All the printing procedures, including any_file_print, personal_letter, and busi_letter are found on page 16 of listing 1. When you look there, you will find that they reference a procedure called fileprint, which begins on page 9 of listing 1 and ends on page 15. The differences in printing the various ways are largely those of handling the different forms of page headers, so a common procedure with a choice of header printing options is employed. The procedure headerprint (pages 10 to 13 of listing 1) within the procedure fileprint contains three detail header printing routines for the various kinds of files.

Much of the styling and detail of a letter can be changed at will by readers who implement a version of this program. These are my own personal choices of how to format distinctive letters of one or more pages, and may not be aesthetically pleasing to others. Knowing the number of choices available and the ease of making changes with a UCSD Pascal system's editor, I fully expect many users of this program to make such changes.

As an afterthought, I put in the final two executable choices of this program. The "T" option is used to invoke a typewriter simulation procedure, typing, as found on pages 17 to 19 of listing 1. This routine displays a menu list of special characters on the main terminal screen, and accepts characters from the screen one by one until a carriage return is received which causes the line to be printed. Figure 3 shows the typing menu as printed from the display, along with a sample line.

The "R" choice is used when preparing personal correspondence in order to place my home address on an envelope. When using blank envelopes, this is done by removing the paper from the printer and putting in envelopes one at a time. For monthly bills where a pre-addressed envelope comes from the source of the bill, I simply put each individual envelope in the printer as I write the checks, leaving the paper in and not bothering with attempting to make the

```
<<< your name here >>>
<<< your street here >>>
<<< your town here >>>
<<< your state, zip here >>>
```

Figure 4: A sample of the simple printout of return address invoked by the "R" option of the main menu.

return address fit the spaces usually provided. ∎

Table 1: A list of all procedures found in listing 1. This listing can be used as an index when studying the program for possible modifications. It was prepared by hand from listing 1.

Procedure	Listing Page	Refers to
setdiablospacing	2	—
diablo	3	setdiablospacing
inttos	4	—
println	4	—
center_the_string	5	—
get_the_date	5	—
getcopyspec	5	—
fix_copyright_tag	6	—
set_up_printer	6	println
open_file_now	6	—
really_initialize	7	setdiablospacing
my_address_lines	9	—
fileprint	9	—
grab_address_lines	9	—
initialize	10	open_file_now, fix_copyright_tag, set_up_printer, grab_address_lines,
headerprint	10	
normal_header	10	setdiablospacing, println, inttos
header_personal_letter	11	setdialospacing, println, my_address_print, center_the_string, inttos
header_business_letter	12	setdiablospacing, println, center_the_string
headerprint [BEGIN...END]	13	normal_headr, header_personal_letter, header_business_letter
checkprocedure	14	println
pagecheck	14	checkprocedure, headerprint
pagebumper	14	pagecheck, println, pagebumper
fileprint [BEGIN...END]	15	initialize, pagebumper, pagecheck, println
namefile	15	—
personal_letter	16	fileprint
busi_letter	16	fileprint
any_file_print	16	fileprint
console_input	16	—
typing	17	
promptings	17	—
typing [BEGIN...END]	17	set_up_printer, promtpings, con, console_input, println,
pagenumber	19	—
procheck	19	—
print_return_address	19	
setup_envelope	19	—
print_return_address [BEGIN...END]	19	setup_envelope, my_address_print
print_menu	20	—
print [BEGIN...END]	20	really_initialize, print_menu, diablo, getcopyspec, any_file_print, procheck, namefile, personal_letter, busi_letter, typing, pagenumber, print_return_address, get_the_date

Listing 1: The PRINT program. This is a complete Pascal program listing for the print program. It was printed by a compiled version customized for the author's personal use. The text printed here is a generic form in which strings like "< < < your name > > >" have been used to indicate places where the program should be changed for the reader's personal use. Note the header information which is repeated at he beginning of each page of listing.

```
PRINT.TEXT         (c) 1979 Carl T Helmers, Jr.      July 22 1979     Page  1
{7/19/79: UCSD Pascal oriented print utility program}
------------------------------------------------------------------------------

(*$R+*)
PROGRAM print ;
{-----------------------------------------------------------------------}
{              P E R S O N A L   P R I N T   U T I L I T Y               }
{                                                                       }
{                author: Carl T. Helmers, Jr.                           }
{                        Editorial Director                             }
{                        BYTE Publications Inc.                         }
{                                                                       }
{                version:  July 19 1979                                 }
{                systems asssumption:  UCSD Pascal Version 1.5          }
{                        running on Northwest Microcomputer Systems     }
{                        model 85/P with Diablo HYTYPE II printer       }
{-----------------------------------------------------------------------}

{ What follow are G L O B A L declarations applicable to the whole program  }
{    In this program, as a general rule most linkages between procedures for }
{    data have been done using these global variables, ignoring the use of   }
{    formal parameters at (perhaps) some risk in understanding on the part of}
{    the reader...                                                          }

TYPE
    string_of_128 = STRING[128];
VAR
    copyright : (my_own,businesz,none);
      cstring : string_of_128;
    file_heading,s,hyphens : string_of_128;
    textfile : FILE OF CHAR;
    pstring,astring,firstline,filename : string_of_128;
    string_nothing : STRING[1];
    apage : INTEGER;
    horiz,verti,c5,c8 :INTEGER;
    pagecount,records : INTEGER;
    line_count,lines_per_page : INTEGER;
    alldone : BOOLEAN;

    which_print_heading : (miscellaneous,a_personal_letter,a_business_letter);
    first_heading_printed : BOOLEAN;
    todays_date : STRING[32];

    correspondent_address : ARRAY[0..4] OF string_of_128;

    we_print_a_program : BOOLEAN;
      c_we_print : STRING[3];
      criterion : INTEGER;

    arraychar: PACKED ARRAY[0..1] OF CHAR;
    anychar : CHAR;
```

168

```
PROCEDURE setdiablospacing(VAR horizontal,vertical : integer);
    { This is a very machine dependent interface program which sets up the
      spacing constants for the Diablo Hytype-II receive-only printer attached
      through a parallel port of the Northwest Microcomputer Systems 85/P
      computer upon which this program was developed.  It assumes that the
      address locations decimal 63520 and 63519 contain the spacing constants
      for horizontal and vertical motion of the print carriage respectively.
    }

    CONST
        vertaddress = 3519;
        horizaddress = 3520;
        bias=30000;
    TYPE
        ptr = ^CHAR;
        memaccess = (pointer,number);
        memory = {variant record used to suppress type checking of addresses}
            RECORD
                CASE memaccess OF
                    pointer : (apointer : ptr);
                    number  : (anumber  : INTEGER)
            END;
    VAR
        i : INTEGER;
        anybyte : memory;

    BEGIN

        {first set up an address as a number }
        anybyte.anumber := vertaddress+(2*bias);
        {then use the pointer variant of that number to change the byte}
        anybyte.apointer^ := chr(vertical);

        {first set up an address as a number }
        anybyte.anumber := horizaddress+(2*bias);
        {then use the pointer variant of that number to change the byte}
        anybyte.apointer^ := chr(horizontal);

    END {setdiablospacing};
```

```
PROCEDURE diablo;
    {  This is a less machine dependent procedure which allows one to set up
       four different variants on the spacing of the printed outputs. All the
       combinations of single or double vertical spacing, 10 or 12 pitch
       horizontal spacing are provided.  "Normal" is single space, 12 pitch
       printing, which is used with a 10 pitch Daisy wheel as, for example, in
       this listing...

       If another printer is used, the semantics of the menu provided in the
       WRITE statements below would have to be rewritten.
    }
VAR
    character : CHAR;
BEGIN {setting up mickey-mouse }
    PAGE(OUTPUT);
    WRITELN('Diablo HYTYPE-II Setup For 85/P & UCSD Pascal');
    WRITELN(' ');
    WRITELN('Pick one of the following options...');
    WRITELN('    S --> normal text');
    WRITELN('    D --> double space');
    WRITELN('    X --> typewriter text');
    WRITELN('    Y --> typewriter double space text');
    WRITELN(' ');
    WRITELN('?');
    READ(KEYBOARD,character);
    WRITELN(character);

    {default diablo spacing is single}
    horiz:=5;
    verti:=8;
    pstring := 'normal text';
    lines_per_page := 58;

    CASE character OF
        'D','d' :
            BEGIN
                verti:=16;
                pstring := 'double spaced normal text';
                lines_per_page := 28
            END;
        'X','x' :
            BEGIN
                horiz:=6;
                verti:=8;
                pstring := 'typewriter text';
                lines_per_page := 58
            END;
        'Y','y' :
            BEGIN
                horiz:=6;
                verti:=16;
                pstring := 'double spaced typewriter text';
                lines_per_page := 28
            END
    END {CASE};

    setdiablospacing (horiz,verti);
    criterion := (3 * lines_per_page) DIV 4
```

```
      END {diablo};


PROCEDURE inttos(VAR i : INTEGER);
      {convert an integer into a string value in global "s" for use by "println"}
      {this procedure may not be absolutely necessary, but was incorporated at  }
      {an early stage in the author's understanding of Pascal as a language.    }
      VAR
          frap : STRING[1];
          txt : string_of_128;
          j : INTEGER;
      BEGIN
          j := i;
          frap := ' ';
          txt := '';
          REPEAT
             frap[1] := CHR(ORD('0')+(j MOD 10));
             txt := CONCAT(frap,txt);
             j := j DIV 10
          UNTIL j = 0;
          s := CONCAT(s,txt);
      END {inttos};


PROCEDURE println {s—>diablo};
      { This procedure is required to allow simultaneous operation of the main
        console device for interactive messages of the program, and the printer
        device (UCSD Pascal Unit 6).  The actual output of this program from some
        file goes to Unit 6, buffered by the global string variable "s".

        The operation of this procedure is functionally identical to the built in
        intrinsic "WRITELN" of the UCSD Pascal implementation.
      }
      VAR
          i : INTEGER;
          chp : PACKED ARRAY[0..127] OF CHAR;
      BEGIN
          FOR i := 1 TO LENGTH(s) DO chp[i-1] := s[i];
          UNITWRITE(6,chp,LENGTH(s),,1);
          chp[0] := CHR(13);
          UNITWRITE(6,chp[0],1,,1)
      END {println };
```

171

```
    PROCEDURE center_the_string;
        { This procedure simply centers the standard global output string "s"
            in an 80 character wide field...
        }
        VAR
            i : INTEGER;
        BEGIN
            IF LENGTH(s) > 79 THEN s := 'String Conversion Error';
            FOR i := 1 TO (80 - LENGTH(s)) DIV 2 DO s := CONCAT(' ',s)
        END;


    PROCEDURE get_the_date;
        { This procedure is used to input the current date for printing with
            the file being transferred...
        }
        BEGIN
            PAGE(OUTPUT);
            WRITELN('Enter today''s date or <return> for null date');
            READLN(astring);
            IF LENGTH(astring)<32 THEN todays_date := astring
        END {get_the_date};


    PROCEDURE getcopyspec {determine copyright message};
        { This procedure is used to modify the default copyright specification,
            which may be "<<< your name >>>", "<<< your company name >>>" or a null
            specification.  Users should modify the two built in strings of this
            listing to reflect their own name and business affiliations.
        }
        BEGIN
            PAGE(OUTPUT);
            WRITELN('Enter copyright choice: B or N (<ret> for personal)');
            READ(KEYBOARD,anychar);
            copyright := my_own;
            IF ((anychar='B') OR (anychar='b')) THEN copyright := businesz;
            IF ((anychar='N') OR (anychar='n')) THEN copyright := none;
            CASE copyright OF
                my_own    : cstring := '<<< your name >>>';
                businesz  : cstring := '<<< your company name >>>';
                none   : cstring := ''
            END {CASE};
            WRITELN('')
        END;
```

```
PROCEDURE fix_copyright_tag;
    { This procedure defines the string named "file_heading" which is used
      for display purposes and reflects the current contents of the
      copyright option chosen...
    }
    BEGIN
        file_heading := CONCAT(filename,'            ');
        IF NOT(copyright=none) THEN
            file_heading := CONCAT(file_heading,'(c) 1979 ')
        ELSE
            file_heading := CONCAT(file_heading,'             ');
        IF copyright=my_own THEN
            file_heading:=CONCAT(file_heading,'<<< your name >>>')
        ELSE
            IF copyright=businesz THEN
                file_heading:=CONCAT(file_heading,
                   '<<< your business name >>>');
        file_heading := CONCAT(file_heading,'      ')
    END {fix_copyright_tag};


PROCEDURE set_up_printer;
    { Ask for and receive an acknowledgement of paper position prior to
      the start of a printing operation.
    }
    BEGIN
        {clear the print buffers}
        s := '';
        println;
        println;
        println;

        {normal interactive query}
        WRITELN('Reset printer to bottom of page then ',
            'type any character');
        READ(KEYBOARD,anychar)
    END {set_up_printer};


PROCEDURE open_file_now;
    { This procedure is used to open the text file which is to be printed
      by the program.  The compiler control toggles "(*$I-*)" and "(*$I+*)"
      are used to suppress automatic error checking during the RESET operation
      so that if an error occurs the program can recover gracefully...
    }
    VAR
        errornumber : INTEGER;
    BEGIN
        records := 0;
        firstline := '';
        {---------------------- BEGIN UNPROTECTED CODE ----------------------}
                                (*$I-*)
        RESET(textfile,filename);
        errornumber := IORESULT;
                                (*$I+*)
        {---------------------- RESUME PROTECTED CODE ----------------------}
        IF errornumber = 0 THEN {file was found in good order }
            BEGIN
                READLN(textfile,firstline);
```

```
                UNITREAD(1{~},arraychar[0],1,,1)
            END

        ELSE {file was non-existent or invalid in some way }
            BEGIN
                WRITELN('File "',filename,'" invalid: result=',errornumber:3);
                WRITELN('Press <sp> to continue');
                READ(KEYBOARD,anychar)
            END

    END {open_file_now};


PROCEDURE really_initialize;
    { As suggested by its name this is the procedure which really initializes
        the whole program's operation.  It is performed once following the start
        of execution, as opposed to other initialization procedures for specific
        routines within the program which may be executed more than once...
    }
    VAR
        i : INTEGER;
    BEGIN
        filename := 'SYSTEM.WRK.TEXT';
        cstring := '<<< your name >>>';
        copyright := my_own;
        todays_date := '?';
        string_nothing := ' ';

        we_print_a_program := TRUE;
            c_we_print := 'YES';

        alldone := FALSE;

        {printer management constants are set up to defaults}
        c5 := 5;
        c8 := 8;
        line_count := 99;
        lines_per_page := 58;
        criterion := 44;
        horiz := 5;
        verti := 8;
        setdiablospacing(horiz,verti);
        pstring := 'normal text';
        pagecount := 0;

        records := 0;
        astring := '';
        firstline := '';
        hyphens := '';
        FOR i := 1 TO 90 DO hyphens := CONCAT(hyphens,'-')
    END {really_initialize};
```

```
PROCEDURE my_address_print;
    { This procedure used by header routines of fileprint, return address
        printer...
    }

    BEGIN
        s := '<<< your name here >>>';
        center_the_string;
        println;                          {1}
        s := '<<< your street here >>>';
        center_the_string;
        println;                          {2}
        s := '<<< your town here >>>';
        center_the_string;
        println;                          {3}
        s := '<<< your state, zip here >>>';
        center_the_string;
        println;                          {4}
        s := '';
        println                           {5}
    END {my_address_print};
```

175

```
PROCEDURE fileprint;

   { This is the master file printing routine, used for "miscellaneous"
     files, as well as personal letters and business letters... The global
     set variable "which_print_heading" controls one of three possible
     headings will be printed on each page.  The global BOOLEAN variable
     "we_print_a_program" controls whether or not the last fourth of a page
     being printed will have a test for the beginning of a new PROCEDURE
     used to automatically generate a skip to the next page.
   }


   PROCEDURE grab_address_lines;
      { When printing either a personal or a company letter, the working
        assumption made is that the text file with the letter begins with
        up to five lines of address information.  This set of lines is read
        at the beginning of a letter printing operation, with the occurrence
        of an asterisk ("*") in the first position of a line acting as a
        premature termination of the address read operation.  The first line
        of the address information will be repeated in any continuation pages
        of a letter printout.
      }
   VAR
       done : BOOLEAN;
       i : INTEGER;

   {read up to five lines of correspondent address from beginning
   of file.  Terminate address scan with a "*" character in a line.}
   BEGIN {grab_address_lines}
       IF (
            (which_print_heading = a_personal_letter)
                    OR
            (which_print_heading = a_business_letter)
           )
       THEN
          BEGIN
             correspondent_address[0] := firstline;
             FOR i := 1 TO 4 DO correspondent_address[i] := '';
             done := FALSE;
             i := 1;
             REPEAT
                BEGIN
                   READLN(textfile,astring);
                   astring := CONCAT(astring,'   ') {guard against nulls};
                   IF ((i<=4) AND (astring[1] <> '*')) THEN
                      correspondent_address[i] := astring
                   ELSE
                      done := TRUE;
                   i := i + 1
                END
             UNTIL done
          END;
   END {grab_address_lines};
```

```
    PROCEDURE initialize {for "fileprint"};
        { This is the procedure which sets up initial conditions when a
            file is to be printed...
        }
        BEGIN
            open_file_now;
            fix_copyright_tag;
            set_up_printer;
            grab_address_lines;
            first_heading := TRUE;
            line_count := 99
        END {initialize for "fileprint"};


    PROCEDURE headerprint;
        { This is the procedure which prints a header which breaks up the
            text into multiple pages...  It is invoked whenever necessary, and
            checks the type of printing operation as determined by the global
            variable "which_print_heading"...  All the headers are printed with
            a "normal" spacing option for the printer.
        }

    PROCEDURE normal_header;
        { This is the header used for most printing operations, including
            the printing of program files...  The printout of this program
            was made using this kind of header...
        }
        VAR
            i : INTEGER;
        BEGIN
            setdiablospacing(horiz,c8);
            s := '';
            IF ((pagecount > 0) AND (line_count<>100)) THEN
                FOR i := 1 TO 2 DO println {s-->diablo};
            pagecount := pagecount +1;
            IF verti = 16 THEN println {s-->diablo};
            println {s-->diablo};
            s := CONCAT(file_heading,todays_date,'     Page  ');
            inttos(pagecount);
            println {s-->diablo};
            s := firstline;
            println {s-->diablo};
            s := hyphens;
            println {s-->diablo};
            s := '';
            println {s-->diablo};
            setdiablospacing(horiz,verti);
            line_count := 0
        END {normal_header};
```

177

```
                PROCEDURE header_personal_letter;
                    { This is the header routine used for personal letters, where on the
                      first time through, a full return address, date and correspondent
                      address are provided.  On second and succeeding headings, only an
                      abbreviated header is used containing the first line of the corre-
                      spondent address, date and page number...
                    }
                VAR
                    i : INTEGER;
                BEGIN {header_personal_letter}
                    setdiablospacing(horiz,c8);
                    s := '';
                    IF ((pagecount > 0) AND (line_count<>100)) THEN
                        FOR i := 1 TO 2 DO println {s-->diablo};
                    pagecount := pagecount +1;
                    IF verti = 16 THEN println {s-->diablo};
                    println {s-->diablo};
                    IF first_heading THEN
                        BEGIN
                          {space down an amount equal to the continuation heading }
                            s := '';
                            println;
                            println;
                            println;
                            println;
                            setdiablospacing(horiz,verti);
                                                          {line count is}
                            my_address_print;               {1-5}
                            s := todays_date;
                            center_the_string;
                            println;                        {6}
                            s := '';
                            println;                        {7}
                            println;                        {8}
                            println;                        {9}
                            s := 'To:';
                            println;                        {10}
                            FOR i := 0 TO 4 DO
                                BEGIN
                                  s := correspondent_address[i];
                                  println                   {11-15}
                                END;
                            s := '';
                            println;                        {16}
                            println;                        {17}
                            println;                        {18}
                            line_count := 18 {lines printed so far}
                        END
                    ELSE
                        BEGIN
                            s := CONCAT('<<< your name >>> to ',correspondent_address[0],'   ',
                                todays_date,'    Page ');
                            inttos(pagecount);
                            println {s-->diablo};
                            s := '';
                            println {s-->diablo};
                            s := hyphens;
                            println {s-->diablo};
                            s := '';
```

```
                    println {s-->diablo};
                    setdiablospacing(horiz,verti);
                    line_count := 0
               END;
          first_heading := FALSE
     END {header_personal_letter};


     PROCEDURE header_business_letter;
          { This is the header routine used for business letters, where on the
            first time through, a full return address, date and correspondent
            address are provided.  On second and succeeding headings, only an
            abbreviated header is used containing the first line of the corre-
            spondent address, date and page number...
          }
          VAR
               i : INTEGER;
          BEGIN {header_business_letter}
             setdiablospacing(horiz,c8);
             s := '';
             IF ((pagecount > 0) AND (line_count<>100)) THEN
                  FOR i := 1 TO 2 DO println {s-->diablo};
             pagecount := pagecount +1;
             IF verti = 16 THEN println {s-->diablo};
             println {s-->diablo};
             IF first_heading THEN
                  BEGIN
                     {space down an amount equal to the continuation heading }
                     s := '';
                     println;
                     println;
                     println;
                     println;
                     setdiablospacing(horiz,verti);
                     {begin the first time heading}
                     s := '<<< your business name >>>';
                     center_the_string;               {line count is}
                     println;                              {1}
                     s := '<<< your business address >>>';
                     center_the_string;
                     println;                              {2}
                     s := '<<< your business town, state, zip >>>';
                     center_the_string;
                     println;                              {3}
                     s := '';
                     println;                              {4}
                     s := '<<< your name >>>';
                     center_the_string;
                     println;                              {5}
                     s := '<<< your title >>>';
                     center_the_string;
                     println;                              {6}
                     s := '';
                     println;                              {7}
                     s := todays_date;
                     center_the_string;
                     println;                              {8}
                     s := '';
                     println;                              {9}
```

```
                    println;                           {10}
                    println;                           {11}
                    s := 'To:';
                    println;                           {12}
                    FOR i := 0 TO 4 DO
                       BEGIN
                          s := correspondent_address[i];
                          println                       {13-17}
                       END;
                    s := '';
                    println;                           {18}
                    println;                           {19}
                    println;                           {20}
                    line_count := 20 {lines printed so far}
                END
             ELSE
                BEGIN
                    s := CONCAT('<<< your name >>> to ',correspondent_address[0],
                       '   ',todays_date,'    Page ');
                    inttos(pagecount);
                    println {s-->diablo};
                    s := '';
                    println {s-->diablo};
                    s := hyphens;
                    println {s-->diablo};
                    s := '';
                    println {s-->diablo};
                    setdiablospacing(horiz,verti);
                    line_count := 0
                END;
             first_heading := FALSE

       END {header_business_letter};


    BEGIN {headerprint};
       IF which_print_heading = miscellaneous
          THEN normal_header
       ELSE
          IF which_print_heading = a_personal_letter
             THEN header_personal_letter
          ELSE
             header_business_letter
    END {headerprint};
```

```
    PROCEDURE checkprocedure;
        { This procedure is used to determine whether the current input line
            contains the keyword "PROCEDURE" in order to perform a rudimentary
            type of "prettyprinting":  a new procedure will  not begin in the
            listing of a "normal" file if it starts more than "criterion"
            down the sheet of paper.
        }
        BEGIN
            IF POS('PROCEDURE',astring) > 0 THEN
                BEGIN
                    s := '';
                    REPEAT
                        BEGIN
                            println;
                            line_count := line_count + 1
                        END
                    UNTIL line_count > lines_per_page
                END
        END {checkprocedure};


    PROCEDURE pagecheck {for "fileprint"};
        { This is the procedure used before every normal "println" call during
            the main portion of a file printing operation, in order to test
            whether a skip to the next page is required.  It invokes the
            "checkprocedure" routine if the Pascal PROGRAM printing option is
            turned on.
        }
        VAR i : INTEGER;
        BEGIN
            line_count := line_count + 1;
            IF
                we_print_a_program
                        AND
                (line_count > criterion)
            THEN checkprocedure;
            IF line_count > lines_per_page THEN headerprint
        END {pagecheck for "fileprint"};


    PROCEDURE pagebumper {for "fileprint"};
        { This procedure implements a rudimentary form of word processing:
            if a "miscellaneous" file format is used, then the standard heading
            field "firstline" can be redefined by an input record with the key
            character "$" in column 2. (This allows it to be wrapped in comments
            braces in a Pascal program.)  For all formats, if the key character
            "#" is found in column 2 of a line, the printing will skip to the
            next page and start a new heading...

            NOTE THIS  P R O C E D U R E   U S E S  R E C U R S I O N !!!!
        }
        VAR
            i : INTEGER;
        BEGIN
            IF LENGTH(astring)<2 THEN astring := CONCAT(astring,' ');
            IF astring[2] = '#' THEN
                BEGIN
                    s := '';
                    WHILE line_count > 0 DO
```

```
                        BEGIN
                            pagecheck;
                            println {s-->diablo}
                        END;
                    READLN(textfile,astring);
                    pagebumper {RECURSIVE CALL}
                END;
            IF astring[2] = '$' THEN
                BEGIN
                    READLN(textfile,firstline);
                    READLN(textfile,astring);
                    pagebumper {RECURSIVE CALL}
                END
        END {pagebumper for "fileprint"};


    BEGIN {the "fileprint" PROCEDURE at last}
        initialize;
        WHILE NOT EOF(textfile) DO
            BEGIN
                READLN(textfile,astring);
                records := records + 1;
                pagebumper;
                pagecheck;
                s := astring;
                println {s-->diablo}
            END;
        s := '';
        line_count := line_count - 5 {adjustment to make it come out even};
        REPEAT
            BEGIN
                println;
                line_count := line_count + 1
            END
        UNTIL line_count > lines_per_page;
        CLOSE(textfile,LOCK)
    END {fileprint};


PROCEDURE namefile;
    { This procedure sets the file name to be printed.  It is always assumed
      that a ".TEXT" extension will be used...
    }
    BEGIN
        PAGE(OUTPUT);
        WRITELN('Enter a new file name to be printed');
        READLN(filename);
        filename := CONCAT(filename,'.TEXT')
    END {namefile};
```

```
PROCEDURE personal_letter;
   BEGIN
      which_print_heading := a_personal_letter;
      fileprint
   END {personal_letter};


PROCEDURE busi_letter;
   BEGIN
      which_print_heading := a_business_letter;
      fileprint
   END {busi_letter};


PROCEDURE any_file_print;
   BEGIN
      which_print_heading := miscellaneous;
      fileprint
   END;


PROCEDURE console_input;
   { This procedure is used to read a single keystroke front the console
      keyboard unit.  It is required because the UCSD Pascal READ(KEYBOARD,
      anychar) intrinsic purges all the normal ASCII control characters...
   }
   VAR
      inch :  PACKED ARRAY[0..0] OF CHAR;
   BEGIN
      UNITREAD(2,inch[0],1,,1);
      WHILE UNITBUSY(2) DO;
      anychar := inch[0]
   END {console_input};
```

```
PROCEDURE typing;
    { This is a self contained procedure to make the terminal keyboard behave
      as a "memory" typewriter.  The contents of the input buffer are printed
      upon receipt of a "<RETURN>" code or upon exceeding an input length of
      96 characters.   The display is used to show the possible special
      function keys as well as the current input line contents... 
    }
    VAR
        ichar : INTEGER;
        itemp : INTEGER;
        line_increment : INTEGER;


    PROCEDURE promptings;
        BEGIN {promptings};
            PAGE(OUTPUT);
            WRITELN('Typing routine...');
            WRITELN('    <return>     = print the current line input');
            WRITELN('    <back space> = delete one character');
            WRITELN('    <ctrl> "I"   = skip to new page');
            WRITELN('    <ctrl> "J"   = delete line');
            WRITELN('    <ctrl> "G"   = confirm line buffer');
            WRITELN('    <esc> to leave typewriter');
            WRITELN('');
            WRITELN(hyphens);
            WRITELN('')
        END;


    BEGIN
        set_up_printer;
        PAGE(OUTPUT);
        line_count := 0;
        IF verti = 16 THEN
            line_increment := 2
        ELSE
            line_increment := 1;
        anychar := ' ';
        s := '';
        promptings;
        UNITCLEAR(2);
        WHILE anychar <> CHR(27) DO
            BEGIN {other than escape <ESC>}

                console_input;

                WRITE(anychar);
                ichar := ORD(anychar);
                IF ichar >= ORD(' ') THEN
                    BEGIN {normal ASCII}
                        string_nothing[1]  := anychar;
                        s := CONCAT(s,string_nothing);
                        IF LENGTH(s) >=  96 THEN ichar := 0 {signal end of line}
                    END {normal ASCII};
                IF ichar < ORD(' ') THEN

                    CASE ichar OF
```

```
                    0 : {line overflow}
                       BEGIN
                          line_count := line_count + line_increment;
                          IF line_count > 66 THEN line_count := 1;
                          println;
                          string_nothing[1] := anychar;
                          s := string_nothing
                       END;

                   10 : {line delete}
                       BEGIN
                          s := '';
                          WRITELN('<<< l i n e   d e l e t e d >>>')
                       END;

                    7 : {bell}
                       BEGIN
                          WRITELN('');
                          WRITELN(s)
                       END;

                    8 : {back space}
                       BEGIN
                          IF LENGTH(s) > 1 THEN
                             BEGIN
                                itemp := LENGTH(s) - 1;
                                s := COPY(s,1,itemp)
                             END
                          ELSE
                             s := ''
                       END;

                    9 : {forms feed}
                       BEGIN
                          line_count := line_count + line_increment;
                          IF line_count > 66 THEN line_count := 1;
                          println;
                          s := '';
                          promptings;
                          WHILE line_count < 66 DO
                             BEGIN
                                line_count := line_count + line_increment;
                                println
                             END
                       END;

                   13 : {print the line}
                       BEGIN
                          line_count := line_count + 1;
                          IF verti > 8 THEN line_count := line_count + 1;
                          IF line_count > 66 THEN line_count := 1;
                          println;
                          s := '';
                          promptings
                       END

                 END {CASE}

           END {other than escape <ESC>};
```

```
            PAGE(OUTPUT)
        END {typing};


PROCEDURE pagenumber;
    BEGIN
        PAGE(OUTPUT);
        WRITELN('Enter starting page number from the following list');
        WRITELN('      <CR>  --> default start from 1');
        WRITELN('      "!"   --> entry of a new starting value');
        WRITELN('      <ESC> --> continue from ',pagecount:4);
        console_input;
        WRITELN(anychar);
        IF ORD(anychar) = 13 THEN
            pagecount := 0 {default to 1}
        ELSE
            BEGIN
                IF anychar = '!' THEN
                    BEGIN
                        WRITELN('');
                        WRITELN('          Enter new page number:');
                        READLN(pagecount);
                        pagecount := pagecount - 1
                    END
            END
    END {pagenumber};


PROCEDURE proccheck;
    BEGIN
        we_print_a_program := NOT we_print_a_program;
        IF we_print_a_program THEN
            c_we_print := 'YES'
        ELSE
            c_we_print := 'NO'
    END;


PROCEDURE print_return_address;
    {Procedure to print return addresses on letter size envelopes}
    VAR
        done : BOOLEAN;

    PROCEDURE setup_envelope;
        BEGIN {setup_envelope};
            WRITELN('Place envelope in printer, then press any character');
            READ(KEYBOARD,anychar);
        END {setup_envelope};


    BEGIN {print_return_address}
        done := FALSE;
        REPEAT
            setup_envelope;
            my_address_print;
            WRITELN('More? <esc> to quit');
            READ(KEYBOARD,anychar);
            IF ORD(anychar) = 27 THEN done:=TRUE
        UNTIL done
```

```
     END {print_return_address};
PROCEDURE print_menu;
    { This is the main function menu for the print utility program
    }
    BEGIN
      PAGE (OUTPUT);
      WRITELN('Carl''s Printing Program... 7/18/79');
      WRITELN('');
      WRITELN('');
      WRITELN('Pick an option from the following list...');
      WRITELN('');
      WRITELN('      D --> printer spacing = ',pstring);
      WRITELN('      # --> set starting page number = ',pagecount:4);
      WRITELN('      N --> file name = ',filename);
      WRITELN('      C --> copyright = ',cstring);
      WRITELN('      Q --> toggle PROCEDURE search option = ',c_we_print);
      WRITELN('      W --> date = ',todays_date);
      WRITELN('');
      WRITELN('      P --> print routine');
      WRITELN('      L --> print as personal letter');
      WRITELN('      B --> print as business letter');
      WRITELN('      T --> enter typewriter routine');
      WRITELN('      R --> prepare return addresses on envelopes');
      WRITELN('');
      WRITELN('Type <esc> to leave the program')
    END {print_menu};


BEGIN {print program main PROCEDURE}
    really_initialize;
    WHILE alldone <> TRUE  DO
      BEGIN
        print_menu;
        READ(KEYBOARD,anychar);
        IF anychar <> CHR(27) THEN
          CASE anychar OF
            'D','d' :diablo;
            'C','c' :getcopyspec;
            'P','p' :any_file_print;
            'Q','q' :proccheck;
            'N','n' :namefile;
            'L','l' :personal_letter;
            'B','b' :busi_letter;
            'T','t' :typing;
            'R','r' :print_return_address;
            'W','w' :get_the_date;
            '#','3' :pagenumber
          END {CASE}
        ELSE
            alldone := TRUE
      END
END.
(*$D+*)
(*$L+*)
```

An Automatic Metric Conversion Program

David A Mundie

Calculators and personal computers have already liberated us from trigonometric and logarithmic tables. It is time they do the same with respect to metric conversion tables. I recently wrote the SUPERMETRIC program shown in listing 1 for just that purpose. (Listing 2 shows a sample run of the program.)

Although my design goals seemed quite modest and straightforward, achieving them turned out to require an astonishing amount of number crunching and devious programming, as the length of the listing testifies. My first requirement was that the program distinguish rigorously between customary units, primary metric units, and secondary metric units. By "primary" metric units I mean the System International (SI) base units such as metre, kilogram, kelvin, and so on, as well as the derived units such as watt, newton, m/s, pascal, and volt. By "secondary" metric units I mean units like °C and km/h which are accepted but not part of SI, along with the formulas for derived units with special names, eg, kg m/s as the formulas for the newton.

This design goal was met by storing the various units and their conversion factors in a table whose structure may most conveniently be understood by examining the "data statements" which generate it in the subroutine INITIALIZE. Each entry in the table contains three items: two units and a conversion factor. The units on the right are all primary units. In the top part of the table (above MAXCUST) the left-hand units are customary, while in the bottom section they are secondary metric units.

The program automatically converts customary and secondary units to primary units. Primary units may be converted to customary by using the "C" command, while the "S" command converts them to secondary units. As it stands now, the program will only convert a given primary unit to the first customary unit it finds in the table. However, it would be a simple matter to add a new command that would allow the user to specify the target unit, "gallon" instead of "fl. ounce," for example. The table is quite easily expanded through the use of additional "data statements."

A second design goal was to have the program automatically add prefixes to metric units as needed, and to adjust inputs with prefixes that are too large or too small. For example, I wanted 5700 kJ to be converted automatically to 5.7 MJ. To this end, the subroutine DEPREFIX removes prefixes from the units input by the user, so that the data is stored internally in unprefixed primary units. The subroutine PREFIX then prints the correctly prefixed measurement. The prefixes themselves are contained in the strings NORMP and SPECP. NORMP contains the normal set of prefixes, each 1000 times larger than the next, as shown in table 1, whereas SPECP stores the special set of prefixes used for volumes and areas, as shown in table 2. Thus 15000 m is converted to 15 km, whereas 15000 m^2 is converted to 1.5 hm^2.

A third design goal was to have the program deal with the problem of precision in a reasonable manner. Nothing is more absurd than to convert 3 square yards to 2.5083821 m^2, although anti-

Power	Prefix	Abbreviation
10^{18}	exa	E
10^{15}	peta	P
10^{12}	tera	T
10^{9}	giga	G
10^{6}	mega	M
10^{3}	kilo	k
10^{-3}	milli	m
10^{-6}	micro	μ
10^{-9}	nano	n
10^{-12}	pico	p
10^{-15}	femto	f
10^{-18}	atto	a

Table 1: Prefixes used by SUPERMETRIC for measurements other than volumes and areas.

Power	Prefix	Abbreviation
10^{3}	kilo	k
10^{2}	hecto	h
10^{1}	deka	da
10^{-1}	deci	d
10^{-2}	centi	c
10^{-3}	milli	m

Table 2: Prefixes used by SUPERMETRIC for volumes and areas.

Correct SI Form	SUPERMETRIC Approximation
μ	u
da	D
.	* (multiplication)
o	$ (degree)
m^2 etc.	m2
Ω	@ (ohm)

Table 3: Differences between SUPER-METRIC and correct System International (SI) symbols.

metric journalists often feign to believe this is correct practice. My approach was to have the program give a converted measurement whose implied error is between 10% and 100% that of the input. This insures that the converted measurement will be at least as precise as the input, but never more than one significant digit more precise. To achieve this goal, the subroutine VALUE reads the measurement which the user enters and calculates the number of significant digits it contains (P). This number is then used to control the number of significant digits in the output. For example, the program automatically converts 3 square yards (implied error ± 0.5 square yard or ± 0.42 m²) to 2.5 m² (implied error ± 0.05 m²). As a convenience to the user, the program will accept numbers with a trailing decimal point and treat all the digits to the left of the decimal point as significant. Thus, although "1000" is treated as having one significant digit, "1000." is treated as having four.

My final design goal was to adhere as closely as possible to standard SI notation within the bounds of the ASCII character set. The points where this goal was not met are shown in table 3. I regret all of these, but had no choice except in the case of the "da" prefix. Since the other deviations were unavoidable, the extra coding needed to handle a 2-character prefix did not seem worthwhile. ∎

The author wishes to thank Joe Berman and Steve Wellons, of the University of Virginia's Microprocessor Laboratory, for their assistance in the preparation of the listings for this article. The listings were done on equipment purchased under NASA contract #NAS1-14862.

Listing 1: The automatic metric conversion program written in UCSD Pascal.

```
PROGRAM supermetrics;
(*$S+*)
CONST
  normp='afpnum kMGTPE';      {normal prefixes}
  specp='mcd Dhk';            {special prefixes for areas and volumes}
  maxentries = 100;
TYPE
  entry = RECORD
             left, right: STRING;
             factor: REAL;
          END;
  index = 0..maxentries;

VAR
  table      :array[index] of entry;
  curtop     :index;      {current top of table}
  current    :index;      {points to current entry}
  maxcust    :index;      {top of customary section of table}
  top        :index;      {permanent top of table}
  leftside   :BOOLEAN;
  finished   :BOOLEAN;
  oldm,oldf  :REAL;
  line       :STRING;     {one line of user input}
  u          :STRING;     {the unit}
  m          :REAL;       {the measurement}
  p          :INTEGER;    {the precision}

{********** mathematical utilities ****************************}

FUNCTION floor(r:REAL): INTEGER;
BEGIN floor:=trunc(r-ord((r<0)and(r<>trunc(r))))
END;

FUNCTION nl(r:REAL):REAL; {Avoids bug in ln function}
BEGIN IF r<1 THEN nl:=-ln(r) ELSE nl:=ln(r)
END;

FUNCTION power(i,j:INTEGER):REAL;
BEGIN power:=exp(nl(i)*j)
END;

FUNCTION log(r:REAL):REAL;
BEGIN log:=nl(abs(r))/nl(10)
END;

FUNCTION lop(r:REAL; p:INTEGER):REAL;
{ Reduce a real to p significant digits }
VAR f:REAL;
BEGIN f:=power(10,floor(log(r))-p+1);
 IF r/f<maxint THEN lop:=f*round(r/f) ELSE lop:=r
END;

FUNCTION norm(r:REAL):REAL;
BEGIN norm:=r/power(10,floor(log(r)))
END;


{********** Convert a string to a real number **********}

FUNCTION value(VAR s:STRING; VAR p:INTEGER):REAL;
CONST
  limit=1.67772E6;        { (2**23)/5) }
  z    =48;               { ord(0) }
VAR
  a,y            :REAL;
  e,i,j,p2       :INTEGER;
  neg,negexp,gtl:BOOLEAN;
  digits         :SET OF CHAR;
BEGIN
  i:=1;p:=0;p2:=0; gtl:=false; digits:=['0'..'9'];
  s:=concat(s,'%'); {safety character}
  a:=0; e:=0; neg:=s[i]='-'; WHILE s[i]=' ' DO i:=i+1;
  IF (s[i]='+')or neg THEN i:=i+1;
  WHILE s[i] in digits DO
    BEGIN
      IF s[i]='0' THEN p2:=p2+1
      ELSE BEGIN p:=p+p2+1; p2:=0; gtl:=true END;
      IF a<limit THEN a:=10*a+ord(s[i])-z ELSE e:=e+1; i:=i+1
    END;
  IF s[i]='.' THEN
    BEGIN p:=p+p2; i:=i+1;
      IF not(s[i] in digits) THEN
        BEGIN insert('0',s,i); i:=i+1
        END
    END;
  p2:=0;
```

```
      WHILE s[i]='0' DO
        BEGIN p2:=p2+1; IF a<limit THEN
          BEGIN a:=10*a+ord(s[i])-z; e:=e-1
          END; i:=i+1
        END;
      IF gt1 THEN p:=p+p2;
      WHILE s[i] in digits DO
        BEGIN p:=p+1;
          IF a<limit THEN
          BEGIN a:=10*a+ord(s[i])-z; e:=e-1
          END; i:=i+1
        END;
      IF s[i] in ['e','E'] THEN
        BEGIN i:=i+1; j:=0; negexp:=(s[i]='-');
          IF(s[i]='+') or negexp THEN i:=i+1;
          WHILE s[i] in digits DO
            BEGIN IF j<limit THEN j:=10*j+ord(s[i])-z; i:=i+1
            END;
          IF negexp THEN e:=e-j ELSE e:=e+j
        END;
    y:=a; IF neg THEN y:=-y;
    IF e<0 THEN value:=y/power(10,-e)
    ELSE IF e<>0 THEN value:=y*power(10,e)
    ELSE value:=y;
    WHILE s[i]=' ' DO i:=i+1; s:=copy(s,i,length(s)-i);
END; {value}


{********** Write a real in appropriate format and return a blank **}

FUNCTION f(r:REAL): CHAR;
CONST
  width  = 22;
VAR
  intpart,decimals,floating:INTEGER;
BEGIN
  intpart:=floor(log(r));
  decimals:=p-intpart-1;
  r:=lop(r,p);
  IF r>10000 or r<0.0001 THEN   {floating point}
    write(r:width)
  ELSE
    IF decimals<=0 THEN   {integer}
      write(round(r): width)
    ELSE   {fixed point}
      write(r:width:decimals);
  f:=' '
END;

{********** Special handling for temperatures ***************}

PROCEDURE temperature(VAR m:REAL; b:BOOLEAN; fact:INTEGER);
VAR
  d:INTEGER;
BEGIN
  d:=p-floor(log(m))-1;
  m:=m+fact*273.15+fact*186.52*ord(b);
  p:=d+floor(log(m))+1
END;

{********** Find u in the table of units *********************}

FUNCTION inlist:BOOLEAN;
VAR t:STRING;

FUNCTION match(s:string):BOOLEAN;
BEGIN match:=(u=s)or(t=s)
END;

BEGIN
  leftside:=true; current:=1;
  t:=u; IF length(t)>1 THEN delete(t,1,1);
  WHILE (not(match(table[current].left))) and(current<=curtop) DO
    current:=current+1;
  IF current<=curtop THEN
    inlist:=true
  ELSE
    BEGIN current:=curtop; leftside:=false;
      WHILE (not(match(table[current].right))) and(current>0)DO
        current:=current-1;
      inlist:=current>0
    END;
END;


{********** Add correct metric prefix **********************}

PROCEDURE prefix(m: REAL; u:STRING);

PROCEDURE pref(p:STRING; fac,term:INTEGER);
VAR
```

```
       i,range: INTEGER;
  BEGIN
    range:=floor(log(m)/fac);
    IF abs(range)>term THEN
      range:=term*(1-2*ord(range<-term));
    m:=m/power(10,fac*range);
    IF range<>0 THEN
      BEGIN
        p:=copy(p,range+term+1,1);
        u:=concat(p,u);
        writeln(f(m),u)
      END
  END;

  BEGIN {prefix}
    IF pos('2',u) =2 THEN pref(specp,2,3)
    ELSE IF pos('3',u)=2 THEN pref(specp,3,3)
    ELSE pref(normp,3,6)
  END;

{********** Convert to primary units *********************}

PROCEDURE primary;
VAR
  oldp:INTEGER;
BEGIN
  WITH table[current] DO
    BEGIN
      IF u='mpg' THEN m:=1/m;
      IF length(u)=2 THEN
        IF(u[1]='$')and(u[2] in ['F','C']) THEN
          temperature(m,u[2]='F',1);
      oldm:=m;
      oldf:=factor;
      oldp:=p;
      p:=p+ord(norm(m)*norm(factor)>=10);
      u:=right;
      m:=m*factor;
      writeln(f(m),u);
      prefix(m,u);
      p:=oldp;
      leftside:=false
    END;
END;

{********** Check metric prefix and adjust if necessary **********}

PROCEDURE normalize(VAR m:REAL; VAR u:STRING);
VAR
  s:STRING;

PROCEDURE depref(p:STRING; fac,term:INTEGER);
VAR
  range,k   :INTEGER;
  needspref:BOOLEAN;
BEGIN
  needspref:=floor(log(m)/fac)<>0;
    IF pos(s,u)=2 THEN
      BEGIN
        range:=term+1;
        FOR k:=1 TO length(p) DO
          IF u[1]=p[k] THEN
            range:=k-term-1;
        IF range+term+1 in [1..term*2+1] THEN
          BEGIN
            m:=m*power(10,fac*range);
            delete(u,1,1);
            writeln(f(m),u)
          END
        ELSE
          writeln('illegal prefix ignored')
      END;
    IF needspref
      THEN
        prefix(m,u)
END;

BEGIN {normalize}
  IF leftside THEN
    s:=table[current].left
  ELSE s:=table[current].right;
  IF pos('2',s)=2 THEN
    depref(specp,2,3)
  ELSE
    IF pos('3',s)=2 THEN
      depref(specp,3,3)
    ELSE depref(normp,3,6)
END;

{********** Convert to customary or secondary units **********}
```

```pascal
          PROCEDURE custandsec(m:REAL);
          VAR
            oldp:INTEGER;
          BEGIN
            WITH table[current] DO
              BEGIN
                oldp:=p;
                p:=p+ord(norm(oldm)*norm(oldf/factor)>=10);
                m:=m/factor;
                IF (u='m3/m') and (current<=maxcust) THEN m:=1/m;
                IF u='K' THEN temperature(m,left[2]='F',-1);
                writeln(f(m),left);
                IF current>maxcust THEN prefix(m,left);
                p:=oldp
              END
          END;

          {********* Set up the table *******************************}

          PROCEDURE initialize;
          PROCEDURE data(l,r:STRING; f:REAL);
          BEGIN
            curtop:=curtop+1;
            WITH table[curtop] DO
              BEGIN
                left:=l;
                right:=r;
                factor:=f;
              END;
          END;

          BEGIN {initialize}
            curtop:=0;
            data('$F','K',5.5556E-1);        data('mpg','m3/m',2.352E-6);
            data('horsepower','W',7.355E2);
            data('inch of mercury','Pa',3.37685E3);
            data('mph','m/s',4.4704E-1);  data('yard','m',9.144E-1);
            data('yard2','m2',8.361274E-1);
            data('acre','m2',4047);          data('barrel','m3',0.159);
            data('kCal','J',4.1868E3);       data('BTU','J',1055);
            data('Curie','Bq',3.7E10);
            maxcust:=curtop;
            data('L','m3',1.0E-3);           data('N/m2','Pa',1);
            data('L/100km','m3/m',1.0E-8);  data('m/h','m/s',2.777E-4);
            data('kW-h','J',3.6E6);
            data('$C','K',1);
            data('N*m','J',1);
            top:=curtop
          END;

          {********* Main subprograms **********************************}

          PROCEDURE commands;
          VAR
            i:INTEGER;
          BEGIN
            CASE line[1] OF
            'f': finished:=true;
            's': IF inlist and (current>maxcust) and not(leftside) THEN
                    custandsec(m);
            'c': BEGIN
                    curtop:=maxcust;
                    IF inlist THEN
                      custandsec(m);
                    curtop:=top
                  END;
            'l': FOR i:=1 TO curtop DO
                    WITH table[i] DO
                       writeln(left,' ',right,' ',factor)
            END;
            writeln
          END;

          PROCEDURE process;
          BEGIN
            m:=value(line,p); u:=line; oldf:=1;
            IF not inlist THEN
              writeln('unit not available')
            ELSE
              BEGIN
                IF (current>maxcust) or (not leftside) THEN
                  normalize(m,u);
                IF leftside THEN
                  primary
              END;
            writeln
          END;

          BEGIN {supermetrics}
            finished:=false;
```

194

```
          initialize;
          writeln('SUPERMETRIC CONVERSION PROGRAM');
          writeln;
          REPEAT
            write('Measure and unit >>');
            readln(line);
            IF line[1] in ['0'..'9','+','-']
              THEN
                 process
              ELSE
                 commands
          UNTIL finished
        END.
```

Listing 2: A sample run of the program shown in listing 1.

```
Measure and unit>>5700 kJ                Measure and unit>>secondary
        5.70000E6 J                              3.00000E5 N*m
        5.7 MJ                                   300 kN*m

Measure and unit>>secondary              Measure and unit>>55 mph
        5.70000E6 N*m                            24.6 m/s
        5.7 MN*m
                                         Measure and unit>>secondary
Measure and unit>>15000 m                        8.90000E4 m/h
        15 km                                    89 km/h

Measure and unit>>15000 m2               Measure and unit>>37 kW-h
        1.5 hm2                                  1.33000E8 J
                                                 133 MJ
Measure and unit>>customary
        3.71 acre                        Measure and unit>>1200 kCal
                                                 5.00000E6 J
Measure and unit>>3 yard2                        5.0 MJ
        2.5 m2
                                         Measure and unit>>29.5 inch of mercury
Measure and unit>>3.0000 yard2                   9.96000E4 Pa
        2.50838 m2                               99.6 kPa

Measure and unit>>5 barrel               Measure and unit>>secondary
        0.8 m3                                   9.96000E4 N/m2
        800 dm3                                  99.6 kN/m2

Measure and unit>>secondary              Measure and unit>>68 $F
        800 L                                    293.2 K

Measure and unit>>38 mpg                 Measure and unit>>secondary
        6.20000E-8 m3/m                          20.0 $C
        62 mm3/m
                                         Measure and unit>>12 $C
Measure and unit>>secondary                      285 K
        6.2 L/100 km
                                         Measure and unit>>customary
Measure and unit>>50 horsepower                  54 $F
        3.70000E3 W
        37 kW                            Measure and unit>>0.005 Curie
                                                 1.85000E8 Bq
Measure and unit>>300 BTU                        185 MBq
        3.00000E5 J
        300 kJ                           Measure and unit>>finished
```

A Computer-Assisted

Dieting Program

David A Mundie

Each spring as I set out to lose my winter fat, I reach for the program shown in listing 1 to decide on a sensible combination of diet and exercise. (A sample run of this program is shown in listing 2.) The program estimates how long a given weight loss will take, based on the person's activity level and food energy intake. Knowing that the unpleasant process will not last forever is a great encouragement.

The program is based on an article by Vincent Antonetti in the American Journal of Clinical Nutrition. In this article, Antonetti shows that the time to go from an original weight W_0 to a final weight W_f is given by

$$\theta = \gamma \int_{W_o}^{W_f} \frac{dW}{(1-\alpha)I - (K_a W + K_b W^n)}$$

where γ is the energy value of one unit of weight gained or lost, α is the specific dynamic action of food, I is the daily food energy intake, n is a constant for estimating the surface area of the body, and K_a and K_b are activity and basal coefficients for the given person, expressed in terms of energy per unit weight per day. This formula is easily solved using the numerical technique known as Simpson's rule.

It is ironic that Antonetti, writing in 1973, felt his formula itself was virtually useless, since people did not have computers in their homes to perform the necessary computations. Nothing speaks more eloquently of how fast the revolution in personal computers has taken place.

To avoid the use of a computer, Antonetti published a massive collection of tables giving selected values of the above formula for various combinations

Listing 1: The computer-assisted dieting program written in UCSD Pascal.

```
PROGRAM diet;
CONST
  gamma=32000;          { 1 kg of body weight = 32000 kJ }
  p=10;                 { number of iterations }
  alpha=0.1;            { specific dynamic action of food }
  n=0.425;              { constant for estimating surface area of body }
  male= 1;
VAR
  theta,               { days for given weight change }
  wo,                  { original weight }
  wf,                  { final weight }
  intake,              { food intake, kJ/d }
  kb,                  { basal coefficient, kJ/(kg*d) }
  ka,                  { activity coefficient, kJ/(kg*d) }
  b,                   { basal metabolic rate, kJ/(m2*h) }
  height,              { in metres }
  age: REAL;
  sex: INTEGER;
  answer:STRING;

FUNCTION find(s:STRING):REAL;
VAR r:REAL;
BEGIN
  write(s,'>>'); readln(r); find:=r
END;

FUNCTION sum:REAL;
VAR
  s:REAL;
  j:INTEGER;

FUNCTION f(j:INTEGER):REAL;

FUNCTION w(j:INTEGER):REAL;
BEGIN
  w:=wo-(j/p)*(wo-wf)
END;

BEGIN {f}
  f:=1/((1-alpha)*intake-(ka*w(j)+kb*exp(n*ln(w(j)))))
END;

BEGIN {sum}
  s:=f(0)+f(p);
  FOR j:=1 TO p-1 DO
    IF odd(j)
      THEN
        s:=s+4*f(j)
      ELSE
        s:=s+2*f(j);
  sum:=s
END;
```

Listing 1, continued:

```
BEGIN {diet}
  writeln;
  writeln('Welcome to the diet!');
  age:=find('Age');
  sex:=round(find('Sex (Male=1)'));
  height:=find('Height in metres');
  IF sex=male
    THEN
      b:=173.8-0.5195*age
    ELSE
      b:=156.36-0.3636*age;
  kb:=4.8*b*exp(0.725*ln(height));
  REPEAT
    writeln;
    writeln('Sample Activity Coefficients:');
    writeln('Sedentary 34, light 40, moderate 53, vigorous 74, severe 113');
    writeln;
    ka:=find('Activity coefficient');
    wo:=find('Initial weight, kg');
    wf:=find('Final weight, kg');
    intake:=find('Daily food intake, kJ');
    theta:=(gamma*(wf-wo)/(3*p))*sum;
    writeln;
    writeln('Time for this weight change is ',round(theta),' days.');
    write('Another?');
    readln(answer)
  UNTIL not(answer[1] in ['y','Y'])
END.
```

Listing 2: A sample run of the program shown in listing 1.

```
Welcome to the diet!
Age>>32
Sex (Male=1)>>1
Height in metres>>1.75

Sample Activity Coefficients:
Sedentary 34, light 40, moderate 53, vigorous 74, severe 113

Activity coefficient>>74
Initial weight, kg>>77
Final weight, kg>>70
Daily food intake, kJ>>5000

Time for this weight change is 28 days.
Another?y

Sample Activity Coefficients:
Sedentary 34, light 40, moderate 53, vigorous 74, severe 113

Activity coefficient>>53
Initial weight, kg>>77
Final weight, kg>>70
Daily food intake, kJ>>5000

Time for this weight change is 35 days.
Another?n
```

of the variables, but my program gives much more accurate answers than any table can. I have converted all measurements to System International (SI) metric units. In particular, food energy is not expressed in kilocalories, but in joules, the only unit of energy in SI. For purposes of conversion and comparison, one "nutritional" calorie (ie 1000 calories) equals about 4.186 kilojoules.

Using the program is quite straightforward, except that the user is required to enter his activity coefficient. This may be estimated from the figures in table 1. The effect of additional exercise may be taken into account using any of the many available tables which give the food energy equivalents for given exercises. For example, if I weigh 60 kg and do 240 kj (57 kilocalories) of running per day, I will raise my activity coefficient by 4. ∎

The author wishes to thank Steve Wellons and Joe Berman of the University of Virginia's Microprocessor Laboratory for their help in making the listings of this program, which were done on equipment purchased under NASA contract #NAS1-14862.

REFERENCES

1. Antonetti, Vincent, "The Equations Governing Weight Change in Human Beings," *The American Journal of Clinical Nutrition,* Volume 26, Number 1, January, 1973.

2. Antonetti, Vincent, *The Computer Diet,* New York, Evans & Company, 1973.

Description	Activity Coefficient kJ/(kg·d)
Inactive: very little standing or walking.	34
Seated most of day: four hours of standing and walking.	40
Stands as often as is seated.	53
Standing and walking most of the day.	74
Very hard physical work.	113

Table 1. Typical values of the Physical Activity Coefficient.

Appendices

Appendix A:

Pascal Run Time Routines (in 8080 Assembly Language) and P-Code to 8080 Assembly Language Translator (in North Star BASIC)

Listing 1: Pascal Run Time Routines (in 8080 Assembly Language)

The run time routines perform the mathematical operations needed by the translated code. They are a collection of subroutines written in assembly language that can be called by a program to perfrom various arithmetic and logical operations. The operations implemented include: a stack, 16 bit addition and subtraction, multiplication and division. The relational operations test for: less than, less than or equal, greater than, greater than or equal conditions. A 16 bit shift routine is also included. The input and output routines are also defined.

```
SYMBOL TABLE
ADD16:1C02    BASE :1A15    BB    :1DF2    BS1  :1A16    CAL   :1AAE
CAL1 :1AA3    CALA :1ADE    D2    :1C8F    D3   :1C96    D4    :1CA5
D4A  :1CAA    DIV16:1C77    DM1   :1C68    DVCK :1C5C    EP1   :1A55
EP1A :1A56    EP2  :1A7D    EP3   :1AB3    EQII :1D07    EQUAL:1CD5
ER1  :1B54    ER2  :1B3D    EXIT  :2028    FALSE:1D02    GETC :1AE2
GETN :1B1B    HEX  :1DCD    HX    :1DDA    IHX  :1DA6    INHEX:1D9E
INP  :2010    INT  :1A27    L9    :1DE1    LESS :1CF0    LIT  :1A20
LOD  :1A52    LOD1 :1A49    LODA  :1ACB    LODX :1A5F    LODX1:1A60
LP   :1C31    LZ   :1B06    MER1  :1B5D    MER2 :1B6B    MUL8 :1C2F
NE   :1D12    NEGB :1BE0    NEGH  :1BD3    NUM  :1B1E    OUTP :200D
OVFL :1BEA    P00  :1BA6    P01   :1C23    P02  :1C0F    P03  :1C15
P04  :1C3C    P05  :1C51    P06   :1CBE    P07  :1CC7    P08  :1CD3
P09  :1CE9    P10  :1D16    P11   :1CED    P12  :1D1D    P13  :1D24
P14  :1D2A    P15  :1D35    P16   :1D40    P17  :1D49    P18  :1D5A
P19  :1D72    P20  :1D7C    P21   :1D86    PNT  :1BF5    POP  :1BBC
POP1 :1BCC    PRINT:1BF3    PUSH  :1BC6    SIGN :1B78    SKIP :1C37
SL1  :1D52    SM1  :1A38    SM2   :1A3E    SR1  :1D64    STK2 :1DF4
STKOV:1A2E    STO  :1A7A    STO1  :1A71    STOA :1AD6    STOX :1A86
STOX1:1A87    SU2  :1C03    SUB1  :1BFF    SUB16:1C18    SYS0 :1AE9
SYS1 :1AF2    SYS2 :1AF9    SYS3  :1B79    SYS4 :1D91    SYS5 :1DC4
SYS8 :1DE7    TRUE :1CF6    WR    :1B9C    Y2   :1AFA    Y2R  :1B43
Y3   :1B8C    Y4   :1D92    Y4E   :1DB9    Y8   :1DE8    YE1  :1B57
```

```
              ; PASCAL RUN-TIME ROUTINES
              ; HY.1  1/30/78   BY  H. YUEN
              ; VERSION 2.0  2/28/78
              ; VERSION 2.1  4/7/78
              INP   EQU  #2010    ; CHAR INPUT ROUTINE IN DOS
              OUTP  EQU  #200D    ; CHAR OUTPUT ROUTINE IN DOS
              EXIT  EQU  #2028    ; RETURN TO DOS
              ;
              ; ON ENTRY: HL -  STACK START ADDR
              ;           DE -  COMP. OF END ADDR
              ;
                    ORG  #1A00
1A00  23            INX  H        ; INITIALIZATION
1A01  22 F2 1D      SHLD BB       ; BASE
1A04  2B            DCX  H
1A05  2B            DCX  H
1A06  EB            XCHG          ; DE USED AS STACK PTR.
1A07  22 F4 1D      SHLD STK2
1A0A  21 05 00      LXI  H,#0005
```

```
1A0D  19              DAD   D         ; (T+3)
1A0E  01 28 20        LXI   B,EXIT    ; EXIT ADDR
1A11  70              MOV   M,B
1A12  23              INX   H
1A13  71              MOV   M,C
1A14  C9              RET
                ;==========
1A15  D5        BASE  PUSH  D
1A16  5E        BS1   MOV   E,M
1A17  2B              DCX   H
1A18  56              MOV   D,M
1A19  EB              XCHG
1A1A  3D              DCR   A
1A1B  C2 16 1A        JNZ   BS1
1A1E  D1              POP   D
1A1F  C9              RET
1A20  EB        LIT   XCHG            ; LOAD LITERAL CONSTANT
1A21  23              INX   H
1A22  70              MOV   M,B
1A23  23              INX   H
1A24  71              MOV   M,C
1A25  EB              XCHG
1A26  C9              RET
1A27  19        INT   DAD   D         ; INCREMENT STACK PTR
1A28  EB              XCHG
1A29  2A F4 1D        LHLD  STK2
1A2C  19              DAD   D
1A2D  D0              RNC
1A2E  21 38 1A  STKOV LXI   H,SM1
1A31  CD F3 1B        CALL  PRINT
1A34  E1              POP   H         ; POP RETURN ADDR
1A35  C3 28 20        JMP   EXIT
1A38  20        SM1   DB    ' STACK'
1A3E  20        SM2   DB    ' OVERFLOW',0D,0A
                ;
1A49  2A F2 1D  LOD1  LHLD  BB
1A4C  CD 15 1A        CALL  BASE
1A4F  C3 55 1A        JMP   EP1
1A52  2A F2 1D  LOD   LHLD  BB        ; LOAD VARIABLE
1A55  13        EP1   INX   D
1A56  09        EP1A  DAD   B
1A57  2B              DCX   H
1A58  7E              MOV   A,M
1A59  12              STAX  D
1A5A  23              INX   H
1A5B  7E              MOV   A,M
1A5C  13              INX   D
1A5D  12              STAX  D
1A5E  C9              RET
1A5F  AF        LODX  XRA   A
1A60  2A F2 1D  LODX1 LHLD  BB        ; LOAD VAR INDEXED
1A63  B7              ORA   A
1A64  C4 15 1A        CNZ   BASE
1A67  09              DAD   B
1A68  EB              XCHG
1A69  4E              MOV   C,M
1A6A  2B              DCX   H
1A6B  46              MOV   B,M
1A6C  EB              XCHG
1A6D  09              DAD   B         ; ADD INDEX
1A6E  C3 56 1A        JMP   EP1A
                ;...
1A71  2A F2 1D  STO1  LHLD  BB
1A74  CD 15 1A        CALL  BASE
1A77  C3 7D 1A        JMP   EP2
1A7A  2A F2 1D  STO   LHLD  BB        ; STORE VARIABLE
1A7D  09        EP2   DAD   B
1A7E  1A              LDAX  D
1A7F  77              MOV   M,A
1A80  2B              DCX   H
1A81  1B              DCX   D
1A82  1A              LDAX  D
```

204

```
1A83   77                      MOV   M,A
1A84   1B                      DCX   D
1A85   C9                      RET
1A86   AF           STOX       XRA   A
1A87   FB           STOX1 XCHG                ; STORE VAR INDEXED
1A88   5F                      MOV   E,M
1A89   2B                      DCX   H
1A8A   56                      MOV   D,M
1A8B   2B                      DCX   H
1A8C   D5                      PUSH  D         ; SAVE VALUE TO BE STORED
1A8D   5F                      MOV   E,M
1A8E   2B                      DCX   H
1A8F   56                      MOV   D,M
1A90   2B                      DCX   H
1A91   EB                      XCHG            ; INDEX IS NOW IN HL
1A92   29                      DAD   H
1A93   09                      DAD   B
1A94   44                      MOV   B,H
1A95   4D                      MOV   C,L
1A96   2A F2 1D                LHLD  RB
1A99   B7                      ORA   A
1A9A   C4 15 1A                CNZ   BASE
1A9D   09                      DAD   B
1A9E   C1                      POP   B         ; RETRIEVE VALUE
1A9F   71                      MOV   M,C
1AA0   2B                      DCX   H
1AA1   70                      MOV   M,B
1AA2   C9                      RET
                    ;...
1AA3   2A F2 1D     CAL1       LHLD  BB
1AA6   44                      MOV   B,H
1AA7   4D                      MOV   C,L        ; SAVE BB IN B,C
1AA8   CD 15 1A                CALL  BASE
1AAB   C3 B3 1A                JMP   EP3
1AAE   2A F2 1D     CAL        LHLD  BB         ; PROC OR FUNC CALL
1AB1   44                      MOV   B,H
1AB2   4D                      MOV   C,L
1AB3   D5           EP3        PUSH  D
1AB4   EB                      XCHG            ; BASE(L) IN D,E
1AB5   23                      INX   H
1AB6   72                      MOV   M,D
1AB7   23                      INX   H
1AB8   73                      MOV   M,E
1AB9   22 F2 1D                SHLD  BB         ; BB=T+1
1ABC   D1                      POP   D          ; RESTORE T
1ABD   23                      INX   H
1ABE   70                      MOV   M,B
1ABF   23                      INX   H
1AC0   71                      MOV   M,C        ; S(T+2)=BB
1AC1   C1                      POP   B          ; GET RETURN ADDR
1AC2   C5                      PUSH  B
1AC3   03                      INX   B
1AC4   03                      INX   B
1AC5   03                      INX   B          ; RET ADDR +3
1AC6   23                      INX   H
1AC7   70                      MOV   M,B
1AC8   23                      INX   H
1AC9   71                      MOV   M,C
1ACA   C9                      RET
                    ;...
1ACB   EB           LODA       XCHG            ; LOAD VAR WITH ABS ADDR
1ACC   5F                      MOV   E,M
1ACD   2B                      DCX   H
1ACE   56                      MOV   D,M
1ACF   36 00                   MVI   M,00
1AD1   1A                      LDAX  D
1AD2   23                      INX   H
1AD3   77                      MOV   M,A
1AD4   EB                      XCHG
1AD5   C9                      RET
                    ;...
1AD6   1A           STOA       LDAX  D          ; STORE VAR WITH ABS ADDR
```

```
1AD7    1B                      DCX   D
1AD8    1B                      DCX   D
1AD9    CD CC 1B                CALL  POP1
1ADC    77                      MOV   M,A
1ADD    C9                      RET
                        ;...
1ADE    CD CC 1B        CALA    CALL  POP1     ; CALL ABS ADDR SUBROUTINE
1AE1    E9                      PCHL
                        ;...
1AE2    CD 10 20        GETC    CALL  INP      ; GET A CHAR
1AE5    47                      MOV   B,A
1AE6    C3 0D 20                JMP   OUTP     ; ECHO THE CHAR
                        ;...
1AE9    13              SYS0    INX   D        ;   [ INCHR ]
1AEA    AF                      XRA   A
1AEB    12                      STAX  D
1AEC    13                      INX   D
1AED    CD E2 1A                CALL  GETC
1AF0    12                      STAX  D
1AF1    C9                      RET
                        ;...
1AF2    1A              SYS1    LDAX  D        ;   [ OUTCHR ]
1AF3    1B                      DCX   D
1AF4    1B                      DCX   D
1AF5    47                      MOV   B,A
1AF6    C3 0D 20                JMP   OUTP
                        ;...
1AF9    D5              SYS2    PUSH  D        ;   [ INNUM ]
1AFA    06 3F           Y2      MVI   B,'?'
1AFC    CD 0D 20                CALL  OUTP
1AFF    50                      MOV   D,B      ; SET INIT FLAG
1B00    AF                      XRA   A
1B01    32 78 1B                STA   SIGN
1B04    67                      MOV   H,A
1B05    6F                      MOV   L,A
1B06    CD E2 1A        LZ      CALL  GETC
1B09    FE 20                   CPI   20
1B0B    CA 06 1B                JZ    LZ       ; SKIP LEADING BLANKS
1B0E    FE 2B                   CPI   '+'
1B10    CA 1B 1B                JZ    GETN
1B13    FE 2D                   CPI   '-'
1B15    C2 1E 1B                JNZ   NUM
1B18    32 78 1B                STA   SIGN
1B1B    CD E2 1A        GETN    CALL  GETC
1B1E    D6 30           NUM     SUI   30
1B20    FA 43 1B                JM    Y2R
1B23    FE 0A                   CPI   0A
1B25    F2 43 1B                JP    Y2R
1B28    5F                      MOV   E,A
1B29    AF                      XRA   A
1B2A    57                      MOV   D,A      ; RESET FLAG
1B2B    29                      DAD   H        ; 2*HL
1B2C    44                      MOV   B,H
1B2D    4D                      MOV   C,L
1B2E    29                      DAD   H
1B2F    8F                      ADC   A
1B30    29                      DAD   H
1B31    8F                      ADC   A
1B32    09                      DAD   B        ; 2*HL+8*HL
1B33    8F                      ADC   A
1B34    19                      DAD   D
1B35    8F                      ADC   A
1B36    C2 3D 1B                JNZ   ER2
1B39    B4                      ORA   H
1B3A    F2 1B 1B                JP    GETN
1B3D    21 6B 1B        ER2     LXI   H,MER2
1B40    C3 57 1B                JMP   YE1
1B43    AF              Y2R     XRA   A
1B44    82                      ADD   D        ; CHECK FLAG
1B45    C2 54 1B                JNZ   ER1
1B48    3A 78 1B                LDA   SIGN
1B4B    B7                      ORA   A
```

206

```
1B4C   C4 D3 1B          CNZ   NEGH          ; NEGATE THE NUM IF SIGN IS '
  -'
1B4F   D1                POP   D
1B50   13                INX   D
1B51   C3 C6 1B          JMP   PUSH
1B54   21 5D 1B    ER1   LXI   H,MER1
1B57   CD F3 1B    YE1   CALL  PRINT
1B5A   C3 FA 1A          JMP   Y2
1B5D   20          MER1  DB    ' INPUT ERROR',0D,0A
1B6B   20          MER2  DB    ' SIZE ERROR',0D,0A
1B78   00          SIGN  DB    00
                   ;...
1B79   CD CC 1B    SYS3  CALL  POP1          ;   [ OUTNUM ]
1B7C   D5                PUSH  D             ; SAVE NEW STK PTR
1B7D   AF                XRA   A
1B7E   3D                DCR   A
1B7F   F5                PUSH  SW            ; PUT -1 & FLAG
1B80   A4                ANA   H             ; TEST SIGN
1B81   F2 8C 1B          JP    Y3
1B84   06 2D             MVI   B,'-'
1B86   CD 0D 20          CALL  OUTP
1B89   CD D3 1B          CALL  NEGH          ; NEGATE THE NUMBER
1B8C   01 0A 00    Y3    LXI   B,#000A
1B8F   CD 77 1C          CALL  DIV16         ; DIVIDE BY 10
1B92   3E 30             MVI   A,30
1B94   83                ADD   E             ; CONVERT TO ASCII
1B95   F5                PUSH  SW            ; SAVE ON STACK (REVERSE ORDER)
1B96   7C                MOV   A,H
1B97   B5                ORA   L
1B98   C2 8C 1B          JNZ   Y3
1B9B   F1                POP   SW
1B9C   47          WR    MOV   B,A
1B9D   CD 0D 20          CALL  OUTP          ; OUTPUT EACH DIGIT
1BA0   F1                POP   SW
1BA1   F2 9C 1B          JP    WR
1BA4   D1                POP   D
1BA5   C9                RET
                   ;...
1BA6   2A F2 1D    P00   LHLD  BB            ; [ PROC RETURN]
1BA9   23                INX   H
1BAA   56                MOV   D,M
1BAB   23                INX   H
1BAC   5E                MOV   E,M
1BAD   EB                XCHG
1BAE   22 F2 1D          SHLD  BB            ; BB=S(T+2)
1BB1   EB                XCHG
1BB2   23                INX   H
1BB3   56                MOV   D,M
1BB4   23                INX   H
1BB5   5E                MOV   E,M           ; P=S(T+3) IN DE
1BB6   01 FA FF          LXI   B,#FFFA       ; 2'S COMP OF -6
1BB9   09                DAD   B             ; T=BB-1
1BBA   EB                XCHG
1BBB   E9                PCHL
                   ;...
1BBC   EB          POP   XCHG
1BBD   4F                MOV   C,M
1BBE   2B                DCX   H
1BBF   46                MOV   B,M           ; S(T) -> B,C
1BC0   2B                DCX   H
1BC1   5F                MOV   E,M
1BC2   2B                DCX   H
1BC3   56                MOV   D,M
1BC4   EB                XCHG                ; S(T-1) -> H,L
1BC5   C9                RET
                   ;....
1BC6   EB          PUSH  XCHG
1BC7   72                MOV   M,D
1BC8   23                INX   H
1BC9   73                MOV   M,E           ; H,L -> S(T)
1BCA   EB                XCHG
```

```
1BCB   C9                  RET
                  ;...
1BCC   EB           POP1   XCHG
1BCD   5E                  MOV   E,M
1BCE   2B                  DCX   H
1BCF   56                  MOV   D,M        ; S(T) -> H,L
1BD0   2B                  DCX   H
1BD1   EB                  XCHG
1BD2   C9                  RFT
                  ;...
1BD3   AF           NEGH   XRA   A          ; NEGATE HL
1BD4   95                  SUB   L
1BD5   6F                  MOV   L,A
1BD6   9C                  SBB   H
1BD7   95                  SUB   L
1BD8   67                  MOV   H,A
1BD9   D6 80               SUI   80
1BDB   B5                  ORA   L
1BDC   C0                  RNZ
1BDD   C3 EA 1B            JMP   OVFL
                  ;...
1BE0   AF           NEGB   XRA   A          ; NEGATE B,C
1BE1   91                  SUB   C
1BE2   4F                  MOV   C,A
1BE3   98                  SBB   B
1BE4   91                  SUB   C
1BE5   47                  MOV   B,A
1BE6   D6 80               SUI   80
1BE8   B1                  ORA   C
1BE9   C0                  RNZ
1BEA   21 3E 1A     OVFL   LXI   H,SM2
1BED   CD F3 1B            CALL  PRINT
1BF0   C3 C6 1B            JMP   PUSH
                  ;
1BF3   0E 0A        PRINT  MVI   C,0A       ; PRINT MESSAGE
1BF5   46           PNT    MOV   B,M
1BF6   23                  INX   H
1BF7   CD 0D 20            CALL  OUTP
1BFA   B9                  CMP   C
1BFB   C2 F5 1B            JNZ   PNT
1BFE   C9                  RET
                  ;...
1BFF   CD E0 1B     SUB1   CALL  NEGB
1C02   78           ADD16  MOV   A,B        ; [16 BIT SIGNED ADD]
1C03   AC           SU2    XRA   H
1C04   09                  DAD   E
1C05   4F                  MOV   C,A
1C06   1F                  RAR
1C07   A9                  XRA   C          ; XOR SIGN OF CARRY
1C08   AC                  XRA   H          ; SIGN OF RESULT
1C09   F2 C6 1B            JP    PUSH
1C0C   C3 EA 1B            JMP   OVFL
                  ;...
1C0F   CD BC 1B     P02    CALL  POP        ; [ ADD ]
1C12   C3 02 1C            JMP   ADD16
                  ;...
1C15   CD BC 1B     P03    CALL  POP
1C18   78           SUB16  MOV   A,B        ; [16 BIT SIGNED SUBTRACT]
1C19   D6 80               SUI   80
1C1B   B1                  ORA   C
1C1C   C2 FF 1B            JNZ   SUB1
1C1F   79                  MOV   A,C
1C20   C3 03 1C            JMP   SU2
                  ;...
1C23   EB           P01    XCHG             ; [ NEGATE ]
1C24   AF                  XRA   A
1C25   96                  SUB   M
1C26   77                  MOV   M,A
1C27   4F                  MOV   C,A
1C28   2B                  DCX   H
1C29   9E                  SBB   M
1C2A   91                  SUB   C
```

```
1C2B   77              MOV   M,A
1C2C   23              INX   H
1C2D   EB              XCHG
1C2E   C9              RET
                ;...
1C2F   16 08    MUL8   MVI   D,08      ; 8-BIT MULTIPLY
1C31   29       LP     DAD   H
1C32   07              RLC
1C33   D2 37 1C        JNC   SKIP
1C36   09              DAD   B
1C37   15       SKIP   DCR   D
1C38   C2 31 1C        JNZ   LP
1C3B   C9              RET
                ;...
1C3C   CD BC 1B P04    CALL  POP       ;   [ MULTIPLY]
1C3F   D5              PUSH  D
1C40   7C              MOV   A,H       ; HIGH BYTE
1C41   5D              MOV   E,L
1C42   21 00 00        LXI   H,#0000
1C45   B7              ORA   A
1C46   C4 2F 1C        CNZ   MUL8
1C49   7B              MOV   A,E       ; LOW BYTE
1C4A   CD 2F 1C        CALL  MUL8
1C4D   D1              POP   D
1C4E   C3 C6 1B        JMP   PUSH
                ;...
1C51   CD BC 1B P05    CALL  POP       ;   [ DIVIDE ]
1C54   D5              PUSH  D
1C55   CD 77 1C        CALL  DIV16
1C58   D1              POP   D
1C59   C3 C6 1B        JMP   PUSH
                ;...
1C5C   21 68 1C DVCK   LXI   H,DM1
1C5F   CD F3 1B        CALL  PRINT
1C62   21 00 00        LXI   H,#0000
1C65   54              MOV   D,H
1C66   5D              MOV   E,L
1C67   C9              RET
1C68   20       DM1    DB    ' DIVIDE CHECK',0D,0A
1C77   78       DIV16  MOV   A,B
1C78   B1              ORA   C
1C79   CA 5C 1C        JZ    DVCK
1C7C   AF              XRA   A
1C7D   80              ADD   B
1C7E   F5              PUSH  SW        ; SAVE SIGN OF DIVISOR
1C7F   F4 E0 1B        CP    NEGB
1C82   AF              XRA   A
1C83   84              ADD   H
1C84   F5              PUSH  SW        ; SAVE SIGN OF DIVIDEND
1C85   FC D3 1B        CM    NEGH
1C88   EB              XCHG            ; DIVIDEND IN DE
1C89   21 00 00        LXI   H,#0000
1C8C   3E 10           MVI   A,10
1C8E   29       D2     DAD   H         ; SHIFT HL
1C8F   EB              XCHG
1C90   29              DAD   H         ; SHIFT DE
1C91   EB              XCHG
1C92   D2 96 1C        JNC   D3
1C95   23              INX   H         ; ADD CARRY FROM DE
1C96   E5       D3     PUSH  H         ; SAVE HL
1C97   09              DAD   B
1C98   D2 A5 1C        JNC   D4
1C9B   1C              INR   E         ; PUT 1 IN LOW ORDER BIT OF DE
1C9C   33              INX   SP        ; THROW AWAY OLD HL
1C9D   33              INX   SP
1C9E   3D              DCR   A
1C9F   C2 8E 1C        JNZ   D2
1CA2   C3 AA 1C        JMP   D4A
1CA5   E1       D4     POP   H         ; GET OLD HL
1CA6   3D              DCR   A
1CA7   C2 8E 1C        JNZ   D2
```

```
1CAA   EB          D4A    XCHG              ; SWITCH QUOT. & REM.
1CAB   C1                 POP   B           ; SIGN OF DIVIDEND
1CAC   F1                 POP   SW          ;  "  DIVISOR
1CAD   A8                 XRA   B
1CAE   FC D3 1B           CM    NEGH
1CB1   7A                 MOV   A,D
1CB2   B3                 ORA   E           ; REMAINDER=0 ?
1CB3   C8                 RZ
1CB4   AF                 XRA   A
1CB5   80                 ADD   B           ; DIVIDEND + ?
1CB6   F0                 RP
1CB7   AF                 XRA   A
1CB8   93                 SUB   E           ; NEGATE THE REMAINDER
1CB9   5F                 MOV   E,A
1CBA   9A                 SBB   D
1CBB   93                 SUB   E
1CBC   57                 MOV   D,A
1CBD   C9                 RET
                   ;...
1CBE   1A          P06    LDAX  D           ; TEST FOR ODD
1CBF   E6 01              ANI   01
1CC1   12                 STAX  D
1CC2   AF                 XRA   A           ; SET HI BYTE TO 0
1CC3   1B                 DCX   D
1CC4   12                 STAX  D
1CC5   13                 INX   D
1CC6   C9                 RET
                   ;...
1CC7   CD BC 1B    P07    CALL  POP         ;  [ MOD ]
1CCA   D5                 PUSH  D
1CCB   CD 77 1C           CALL  DIV16
1CCE   EB                 XCHG              ; PUT REMAINDER IN HL
1CCF   D1                 POP   D
1CD0   C3 C6 1B           JMP   PUSH
                   ;...
1CD3   3E 01       P08    MVI   A,01        ; TEST FOR =
                   ;...
1CD5   F5          EQUAL  PUSH  SW          ; SAVE FLAG
1CD6   CD BC 1B           CALL  POP
1CD9   AF                 XRA   A
1CDA   12                 STAX  D           ; PUT 0 IN HI BYTE
1CDB   13                 INX   D
1CDC   7D                 MOV   A,L
1CDD   B9                 CMP   C
1CDE   C2 02 1D           JNZ   FALSE
1CE1   7C                 MOV   A,H
1CE2   B8                 CMP   B
1CE3   C2 02 1D           JNZ   FALSE
1CE6   F1          TRUE   POP   SW
1CE7   12                 STAX  D
1CE8   C9                 RET
                   ;...
1CE9   AF          P09    XRA   A           ; TEST FOR <>
1CEA   C3 D5 1C           JMP   EQUAL
                   ;...
1CED   06 00       P11    MVI   B,00        ; TEST FOR >=
1CEF   48                 MOV   C,B         ; (OPPOSITE OF P10)
1CF0   C5          LESS   PUSH  B           ; SAVE FLAG
1CF1   CD BC 1B           CALL  POP
1CF4   AF                 XRA   A
1CF5   12                 STAX  D           ; PUT 0 IN HI BYTE
1CF6   13                 INX   D
1CF7   7C                 MOV   A,H
1CF8   B8                 CMP   B
1CF9   CA 07 1D           JZ    EQH
1CFC   1F                 RAR               ; GET CARRY IN MSB
1CFD   AC                 XRA   H
1CFE   A8                 XRA   B
1CFF   FA E6 1C           JM    TRUE
1D02   F1          FALSE  POP   SW
1D03   EE 01              XRI   01          ; COMPLEMENT FLAG
1D05   12                 STAX  D
```

```
1D06    C9                  RET
1D07    7D          EQH     MOV  A,L
1D08    B9                  CMP  C
1D09    DA E6 1C            JC   TRUE
1D0C    C1                  POP  B          ; RETRIEVE FLAG
1D0D    78                  MOV  A,B
1D0E    C2 12 1D            JNZ  NE         ; L <> C
1D11    A9                  XRA  C          ; HL=BC
1D12    EE 01       NE      XRI  01
1D14    12                  STAX D
1D15    C9                  RET
                    ;...
1D16    06 01       P10     MVI  B,01       ; TEST FOR <
1D18    0E 00               MVI  C,00
1D1A    C3 F0 1C            JMP  LESS
                    ;...
1D1D    06 00       P12     MVI  B,00       ; TEST FOR >
1D1F    0E 01               MVI  C,01       ; (OPPOSITE OF P13)
1D21    C3 F0 1C            JMP  LESS
                    ;...
1D24    06 01       P13     MVI  B,01       ; TEST FOR <=
1D26    48                  MOV  C,B
1D27    C3 F0 1C            JMP  LESS
                    ;....
1D2A    CD BC 1B    P14     CALL POP        ;    [OR]
1D2D    7C                  MOV  A,H
1D2E    B0                  ORA  B
1D2F    12                  STAX D
1D30    7D                  MOV  A,L
1D31    B1                  ORA  C
1D32    13                  INX  D
1D33    12                  STAX D
1D34    C9                  RET
                    ;....
1D35    CD BC 1B    P15     CALL POP        ;    [AND]
1D38    7C                  MOV  A,H
1D39    A0                  ANA  B
1D3A    12                  STAX D
1D3B    7D                  MOV  A,L
1D3C    A1                  ANA  C
1D3D    13                  INX  D
1D3E    12                  STAX D
1D3F    C9                  RET
                    ;....
1D40    1A          P16     LDAX D          ;    [COMPLEMENT]
1D41    2F                  CMA
1D42    12                  STAX D
1D43    1B                  DCX  D
1D44    1A                  LDAX D
1D45    2F                  CMA
1D46    12                  STAX D
1D47    13                  INX  D
1D48    C9                  RET
                    ;....
1D49    CD BC 1B    P17     CALL POP        ;    [SHL]
1D4C    AF                  XRA  A
1D4D    81                  ADD  C
1D4E    C8                  RZ
1D4F    FA 64 1D            JM   SR1
1D52    29          SL1     DAD  H          ; SHIFT LEFT
1D53    3D                  DCR  A
1D54    C2 52 1D            JNZ  SL1
1D57    C3 C6 1B            JMP  PUSH
                    ;....
1D5A    CD BC 1B    P18     CALL POP        ;    [SHR]
1D5D    AF                  XRA  A
1D5E    91                  SUB  C
1D5F    C8                  RZ
1D60    F2 52 1D            JP   SL1
1D63    4F                  MOV  C,A
1D64    AF          SR1     XRA  A
1D65    B4                  ORA  H          ; CLEAR CARRY
```

```
1D66   1F                 RAR              ;  SHIFT RIGHT
1D67   67                 MOV   H,A
1D68   7D                 MOV   A,L
1D69   1F                 RAR
1D6A   6F                 MOV   L,A
1D6B   0C                 INR   C
1D6C   C2 64 1D           JNZ   SR1
1D6F   C3 C6 1B           JMP   PUSH
                 ;...
1D72   1A        P19      LDAX  D          ;   [ INC ]
1D73   C6 01              ADI   01
1D75   12                 STAX  D
1D76   D0                 RNC
1D77   62                 MOV   H,D
1D78   6B                 MOV   L,F
1D79   2B                 DCX   H
1D7A   34                 INR   M          ;  INCREMENT HI BYTE BY 1
1D7B   C9                 RET
                 ;...
1D7C   1A        P20      LDAX  D          ;   [ DEC ]
1D7D   D6 01              SUI   01
1D7F   12                 STAX  D
1D80   D0                 RNC
1D81   62                 MOV   H,D
1D82   6B                 MOV   L,E
1D83   2B                 DCX   H
1D84   35                 DCR   M          ;  DECREMENT HI BYTE BY 1
1D85   C9                 RET
                 ;...
1D86   62        P21      MOV   H,D        ;   [ COPY ]
1D87   6B                 MOV   L,F
1D88   13                 INX   D
1D89   2B                 DCX   H
1D8A   7E                 MOV   A,M
1D8B   12                 STAX  D
1D8C   13                 INX   D
1D8D   23                 INX   H
1D8E   7F                 MOV   A,M
1D8F   12                 STAX  D
1D90   C9                 RET
                 ;...
1D91   13        SYS4     INX   D          ;   [ INHEX ]
1D92   CD 9E 1D  Y4       CALL  INHE
1D95   81                 ADD   C
1D96   12                 STAX  D
1D97   CD 9E 1D           CALL  INHEX
1D9A   81                 ADD   C
1D9B   13                 INX   D
1D9C   12                 STAX  D
1D9D   C9                 RET
1D9E   CD A6 1D  INHEX    CALL  IHX        ;  INPUT 2 HEX DIGITS
1DA1   07                 RLC
1DA2   07                 RLC
1DA3   07                 RLC
1DA4   07                 RLC
1DA5   4F                 MOV   C,A        ;  SAVE HI ORDER HEX DIGIT (SHIFTED)
1DA6   CD E2 1A  IHX      CALL  GETC
1DA9   D6 30              SUI   30
1DAB   FA B9 1D           JM    Y4E
1DAE   FE 0A              CPI   0A
1DB0   F8                 RM
1DB1   D6 07              SUI   07
1DB3   FA B9 1D           JM    Y4E
1DB6   FE 10              CPI   10
1DB8   F8                 RM
1DB9   21 5D 1B  Y4E      LXI   H,MER1
1DBC   CD F3 1B           CALL  PRINT
1DBF   E1                 POP   H
1DC0   E1                 POP   H
1DC1   C3 92 1D           JMP   Y4
```

```
1DC4    1A              SYS5    LDAX    D           ;    [ OUTHEX ]
1DC5    6F                      MOV     L,A         ; SAVE LOW ORDER BYTE
1DC6    1B                      DCX     D
1DC7    1A                      LDAX    D
1DC8    1B                      DCX     D
1DC9    CD CD 1D                CALL    HEX
1DCC    7D                      MOV     A,L
1DCD    4F              HEX     MOV     C,A
1DCE    E6 F0                   ANI     F0          ; HI ORDER HEX DIGIT
1DD0    0F                      RRC
1DD1    0F                      RRC
1DD2    0F                      RRC
1DD3    0F                      RRC
1DD4    CD DA 1D                CALL    HX
1DD7    79                      MOV     A,C
1DD8    E6 0F                   ANI     0F          ; LO ORDER HEX DIGIT
1DDA    FE 0A           HX      CPI     0A
1DDC    FA E1 1D                JM      L9
1DDF    C6 07                   ADI     07
1DE1    C6 30           L9      ADI     30          ; CONVERT TO ASCII
1DE3    47                      MOV     B,A
1DE4    C3 0D 20                JMP     OUTP
                        ;...
1DE7    E1              SYS8    POP     H           ;    [ OUTSTR ]
1DE8    46              Y8      MOV     B,M
1DE9    CD 0D 20                CALL    OUTP
1DEC    23                      INX     H
1DED    0D                      DCR     C           ; CHAR COUNT
1DEE    C2 E8 1D                JNZ     Y8
1DF1    E9                      PCHL                ; JUMP TO LOC FOLLOWING STRING
                        ;...
1DF2    00 00           BB      DW                  ; BASE ADDR
1DF4    00 00           STK2    DW                  ; COMPLEMENT OF STACK END ADDR

                                END
```

Listing 2: P-Code to 8080 Assembly Language Translator

The p-code to 8080 translator is written in North Star BASIC. The p-codes are usually translated into subroutine calls to the appropriate run time routine. In this way, a pseudo-macroassembler is used. The translator also performs a crude form of 8080 code optimization which is discussed in table 4 of part 3.

```
LIST

5REM..LAST MOD 5/21/78
10REM..P-CODE TO 8080 TRANSLATOR
20REM  HY.1 2/5/78   BY  F. YUEN
25REM  HY.2 3/23/78
30 DIM A$(4),B$(4),H0$(16),B0$(4)
40 S1=500:S2=400
50 DIM T$(S1):REM..TABLE OF REFERENCES
60 DIM D$(S2):REM..8080 ADDR OF P-CODE LABELS
65 DIM E(S2):REM..TABLE OF FORWARD REF
68 DIM W$(36),Z$(88):O2=21
70 DIM Y1(15),Y2(15),Y$(60)
75 DIM Z1(30),Z2(30)
78 H0$="0123456789ABCDEF"
80REM..        LIT LOD LD1 LDX LX1 LDA STO ST1
82 Y$(1,32)="1A201A521A491A5F1A601ACB1A7A1A71"
84REM..        STX SX1 STA CAL CL1 CLA INT
86Y$(33,60)="1A861A871AD61AAE1AA31ADE1A27"
90REM..P00,P01,..P21
94 Z$(1,32)= "1BA61C231C0F1C151C3C1C511CBE1CC7"
96 Z$(33,64)="1CD31CE91D161CED1D1D1D241D2A1D35"
98 Z$(65,88)="1D401D491D5A1D721D7C1D86"
99REM..SYS0,..SYS8
100 W$(1,24)="1AE91AF21AF91B791D911DC4"
102 W$(33,36)="1DE7"
103REM===========
105REM SETUP ADDR OF ENTRY PT IN RUN-TIME ROUTINE
106REM===========
110 M=0:FOR K=1 TO 60 STEP 4
112 M=M+1:Y2(M)=FND(Y$(K,K+1),2)+X
113 Y1(M)=FND(Y$(K+2,K+3),2)+X:NEXT
114 M=0:FOR K=1 TO 88 STEP 4
115 Z2(M)=FND(Z$(K,K+1),2)+X
116 Z1(M)=FND(Z$(K+2,K+3),2)+X
117 M=M+1:NEXT
118 M=O2+1:FOR K=1 TO 36 STEP 4
119 Z2(M)=FND(W$(K,K+1),2)+X
120 Z1(M)=FND(W$(K+2,K+3),2)+X
122 M=M+1:NEXT:GOTO 300
123REM===========
125REM..CONVERT HEX TO DECIMAL
130 DEF FND(H1$,L)
135 N=0:FOR I=1 TO L
140 J=ASC(H1$(I,I))-48
145 IF J>9 THEN J=J-7
150 N=N*16+J:NEXT:RETURN N
160 FNEND
165REM..CONVERT INTEGER TO HEX
```

```
170 DEF FNH$(L)
175 R=INT(L/16)+1:S=L-R*16+17
180 RETURN H0$(R,R)+H0$(S,S)
185 FNEND
190REM..CODE GENERATOR
200 DEF FNG(O,M,N)
210 FILL P,O:FILL P+1,M
220 FILL P+2,N:RETURN P+3
230 FNEND
240REM..CODE GENERATOR 2
250 DEF FNQ(O,M)
260 FILL P,O:FILL P+1,Y1(M)
270 FILL P+2,Y2(M):RFTURN P+3
280 FNEND
285REM============
290REM
300 PRINT"*** P-CODE TO 8080 TRANSLATION ***"
302 INPUT"ADDR (HEX) OF PAS.LIB:",B0$
304 IF B0$="" THEN B0$="1A00"
306 X=FND(B0$,4)-FND("1A00",4)
310 INPUT"ADDR (HEX) OF P-CODE:",A$
315 IF A$="" THEN A$="9800"
320 X=FND(A$,4):X0=X
330 INPUT"ADDR (HEX) OF OUTPUT 8080 PGM:",B$
335 IF B$="" THEN B$="9000":P0=FND(B$,4)
340 INPUT"STACK START ADDR (HEX):",B$
345 IF B$<>"" THEN 360
350 PRINT"DEFAULT STACK ADDRESSES USED"
355 A$="9FFF":GOTO 365
360 INPUT"STACK END ADDR (HEX):",A$
365 K=65536-FND(A$,4)
370 J=INT(K/256):I=K-J*256
375 P=P0+3:P=FNG(17,I,J)
380 P=FNG(205,FND(B0$(3,4),2),FND(B0$(1,2),2))
385 B0$=B$
388REM=========
390REM..1ST PASS..PICK UP LABELS
400 W=1:REM..TABLE PTR
420 J=EXAM(X):IF J=255 THEN 470
430 X=X+4:IF J<4 THEN 420
435 IF J=5 OR J>7 THEN 420
440 T$(W,W+1)=CHR$(EXAM(X-1))+CHR$(EXAM(X-2))
450 W=W+2:GOTO 420
470 PRINT(W-1)/2," REFERENCES":W=W-2
472REM===
475REM..PRE-COMPRESS TABLE
477REM COMPARE ITEM WITH LAST 3 ENTRIES, DELETE IF =
480 IF W<160 THEN 500
482 J=5:FOR I=7 TO W STEP 2
484 FOR K=J-4 TO J STEP 2
486 IF T$(I,I+1)=T$(K,K+1) THEN EXIT 490
488 NEXT:J=J+2:T$(J,J+1)=T$(I,I+1)
490 NEXT:W=J
492REM===
495REM..BUBBLE SORT
500 FOR I=1 TO W-2 STEP 2:A$="0"
510 FOR J=W-2 TO I STEP -2
520 IF T$(J,J+1)<=T$(J+2,J+3) THEN 550
530 B$=T$(J,J+1):T$(J,J+1)=T$(J+2,J+3)
540 T$(J+2,J+3)=B$:A$="1"
550 NEXT:IF A$="0" THEN EXIT 600
560 NEXT
565REM===
570REM..REPACK TABLE
600 J=1:FOR I=3 TO W STEP 2
610 IF T$(I,I+1)=T$(J,J+1) THEN 630
620 J=J+2:T$(J,J+1)=T$(I,I+1)
630 NEXT:W0=J
640 T$(J+2,J+3)=CHR$(255)+CHR$(255)
660 FOR I=1 TO J STEP 2
670 D$(I,I+1)="   ":NEXT
680 PRINT(J+1)/2," ACTUAL LABELS"
```

```
685REM==========
690REM..2ND PASS..TRANSLATE
700 X=X0-4:K=-1:G=0
702 K1=0:L1=0
705 U=ASC(T$(2,2)):W=1:M=15
710 X=X+4:K=K+1:R0=0
711 J=INT(P/256):I=P-J*256
712 M=M+1:IF M<=14 THEN 715
714 PRINT:PRINT%4I,K,"   ",FNH$(J),:M=0
715 PRINTFNH$(I)," ",
716 F=EXAM(X)
720 C1=EXAM(X+2):C2=EXAM(X+3)
725 IF K<U THEN 765
740 D$(W,W+1)=CHR$(I)+CHR$(J)
750 W=W+2:R0=1:REM R0=1 MEANS INSTR. REFERENCED
760 U=ASC(T$(W,W))*256+ASC(T$(W+1,W+1))
765 V=0:IF F<=8 THEN 780
770 V=1:F=F-16:REM..INDEX ADDR
775 IF F>8 THEN 1700
778REM.........LIT.OPR.LOD.STO..CAL..INT..JMP..JPC..CSP.
780 ON F+1 GOTO 800,850,900,1100,1200,1500,1250,1550,1600
790REM===
800 IF C1+C2=0 THEN 830:REM..LIT
810 P=FNG(1,C1,C2)
820 P=FNQ(205,1):GOTO 710
830 P=FNG(175,19,18)
840 P=FNG(19,18,0)-1:GOTO 710
845REM===
850 J=205:IF C1>3 THEN 890:REM..OPR
855 IF C1=0 THEN 885
860 IF EXAM(X-4)<>0 THEN 890:REM LAST INSTR. =LIT ?
862 IF C1>1 THEN 870:REM LAST CODE = NEGATE ?
864 J=P-5:FILL J,256-EXAM(J)
866 FILL J+1,255-EXAM(J+1):GOTO 710
870 IF EXAM(X-1)>0 THEN 890
872 L=EXAM(X-2):IF L>3 THEN 890
874 P=P-6:N=17+C1:REM CONVERT ADD TO INC, SUB TO DEC
876 FOR I=1 TO L
878 P=FNG(J,Z1(N),Z2(N))
880 NEXT:GOTO 710
885 J=195:REM JMP
890 P=FNG(J,Z1(C1),Z2(C1)):GOTO 710
895REM===
900 F=2:REM..LOD
902 IF R0 OR V THEN 925
904 IF K>K1+1 OR L<>L1 THEN 925
906 IF C1<>EXAM(X-2) OR C2<>EXAM(X-1) THEN 925
910 K1=K:IF EXAM(X-4)=2 THEN 920:REM LAST CODE = LOD ?
915 P=FNG(19,19,0)-1:GOTO 710
920 P=FNG(205,Z1(21),Z2(21)):GOTO 710
925 J=4:L=EXAM(X+1):IF L=255 THEN 1040
930 GOSUB 1450:REM..GET 2A
940 P=FNG(1,C1,C2)
950 J=2:IF V THEN 960
955 J=0:K1=K:L1=L:REM..NON-INDEXED LOD OR STO
960 IF L=0 THEN 1040
1030 J=J+1:P=FNG(62,L,0)-1
1040 P=FNQ(205,F+J):GOTO 710
1090REM===
1100 F=7:GOTO 925:REM..STO
1190REM===
1200 L=EXAM(X+1):IF L>0 THEN 1225:REM..CAL
1210 P=FNQ(205,12)
1220 GOTO 1260
1225 IF L<255 THEN 1230
1227 P=FNQ(205,14):GOTO 710
1230 P=FNG(62,L,0)-1
1240 P=FNQ(205,13):GOTO 1260
1245REM===
1250 IF C1+C2*256=K+1 THEN 710:REM..JMP
1260 GOSUB 1300
1270 P=FNG(195,I,J):GOTO 710
```

216

```
1280REM=====
1290REM...TABLE LOOKUP, RETURNS ADDR IN I,J
1300 A$=CHR$(C2)+CHR$(C1)
1310 I=1:J=W0:REM..BINARY SEARCH
1320 N=INT((I+J)/4)*2+1
1330 IF A$=T$(N,N+1) THEN 1360
1340 IF A$>T$(N,N+1) THEN I=N+2 ELSE J=N-2
1350 IF I<=J THEN 1320
1360 IF D$(N,N+1)<>"  " THEN 1400
1370 G=G+1:E(G)=P+1:REM..FORWARD REF
1390 J=INT(N/256):I=N-J*256:RETURN
1400 I=ASC(D$(N,N)):J=ASC(D$(N+1,N+1)):RETURN
1440REM=====
1450 C1=C1+C1:C2=C2+C2:REM..2A
1460 IF C1<256 THEN 1480
1470 C1=C1-256:C2=C2+1
1480 IF C2>256 THEN C2=C2-256:RETURN
1490REM===
1500 IF C1+C2=0 THEN 710:REM..INT
1505 GOSUB 1450:N=C1+C2*256
1510 IF N>4 AND N<65530 THEN 1530
1515 J=19:IF N<=4 THEN 1520:N=65536-N:J=27
1520 FOR I=1 TO N/2:P=FNG(J,J,0)-1
1525 NEXT:GOTO 710
1530 P=FNG(33,C1,C2)
1535 P=FNQ(205,15):GOTO 710
1540REM===
1550 IF C1+C2*256=K+1 THEN 710:REM..JPC
1555 P=FNG(26,27,27)
1560 FILL P,31:P=P+1:REM..RAR
1570 GOSUB 1300:N=210
1575 IF EXAM(X+1)>0 THEN N=218
1580 P=FNG(N,I,J):GOTO 710
1590REM===
1600 I=C1+O2+1:REM..CSP
1605 IF C1=8 THEN 1620
1610 P=FNG(205,Z1(I),Z2(I)):GOTO 710
1620 J=EXAM(X-2):REM GET LENGTH OF STRING
1625 P=P-J*6-6:X1=X-J*4-2:REM BACK UP
1630 P=FNG(14,J,0)-1
1632 P=FNG(205,Z1(I),Z2(I))
1635 FOR I=1 TO J
1640 FILL P,EXAM(X1)
1645 P=P+1:X1=X1+4
1650 NEXT:GOTO 710
1700 PRINT:PRINT"   ",G," FORWARD REFERENCES"
1710 P1=P
1770REM============
1775REM..3RD PASS..FIXUP FOR. REF.
1780 FOR N=1 TO G
1790 P=E(N)
1800 J=EXAM(P)+EXAM(P+1)*256
1810 FILL P,ASC(D$(J,J))
1820 FILL P+1,ASC(D$(J+1,J+1))
1830 NEXT
1840REM..SETUP STACK ADDR
1850 IF B0$="" THEN P=P1 ELSE P=FND(B0$,4)
1860 J=INT(P/256):I=P-J*256
1870 P=P0:P=FNG(33,I,J)
1940 PRINT"P-CODE..",K," INSTRUCTIONS"
1950 PRINT"8080..",P1-P0," BYTES"
1960 PRINT"P-CODE:8080 =",(P1-P0)/(K*4)
1970 PRINT"* END TRANSLATION *"
1980 PRINTCHR$(129):REM..TURNOFF PRINTER
2000 END
READY
```

Appendix B:

"Tiny" Pascal 8080 Assembly Language

Listing 1: A Sample Compilation in "Tiny" Pascal

```
0010  }PROGRAM DECODE}
0020  CONST STOP=%FF; EXIT=%6946;
0030  VAR STADR, INDX, NUM: INTEGER;
0040  PROC CRLF;
0050    BEGIN WRITE (13) END;
0060  PROC FMT (VAL, LEN);
0070    VAR I, J: INTEGER;
0080    BEGIN }FMT}
0090    J := VAL;
0100    FOR I := 2 + (J=0) TO LEN DO
0110      IF J=0 THEN WRITE (32) ELSE J := J DIV 10;
0120    IF J>9 THEN WRITE ('&');
0130    WRITE (VAL#)
0140  END }FMT};
0150  BEGIN }MAIN}
0160    WRITE (12, 'START DECODING AT '); READ (STADR%); CRLF;
0170    CRLF; INDX := 0;
0180    WHILE (STADR < %6900) AND (MEM[STADR] <> STOP) DO
0190      BEGIN FMT (INDX, 10); WRITE ('   '); INDX := INDX + 1;
0200      NUM := MEM[STADR];
0210      CASE NUM OF
0220      0     : WRITE ('LIT');
0230      1     : WRITE ('OPR');
0240      2,%12: WRITE ('LOD');
0250      3,%13: WRITE ('STO');
0260      4     : WRITE ('CAL');
0270      5     : WRITE ('INT');
0280      6     : WRITE ('JMP');
0290      7     : WRITE ('JPC');
0300      8     : WRITE ('CSP')
0310      ELSE BEGIN WRITE ('ILL'); MEM[STADR] := STOP END
0320      END; }CASE}
0330      IF (NUM=%12) OR (NUM=%13) THEN WRITE ('X')
0340        ELSE WRITE (32); WRITE (32);
0350      WRITE (MEM[STADR+1]#,',');
0360      NUM := MEM[STADR+3] SHL 8 + MEM[STADR+2];
0370      WRITE (NUM#); CRLF;
0380      IF INDX MOD 15 = 0 THEN BEGIN
0390        READ (NUM); IF NUM=%18 THEN CALL(EXIT) END;
0400      IF MEM[STADR] <> STOP THEN STADR := STADR + 4;
0410    END; }WHILE}
0420  END. }MAIN}

>


P-CODE STARTS AT 2C00H
WANT CODE PRINTED? Y
    0  $DCOD$
    0  }PROGRAM DECODE}
    0  CONST STOP=%FF; EXIT=%6946;
               0  JMP    0  0
    1  VAR STADR, INDX, NUM: INTEGER;
    1  PROC CRLF;
    1    BEGIN WRITE (13) END;
               1  JMP    0  0
ADDR AT 1 CHANGED TO 2
               2  INT    0  0
               3  LIT    0  13
               4  CSP    0  1
               5  OPR    0  0
    6  PROC FMT (VAL, LEN);
```

```
  6    VAR I, J: INTEGER;
               6    JMP    0    0
  7    BEGIN }FMT}
  7    J := VAL;
ADDR AT 6 CHANGED TO 7
               7    INT    0    2
               8    LOD    0    -5
               9    STO    0    1
 10    FOR I := 2 + (J=0) TO LEN DO
              10    LIT    0    2
              11    LOD    0    1
              12    LIT    0    0
              13    OPR    0    8
              14    OPR    0    2
              15    STO    0    0
              16    LOD    0    -4
              17    OPR    0    21
              18    LOD    0    0
              19    OPR    0    11
              20    JPC    0    0
 21    IF J=0 THEN WRITE (32) ELSE J := J DIV 10;
              21    LOD    0    1
              22    LIT    0    0
              23    OPR    0    8
              24    JPC    0    0
              25    LIT    0    32
              26    CSP    0    1
              27    JMP    0    0
ADDR AT 24 CHANGED TO 28
              28    LOD    0    1
              29    LIT    0    10
              30    OPR    0    5
              31    STO    0    1
ADDR AT 27 CHANGED TO 32
              32    LOD    0    0
              33    OPR    0    19
              34    STO    0    0
              35    JMP    0    17
ADDR AT 20 CHANGED TO 36
              36    INT    0    -1
 37    IF J>9 THEN WRITE ('&');
              37    LOD    0    1
              38    LIT    0    9
              39    OPR    0    12
              40    JPC    0    0
              41    LIT    0    38
              42    CSP    0    1
ADDR AT 40 CHANGED TO 43
 43    WRITE (VAL#)
              43    LOD    0    -5
              44    CSP    0    3
 45    END }FMT};
              45    OPR    0    0
 46    BEGIN }MAIN}
 46    WRITE (12, 'START DECODING AT '); READ (STADR%); CRLF;
ADDR AT 0 CHANGED TO 46
              46    INT    0    3
              47    LIT    0    12
              48    CSP    0    1
              49    LIT    0    83
              50    LIT    0    84
              51    LIT    0    65
              52    LIT    0    82
              53    LIT    0    84
              54    LIT    0    32
              55    LIT    0    68
              56    LIT    0    69
              57    LIT    0    67
```

```
               58   LIT    0    79
               59   LIT    0    68
               60   LIT    0    73
               61   LIT    0    78
               62   LIT    0    71
               63   LIT    0    32
               64   LIT    0    65
               65   LIT    0    84
               66   LIT    0    32
               67   LIT    0    18
               68   CSP    0    8
               69   CSP    0    4
               70   STO    0    0
               71   CAL    0    2
 72     CRLF; INDX := 0;
               72   CAL    0    2
               73   LIT    0    0
               74   STO    0    1
 75     WHILE (STADR < %6900) AND (MEM[STADR] <> STOP) DO
               75   LOD    0    0
               76   LIT    0    26880
               77   OPR    0    10
               78   LOD    0    0
               79   LOD    255  0
               80   LIT    0    255
               81   OPR    0    9
               82   OPR    0    15
               83   JPC    0    0
 84     BEGIN FMT (INDX, 10); WRITE ('    '); INDX := INDX + 1;
               84   LOD    0    1
               85   LIT    0    10
               86   CAL    0    7
               87   INT    0    -2
               88   LIT    0    32
               89   LIT    0    32
               90   LIT    0    32
               91   LIT    0    3
               92   CSP    0    8
               93   LOD    0    1
               94   LIT    0    1
               95   OPR    0    2
               96   STO    0    1
 97     NUM := MEM[STADR];
               97   LOD    0    0
               98   LOD    255  0
               99   STO    0    2
100     CASE NUM OF
              100   LOD    0    2
101      0     : WRITE ('LIT');
              101   OPR    0    21
              102   LIT    0    0
              103   OPR    0    8
              104   JPC    0    0
              105   LIT    0    76
              106   LIT    0    73
              107   LIT    0    84
              108   LIT    0    3
              109   CSP    0    8
              110   JMP    0    0
ADDR AT 104 CHANGED TO 111
111      1     : WRITE ('OPR');
              111   OPR    0    21
              112   LIT    0    1
              113   OPR    0    8
              114   JPC    0    0
              115   LIT    0    79
              116   LIT    0    80
              117   LIT    0    82
```

```
                    118    LIT    0    3
                    119    CSP    0    8
                    120    JMP    0    0
ADDR AT 114 CHANGED TO 121
  121        2,%12:  WRITE ('LOD');
                    121    OPR    0    21
                    122    LIT    0    2
                    123    OPR    0    8
                    124    JPC    1    0
                    125    OPR    0    21
                    126    LIT    0    18
                    127    OPR    0    8
                    128    JPC    0    0
ADDR AT 124 CHANGED TO 129
                    129    LIT    0    76
                    130    LIT    0    79
                    131    LIT    0    68
                    132    LIT    0    3
                    133    CSP    0    8
                    134    JMP    0    0
ADDR AT 128 CHANGED TO 135
  135        3,%13:  WRITE ('STO');
                    135    OPR    0    21
                    136    LIT    0    3
                    137    OPR    0    8
                    138    JPC    1    0
                    139    OPR    0    21
                    140    LIT    0    19
                    141    OPR    0    8
                    142    JPC    0    0
ADDR AT 138 CHANGED TO 143
                    143    LIT    0    83
                    144    LIT    0    84
                    145    LIT    0    79
                    146    LIT    0    3
                    147    CSP    0    8
                    148    JMP    0    0
ADDR AT 142 CHANGED TO 149
  149        4    :  WRITE ('CAL');
                    149    OPR    0    21
                    150    LIT    0    4
                    151    OPR    0    8
                    152    JPC    0    0
                    153    LIT    0    67
                    154    LIT    0    65
                    155    LIT    0    76
                    156    LIT    0    3
                    157    CSP    0    8
                    158    JMP    0    0
ADDR AT 152 CHANGED TO 159
  159        5    :  WRITE ('INT');
                    159    OPR    0    21
                    160    LIT    0    5
                    161    OPR    0    8
                    162    JPC    0    0
                    163    LIT    0    73
                    164    LIT    0    78
                    165    LIT    0    84
                    166    LIT    0    3
                    167    CSP    0    8
                    168    JMP    0    0
ADDR AT 162 CHANGED TO 169
  169        6    :  WRITE ('JMP');
                    169    OPR    0    21
                    170    LIT    0    6
                    171    OPR    0    8
                    172    JPC    0    0
                    173    LIT    0    74
```

```
              174    LIT     0   77
              175    LIT     0   80
              176    LIT     0   3
              177    CSP     0   8
              178    JMP     0   0
ADDR AT 172 CHANGED TO 179
 179       7     : WRITE ('JPC');
              179    OPR     0   21
              180    LIT     0   7
              181    OPR     0   8
              182    JPC     0   0
              183    LIT     0   74
              184    LIT     0   80
              185    LIT     0   67
              186    LIT     0   3
              187    CSP     0   8
              188    JMP     0   0
ADDR AT 182 CHANGED TO 189
 189       8     : WRITE ('CSP')
              189    OPR     0   21
              190    LIT     0   8
              191    OPR     0   8
              192    JPC     0   0
              193    LIT     0   67
              194    LIT     0   83
              195    LIT     0   80
              196    LIT     0   3
              197    CSP     0   8
 198      ELSE BEGIN WRITE ('ILL'); MEM[STADR] := STOP END
              198    JMP     0   0
ADDR AT 192 CHANGED TO 199
              199    LIT     0   73
              200    LIT     0   76
              201    LIT     0   76
              202    LIT     0   3
              203    CSP     0   8
              204    LOD     0   0
              205    LIT     0   255
              206    STO    255  0
 207      END; }CASE}
ADDR AT 198 CHANGED TO 207
ADDR AT 188 CHANGED TO 207
ADDR AT 178 CHANGED TO 207
ADDR AT 168 CHANGED TO 207
ADDR AT 158 CHANGED TO 207
ADDR AT 148 CHANGED TO 207
ADDR AT 134 CHANGED TO 207
ADDR AT 120 CHANGED TO 207
ADDR AT 110 CHANGED TO 207
              207    INT     0   -1
 208      IF (NUM=%12) OR (NUM=%13) THEN WRITE ('X')
              208    LOD     0   2
              209    LIT     0   18
              210    OPR     0   8
              211    LOD     0   2
              212    LIT     0   19
              213    OPR     0   8
              214    OPR     0   14
              215    JPC     0   0
              216    LIT     0   88
              217    CSP     0   1
 218      ELSE WRITE (32); WRITE (32);
              218    JMP     0   0
ADDR AT 215 CHANGED TO 219
              219    LIT     0   32
              220    CSP     0   1
ADDR AT 218 CHANGED TO 221
              221    LIT     0   32
```

```
           222    CSP     0    1
 223      WRITE (MEM[STADR+1]#,',');
           223    LOD     0    0
           224    LIT     0    1
           225    OPR     0    2
           226    LOD    255   0
           227    CSP     0    3
           228    LIT     0    44
           229    CSP     0    1
 230      NUM := MEM[STADR+3] SHL 8 + MEM[STADR+2];
           230    LOD     0    0
           231    LIT     0    3
           232    OPR     0    2
           233    LOD    255   0
           234    LIT     0    8
           235    OPR     0    17
           236    LOD     0    0
           237    LIT     0    2
           238    OPR     0    2
           239    LOD    255   0
           240    OPR     0    2
           241    STO     0    2
 242      WRITE (NUM#); CRLF;
           242    LOD     0    2
           243    CSP     0    3
           244    CAL     0    2
 245      IF INDX MOD 15 = 0 THEN BEGIN
           245    LOD     0    1
           246    LIT     0    15
           247    OPR     0    7
           248    LIT     0    0
           249    OPR     0    8
           250    JPC     0    0
 251      READ (NUM); IF NUM=%18 THEN CALL(EXIT) END;
           251    CSP     0    0
           252    STO     0    2
           253    LOD     0    2
           254    LIT     0    24
           255    OPR     0    8
           256    JPC     0    0
           257    LIT     0    26950
           258    CAL    255   0
ADDR AT 256 CHANGED TO 259
ADDR AT 250 CHANGED TO 259
 259      IF MEM[STADR] <> STOP THEN STADR := STADR + 4;
           259    LOD     0    0
           260    LOD    255   0
           261    LIT     0    255
           262    OPR     0    9
           263    JPC     0    0
           264    LOD     0    0
           265    LIT     0    4
           266    OPR     0    2
           267    STO     0    0
ADDR AT 263 CHANGED TO 268
 268    END; }WHILE}
           268    JMP     0    75
ADDR AT 83 CHANGED TO 269
 269   END. }MAIN}
           269    OPR     0    0
FILE ENDS AT 3039
INTERPRET(I), OR TRANSLATE(T)? T
G
```

```
***** P-CODE TO 8080 TRANSLATION *****
        ADDRESS OF RUNTIME MODULE? %6900
        P-CODE START ADDRESS? %2C00
        OBJECT-CODE START ADDRESS? %1000
        STACK START ADDRESS? %0000  ← DEFAULTS USED

40 REFERENCES
27 DIFFERENT LABELS

    0   100F 12 12 12 18 1B 1E 1E 22 28 2E 34 3A 3F 42 45 4B 51 54 5A
   20   105D 64 6A 6F 72 79 7F 82 85 8B 91 94 9A A0 A3 A9 AC AE B4 BA
   40   10BD C4 CA CD D3 D6 D9 DF E5 E8 EE F4 FA 00 06 0C 12 18 1E 24
   60   112A 30 36 3C 42 48 4E 54 5A FF 02 08 0E 14 19 1F 25 2B 2E 34
   80   1137 3D 40 43 4A 50 56 5C 60 66 6C 72 78 68 6E 74 71 77 7D 80
  100   1186 88 8B 90 93 9A A0 A6 AC B2 A2 A5 A8 AE B1 B8 BE C4 CA D0
  120   11C0 C3 C6 CC CF D6 D9 DF E2 E9 EF F5 FB 01 F1 F4 F7 FD 00 07
  140   120A 10 13 1A 20 26 2C 32 22 25 28 2E 31 38 3E 44 4A 50 40 43
  160   1246 4C 4F 56 5C 62 68 6E 5E 61 64 6A 6D 74 7A 80 86 8C 7C 7F
  180   1282 88 8B 92 98 9E A4 AA 9A 9D A0 A6 A9 B0 B6 BC C2 C8 B8 BB
  200   12C1 C7 CD D3 C3 C9 CF D2 D4 DA E0 E3 E9 EF F2 F5 FC 02 05 08
  220   130E 11 17 1A 20 26 23 26 29 2F 32 38 3E 41 44 4A 4D 53 59 59
  240   135C 5F 65 67 6A 70 76 7C 7F 84 87 8E 91 97 99 9F A2 A9 AF B2
  260   13B8 BB C1 C4 CB D1 D7 DA E0 E3 E6
31 FORWARD REFERENCES

270 P-CODES TRANSLATED (TOTAL 0438H BYTES)
03E6H BYTES OF OBJECT CODE PRODUCED - CODE ENDS AT 13E6



1000 AF D3 04 31 00 10 21 E6 13 11 01 97 CD 00 69 C3
1010 D9 10 01 0D 00 CD 6C 6B CD 00 6B C3 25 6C 13 13
1020 13 13 01 F6 FF CD 8D 6B 01 02 00 CD B5 6B 01 02
1030 00 CD 6C 6B 01 02 00 CD 8D 6B AF 13 12 13 12 CD
1040 B0 6C CD 4E 6C 01 00 00 CD B5 6B 01 F8 FF CD 8D
1050 6B CD 60 6D 01 00 00 CD 8D 6B CD CA 6C 1A 1B 1B
1060 1F D2 AC 10 01 02 00 CD 8D 6B AF 13 12 13 12 CD
1070 B0 6C 1A 1B 1B 1F D2 85 10 01 20 00 CD 6C 6B CD
1080 00 6B C3 9A 10 01 02 00 CD 8D 6B 01 0A 00 CD 6C
1090 6B CD 90 6C 01 02 00 CD B5 6B 01 00 00 CD 8D 6B
10A0 CD 4C 6D 01 00 00 CD B5 6B C3 51 10 1B 1B 01 02
10B0 00 CD 8D 6B 01 09 00 CD 6C 6B CD F9 6C 1A 1B 1B
10C0 1F D2 CD 10 01 26 00 CD 6C 6B CD 00 6B 01 F6 FF
10D0 CD 8D 6B CD 10 6B C3 25 6C 21 06 00 CD 73 6B 01
10E0 0C 00 CD 6C 6B CD 00 6B 0E 12 CD 52 6B 53 54 41
10F0 52 54 20 44 45 43 4F 44 49 4E 47 20 41 54 20 CD
1100 3C 6B 01 00 00 CD B5 6B CD E9 6B C3 12 10 CD E9
1110 6B C3 12 10 AF 13 12 13 12 01 02 00 CD B5 6B 01
1120 00 00 CD 8D 6B 01 00 69 CD 6C 6B CD F3 6C 01 00
1130 00 CD 8D 6B CD 0E 6C 01 FF 00 CD 6C 6B CD C6 6C
1140 CD 0F 6D 1A 1B 1B 1F D2 E3 13 01 02 00 CD 8D 6B
1150 01 0A 00 CD 6C 6B CD E9 6B C3 1E 10 1B 1B 1B 1B
1160 0E 03 CD 52 6B 20 20 20 01 02 00 CD 8D 6B CD 4C
1170 6D 01 02 00 CD B5 6B 01 00 00 CD 8D 6B CD 0E 6C
1180 01 04 00 CD B5 6B 13 13 CD 60 6D AF 13 12 13 12
1190 CD B0 6C 1A 1B 1B 1F D2 A5 11 0E 03 CD 52 6B 4C
11A0 49 54 C3 D2 12 CD 60 6D 01 01 00 CD 6C 6B CD B0
11B0 6C 1A 1B 1B 1F D2 C3 11 0E 03 CD 52 6B 4F 50 52
11C0 C3 D2 12 CD 60 6D 01 02 00 CD 6C 6B CD B0 6C 1A
11D0 1B 1B 1F DA E9 11 CD 60 6D 01 12 00 CD 6C 6B CD
11E0 B0 6C 1A 1B 1B 1F D2 F4 11 0E 03 CD 52 6B 4C 4F
11F0 44 C3 D2 12 CD 60 6D 01 03 00 CD 6C 6B CD B0 6C
1200 1A 1B 1B 1F DA 1A 12 CD 60 6D 01 13 00 CD 6C 6B
1210 CD B0 6C 1A 1B 1B 1F D2 25 12 0E 03 CD 52 6B 53
1220 54 4F C3 D2 12 CD 60 6D 01 04 00 CD 6C 6B CD B0
1230 6C 1A 1B 1B 1F D2 43 12 0E 03 CD 52 6B 43 41 4C
1240 C3 D2 12 CD 60 6D 01 05 00 CD 6C 6B CD B0 6C 1A
```

227

```
1250  1B 1B 1F D2 61 12 0E 03 CD 52 6B 49 4E 54 C3 D2
1260  12 CD 60 6D 01 06 00 CD 6C 6B CD B0 6C 1A 1B 1B
1270  1F D2 7F 12 0E 03 CD 52 6B 4A 4D 50 C3 D2 12 CD
1280  60 6D 01 07 00 CD 6C 6B CD B0 6C 1A 1B 1B 1F D2
1290  9D 12 0E 03 CD 52 6B 4A 50 43 C3 D2 12 CD 60 6D
12A0  01 08 00 CD 6C 6B CD B0 6C 1A 1B 1B 1F D2 BB 12
12B0  0E 03 CD 52 6B 43 53 50 C3 D2 12 0E 03 CD 52 6B
12C0  49 4C 4C 01 00 00 CD 8D 6B 01 FF 00 CD 6C 6B CD
12D0  19 6C 1B 1B 01 04 00 CD 8D 6B 01 12 00 CD 6C 6B
12E0  CD B0 6C 01 04 00 CD 8D 6B 01 13 00 CD 6C 6B CD
12F0  B0 6C CD 04 6D 1A 1B 1B 1F D2 08 13 01 58 00 CD
1300  6C 6B CD 00 6B C3 11 13 01 20 00 CD 6C 6B CD 00
1310  6B 01 20 00 CD 6C 6B CD 00 6B 01 00 00 CD 8D 6B
1320  CD 4C 6D CD 0E 6C CD 10 6B 01 2C 00 CD 6C 6B CD
1330  00 6B 01 00 00 CD 8D 6B CD 4C 6D CD 4C 6D CD 4C
1340  6D CD 0E 6C 01 08 00 CD 6C 6B CD 23 6D 01 00 00
1350  CD 8D 6B CD 4C 6D CD 4C 6D CD 0E 6C CD 4E 6C 01
1360  04 00 CD B5 6B 13 13 CD 10 6B CD E9 6B C3 12 10
1370  01 02 00 CD 8D 6B 01 0F 00 CD 6C 6B CD A4 6C AF
1380  13 12 13 12 CD B0 6C 1A 1B 1B 1F D2 B2 13 CD F7
1390  6A 01 04 00 CD B5 6B 13 13 01 18 00 CD 6C 6B CD
13A0  B0 6C 1A 1B 1B 1F D2 B2 13 01 46 69 CD 6C 6B CD
13B0  21 6C 01 00 00 CD 8D 6B CD 0E 6C 01 FF 00 CD 6C
13C0  6B CD C6 6C 1A 1B 1B 1F D2 E0 13 01 00 00 CD 8D
13D0  6B 01 04 00 CD 6C 6B CD 4E 6C 01 00 00 CD B5 6B
13E0  C3 1F 11 C3 25 6C 20
>
```

```
1000  AF            0010  Z1000H  XRA      A
1001  D3 04         0020          OUT      004H
1003  31 00 10      0030          LXI      P,01000H
1006  21 E6 13      0040          LXI      H,013E6H
1009  11 01 97      0050          LXI      D,09701H
100C  CD 00 69      0060          CALL     06900H
100F  C3 D9 10      0070          JMP      010D9H
1012  01 0D 00      0080  Z1012H  LXI      B,0000DH
1015  CD 6C 6B      0090          CALL     06B6CH
1018  CD 00 6B      0100          CALL     06B00H
101B  C3 25 6C      0110          JMP      06C25H
101E  13            0120  Z101EH  INX      D
101F  13            0130          INX      D
1020  13            0140          INX      D
1021  13            0150          INX      D
1022  01 F6 FF      0160          LXI      B,0FFF6H
1025  CD 8D 6B      0170          CALL     06B8DH
1028  01 02 00      0180          LXI      B,00002H
102B  CD B5 6B      0190          CALL     06BB5H
102E  01 02 00      0200          LXI      B,00002H
1031  CD 6C 6B      0210          CALL     06B6CH
1034  01 02 00      0220          LXI      B,00002H
1037  CD 8D 6B      0230          CALL     06B8DH
103A  AF            0240          XRA      A
103B  13            0250          INX      D
103C  12            0260          STAX     D
103D  13            0270          INX      D
103E  12            0280          STAX     D
103F  CD B0 6C      0290          CALL     06CB0H
1042  CD 4E 6C      0300          CALL     06C4EH
1045  01 00 00      0310          LXI      B,00000H
1048  CD B5 6B      0320          CALL     06BB5H
104B  01 F8 FF      0330          LXI      B,0FFF8H
104E  CD 8D 6B      0340          CALL     06B8DH
1051  CD 60 6D      0350  Z1051H  CALL     06D60H
1054  01 00 00      0360          LXI      B,00000H
1057  CD 8D 6B      0370          CALL     06B8DH
105A  CD CA 6C      0380          CALL     06CCAH
105D  1A            0390          LDAX     D
105E  1B            0400          DCX      D
```

105F	1B	0410		DCX	D
1060	1F	0420		RAR	
1061	D2 AC 10	0430		JNC	010ACH
1064	01 02 00	0440		LXI	B,00002H
1067	CD 8D 6B	0450		CALL	06B8DH
106A	AF	0460		XRA	A
106B	13	0470		INX	D
106C	12	0480		STAX	D
106D	13	0490		INX	D
106E	12	0500		STAX	D
106F	CD B0 6C	0510		CALL	06CB0H
1072	1A	0520		LDAX	D
1073	1B	0530		DCX	D
1074	1B	0540		DCX	D
1075	1F	0550		RAR	
1076	D2 85 10	0560		JNC	01085H
1079	01 20 00	0570		LXI	B,00020H
107C	CD 6C 6B	0580		CALL	06B6CH
107F	CD 00 6B	0590		CALL	06B00H
1082	C3 9A 10	0600		JMP	0109AH
1085	01 02 00	0610	Z1085H	LXI	B,00002H
1088	CD 8D 6B	0620		CALL	06B8DH
108B	01 0A 00	0630		LXI	B,0000AH
108E	CD 6C 6B	0640		CALL	06B6CH
1091	CD 90 6C	0650		CALL	06C90H
1094	01 02 00	0660		LXI	B,00002H
1097	CD B5 6B	0670		CALL	06BB5H
109A	01 00 00	0680	Z109AH	LXI	B,00000H
109D	CD 8D 6B	0690		CALL	06B8DH
10A0	CD 4C 6D	0700		CALL	06D4CH
10A3	01 00 00	0710		LXI	B,00000H
10A6	CD B5 6B	0720		CALL	06BB5H
10A9	C3 51 10	0730		JMP	01051H
10AC	1B	0740	Z10ACH	DCX	D
10AD	1B	0750		DCX	D
10AE	01 02 00	0760		LXI	B,00002H
10B1	CD 8D 6B	0770		CALL	06B8DH
10B4	01 09 00	0780		LXI	B,00009H
10B7	CD 6C 6B	0790		CALL	06B6CH
10BA	CD F9 6C	0800		CALL	06CF9H
10BD	1A	0810		LDAX	D
10BE	1B	0820		DCX	D
10BF	1B	0830		DCX	D
10C0	1F	0840		RAR	
10C1	D2 CD 10	0850		JNC	010CDH
10C4	01 26 00	0860		LXI	B,00026H
10C7	CD 6C 6B	0870		CALL	06B6CH
10CA	CD 00 6B	0880		CALL	06B00H
10CD	01 F6 FF	0890	Z10CDH	LXI	B,0FFF6H
10D0	CD 8D 6B	0900		CALL	06B8DH
10D3	CD 10 6B	0910		CALL	06B10H
10D6	C3 25 6C	0920		JMP	06C25H
10D9	21 06 00	0930	Z10D9H	LXI	H,00006H
10DC	CD 73 6B	0940		CALL	06B73H
10DF	01 0C 00	0950		LXI	B,0000CH
10E2	CD 6C 6B	0960		CALL	06B6CH
10E5	CD 00 6B	0970		CALL	06B00H
10E8	0E 12	0980		MVI	C,012H
10EA	CD 52 6B	0990		CALL	06B52H
10ED	53	1000		MOV	D,E S
10EE	54	1010		MOV	D,H T
10EF	41	1020		MOV	B,C A
10F0	52	1030		MOV	D,D R
10F1	54	1040		MOV	D,H T
10F2	20	1050		DB	020H
10F3	44	1060		MOV	B,H D
10F4	45	1070		MOV	B,L E
10F5	43	1080		MOV	B,E C

```
10F6  4F              1090        MOV     C,A       O
10F7  44              1100        MOV     B,H       D
10F8  49              1110        MOV     C,C       I
10F9  4E              1120        MOV     C,M       N
10FA  47              1130        MOV     B,A       G
10FB  20              1140        DB      020H
10FC  41              1150        MOV     B,C       A
10FD  54              1160        MOV     D,H       T
10FE  20              1170        DB      020H
10FF  CD 3C 6B        1180        CALL    06B3CH
1102  01 00 00        1190        LXI     B,00000H
1105  CD B5 6B        1200        CALL    06BB5H
1108  CD E9 6B        1210        CALL    06BE9H
110B  C3 12 10        1220        JMP     01012H
110E  CD E9 6B        1230        CALL    06BE9H
1111  C3 12 10        1240        JMP     01012H
1114  AF              1250        XRA     A
1115  13              1260        INX     D
1116  12              1270        STAX    D
1117  13              1280        INX     D
1118  12              1290        STAX    D
1119  01 02 00        1300        LXI     B,00002H
111C  CD B5 6B        1310        CALL    06BB5H
111F  01 00 00        1320  Z111FH LXI    B,00000H
1122  CD 8D 6B        1330        CALL    06B8DH
1125  01 00 69        1340        LXI     B,06900H
1128  CD 6C 6B        1350        CALL    06B6CH
112B  CD F3 6C        1360        CALL    06CF3H
112E  01 00 00        1370        LXI     B,00000H
1131  CD 8D 6B        1380        CALL    06B8DH
1134  CD 0E 6C        1390        CALL    06C0EH
1137  01 FF 00        1400        LXI     B,000FFH
113A  CD 6C 6B        1410        CALL    06B6CH
113D  CD C6 6C        1420        CALL    06CC6H
1140  CD 0F 6D        1430        CALL    06D0FH
1143  1A              1440        LDAX    D
1144  1B              1450        DCX     D
1145  1B              1460        DCX     D
1146  1F              1470        RAR
1147  D2 E3 13        1480        JNC     013E3H
114A  01 02 00        1490        LXI     B,00002H
114D  CD 8D 6B        1500        CALL    06B8DH
1150  01 0A 00        1510        LXI     B,0000AH
1153  CD 6C 6B        1520        CALL    06B6CH
1156  CD E9 6B        1530        CALL    06BE9H
1159  C3 1E 10        1540        JMP     0101EH
115C  1B              1550        DCX     D
115D  1B              1560        DCX     D
115E  1B              1570        DCX     D
115F  1B              1580        DCX     D
1160  0E 03           1590        MVI     C,003H
1162  CD 52 6B        1600        CALL    06B52H
1165  20              1610        DB      020H
1166  20              1620        DB      020H
1167  20              1630        DB      020H
1168  01 02 00        1640        LXI     B,00002H
116B  CD 8D 6B        1650        CALL    06B8DH
116E  CD 4C 6D        1660        CALL    06D4CH
1171  01 02 00        1670        LXI     B,00002H
1174  CD B5 6B        1680        CALL    06BB5H
1177  01 00 00        1690        LXI     B,00000H
117A  CD 8D 6B        1700        CALL    06B8DH
117D  CD 0E 6C        1710        CALL    06C0EH
1180  01 04 00        1720        LXI     B,00004H
1183  CD B5 6B        1730        CALL    06BB5H
1186  13              1740        INX     D
1187  13              1750        INX     D
1188  CD 60 6D        1760        CALL    06D60H
```

```
118B AF              1770         XRA     A
118C 13              1780         INX     D
118D 12              1790         STAX    D
118E 13              1800         INX     D
118F 12              1810         STAX    D
1190 CD B0 6C        1820         CALL    06CB0H
1193 1A              1830         LDAX    D
1194 1B              1840         DCX     D
1195 1B              1850         DCX     D
1196 1F              1860         RAR
1197 D2 A5 11        1870         JNC     011A5H
119A 0E 03           1880         MVI     C,003H
119C CD 52 6B        1890         CALL    06B52H
119F 4C              1900         MOV     C,H
11A0 49              1910         MOV     C,C
11A1 54              1920         MOV     D,H
11A2 C3 D2 12        1930         JMP     012D2H
11A5 CD 60 6D        1940  Z11A5H CALL    06D60H
11A8 01 01 00        1950         LXI     B,00001H
11AB CD 6C 6B        1960         CALL    06B6CH
11AE CD B0 6C        1970         CALL    06CB0H
11B1 1A              1980         LDAX    D
11B2 1B              1990         DCX     D
11B3 1B              2000         DCX     D
11B4 1F              2010         RAR
11B5 D2 C3 11        2020         JNC     011C3H
11B8 0E 03           2030         MVI     C,003H
11BA CD 52 6B        2040         CALL    06B52H
11BD 4F              2050         MOV     C,A       O
11BE 50              2060         MOV     D,B       P
11BF 52              2070         MOV     D,D       R
11C0 C3 D2 12        2080         JMP     012D2H
11C3 CD 60 6D        2090  Z11C3H CALL    06D60H
11C6 01 02 00        2100         LXI     B,00002H
11C9 CD 6C 6B        2110         CALL    06B6CH
11CC CD B0 6C        2120         CALL    06CB0H
11CF 1A              2130         LDAX    D
11D0 1B              2140         DCX     D
11D1 1B              2150         DCX     D
11D2 1F              2160         RAR
11D3 DA E9 11        2170         JC      011E9H
11D6 CD 60 6D        2180         CALL    06D60H
11D9 01 12 00        2190         LXI     B,00012H
11DC CD 6C 6B        2200         CALL    06B6CH
11DF CD B0 6C        2210         CALL    06CB0H
11E2 1A              2220         LDAX    D
11E3 1B              2230         DCX     D
11E4 1B              2240         DCX     D
11E5 1F              2250         RAR
11E6 D2 F4 11        2260         JNC     011F4H
11E9 0E 03           2270  Z11E9H MVI     C,003H
11EB CD 52 6B        2280         CALL    06B52H
11EE 4C              2290         MOV     C,H       L
11EF 4F              2300         MOV     C,A       O
11F0 44              2310         MOV     B,H       D
11F1 C3 D2 12        2320         JMP     012D2H
11F4 CD 60 6D        2330  Z11F4H CALL    06D60H
11F7 01 03 00        2340         LXI     B,00003H
11FA CD 6C 6B        2350         CALL    06B6CH
11FD CD B0 6C        2360         CALL    06CB0H
1200 1A              2370         LDAX    D
1201 1B              2380         DCX     D
1202 1B              2390         DCX     D
1203 1F              2400         RAR
1204 DA 1A 12        2410         JC      0121AH
1207 CD 60 6D        2420         CALL    06D60H
120A 01 13 00        2430         LXI     B,00013H
120D CD 6C 6B        2440         CALL    06B6CH
```

```
1210 CD B0 6C    2450              CALL    06CB0H
1213 1A          2460              LDAX    D
1214 1B          2470              DCX     D
1215 1B          2480              DCX     D
1216 1F          2490              RAR
1217 D2 25 12    2500              JNC     01225H
121A 0E 03       2510    Z121AH    MVI     C,003H
121C CD 52 6B    2520              CALL    06B52H
121F 53          2530              MOV     D,E     S
1220 54          2540              MOV     D,H     T
1221 4F          2550              MOV     C,A     O
1222 C3 D2 12    2560              JMP     012D2H
1225 CD 60 6D    2570    Z1225H    CALL    06D60H
1228 01 04 00    2580              LXI     B,00004H
122B CD 6C 6B    2590              CALL    06B6CH
122E CD B0 6C    2600              CALL    06CB0H
1231 1A          2610              LDAX    D
1232 1B          2620              DCX     D
1233 1B          2630              DCX     D
1234 1F          2640              RAR
1235 D2 43 12    2650              JNC     01243H
1238 0E 03       2660              MVI     C,003H
123A CD 52 6B    2670              CALL    06B52H
123D 43          2680              MOV     B,E     C
123E 41          2690              MOV     B,C     A
123F 4C          2700              MOV     C,H     L
1240 C3 D2 12    2710              JMP     012D2H
1243 CD 60 6D    2720    Z1243H    CALL    06D60H
1246 01 05 00    2730              LXI     B,00005H
1249 CD 6C 6B    2740              CALL    06B6CH
124C CD B0 6C    2750              CALL    06CB0H
124F 1A          2760              LDAX    D
1250 1B          2770              DCX     D
1251 1B          2780              DCX     D
1252 1F          2790              RAR
1253 D2 61 12    2800              JNC     01261H
1256 0E 03       2810              MVI     C,003H
1258 CD 52 6B    2820              CALL    06B52H
125B 49          2830              MOV     C,C     I
125C 4E          2840              MOV     C,M     N
125D 54          2850              MOV     D,H     T
125E C3 D2 12    2860              JMP     012D2H
1261 CD 60 6D    2870    Z1261H    CALL    06D60H
1264 01 06 00    2880              LXI     B,00006H
1267 CD 6C 6B    2890              CALL    06B6CH
126A CD B0 6C    2900              CALL    06CB0H
126D 1A          2910              LDAX    D
126E 1B          2920              DCX     D
126F 1B          2930              DCX     D
1270 1F          2940              RAR
1271 D2 7F 12    2950              JNC     0127FH
1274 0E 03       2960              MVI     C,003H
1276 CD 52 6B    2970              CALL    06B52H
1279 4A          2980              MOV     C,D     J
127A 4D          2990              MOV     C,L     M
127B 50          3000              MOV     D,B     P
127C C3 D2 12    3010              JMP     012D2H
127F CD 60 6D    3020    Z127FH    CALL    06D60H
1282 01 07 00    3030              LXI     B,00007H
1285 CD 6C 6B    3040              CALL    06B6CH
1288 CD B0 6C    3050              CALL    06CB0H
128B 1A          3060              LDAX    D
128C 1B          3070              DCX     D
128D 1B          3080              DCX     D
128E 1F          3090              RAR
128F D2 9D 12    3100              JNC     0129DH
1292 0E 03       3110              MVI     C,003H
1294 CD 52 6B    3120              CALL    06B52H
1297 4A          3130              MOV     C,D     J
```

```
1298 50              3140              MOV     D,B      P
1299 43              3150              MOV     B,E      C
129A C3 D2 12        3160              JMP     012D2H
129D CD 60 6D        3170    Z129DH    CALL    06D60H
12A0 01 08 00        3180              LXI     B,00008H
12A3 CD 6C 6B        3190              CALL    06B6CH
12A6 CD B0 6C        3200              CALL    06CB0H
12A9 1A              3210              LDAX    D
12AA 1B              3220              DCX     D
12AB 1B              3230              DCX     D
12AC 1F              3240              RAR
12AD D2 BB 12        3250              JNC     012BBH
12B0 0E 03           3260              MVI     C,003H
12B2 CD 52 6B        3270              CALL    06B52H
12B5 43              3280              MOV     B,E      C
12B6 53              3290              MOV     D,E      S
12B7 50              3300              MOV     D,B      P
12B8 C3 D2 12        3310              JMP     012D2H
12BB 0E 03           3320    Z12BBH    MVI     C,003H
12BD CD 52 6B        3330              CALL    06B52H
12C0 49              3340              MOV     C,C      I
12C1 4C              3350              MOV     C,H      L
12C2 4C              3360              MOV     C,H      L
12C3 01 00 00        3370              LXI     B,00000H
12C6 CD 8D 6B        3380              CALL    06B8DH
12C9 01 FF 00        3390              LXI     B,000FFH
12CC CD 6C 6B        3400              CALL    06B6CH
12CF CD 19 6C        3410              CALL    06C19H
12D2 1B              3420    Z12D2H    DCX     D
12D3 1B              3430              DCX     D
12D4 01 04 00        3440              LXI     B,00004H
12D7 CD 8D 6B        3450              CALL    06B8DH
12DA 01 12 00        3460              LXI     B,00012H
12DD CD 6C 6B        3470              CALL    06B6CH
12E0 CD B0 6C        3480              CALL    06CB0H
12E3 01 04 00        3490              LXI     B,00004H
12E6 CD 8D 6B        3500              CALL    06B8DH
12E9 01 13 00        3510              LXI     B,00013H
12EC CD 6C 6B        3520              CALL    06B6CH
12EF CD B0 6C        3530              CALL    06CB0H
12F2 CD 04 6D        3540              CALL    06D04H
12F5 1A              3550              LDAX    D
12F6 1B              3560              DCX     D
12F7 1B              3570              DCX     D
12F8 1F              3580              RAR
12F9 D2 08 13        3590              JNC     01308H
12FC 01 58 00        3600              LXI     B,00058H
12FF CD 6C 6B        3610              CALL    06B6CH
1302 CD 00 6B        3620              CALL    06B00H
1305 C3 11 13        3630              JMP     01311H
1308 01 20 00        3640    Z1308H    LXI     B,00020H
130B CD 6C 6B        3650              CALL    06B6CH
130E CD 00 6B        3660              CALL    06B00H
1311 01 20 00        3670    Z1311H    LXI     B,00020H
1314 CD 6C 6B        3680              CALL    06B6CH
1317 CD 00 6B        3690              CALL    06B00H
131A 01 00 00        3700              LXI     B,00000H
131D CD 8D 6B        3710              CALL    06B8DH
1320 CD 4C 6D        3720              CALL    06D4CH
1323 CD 0E 6C        3730              CALL    06C0EH
1326 CD 10 6B        3740              CALL    06B10H
1329 01 2C 00        3750              LXI     B,0002CH
132C CD 6C 6B        3760              CALL    06B6CH
132F CD 00 6B        3770              CALL    06B00H
1332 01 00 00        3780              LXI     B,00000H
1335 CD 8D 6B        3790              CALL    06B8DH
1338 CD 4C 6D        3800              CALL    06D4CH
133B CD 4C 6D        3810              CALL    06D4CH
133E CD 4C 6D        3820              CALL    06D4CH
```

1341	CD 0E 6C	3830		CALL	06C0EH
1344	01 08 00	3840		LXI	B,00008H
1347	CD 6C 6B	3850		CALL	06B6CH
134A	CD 23 6D	3860		CALL	06D23H
134D	01 00 00	3870		LXI	B,00000H
1350	CD 8D 6B	3880		CALL	06B8DH
1353	CD 4C 6D	3890		CALL	06D4CH
1356	CD 4C 6D	3900		CALL	06D4CH
1359	CD 0E 6C	3910		CALL	06C0EH
135C	CD 4E 6C	3920		CALL	06C4EH
135F	01 04 00	3930		LXI	B,00004H
1362	CD B5 6B	3940		CALL	06BB5H
1365	13	3950		INX	D
1366	13	3960		INX	D
1367	CD 10 6B	3970		CALL	06B10H
136A	CD E9 6B	3980		CALL	06BE9H
136D	C3 12 10	3990		JMP	01012H
1370	01 02 00	4000		LXI	B,00002H
1373	CD 8D 6B	4010		CALL	06B8DH
1376	01 0F 00	4020		LXI	B,0000FH
1379	CD 6C 6B	4030		CALL	06B6CH
137C	CD A4 6C	4040		CALL	06CA4H
137F	AF	4050		XRA	A
1380	13	4060		INX	D
1381	12	4070		STAX	D
1382	13	4080		INX	D
1383	12	4090		STAX	D
1384	CD B0 6C	4100		CALL	06CB0H
1387	1A	4110		LDAX	D
1388	1B	4120		DCX	D
1389	1B	4130		DCX	D
138A	1F	4140		RAR	
138B	D2 B2 13	4150		JNC	013B2H
138E	CD F7 6A	4160		CALL	06AF7H
1391	01 04 00	4170		LXI	B,00004H
1394	CD B5 6B	4180		CALL	06BB5H
1397	13	4190		INX	D
1398	13	4200		INX	D
1399	01 18 00	4210		LXI	B,00018H
139C	CD 6C 6B	4220		CALL	06B6CH
139F	CD B0 6C	4230		CALL	06CB0H
13A2	1A	4240		LDAX	D
13A3	1B	4250		DCX	D
13A4	1B	4260		DCX	D
13A5	1F	4270		RAR	
13A6	D2 B2 13	4280		JNC	013B2H
13A9	01 46 69	4290		LXI	B,06946H
13AC	CD 6C 6B	4300		CALL	06B6CH
13AF	CD 21 6C	4310		CALL	06C21H
13B2	01 00 00	4320	Z13B2H	LXI	B,00000H
13B5	CD 8D 6B	4330		CALL	06B8DH
13B8	CD 0E 6C	4340		CALL	06C0EH
13BB	01 FF 00	4350		LXI	B,000FFH
13BE	CD 6C 6B	4360		CALL	06B6CH
13C1	CD C6 6C	4370		CALL	06CC6H
13C4	1A	4380		LDAX	D
13C5	1B	4390		DCX	D
13C6	1B	4400		DCX	D
13C7	1F	4410		RAR	
13C8	D2 E0 13	4420		JNC	013E0H
13CB	01 00 00	4430		LXI	B,00000H
13CE	CD 8D 6B	4440		CALL	06B8DH
13D1	01 04 00	4450		LXI	B,00004H
13D4	CD 6C 6B	4460		CALL	06B6CH
13D7	CD 4E 6C	4470		CALL	06C4EH
13DA	01 00 00	4480		LXI	B,00000H
13DD	CD B5 6B	4490		CALL	06BB5H
13E0	C3 1F 11	4500	Z13E0H	JMP	0111FH
13E3	C3 25 6C	4510	Z13E3H	JMP	06C25H

Listing 2: 8080 Run Time Routines for Pascal Object Code

```
0000                    0010 * RUN-TIME ROUTINES FOR PASCAL OBJECT CODE
0000                    0020 ORGA EQU 6900H
0000                    0030   ORG ORGA
6900 C3 6F 6D           0040 RUN JMP ORGA+46FH
6903                    0050 WHO EQU 0C20H
6903                    0060 INP EQU WHO
6903                    0070 WH1 EQU 0C24H
6903                    0080 OUTP EQU WH1
6903                    0090 CRLF EQU 9F8H
6903                    0100 CROUT EQU CRLF
6903                    0110 OSEQ EQU 5ADH
6903                    0120 BYTE1 EQU 0A11H
6903                    0130 DEOUT1 EQU 0A0CH
6903                    0140 BLK1 EQU 0A02H
6903                    0150 CLEAR EQU 9FDH
6903                    0160 POS EQU 0C0EH
6903                    0170 POS1 EQU 727FH
6903                    0180 MENTR EQU 7390H
6903                    0190 ABUF DS 7
690A                    0200 SFLG DS 1
690B                    0210 SIGN EQU SFLG
690B                    0220 STK2 DS 2
690D                    0230 BB DS 2
690F 20 53 54 41        0240 SM1 DB ' STACK'
6915 20 4F 56 45        0250 SM2 DB ' OVERFLOW'
691E 0D                 0260   DB 13
691F 20 49 4E 50        0270 MER1 DB ' INPUT ERROR'
692B 0D                 0280   DB 13
692C 20 53 49 5A        0290 MER2 DB ' SIZE ERROR'
6937 0D                 0300   DB 13
6938 20 44 49 56        0310 DM1 DB ' DIVIDE CHECK'
6945 0D                 0320   DB 13
6946 CD F8 09           0330 EXIT CALL CRLF
6949 2A 0E 0C           0340   LHLD POS
694C 22 7F 72           0350   SHLD POS1
694F C3 90 73           0360   JMP MENTR
6952 CD AD 05           0370 PRINT CALL OSEQ
6955 C3 F8 09           0380   JMP CRLF
6958 EB                 0390 POP XCHG
6959 4E                 0400   MOV C,M
695A 2B                 0410   DCX H
695B 46                 0420   MOV B,M
695C 2B                 0430   DCX H
695D 5E                 0440   MOV E,M
695E 2B                 0450   DCX H
695F 56                 0460   MOV D,M
6960 EB                 0470   XCHG
6961 C9                 0480   RET
6962 EB                 0490 PUSH XCHG
6963 72                 0500   MOV M,D
6964 23                 0510   INX H
6965 73                 0520   MOV M,E
6966 EB                 0530   XCHG
6967 C9                 0540   RET
6968 EB                 0550 POP1 XCHG
6969 5E                 0560   MOV E,M
696A 2B                 0570   DCX H
696B 56                 0580   MOV D,M
696C 2B                 0590   DCX H
696D EB                 0600   XCHG
696E C9                 0610   RET
696F AF                 0620 NEGH XRA A
```

```
6970 95        0630    SUB L
6971 6F        0640    MOV L,A
6972 9C        0650    SBB H
6973 95        0660    SUB L
6974 67        0670    MOV H,A
6975 D6 50     0680    SUI 80
6977 B5        0690    ORA L
6978 C0        0700    RNZ
6979 21 15 69  0710 OVFL LXI H,SM2
697C CD 52 69  0720    CALL PRINT
697F C3 62 69  0730    JMP PUSH
6982 AF        0740 NEGB XRA A
6983 91        0750    SUB C
6984 4F        0760    MOV C,A
6985 98        0770    SBB B
6986 91        0780    SUB C
6987 47        0790    MOV B,A
6988 D6 50     0800    SUI 80
698A B1        0810    ORA C
698B C0        0820    RNZ
698C C3 79 69  0830    JMP OVFL
698F 7A        0840 CMD MOV A,D
6990 2F        0850    CMA
6991 57        0860    MOV D,A
6992 7B        0870    MOV A,E
6993 2F        0880    CMA
6994 5F        0890    MOV E,A
6995 13        0900    INX D
6996 C9        0910    RET
6997 CD 20 0C  0920 GETC CALL WHO
699A 47        0930    MOV B,A
699B C3 24 0C  0940    JMP WH1
699E 21 03 69  0950 READ LXI H,ABUF
69A1 0E 00     0960    MVI C,0
69A3 CD 20 0C  0970 RLP CALL WHO
69A6 FE 7F     0980    CPI 7FH
69A8 CA D4 69  0990    JZ RUB
69AB FE 18     1000    CPI 18H
69AD CA E3 69  1010    JZ CAN
69B0 FE 0D     1020    CPI 0DH
69B2 CA B8 69  1030    JZ $+3
69B5 CD 24 0C  1040    CALL WH1
69B8 77        1050    MOV M,A
69B9 23        1060    INX H
69BA 0C        1070    INR C
69BB FE 0D     1080    CPI 0DH
69BD C8        1090    RZ
69BE 79        1100    MOV A,C
69BF FE 06     1110    CPI 6
69C1 C2 A3 69  1120    JNZ RLP
69C4 CD 20 0C  1130    CALL WHO
69C7 FE 7F     1140    CPI 7FH
69C9 CA D4 69  1150    JZ RUB
69CC FE 18     1160    CPI 18H
69CE CA E3 69  1170    JZ CAN
69D1 36 0D     1180    MVI M,0DH
69D3 C9        1190    RET
69D4 79        1200 RUB MOV A,C
69D5 B7        1210    ORA A
69D6 CA A3 69  1220    JZ RLP
69D9 3E 7F     1230    MVI A,7FH
69DB CD 24 0C  1240    CALL WH1
69DE 0D        1250    DCR C
69DF 2B        1260    DCX H
69E0 C3 A3 69  1270    JMP RLP
69E3 79        1280 CAN MOV A,C
69E4 B7        1290    ORA A
69E5 CA A3 69  1300    JZ RLP
69E8 3E 7F     1310    MVI A,7FH
69EA CD 24 0C  1320    CALL WH1
69ED 2B        1330    DCX H
69EE 0D        1340    DCR C
69EF C3 E3 69  1350    JMP CAN
69F2 D6 30     1360 DIGIT SUI 30H
69F4 D8        1370    RC

69F5 FE 0A     1380    CPI 0AH
69F7 3F        1390    CMC
69F8 C9        1400    RET
69F9 E5        1410 DECIN PUSH H
69FA C5        1420    PUSH B
69FB AF        1430    XRA A
69FC 32 0A 69  1440    STA SFLG
69FF 3E 23     1450    MVI A,'#'
6A01 CD 24 0C  1460    CALL WH1
6A04 CD 9E 69  1470    CALL READ
6A07 21 00 00  1480    LXI H,0
6A0A 01 03 69  1490    LXI B,ABUF
6A0D 0A        1500    LDAX B
6A0E 03        1510    INX B
6A0F FE 2D     1520    CPI '-'
6A11 C2 19 6A  1530    JNZ DECIL+2
6A14 32 0A 69  1540    STA SFLG
6A17 0A        1550 DECIL LDAX B
6A18 03        1560    INX B
6A19 CD F2 69  1570    CALL DIGIT
6A1C DA 31 6A  1580    JC DECID
6A1F 5D        1590    MOV E,L
6A20 54        1600    MOV D,H
6A21 29        1610    DAD H
6A22 29        1620    DAD H
6A23 19        1630    DAD D
6A24 29        1640    DAD H
6A25 85        1650    ADD L
6A26 6F        1660    MOV L,A
6A27 D2 17 6A  1670    JNC DECIL
6A2A 24        1680    INR H
6A2B FA 47 6A  1690    JM ER2
6A2E C3 17 6A  1700    JMP DECIL
6A31 FE DD     1710 DECID CPI 13-48
6A33 C2 41 6A  1720    JNZ ER1
6A36 EB        1730    XCHG
6A37 C1        1740    POP B
6A38 E1        1750    POP H
6A39 3A 0A 69  1760    LDA SFLG
6A3C B7        1770    ORA A
6A3D C8        1780    RZ
6A3E C3 8F 69  1790    JMP CMD
6A41 21 1F 69  1800 ER1 LXI H,MER1
6A44 C3 4A 6A  1810    JMP $+3
6A47 21 2C 69  1820 ER2 LXI H,MER2
6A4A CD 52 69  1830    CALL PRINT
6A4D C3 FB 69  1840    JMP DECIN+2
6A50 E5        1850 HEXIN PUSH H
6A51 C5        1860    PUSH B
6A52 AF        1870    XRA A
6A53 32 0A 69  1880    STA SFLG
6A56 3E 25     1890    MVI A,'%'
6A58 CD 24 0C  1900    CALL WH1
6A5B CD 9E 69  1910    CALL READ
6A5E 21 00 00  1920    LXI H,0
6A61 01 03 69  1930    LXI B,ABUF
6A64 0A        1940    LDAX B
6A65 03        1950    INX B
6A66 FE 2D     1960    CPI '-'
6A68 C2 70 6A  1970    JNZ HEXIL+2
6A6B 32 0A 69  1980    STA SFLG
6A6E 0A        1990 HEXIL LDAX B
6A6F 03        2000    INX B
6A70 CD F2 69  2010    CALL DIGIT
6A73 D2 82 6A  2020    JNC HEX16
6A76 D6 07     2030    SUI 7
6A78 FE 0A     2040    CPI 0AH
6A7A DA 8F 6A  2050    JC HEXID
6A7D FE 10     2060    CPI 10H
6A7F D2 8F 6A  2070    JNC HEXID
6A82 29        2080 HEX16 DAD H
6A83 29        2090    DAD H
6A84 29        2100    DAD H
6A85 29        2110    DAD H
6A86 85        2120    ADD L
```

6A87 6F	2130 MOV L,A	6B02 1B	2880 DCX D
6A88 D2 6E 6A	2140 JNC HEXIL	6B03 C3 24 0C	2890 JMP OUTP
6A8B 24	2150 INR H	6B06 D5	2900 SYS2 PUSH D
6A8C C3 6E 6A	2160 JMP HEXIL	6B07 CD F9 69	2910 CALL DECIN
6A8F FE D6	2170 HEXID CPI 13-37H	6B0A EB	2920 XCHG
6A91 C2 9F 6A	2180 JNZ HER1	6B0B D1	2930 POP D
6A94 EB	2190 XCHG	6B0C 13	2940 INX D
6A95 C1	2200 POP B	6B0D C3 62 69	2950 JMP PUSH
6A96 E1	2210 POP H	6B10 CD 68 69	2960 SYS3 CALL POP1
6A97 3A 0A 69	2220 LDA SFLG	6B13 D5	2970 PUSH D
6A9A B7	2230 ORA A	6B14 AF	2980 XRA A
6A9B C8	2240 RZ	6B15 3D	2990 DCR A
6A9C C3 8F 69	2250 JMP CMD	6B16 F5	3000 PUSH P
6A9F 21 1F 69	2260 HER1 LXI H,MER1	6B17 A4	3010 ANA H
6AA2 CD 52 69	2270 CALL PRINT	6B18 F2 23 6B	3020 JP Y3
6AA5 C3 52 6A	2280 JMP HEXIN+2	6B1B 3E 2D	3030 MVI A,'-'
6AA8 21 38 69	2290 DVCK LXI H,DM1	6B1D CD 24 0C	3040 CALL OUTP
6AAB CD 52 69	2300 CALL PRINT	6B20 CD 6F 69	3050 CALL NEGH
6AAE 21 00 00	2310 LXI H,0	6B23 01 0A 00	3060 Y3 LXI B,10
6AB1 54	2320 MOV D,H	6B26 CD B4 6A	3070 CALL DIV16
6AB2 5D	2330 MOV E,L	6B29 3E 30	3080 MVI A,30H
6AB3 C9	2340 RET	6B2B 83	3090 ADD E
6AB4 78	2350 DIV16 MOV A,B	6B2C F5	3100 PUSH P
6AB5 B1	2360 ORA C	6B2D 7C	3110 MOV A,H
6AB6 CA A8 6A	2370 JZ DVCK	6B2E B5	3120 ORA L
6AB9 AF	2380 XRA A	6B2F C2 23 6B	3130 JNZ Y3
6ABA 80	2390 ADD B	6B32 F1	3140 POP P
6ABB F5	2400 PUSH P	6B33 CD 24 0C	3150 WR CALL OUTP
6ABC F4 82 69	2410 CP NEGB	6B36 F1	3160 POP P
6ABF AF	2420 XRA A	6B37 F2 33 6B	3170 JP WR
6AC0 84	2430 ADD H	6B3A D1	3180 POP D
6AC1 F5	2440 PUSH P	6B3B C9	3190 RET
6AC2 FC 6F 69	2450 CM NEGH	6B3C D5	3200 SYS4 PUSH D
6AC5 EB	2460 XCHG	6B3D CD 50 6A	3210 CALL HEXIN
6AC6 21 00 00	2470 LXI H,0	6B40 EB	3220 XCHG
6AC9 3E 10	2480 MVI A,10H	6B41 D1	3230 POP D
6ACB 29	2490 D2 DAD H	6B42 13	3240 INX D
6ACC EB	2500 XCHG	6B43 C3 62 69	3250 JMP PUSH
6ACD 29	2510 DAD H	6B46 1A	3260 SYS5 LDAX D
6ACE EB	2520 XCHG	6B47 6F	3270 MOV L,A
6ACF D2 D3 6A	2530 JNC D3	6B48 1B	3280 DCX D
6AD2 23	2540 INX H	6B49 1A	3290 LDAX D
6AD3 E5	2550 D3 PUSH H	6B4A 1B	3300 DCX D
6AD4 09	2560 DAD B	6B4B CD 11 0A	3310 CALL BYTE1
6AD5 D2 E2 6A	2570 JNC D4	6B4E 7D	3320 MOV A,L
6AD8 1C	2580 INR E	6B4F C3 11 0A	3330 JMP BYTE1
6AD9 33	2590 INX P	6B52 E1	3340 SYS8 POP H
6ADA 33	2600 INX P	6B53 7E	3350 MOV A,M
6ADB 3D	2610 DCR A	6B54 CD 24 0C	3360 CALL OUTP
6ADC C2 CB 6A	2620 JNZ D2	6B57 23	3370 INX H
6ADF C3 E7 6A	2630 JMP D4A	6B58 0D	3380 DCR C
6AE2 E1	2640 D4 POP H	6B59 C2 53 6B	3390 JNZ SYS8+1
6AE3 3D	2650 DCR A	6B5C E9	3400 PCHL
6AE4 C2 CB 6A	2660 JNZ D2	6B5D D5	0010 BASE PUSH D
6AE7 EB	2670 D4A XCHG	6B5E 11 FA FF	0020 BS1 LXI D,-6
6AE8 C1	2680 POP B	6B61 19	0030 DAD D
6AE9 F1	2690 POP P	6B62 5E	0040 MOV E,M
6AEA A8	2700 XRA B	6B63 2B	0050 DCX H
6AEB FC 6F 69	2710 CM NEGH	6B64 56	0060 MOV D,M
6AEE 7A	2720 MOV A,D	6B65 EB	0070 XCHG
6AEF B3	2730 ORA E	6B66 3D	0080 DCR A
6AF0 C8	2740 RZ	6B67 C2 5E 6B	0090 JNZ BS1
6AF1 AF	2750 XRA A	6B6A D1	0100 POP D
6AF2 80	2760 ADD B	6B6B C9	0110 RET
6AF3 F0	2770 RP	6B6C EB	0120 LIT XCHG
6AF4 C3 8F 69	2780 JMP CMD	6B6D 23	0130 INX H
6AF7 13	2790 SYS0 INX D	6B6E 70	0140 MOV M,B
6AF8 AF	2800 XRA A	6B6F 23	0150 INX H
6AF9 12	2810 STAX D	6B70 71	0160 MOV M,C
6AFA 13	2820 INX D	6B71 EB	0170 XCHG
6AFB CD 20 0C	2830 CALL INP	6B72 C9	0180 RET
6AFE 12	2840 STAX D	6B73 19	0190 INT DAD D
6AFF C9	2850 RET	6B74 EB	0200 XCHG
6B00 1A	2860 SYS1 LDAX D	6B75 2A 0B 69	0210 LHLD STK2
6B01 1B	2870 DCX D	6B78 19	0220 DAD D

```
6B79 D0           0230  RNC
6B7A 21 0F 69     0240  STKOV LXI H,SM1
6B7D CD 52 69     0250        CALL PRINT
6B80 E1           0260        POP H
6B81 C3 46 69     0270        JMP EXIT
6B84 2A 0D 69     0280  LOD1  LHLD BB
6B87 CD 5D 6B     0290        CALL BASE
6B8A C3 90 6B     0300        JMP $+3
6B8D 2A 0D 69     0310  LOD   LHLD BB
6B90 13           0320        INX D
6B91 09           0330        DAD B
6B92 2B           0340        DCX H
6B93 7E           0350        MOV A,M
6B94 12           0360        STAX D
6B95 23           0370        INX H
6B96 7E           0380        MOV A,M
6B97 13           0390        INX D
6B98 12           0400        STAX D
6B99 C9           0410        RET
6B9A AF           0420  LODX  XRA A
6B9B 2A 0D 69     0430  LODX1 LHLD BB
6B9E B7           0440        ORA A
6B9F C4 5D 6B     0450        CNZ BASE
6BA2 09           0460        DAD B
6BA3 EB           0470        XCHG
6BA4 4E           0480        MOV C,M
6BA5 2B           0490        DCX H
6BA6 46           0500        MOV B,M
6BA7 EB           0510        XCHG
6BA8 09           0520        DAD B
6BA9 C3 91 6B     0530        JMP LOD+4
6BAC 2A 0D 69     0540  STO1  LHLD BB
6BAF CD 5D 6B     0550        CALL BASE
6BB2 C3 B8 6B     0560        JMP $+3
6BB5 2A 0D 69     0570  STO   LHLD BB
6BB8 09           0580        DAD B
6BB9 1A           0590        LDAX D
6BBA 77           0600        MOV M,A
6BBB 2B           0610        DCX H
6BBC 1B           0620        DCX D
6BBD 1A           0630        LDAX D
6BBE 77           0640        MOV M,A
6BBF 1B           0650        DCX D
6BC0 C9           0660        RET
6BC1 AF           0670  STOX  XRA A
6BC2 EB           0680  STOX1 XCHG
6BC3 5E           0690        MOV E,M
6BC4 2B           0700        DCX H
6BC5 56           0710        MOV D,M
6BC6 2B           0720        DCX H
6BC7 D5           0730        PUSH D
6BC8 5E           0740        MOV E,M
6BC9 2B           0750        DCX H
6BCA 56           0760        MOV D,M
6BCB 2B           0770        DCX H
6BCC EB           0780        XCHG
6BCD 29           0790        DAD H
6BCE 09           0800        DAD B
6BCF 44           0810        MOV B,H
6BD0 4D           0820        MOV C,L
6BD1 2A 0D 69     0830        LHLD BB
6BD4 B7           0840        ORA A
6BD5 C4 5D 6B     0850        CNZ BASE
6BD8 09           0860        DAD B
6BD9 C1           0870        POP B
6BDA 71           0880        MOV M,C
6BDB 2B           0890        DCX H
6BDC 70           0900        MOV M,B
6BDD C9           0910        RET
6BDE 2A 0D 69     0920  CAL1  LHLD BB
6BE1 44           0930        MOV B,H
6BE2 4D           0940        MOV C,L
6BE3 CD 5D 6B     0950        CALL BASE
6BE6 C3 EE 6B     0960        JMP $+5
6BE9 2A 0D 69     0970  CAL   LHLD BB
6BEC 44           0980        MOV B,H
6BED 4D           0990        MOV C,L
6BEE D5           1000        PUSH D
6BEF EB           1010        XCHG
6BF0 23           1020        INX H
6BF1 72           1030        MOV M,D
6BF2 23           1040        INX H
6BF3 73           1050        MOV M,E
6BF4 D1           1060        POP D
6BF5 13           1070        INX D
6BF6 13           1080        INX D
6BF7 13           1090        INX D
6BF8 13           1100        INX D
6BF9 13           1110        INX D
6BFA 13           1120        INX D
6BFB 23           1130        INX H
6BFC 70           1140        MOV M,B
6BFD 23           1150        INX H
6BFE 71           1160        MOV M,C
6BFF C1           1170        POP B
6C00 C5           1180        PUSH B
6C01 03           1190        INX B
6C02 03           1200        INX B
6C03 03           1210        INX B
6C04 23           1220        INX H
6C05 70           1230        MOV M,B
6C06 23           1240        INX H
6C07 71           1250        MOV M,C
6C08 23           1260        INX H
6C09 23           1270        INX H
6C0A 22 0D 69     1280        SHLD BB
6C0D C9           1290        RET
6C0E EB           1300  LODA  XCHG
6C0F 5E           1310        MOV E,M
6C10 2B           1320        DCX H
6C11 56           1330        MOV D,M
6C12 36 00        1340        MVI M,0
6C14 1A           1350        LDAX D
6C15 23           1360        INX H
6C16 77           1370        MOV M,A
6C17 EB           1380        XCHG
6C18 C9           1390        RET
6C19 1A           1400  STOA  LDAX D
6C1A 1B           1410        DCX D
6C1B 1B           1420        DCX D
6C1C CD 68 69     1430        CALL POP1
6C1F 77           1440        MOV M,A
6C20 C9           1450        RET
6C21 CD 68 69     1460  CALA  CALL POP1
6C24 E9           1470        PCHL
6C25 2A 0D 69     1480  POO   LHLD BB
6C28 11 FB FF     1490        LXI D,-5
6C2B 19           1500        DAD D
6C2C 56           1510        MOV D,M
6C2D 23           1520        INX H
6C2E 5E           1530        MOV E,M
6C2F EB           1540        XCHG
6C30 22 0D 69     1550        SHLD BB
6C33 EB           1560        XCHG
6C34 23           1570        INX H
6C35 56           1580        MOV D,M
6C36 23           1590        INX H
6C37 5E           1600        MOV E,M
6C38 01 FA FF     1610        LXI B,-6
6C3B 09           1620        DAD B
6C3C EB           1630        XCHG
6C3D E9           1640        PCHL
6C3E CD 82 69     1650  SUB1  CALL NEGB
6C41 78           1660  ADD16 MOV A,B
6C42 AC           1670  SU2   XRA H
6C43 09           1680        DAD B
6C44 4F           1690        MOV C,A
6C45 1F           1700        RAR
6C46 A9           1710        XRA C
6C47 AC           1720        XRA H
```

```
6C48 F2 62 69    1730    JP   PUSH
6C4B C3 79 69    1740    JMP  OVFL
6C4E CD 58 69    1750 P02 CALL POP
6C51 C3 41 6C    1760    JMP  ADD16
6C54 CD 58 69    1770 P03 CALL POP
6C57 78          1780 SUB16 MOV A,B
6C58 D6 50       1790    SUI  80
6C5A B1          1800    ORA  C
6C5B C2 3E 6C    1810    JNZ  SUB1
6C5E 79          1820    MOV  A,C
6C5F C3 42 6C    1830    JMP  SU2
6C62 EB          1840 P01 XCHG
6C63 AF          1850    XRA  A
6C64 96          1860    SUB  M
6C65 77          1870    MOV  M,A
6C66 4F          1880    MOV  C,A
6C67 2B          1890    DCX  H
6C68 9E          1900    SBB  M
6C69 91          1910    SUB  C
6C6A 77          1920    MOV  M,A
6C6B 23          1930    INX  H
6C6C EB          1940    XCHG
6C6D C9          1950    RET
6C6E 16 08       1960 MUL8 MVI D,8
6C70 29          1970    DAD  H
6C71 07          1980    RLC
6C72 D2 76 6C    1990    JNC  $+1
6C75 09          2000    DAD  B
6C76 15          2010    DCR  D
6C77 C2 70 6C    2020    JNZ  MUL8+2
6C7A C9          2030    RET
6C7B CD 58 69    2040 P04 CALL POP
6C7E D5          2050    PUSH D
6C7F 7C          2060    MOV  A,H
6C80 5D          2070    MOV  E,L
6C81 21 00 00    2080    LXI  H,0
6C84 B7          2090    ORA  A
6C85 C4 6E 6C    2100    CNZ  MUL8
6C88 7B          2110    MOV  A,E
6C89 CD 6E 6C    2120    CALL MUL8
6C8C D1          2130    POP  D
6C8D C3 62 69    2140    JMP  PUSH
6C90 CD 58 69    2150 P05 CALL POP
6C93 D5          2160    PUSH D
6C94 CD B4 6A    2170    CALL DIV16
6C97 D1          2180    POP  D
6C98 C3 62 69    2190    JMP  PUSH
6C9B 1A          2200 P06 LDAX D
6C9C E6 01       2210    ANI  1
6C9E 12          2220    STAX D
6C9F AF          2230    XRA  A
6CA0 1B          2240    DCX  D
6CA1 12          2250    STAX D
6CA2 13          2260    INX  D
6CA3 C9          2270    RET
6CA4 CD 58 69    2280 P07 CALL POP
6CA7 D5          2290    PUSH D
6CA8 CD B4 6A    2300    CALL DIV16
6CAB EB          2310    XCHG
6CAC D1          2320    POP  D
6CAD C3 62 69    2330    JMP  PUSH
6CB0 3E 01       2340 P08 MVI A,1
6CB2 F5          2350 EQUAL PUSH P
6CB3 CD 58 69    2360    CALL POP
6CB6 AF          2370    XRA  A
6CB7 12          2380    STAX D
6CB8 13          2390    INX  D
6CB9 7D          2400    MOV  A,L
6CBA B9          2410    CMP  C
6CBB C2 DF 6C    2420    JNZ  FALSE
6CBE 7C          2430    MOV  A,H
6CBF B8          2440    CMP  B
6CC0 C2 DF 6C    2450    JNZ  FALSE
6CC3 F1          2460 TRUE POP P
6CC4 12          2470    STAX D

6CC5 C9          2480    RET
6CC6 AF          2490 P09 XRA A
6CC7 C3 B2 6C    2500    JMP  EQUAL
6CCA 06 00       2510 P11 MVI B,0
6CCC 48          2520    MOV  C,B
6CCD C5          2530 LESS PUSH B
6CCE CD 58 69    2540    CALL POP
6CD1 AF          2550    XRA  A
6CD2 12          2560    STAX D
6CD3 13          2570    INX  D
6CD4 7C          2580    MOV  A,H
6CD5 B8          2590    CMP  B
6CD6 CA E4 6C    2600    JZ   EQH
6CD9 1F          2610    RAR
6CDA AC          2620    XRA  H
6CDB A8          2630    XRA  B
6CDC FA C3 6C    2640    JM   TRUE
6CDF F1          2650 FALSE POP P
6CE0 EE 01       2660    XRI  1
6CE2 12          2670    STAX D
6CE3 C9          2680    RET
6CE4 7D          2690 EQH MOV A,L
6CE5 B9          2700    CMP  C
6CE6 DA C3 6C    2710    JC   TRUE
6CE9 C1          2720    POP  B
6CEA 78          2730    MOV  A,B
6CEB C2 EF 6C    2740    JNZ  $+1
6CEE A9          2750    XRA  C
6CEF EE 01       2760    XRI  1
6CF1 12          2770    STAX D
6CF2 C9          2780    RET
6CF3 01 00 01    2790 P10 LXI B,100H
6CF6 C3 CD 6C    2800    JMP  LESS
6CF9 01 01 00    2810 P12 LXI B,1
6CFC C3 CD 6C    2820    JMP  LESS
6CFF 06 01       2830 P13 MVI B,1
6D01 C3 CC 6C    2840    JMP  LESS-1
6D04 CD 58 69    2850 P14 CALL POP
6D07 7C          2860    MOV  A,H
6D08 B0          2870    ORA  B
6D09 12          2880    STAX D
6D0A 7D          2890    MOV  A,L
6D0B B1          2900    ORA  C
6D0C 13          2910    INX  D
6D0D 12          2920    STAX D
6D0E C9          2930    RET
6D0F CD 58 69    2940 P15 CALL POP
6D12 7C          2950    MOV  A,H
6D13 A0          2960    ANA  B
6D14 12          2970    STAX D
6D15 7D          2980    MOV  A,L
6D16 A1          2990    ANA  C
6D17 13          3000    INX  D
6D18 12          3010    STAX D
6D19 C9          3020    RET
6D1A 1A          3030 P16 LDAX D
6D1B 2F          3040    CMA
6D1C 12          3050    STAX D
6D1D 1B          3060    DCX  D
6D1E 1A          3070    LDAX D
6D1F 2F          3080    CMA
6D20 12          3090    STAX D
6D21 13          3100    INX  D
6D22 C9          3110    RET
6D23 CD 58 69    3120 P17 CALL POP
6D26 AF          3130    XRA  A
6D27 81          3140    ADD  C
6D28 CA 62 69    3150    JZ   PUSH
6D2B FA 42 6D    3160    JM   SR1
6D2E 29          3170 SL1 DAD H
6D2F 3D          3180    DCR  A
6D30 C2 2E 6D    3190    JNZ  SL1
6D33 C3 62 69    3200    JMP  PUSH
6D36 CD 58 69    3210 P18 CALL POP
6D39 AF          3220    XRA  A
```

```
6D3A 91          3230       SUB  C
6D3B CA 62 69    3240       JZ   PUSH
6D3E F2 2E 6D    3250       JP   SL1
6D41 4F          3260       MOV  C,A
6D42 AF          3270  SR1  XRA  A
6D43 B4          3280       ORA  H
6D44 1F          3290       RAR
6D45 67          3300       MOV  H,A
6D46 7D          3310       MOV  A,L
6D47 1F          3320       RAR
6D48 6F          3330       MOV  L,A
6D49 0C          3340       INR  C
6D4A C2 42 6D    3350       JNZ  SR1
6D4D C3 62 69    3360       JMP  PUSH
6D50 1A          3370  P19  LDAX D
6D51 C6 01       3380       ADI  1
6D53 12          3390       STAX D
6D54 D0          3400       RNC
6D55 62          3410       MOV  H,D
6D56 6B          3420       MOV  L,E
6D57 2B          3430       DCX  H
6D58 34          3440       INR  M
6D59 C9          3450       RET
6D5A 1A          3460  P20  LDAX D
6D5B D6 01       3470       SUI  1
6D5D 12          3480       STAX D
6D5E D0          3490       RNC
6D5F 62          3500       MOV  H,D
6D60 6B          3510       MOV  L,E
6D61 2B          3520       DCX  H
6D62 35          3530       DCR  M
6D63 C9          3540       RET
6D64 62          3550  P21  MOV  H,D
6D65 6B          3560       MOV  L,E
6D66 13          3570       INX  D
6D67 2B          3580       DCX  H
6D68 7E          3590       MOV  A,M
6D69 12          3600       STAX D
6D6A 13          3610       INX  D
6D6B 23          3620       INX  H
6D6C 7E          3630       MOV  A,M
6D6D 12          3640       STAX D
6D6E C9          3650       RET
6D6F AF          3660  INIT XRA  A
6D70 D3 04       3670       OUT  4
6D72 E5          3680       PUSH H
6D73 2A 7F 72    3690       LHLD POS1
6D76 22 0E 0C    3700       SHLD POS
6D79 E1          3710       POP  H
6D7A 01 07 00    3720       LXI  B,7
6D7D 09          3730       DAD  B
6D7E 22 0D 69    3740       SHLD BB
6D81 2B          3750       DCX  H
6D82 2B          3760       DCX  H
6D83 EB          3770       XCHG
6D84 22 0B 69    3780       SHLD STK2
6D87 6B          3790       MOV  L,E
6D88 62          3800       MOV  H,D
6D89 01 46 69    3810       LXI  B,EXIT
6D8C 71          3820       MOV  M,C
6D8D 2B          3830       DCX  H
6D8E 70          3840       MOV  M,B
6D8F C9          3850       RET
6D90             3860  RUNEND EQU $-1
```

Listing 3: P-Code to 8080 Translator Routines

```
6D90                          0010 * P-CODE TO 8080 TRANSLATOR
6D90                          0020 ORGA2 EQU 5A00H
6D90                          0030   ORG ORGA2
5A00  C3 F7 64                0040 TRANS JMP ORGA2+0AF7H
5A03                          0050 O2 EQU 21
5A03                          0060 S1 EQU 500
5A03                          0070 S2 EQU 400
5A03                          0080 PCDEF EQU 2C00H
5A03                          0090 OBDEF EQU 1000H
5A03                          0100 STK1 EQU 0
5A03                          0110 STAK2 EQU RUN-1
5A03                          0120 TST DS S1+1
5BF8                          0130 DST DS S2+1
5D89                          0140 EA DS S2+2
5F1B                          0150 Y12 DS 30
5F39                          0160 Z12 DS 58
5F73                          0170 AST DS 2
5F75                          0180 BOST DS 2
5F77                          0190 X DS 2
5F79                          0200 X0 DS 2
5F7B                          0210 X1 DS 2
5F7D                          0220 PT DS 2
5F7F                          0230 P0 DS 2
5F81                          0240 P1 DS 2
5F83                          0250 C1 DS 1
5F84                          0260 C2 DS 1
5F85                          0270 F DS 1
5F86                          0280 R0 DS 1
5F87                          0290 V DS 1
5F88                          0300 ML DS 1
5F89                          0310 G DS 2
5F8B                          0320 I DS 2
5F8D                          0330 J DS 2
5F8F                          0340 K DS 2
5F91                          0350 K1 DS 2
5F93                          0360 L0 DS 2
5F95                          0370 L1 DS 2
5F97                          0380 N DS 2
5F99                          0390 U DS 2
5F9B                          0400 W DS 2
5F9D                          0410 W0 DS 2
5F9F  6C 02                   0420 YST DW LIT-RUN
5FA1  8D 02                   0430   DW LOD-RUN
5FA3  84 02                   0440   DW LOD1-RUN
5FA5  9A 02                   0450   DW LODX-RUN
5FA7  9B 02                   0460   DW LODX1-RUN
5FA9  0E 03                   0470   DW LODA-RUN
5FAB  B5 02                   0480   DW STO-RUN
5FAD  AC 02                   0490   DW STO1-RUN
5FAF  C1 02                   0500   DW STOX-RUN
5FB1  C2 02                   0510   DW STOX1-RUN
5FB3  19 03                   0520   DW STOA-RUN
5FB5  E9 02                   0530   DW CAL-RUN
5FB7  DE 02                   0540   DW CAL1-RUN
5FB9  21 03                   0550   DW CALA-RUN
5FBB  73 02                   0560   DW INT-RUN
5FBD  25 03                   0570 ZST DW P00-RUN
5FBF  62 03                   0580   DW P01-RUN
5FC1  4E 03                   0590   DW P02-RUN
5FC3  54 03                   0600   DW P03-RUN
5FC5  7B 03                   0610   DW P04-RUN
5FC7  90 03                   0620   DW P05-RUN
5FC9  9B 03                   0630   DW P06-RUN
```

```
5FCB A4 03          0640     DW P07-RUN
5FCD B0 03          0650     DW P08-RUN
5FCF C6 03          0660     DW P09-RUN
5FD1 F3 03          0670     DW P10-RUN
5FD3 CA 03          0680     DW P11-RUN
5FD5 F9 03          0690     DW P12-RUN
5FD7 FF 03          0700     DW P13-RUN
5FD9 04 04          0710     DW P14-RUN
5FDB 0F 04          0720     DW P15-RUN
5FDD 1A 04          0730     DW P16-RUN
5FDF 23 04          0740     DW P17-RUN
5FE1 36 04          0750     DW P18-RUN
5FE3 50 04          0760     DW P19-RUN
5FE5 5A 04          0770     DW P20-RUN
5FE7 64 04          0780     DW P21-RUN
5FE9 F7 01          0790     DW SYS0-RUN
5FEB 00 02          0800     DW SYS1-RUN
5FED 06 02          0810     DW SYS2-RUN
5FEF 10 02          0820     DW SYS3-RUN
5FF1 3C 02          0830     DW SYS4-RUN
5FF3 46 02          0840     DW SYS5-RUN
5FF5 52 02          0850     DW SYS8-RUN
5FF7 0C             0860 GOMSG DB 12
5FF8 2A 2A 2A 2A    0870     DB '***** P-CODE TO 8080  TRANSLATION *****'
601E 0D             0880     DB 13
601F 09             0890     DB 9
6020 41 44 44 52    0900     DB 'ADDRESS OF RUNTIME MODULE? '
603B 0D             0910     DB 13
603C 00 69          0920     DW RUN
603E 09             0930 PCMSG DB 9
603F 50 2D 43 4F    0940     DB 'P-CODE START ADDRESS? '
6055 0D             0950     DB 13
6056 00 2C          0960     DW PCDEF
6058 09             0970 DSTMSG DB 9
6059 4F 42 4A 45    0980     DB 'OBJECT-CODE START ADDRESS? '
6074 0D             0990     DB 13
6075 00 10          1000     DW OBDEF
6077 09             1010 STKMS1 DB 9
6078 53 54 41 43    1020     DB 'STACK START ADDRESS? '
608D 0D             1030     DB 13
608E 00 00          1040     DW STK1
6090 FF 68          1050     DW STAK2
6092 09             1060 STKMS2 DB 9
6093 53 54 41 43    1070     DB 'STACK END ADDRESS? '
60A6 0D             1080     DB 13
60A7 FF 68          1090     DW STAK2
60A9 20 52 45 46    1100 REFMSG DB ' REFERENCES'
60B4 0D             1110     DB 13
60B5 20 44 49 46    1120 LABMSG DB ' DIFFERENT LABELS'
60C6 0D             1130     DB 13
60C7 20 46 4F 52    1140 FWDMSG DB ' FORWARD REFERENCES'
60DA 0D             1150     DB 13
60DB 20 50 2D 43    1160 FINMSG DB ' P-CODES TRANSLATED ( TOTAL '
60F6 0D             1170     DB 13
60F7 48 20 42 59    1180     DB 'H BYTES)'
60FF 0D             1190     DB 13
6100 48 20 42 59    1200     DB 'H BYTES OF OBJECT CODE PRODUCED - CODE E
NDS AT '
612F 0D             1210     DB 13
6130 7C             1220 HDCMP MOV A,H
6131 BA             1230     CMP D
6132 C0             1240     RNZ
6133 7D             1250     MOV A,L
6134 93             1260     SUB E
6135 C8             1270     RZ
6136 1F             1280     RAR
6137 B7             1290     ORA A
6138 17             1300     RAL
6139 F8             1310     RM
613A AF             1320     XRA A
613B 3C             1330     INR A
613C C9             1340     RET
613D CD AD 05       1350 ADDRIN CALL OSEQ
6140 E5             1360     PUSH H
6141 CD 50 6A       1370     CALL HEXIN
```

6144 E1	1380	POP H	
6145 7B	1390	MOV A,E	
6146 B2	1400	ORA D	
6147 F5	1410	PUSH P	
6148 C2 52 61	1420	JNZ $+7	
614B 23	1430	INX H	
614C 5E	1440	MOV E,M	
614D 23	1450	INX H	
614E 56	1460	MOV D,M	
614F CD 0C 0A	1470	CALL DEOUT1	
6152 CD F8 09	1480	CALL CRLF	
6155 F1	1490	POP P	
6156 EB	1500	XCHG	
6157 C9	1510	RET	
6158 2A 7D 5F	1520	FNG LHLD PT	
615B 70	1530	MOV M,B	
615C 23	1540	INX H	
615D 71	1550	MOV M,C	
615E 23	1560	INX H	
615F 72	1570	MOV M,D	
6160 23	1580	INX H	
6161 22 7D 5F	1590	SHLD PT	
6164 C9	1600	RET	
6165 21 1B 5F	1610	FNQ LXI H,Y12	
6168 3D	1620	DCR A	
6169 87	1630	ADD A	
616A 85	1640	ADD L	
616B 6F	1650	MOV L,A	
616C D2 70 61	1660	JNC $+1	
616F 24	1670	INR H	
6170 4E	1680	MOV C,M	
6171 23	1690	INX H	
6172 56	1700	MOV D,M	
6173 C3 58 61	1710	JMP FNG	
6176	1720	* LIT	
6176 21 83 5F	1730	L800 LXI H,C1	
6179 7E	1740	MOV A,M	
617A 23	1750	INX H	
617B B6	1760	ORA M	
617C CA 8E 61	1770	JZ L830	
617F 56	1780	MOV D,M	
6180 2B	1790	DCX H	
6181 4E	1800	MOV C,M	
6182 06 01	1810	MVI B,1	
6184 CD 58 61	1820	CALL FNG	
6187 3E 01	1830	MVI A,1	
6189 06 CD	1840	MVI B,205	
618B C3 65 61	1850	JMP FNQ	
618E 01 13 AF	1860	L830 LXI B,0AF13H	
6191 16 12	1870	MVI D,18	
6193 CD 58 61	1880	CALL FNG	
6196 01 12 13	1890	LXI B,1312H	
6199 16 00	1900	MVI D,0	
619B CD 58 61	1910	CALL FNG	
619E 2B	1920	DCX H	
619F 22 7D 5F	1930	SHLD PT	
61A2 C9	1940	RET	
61A3	1950	* OPR	
61A3 21 CD 00	1960	L850 LXI H,205	
61A6 22 8D 5F	1970	SHLD J	
61A9 3A 83 5F	1980	LDA C1	
61AC FE 04	1990	CPI 4	
61AE F2 0F 62	2000	JP L890	
61B1 B7	2010	ORA A	
61B2 CA 09 62	2020	JZ L885	
61B5 2A 77 5F	2030	LHLD X	
61B8 2B	2040	DCX H	
61B9 2B	2050	DCX H	
61BA 2B	2060	DCX H	
61BB 2B	2070	DCX H	
61BC 7E	2080	MOV A,M	
61BD B7	2090	ORA A	
61BE C2 0F 62	2100	JNZ L890	
61C1 3A 83 5F	2110	LDA C1	
61C4 FE 02	2120	CPI 2	

61C6 F2 DD 61	2130	JP L870	
61C9 2A 7D 5F	2140	LHLD PT	
61CC 2B	2150	DCX H	
61CD 2B	2160	DCX H	
61CE 2B	2170	DCX H	
61CF 2B	2180	DCX H	
61D0 2B	2190	DCX H	
61D1 7E	2200	MOV A,M	
61D2 2F	2210	CMA	
61D3 C6 01	2220	ADI 1	
61D5 77	2230	MOV M,A	
61D6 23	2240	INX H	
61D7 7E	2250	MOV A,M	
61D8 2F	2260	CMA	
61D9 CE 00	2270	ACI 0	
61DB 77	2280	MOV M,A	
61DC C9	2290	RET	
61DD 2A 77 5F	2300	L870 LHLD X	
61E0 2B	2310	DCX H	
61E1 7E	2320	MOV A,M	
61E2 B7	2330	ORA A	
61E3 C2 0F 62	2340	JNZ L890	
61E6 2B	2350	DCX H	
61E7 7E	2360	MOV A,M	
61E8 FE 04	2370	CPI 4	
61EA F2 0F 62	2380	JP L890	
61ED 5F	2390	MOV E,A	
61EE 2A 7D 5F	2400	LHLD PT	
61F1 01 FA FF	2410	LXI B,-6	
61F4 09	2420	DAD B	
61F5 22 7D 5F	2430	SHLD PT	
61F8 2A 8D 5F	2440	LHLD J	
61FB 45	2450	MOV B,L	
61FC 3A 83 5F	2460	LDA C1	
61FF C6 21	2470	ADI 33	
6201 CD 65 61	2480	CALL FNQ	
6204 1D	2490	DCR E	
6205 C2 FC 61	2500	JNZ $-12	
6208 C9	2510	RET	
6209 21 C3 00	2520	L885 LXI H,195	
620C C3 12 62	2530	JMP $+3	
620F 2A 8D 5F	2540	L890 LHLD J	
6212 45	2550	MOV B,L	
6213 3A 83 5F	2560	LDA C1	
6216 C6 10	2570	ADI 16	
6218 C3 65 61	2580	JMP FNQ	
621B	2590	* LOD	
621B 3E 02	2600	L900 MVI A,2	
621D 32 85 5F	2610	STA F	
6220 21 04 00	2620	L925 LXI H,4	
6223 22 8D 5F	2630	SHLD J	
6226 2A 77 5F	2640	LHLD X	
6229 23	2650	INX H	
622A 6E	2660	MOV L,M	
622B 26 00	2670	MVI H,0	
622D 22 93 5F	2680	SHLD L0	
6230 7D	2690	MOV A,L	
6231 3C	2700	INR A	
6232 CA DF 62	2710	JZ L1040	
6235 3A 85 5F	2720	LDA F	
6238 FE 02	2730	CPI 2	
623A C2 9D 62	2740	JNZ L930	
623D 3A 86 5F	2750	LDA R0	
6240 47	2760	MOV B,A	
6241 3A 87 5F	2770	LDA V	
6244 B0	2780	ORA B	
6245 C2 9D 62	2790	JNZ L930	
6248 2A 91 5F	2800	LHLD K1	
624B 23	2810	INX H	
624C EB	2820	XCHG	
624D 2A 8F 5F	2830	LHLD K	
6250 CD 30 61	2840	CALL HDCMP	
6253 CA 59 62	2850	JZ $+3	
6256 F2 9D 62	2860	JP L930	
6259 2A 95 5F	2870	LHLD L1	

625C EB	2880 XCHG	62FC C2 09 63	0110 JNZ L1225
625D 2A 93 5F	2890 LHLD L0	62FF 06 CD	0120 MVI B,205
6260 CD 30 61	2900 CALL HDCMP	6301 3E 0C	0130 MVI A,12
6263 C2 9D 62	2910 JNZ L930	6303 CD 65 61	0140 CALL FNQ
6266 2A 77 5F	2920 LHLD X	6306 C3 39 63	0150 JMP L1260
6269 2B	2930 DCX H	6309 3C	0160 L1225 INR A
626A 3A 84 5F	2940 LDA C2	630A C2 14 63	0170 JNZ L1230
626D BE	2950 CMP M	630D 06 CD	0180 MVI B,205
626E C2 9D 62	2960 JNZ L930	630F 3E 0E	0190 MVI A,14
6271 2B	2970 DCX H	6311 C3 65 61	0200 JMP FNQ
6272 3A 83 5F	2980 LDA C1	6314 06 3E	0210 L1230 MVI B,62
6275 BE	2990 CMP M	6316 3A 93 5F	0220 LDA L0
6276 C2 9D 62	3000 JNZ L930	6319 4F	0230 MOV C,A
6279 E5	3010 PUSH H	631A 16 00	0240 MVI D,0
627A 2A 8F 5F	3020 LHLD K	631C CD 58 61	0250 CALL FNG
627D 22 91 5F	3030 SHLD K1	631F 2B	0260 DCX H
6280 E1	3040 POP H	6320 22 7D 5F	0270 SHLD PT
6281 2B	3050 DCX H	6323 06 CD	0280 MVI B,205
6282 2B	3060 DCX H	6325 3E 0D	0290 MVI A,13
6283 7E	3070 MOV A,M	6327 CD 65 61	0300 CALL FNQ
6284 FE 02	3080 CPI 2	632A C3 39 63	0310 JMP L1260
6286 CA 96 62	3090 JZ L920	632D	0320 * JMP
6289 01 13 13	3100 LXI B,1313H	632D 2A 8F 5F	0330 L1250 LHLD K
628C 16 00	3110 MVI D,0	6330 23	0340 INX H
628E CD 58 61	3120 CALL FNG	6331 EB	0350 XCHG
6291 2B	3130 DCX H	6332 2A 83 5F	0360 LHLD C1
6292 22 7D 5F	3140 SHLD PT	6335 CD 30 61	0370 CALL HDCMP
6295 C9	3150 RET	6338 C8	0380 RZ
6296 06 CD	3160 L920 MVI B,205	6339 CD 49 63	0390 L1260 CALL S1300
6298 3E 25	3170 MVI A,37	633C 06 C3	0400 MVI B,195
629A C3 65 61	3180 JMP FNQ	633E 3A 8B 5F	0410 LDA I
629D 2A 83 5F	3190 L930 LHLD C1	6341 4F	0420 MOV C,A
62A0 29	3200 DAD H	6342 3A 8D 5F	0430 LDA J
62A1 06 01	3210 MVI B,1	6345 57	0440 MOV D,A
62A3 4D	3220 MOV C,L	6346 C3 58 61	0450 JMP FNG
62A4 54	3230 MOV D,H	6349 2A 83 5F	0460 S1300 LHLD C1
62A5 CD 58 61	3240 CALL FNG	634C 22 73 5F	0470 SHLD AST
62A8 21 02 00	3250 LXI H,2	634F 21 01 00	0480 LXI H,1
62AB 22 8D 5F	3260 SHLD J	6352 22 8B 5F	0490 SHLD I
62AE 3A 87 5F	3270 LDA V	6355 2A 9D 5F	0500 LHLD W0
62B1 B7	3280 ORA A	6358 22 8D 5F	0510 SHLD J
62B2 2A 93 5F	3290 LHLD L0	635B 2A 8B 5F	0520 L1320 LHLD I
62B5 7D	3300 MOV A,L	635E EB	0530 XCHG
62B6 C2 C8 62	3310 JNZ L960	635F 2A 8D 5F	0540 LHLD J
62B9 22 95 5F	3320 SHLD L1	6362 19	0550 DAD D
62BC 21 00 00	3330 LXI H,0	6363 AF	0560 XRA A
62BF 22 8D 5F	3340 SHLD J	6364 B4	0570 ORA H
62C2 2A 8F 5F	3350 LHLD K	6365 1F	0580 RAR
62C5 22 91 5F	3360 SHLD K1	6366 67	0590 MOV H,A
62C8 B7	3370 L960 ORA A	6367 7D	0600 MOV A,L
62C9 CA DF 62	3380 JZ L1040	6368 1F	0610 RAR
62CC 2A 8D 5F	3390 LHLD J	6369 F6 01	0620 ORI 1
62CF 23	3400 INX H	636B 6F	0630 MOV L,A
62D0 22 8D 5F	3410 SHLD J	636C 22 97 5F	0640 SHLD N
62D3 06 3E	3420 MVI B,62	636F 11 03 5A	0650 LXI D,TST
62D5 4F	3430 MOV C,A	6372 19	0660 DAD D
62D6 16 00	3440 MVI D,0	6373 5E	0670 MOV E,M
62D8 CD 58 61	3450 CALL FNG	6374 23	0680 INX H
62DB 2B	3460 DCX H	6375 56	0690 MOV D,M
62DC 22 7D 5F	3470 SHLD PT	6376 2A 73 5F	0700 LHLD AST
62DF 3A 85 5F	3480 L1040 LDA F	6379 CD 30 61	0710 CALL HDCMP
62E2 2A 8D 5F	3490 LHLD J	637C CA A2 63	0720 JZ L1360
62E5 85	3500 ADD L	637F F2 8D 63	0730 JP $+11
62E6 06 CD	3510 MVI B,205	6382 2A 97 5F	0740 LHLD N
62E8 C3 65 61	3520 JMP FNQ	6385 2B	0750 DCX H
62EB	0010 * STO	6386 2B	0760 DCX H
62EB 3E 07	0020 L1100 MVI A,7	6387 22 8D 5F	0770 SHLD J
62ED 32 85 5F	0030 STA F	638A C3 95 63	0780 JMP L1350
62F0 C3 20 62	0040 JMP L925	638D 2A 97 5F	0790 LHLD N
62F3	0050 * CAL	6390 23	0800 INX H
62F3 2A 77 5F	0060 L1200 LHLD X	6391 23	0810 INX H
62F6 23	0070 INX H	6392 22 8B 5F	0820 SHLD I
62F7 7E	0080 MOV A,M	6395 2A 8B 5F	0830 L1350 LHLD I
62F8 32 93 5F	0090 STA L0	6398 EB	0840 XCHG
62FB B7	0100 ORA A	6399 2A 8D 5F	0850 LHLD J

639C CD 30 61	0860 CALL HDCMP	642D B4	1610 ORA H
639F F2 5B 63	0870 JP L1320	642E C8	1620 RZ
63A2 2A 97 5F	0880 L1360 LHLD N	642F E5	1630 PUSH H
63A5 11 F8 5B	0890 LXI D,DST	6430 2A 8D 5F	1640 LHLD J
63A8 19	0900 DAD D	6433 45	1650 MOV B,L
63A9 5E	0910 MOV E,M	6434 4D	1660 MOV C,L
63AB 56	0920 INX H	6435 16 00	1670 MVI D,0
63AC 21 20 20	0930 MOV D,M	6437 CD 58 61	1680 CALL FNG
63AF CD 30 61	0940 LXI H,2020H	643A 2B	1690 DCX H
63B2 C2 E0 63	0950 CALL HDCMP	643B 22 7D 5F	1700 SHLD PT
63B5 2A 89 5F	0960 JNZ L1400	643E E1	1710 POP H
63B8 23	0970 LHLD G	643F 2B	1720 DCX H
63B9 22 89 5F	0980 INX H	6440 2B	1730 DCX H
63BC 29	0990 SHLD G	6441 C3 2C 64	1740 JMP L1521
63BD 11 89 5D	1000 DAD H	6444 4D	1750 L1530 MOV C,L
63C0 19	1010 LXI D,EA	6445 54	1760 MOV D,H
63C1 EB	1020 DAD D	6446 06 21	1770 MVI B,33
63C2 2A 7D 5F	1030 XCHG	6448 CD 58 61	1780 CALL FNG
63C5 23	1040 LHLD PT	644B 06 CD	1790 MVI B,205
63C6 EB	1050 INX H	644D 3E 0F	1800 MVI A,15
63C7 73	1060 XCHG	644F C3 65 61	1810 JMP FNQ
63C8 23	1070 MOV M,E	6452	1820 * JPC
63C9 72	1080 INX H	6452 2A 8F 5F	1830 L1550 LHLD K
63CA 2A 97 5F	1090 MOV M,D	6455 23	1840 INX H
63CD 6C	1100 LHLD N	6456 EB	1850 XCHG
63CE 26 00	1110 MOV L,H	6457 2A 83 5F	1860 LHLD C1
63D0 22 8D 5F	1120 MVI H,0	645A CD 30 61	1870 CALL HDCMP
63D3 65	1130 SHLD J	645D C8	1880 RZ
63D4 CD 6F 69	1140 MOV H,L	645E 06 1A	1890 MVI B,26
63D7 EB	1150 CALL NEGH	6460 0E 1B	1900 MVI C,27
63D8 2A 97 5F	1160 XCHG	6462 51	1910 MOV D,C
63DB 19	1170 LHLD N	6463 CD 58 61	1920 CALL FNG
63DC 22 8B 5F	1180 DAD D	6466 36 1F	1930 MVI M,31
63DF C9	1190 SHLD I	6468 23	1940 INX H
63E0 2A 97 5F	1200 RET	6469 22 7D 5F	1950 SHLD PT
63E3 11 F8 5B	1210 L1400 LHLD N	646C CD 49 63	1960 CALL S1300
63E6 19	1220 LXI D,DST	646F 06 D2	1970 MVI B,210
63E7 5E	1230 DAD D	6471 2A 77 5F	1980 LHLD X
63E8 23	1240 MOV E,M	6474 23	1990 INX H
63E9 6E	1250 INX H	6475 7E	2000 MOV A,M
63EA 26 00	1260 MOV L,M	6476 3D	2010 DCR A
63EC 22 8D 5F	1270 MVI H,0	6477 FA 7C 64	2020 JM $+2
63EF 6B	1280 SHLD J	647A 06 DA	2030 MVI B,218
63F0 22 8B 5F	1290 MOV L,E	647C 3A 8B 5F	2040 LDA I
63F3 C9	1300 SHLD I	647F 4F	2050 MOV C,A
63F4	1310 RET	6480 3A 8D 5F	2060 LDA J
63F4 2A 83 5F	1320 * INT	6483 57	2070 MOV D,A
63F7 7D	1330 L1500 LHLD C1	6484 C3 58 61	2080 JMP FNG
63F8 B4	1340 MOV A,L	6487	2090 * CSP
63F9 C8	1350 ORA H	6487 3A 83 5F	2100 L1600 LDA C1
63FA 29	1360 RZ	648A C6 15	2110 ADI 02
63FB 11 04 00	1370 DAD H	648C 3C	2120 INR A
63FE CD 30 61	1380 LXI D,4 ┐ *	648D F5	2130 PUSH P
6401 CA 10 64	1390 CALL HDCMP	648E 3A 83 5F	2140 LDA C1
6404 EA 10 64	1400 JZ L1515	6491 FE 08	2150 CPI 8
6407 11 FA FF	1410 JM L1515	6493 CA 9E 64	2160 JZ L1620
640A CD 30 61	1420 LXI D,-6	6496 F1	2170 POP P
640D DA 44 64	1430 CALL HDCMP	6497 C6 10	2180 ADI 16
6410 EB	1440 JC L1530 ┘	6499 06 CD	2190 MVI B,205
6411 21 13 00	1450 L1515 XCHG	649B C3 65 61	2200 JMP FNQ
6414 22 8D 5F	1460 LXI H,19	649E 2A 77 5F	2210 L1620 LHLD X
6417 EB	1470 SHLD J	64A1 2B	2220 DCX H
6418 7C	1480 XCHG	64A2 2B	2230 DCX H
6419 B7	1490 MOV A,H	64A3 6E	2240 MOV L,M
641A F2 28 64	1500 ORA A	64A4 26 00	2250 MVI H,0
641D CD 6F 69	1510 JP L1520	64A6 22 8D 5F	2260 SHLD J
6420 EB	1520 CALL NEGH	64A9 CD 6F 69	2270 CALL NEGH
6421 21 1B 00	1530 XCHG	64AC 29	2280 DAD H
6424 22 8D 5F	1540 LXI H,27	64AD 5D	2290 MOV E,L
6427 EB	1550 SHLD J	64AE 54	2300 MOV D,H
6428 7D	1560 XCHG	64AF 29	2310 DAD H
6429 E6 FE	1570 L1520 MOV A,L	64B0 E5	2320 PUSH H
642B 6F	1580 ANI 0FEH	64B1 19	2330 DAD D
642C 7D	1590 MOV L,A	64B2 11 FA FF	2340 LXI D,-6
	1600 L1521 MOV A,L	64B5 19	2350 DAD D

*See author's note page 93

```
64B6 EB          2360 XCHG             6535 E1          3110 POP H
64B7 2A 7D 5F    2370 LHLD PT          6536 21 3E 60    3120 LXI H,PCMSG
64BA 19          2380 DAD D            6539 CD 3D 61    3130 CALL ADDRIN
64BB 22 7D 5F    2390 SHLD PT          653C 22 77 5F    3140 SHLD X
64BE D1          2400 POP D            653F 22 79 5F    3150 SHLD X0
64BF 2A 77 5F    2410 LHLD X           6542 21 58 60    3160 LXI H,DSTMSG
64C2 19          2420 DAD D            6545 CD 3D 61    3170 CALL ADDRIN
64C3 2B          2430 DCX H            6548 22 7F 5F    3180 SHLD P0
64C4 2B          2440 DCX H            654B 22 7D 5F    3190 SHLD PT
64C5 22 7B 5F    2450 SHLD X1          654E 01 D3 AF    3200 LXI B,0AFD3H
64C8 06 0E       2460 MVI B,14         6551 16 04       3210 MVI D,4
64CA 3A 8D 5F    2470 LDA J            6553 CD 58 61    3220 CALL FNG
64CD 4F          2480 MOV C,A          6556 01 00 31    3230 LXI B,3100H
64CE 16 00       2490 MVI D,0          6559 16 10       3240 MVI D,10H
64D0 CD 58 61    2500 CALL FNG         655B CD 58 61    3250 CALL FNG
64D3 2B          2510 DCX H            655E 21 77 60    3260 LXI H,STKMS1
64D4 22 7D 5F    2520 SHLD PT          6561 CD 3D 61    3270 CALL ADDRIN
64D7 F1          2530 POP P            6564 E5          3280 PUSH H
64D8 C6 0E       2540 ADI 14           6565 C2 71 65    3290 JNZ $+9
64DA 06 CD       2550 MVI B,205        6568 EB          3300 XCHG
64DC CD 65 61    2560 CALL FNQ         6569 23          3310 INX H
64DF EB          2570 XCHG             656A 5E          3320 MOV E,M
64E0 3A 8D 5F    2580 LDA J            656B 23          3330 INX H
64E3 4F          2590 MOV C,A          656C 56          3340 MOV D,M
64E4 2A 7B 5F    2600 LHLD X1          656D EB          3350 XCHG
64E7 7E          2610 L1640 MOV A,M    656E C3 77 65    3360 JMP $+6
64E8 12          2620 STAX D           6571 21 92 60    3370 LXI H,STKMS2
64E9 13          2630 INX D            6574 CD 3D 61    3380 CALL ADDRIN
64EA 23          2640 INX H            6577 CD F8 09    3390 CALL CRLF
64EB 23          2650 INX H            657A CD 6F 69    3400 CALL NEGH
64EC 23          2660 INX H            657D 06 11       3410 MVI B,17
64ED 23          2670 INX H            657F 4D          3420 MOV C,L
64EE 0D          2680 DCR C            6580 54          3430 MOV D,H
64EF C2 E7 64    2690 JNZ L1640        6581 2A 7D 5F    3440 LHLD PT
64F2 EB          2700 XCHG             6584 23          3450 INX H
64F3 22 7D 5F    2710 SHLD PT          6585 23          3460 INX H
64F6 C9          2720 RET              6586 23          3470 INX H
64F7            2730 * MAIN PROGRAM    6587 22 7D 5F    3480 SHLD PT
64F7 AF          2740 BEGIN XRA A      658A CD 58 61    3490 CALL FNG
64F8 D3 04       2750 OUT 4            658D 2A 75 5F    3500 LHLD BOST
64FA 21 03 5A    2760 LXI H,TST        6590 06 CD       3510 MVI B,205
64FD 11 9C 05    2770 LXI D,YST-TST    6592 4D          3520 MOV C,L
6500 36 00       2780 ZERO MVI M,0     6593 54          3530 MOV D,H
6502 23          2790 INX H            6594 CD 58 61    3540 CALL FNG
6503 1B          2800 DCX D            6597 E1          3550 POP H
6504 7B          2810 MOV A,E          6598 22 75 5F    3560 SHLD BOST
6505 B2          2820 ORA D            659B            0010 * FIRST PASS
6506 C2 00 65    2830 JNZ ZERO         659B 21 01 00    0020 L400 LXI H,1
6509 21 F7 5F    2840 LXI H,GOMSG      659E 22 9B 5F    0030 SHLD W
650C CD AD 05    2850 CALL OSEQ        65A1 2A 77 5F    0040 LHLD X
650F CD F8 09    2860 CALL CRLF        65A4 7E          0050 L420 MOV A,M
6512 23          2870 INX H            65A5 3C          0060 INR A
6513 CD 3D 61    2880 CALL ADDRIN      65A6 CA D6 65    0070 JZ L470
6516 22 75 5F    2890 SHLD BOST        65A9 23          0080 INX H
6519 E5          2900 PUSH H           65AA 23          0090 INX H
651A 11 1B 5F    2910 LXI D,Y12        65AB 23          0100 INX H
651D 21 9F 5F    2920 LXI H,YST        65AC 23          0110 INX H
6520 3E 2C       2930 MVI A,44         65AD 3D          0120 DCR A
6522 4E          2940 SETL MOV C,M     65AE FE 04       0130 CPI 4
6523 23          2950 INX H            65B0 DA A4 65    0140 JC L420
6524 46          2960 MOV B,M          65B3 FE 05       0150 CPI 5
6525 23          2970 INX H            65B5 CA A4 65    0160 JZ L420
6526 E3          2980 XTHL             65B8 FE 08       0170 CPI 8
6527 E5          2990 PUSH H           65BA D2 A4 65    0180 JNC L420
6528 09          3000 DAD B            65BD E5          0190 PUSH H
6529 EB          3010 XCHG             65BE 2B          0200 DCX H
652A 73          3020 MOV M,E          65BF 46          0210 MOV B,M
652B 23          3030 INX H            65C0 2B          0220 DCX H
652C 72          3040 MOV M,D          65C1 4E          0230 MOV C,M
652D 23          3050 INX H            65C2 2A 9B 5F    0240 LHLD W
652E EB          3060 XCHG             65C5 23          0250 INX H
652F E1          3070 POP H            65C6 23          0260 INX H
6530 E3          3080 XTHL             65C7 22 9B 5F    0270 SHLD W
6531 3D          3090 DCR A            65CA 11 03 5A    0280 LXI D,TST
6532 C2 22 65    3100 JNZ SETL         65CD 19          0290 DAD D
```

```
65CE 2B        0300  DCX  H            6645 C3 49 66   1050  JMP L490
65CF 70        0310  MOV  M,B          6648 E1         1060  L489 POP H
65D0 2B        0320  DCX  H            6649 C1         1070  L490 POP B
65D1 71        0330  MOV  M,C          664A 59         1080  MOV  E,C
65D2 E1        0340  POP  H            664B 50         1090  MOV  D,B
65D3 C3 A4 65  0350  JMP  L420         664C 2A 8B 5F   1100  LHLD I
65D6 22 77 5F  0360  L470 SHLD X       664F CD 30 61   1110  CALL HDCMP
65D9 2A 9B 5F  0370  LHLD W            6652 C2 09 66   1120  JNZ L483
65DC 2B        0380  DCX  H            6655 2A 8D 5F   1130  LHLD J
65DD AF        0390  XRA  A            6658 22 9B 5F   1140  SHLD W
65DE B4        0400  ORA  H            665B 2B         1150  L500 DCX H
65DF 1F        0410  RAR               665C 2B         1160  DCX  H
65E0 57        0420  MOV  D,A          665D 4D         1170  MOV  C,L
65E1 7D        0430  MOV  A,L          665E 44         1180  MOV  B,H
65E2 1F        0440  RAR               665F 21 01 00   1190  LXI  H,1
65E3 5F        0450  MOV  E,A          6662 22 8B 5F   1200  L505 SHLD I
65E4 EB        0460  XCHG              6665 59         1210  MOV  E,C
65E5 CD 13 6B  0470  CALL SYS3+3       6666 50         1220  MOV  D,B
65E8 EB        0480  XCHG              6667 CD 30 61   1230  CALL HDCMP
65E9 2B        0490  DCX  H            666A CA 70 66   1240  JZ  $+3
65EA 22 9B 5F  0500  SHLD W            666D F2 C1 66   1250  JP  L600
65ED EB        0510  XCHG              6670 AF         1260  XRA  A
65EE 21 A9 60  0520  LXI  H,REFMSG     6671 32 73 5F   1270  STA AST
65F1 CD AD 05  0530  CALL OSEQ         6674 EB         1280  XCHG
65F4 CD F8 09  0540  CALL CRLF         6675 22 8D 5F   1290  L515 SHLD J
65F7 EB        0550  XCHG              6678 EB         1300  XCHG
65F8 11 A0 00  0560  LXI  D,160        6679 2A 8B 5F   1310  LHLD I
65FB CD 30 61  0570  CALL HDCMP        667C CD 30 61   1320  CALL HDCMP
65FE DA 5B 66  0580  JC  L500          667F CA 85 66   1330  JZ  $+3
6601          0590  * PRE-COMPRESSION  6682 F2 B2 66   1340  JP  L555
6601 44        0600  MOV  B,H          6685 21 03 5A   1350  LXI  H,TST
6602 4D        0610  MOV  C,L          6688 19         1360  DAD  D
6603 21 05 00  0620  LXI  H,5          6689 5E         1370  MOV  E,M
6606 22 8D 5F  0630  SHLD J            668A 23         1380  INX  H
6609 23        0640  L483 INX H        668B 56         1390  MOV  D,M
660A 23        0650  INX  H            668C 23         1400  INX  H
660B 22 8B 5F  0660  SHLD I            668D 7E         1410  MOV  A,M
660E C5        0670  PUSH B            668E 23         1420  INX  H
660F 0E 03     0680  MVI  C,3          668F E5         1430  PUSH H
6611 2A 8D 5F  0690  LHLD J            6690 66         1440  MOV  H,M
6614 2B        0700  DCX  H            6691 6F         1450  MOV  L,A
6615 2B        0710  DCX  H            6692 EB         1460  XCHG
6616 2B        0720  DCX  H            6693 CD 30 61   1470  CALL HDCMP
6617 2B        0730  DCX  H            6696 DA A9 66   1480  JC  L550
6618 E5        0740  L486 PUSH H       6699 EB         1490  XCHG
6619 2A 8B 5F  0750  LHLD I            669A E3         1500  XTHL
661C 11 03 5A  0760  LXI  D,TST        669B 72         1510  MOV  M,D
661F 19        0770  DAD  D            669C 2B         1520  DCX  H
6620 7E        0780  MOV  A,M          669D 73         1530  MOV  M,E
6621 23        0790  INX  H            669E D1         1540  POP  D
6622 66        0800  MOV  H,M          669F 2B         1550  DCX  H
6623 6F        0810  MOV  L,A          66A0 72         1560  MOV  M,D
6624 E3        0820  XTHL              66A1 2B         1570  DCX  H
6625 EB        0830  XCHG              66A2 73         1580  MOV  M,E
6626 19        0840  DAD  D            66A3 3E FF      1590  MVI  A,-1
6627 7E        0850  MOV  A,M          66A5 32 73 5F   1600  STA AST
6628 23        0860  INX  H            66A8 E5         1610  PUSH H
6629 66        0870  MOV  H,M          66A9 E1         1620  L550 POP H
662A 6F        0880  MOV  L,A          66AA 2A 8D 5F   1630  LHLD J
662B EB        0890  XCHG              66AD 2B         1640  DCX  H
662C E3        0900  XTHL              66AE 2B         1650  DCX  H
662D CD 30 61  0910  CALL HDCMP        66AF C3 75 66   1660  JMP L515
6630 CA 48 66  0920  JZ  L489          66B2 3A 73 5F   1670  L555 LDA AST
6633 EB        0930  XCHG              66B5 B7         1680  ORA  A
6634 E1        0940  POP  H            66B6 CA C1 66   1690  JZ  L600
6635 23        0950  INX  H            66B9 2A 8B 5F   1700  LHLD I
6636 23        0960  INX  H            66BC 23         1710  INX  H
6637 0D        0970  DCR  C            66BD 23         1720  INX  H
6638 C2 18 66  0980  JNZ L486          66BE C3 62 66   1730  JMP L505
663B 22 8D 5F  0990  SHLD J            66C1 21 01 00   1740  L600 LXI H,1
663E 01 03 5A  1000  LXI  B,TST        66C4 22 8D 5F   1750  SHLD J
6641 09        1010  DAD  B            66C7 21 03 00   1760  LXI  H,3
6642 73        1020  MOV  M,E          66CA 22 8B 5F   1770  L605 SHLD I
6643 23        1030  INX  H            66CD EB         1780  XCHG
6644 72        1040  MOV  M,D          66CE 2A 9B 5F   1790  LHLD W
```

```
66D1 CD 30 61   1800      CALL HDCMP
66D4 FA 0A 67   1810      JM L635
66D7 21 03 5A   1820      LXI H,TST
66DA 19         1830      DAD D
66DB 5E         1840      MOV E,M
66DC 23         1850      INX H
66DD 56         1860      MOV D,M
66DE 23         1870      INX H
66DF D5         1880      PUSH D
66E0 2A 8D 5F   1890      LHLD J
66E3 11 03 5A   1900      LXI D,TST
66E6 19         1910      DAD D
66E7 5E         1920      MOV E,M
66E8 23         1930      INX H
66E9 56         1940      MOV D,M
66EA E1         1950      POP H
66EB CD 30 61   1960      CALL HDCMP
66EE CA 02 67   1970      JZ L630
66F1 E5         1980      PUSH H
66F2 2A 8D 5F   1990      LHLD J
66F5 23         2000      INX H
66F6 23         2010      INX H
66F7 22 8D 5F   2020      SHLD J
66FA 11 03 5A   2030      LXI D,TST
66FD 19         2040      DAD D
66FE D1         2050      POP D
66FF 73         2060      MOV M,E
6700 23         2070      INX H
6701 72         2080      MOV M,D
6702 2A 8B 5F   2090  L630 LHLD I
6705 23         2100      INX H
6706 23         2110      INX H
6707 C3 CA 66   2120      JMP L605
670A 2A 8D 5F   2130  L635 LHLD J
670D 22 9D 5F   2140      SHLD WO
6710 23         2150      INX H ┐ *
6711 23         2160      INX H │
6712 36 FF      2170      MVI M,-1
6714 23         2180      INX H │
6715 36 FF      2190      MVI M,-1
6717 2A 8D 5F   2200      LHLD J ┘
671A 29         2210      DAD H
671B EB         2220      XCHG
671C 21 F9 5B   2230      LXI H,DST+1
671F 36 20      2240  L670 MVI M,'
6721 23         2250      INX H
6722 1B         2260      DCX D
6723 7B         2270      MOV A,E
6724 B2         2280      ORA D
6725 C2 1F 67   2290      JNZ L670
6728 2A 8D 5F   2300      LHLD J
672B 23         2310      INX H
672C AF         2320      XRA A
672D B4         2330      ORA H
672E 1F         2340      RAR
672F 67         2350      MOV H,A
6730 7D         2360      MOV A,L
6731 1F         2370      RAR
6732 6F         2380      MOV L,A
6733 CD 13 6B   2390      CALL SYS3+3
6736 21 B5 60   2400      LXI H,LABMSG
6739 CD AD 05   2410      CALL OSEQ
673C CD F8 09   2420      CALL CROUT
673F            2430      * PASS 1 ENDS
673F 2A 79 5F   2440      LHLD X0
6742 2B         2450      DCX H
6743 2B         2460      DCX H
6744 2B         2470      DCX H
6745 2B         2480      DCX H
6746 22 77 5F   2490      SHLD X
6749 21 FF FF   2500      LXI H,-1
674C 22 8F 5F   2510      SHLD K
674F 23         2520      INX H
6750 22 89 5F   2530      SHLD G
6753 22 91 5F   2540      SHLD K1

6756 22 95 5F   2550      SHLD L1
6759 23         2560      INX H
675A 22 9B 5F   2570      SHLD W
675D 21 03 5A   2580      LXI H,TST
6760 23         2590      INX H
6761 6E         2600      MOV L,M
6762 26 00      2610      MVI H,0
6764 22 99 5F   2620      SHLD U
6767 3E 14      2630      MVI A,20
6769 32 88 5F   2640      STA ML
676C 21 6C 67   2650  L710 LXI H,L710
676F E5         2660      PUSH H
6770 2A 77 5F   2670      LHLD X
6773 23         2680      INX H
6774 23         2690      INX H
6775 23         2700      INX H
6776 23         2710      INX H
6777 22 77 5F   2720      SHLD X
677A 2A 8F 5F   2730      LHLD K
677D 23         2740      INX H
677E 22 8F 5F   2750      SHLD K
6781 AF         2760      XRA A
6782 32 86 5F   2770      STA R0
6785 2A 7D 5F   2780      LHLD PT
6788 3A 88 5F   2790      LDA ML
678B 3C         2800      INR A
678C FE 14      2810      CPI 20
678E DA CF 67   2820      JC L715
6791 CD F8 09   2830      CALL CRLF
6794 EB         2840      XCHG
6795 2A 8F 5F   2850      LHLD K
6798 EB         2860      XCHG
6799 E5         2870      PUSH H
679A 21 E7 03   2880      LXI H,999
679D CD 30 61   2890      CALL HDCMP
67A0 DA BE 67   2900      JC CSYS
67A3 CD 02 0A   2910      CALL BLK1
67A6 21 63 00   2920      LXI H,99
67A9 CD 30 61   2930      CALL HDCMP
67AC DA BE 67   2940      JC CSYS
67AF CD 02 0A   2950      CALL BLK1
67B2 21 09 00   2960      LXI H,9
67B5 CD 30 61   2970      CALL HDCMP
67B8 DA BE 67   2980      JC CSYS
67BB CD 02 0A   2990      CALL BLK1
67BE E1         3000  CSYS POP H
67BF EB         3010      XCHG
67C0 CD 13 6B   3020      CALL SYS3+3
67C3 EB         3030      XCHG
67C4 CD 02 0A   3040      CALL BLK1
67C7 CD 02 0A   3050      CALL BLK1
67CA 7C         3060      MOV A,H
67CB CD 11 0A   3070      CALL BYTE1
67CE AF         3080      XRA A
67CF 32 88 5F   3090  L715 STA ML
67D2 7D         3100      MOV A,L
67D3 CD 11 0A   3110      CALL BYTE1
67D6 CD 02 0A   3120      CALL BLK1
67D9 2A 77 5F   3130      LHLD X
67DC 7E         3140      MOV A,M
67DD 32 85 5F   3150      STA F
67E0 23         3160      INX H
67E1 23         3170      INX H
67E2 7E         3180      MOV A,M
67E3 32 83 5F   3190      STA C1
67E6 23         3200      INX H
67E7 7E         3210      MOV A,M
67E8 32 84 5F   3220      STA C2
67EB 2A 99 5F   3230      LHLD U
67EE EB         3240      XCHG
67EF 2A 8F 5F   3250      LHLD K
67F2 CD 30 61   3260      CALL HDCMP
67F5 C2 20 68   3270      JNZ L765
67F8 2A 9B 5F   3280      LHLD W
67FB 23         3290      INX H
```

*See author's note page 93

```
67FC 23              3300     INX H
67FD 22 9B 5F        3310     SHLD W
6800 11 F8 5B        3320     LXI D,DST
6803 19              3330     DAD D
6804 EB              3340     XCHG
6805 2A 7D 5F        3350     LHLD PT
6808 EB              3360     XCHG
6809 2B              3370     DCX H
680A 72              3380     MOV M,D
680B 2B              3390     DCX H
680C 73              3400     MOV M,E
680D 3E 01           3410     MVI A,1
680F 32 86 5F        3420     STA R0
6812 2A 9B 5F        3430     LHLD W
6815 11 03 5A        3440     LXI D,TST
6818 19              3450     DAD D
6819 5E              3460     MOV E,M
681A 23              3470     INX H
681B 56              3480     MOV D,M
681C EB              3490     XCHG
681D 22 99 5F        3500     SHLD U
6820 AF              3510 L765 XRA A
6821 32 87 5F        3520     STA V
6824 3A 85 5F        3530     LDA F
6827 FE 09           3540     CPI 9
6829 DA 35 68        3550     JC L780
682C D6 10           3560     SUI 16
682E 32 85 5F        3570     STA F
6831 21 87 5F        3580     LXI H,V
6834 34              3590     INR M
6835 B7              3600 L780 ORA A
6836 CA 76 61        3610     JZ L800
6839 3D              3620     DCR A
683A CA A3 61        3630     JZ L850
683D 3D              3640     DCR A
683E CA 1B 62        3650     JZ L900
6841 3D              3660     DCR A
6842 CA EB 62        3670     JZ L1100
6845 3D              3680     DCR A
6846 CA F3 62        3690     JZ L1200
6849 3D              3700     DCR A
684A CA F4 63        3710     JZ L1500
684D 3D              3720     DCR A
684E CA 2D 63        3730     JZ L1250
6851 3D              3740     DCR A
6852 CA 52 64        3750     JZ L1550
6855 3D              3760     DCR A
6856 CA 87 64        3770     JZ L1600
6859                 0010 * FORWARD REFERENCE CORRECTION
6859 E1              0020 L1700 POP H
685A CD F8 09        0030     CALL CRLF
685D 2A 89 5F        0040     LHLD G
6860 5D              0050     MOV E,L
6861 54              0060     MOV D,H
6862 CD 13 6B        0070     CALL SYS3+3
6865 21 C7 60        0080     LXI H,FWDMSG
6868 CD AD 05        0090     CALL OSEQ
686B CD F8 09        0100     CALL CRLF
686E 2A 7D 5F        0110     LHLD PT
6871 22 81 5F        0120     SHLD P1
6874 21 89 5D        0130     LXI H,EA
6877 E5              0140     PUSH H
6878 19              0150     DAD D
6879 19              0160     DAD D
687A 23              0170     INX H
687B 23              0180     INX H
687C EB              0190     XCHG
687D E1              0200     POP H
687E 23              0210 L1780 INX H
687F 23              0220     INX H
6880 CD 30 61        0230     CALL HDCMP
6883 D2 A1 68        0240     JNC L1850
6886 E5              0250     PUSH H
6887 D5              0260     PUSH D
6888 5E              0270     MOV E,M
```

```
6889 23              0280    INX  H
688A 56              0290    MOV  D,M
688B EB              0300    XCHG
688C E5              0310    PUSH H
688D 5E              0320    MOV  E,M
688E 23              0330    INX  H
688F 56              0340    MOV  D,M
6890 EB              0350    XCHG
6891 11 F8 5B        0360    LXI  D,DST
6894 19              0370    DAD  D
6895 5E              0380    MOV  E,M
6896 23              0390    INX  H
6897 56              0400    MOV  D,M
6898 E1              0410    POP  H
6899 73              0420    MOV  M,E
689A 23              0430    INX  H
689B 72              0440    MOV  M,D
689C D1              0450    POP  D
689D E1              0460    POP  H
689E C3 7E 68        0470    JMP  L1780
68A1 2A 75 5F        0480 L1850 LHLD BOST
68A4 7C              0490    MOV  A,H
68A5 B5              0500    ORA  L
68A6 C2 AC 68        0510    JNZ  $+3
68A9 2A 81 5F        0520    LHLD P1
68AC 4D              0530    MOV  C,L
68AD 54              0540    MOV  D,H
68AE 06 21           0550    MVI  B,33
68B0 2A 7F 5F        0560    LHLD P0
68B3 23              0570    INX  H
68B4 23              0580    INX  H
68B5 23              0590    INX  H
68B6 23              0600    INX  H
68B7 23              0610    INX  H
68B8 23              0620    INX  H
68B9 22 7D 5F        0630    SHLD PT
68BC CD 58 61        0640    CALL FNG
68BF CD F8 09        0650    CALL CRLF
68C2 2A 8F 5F        0660    LHLD K
68C5 5D              0670    MOV  E,L
68C6 54              0680    MOV  D,H
68C7 CD 13 6B        0690    CALL SYS3+3
68CA 21 DB 60        0700    LXI  H,FINMSG
68CD CD AD 05        0710    CALL OSEQ
68D0 23              0720    INX  H
68D1 EB              0730    XCHG
68D2 29              0740    DAD  H
68D3 29              0750    DAD  H
68D4 EB              0760    XCHG
68D5 CD 0C 0A        0770    CALL DEOUT1
68D8 CD AD 05        0780    CALL OSEQ
68DB CD F8 09        0790    CALL CRLF
68DE 23              0800    INX  H
68DF E5              0810    PUSH H
68E0 2A 7F 5F        0820    LHLD P0
68E3 CD 6F 69        0830    CALL NEGH
68E6 EB              0840    XCHG
68E7 2A 81 5F        0850    LHLD P1
68EA EB              0860    XCHG
68EB 19              0870    DAD  D
68EC EB              0880    XCHG
68ED CD 0C 0A        0890    CALL DEOUT1
68F0 E3              0900    XTHL
68F1 CD AD 05        0910    CALL OSEQ
68F4 D1              0920    POP  D
68F5 CD 0C 0A        0930    CALL DEOUT1
68F8 CD F8 09        0940    CALL CRLF
68FB C3 46 69        0950    JMP  EXIT
68FE                 0960 LSTBYT EQU $-1
```

Symbol	Addr	Symbol	Addr	Symbol	Addr	Symbol	Addr
ORGA	6900	RUN	6900	WHO	0C20	INP	0C20
WH1	0C24	OUTP	0C24	CRLF	09F8	CROUT	09F8
OSEQ	05AD	BYTE1	0A11	DEOUT1	0A0C	BLK1	0A02
CLEAR	09FD	POS	0C0E	POS1	727F	MENTR	7390
ABUF	6903	SFLG	690A	SIGN	690A	STK2	690B
BB	690D	SM1	690F	SM2	6915	MER1	691F
MER2	692C	DM1	6938	EXIT	6946	PRINT	6952
POP	6958	PUSH	6962	POP1	6968	NEGH	696F
OVFL	6979	NEGB	6982	CMD	698F	GETC	6997
READ	699E	RLP	69A3	RUB	69D4	CAN	69E3
DIGIT	69F2	DECIN	69F9	DECIL	6A17	DECID	6A31
ER1	6A41	ER2	6A47	HEXIN	6A50	HEXIL	6A6E
HEX16	6A82	HEXID	6A8F	HER1	6A9F	DVCK	6AA8
DIV16	6AB4	D2	6ACB	D3	6AD3	D4	6AE2
D4A	6AE7	SYS0	6AF7	SYS1	6B00	SYS2	6B06
SYS3	6B10	Y3	6B23	WR	6B33	SYS4	6B3C
SYS5	6B46	SYS8	6B52	BASE	6B5D	BS1	6B5E
LIT	6B6C	INT	6B73	STKOV	6B7A	LOD1	6B84
LOD	6B8D	LODX	6B9A	LODX1	6B9B	STO1	6BAC
STO	6BB5	STOX	6BC1	STOX1	6BC2	CAL1	6BDE
CAL	6BE9	LODA	6C0E	STOA	6C19	CALA	6C21
P00	6C25	SUB1	6C3E	ADD16	6C41	SU2	6C42
P02	6C4E	P03	6C54	SUB16	6C57	P01	6C62
MUL8	6C6E	P04	6C7B	P05	6C90	P06	6C9B
P07	6CA4	P08	6CB0	EQUAL	6CB2	TRUE	6CC3
P09	6CC6	P11	6CCA	LESS	6CCD	FALSE	6CDF
EQH	6CE4	P10	6CF3	P12	6CF9	P13	6CFF
P14	6D04	P15	6D0F	P16	6D1A	P17	6D23
SL1	6D2E	P18	6D36	SR1	6D42	P19	6D50
P20	6D5A	P21	6D64	INIT	6D6F	RUNEND	6D8F
ORGA2	5A00	TRANS	5A00	02	0015	S1	01F4
S2	0190	PCDEF	2C00	OBDEF	1000	STK1	0000
STAK2	68FF	TST	5A03	DST	5BF8	EA	5D89
Y12	5F1B	Z12	5F39	AST	5F73	BOST	5F75
X	5F77	X0	5F79	X1	5F7B	PT	5F7D
P0	5F7F	P1	5F81	C1	5F83	C2	5F84
F	5F85	R0	5F86	V	5F87	ML	5F88
G	5F89	I	5F8B	J	5F8D	K	5F8F
K1	5F91	L0	5F93	L1	5F95	N	5F97
U	5F99	W	5F9B	W0	5F9D	YST	5F9F
ZST	5FBD	GOMSG	5FF7	PCMSG	603E	DSTMSG	6058
STKMS1	6077	STKMS2	6092	REFMSG	60A9	LABMSG	60B5
FWDMSG	60C7	FINMSG	60DB	HDCMP	6130	ADDRIN	613D
FNG	6158	FNQ	6165	L800	6176	L830	618E
L850	61A3	L870	61DD	L885	6209	L890	620F
L900	621B	L925	6220	L920	6296	L930	629D
L960	62C8	L1040	62DF	L1100	62EB	L1200	62F3
L1225	6309	L1230	6314	L1250	632D	L1260	6339
S1300	6349	L1330	635B	L1350	6395	L1360	63A2
L1400	63E0	L1500	63F4	L1515	6410	L1520	6428
L1521	642C	L1530	6444	L1550	6452	L1600	6487
L1620	649E	L1640	64E7	BEGIN	64F7	ZERO	6500
SETL	6522	L400	659B	L420	65A4	L470	65D6
L483	6609	L486	6618	L489	6648	L490	6649
L500	665B	L505	6662	L515	6675	L550	66A9
L555	66B2	L600	66C1	L605	66CA	L630	6702
L635	670A	L670	671F	L710	676C	CSYS	67BE
L715	67CF	L765	6820	L780	6835	L1700	6859
L1780	687E	L1850	68A1	LSTBYT	68FD		

251

Listing 4: P-Code Interpreter

```
5000                    0010 *P-CODE INTERPRETER
5000                    0020 * 1979-I-23
5000                    0030 ORGA EQU 5000H
5000                    0040  ORG ORGA
5000 C3 D1 5C           0050 COLDST JMP ORGA+OCD1H
5003 C3 62 5E           0060 WARMST JMP ORGA+OE62H
5006                    0070 U EQU 13
5006                    0080 WHO EQU OC20H
5006                    0090 WH1 EQU OC24H
5006                    0100 BLK1 EQU OA02H
5006                    0110 DEOUT1 EQU OAOCH
5006                    0120 OSEQ EQU 05ADH
5006                    0130 BPLIM EQU 5
5006                    0140 SIZE EQU 500
5006                    0150 SIZE1 EQU 480
5006                    0160 Z DS 2
5008                    0170 IP DS 2
500A                    0180 BASED DS 2
500C                    0190 T DS 2
500E                    0200 BP DS 2
5010                    0210 PO DS 2
5012                    0220 TP DS 2
5014                    0230 CMND DS 2
5016                    0240 I DS 2
5018                    0250 J DS 2
501A                    0260 K DS 2
501C                    0270 STOP DS 2
501E                    0280 N DS 2
5020                    0290 S DS SIZE+SIZE+2
540A                    0300 TRACE DS U+U+2
5426                    0310 MN DS 54
545C                    0320 BREAK DS BPLIM+BPLIM+2
5468                    0330 B1 DS 2
546A                    0340 X DS 2
546C                    0350 EA DS 2
546E                    0360 EL DS 2
5470                    0370 F DS 2
5472                    0380 IDX DS 2
5474                    0390 RES DS 2
5476                    0400 SFLG DS 1
5477                    0410 ABUF DS 7
547E 49 4C 4C 45        0420 ILLOPC DB 'ILLEGAL OPCODE'
548C OD                 0430  DB ODH
548D 49 4C 4C 45        0440 ILLOPR DB 'ILLEGAL OPERAND'
549C OD                 0450  DB ODH
549D 53  4 41 43        0460 STOVFL DB 'STACK OVERFLOW'
54AB OD                 0470  DB ODH
54AC 49 4C 4C 45        0480 ILLCSP DB 'ILLEGAL CSP'
54B7 OD                 0490  DB ODH
54B8 20 42 52 45        0500 BREAKM DB ' BREAK:'
54BF OD                 0510  DB ODH
54C0 53 54 41 52        0520 ADDRM DB 'START ADDRESS? '
54CF OD                 0530  DB ODH
54D0 20 20 50 20        0540 XMSG DB '  P ='
54D5 OD                 0550  DB ODH
54D6 20 42 20 3D        0560  DB ' B ='
54DA OD                 0570  DB ODH
54DB 20 54 20 3D        0580  DB ' T ='
54DF OD                 0590  DB ODH
54E0 20 53 5B 54        0600  DB ' S[T] ='
54E7 OD                 0610  DB ODH
54E8 20 53 5B 54        0620  DB ' S[T-1] ='
54F1 OD                 0630  DB ODH
```

```
54F2 20 2A 20 54    0640 TRCMSG DB ' * TRACE *'
54FC 0D             0650    DB 0DH
54FD 45 4E 44 20    0660 FINMSG DB 'END OF EXECUTION'
550D 0D             0670    DB 0DH
550E 4C 49 54 4F    0680 MNEM DB 'LITOPRLODSTOCALINTJMPJPCCSP'
5529 2A 0C 50       0690 TM1 LHLD T
552C 2B             0700    DCX H
552D 22 0C 50       0710    SHLD T
5530 C9             0720    RET
5531 2A 0C 50       0730 STGET LHLD T
5534 EB             0740    XCHG
5535 21 20 50       0750    LXI H,S
5538 E5             0760 ARRAY PUSH H
5539 6B             0770    MOV L,E
553A 62             0780    MOV H,D
553B 19             0790    DAD D
553C EB             0800    XCHG
553D E1             0810    POP H
553E 19             0820    DAD D
553F 5E             0830    MOV E,M
5540 23             0840    INX H
5541 56             0850    MOV D,M
5542 2B             0860    DCX H
5543 C9             0870    RET
5544 7B             0880 CMD MOV A,E
5545 2F             0890    CMA
5546 C6 01          0900    ADI 1
5548 5F             0910    MOV E,A
5549 7A             0920    MOV A,D
554A 2F             0930    CMA
554B CE 00          0940    ACI 0
554D 57             0950    MOV D,A
554E C9             0960    RET
554F C5             0970 SHL PUSH B
5550 4F             0980    MOV C,A
5551 29             0990 SH1 DAD H
5552 0D             1000    DCR C
5553 C2 51 55       1010    JNZ SH1
5556 C1             1020    POP B
5557 C9             1030    RET
5558 78             1040 BHCMP MOV A,B
5559 BC             1050    CMP H
555A C0             1060    RNZ
555B 79             1070    MOV A,C
555C 95             1080    SUB L
555D C8             1090    RZ
555E 1F             1100    RAR
555F B7             1110    ORA A
5560 17             1120    RAL
5561 F8             1130    RM
5562 AF             1140    XRA A
5563 3C             1150    INR A
5564 C9             1160    RET
5565 CD 31 55       1170 COMP CALL STGET
5568 42             1180    MOV B,D
5569 4B             1190    MOV C,E
556A CD 29 55       1200    CALL TM1
556D CD 31 55       1210    CALL STGET
5570 EB             1220    XCHG
5571 CD 58 55       1230    CALL BHCMP
5574 EB             1240    XCHG
5575 11 00 00       1250    LXI D,0
5578 C9             1260    RET
5579 21 77 54       1270 READ LXI H,ABUF
557C 0E 00          1280    MVI C,0
557E CD 20 0C       1290 RLP CALL WH0
5581 FE 7F          1300    CPI 7FH
5583 CA AF 55       1310    JZ RUB
5586 FE 18          1320    CPI 18H
5588 CA BE 55       1330    JZ CAN
558B FE 0D          1340    CPI 0DH
558D CA 93 55       1350    JZ $+3
5590 CD 24 0C       1360    CALL WH1
5593 77             1370    MOV M,A
5594 23             1380    INX H
```

```
5595 0C          1390       INR  C
5596 FE 0D       1400       CPI  0DH
5598 C8          1410       RZ
5599 79          1420       MOV  A,C
559A FE 06       1430       CPI  6
559C C2 7E 55    1440       JNZ  RLP
559F CD 20 0C    1450       CALL WH0
55A2 FE 7F       1460       CPI  7FH
55A4 CA AF 55    1470       JZ   RUB
55A7 FE 18       1480       CPI  18H
55A9 CA BE 55    1490       JZ   CAN
55AC 36 0D       1500       MVI  M,0DH
55AE C9          1510       RET
55AF 79          1520  RUB  MOV  A,C
55B0 B7          1530       ORA  A
55B1 CA 7E 55    1540       JZ   RLP
55B4 3E 7F       1550       MVI  A,7FH
55B6 CD 24 0C    1560       CALL WH1
55B9 0D          1570       DCR  C
55BA 2B          1580       DCX  H
55BB C3 7E 55    1590       JMP  RLP
55BE 79          1600  CAN  MOV  A,C
55BF B7          1610       ORA  A
55C0 CA 7E 55    1620       JZ   RLP
55C3 3E 7F       1630       MVI  A,7FH
55C5 CD 24 0C    1640       CALL WH1
55C8 2B          1650       DCX  H
55C9 0D          1660       DCR  C
55CA C3 BE 55    1670       JMP  CAN
55CD D6 30       1680  DIGIT SUI 30H
55CF D8          1690       RC
55D0 FE 0A       1700       CPI  0AH
55D2 3F          1710       CMC
55D3 C9          1720       RET
55D4 AF          1730  DECIN XRA A
55D5 32 76 54    1740       STA  SFLG
55D8 E5          1750       PUSH H
55D9 C5          1760       PUSH B
55DA 3E 23       1770       MVI  A,'#'
55DC CD 24 0C    1780       CALL WH1
55DF CD 79 55    1790       CALL READ
55E2 21 00 00    1800       LXI  H,0
55E5 01 77 54    1810       LXI  B,ABUF
55E8 0A          1820       LDAX B
55E9 03          1830       INX  B
55EA FE 2D       1840       CPI  '-'
55EC C2 F4 55    1850       JNZ  DECIL+2
55EF 32 76 54    1860       STA  SFLG
55F2 0A          1870  DECIL LDAX B
55F3 03          1880       INX  B
55F4 CD CD 55    1890       CALL DIGIT
55F7 DA 09 56    1900       JC   DECID
55FA 5D          1910       MOV  E,L
55FB 54          1920       MOV  D,H
55FC 29          1930       DAD  H
55FD 29          1940       DAD  H
55FE 19          1950       DAD  D
55FF 29          1960       DAD  H
5600 85          1970       ADD  L
5601 6F          1980       MOV  L,A
5602 D2 F2 55    1990       JNC  DECIL
5605 24          2000       INR  H
5606 C3 F2 55    2010       JMP  DECIL
5609 EB          2020  DECID XCHG
560A C1          2030       POP  B
560B E1          2040       POP  H
560C 3A 76 54    2050       LDA  SFLG
560F B7          2060       ORA  A
5610 C8          2070       RZ
5611 C3 44 55    2080       JMP  CMD
5614 AF          2090  HEXIN XRA A
5615 32 76 54    2100       STA  SFLG
5618 E5          2110       PUSH H
5619 C5          2120       PUSH B
561A 3E 25       2130       MVI  A,'%'

561C CD 24 0C    2140       CALL WH1
561F CD 79 55    2150       CALL READ
5622 21 00 00    2160       LXI  H,0
5625 01 77 54    2170       LXI  B,ABUF
5628 0A          2180       LDAX B
5629 03          2190       INX  B
562A FE 2D       2200       CPI  '-'
562C C2 34 56    2210       JNZ  HEXIL+2
562F 32 76 54    2220       STA  SFLG
5632 0A          2230  HEXIL LDAX B
5633 03          2240       INX  B
5634 CD CD 55    2250       CALL DIGIT
5637 D2 46 56    2260       JNC  HEX16
563A D6 07       2270       SUI  7
563C FE 0A       2280       CPI  0AH
563E DA 53 56    2290       JC   HEXID
5641 FE 10       2300       CPI  10H
5643 D2 53 56    2310       JNC  HEXID
5646 29          2320  HEX16 DAD H
5647 29          2330       DAD  H
5648 29          2340       DAD  H
5649 29          2350       DAD  H
564A 85          2360       ADD  L
564B 6F          2370       MOV  L,A
564C D2 32 56    2380       JNC  HEXIL
564F 24          2390       INR  H
5650 C3 32 56    2400       JMP  HEXIL
5653 EB          2410  HEXID XCHG
5654 C1          2420       POP  B
5655 E1          2430       POP  H
5656 3A 76 54    2440       LDA  SFLG
5659 B7          2450       ORA  A
565A C8          2460       RZ
565B C3 44 55    2470       JMP  CMD
565E 06 00       2480  DCALC MVI B,0
5660 19          2490       DAD  D
5661 04          2500       INR  B
5662 7C          2510       MOV  A,H
5663 B7          2520       ORA  A
5664 F2 60 56    2530       JP   $-7
5667 CD 44 55    2540       CALL CMD
566A 19          2550       DAD  D
566B 05          2560       DCR  B
566C 78          2570       MOV  A,B
566D B9          2580       CMP  C
566E C8          2590       RZ
566F 0D          2600       DCR  C
5670 C6 30       2610       ADI  30H
5672 C9          2620       RET
5673 7A          2630  DECOUT MOV A,D
5674 B7          2640       ORA  A
5675 F2 80 56    2650       JP   CDEC
5678 3E 2D       2660       MVI  A,'-'
567A CD 24 0C    2670       CALL WH1
567D CD 44 55    2680       CALL CMD
5680 E5          2690  CDEC  PUSH H
5681 21 77 54    2700       LXI  H,ABUF
5684 E5          2710       PUSH H
5685 EB          2720       XCHG
5686 11 F0 D8    2730       LXI  D,-10000
5689 0E 00       2740       MVI  C,0
568B CD 5E 56    2750       CALL DCALC
568E CA 95 56    2760       JZ   $+4
5691 E3          2770       XTHL
5692 77          2780       MOV  M,A
5693 23          2790       INX  H
5694 E3          2800       XTHL
5695 11 18 FC    2810       LXI  D,-1000
5698 CD 5E 56    2820       CALL DCALC
569B CA A2 56    2830       JZ   $+4
569E E3          2840       XTHL
569F 77          2850       MOV  M,A
56A0 23          2860       INX  H
56A1 E3          2870       XTHL
56A2 11 9C FF    2880       LXI  D,-100
```

```
56A5 CD 5E 56      2890      CALL DCALC
56A8 CA AF 56      2900      JZ $+4
56AB E3            2910      XTHL
56AC 77            2920      MOV M,A
56AD 23            2930      INX H
56AE E3            2940      XTHL
56AF 11 F6 FF      2950      LXI D,-10
56B2 CD 5E 56      2960      CALL DCALC
56B5 CA BC 56      2970      JZ $+4
56B8 E3            2980      XTHL
56B9 77            2990      MOV M,A
56BA 23            3000      INX H
56BB E3            3010      XTHL
56BC 7D            3020      MOV A,L
56BD E1            3030      POP H
56BE C6 30         3040      ADI 30H
56C0 77            3050      MOV M,A
56C1 23            3060      INX H
56C2 36 0D         3070      MVI M,0DH
56C4 21 77 54      3080      LXI H,ABUF
56C7 CD AD 05      3090      CALL OSEQ
56CA E1            3100      POP H
56CB C9            3110      RET
56CC               3120      HEXOUT EQU DEOUT1

56CC 2A 0A 50      0010      BASE LHLD BASEB
56CF 22 68 54      0020      SHLD B1
56D2 7B            0030      BA1 MOV A,E
56D3 B2            0040      ORA D
56D4 CA EE 56      0050      JZ BA2
56D7 D5            0060      PUSH D
56D8 2A 68 54      0070      LHLD B1
56DB 2B            0080      DCX H
56DC 2B            0090      DCX H
56DD 2B            0100      DCX H
56DE EB            0110      XCHG
56DF 21 20 50      0120      LXI H,S
56E2 CD 38 55      0130      CALL ARRAY
56E5 EB            0140      XCHG
56E6 22 68 54      0150      SHLD B1
56E9 D1            0160      POP D
56EA 1B            0170      DCX D
56EB C3 D2 56      0180      JMP BA1
56EE 2A 68 54      0190      BA2 LHLD B1
56F1 EB            0200      XCHG
56F2 C9            0210      RET
56F3 21 00 00      0220      INIT LXI H,0
56F6 22 08 50      0230      SHLD IP
56F9 22 1C 50      0240      SHLD STOP
56FC 22 10 50      0250      SHLD P0
56FF 22 1A 50      0260      SHLD K
5702 22 22 50      0270      SHLD S+2
5705 22 24 50      0280      SHLD S+4
5708 2B            0290      DCX H
5709 22 26 50      0300      SHLD S+6
570C 21 03 00      0310      LXI H,3
570F 22 0C 50      0320      SHLD T
5712 2C            0330      INR L
5713 22 0A 50      0340      SHLD BASEB
5716 21 0D 00      0350      LXI H,U
5719 22 12 50      0360      SHLD TP
571C 29            0370      DAD H
571D EB            0380      XCHG
571E 21 0A 54      0390      LXI H,TRACE
5721 36 FF         0400      INI1 MVI M,-1
5723 23            0410      INX H
5724 1B            0420      DCX D
5725 7B            0430      MOV A,E
5726 B2            0440      ORA D
5727 C2 21 57      0450      JNZ INI1
572A C9            0460      RET
572B               0470      CRLF EQU 09F8H
572B               0480      *CODE FOR CASES OF EA IN CASF1
572B 2A 0A 50      0490      EA1C0 LHLD BASEB
572E 2B            0500      DCX H
```

255

572F 2B	0510 DCX H	57B6 EB	1260 XCHG
5730 2B	0520 DCX H	57B7 29	1270 DAD H
5731 2B	0530 DCX H	57B8 EB	1280 XCHG
5732 22 0C 50	0540 SHLD T	57B9 0D	1290 DCR C
5735 23	0550 INX H	57BA C2 B1 57	1300 JNZ X8BL
5736 23	0560 INX H	57BD C9	1310 RET
5737 EB	0570 XCHG	57BE CD 31 55	1320 EA1C5 CALL STGET
5738 21 20 50	0580 LXI H,S	57C1 7B	1330 MOV A,E
573B CD 38 55	0590 CALL ARRAY	57C2 B2	1340 ORA D
573E EB	0600 XCHG	57C3 C2 CC 57	1350 JNZ NOT0
573F 22 0A 50	0610 SHLD BASEB	57C6 21 8D 54	1360 LXI H,ILLOPR
5742 13	0620 INX D	57C9 C3 13 59	1370 JMP ERR
5743 13	0630 INX D	57CC AF	1380 NOT0 XRA A
5744 1A	0640 LDAX D	57CD 32 76 54	1390 STA SFLG
5745 32 08 50	0650 STA IP	57D0 CD 73 57	1400 CALL SIGND
5748 13	0660 INX D	57D3 D5	1410 PUSH D
5749 1A	0670 LDAX D	57D4 CD 29 55	1420 CALL TM1
574A 32 09 50	0680 STA IP+1	57D7 CD 31 55	1430 CALL STGET
574D C9	0690 RET	57DA CD 73 57	1440 CALL SIGND
574E CD 31 55	0700 EA1C1 CALL STGET	57DD 42	1450 MOV B,D
5751 CD 44 55	0710 CALL CMD	57DE 4B	1460 MOV C,E
5754 73	0720 MOV M,E	57DF D1	1470 POP D
5755 23	0730 INX H	57E0 E5	1480 PUSH H
5756 72	0740 MOV M,D	57E1 21 00 00	1490 LXI H,0
5757 C9	0750 RET	57E4 22 74 54	1500 SHLD RES
5758 CD 31 55	0760 EA1C2 CALL STGET	57E7 EB	1510 EA1C5L XCHG
575B 42	0770 MOV B,D	57E8 CD 58 55	1520 CALL BHCMP
575C 4B	0780 MOV C,E	57EB FA 28 58	1530 JM EA1C5D
575D CD 29 55	0790 CALL TM1	57EE 5D	1540 MOV E,L
5760 CD 31 55	0800 CALL STGET	57EF 54	1550 MOV D,H
5763 EB	0810 XCHG	57F0 E5	1560 PUSH H
5764 09	0820 DAD B	57F1 21 01 00	1570 LXI H,1
5765 EB	0830 XCHG	57F4 E3	1580 XTHL
5766 73	0840 MOV M,E	57F5 CD 58 55	1590 C5I CALL BHCMP
5767 23	0850 INX H	57F8 FA 02 58	1600 JM C5ID
5768 72	0860 MOV M,D	57FB 29	1610 DAD H
5769 C9	0870 RET	57FC E3	1620 XTHL
576A CD 31 55	0880 EA1C3 CALL STGET	57FD 29	1630 DAD H
576D CD 44 55	0890 CALL CMD	57FE E3	1640 XTHL
5770 C3 5B 57	0900 JMP EA1C2+3	57FF C3 F5 57	1650 JMP C5I
5773 7A	0910 SIGND MOV A,D	5802 37	1660 C5ID STC
5774 E6 80	0920 ANI 80H	5803 3F	1670 CMC
5776 C8	0930 RZ	5804 7C	1680 MOV A,H
5777 3A 76 54	0940 LDA SFLG	5805 1F	1690 RAR
577A 2F	0950 CMA	5806 67	1700 MOV H,A
577B 32 76 54	0960 STA SFLG	5807 7D	1710 MOV A,L
577E C3 44 55	0970 JMP CMD	5808 1F	1720 RAR
5781 CD 31 55	0980 EA1C4 CALL STGET	5809 6F	1730 MOV L,A
5784 AF	0990 XRA A	580A EB	1740 XCHG
5785 32 76 54	1000 STA SFLG	580B CD 44 55	1750 CALL CMD
5788 CD 73 57	1010 CALL SIGND	580E EB	1760 XCHG
578B 42	1020 MOV B,D	580F 09	1770 DAD B
578C 4B	1030 MOV C,E	5810 44	1780 MOV B,H
578D CD 29 55	1040 CALL TM1	5811 4D	1790 MOV C,L
5790 CD 31 55	1050 CALL STGET	5812 E1	1800 POP H
5793 CD 73 57	1060 CALL SIGND	5813 EB	1810 XCHG
5796 E5	1070 PUSH H	5814 E5	1820 PUSH H
5797 21 00 00	1080 LXI H,0	5815 2A 74 54	1830 LHLD RES
579A 79	1090 MOV A,C	5818 37	1840 STC
579B CD AF 57	1100 CALL X8BIT	5819 3F	1850 CMC
579E 78	1110 MOV A,B	581A 7A	1860 MOV A,D
579F CD AF 57	1120 CALL X8BIT	581B 1F	1870 RAR
57A2 EB	1130 EA1C4D XCHG	581C 57	1880 MOV D,A
57A3 3A 76 54	1140 LDA SFLG	581D 7B	1890 MOV A,E
57A6 B7	1150 ORA A	581E 1F	1900 RAR
57A7 C4 44 55	1160 CNZ CMD	581F 5F	1910 MOV E,A
57AA E1	1170 POP H	5820 19	1920 DAD D
57AB 73	1180 MOV M,E	5821 22 74 54	1930 SHLD RES
57AC 23	1190 INX H	5824 D1	1940 POP D
57AD 72	1200 MOV M,D	5825 C3 E7 57	1950 JMP EA1C5L
57AE C9	1210 RET	5828 E1	1960 EA1C5D POP H
57AF 0E 08	1220 X8BIT MVI C,8	5829 E5	1970 PUSH H
57B1 1F	1230 X8BL RAR	582A 23	1980 INX H
57B2 D2 B6 57	1240 JNC $+1	582B 7E	1990 MOV A,M
57B5 19	1250 DAD D	582C B7	2000 ORA A

256

```
582D  2A 74 54    2010    LHLD RES
5830  F2 A2 57    2020    JP EA1C4D
5833  59          2030    MOV E,C
5834  50          2040    MOV D,B
5835  CD 44 55    2050    CALL CMD
5838  42          2060    MOV B,D
5839  4B          2070    MOV C,E
583A  C3 A2 57    2080    JMP EA1C4D
583D  CD 31 55    2090    EA1C6 CALL STGET
5840  3E 01       2100    MVI A,1
5842  A3          2110    ANA E
5843  77          2120    MOV M,A
5844  23          2130    INX H
5845  36 00       2140    MVI M,0
5847  C9          2150    RET
5848  CD BE 57    2160    EA1C7 CALL EA1C5
584B  70          2170    MOV M,B
584C  2B          2180    DCX H
584D  71          2190    MOV M,C
584E  C9          2200    RET
584F  CD 65 55    2210    EA1C8 CALL COMP
5852  C2 56 58    2220    JNZ NO
5855  1C          2230    YES INR E
5856  73          2240    NO MOV M,E
5857  23          2250    INX H
5858  72          2260    MOV M,D
5859  C9          2270    RET
585A  CD 65 55    2280    EA1C9 CALL COMP
585D  CA 56 58    2290    JZ NO
5860  C3 55 58    2300    JMP YES
5863  CD 65 55    2310    EA1C10 CALL COMP
5866  CA 56 58    2320    JZ NO
5869  FA 56 58    2330    JM NO
586C  C3 55 58    2340    JMP YES
586F  CD 65 55    2350    EA1C11 CALL COMP
5872  CA 55 58    2360    JZ YES
5875  FA 55 58    2370    JM YES
5878  C3 56 58    2380    JMP NO
587B  CD 65 55    2390    EA1C12 CALL COMP
587E  FA 55 58    2400    JM YES
5881  C3 56 58    2410    JMP NO
5884  CD 65 55    2420    EA1C13 CALL COMP
5887  FA 56 58    2430    JM NO
588A  C3 55 58    2440    JMP YES
588D  CD 31 55    2450    EA1C14 CALL STGET
5890  42          2460    MOV B,D
5891  4B          2470    MOV C,E
5892  CD 29 55    2480    CALL TM1
5895  CD 31 55    2490    CALL STGET
5898  79          2500    MOV A,C
5899  B3          2510    ORA E
589A  77          2520    MOV M,A
589B  23          2530    INX H
589C  78          2540    MOV A,B
589D  B2          2550    ORA D
589E  77          2560    MOV M,A
589F  C9          2570    RET
58A0  CD 31 55    2580    EA1C15 CALL STGET
58A3  42          2590    MOV B,D
58A4  4B          2600    MOV C,E
58A5  CD 29 55    2610    CALL TM1
58A8  CD 31 55    2620    CALL STGET
58AB  79          2630    MOV A,C
58AC  A3          2640    ANA E
58AD  77          2650    MOV M,A
58AE  23          2660    INX H
58AF  78          2670    MOV A,B
58B0  A2          2680    ANA D
58B1  77          2690    MOV M,A
58B2  C9          2700    RET
58B3  CD 31 55    2710    EA1C16 CALL STGET
58B6  7B          2720    MOV A,E
58B7  2F          2730    CMA
58B8  77          2740    MOV M,A
58B9  23          2750    INX H
```

```
58BA  7A            2760        MOV A,D
58BB  2F            2770        CMA
58BC  77            2780        MOV M,A
58BD  C9            2790        RET
58BE  CD 31 55      2800 EA1C17 CALL STGET
58C1  7B            2810        MOV A,E
58C2  E6 0F         2820        ANI 0FH
58C4  4F            2830        MOV C,A
58C5  CD 29 55      2840        CALL TM1
58C8  CD 31 55      2850        CALL STGET
58CB  EB            2860        XCHG
58CC  79            2870        MOV A,C
58CD  CD 4F 55      2880        CALL SHL
58D0  EB            2890        XCHG
58D1  73            2900        MOV M,E
58D2  23            2910        INX H
58D3  72            2920        MOV M,D
58D4  C9            2930        RET
58D5  CD 31 55      2940 EA1C18 CALL STGET
58D8  7B            2950        MOV A,E
58D9  E6 0F         2960        ANI 0FH
58DB  4F            2970        MOV C,A
58DC  CD 29 55      2980        CALL TM1
58DF  CD 31 55      2990        CALL STGET
58E2  79            3000 SHR    MOV A,C
58E3  B7            3010        ORA A
58E4  CA F7 58      3020        JZ EA1C19+4
58E7  7A            3030        MOV A,D
58E8  37            3040        STC
58E9  3F            3050        CMC
58EA  1F            3060        RAR
58EB  57            3070        MOV D,A
58EC  7B            3080        MOV A,E
58ED  1F            3090        RAR
58EE  5F            3100        MOV E,A
58EF  0D            3110        DCR C
58F0  C3 E2 58      3120        JMP SHR
58F3  CD 31 55      3130 EA1C19 CALL STGET
58F6  13            3140        INX D
58F7  73            3150        MOV M,E
58F8  23            3160        INX H
58F9  72            3170        MOV M,D
58FA  C9            3180        RET
58FB  CD 31 55      3190 EA1C20 CALL STGET
58FE  1B            3200        DCX D
58FF  73            3210        MOV M,E
5900  23            3220        INX H
5901  72            3230        MOV M,D
5902  C9            3240        RET
5903  CD 31 55      3250 EA1C21 CALL STGET
5906  23            3260        INX H
5907  23            3270        INX H
5908  73            3280        MOV M,E
5909  23            3290        INX H
590A  72            3300        MOV M,D
590B  2A 0C 50      3310        LHLD T
590E  23            3320        INX H
590F  22 0C 50      3330        SHLD T
5912  C9            3340        RET
5913  CD AD 05      3350 ERR    CALL OSEQ
5916  CD F8 09      3360        CALL CRLF
5919  21 01 00      3370        LXI H,1
591C  22 1C 50      3380        SHLD STOP
591F  C9            3390        RET
5920                3400 *CODE FOR CASES OF EA IN CASF8
5920  2A 0C 50      3410 EA2C0  LHLD T
5923  23            3420        INX H
5924  22 0C 50      3430        SHLD T
5927  CD 31 55      3440        CALL STGET
592A  CD 20 0C      3450        CALL WH0
592D  77            3460        MOV M,A
592E  23            3470        INX H
592F  36 00         3480        MVI M,0
5931  C9            3490        RET
5932  CD 31 55      3500 EA2C1  CALL STGET
```

```
5935 7B              3510 MOV A,E              59C8 CA 3D 58    0300 JZ EA1C6
5936 CD 24 0C        3520 CALL WH1            59CB 3D           0310 DCR A
5939 C3 29 55        3530 JMP TM1             59CC CA 48 58    0320 JZ EA1C7
593C 2A 0C 50        3540 EA2C2 LHLD T        59CF 3D           0330 DCR A
593F 23              3550 INX H               59D0 CA 4F 58    0340 JZ EA1C8
5940 22 0C 50        3560 SHLD T              59D3 3D           0350 DCR A
5943 CD 31 55        3570 CALL STGET          59D4 CA 5A 58    0360 JZ EA1C9
5946 CD D4 55        3580 CALL DECIN          59D7 3D           0370 DCR A
5949 73              3590 MOV M,E             59D8 CA 63 58    0380 JZ EA1C10
594A 23              3600 INX H               59DB 3D           0390 DCR A
594B 72              3610 MOV M,D             59DC CA 6F 58    0400 JZ EA1C11
594C C9              3620 RET                 59DF 3D           0410 DCR A
594D CD 31 55        3630 EA2C3 CALL STGET    59E0 CA 7B 58    0420 JZ EA1C12
5950 CD 73 56        3640 CALL DECOUT         59E3 3D           0430 DCR A
5953 C3 29 55        3650 JMP TM1             59E4 CA 84 58    0440 JZ EA1C13
5956 2A 0C 50        3660 EA2C4 LHLD T        59E7 3D           0450 DCR A
5959 23              3670 INX H               59E8 CA 8D 58    0460 JZ EA1C14
595A 22 0C 50        3680 SHLD T              59EB 3D           0470 DCR A
595D CD 31 55        3690 CALL STGET          59EC CA A0 58    0480 JZ EA1C15
5960 CD 14 56        3700 CALL HEXIN          59EF 3D           0490 DCR A
5963 73              3710 MOV M,E             59F0 CA B3 58    0500 JZ EA1C16
5964 23              3720 INX H               59F3 3D           0510 DCR A
5965 72              3730 MOV M,D             59F4 CA BE 58    0520 JZ EA1C17
5966 C9              3740 RET                 59F7 3D           0530 DCR A
5967 CD 31 55        3750 EA2C5 CALL STGET    59F8 CA D5 58    0540 JZ EA1C18
596A CD 0C 0A        3760 CALL HEXOUT         59FB 3D           0550 DCR A
596D C3 29 55        3770 JMP TM1             59FC CA F3 58    0560 JZ EA1C19
5970 CD 31 55        3780 EA2C8 CALL STGET    59FF 3D           0570 DCR A
5973 2A 0C 50        3790 LHLD T              5A00 CA FB 58    0580 JZ EA1C20
5976 CD 44 55        3800 CALL CMD            5A03 3D           0590 DCR A
5979 19              3810 DAD D               5A04 CA 03 59    0600 JZ EA1C21
597A 22 0C 50        3820 SHLD T              5A07 21 8D 54    0610 LXI H,ILLOPR
597D CD 44 55        3830 CALL CMD            5A0A C3 13 59    0620 JMP ERR
5980 D5              3840 PUSH D              5A0D 2A 6A 54    0630 CASF2 LHLD X
5981 CD 31 55        3850 CALL STGET          5A10 23           0640 INX H
5984 D1              3860 POP D               5A11 6E           0650 MOV L,M
5985 7E              3870 EA2C8L MOV A,M      5A12 26 00        0660 MVI H,0
5986 23              3880 INX H               5A14 22 6E 54    0670 SHLD EL
5987 23              3890 INX H               5A17 7D           0680 MOV A,L
5988 CD 24 0C        3900 CALL WH1            5A18 3C           0690 INR A
598B 1B              3910 DCX D               5A19 CA 53 5A    0700 JZ F2FF
598C 7B              3920 MOV A,E             5A1C 2A 72 54    0710 LHLD IDX
598D B2              3930 ORA D               5A1F 7D           0720 MOV A,L
598E C2 85 59        3940 JNZ EA2C8L          5A20 B7           0730 ORA A
5991 C3 29 55        3950 JMP TM1             5A21 CA 31 5A    0740 JZ F20
                                             5A24 CD 31 55    0750 CALL STGET
5994                 0010 *CASES OF F IN EXEC 5A27 2A 6C 54    0760 LHLD EA
5994 2A 0C 50        0020 CASF0 LHLD T        5A2A 19           0770 DAD D
5997 23              0030 INX H               5A2B 22 6C 54    0780 SHLD EA
5998 22 0C 50        0040 SHLD T              5A2E C3 38 5A    0790 JMP F21
599B EB              0050 XCHG                5A31 2A 0C 50    0800 F20 LHLD T
599C 21 20 50        0060 LXI H,S             5A34 23           0810 INX H
599F CD 38 55        0070 CALL ARRAY          5A35 22 0C 50    0820 SHLD T
59A2 EB              0080 XCHG                5A38 2A 6E 54    0830 F21 LHLD EL
59A3 2A 6C 54        0090 LHLD EA             5A3B EB           0840 XCHG
59A6 EB              0100 XCHG                5A3C CD CC 56    0850 CALL BASE
59A7 73              0110 MOV M,E             5A3F 2A 6C 54    0860 LHLD EA
59A8 23              0120 INX H               5A42 19           0870 DAD D
59A9 72              0130 MOV M,D             5A43 EB           0880 XCHG
59AA C9              0140 RET                 5A44 21 20 50    0890 LXI H,S
59AB 2A 6C 54        0150 CASF1 LHLD EA       5A47 CD 38 55    0900 CALL ARRAY
59AE 7D              0160 MOV A,L             5A4A D5           0910 PUSH D
59AF B7              0170 ORA A               5A4B CD 31 55    0920 CALL STGET
59B0 CA 2B 57        0180 JZ EA1C0            5A4E D1           0930 POP D
59B3 3D              0190 DCR A               5A4F 73           0940 MOV M,E
59B4 CA 4E 57        0200 JZ EA1C1            5A50 23           0950 INX H
59B7 3D              0210 DCR A               5A51 72           0960 MOV M,D
59B8 CA 58 57        0220 JZ EA1C2            5A52 C9           0970 RET
59BB 3D              0230 DCR A               5A53 CD 31 55    0980 F2FF CALL STGET
59BC CA 6A 57        0240 JZ EA1C3            5A56 1A           0990 LDAX D
59BF 3D              0250 DCR A               5A57 77           1000 MOV M,A
59C0 CA 81 57        0260 JZ EA1C4            5A58 23           1010 INX H
59C3 3D              0270 DCR A               5A59 36 00        1020 MVI M,0
59C4 CA BE 57        0280 JZ EA1C5            5A5B C9           1030 RET
59C7 3D              0290 DCR A               5A5C 2A 6A 54    1040 CASF3 LHLD X
```

5A5F	23	1050	INX H
5A60	6E	1060	MOV L,M
5A61	26 00	1070	MVI H,0
5A63	22 6E 54	1080	SHLD EL
5A66	7D	1090	MOV A,L
5A67	3C	1100	INR A
5A68	CA A7 5A	1110	JZ F3FF
5A6B	2A 72 54	1120	LHLD IDX
5A6E	7D	1130	MOV A,L
5A6F	B7	1140	ORA A
5A70	F5	1150	PUSH P
5A71	CA 86 5A	1160	JZ F30
5A74	2A 0C 50	1170	LHLD T
5A77	2B	1180	DCX H
5A78	EB	1190	XCHG
5A79	21 20 50	1200	LXI H,S
5A7C	CD 38 55	1210	CALL ARRAY
5A7F	2A 6C 54	1220	LHLD EA
5A82	19	1230	DAD D
5A83	22 6C 54	1240	SHLD EA
5A86	CD 31 55	1250	F30 CALL STGET
5A89	D5	1260	PUSH D
5A8A	2A 6E 54	1270	LHLD EL
5A8D	EB	1280	XCHG
5A8E	CD CC 56	1290	CALL BASE
5A91	2A 6C 54	1300	LHLD EA
5A94	19	1310	DAD D
5A95	EB	1320	XCHG
5A96	21 20 50	1330	LXI H,S
5A99	CD 38 55	1340	CALL ARRAY
5A9C	D1	1350	POP D
5A9D	73	1360	MOV M,E
5A9E	23	1370	INX H
5A9F	72	1380	MOV M,D
5AA0	F1	1390	POP P
5AA1	C4 29 55	1400	CNZ TM1
5AA4	C3 29 55	1410	JMP TM1
5AA7	CD 31 55	1420	F3FF CALL STGET
5AAA	4B	1430	MOV C,E
5AAB	CD 29 55	1440	CALL TM1
5AAE	CD 31 55	1450	CALL STGET
5AB1	EB	1460	XCHG
5AB2	71	1470	MOV M,C
5AB3	C3 29 55	1480	JMP TM1
5AB6	2A 6A 54	1490	CASF4 LHLD X
5AB9	23	1500	INX H
5ABA	6E	1510	MOV L,M
5ABB	26 00	1520	MVI H,0
5ABD	22 6E 54	1530	SHLD EL
5AC0	7D	1540	MOV A,L
5AC1	3C	1550	INR A
5AC2	CA FF 5A	1560	JZ F4FF
5AC5	EB	1570	XCHG
5AC6	CD CC 56	1580	CALL BASE
5AC9	D5	1590	PUSH D
5ACA	2A 0C 50	1600	LHLD T
5ACD	23	1610	INX H
5ACE	EB	1620	XCHG
5ACF	21 20 50	1630	LXI H,S
5AD2	CD 38 55	1640	CALL ARRAY
5AD5	D1	1650	POP D
5AD6	73	1660	MOV M,E
5AD7	23	1670	INX H
5AD8	72	1680	MOV M,D
5AD9	23	1690	INX H
5ADA	EB	1700	XCHG
5ADB	2A 0A 50	1710	LHLD BASEB
5ADE	EB	1720	XCHG
5ADF	73	1730	MOV M,E
5AE0	23	1740	INX H
5AE1	72	1750	MOV M,D
5AE2	23	1760	INX H
5AE3	EB	1770	XCHG
5AE4	2A 08 50	1780	LHLD IP
5AE7	EB	1790	XCHG
5AE8	73	1800	MOV M,E
5AE9	23	1810	INX H
5AEA	72	1820	MOV M,D
5AEB	2A 0C 50	1830	LHLD T
5AEE	23	1840	INX H
5AEF	23	1850	INX H
5AF0	23	1860	INX H
5AF1	22 0C 50	1870	SHLD T
5AF4	23	1880	INX H
5AF5	22 0A 50	1890	SHLD BASEB
5AF8	2A 6C 54	1900	LHLD EA
5AFB	22 08 50	1910	SHLD IP
5AFE	C9	1920	RET
5AFF	CD 31 55	1930	F4FF CALL STGET
5B02	21 29 55	1940	LXI H,TM1
5B05	E5	1950	PUSH H
5B06	EB	1960	XCHG
5B07	E9	1970	PCHL
5B08	2A 6C 54	1980	CASF5 LHLD EA
5B0B	EB	1990	XCHG
5B0C	CD 44 55	2000	CALL CMD
5B0F	2A E0 01	2010	LHLD SIZE1
5B12	19	2020	DAD D
5B13	4D	2030	MOV C,L
5B14	44	2040	MOV B,H
5B15	2A 0C 50	2050	LHLD T
5B18	CD 58 55	2060	CALL BHCMP
5B1B	FA 27 5B	2070	JM OVER
5B1E	EB	2080	XCHG
5B1F	2A 6C 54	2090	LHLD EA
5B22	19	2100	DAD D
5B23	22 0C 50	2110	SHLD T
5B26	C9	2120	RET
5B27	21 9D 54	2130	OVER LXI H,STOVFL
5B2A	C3 13 59	2140	JMP ERR
5B2D	2A 6C 54	2150	CASF6 LHLD EA
5B30	22 08 50	2160	SHLD IP
5B33	C9	2170	RET
5B34	2A 6A 54	2180	CASF7 LHLD X
5B37	23	2190	INX H
5B38	4E	2200	MOV C,M
5B39	CD 31 55	2210	CALL STGET
5B3C	7B	2220	MOV A,E
5B3D	E6 01	2230	ANI 1
5B3F	B9	2240	CMP C
5B40	C2 29 55	2250	JNZ TM1
5B43	2A 6C 54	2260	LHLD EA
5B46	22 08 50	2270	SHLD IP
5B49	C3 29 55	2280	JMP TM1
5B4C	2A 6C 54	2290	CASF8 LHLD EA
5B4F	7D	2300	MOV A,L
5B50	B7	2310	ORA A
5B51	CA 20 59	2320	JZ EA2C0
5B54	3D	2330	DCR A
5B55	CA 32 59	2340	JZ EA2C1
5B58	3D	2350	DCR A
5B59	CA 3C 59	2360	JZ EA2C2
5B5C	3D	2370	DCR A
5B5D	CA 4D 59	2380	JZ EA2C3
5B60	3D	2390	DCR A
5B61	CA 56 59	2400	JZ EA2C4
5B64	3D	2410	DCR A
5B65	CA 67 59	2420	JZ EA2C5
5B68	D6 03	2430	SUI 3
5B6A	CA 70 59	2440	JZ EA2C8
5B6D	21 AC 54	2450	LXI H,ILLCSF
5B70	C3 13 59	2460	JMP ERR
5B73	2A 08 50	2470	EXEC LHLD IP
5B76	3E 02	2480	MVI A,2
5B78	CD 4F 55	2490	CALL SHL
5B7B	EB	2500	XCHG
5B7C	2A 06 50	2510	LHLD Z
5B7F	19	2520	DAD D
5B80	22 6A 54	2530	SHLD X
5B83	23	2540	INX H

```
5B84 23
5B85 7E
5B86 23
5B87 66
5B88 6F
5B89 22 6C 54
5B8C 2A 12 50
5B8F 23
5B90 3E 0D
5B92 BD
5B93 D2 99 5B
5B96 21 00 00
5B99 22 12 50
5B9C EB
5B9D 21 0A 54
5BA0 CD 38 55
5BA3 EB
5BA4 2A 08 50
5BA7 EB
5BA8 73
5BA9 23
5BAA 72
5BAB EB
5BAC 23
5BAD 22 08 50
5BB0 22 10 50
5BB3 2A 1A 50
5BB6 23
5BB7 22 1A 50
5BBA 2A 6A 54
5BBD 6E
5BBE 26 00
5BC0 22 70 54
5BC3 3E 08
5BC5 BD
5BC6 DA D1 5B
5BC9 2E 00
5BCB 22 72 54
5BCE C3 E0 5B
5BD1 2E 01
5BD3 22 72 54
5BD6 2A 70 54
5BD9 11 F0 FF
5BDC 19
5BDD 22 70 54
5BE0 2A 70 54
5BE3 7D
5BE4 B7
5BE5 CA 94 59
5BE8 3D
5BE9 CA AB 59
5BEC 3D
5BED CA 0D 5A
5BF0 3D
5BF1 CA 5C 5A
5BF4 3D
5BF5 CA B6 5A
5BF8 3D
5BF9 CA 08 5B
5BFC 3D
5BFD CA 2D 5B
5C00 3D
5C01 CA 34 5B
5C04 3D
5C05 CA 4C 5B
5C08 21 7E 54
5C0B C3 13 59

5C0E D5
5C0F EB
5C10 3E 02
5C12 CD 4F 55
5C15 EB
5C16 2A 06 50
5C19 19
```

```
2550    INX H
2560    MOV A,M
2570    INX H
2580    MOV H,M
2590    MOV L,A
2600    SHLD EA
2610    LHLD TP
2620    INX H
2630    MVI A,U
2640    CMP L
2650    JNC $+3
2660    LXI H,0
2670    SHLD TP
2680    XCHG
2690    LXI H,TRACE
2700    CALL ARRAY
2710    XCHG
2720    LHLD IP
2730    XCHG
2740    MOV M,E
2750    INX H
2760    MOV M,D
2770    XCHG
2780    INX H
2790    SHLD IP
2800    SHLD P0
2810    LHLD K
2820    INX H
2830    SHLD K
2840    LHLD X
2850    MOV L,M
2860    MVI H,0
2870    SHLD F
2880    MVI A,8
2890    CMP L
2900    JC FBIGR8
2910    MVI L,0
2920    SHLD IDX
2930    JMP CASF
2940 FBIGR8 MVI L,1
2950    SHLD IDX
2960    LHLD F
2970    LXI D,-16
2980    DAD D
2990    SHLD F
3000 CASF LHLD F
3010    MOV A,L
3020    ORA A
3030    JZ CASF0
3040    DCR A
3050    JZ CASF1
3060    DCR A
3070    JZ CASF2
3080    DCR A
3090    JZ CASF3
3100    DCR A
3110    JZ CASF4
3120    DCR A
3130    JZ CASF5
3140    DCR A
3150    JZ CASF6
3160    DCR A
3170    JZ CASF7
3180    DCR A
3190    JZ CASF8
3200    LXI H,ILLOPC
3210    JMP ERR

0010 CODE PUSH D
0020    XCHG
0030    MVI A,2
0040    CALL SHL
0050    XCHG
0060    LHLD Z
0070    DAD D
```

```
5C1A 22 6A 54
5C1D 7E
5C1E 6F
5C1F 26 00
5C21 29
5C22 85
5C23 6F
5C24 D2 28 5C
5C27 24
5C28 22 1E 50
5C2B 01 18 00
5C2E CD 58 55
5C31 3E 20
5C33 F2 42 5C
5C36 2A 1E 50
5C39 01 D0 FF
5C3C 09
5C3D 22 1E 50
5C40 3E 58
5C42 F5
5C43 CD 02 0A
5C46 CD 02 0A
5C49 F1
5C4A D1
5C4B F5
5C4C CD 73 56
5C4F CD 02 0A
5C52 CD 02 0A
5C55 2A 1E 50
5C58 EB
5C59 21 0E 55
5C5C 19
5C5D 7E
5C5E 23
5C5F CD 24 0C
5C62 7E
5C63 23
5C64 CD 24 0C
5C67 7E
5C68 CD 24 0C
5C6B F1
5C6C CD 24 0C
5C6F CD 02 0A
5C72 2A 6A 54
5C75 23
5C76 5E
5C77 16 00
5C79 CD 73 56
5C7C 3E 2C
5C7E CD 24 0C
5C81 23
5C82 5E
5C83 23
5C84 56
5C85 CD 73 56
5C88 C3 F8 09
5C8B 2A 08 50
5C8E 7C
5C8F B7
5C90 FA CA 5C
5C93 EB
5C94 2A 0E 50
5C97 7C
5C98 B5
5C99 C8
5C9A D5
5C9B 01 01 00
5C9E 59
5C9F 50
5CA0 21 5C 54
5CA3 CD 38 55
5CA6 E1
5CA7 E5
5CA8 CD 44 55
5CAB 19
```

```
0080    SHLD X
0090    MOV A,M
0100    MOV L,A
0110    MVI H,0
0120    DAD H
0130    ADD L
0140    MOV L,A
0150    JNC $+1
0160    INR H
0170    SHLD N
0180    LXI B,24
0190    CALL BHCMP
0200    MVI A,' '
0210    JP WRTCD
0220    LHLD N
0230    LXI B,-48
0240    DAD B
0250    SHLD N
0260    MVI A,'X'
0270 WRTCD PUSH P
0280    CALL BLK1
0290    CALL BLK1
0300    POP P
0310    POP D
0320    PUSH P
0330    CALL DECOUT
0340    CALL BLK1
0350    CALL BLK1
0360    LHLD N
0370    XCHG
0380    LXI H,MNEM
0390    DAD D
0400    MOV A,M
0410    INX H
0420    CALL WH1
0430    MOV A,M
0440    INX H
0450    CALL WH1
0460    MOV A,M
0470    CALL WH1
0480    POP P
0490    CALL WH1
0500    CALL BLK1
0510    LHLD X
0520    INX H
0530    MOV E,M
0540    MVI D,0
0550    CALL DECOUT
0560    MVI A,','
0570    CALL WH1
0580    INX H
0590    MOV E,M
0600    INX H
0610    MOV D,M
0620    CALL DECOUT
0630    JMP CRLF
0640 CKBP LHLD IP
0650    MOV A,H
0660    ORA A
0670    JM PLT0
0680    XCHG
0690    LHLD BP
0700    MOV A,H
0710    ORA L
0720    RZ
0730    PUSH D
0740    LXI B,1
0750 CKBPL MOV E,C
0760    MOV D,B
0770    LXI H,BREAK
0780    CALL ARRAY
0790    POP H
0800    PUSH H
0810    CALL CMD
0820    DAD D
```

```
5CAC 7C          0830       MOV A,H          5D50 CD 73 56    1580       CALL DECOUT
5CAD B5          0840       ORA L            5D53 CD AD 05    1590       CALL OSEQ
5CAE CA C0 5C    0850       JZ BFND          5D56 23          1600       INX H
5CB1 03          0860       INX B            5D57 E5          1610       PUSH H
5CB2 2A 0E 50    0870       LHLD BP          5D58 CD 31 55    1620       CALL STGET
5CB5 CD 58 55    0880       CALL BHCMP       5D5B CD 73 56    1630       CALL DECOUT
5CB8 FA 9E 5C    0890       JM CKBPL         5D5E E1          1640       POP H
5CBB CA 9E 5C    0900       JZ CKBPL         5D5F CD AD 05    1650       CALL OSEQ
5CBE E1          0910       POP H            5D62 2A 0C 50    1660       LHLD T
5CBF C9          0920       RET              5D65 2B          1670       DCX H
5CC0 21 B8 54    0930 BFND  LXI H,BREAKM     5D66 EB          1680       XCHG
5CC3 CD AD 05    0940       CALL OSEQ        5D67 21 20 50    1690       LXI H,S
5CC6 D1          0950       POP D            5D6A CD 38 55    1700       CALL ARRAY
5CC7 CD 0E 5C    0960       CALL CODE        5D6D CD 73 56    1710       CALL DECOUT
5CCA 21 01 00    0970 PLT0  LXI H,1          5D70 C3 F8 09    1720       JMP CRLF
5CCD 22 1C 50    0980       SHLD STOP        5D73 CD F3 56    1730 CMG   CALL INIT
5CD0 C9          0990       RET              5D76 C3 13 5D    1740       JMP CMRL
5CD1 31 00 10    1000 MAIN  LXI P,1000H      5D79 21 F2 54    1750 CMT   LXI H,TRCMSG
5CD4 AF          1010       XRA A            5D7C CD AD 05    1760       CALL OSEQ
5CD5 D3 04       1020       OUT 4            5D7F CD F8 09    1770       CALL CRLF
5CD7 21 26 54    1030       LXI H,MN         5D82 0E 0E       1780       MVI C,U+1
5CDA 11 0E 55    1040       LXI D,MNEM       5D84 2A 12 50    1790 CMTL  LHLD TP
5CDD 0E 1B       1050       MVI C,27         5D87 23          1800       INX H
5CDF 1A          1060 MNLP  LDAX D           5D88 3E 0D       1810       MVI A,U
5CE0 13          1070       INX D            5D8A BD          1820       CMP L
5CE1 77          1080       MOV M,A          5D8B D2 91 5D    1830       JNC $+3
5CE2 23          1090       INX H            5D8E 21 00 00    1840       LXI H,0
5CE3 36 00       1100       MVI M,0          5D91 22 12 50    1850       SHLD TP
5CE5 23          1110       INX H            5D94 EB          1860       XCHG
5CE6 0D          1120       DCR C            5D95 21 0A 54    1870       LXI H,TRACE
5CE7 C2 DF 5C    1130       JNZ MNLP         5D98 CD 38 55    1880       CALL ARRAY
5CEA 21 C0 54    1140       LXI H,ADDRM      5D9B 7A          1890       MOV A,D
5CED CD AD 05    1150       CALL OSEQ        5D9C B7          1900       ORA A
5CF0 CD 14 56    1160       CALL HEXIN       5D9D FA A5 5D    1910       JM $+5
5CF3 EB          1170       XCHG             5DA0 C5          1920       PUSH B
5CF4 22 06 50    1180       SHLD Z           5DA1 CD 0E 5C    1930       CALL CODE
5CF7 CD F8 09    1190       CALL CRLF        5DA4 C1          1940       POP B
5CFA CD F3 56    1200       CALL INIT        5DA5 0D          1950       DCR C
5CFD 2A 08 50    1210       LHLD IP          5DA6 C2 84 5D    1960       JNZ CMTL
5D00 EB          1220       XCHG             5DA9 C9          1970       RET
5D01 CD 0E 5C    1230       CALL CODE        5DAA CD D4 55    1980 CMK   CALL DECIN
5D04 21 00 00    1240       LXI H,0          5DAD 0E 07       1990       MVI C,7
5D07 22 0E 50    1250       SHLD BP          5DAF C5          2000 CMKL  PUSH B
5D0A C3 62 5E    1260       JMP BEGIN        5DB0 D5          2010       PUSH D
5D0D 21 00 00    1270 CMR   LXI H,0          5DB1 21 20 50    2020       LXI H,S
5D10 22 1C 50    1280       SHLD STOP        5DB4 CD 38 55    2030       CALL ARRAY
5D13 CD 73 5B    1290 CMRL  CALL EXEC        5DB7 CD 02 0A    2040       CALL BLK1
5D16 CD 8B 5C    1300       CALL CKBP        5DBA CD 02 0A    2050       CALL BLK1
5D19 3A 1C 50    1310       LDA STOP         5DBD CD 73 56    2060       CALL DECOUT
5D1C B7          1320       ORA A            5DC0 CD F8 09    2070       CALL CRLF
5D1D CA 13 5D    1330       JZ CMRL          5DC3 D1          2080       POP D
5D20 C9          1340       RET              5DC4 C1          2090       POP B
5D21 CD 73 5B    1350 CMS   CALL EXEC        5DC5 13          2100       INX D
5D24 2A 08 50    1360       LHLD IP          5DC6 0D          2110       DCR C
5D27 EB          1370       XCHG             5DC7 C2 AF 5D    2120       JNZ CMKL
5D28 CD 0E 5C    1380       CALL CODE        5DCA C9          2130       RET
5D2B C9          1390       RET              5DCB 01 05 00    2140 CMB   LXI B,BFLIM
5D2C 21 D0 54    1400 CMX   LXI H,XMSG       5DCE 2A 0E 50    2150       LHLD BP
5D2F CD AD 05    1410       CALL OSEQ        5DD1 CD 58 55    2160       CALL BHCMP
5D32 23          1420       INX H            5DD4 C8          2170       RZ
5D33 EB          1430       XCHG             5DD5 F8          2180       RM
5D34 2A 08 50    1440       LHLD IP          5DD6 23          2190       INX H
5D37 EB          1450       XCHG             5DD7 22 0E 50    2200       SHLD BP
5D38 CD 73 56    1460       CALL DECOUT      5DDA EB          2210       XCHG
5D3B CD AD 05    1470       CALL OSEQ        5DDB D5          2220       PUSH D
5D3E 23          1480       INX H            5DDC CD 73 56    2230       CALL DECOUT
5D3F EB          1490       XCHG             5DDF 3E 3A       2240       MVI A,':'
5D40 2A 0A 50    1500       LHLD BASEB       5DE1 CD 24 0C    2250       CALL WH1
5D43 EB          1510       XCHG             5DE4 CD 02 0A    2260       CALL BLK1
5D44 CD 73 56    1520       CALL DECOUT      5DE7 D1          2270       POP D
5D47 CD AD 05    1530       CALL OSEQ        5DE8 21 5C 54    2280       LXI H,BREAK
5D4A 23          1540       INX H            5DEB CD 38 55    2290       CALL ARRAY
5D4B EB          1550       XCHG             5DEE CD D4 55    2300       CALL DECIN
5D4C 2A 0C 50    1560       LHLD T           5DF1 73          2310       MOV M,E
5D4F EB          1570       XCHG             5DF2 23          2320       INX H
```

```
5DF3  72            2330  MOV  M,D          5E8D  CA F7 5D    3080  JZ  CMC
5DF4  C3 F8 09      2340  JMP  CRLF         5E90  D6 02       3090  SUI 2
5DF7  21 00 00      2350  CMC LXI H,0       5E92  CA 1F 5E    3100  JZ  CME
5DFA  22 0E 50      2360  SHLD BP           5E95  D6 02       3110  SUI 2
5DFD  C9            2370  RET               5E97  CA 73 5D    3120  JZ  CMG
5DFE  2A 0E 50      2380  CMY LHLD BP       5E9A  D6 04       3130  SUI 4
5E01  7D            2390  MOV  A,L          5E9C  CA AA 5D    3140  JZ  CMK
5E02  B4            2400  ORA  H            5E9F  D6 03       3150  SUI 3
5E03  C8            2410  RZ                5EA1  CA 36 5E    3160  JZ  CMN
5E04  4D            2420  MOV  C,L          5EA4  D6 03       3170  SUI 3
5E05  21 5E 54      2430  LXI  H,BREAK+2    5EA6  CA 42 5E    3180  JZ  CMQ
5E08  C5            2440  CMYL PUSH B       5EA9  3D          3190  DCR A
5E09  5E            2450  MOV  E,M          5EAA  CA 0D 5D    3200  JZ  CMR
5E0A  23            2460  INX  H            5EAD  3D          3210  DCR A
5E0B  56            2470  MOV  D,M          5EAE  CA 21 5D    3220  JZ  CMS
5E0C  23            2480  INX  H            5EB1  3D          3230  DCR A
5E0D  CD 02 0A      2490  CALL BLK1         5EB2  CA 79 5D    3240  JZ  CMT
5E10  CD 02 0A      2500  CALL BLK1         5EB5  3D          3250  DCR A
5E13  CD 73 56      2510  CALL DECOUT       5EB6  CA 26 5E    3260  JZ  CMU
5E16  CD F8 09      2520  CALL CRLF         5EB9  D6 03       3270  SUI 3
5E19  C1            2530  POP  B            5EBB  CA 2C 5D    3280  JZ  CMX
5E1A  0D            2540  DCR  C            5EBE  3D          3290  DCR A
5E1B  C2 08 5E      2550  JNZ  CMYL         5EBF  CA FE 5D    3300  JZ  CMY
5E1E  C9            2560  RET               5EC2  3E 3F       3310  MVI A,'?'
5E1F  CD D4 55      2570  CME CALL DECIN    5EC4  CD 24 0C    3320  CALL WH1
5E22  CD 0E 5C      2580  CALL CODE         5EC7  CD 24 0C    3330  CALL WH1
5E25  C9            2590  RET               5ECA  CD F8 09    3340  CALL CRLF
5E26  2A 10 50      2600  CMU LHLD P0       5ECD  C3 74 5E    3350  JMP PROMPT
5E29  2B            2610  DCX  H            5ED0              3360  LB EQU $-1
5E2A  7C            2620  MOV  A,H
5E2B  B5            2630  ORA  L
5E2C  C8            2640  RZ
5E2D  F8            2650  RM
5E2E  22 10 50      2660  SHLD P0
5E31  EB            2670  XCHG
5E32  CD 0E 5C      2680  CALL CODE
5E35  C9            2690  RET
5E36  2A 10 50      2700  CMN LHLD P0
5E39  23            2710  INX  H
5E3A  22 10 50      2720  SHLD P0
5E3D  EB            2730  XCHG
5E3E  CD 0E 5C      2740  CALL CODE
5E41  C9            2750  RET
5E42  21 FF FF      2760  CMQ LXI H,-1
5E45  22 08 50      2770  SHLD IP
5E48  C9            2780  RET
5E49  CD F8 09      2790  FINISH CALL CRLF
5E4C  21 FD 54      2800  LXI  H,FINMSG
5E4F  CD AD 05      2810  CALL OSEQ
5E52  2A 1A 50      2820  LHLD K
5E55  EB            2830  XCHG
5E56  CD 73 56      2840  CALL DECOUT
5E59  CD F8 09      2850  CALL CRLF
5E5C  CD 20 0C      2860  CALL WH0
5E5F  C3 90 73      2870  JMP 7390H
5E62  31 00 10      2880  BEGIN LXI P,1000H
5E65  AF            2890  XRA  A
5E66  D3 04         2900  OUT 4
5E68  2A 08 50      2910  LHLD IP
5E6B  7C            2920  MOV  A,H
5E6C  B7            2930  ORA  A
5E6D  FA 49 5E      2940  JM FINISH
5E70  21 62 5E      2950  LXI  H,BEGIN
5E73  E5            2960  PUSH H
5E74  3E 3E         2970  PROMPT MVI A,'>'
5E76  CD 24 0C      2980  CALL WH1
5E79  CD 20 0C      2990  CALL WH0
5E7C  CD 24 0C      3000  CALL WH1
5E7F  F5            3010  PUSH P
5E80  CD F8 09      3020  CALL CRLF
5E83  F1            3030  POP  P
5E84  32 14 50      3040  STA CMND
5E87  D6 42         3050  SUI 'B'
5E89  CA CB 5D      3060  JZ CMB
5E8C  3D            3070  DCR A
```

ORGA	5000	READ	5579	EA2C0	5920
COLDST	5000	RLP	557E	EA2C1	5932
WARMST	5003	RUB	55AF	EA2C2	593C
U	000D	CAN	55BE	EA2C3	594D
WH0	0C20	DIGIT	55CD	EA2C4	5956
WH1	0C24	DECIN	55D4	EA2C5	5967
BLK1	0A02	DECIL	55F2	EA2C8	5970
DEQUT1	0A0C	DECID	5609	EA2C8L	5985
OSEQ	05AD	HEXIN	5614	CASF0	5994
BPLIM	0005	HEXIL	5632	CASF1	59AB
SIZE	01F4	HEX16	5646	CASF2	5A0D
SIZE1	01E0	HEXID	5653	F20	5A31
Z	5006	DCALC	565E	F21	5A38
IP	5008	DECOUT	5673	F2FF	5A53
BASEB	500A	CDEC	5680	CASF3	5A5C
T	500C	HEXOUT	0A0C	F30	5A86
BP	500E	BASE	56CC	F3FF	5AA7
P0	5010	BA1	56D2	CASF4	5AB6
TP	5012	BA2	56EE	F4FF	5AFF
CMND	5014	INIT	56F3	CASF5	5B08
I	5016	INI1	5721	OVER	5B27
J	5018	CRLF	09F8	CASF6	5B2D
K	501A	EA1C0	572B	CASF7	5B34
STOP	501C	EA1C1	574E	CASF8	5B4C
N	501E	EA1C2	5758	EXEC	5B73
S	5020	EA1C3	576A	FBIGR8	5BD1
TRACE	540A	SIGND	5773	CASF	5BE0
MN	5426	EA1C4	5781	CODE	5C0E
BREAK	545C	EA1C4D	57A2	WRTCD	5C42
B1	5468	X8BIT	57AF	CKBP	5C8B
X	546A	X8BL	57B1	CKBPL	5C9E
EA	546C	EA1C5	57BE	BFND	5CC0
EL	546E	NOT0	57CC	PLT0	5CCA
F	5470	EA1C5L	57E7	MAIN	5CD1
IDX	5472	C5I	57F5	MNLP	5CDF
RES	5474	C5ID	5802	CMR	5D0D
SFLG	5476	EA1C5D	5828	CMRL	5D13
ABUF	5477	EA1C6	583D	CMS	5D21
ILLOPC	547E	EA1C7	5848	CMX	5D2C
ILLOPR	548D	EA1C8	584F	CMG	5D73
STOVFL	549D	YES	5855	CMT	5D79
ILLCSP	54AC	NO	5856	CMTL	5D84
BREAKM	54B8	EA1C9	585A	CMK	5DAA
ADDRM	54C0	EA1C10	5863	CMKL	5DAF
XMSG	54D0	EA1C11	586F	CMB	5DCB
TRCMSG	54F2	EA1C12	587B	CMC	5DF7
FINMSG	54FD	EA1C13	5884	CMY	5DFE
MNEM	550E	EA1C14	588D	CMYL	5E08
TM1	5529	EA1C15	58A0	CME	5E1F
STGET	5531	EA1C16	58B3	CMU	5E26
ARRAY	5538	EA1C17	58BE	CMN	5E36
CMD	5544	EA1C18	58D5	CMQ	5E42
SHL	554F	SHR	58E2	FINISH	5E49
SH1	5551	EA1C19	58F3	BEGIN	5E62
BHCMP	5558	EA1C20	58FB	PROMPT	5E74
COMP	5565	EA1C21	5903	LB	5ECF
		ERR	5913		

Listing 5: Pascal to P-Code Interpreter

```
4F00                    0010 * PASCAL-TO-P-CODE COMPILER (FROM BASIC)
4F00                    0020 * 1978-XII-18
4F00                    0030 ORGA EQU 4F00H
4F00                    0040   ORG ORGA
4F00  C3 E0 6C          0050 START JMP ORGA+1DE0H (RUN)
4F03  C3 68 69          0060 F3490 JMP ORGA+1A68H (S3490)
4F06  C3 E5 64          0070 F4290 JMP ORGA+15E5H (L4290)
4F09  C3 48 6B          0080 F5340 JMP ORGA+1C48H (S5340)
4F0C                    0090 PCODES EQU 2C00H
4F0C                    0100 MEMLIM EQU ORGA-1
4F0C                    0110 SRCFIL EQU 1000H
4F0C                    0120 N0 EQU 32
4F0C                    0130 T0 EQU 50
4F0C                    0140 N1 EQU 32767
4F0C                    0150 N2 EQU 8
4F0C                    0160 TST DS 400
509C                    0170 T0ST DS T0
50CE                    0180 LST DS 64
510E                    0190 AST DS N2+4
511A                    0200 BST DS N2
5122                    0210 S DS 200
51EA                    0220 SST DS 100
524E                    0230 CST DS 80
529E                    0240 OST DS 8
52A6                    0250 T1 DS T0+T0+2
530C                    0260 T2 DS T0+T0+2
5372                    0270 T3 DS T0+T0+2
53D8                    0280 XST DS 1
53D9                    0290 FNE1ST DS 5
53DE                    0300 YST DS 5
53E3                    0310 S0ST DS 5
53E8                    0320 KST DS 5
53ED                    0330 ZST DS 5
53F2                    0340 FPTR DS 2
53F4                    0350 BOFP DS 2
53F6                    0360 EOFP DS 2
53F8                    0370 P7 DS 2
53FA                    0380 P8 DS 2
53FC                    0390 P9 DS 2
53FE                    0400 Q9 DS 2
5400                    0410 S9 DS 2
5402                    0420 F5 DS 2
5404                    0430 Y9 DS 2
5406                    0440 Z DS 2
5408                    0450 C0 DS 2
540A                    0460 E9 DS 2
540C                    0470 L0 DS 2
540E                    0480 C1 DS 2
5410                    0490 K DS 2
5412                    0500 T DS 2
5414                    0510 I DS 2
5416                    0520 J DS 2
5418                    0530 N3 DS 2
541A                    0540 X DS 2
541C                    0550 I1 DS 2
541E                    0560 I2 DS 2
5420                    0570 L1 DS 2
5422                    0580 F9 DS 2
5424                    0590 L00 DS 2
5426                    0600 K1 DS 2
5428                    0610 K2 DS 2
542A                    0620 K3 DS 2
542C                    0630 D0 DS 2
```

```
542E                    0640 N DS 2
5430                    0650 NCHR DS 1
5431                    0660 ADDS DS 2
5433 41 4E 44 20        0670 WOST DB 'AND  ARRAYBEGINCALL CASE CONSTDIV  D
O  '
545B 44 4F 57 4E        0680      DB 'DOWNTELSE END  FOR  FUNC IF   INTEGMEM
'
5483 4D 4F 44 20        0690      DB 'MOD  NOT  OF   OR   PROC READ REPEASHL
'
54AB 53 48 52 20        0700      DB 'SHR  THEN TO   TYPE UNTILVAR  WHILEWRITE
'
54D3 49 44 45 4E        0710 IDENT DB 'IDENT'
54D8 4E 55 4D 20        0720 NUM DB 'NUM  '
54DD 53 54 52 20        0730 STR DB 'STR  '
54E2 4C 49 54 4F        0740 MST DB 'LITOPRLODSTOCALINTJMPJPCCSP'
54FD 50 2D 43 4F        0750 L250 DB 'P-CODE STARTS AT 2C00H'
5513 0D                 0760      DB 0DH
5514 57 41 4E 54        0770 L280 DB 'WANT CODE PRINTED? '
5527 0D                 0780      DB 0DH
5528 46 49 4C 45        0790 L339 DB 'FILE ENDS AT '
5535 0D                 0800      DB 0DH
5536 49 4E 54 45        0810 L340 DB 'INTERPRET(I), OR TRANSLATE(T)? '
5555 0D                 0820      DB 0DH
5556 4C 44 47 4F        0830 L360 DB 'LDGO INTRP :0'
5563 4C 44 47 4F        0840 L370 DB 'LDGO TRANS :0'
5570 4D 45 4D 20        0850 L710 DB 'MEM FULL'
5578 0D                 0860      DB 0DH
5579 43 4F 4E 53        0870 L720 DB 'CONST EXPECTED'
5587 0D                 0880      DB 0DH
5588 22 3D 22 20        0890 L730 DB '"=" EXPECTED'
5594 0D                 0900      DB 0DH
5595 49 44 45 4E        0910 L740 DB 'IDENTIFIER EXPECTED'
55A8 0D                 0920      DB 0DH
55A9 22 3B 22 20        0930 L750 DB '";" OR ":" MISSING'
55BB 0D                 0940      DB 0DH
55BC 22 2E 22 20        0950 L760 DB '"." EXPECTED'
55C8 0D                 0960      DB 0DH
55C9 22 3B 22 20        0970 L770 DB '";" MISSING'
55D4 0D                 0980      DB 0DH
55D5 55 4E 44 45        0990 L780 DB 'UNDECLARED IDENT'
55E5 0D                 1000      DB 0DH
55E6 49 4C 4C 45        1010 L790 DB 'ILLEGAL IDENT'
55F3 0D                 1020      DB 0DH
55F4 22 3A 3D 22        1030 L800 DB '":=" EXPECTED'
5601 0D                 1040      DB 0DH
5602 22 54 48 45        1050 L810 DB '"THEN" EXPECTED'
5611 0D                 1060      DB 0DH
5612 22 3B 22 20        1070 L820 DB '";" OR "END" EXPECTED'
5627 0D                 1080      DB 0DH
5628 22 44 4F 22        1090 L830 DB '"DO" EXPECTED'
5635 0D                 1100      DB 0DH
5636 49 4E 43 4F        1110 L840 DB 'INCORRECT SYMBOL'
5646 0D                 1120      DB 0DH
5647 52 45 4C 41        1130 L850 DB 'RELATIONAL OPERATOR EXPECTED'
5663 0D                 1140      DB 0DH
5664 55 53 45 20        1150 L860 DB 'USE OF PROC IDENT IN EXPR'
567D 0D                 1160      DB 0DH
567E 22 29 22 20        1170 L870 DB '")" EXPECTED'
568A 0D                 1180      DB 0DH
568B 49 4C 4C 45        1190 L880 DB 'ILLEGAL FACTOR'
5699 0D                 1200      DB 0DH
569A 22 42 45 47        1210 L890 DB '"BEGIN" EXPECTED'
56AA 0D                 1220      DB 0DH
56AB 22 4F 46 22        1230 L900 DB '"OF" EXPECTED'
56B8 0D                 1240      DB 0DH
56B9 49 4C 4C 45        1250 L910 DB 'ILLEGAL HEX CONST'
56CA 0D                 1260      DB 0DH
56CB 22 54 4F 22        1270 L920 DB '"TO" OR "DOWNTO" EXPECTED'
56E4 0D                 1280      DB 0DH
56E5 4E 55 4D 42        1290 L930 DB 'NUMBER OUT OF RANGE'
56F8 0D                 1300      DB 0DH
56F9 22 28 22 20        1310 L940 DB '"(" EXPECTED'
5705 0D                 1320      DB 0DH
5706 22 5B 22 20        1330 L950 DB '"[" EXPECTED'
5712 0D                 1340      DB 0DH
```

```
5713 22 5D 22 20    1350 L960 DB '"]" EXPECTED'
571F 0D             1360      DB 0DH
5720 50 41 52 41    1370 L970 DB 'PARAMETERS MISMATCHED'
5735 0D             1380      DB 0DH
5736 44 41 54 41    1390 L980 DB 'DATA TYPE NOT RECOGNIZED'
574E 0D             1400      DB 0DH
574F 42 55 47       1410 L990 DB 'BUG'
5752 0D             1420      DB 0DH
5753 41 44 44 52    1430 L6570 DB 'ADDR AT'
575A 0D             1440      DB 0DH
575B 43 48 41 4E    1450      DB 'CHANGED TO'
5765 0D             1460      DB 0DH
5766 70 55          1470 ETAB DW L710
5768 79 55          1480      DW L720
576A 88 55          1490      DW L730
576C 95 55          1500      DW L740
576E A9 55          1510      DW L750
5770 4F 57          1520      DW L990
5772 4F 57          1530      DW L990
5774 4F 57          1540      DW L990
5776 BC 55          1550      DW L760
5778 C9 55          1560      DW L770
577A D5 55          1570      DW L780
577C E6 55          1580      DW L790
577E F4 55          1590      DW L800
5780 4F 57          1600      DW L990
5782 4F 57          1610      DW L990
5784 02 56          1620      DW L810
5786 12 56          1630      DW L820
5788 28 56          1640      DW L830
578A 36 56          1650      DW L840
578C 47 56          1660      DW L850
578E 64 56          1670      DW L860
5790 7E 56          1680      DW L870
5792 8B 56          1690      DW L880
5794 4F 57          1700      DW L990
5796 9A 56          1710      DW L890
5798 AB 56          1720      DW L900
579A B9 56          1730      DW L910
579C CB 56          1740      DW L920
579E 4F 57          1750      DW L990
57A0 E5 56          1760      DW L930
57A2 F9 56          1770      DW L940
57A4 4F 57          1780      DW L990
57A6 06 57          1790      DW L950
57A8 13 57          1800      DW L960
57AA 20 57          1810      DW L970
57AC 36 57          1820      DW L980
57AE 20 20 20 20    1830 L1300 DB
57BA                1840 WH0 EQU 0C20H
57BA                1850 WH1 EQU 0C24H
57BA                1860 MOVE EQU 100H
57BA                1870 OSEQ EQU 5ADH
57BA                1880 CROUT EQU 09F8H
57BA                1890 CRLF EQU CROUT
57BA                1900 CLEAR EQU 09FDH
57BA                1910 KBUF EQU 0C0CH
57BA                1920 FLAG EQU 0
57BA                1930 BLK1 EQU 0A02H
57BA                1940 DEOUT EQU 0A0CH
57BA E5             1950 ARRAY PUSH H
57BB 6B             1960      MOV L,E
57BC 62             1970      MOV H,D
57BD 19             1980      DAD D
57BE EB             1990      XCHG
57BF E1             2000      POP H
57C0 19             2010      DAD D
57C1 5E             2020      MOV E,M
57C2 23             2030      INX H
57C3 56             2040      MOV D,M
57C4 2B             2050      DCX H
57C5 C9             2060      RET
57C6 7B             2070 CMD MOV A,E
57C7 2F             2080      CMA
57C8 C6 01          2090      ADI 1
```

```
57CA 5F           2100       MOV  E,A          5841 C6 30        2850       ADI  30H
57CB 7A           2110       MOV  A,D          5843 C9           2860       RET
57CC 2F           2120       CMA               5844 D5           2870 DECPR PUSH D
57CD CE 00        2130       ACI  0            5845 E5           2880       PUSH H
57CF 57           2140       MOV  D,A          5846 21 9E 52     2890       LXI  H,OST
57D0 C9           2150       RET               5849 7A           2900       MOV  A,D
57D1 78           2160 BHCMP MOV  A,B          584A B7           2910       ORA  A
57D2 BC           2170       CMP  H            584B F5           2920       PUSH P
57D3 C0           2180       RNZ               584C F2 55 58     2930       JP   CDEC
57D4 79           2190       MOV  A,C          584F 36 2D        2940       MVI  M,'-'
57D5 95           2200       SUB  L            5851 23           2950       INX  H
57D6 C8           2210       RZ                5852 CD C6 57     2960       CALL CMD
57D7 1F           2220       RAR               5855 E5           2970 CDEC  PUSH H
57D8 B7           2230       ORA  A            5856 0E 00        2980       MVI  C,0
57D9 17           2240       RAL               5858 EB           2990       XCHG
57DA F8           2250       RM                5859 11 F0 D8     3000       LXI  D,-10000
57DB AF           2260       XRA  A            585C CD 2F 58     3010       CALL DCALC
57DC 3C           2270       INR  A            585F CA 66 58     3020       JZ   $+4
57DD C9           2280       RET               5862 E3           3030       XTHL
57DE 21 3F 00     2290 READ  LXI  H,63         5863 77           3040       MOV  M,A
57E1 11 CE 50     2300       LXI  D,LST        5864 23           3050       INX  H
57E4 01 00 00     2310       LXI  B,0          5865 E3           3060       XTHL
57E7 CD 20 0C     2320 RELP  CALL WHO          5866 11 18 FC     3070       LXI  D,-1000
57EA FE 18        2330       CPI  18H          5869 CD 2F 58     3080       CALL DCALC
57EC CA 1F 58     2340       JZ   CAN          586C CA 73 58     3090       JZ   $+4
57EF FE 7F        2350       CPI  7FH          586F E3           3100       XTHL
57F1 CA 0F 58     2360       JZ   RUB          5870 77           3110       MOV  M,A
57F4 CD 24 0C     2370       CALL WH1          5871 23           3120       INX  H
57F7 FE 0D        2380       CPI  0DH          5872 E3           3130       XTHL
57F9 CA 05 58     2390       JZ   CRF          5873 11 9C FF     3140       LXI  D,-100
57FC 12           2400       STAX D            5876 CD 2F 58     3150       CALL DCALC
57FD 13           2410       INX  D            5879 CA 80 58     3160       JZ   $+4
57FE 03           2420       INX  B            587C E3           3170       XTHL
57FF 2B           2430       DCX  H            587D 77           3180       MOV  M,A
5800 7C           2440       MOV  A,H          587E 23           3190       INX  H
5801 B5           2450       ORA  L            587F E3           3200       XTHL
5802 C2 E7 57     2460       JNZ  RELP         5880 11 F6 FF     3210       LXI  D,-10
5805 3E 20        2470 CRF   MVI  A,20H        5883 CD 2F 58     3220       CALL DCALC
5807 12           2480       STAX D            5886 CA 8D 58     3230       JZ   $+4
5808 03           2490       INX  B            5889 E3           3240       XTHL
5809 69           2500       MOV  L,C          588A 77           3250       MOV  M,A
580A 60           2510       MOV  H,B          588B 23           3260       INX  H
580B 22 24 54     2520       SHLD L00          588C E3           3270       XTHL
580E C9           2530       RET               588D 7D           3280       MOV  A,L
580F 78           2540 RUB   MOV  A,B          588E E1           3290       POP  H
5810 B1           2550       ORA  C            588F C6 30        3300       ADI  30H
5811 CA E7 57     2560       JZ   RELP         5891 77           3310       MOV  M,A
5814 1B           2570       DCX  D            5892 23           3320       INX  H
5815 0B           2580       DCX  B            5893 0D           3330       DCR  C
5816 23           2590       INX  H            5894 36 0D        3340       MVI  M,0DH
5817 3E 7F        2600       MVI  A,7FH        5896 F1           3350       POP  P
5819 CD 24 0C     2610       CALL WH1          5897 F2 9B 58     3360       JP   $+1
581C C3 E7 57     2620       JMP  RELP         589A 0D           3370       DCR  C
581F 78           2630 CAN   MOV  A,B          589B E1           3380       POP  H
5820 B1           2640       ORA  C            589C D1           3390       POP  D
5821 CA E7 57     2650       JZ   RELP         589D C9           3400       RET
5824 3E 7F        2660       MVI  A,7FH
5826 CD 24 0C     2670       CALL WH1          589E CD 44 58     0010 DECOUT CALL DECPR
5829 1B           2680       DCX  D            58A1 CD 02 0A     0020       CALL BLK1
582A 0B           2690       DCX  B            58A4 C3 C8 58     0030       JMP  OPUT
582B 23           2700       INX  H            58A7 F5           0040 DECFMT PUSH P
582C C3 1F 58     2710       JMP  CAN          58A8 CD 44 58     0050       CALL DECPR
582F 06 00        2720 DCALC MVI  B,0          58AB F1           0060       POP  P
5831 19           2730       DAD  D            58AC 0D           0070       DCR  C
5832 04           2740       INR  B            58AD 81           0080       ADD  C
5833 7C           2750       MOV  A,H          58AE CA C8 58     0090       JZ   OPUT
5834 B7           2760       ORA  A            58B1 F2 C0 58     0100       JP   FILL
5835 F2 31 58     2770       JP   $-7          58B4 91           0110       SUB  C
5838 CD C6 57     2780       CALL CMD          58B5 4F           0120       MOV  C,A
583B 19           2790       DAD  D            58B6 3E 2A        0130       MVI  A,'*'
583C 05           2800       DCR  B            58B8 CD 24 0C     0140 FMLP  CALL WH1
583D 78           2810       MOV  A,B          58BB 0C           0150       INR  C
583E B9           2820       CMP  C            58BC C2 B8 58     0160       JNZ  FMLP
583F C8           2830       RZ                58BF C9           0170       RET
5840 0D           2840       DCR  C            58C0 2F           0180 FILL  CMA
```

```
58C1  3C              0190       INR A
58C2  4F              0200       MOV C,A
58C3  3E 20           0210       MVI A,' '
58C5  CD B8 58        0220       CALL FMLP
58C8  E5              0230  OPUT PUSH H
58C9  21 9E 52        0240       LXI H,OST
58CC  CD AD 05        0250       CALL OSEQ
58CF  E1              0260       POP H
58D0  C3 02 0A        0270       JMP BLK1
58D3  2A 08 54        0280  S1030 LHLD CO
58D6  4D              0290       MOV C,L
58D7  44              0300       MOV B,H
58D8  2A 24 54        0310       LHLD LOO
58DB  CD D1 57        0320       CALL BHCMP
58DE  DA E7 58        0330       JC $+6
58E1  CD F7 58        0340       CALL S1090
58E4  C3 D3 58        0350       JMP S1030
58E7  69              0360       MOV L,C
58E8  60              0370       MOV H,B
58E9  23              0380       INX H
58EA  22 08 54        0390       SHLD CO
58ED  2B              0400       DCX H
58EE  11 CE 50        0410       LXI D,LST
58F1  19              0420       DAD D
58F2  7E              0430       MOV A,M
58F3  32 D8 53        0440       STA XST
58F6  C9              0450       RET
58F7  2A 0E 54        0460  S1090 LHLD C1
58FA  EB              0470       XCHG
58FB  3E 05           0480       MVI A,5
58FD  CD A7 58        0490       CALL DECFMT
5900  3A 03 54        0500       LDA F5+1
5903  B7              0510       ORA A
5904  FA 20 59        0520       JM L1160
5907  CD DE 57        0530  L1110 CALL READ
590A  3A 24 54        0540       LDA LOO
590D  3D              0550       DCR A
590E  CA F7 58        0560       JZ S1090
5911  3A CE 50        0570       LDA LST
5914  FE 24           0580       CPI '$'
5916  CA 60 59        0590       JZ L1210
5919  21 00 00        0600       LXI H,0
591C  22 08 54        0610       SHLD CO
591F  C9              0620       RET
5920  2A F2 53        0630  L1160 LHLD FPTR
5923  7E              0640       MOV A,M
5924  FE 01           0650       CPI 1
5926  C2 3A 59        0660       JNZ L1190
5929  21 00 00        0670       LXI H,0
592C  22 02 54        0680       SHLD F5
592F  21 0D 0C        0690       LXI H,KBUF+1
5932  36 24           0700       MVI M,'$'
5934  2B              0710       DCX H
5935  36 00           0720       MVI M,FLAG
5937  C3 07 59        0730       JMP L1110
593A  11 05 00        0740  L1190 LXI D,5
593D  19              0750       DAD D
593E  11 CE 50        0760       LXI D,LST
5941  01 00 00        0770       LXI B,0
5944  7E              0780  IFLP MOV A,M
5945  12              0790       STAX D
5946  CD 24 0C        0800       CALL WH1
5949  23              0810       INX H
594A  13              0820       INX D
594B  03              0830       INX B
594C  FE 0D           0840       CPI 0DH
594E  C2 44 59        0850       JNZ IFLP
5951  1B              0860       DCX D
5952  3E 20           0870       MVI A,20H
5954  12              0880       STAX D
5955  22 F2 53        0890       SHLD FPTR
5958  69              0900       MOV L,C
5959  60              0910       MOV H,B
595A  22 24 54        0920       SHLD LOO
595D  C3 0A 59        0930       JMP L1110+3
```

```
5960  21 FF FF     0940  L1210 LXI H,-1
5963  22 02 54     0950        SHLD F5
5966  21 CF 50     0960        LXI H,LST+1
5969  11 54 0C     0970        LXI D,0C54H
596C  01 FB FF     0980        LXI B,-5
596F  CD 00 01     0990        CALL MOVE
5972  2A F4 53     1000        LHLD BOFP
5975  22 F2 53     1010        SHLD FPTR
5978  22 6A 0C     1020        SHLD 0C6AH
597B  21 89 59     1030        LXI H,$+11
597E  22 6C 0C     1040        SHLD 0C6CH
5981  3E 49        1050        MVI A,'I'
5983  32 73 0C     1060        STA 0C73H
5986  C3 9A 59     1070        JMP READO
5989  2A 7F 72     1080        LHLD 727FH
598C  22 0E 0C     1090        SHLD 0C0EH
598F  2A 6E 0C     1100        LHLD 0C6EH
5992  36 01        1110        MVI M,1
5994  22 F6 53     1120        SHLD EOFP
5997  C3 F7 58     1130        JMP S1090
599A                1140  MENTR EQU 7390H
599A  2A BC 73     1150  READO LHLD MENTR+2CH
599D  36 4C        1160        MVI M,'L'
599F  23           1170        INX H
59A0  36 4F        1180        MVI M,'O'
59A2  23           1190        INX H
59A3  36 20        1200        MVI M,' '
59A5  23           1210        INX H
59A6  EB           1220        XCHG
59A7  21 54 0C     1230        LXI H,0C54H
59AA  01 FB FF     1240        LXI B,-5
59AD  CD 00 01     1250        CALL MOVE
59B0  EB           1260        XCHG
59B1  36 20        1270        MVI M,' '
59B3  23           1280        INX H
59B4  36 2E        1290        MVI M,'.'
59B6  23           1300        INX H
59B7  36 20        1310        MVI M,' '
59B9  23           1320        INX H
59BA  EB           1330        XCHG
59BB  2A 6A 0C     1340        LHLD 0C6AH
59BE  4D           1350        MOV C,L
59BF  7C           1360        MOV A,H
59C0  CD F9 59     1370        CALL BINH
59C3  2B           1380        DCX H
59C4  7E           1390        MOV A,M
59C5  12           1400        STAX D
59C6  13           1410        INX D
59C7  23           1420        INX H
59C8  7E           1430        MOV A,M
59C9  12           1440        STAX D
59CA  13           1450        INX D
59CB  79           1460        MOV A,C
59CC  CD F9 59     1470        CALL BINH
59CF  2B           1480        DCX H
59D0  7E           1490        MOV A,M
59D1  12           1500        STAX D
59D2  13           1510        INX D
59D3  23           1520        INX H
59D4  7E           1530        MOV A,M
59D5  12           1540        STAX D
59D6  13           1550        INX D
59D7  3E 0D        1560        MVI A,0DH
59D9  12           1570        STAX D
59DA  21 90 73     1580        LXI H,MENTR
59DD  22 BA 73     1590        SHLD MENTR+2AH
59E0  2A 0E 0C     1600        LHLD 0C0EH
59E3  22 7F 72     1610        SHLD 727FH
59E6  F3           1620        DI
59E7  2A BC 73     1630        LHLD MENTR+2CH
59EA  CD C2 73     1640        CALL MENTR+32H
59ED  2A B0 73     1650        LHLD MENTR+20H
59F0  2B           1660        DCX H
59F1  22 6E 0C     1670        SHLD 0C6EH
59F4  2A 6C 0C     1680        LHLD 0C6CH
```

```
59F7 FB           1690      EI
59F8 E9           1700      PCHL
59F9 21 31 54     1710 BINH LXI H,ADDS
59FC 47           1720      MOV B,A
59FD 1F           1730      RAR
59FE 1F           1740      RAR
59FF 1F           1750      RAR
5A00 1F           1760      RAR
5A01 CD 0C 5A     1770      CALL BIN1
5A04 77           1780      MOV M,A
5A05 23           1790      INX H
5A06 78           1800      MOV A,B
5A07 CD 0C 5A     1810      CALL BIN1
5A0A 77           1820      MOV M,A
5A0B C9           1830      RET
5A0C E6 0F        1840 BIN1 ANI 0FH
5A0E C6 30        1850      ADI 30H
5A10 FE 3A        1860      CPI '9'+1
5A12 D8           1870      RC
5A13 C6 07        1880      ADI 7
5A15 C9           1890      RET
5A16 2A A6 52     1900 S1960 LHLD T1
5A19 23           1910      INX H
5A1A 22 A6 52     1920      SHLD T1
5A1D 2B           1930      DCX H
5A1E 29           1940      DAD H
5A1F 29           1950      DAD H
5A20 29           1960      DAD H
5A21 11 0C 4F     1970      LXI D,TST
5A24 19           1980      DAD D
5A25 11 0E 51     1990      LXI D,AST
5A28 01 F8 FF     2000      LXI B,-8
5A2B EB           2010      XCHG
5A2C CD 00 01     2020      CALL MOVE
5A2F 2A A6 52     2030      LHLD T1
5A32 E5           2040      PUSH H
5A33 11 9C 50     2050      LXI D,TOST
5A36 19           2060      DAD D
5A37 2B           2070      DCX H
5A38 3A E8 53     2080      LDA KST
5A3B 77           2090      MOV M,A
5A3C E1           2100      POP H
5A3D FE 43        2110      CPI 'C'
5A3F C2 52 5A     2120      JNZ L2010
5A42 11 0C 53     2130      LXI D,T2
5A45 EB           2140      XCHG
5A46 CD BA 57     2150      CALL ARRAY
5A49 EB           2160      XCHG
5A4A 2A 18 54     2170      LHLD N3
5A4D EB           2180      XCHG
5A4E 73           2190      MOV M,E
5A4F 23           2200      INX H
5A50 72           2210      MOV M,D
5A51 C9           2220      RET
5A52 11 A6 52     2230 L2010 LXI D,T1
5A55 EB           2240      XCHG
5A56 CD BA 57     2250      CALL ARRAY
5A59 EB           2260      XCHG
5A5A 2A 20 54     2270      LHLD L1
5A5D EB           2280      XCHG
5A5E 73           2290      MOV M,E
5A5F 23           2300      INX H
5A60 72           2310      MOV M,D
5A61 3A E8 53     2320      LDA KST
5A64 FE 56        2330      CPI 'V'
5A66 C0           2340      RNZ
5A67 3A 22 54     2350      LDA F9
5A6A B7           2360      ORA A
5A6B C8           2370      RZ
5A6C 2A A6 52     2380      LHLD T1
5A6F 11 0C 53     2390      LXI D,T2
5A72 EB           2400      XCHG
5A73 CD BA 57     2410      CALL ARRAY
5A76 EB           2420      XCHG
5A77 2A 2C 54     2430      LHLD D0

5A7A EB           2440      XCHG
5A7B 73           2450      MOV M,E
5A7C 23           2460      INX H
5A7D 72           2470      MOV M,D
5A7E EB           2480      XCHG
5A7F 23           2490      INX H
5A80 22 2C 54     2500      SHLD D0
5A83 C9           2510      RET
5A84 0E 05        2520 STCMP MVI C,5
5A86 C3 A1 5A     2530      JMP SEAR
5A89 2A 31 54     2540 COMS LHLD ADDS
5A8C 3A 30 54     2550      LDA NCHR
5A8F 4F           2560      MOV C,A
5A90 D5           2570      PUSH D
5A91 CD A1 5A     2580      CALL SEAR
5A94 C2 99 5A     2590      JNZ $+2
5A97 D1           2600      POP D
5A98 C9           2610      RET
5A99 E3           2620      XTHL
5A9A E1           2630      POP H
5A9B 05           2640      DCR B
5A9C C2 89 5A     2650      JNZ COMS
5A9F 04           2660      INR B
5AA0 C9           2670      RET
5AA1 1A           2680 SEAR LDAX D
5AA2 BE           2690      CMP M
5AA3 C2 B0 5A     2700      JNZ INCA
5AA6 FE 20        2710      CPI ' '
5AA8 C8           2720      RZ
5AA9 23           2730      INX H
5AAA 13           2740      INX D
5AAB 0D           2750      DCR C
5AAC C2 A1 5A     2760      JNZ SEAR
5AAF C9           2770      RET
5AB0 13           2780 INCA INX D
5AB1 0D           2790      DCR C
5AB2 C2 B0 5A     2800      JNZ INCA
5AB5 0C           2810      INR C
5AB6 C9           2820      RET
5AB7 2A A6 52     2830 S2060 LHLD T1
5ABA 22 14 54     2840      SHLD I
5ABD 7C           2850      MOV A,H
5ABE B5           2860      ORA L
5ABF C2 C4 5A     2870      JNZ $+2
5AC2 3C           2880      INR A
5AC3 C9           2890      RET
5AC4 2B           2900      DCX H
5AC5 29           2910      DAD H
5AC6 29           2920      DAD H
5AC7 29           2930      DAD H
5AC8 11 0C 4F     2940      LXI D,TST
5ACB 19           2950      DAD D
5ACC 11 0E 51     2960      LXI D,AST
5ACF 0E 08        2970      MVI C,8
5AD1 CD A1 5A     2980      CALL SEAR
5AD4 2A 14 54     2990      LHLD I
5AD7 C8           3000      RZ
5AD8 2B           3010      DCX H
5AD9 C3 BA 5A     3020      JMP S2060+3

5ADC 3A D8 53     0010 S1240 LDA XST
5ADF FE 20        0020      CPI 20H
5AE1 C2 EA 5A     0030      JNZ L1280
5AE4 CD D3 58     0040      CALL S1030
5AE7 C3 DC 5A     0050      JMP S1240
5AEA FE 41        0060 L1280 CPI 'A'
5AEC DA DE 5B     0070      JC L1460
5AEF FE 5B        0080      CPI 'Z'+1
5AF1 D2 DE 5B     0090      JNC L1460
5AF4 21 00 00     0100      LXI H,0
5AF7 22 10 54     0110      SHLD K
5AFA 21 AE 57     0120      LXI H,L1300
5AFD 11 0E 51     0130      LXI D,AST
5B00 01 F4 FF     0140      LXI B,-12
5B03 CD 00 01     0150      CALL MOVE
```

```
5B06  2A  10  54        0160  L1310  LHLD  K
5B09  4D                0170         MOV   C,L
5B0A  44                0180         MOV   B,H
5B0B  21  08  00        0190         LXI   H,8
5B0E  CD  D1  57        0200         CALL  BHCMP
5B11  D2  23  5B        0210         JNC   L1330
5B14  60                0220         MOV   H,B
5B15  69                0230         MOV   L,C
5B16  23                0240         INX   H
5B17  22  10  54        0250         SHLD  K
5B1A  2B                0260         DCX   H
5B1B  11  0E  51        0270         LXI   D,AST
5B1E  19                0280         DAD   D
5B1F  3A  D8  53        0290         LDA   XST
5B22  77                0300         MOV   M,A
5B23  CD  D3  58        0310  L1330  CALL  S1030
5B26  6F                0320         MOV   L,A
5B27  26  00            0330         MVI   H,0
5B29  22  12  54        0340         SHLD  T
5B2C  FE  30            0350         CPI   '0'
5B2E  DA  40  5B        0360         JC    L1360
5B31  FE  3A            0370         CPI   '9'+1
5B33  DA  06  5B        0380         JC    L1310
5B36  FE  41            0390         CPI   'A'
5B38  DA  40  5B        0400         JC    L1360
5B3B  FE  5B            0410         CPI   'Z'+1
5B3D  DA  06  5B        0420         JC    L1310
5B40  21  01  00        0430  L1360  LXI   H,1
5B43  22  14  54        0440         SHLD  I
5B46  21  9C  00        0450         LXI   H,N0+N0+N0+N0+N0-4
5B49  22  16  54        0460         SHLD  J
5B4C  21  0E  51        0470         LXI   H,AST
5B4F  11  1A  51        0480         LXI   D,BST
5B52  01  F8  FF        0490         LXI   B,-8
5B55  CD  00  01        0500         CALL  MOVE
5B58  2A  14  54        0510  L1390  LHLD  I
5B5B  EB                0520         XCHG
5B5C  2A  16  54        0530         LHLD  J
5B5F  19                0540         DAD   D
5B60  11  F6  FF        0550         LXI   D,-10
5B63  01  FF  FF        0560         LXI   B,-1
5B66  19                0570  DIVL   DAD   D
5B67  03                0580         INX   B
5B68  7C                0590         MOV   A,H
5B69  B7                0600         ORA   A
5B6A  F2  66  5B        0610         JP    DIVL
5B6D  69                0620         MOV   L,C
5B6E  60                0630         MOV   H,B
5B6F  29                0640         DAD   H
5B70  29                0650         DAD   H
5B71  09                0660         DAD   B
5B72  23                0670         INX   H
5B73  22  10  54        0680         SHLD  K
5B76  2B                0690         DCX   H
5B77  11  33  54        0700         LXI   D,WOST
5B7A  19                0710         DAD   D
5B7B  11  ED  53        0720         LXI   D,ZST
5B7E  01  FB  FF        0730         LXI   B,-5
5B81  CD  00  01        0740         CALL  MOVE
5B84  21  FB  FF        0750         LXI   H,-5
5B87  19                0760         DAD   D
5B88  11  1A  51        0770         LXI   D,BST
5B8B  0E  05            0780         MVI   C,5
5B8D  1A                0790  L1400  LDAX  D
5B8E  BE                0800         CMP   M
5B8F  C2  98  5B        0810         JNZ   L1410
5B92  23                0820         INX   H
5B93  13                0830         INX   D
5B94  0D                0840         DCR   C
5B95  C2  8D  5B        0850         JNZ   L1400
5B98  CC  C8  5B        0860  L1410  CZ    JKM5
5B9B  FC  C8  5B        0870         CM    JKM5
5B9E  F4  D3  5B        0880         CP    IKP5
5BA1  2A  16  54        0890         LHLD  J
5BA4  4D                0900         MOV   C,L
```

```
5BA5 44           0910       MOV  B,H
5BA6 2A 14 54     0920       LHLD I
5BA9 CD D1 57     0930       CALL BHCMP
5BAC F2 5B 5B     0940       JP   L1390+3
5BAF 11 FB FF     0950       LXI  D,-5
5BB2 19           0960       DAD  D
5BB3 CD D1 57     0970       CALL BHCMP
5BB6 21 1A 51     0980       LXI  H,BST
5BB9 FA BF 5B     0990       JM   $+3
5BBC 21 D3 54     1000       LXI  H,IDENT
5BBF 11 E3 53     1010       LXI  D,SOST
5BC2 01 FB FF     1020       LXI  B,-5
5BC5 C3 00 01     1030       JMP  MOVE
5BC8 2A 10 54     1040 JKM5  LHLD K
5BCB 11 FB FF     1050       LXI  D,-5
5BCE 19           1060       DAD  D
5BCF 22 16 54     1070       SHLD J
5BD2 C9           1080       RET
5BD3 2A 10 54     1090 IKP5  LHLD K
5BD6 11 05 00     1100       LXI  D,5
5BD9 19           1110       DAD  D
5BDA 22 14 54     1120       SHLD I
5BDD C9           1130       RET
5BDE 21 ED 53     1140 L1460 LXI  H,ZST
5BE1 3A D8 53     1150       LDA  XST
5BE4 FE 30        1160       CPI  '0'
5BE6 DA 42 5C     1170       JC   L1580
5BE9 FE 3A        1180       CPI  '9'+1
5BEB D2 42 5C     1190       JNC  L1580
5BEE 77           1200 L1500 MOV  M,A
5BEF 23           1210       INX  H
5BF0 E5           1220       PUSH H
5BF1 CD D3 58     1230       CALL S1030
5BF4 E1           1240       POP  H
5BF5 FE 30        1250       CPI  '0'
5BF7 DA FF 5B     1260       JC   $+5
5BFA FE 3A        1270       CPI  '9'+1
5BFC DA EE 5B     1280       JC   L1500
5BFF 11 ED 53     1290       LXI  D,ZST
5C02 CD C6 57     1300       CALL CMD
5C05 19           1310       DAD  D
5C06 4D           1320       MOV  C,L
5C07 44           1330       MOV  B,H
5C08 21 00 00     1340       LXI  H,0
5C0B 11 ED 53     1350       LXI  D,ZST
5C0E 1A           1360 L1530 LDAX D
5C0F 13           1370       INX  D
5C10 D6 30        1380       SUI  30H
5C12 D5           1390       PUSH D
5C13 5D           1400       MOV  E,L
5C14 54           1410       MOV  D,H
5C15 29           1420       DAD  H
5C16 29           1430       DAD  H
5C17 19           1440       DAD  D
5C18 29           1450       DAD  H
5C19 5F           1460       MOV  E,A
5C1A 16 00        1470       MVI  D,0
5C1C 19           1480       DAD  D
5C1D D1           1490       POP  D
5C1E 0B           1500       DCX  B
5C1F 79           1510       MOV  A,C
5C20 B0           1520       ORA  B
5C21 C2 0E 5C     1530       JNZ  L1530
5C24 22 18 54     1540       SHLD N3
5C27 01 FF 7F     1550       LXI  B,N1
5C2A CD D1 57     1560       CALL BHCMP
5C2D D2 36 5C     1570       JNC  NOK
5C30 21 1E 00     1580       LXI  H,30
5C33 C3 57 5D     1590       JMP  FNE
5C36 21 D8 54     1600 NOK   LXI  H,NUM
5C39 11 E3 53     1610       LXI  D,SOST
5C3C 01 FB FF     1620       LXI  B,-5
5C3F C3 00 01     1630       JMP  MOVE
5C42 21 E3 53     1640 L1580 LXI  H,SOST
5C45 FE 3A        1650       CPI  ':'

5C47 C2 61 5C     1660       JNZ  L1640
5C4A E5           1670       PUSH H
5C4B CD D3 58     1680       CALL S1030
5C4E E1           1690       POP  H
5C4F FE 3D        1700       CPI  '='
5C51 36 3A        1710       MVI  M,':'
5C53 23           1720       INX  H
5C54 CA 5A 5C     1730       JZ   L1620
5C57 36 20        1740       MVI  M,' '
5C59 C9           1750       RET
5C5A 77           1760 L1620 MOV  M,A
5C5B 23           1770       INX  H
5C5C 36 20        1780       MVI  M,' '
5C5E C3 D3 58     1790       JMP  S1030
5C61 FE 3C        1800 L1640 CPI  '<'
5C63 C2 81 5C     1810       JNZ  L1710
5C66 77           1820       MOV  M,A
5C67 23           1830       INX  H
5C68 E5           1840       PUSH H
5C69 CD D3 58     1850       CALL S1030
5C6C E1           1860       POP  H
5C6D FE 3E        1870       CPI  '>'
5C6F CA 7A 5C     1880       JZ   L1690
5C72 FE 3D        1890       CPI  '='
5C74 CA 7A 5C     1900       JZ   L1690
5C77 36 20        1910       MVI  M,' '
5C79 C9           1920       RET
5C7A 77           1930 L1690 MOV  M,A
5C7B 23           1940       INX  H
5C7C 36 20        1950       MVI  M,' '
5C7E C3 D3 58     1960       JMP  S1030
5C81 FE 3E        1970 L1710 CPI  '>'
5C83 C2 95 5C     1980       JNZ  L1750
5C86 77           1990       MOV  M,A
5C87 23           2000       INX  H
5C88 E5           2010       PUSH H
5C89 CD D3 58     2020       CALL S1030
5C8C E1           2030       POP  H
5C8D FE 3D        2040       CPI  '='
5C8F CA 7A 5C     2050       JZ   L1690
5C92 36 20        2060       MVI  M,' '
5C94 C9           2070       RET
5C95 FE 27        2080 L1750 CPI  ''''
5C97 C2 CA 5C     2090       JNZ  L1790
5C9A 21 DD 54     2100       LXI  H,STR
5C9D 11 E3 53     2110       LXI  D,SOST
5CA0 01 FB FF     2120       LXI  B,-5
5CA3 CD 00 01     2130       CALL MOVE
5CA6 21 4E 52     2140       LXI  H,CST
5CA9 E5           2150 L1770 PUSH H
5CAA CD D3 58     2160       CALL S1030
5CAD E1           2170       POP  H
5CAE FE 27        2180       CPI  ''''
5CB0 CA B8 5C     2190       JZ   QFND
5CB3 77           2200       MOV  M,A
5CB4 23           2210       INX  H
5CB5 C3 A9 5C     2220       JMP  L1770
5CB8 E5           2230 QFND  PUSH H
5CB9 CD D3 58     2240       CALL S1030
5CBC E1           2250       POP  H
5CBD FE 27        2260       CPI  ''''
5CBF C2 C7 5C     2270       JNZ  L1780
5CC2 77           2280       MOV  M,A
5CC3 23           2290       INX  H
5CC4 C3 A9 5C     2300       JMP  L1770
5CC7 36 20        2310 L1780 MVI  M,' '
5CC9 C9           2320       RET
5CCA FE 7D        2330 L1790 CPI  '}'
5CCC C2 DD 5C     2340       JNZ  L1820
5CCF CD D3 58     2350 COM   CALL S1030
5CD2 FE 7D        2360       CPI  '}'
5CD4 C2 CF 5C     2370       JNZ  COM
5CD7 CD D3 58     2380       CALL S1030
5CDA C3 DC 5A     2390       JMP  S1240
5CDD FE 25        2400 L1820 CPI  '%'
```

```
5CDF C2 2E 5D    2410       JNZ L1930
5CE2 21 D8 54    2420       LXI H,NUM
5CE5 11 E3 53    2430       LXI D,SOST
5CE8 01 FB FF    2440       LXI B,-5
5CEB CD 00 01    2450       CALL MOVE
5CEE 21 00 00    2460       LXI H,0
5CF1 4D          2470       MOV C,L
5CF2 E5          2480 HXI   PUSH H
5CF3 C5          2490       PUSH B
5CF4 CD D3 58    2500       CALL S1030
5CF7 C1          2510       POP B
5CF8 E1          2520       POP H
5CF9 D6 30       2530       SUI '0'
5CFB DA 19 5D    2540       JC L1910
5CFE FE 0A       2550       CPI 10
5D00 DA 0F 5D    2560       JC L1880
5D03 D6 07       2570       SUI 7
5D05 FE 0A       2580       CPI 10
5D07 DA 19 5D    2590       JC L1910
5D0A FE 10       2600       CPI 16
5D0C D2 19 5D    2610       JNC L1910
5D0F 29          2620 L1880 DAD H
5D10 29          2630       DAD H
5D11 29          2640       DAD H
5D12 29          2650       DAD H
5D13 85          2660       ADD L
5D14 6F          2670       MOV L,A
5D15 0C          2680       INR C
5D16 C3 F2 5C    2690       JMP HXI
5D19 22 18 54    2700 L1910 SHLD N3
5D1C 21 1B 00    2710       LXI H,27
5D1F 79          2720       MOV A,C
5D20 FE 05       2730       CPI 5
5D22 D2 57 5D    2740       JNC FNE
5D25 B7          2750       ORA A
5D26 C0          2760       RNZ
5D27 21 25 20    2770       LXI H,' %'
5D2A 22 E3 53    2780       SHLD SOST
5D2D C9          2790       RET
5D2E 21 E3 53    2800 L1930 LXI H,SOST
5D31 77          2810       MOV M,A
5D32 23          2820       INX H
5D33 36 20       2830       MVI M,' '
5D35 C3 D3 58    2840       JMP S1030
5D38 E5          2850 FNE2  PUSH H
5D39 CD DC 5A    2860       CALL S1240
5D3C E1          2870       POP H
5D3D E5          2880 FNE1  PUSH H
5D3E 11 E3 53    2890       LXI D,SOST
5D41 21 D9 53    2900       LXI H,FNE1ST
5D44 CD 84 5A    2910       CALL STCMP
5D47 E1          2920       POP H
5D48 C2 57 5D    2930       JNZ FNE
5D4B 21 AE 57    2940 BLST  LXI H,L1300
5D4E 11 D9 53    2950       LXI D,FNE1ST
5D51 01 FB FF    2960       LXI B,-5
5D54 C3 00 01    2970       JMP MOVE
5D57 E5          2980 FNE   PUSH H
5D58 2B          2990       DCX H
5D59 29          3000       DAD H
5D5A 11 66 57    3010       LXI D,ETAB
5D5D 19          3020       DAD D
5D5E 7E          3030       MOV A,M
5D5F 23          3040       INX H
5D60 66          3050       MOV H,M
5D61 6F          3060       MOV L,A
5D62 E3          3070       XTHL
5D63 E5          3080       PUSH H
5D64 2A 08 54    3090       LHLD C0
5D67 11 04 00    3100       LXI D,4
5D6A 19          3110       DAD D
5D6B CD 02 0A    3120 FL    CALL BLK1
5D6E 2B          3130       DCX H
5D6F 7D          3140       MOV A,L
5D70 B4          3150       ORA H

5D71 C2 6B 5D    3160       JNZ FL
5D74 3E 5E       3170       MVI A,'↑'
5D76 CD 24 0C    3180       CALL WH1
5D79 CD 02 0A    3190       CALL BLK1
5D7C E1          3200       POP H
5D7D EB          3210       XCHG
5D7E CD 9E 58    3220       CALL DECOUT
5D81 CD F8 09    3230       CALL CRLF
5D84 E1          3240       POP H
5D85 CD AD 05    3250       CALL OSEQ
5D88 CD F8 09    3260       CALL CRLF
5D8B CD 20 0C    3270       CALL WH0
5D8E 2A 0E 0C    3280       LHLD 0C0EH
5D91 22 7F 72    3290       SHLD 727FH
5D94 C3 90 73    3300       JMP 7390H
5D97 3E 20       3310 FNG   MVI A,'
5D99 32 1A 51    3320       STA BST
5D9C 2A FE 53    3330       LHLD Q9
5D9F D5          3340       PUSH D
5DA0 EB          3350       XCHG
5DA1 2A FC 53    3360       LHLD P9
5DA4 23          3370       INX H
5DA5 23          3380       INX H
5DA6 23          3390       INX H
5DA7 23          3400       INX H
5DA8 CD C6 57    3410       CALL CMD
5DAB 19          3420       DAD D
5DAC 7C          3430       MOV A,H
5DAD B7          3440       ORA A
5DAE 21 01 00    3450       LXI H,1
5DB1 F2 57 5D    3460       JP FNE
5DB4 2A FC 53    3470       LHLD P9
5DB7 D1          3480       POP D
5DB8 70          3490       MOV M,B
5DB9 23          3500       INX H
5DBA 71          3510       MOV M,C
5DBB 23          3520       INX H
5DBC 73          3530       MOV M,E
5DBD 23          3540       INX H
5DBE 72          3550       MOV M,D
5DBF 23          3560       INX H
5DC0 22 FC 53    3570       SHLD P9
5DC3 3A 04 54    3580       LDA Y9
5DC6 B7          3590       ORA A
5DC7 C2 14 5E    3600       JNZ L6400
5DCA 78          3610       MOV A,B
5DCB FE 10       3620       CPI 16
5DCD DA D8 5D    3630       JC L6390
5DD0 D6 10       3640       SUI 16
5DD2 47          3650       MOV B,A
5DD3 3E 58       3660       MVI A,'X'
5DD5 32 1A 51    3670       STA BST
5DD8 78          3680 L6390 MOV A,B
5DD9 87          3690       ADD A
5DDA 80          3700       ADD B
5DDB 47          3710       MOV B,A
5DDC 2A 0E 54    3720       LHLD C1
5DDF D5          3730       PUSH D
5DE0 C5          3740       PUSH B
5DE1 EB          3750       XCHG
5DE2 3E 10       3760       MVI A,16
5DE4 CD A7 58    3770       CALL DECFMT
5DE7 CD 02 0A    3780       CALL BLK1
5DEA C1          3790       POP B
5DEB 21 E2 54    3800       LXI H,MST
5DEE 58          3810       MOV E,B
5DEF 16 00       3820       MVI D,0
5DF1 19          3830       DAD D
5DF2 7E          3840       MOV A,M
5DF3 CD 24 0C    3850       CALL WH1
5DF6 23          3860       INX H
5DF7 7E          3870       MOV A,M
5DF8 CD 24 0C    3880       CALL WH1
5DFB 23          3890       INX H
5DFC 7E          3900       MOV A,M
```

```
5DFD CD 24 0C    3910 L       CALL WH1
5E00 3A 1A 51    3920         LDA  BST
5E03 CD 24 0C    3930         CALL WH1
5E06 CD 02 0A    3940         CALL BLK1
5E09 59          3950         MOV  E,C
5E0A CD 9E 58    3960         CALL DECOUT
5E0D D1          3970         POP  D
5E0E CD 9E 58    3980         CALL DECOUT
5E11 CD F8 09    3990         CALL CRLF
5E14 2A 0E 54    4000 L6400   LHLD C1
5E17 23          4010         INX  H
5E18 22 0E 54    4020         SHLD C1
5E1B C9          4030         RET

5E1C CD 8F 5E    0010 S6520   CALL S6150
5E1F 2A 1A 54    0020 L6540   LHLD X
5E22 29          0030         DAD  H
5E23 29          0040         DAD  H
5E24 EB          0050         XCHG
5E25 2A F8 53    0060         LHLD P7
5E28 19          0070         DAD  D
5E29 22 2E 54    0080         SHLD N
5E2C EB          0090         XCHG
5E2D 2A 0E 54    0100         LHLD C1
5E30 EB          0110         XCHG
5E31 23          0120         INX  H
5E32 23          0130         INX  H
5E33 73          0140         MOV  M,E
5E34 23          0150         INX  H
5E35 72          0160         MOV  M,D
5E36 2A 04 54    0170         LHLD Y9
5E39 7C          0180         MOV  A,H
5E3A B5          0190         ORA  L
5E3B C0          0200         RNZ
5E3C 21 53 57    0210         LXI  H,L6570
5E3F CD AD 05    0220         CALL OSEQ
5E42 23          0230         INX  H
5E43 E5          0240         PUSH H
5E44 2A 1A 54    0250         LHLD X
5E47 EB          0260         XCHG
5E48 CD 9E 58    0270         CALL DECOUT
5E4B E1          0280         POP  H
5E4C CD AD 05    0290         CALL OSEQ
5E4F 2A 0E 54    0300         LHLD C1
5E52 EB          0310         XCHG
5E53 CD 9E 58    0320         CALL DECOUT
5E56 C3 F8 09    0330         JMP  CRLF
5E59 21 E3 53    0340 CKRES   LXI  H,SOST
5E5C 22 31 54    0350         SHLD ADDS
5E5F 3E 05       0360         MVI  A,5
5E61 32 30 54    0370         STA  NCHR
5E64 06 23       0380         MVI  B,35
5E66 11 33 54    0390         LXI  D,WOST
5E69 CD 89 5A    0400         CALL COMS
5E6C C0          0410         RNZ
5E6D 21 33 54    0420         LXI  H,WOST
5E70 EB          0430         XCHG
5E71 CD C6 57    0440         CALL CMD
5E74 19          0450         DAD  D
5E75 AF          0460         XRA  A
5E76 C9          0470         RET
5E77 2A 00 54    0480 S6120   LHLD S9
5E7A 23          0490         INX  H
5E7B 22 00 54    0500         SHLD S9
5E7E 2B          0510         DCX  H
5E7F EB          0520         XCHG
5E80 21 22 51    0530         LXI  H,S
5E83 CD BA 57    0540         CALL ARRAY
5E86 EB          0550         XCHG
5E87 2A 1A 54    0560         LHLD X
5E8A EB          0570         XCHG
5E8B 73          0580         MOV  M,E
5E8C 23          0590         INX  H
5E8D 72          0600         MOV  M,D
5E8E C9          0610         RET

5E8F 2A 00 54    0620 S6150   LHLD S9
5E92 2B          0630         DCX  H
5E93 22 00 54    0640         SHLD S9
5E96 EB          0650         XCHG
5E97 21 22 51    0660         LXI  H,S
5E9A CD BA 57    0670         CALL ARRAY
5E9D EB          0680         XCHG
5E9E 22 1A 54    0690         SHLD X
5EA1 C9          0700         RET
5EA2 2A FA 53    0710 S6180   LHLD P8
5EA5 22 1A 54    0720         SHLD X
5EA8 CD 77 5E    0730         CALL S6120
5EAB 21 DE 53    0740         LXI  H,YST
5EAE 01 00 00    0750         LXI  B,0
5EB1 7E          0760 L6190   MOV  A,M
5EB2 FE 20       0770         CPI  20H
5EB4 CA C1 5E    0780         JZ   L6200
5EB7 12          0790         STAX D
5EB8 23          0800         INX  H
5EB9 13          0810         INX  D
5EBA 0B          0820         DCX  B
5EBB 79          0830         MOV  A,C
5EBC FE FB       0840         CPI  -5
5EBE C2 B1 5E    0850         JNZ  L6190
5EC1 EB          0860 L6200   XCHG
5EC2 22 FA 53    0870         SHLD P8
5EC5 69          0880         MOV  L,C
5EC6 60          0890         MOV  H,B
5EC7 22 1A 54    0900         SHLD X
5ECA C3 77 5E    0910         JMP  S6120
5ECD CD 8F 5E    0920 S6240   CALL S6150
5ED0 4D          0930         MOV  C,L
5ED1 44          0940         MOV  B,H
5ED2 CD 8F 5E    0950         CALL S6150
5ED5 22 FA 53    0960         SHLD P8
5ED8 11 DE 53    0970         LXI  D,YST
5EDB C5          0980         PUSH B
5EDC 79          0990         MOV  A,C
5EDD B0          1000         ORA  B
5EDE C4 00 01    1010         CNZ  MOVE
5EE1 C1          1020         POP  B
5EE2 EB          1030         XCHG
5EE3 79          1040         MOV  A,C
5EE4 FE FB       1050 L6270   CPI  -5
5EE6 C8          1060         RZ
5EE7 36 20       1070         MVI  M,' '
5EE9 23          1080         INX  H
5EEA 3D          1090         DCR  A
5EEB C3 E4 5E    1100         JMP  L6270
5EEE 21 D3 54    1110 S2180   LXI  H,IDENT
5EF1 11 D9 53    1120         LXI  D,FNE1ST
5EF4 01 FB FF    1130         LXI  B,-5
5EF7 CD 00 01    1140         CALL MOVE
5EFA 21 04 00    1150         LXI  H,4
5EFD CD 3D 5D    1160         CALL FNE1
5F00 21 3D 20    1170         LXI  H,' ='
5F03 22 D9 53    1180         SHLD FNE1ST
5F06 21 03 00    1190         LXI  H,3
5F09 CD 38 5D    1200         CALL FNE2
5F0C CD DC 5A    1210         CALL S1240
5F0F 3A E3 53    1220         LDA  SOST
5F12 FE 2D       1230         CPI  '-'
5F14 F5          1240         PUSH P
5F15 CC DC 5A    1250         CZ   S1240
5F18 CD 35 5F    1260         CALL S2240
5F1B F1          1270         POP  P
5F1C C2 2A 5F    1280         JNZ  $+11
5F1F 2A 18 54    1290         LHLD N3
5F22 EB          1300         XCHG
5F23 CD C6 57    1310         CALL CMD
5F26 EB          1320         XCHG
5F27 22 18 54    1330         SHLD N3
5F2A 3E 43       1340         MVI  A,'C'
5F2C 32 E8 53    1350         STA  KST
5F2F CD 16 5A    1360         CALL S1960
```

5F32 C3 DC 5A	1370	JMP S1240
5F35 21 E3 53	1380 S2240	LXI H,SOST
5F38 11 D8 54	1390	LXI D,NUM
5F3B CD 84 5A	1400	CALL STCMP
5F3E C8	1410	RZ
5F3F 21 E3 53	1420	LXI H,SOST
5F42 11 D3 54	1430	LXI D,IDENT
5F45 CD 84 5A	1440	CALL STCMP
5F48 CA 67 5F	1450	JZ L2290
5F4B 21 DD 54	1460	LXI H,STR
5F4E 11 D9 53	1470	LXI D,FNE1ST
5F51 01 FB FF	1480	LXI B,-5
5F54 CD 00 01	1490	CALL MOVE
5F57 21 02 00	1500	LXI H,2
5F5A CD 3D 5D	1510	CALL FNE1
5F5D 3A 4E 52	1520	LDA CST
5F60 6F	1530	MOV L,A
5F61 26 00	1540	MVI H,0
5F63 22 18 54	1550	SHLD N3
5F66 C9	1560	RET
5F67 CD B7 5A	1570 L2290	CALL S2060
5F6A 2A 14 54	1580	LHLD I
5F6D EB	1590	XCHG
5F6E 21 02 00	1600	LXI H,2
5F71 7B	1610	MOV A,E
5F72 B2	1620	ORA D
5F73 CA 57 5D	1630	JZ FNE
5F76 E5	1640	PUSH H
5F77 21 9C 50	1650	LXI H,TOST
5F7A 19	1660	DAD D
5F7B 2B	1670	DCX H
5F7C 7E	1680	MOV A,M
5F7D E1	1690	POP H
5F7E FE 43	1700	CPI 'C'
5F80 C2 57 5D	1710	JNZ FNE
5F83 21 0C 53	1720	LXI H,T2
5F86 CD BA 57	1730	CALL ARRAY
5F89 EB	1740	XCHG
5F8A 22 18 54	1750	SHLD N3
5F8D C9	1760	RET
5F8E 21 D3 54	1770 S2340	LXI H,IDENT
5F91 11 D9 53	1780	LXI D,FNE1ST
5F94 01 FB FF	1790	LXI B,-5
5F97 CD 00 01	1800	CALL MOVE
5F9A 21 04 00	1810	LXI H,4
5F9D CD 3D 5D	1820	CALL FNE1
5FA0 3E 56	1830	MVI A,'V'
5FA2 32 E8 53	1840	STA KST
5FA5 CD 16 5A	1850	CALL S1960
5FA8 C3 DC 5A	1860	JMP S1240
5FAB 3A E3 53	1870 S2380	LDA SOST
5FAE FE 2B	1880	CPI '+'
5FB0 CA B8 5F	1890	JZ L2420
5FB3 FE 2D	1900	CPI '-'
5FB5 C2 2B 60	1910	JNZ L2590
5FB8 32 DE 53	1920 L2420	STA YST
5FBB 3E 20	1930	MVI A,' '
5FBD 32 DF 53	1940	STA YST+1
5FC0 CD A2 5E	1950	CALL S6180
5FC3 CD DC 5A	1960	CALL S1240
5FC6 CD 31 60	1970	CALL S2610
5FC9 CD CD 5E	1980	CALL S6240
5FCC 3A DE 53	1990	LDA YST
5FCF FE 2D	2000	CPI '-'
5FD1 C2 DD 5F	2010	JNZ L2460
5FD4 11 01 00	2020	LXI D,1
5FD7 01 00 01	2030	LXI B,100H
5FDA CD 97 5D	2040	CALL FNG
5FDD 3A E3 53	2050 L2460	LDA SOST
5FE0 FE 2B	2060	CPI '+'
5FE2 CA F7 5F	2070	JZ L2500
5FE5 FE 2D	2080	CPI '-'
5FE7 CA F7 5F	2090	JZ L2500
5FEA 21 92 54	2100	LXI H,WOST+95
5FED 11 E3 53	2110	LXI D,SOST
5FF0 CD 84 5A	2120	CALL STCMP
5FF3 CA F7 5F	2130	JZ L2500
5FF6 C9	2140	RET
5FF7 21 E3 53	2150 L2500	LXI H,SOST
5FFA 11 DE 53	2160	LXI D,YST
5FFD 01 FB FF	2170	LXI B,-5
6000 CD 00 01	2180	CALL MOVE
6003 CD A2 5E	2190	CALL S6180
6006 CD DC 5A	2200	CALL S1240
6009 CD 31 60	2210	CALL S2610
600C CD CD 5E	2220	CALL S6240
600F 01 00 01	2230	LXI B,100H
6012 11 03 00	2240	LXI D,3
6015 3A DE 53	2250	LDA YST
6018 FE 2D	2260	CPI '-'
601A CA 25 60	2270	JZ L2560
601D 1D	2280	DCR E
601E FE 2B	2290	CPI '+'
6020 CA 25 60	2300	JZ L2560
6023 1E 0E	2310	MVI E,14
6025 CD 97 5D	2320 L2560	CALL FNG
6028 C3 DD 5F	2330	JMP L2460
602B CD 31 60	2340 L2590	CALL S2610
602E C3 DD 5F	2350	JMP L2460
6031 CD B5 60	2360 S2610	CALL S2850
6034 3A E3 53	2370 L2630	LDA SOST
6037 FE 2A	2380	CPI '*'
6039 CA 57 60	2390	JZ L2700
603C CD 59 5E	2400	CALL CKRES
603F C0	2410	RNZ
6040 AF	2420	XRA A
6041 85	2430	ADD L
6042 CA 57 60	2440	JZ L2700
6045 D6 1E	2450	SUI 30
6047 CA 57 60	2460	JZ L2700
604A D6 32	2470	SUI 50
604C CA 57 60	2480	JZ L2700
604F D6 23	2490	SUI 35
6051 CA 57 60	2500	JZ L2700
6054 D6 05	2510	SUI 5
6056 C0	2520	RNZ
6057 21 E3 53	2530 L2700	LXI H,SOST
605A 11 DE 53	2540	LXI D,YST
605D 01 FB FF	2550	LXI B,-5
6060 CD 00 01	2560	CALL MOVE
6063 CD A2 5E	2570	CALL S6180
6066 CD DC 5A	2580	CALL S1240
6069 CD B5 60	2590	CALL S2850
606C CD CD 5E	2600	CALL S6240
606F 01 00 01	2610	LXI B,100H
6072 11 04 00	2620	LXI D,4
6075 3A DE 53	2630	LDA YST
6078 FE 2A	2640	CPI '*'
607A CA AF 60	2650	JZ L2830
607D C5	2660	PUSH B
607E D5	2670	PUSH D
607F 21 DE 53	2680	LXI H,YST
6082 CD 5C 5E	2690	CALL CKRES+3
6085 D1	2700	POP D
6086 C1	2710	POP B
6087 AF	2720	XRA A
6088 85	2730	ADD L
6089 C2 92 60	2740	JNZ L2730
608C 11 0F 00	2750	LXI D,15
608F C3 AF 60	2760	JMP L2830
6092 D6 1E	2770 L2730	SUI 30
6094 C2 9B 60	2780	JNZ L2740
6097 13	2790	INX D
6098 C3 AF 60	2800	JMP L2830
609B D6 32	2810 L2740	SUI 50
609D C2 A6 60	2820	JNZ L2760
60A0 11 07 00	2830	LXI D,7
60A3 C3 AF 60	2840	JMP L2830
60A6 11 11 00	2850 L2760	LXI D,'·'
60A9 D6 23	2860	SUI 35

```
60AB  CA AF 60      2870        JZ   L2830
60AE  13            2880        INX  D
60AF  CD 97 5D      2890 L2830  CALL FNG
60B2  C3 34 60      2900        JMP  L2630
60B5  3A E3 53      2910 S2850  LDA  S0ST

60B8  FE 28         0010        CPI  '('
60BA  CA 73 61      0020        JZ   L3100
60BD  CD 59 5E      0030        CALL CKRES
60C0  C2 DD 60      0040        JNZ  L2920
60C3  3E AA         0050        MVI  A,170
60C5  95            0060        SUB  L
60C6  CA 6A 61      0070        JZ   L3080
60C9  D6 05         0080        SUI  5
60CB  CA 5D 61      0090        JZ   L3060
60CE  D6 05         0100        SUI  5
60D0  CA E3 60      0110        JZ   L2940
60D3  D6 4B         0120        SUI  75
60D5  CA FF 61      0130        JZ   L3260
60D8  D6 0A         0140        SUI  10
60DA  CA 87 61      0150        JZ   L3140
60DD  21 17 00      0160 L2920  LXI  H,23
60E0  C3 57 5D      0170        JMP  FNE
60E3  CD B7 5A      0180 L2940  CALL S2060
60E6  7C            0190        MOV  A,H
60E7  B5            0200        ORA  L
60E8  C2 F1 60      0210        JNZ  $+6
60EB  21 0B 00      0220        LXI  H,11
60EE  C3 57 5D      0230        JMP  FNE
60F1  2B            0240        DCX  H
60F2  11 9C 50      0250        LXI  D,TOST
60F5  19            0260        DAD  D
60F6  7E            0270        MOV  A,M
60F7  FE 50         0280        CPI  'P'
60F9  C2 02 61      0290        JNZ  L2970
60FC  21 15 00      0300        LXI  H,21
60FF  C3 57 5D      0310        JMP  FNE
6102  FE 59         0320 L2970  CPI  'Y'
6104  C2 1A 61      0330        JNZ  L3000
6107  01 00 05      0340        LXI  B,500H
610A  11 01 00      0350        LXI  D,1
610D  CD 97 5D      0360        CALL FNG
6110  2A 14 54      0370        LHLD I
6113  2B            0380        DCX  H
6114  22 14 54      0390        SHLD I
6117  C3 06 4F      0400        JMP  F4290
611A  FE 41         0410 L3000  CPI  'A'
611C  CA B1 61      0420        JZ   L3190
611F  FE 43         0430        CPI  'C'
6121  C2 37 61      0440        JNZ  L3030
6124  2A 14 54      0450        LHLD I
6127  EB            0460        XCHG
6128  21 0C 53      0470        LXI  H,T2
612B  CD BA 57      0480        CALL ARRAY
612E  01 00 00      0490        LXI  B,0
6131  CD 97 5D      0500        CALL FNG
6134  C3 DC 5A      0510        JMP  S1240
6137  2A 14 54      0520 L3030  LHLD I
613A  EB            0530        XCHG
613B  21 0C 53      0540        LXI  H,T2
613E  CD BA 57      0550        CALL ARRAY
6141  D5            0560        PUSH D
6142  2A 14 54      0570        LHLD I
6145  EB            0580        XCHG
6146  21 A6 52      0590        LXI  H,T1
6149  CD BA 57      0600        CALL ARRAY
614C  CD C6 57      0610        CALL CMD
614F  2A 20 54      0620        LHLD L1
6152  19            0630        DAD  D
6153  4D            0640        MOV  C,L
6154  06 02         0650        MVI  B,2
6156  D1            0660        POP  D
6157  CD 97 5D      0670        CALL FNG
615A  C3 DC 5A      0680        JMP  S1240
615D  2A 18 54      0690 L3060  LHLD N3

6160  EB            0700        XCHG
6161  01 00 00      0710        LXI  B,0
6164  CD 97 5D      0720        CALL FNG
6167  C3 DC 5A      0730        JMP  S1240
616A  3A 4E 52      0740 L3080  LDA  CST
616D  5F            0750        MOV  E,A
616E  16 00         0760        MVI  D,0
6170  C3 61 61      0770        JMP  L3060+4
6173  CD DC 5A      0780 L3100  CALL S1240
6176  CD 0E 62      0790        CALL S3290
6179  3A E3 53      0800        LDA  S0ST
617C  FE 29         0810        CPI  ' )'
617E  CA DC 5A      0820        JZ   S1240
6181  21 16 00      0830        LXI  H,22
6184  C3 57 5D      0840        JMP  FNE
6187  21 5B 20      0850 L3140  LXI  H,' ['
618A  22 D9 53      0860        SHLD FNE1ST
618D  21 21 00      0870        LXI  H,33
6190  CD 38 5D      0880        CALL FNE2
6193  CD DC 5A      0890        CALL S1240
6196  CD 0E 62      0900        CALL S3290
6199  21 5D 20      0910        LXI  H,' ]'
619C  22 D9 53      0920        SHLD FNE1ST
619F  21 22 00      0930        LXI  H,34
61A2  CD 3D 5D      0940        CALL FNE1
61A5  01 FF 02      0950        LXI  B,2FFH
61A8  11 00 00      0960        LXI  D,0
61AB  CD 97 5D      0970        CALL FNG
61AE  C3 DC 5A      0980        JMP  S1240
61B1  2A 14 54      0990 L3190  LHLD I
61B4  22 1A 54      1000        SHLD X
61B7  CD 77 5E      1010        CALL S6120
61BA  21 5B 20      1020        LXI  H,' ['
61BD  22 D9 53      1030        SHLD FNE1ST
61C0  21 21 00      1040        LXI  H,33
61C3  CD 38 5D      1050        CALL FNE2
61C6  CD DC 5A      1060        CALL S1240
61C9  CD 0E 62      1070        CALL S3290
61CC  21 5D 20      1080        LXI  H,' ]'
61CF  22 D9 53      1090        SHLD FNE1ST
61D2  21 22 00      1100        LXI  H,34
61D5  CD 3D 5D      1110        CALL FNE1
61D8  CD 8F 5E      1120        CALL S6150
61DB  2A 1A 54      1130        LHLD X
61DE  EB            1140        XCHG
61DF  21 A6 52      1150        LXI  H,T1
61E2  CD BA 57      1160        CALL ARRAY
61E5  CD C6 57      1170        CALL CMD
61E8  2A 20 54      1180        LHLD L1
61EB  19            1190        DAD  D
61EC  4D            1200        MOV  C,L
61ED  06 12         1210        MVI  B,18
61EF  2A 1A 54      1220        LHLD X
61F2  EB            1230        XCHG
61F3  21 0C 53      1240        LXI  H,T2
61F6  CD BA 57      1250        CALL ARRAY
61F9  CD 97 5D      1260        CALL FNG
61FC  C3 DC 5A      1270        JMP  S1240
61FF  CD DC 5A      1280 L3260  CALL S1240
6202  CD B5 60      1290        CALL S2850
6205  11 10 00      1300        LXI  D,16
6208  01 00 01      1310        LXI  B,100H
620B  C3 97 5D      1320        JMP  FNG
620E  CD AB 5F      1330 S3290  CALL S2380
6211  2A E3 53      1340        LHLD S0ST
6214  11 08 00      1350        LXI  D,8
6217  44            1360        MOV  B,H
6218  4D            1370        MOV  C,L
6219  21 3D 20      1380        LXI  H,' ='
621C  CD 43 62      1390        CALL BHCMPJ
621F  13            1400        INX  D
6220  21 3C 3E      1410        LXI  H,'><'
6223  CD 43 62      1420        CALL BHCMPJ
6226  13            1430        INX  D
6227  21 3C 20      1440        LXI  H,' <'
```

```
622A CD 43 62   1450  CALL BHCMPJ
622D 13         1460  INX D
622E 21 3E 3D   1470  LXI H,'=>'
6231 CD 43 62   1480  CALL BHCMPJ
6234 13         1490  INX D
6235 21 3E 20   1500  LXI H,' >'
6238 CD 43 62   1510  CALL BHCMPJ
623B 13         1520  INX D
623C 21 3C 3D   1530  LXI H,'=<'
623F CD 43 62   1540  CALL BHCMPJ
6242 C9         1550  RET
6243 CD D1 57   1560  BHCMPJ CALL BHCMP
6246 C0         1570  RNZ
6247 E1         1580  POP H
6248 D5         1590  PUSH D
6249 21 E3 53   1600  LXI H,SOST
624C 11 DE 53   1610  LXI D,YST
624F 01 FB FF   1620  LXI B,-5
6252 CD 00 01   1630  CALL MOVE
6255 CD A2 5E   1640  CALL S6180
6258 CD DC 5A   1650  CALL S1240
625B CD AB 5F   1660  CALL S2380
625E CD CD 5E   1670  CALL S6240
6261 D1         1680  POP D
6262 01 00 01   1690  LXI B,100H
6265 C3 97 5D   1700  JMP FNG
6268 CD B7 5A   1710  L3630 CALL S2060
626B CA 74 62   1720  JZ L3650
626E 21 0B 00   1730  LXI H,11
6271 C3 57 5D   1740  JMP FNE
6274 11 9C 50   1750  L3650 LXI D,TOST
6277 19         1760  DAD D
6278 2B         1770  DCX H
6279 7E         1780  MOV A,M
627A FE 41      1790  CPI 'A'
627C CA 94 62   1800  JZ L3700
627F FE 56      1810  CPI 'V'
6281 CA C7 62   1820  JZ L3760
6284 FE 59      1830  CPI 'Y'
6286 CA C7 62   1840  JZ L3760
6289 FE 50      1850  CPI 'P'
628B CA 06 4F   1860  JZ F4290
628E 21 0C 00   1870  LXI H,12
6291 C3 57 5D   1880  JMP FNE
6294 2A 14 54   1890  L3700 LHLD I
6297 22 1A 54   1900  SHLD X
629A CD 77 5E   1910  CALL S6120
629D 21 10 00   1920  LXI H,16
62A0 22 1A 54   1930  SHLD X
62A3 CD 77 5E   1940  CALL S6120
62A6 21 5B 20   1950  LXI H,' ['
62A9 22 D9 53   1960  SHLD FNE1ST
62AC 21 21 00   1970  LXI H,33
62AF CD 38 5D   1980  CALL FNE2
62B2 CD DC 5A   1990  CALL S1240
62B5 CD 0E 62   2000  CALL S3290
62B8 21 5D 20   2010  LXI H,' ]'
62BB 22 D9 53   2020  SHLD FNE1ST
62BE 21 22 00   2030  LXI H,34
62C1 CD 3D 5D   2040  CALL FNE1
62C4 C3 D9 62   2050  JMP L3780
62C7 2A 14 54   2060  L3760 LHLD I
62CA 22 1A 54   2070  SHLD X
62CD CD 77 5E   2080  CALL S6120
62D0 21 00 00   2090  LXI H,0
62D3 22 1A 54   2100  SHLD X
62D6 CD 77 5E   2110  CALL S6120
62D9 CD DC 5A   2120  L3780 CALL S1240
62DC 2A E3 53   2130  LHLD SOST
62DF 01 3A 3D   2140  LXI B,'=:'
62E2 CD D1 57   2150  CALL BHCMP
62E5 CA EE 62   2160  JZ L3810
62E8 21 0D 00   2170  LXI H,13
62EB C3 57 5D   2180  JMP FNE
62EE CD DC 5A   2190  L3810 CALL S1240
62F1 CD 0E 62   2200  CALL S3290
62F4 CD 8F 5E   2210  CALL S6150
62F7 2A 1A 54   2220  LHLD X
62FA 22 10 54   2230  SHLD K
62FD CD 8F 5E   2240  CALL S6150
6300 3A 10 54   2250  LDA K
6303 C6 03      2260  ADI 3
6305 47         2270  MOV B,A
6306 2A 1A 54   2280  LHLD X
6309 EB         2290  XCHG
630A 21 A6 52   2300  LXI H,T1
630D CD BA 57   2310  CALL ARRAY
6310 CD C6 57   2320  CALL CMD
6313 2A 20 54   2330  LHLD L1
6316 19         2340  DAD D
6317 4D         2350  MOV C,L
6318 2A 1A 54   2360  LHLD X
631B EB         2370  XCHG
631C 21 0C 53   2380  LXI H,T2
631F CD BA 57   2390  CALL ARRAY
6322 C3 97 5D   2400  JMP FNG
6325 21 28 20   2410  L3870 LXI H,' ('
6328 22 D9 53   2420  SHLD FNE1ST
632B 21 1F 00   2430  LXI H,31
632E CD 38 5D   2440  CALL FNE2
6331 CD DC 5A   2450  L3880 CALL S1240
6334 E5         2460  PUSH H
6335 21 DD 54   2470  LXI H,STR
6338 11 E3 53   2480  LXI D,SOST
633B CD 84 5A   2490  CALL STCMP
633E E1         2500  POP H
633F C2 99 63   2510  JNZ L3950
6342 11 4E 52   2520  LXI D,CST
6345 CD C6 57   2530  CALL CMD
6348 19         2540  DAD D
6349 7D         2550  MOV A,L
634A FE 01      2560  CPI 1
634C C2 66 63   2570  JNZ L3910
634F 01 00 00   2580  LXI B,0
6352 3A 4E 52   2590  LDA CST
6355 5F         2600  MOV E,A
6356 51         2610  MOV D,C
6357 CD 97 5D   2620  CALL FNG
635A 01 00 08   2630  LXI B,800H
635D 11 01 00   2640  LXI D,1
6360 CD 97 5D   2650  CALL FNG
6363 C3 93 63   2660  JMP L3940
6366 21 4E 52   2670  L3910 LXI H,CST
6369 5F         2680  MOV E,A
636A 16 00      2690  MVI D,0
636C D5         2700  PUSH D
636D E5         2710  L3920 PUSH H
636E F5         2720  PUSH P
636F 7E         2730  MOV A,M
6370 01 00 00   2740  LXI B,0
6373 51         2750  MOV D,C
6374 5F         2760  MOV E,A
6375 CD 97 5D   2770  CALL FNG
6378 F1         2780  POP P
6379 3D         2790  DCR A
637A CA 82 63   2800  JZ L3930
637D E1         2810  POP H
637E 23         2820  INX H
637F C3 6D 63   2830  JMP L3920
6382 D1         2840  L3930 POP D
6383 D1         2850  POP D
6384 01 00 00   2860  LXI B,0
6387 CD 97 5D   2870  CALL FNG
638A 01 00 08   2880  LXI B,800H
638D 11 08 00   2890  LXI D,8
6390 CD 97 5D   2900  CALL FNC
6393 CD DC 5A   2910  L3940 CALL S1240
6396 C3 C3 63   2920  JMP L4000
6399 CD 0E 62   2930  L3950 CALL S3290
639C 21 01 00   2940  LXI H,1
```

```
639F 3A E3 53   2950        LDA SOST
63A2 FE 23      2960        CPI '#'
63A4 CA AE 63   2970        JZ L3980-2
63A7 FE 25      2980        CPI '%'
63A9 C2 B0 63   2990        JNZ L3980
63AC 23         3000        INX H
63AD 23         3010        INX H
63AE 23         3020        INX H
63AF 23         3030        INX H
63B0 22 10 54   3040  L3980 SHLD K
63B3 7D         3050        MOV A,L
63B4 FE 02      3060        CPI 2
63B6 F4 DC 5A   3070        CP S1240
63B9 2A 10 54   3080  L3990 LHLD K
63BC EB         3090        XCHG
63BD 01 00 08   3100        LXI B,800H
63C0 CD 97 5D   3110        CALL FNG
63C3 3A E3 53   3120  L4000 LDA SOST
63C6 FE 2C      3130        CPI ','
63C8 CA 31 63   3140        JZ L3880
63CB 21 29 20   3150        LXI H,' )'
63CE 22 D9 53   3160        SHLD FNE1ST
63D1 21 16 00   3170        LXI H,22
63D4 CD 3D 5D   3180        CALL FNE1
63D7 C3 DC 5A   3190        JMP S1240
63DA 21 28 20   3200  L4040 LXI H,' ('
63DD 22 D9 53   3210        SHLD FNE1ST
63E0 21 1F 00   3220        LXI H,31
63E3 CD 38 5D   3230        CALL FNE2
63E6 21 D3 54   3240  L4050 LXI H,IDENT
63E9 11 D9 53   3250        LXI D,FNE1ST
63EC 01 FB FF   3260        LXI B,-5
63EF CD 00 01   3270        CALL MOVE
63F2 21 04 00   3280        LXI H,4
63F5 CD 38 5D   3290        CALL FNE2
63F8 CD B7 5A   3300        CALL S2060
63FB 7C         3310        MOV A,H
63FC B5         3320        ORA L
63FD C2 06 64   3330        JNZ L4070
6400 21 0B 00   3340        LXI H,11
6403 C3 57 5D   3350        JMP FNE
6406 22 1A 54   3360  L4070 SHLD X
6409 CD 77 5E   3370        CALL S6120
640C 2A 14 54   3380        LHLD I
640F 11 9C 50   3390        LXI D,TOST
6412 19         3400        DAD D
6413 2B         3410        DCX H
6414 7E         3420        MOV A,M
6415 FE 41      3430        CPI 'A'
6417 CA 94 64   3440        JZ L4190
641A FE 56      3450        CPI 'V'
641C CA 25 64   3460        JZ L4090
641F 21 04 00   3470        LXI H,4
6422 C3 57 5D   3480        JMP FNE
6425 21 00 00   3490  L4090 LXI H,0
6428 22 0C 54   3500        SHLD L0
642B CD DC 5A   3510  L4100 CALL S1240
642E 21 00 00   3520        LXI H,0
6431 3A E3 53   3530        LDA SOST
6434 FE 23      3540        CPI '#'
6436 CA 40 64   3550        JZ L4130-2
6439 FE 25      3560        CPI '%'
643B C2 42 64   3570        JNZ L4130
643E 23         3580        INX H
643F 23         3590        INX H
6440 23         3600        INX H
6441 23         3610        INX H
6442 22 10 54   3620  L4130 SHLD K
6445 01 00 08   3630        LXI B,800H
6448 EB         3640        XCHG
6449 CD 97 5D   3650        CALL FNG
644C 2A 10 54   3660        LHLD K
644F 7D         3670        MOV A,L
6450 B4         3680        ORA H
6451 C4 DC 5A   3690        CNZ S1240

6454 CD 8F 5E   3700        CALL S6150
6457 2A 0C 54   3710        LHLD L0
645A 23         3720        INX H
645B 23         3730        INX H
645C 23         3740        INX H
645D 45         3750        MOV B,L
645E 2A 1A 54   3760        LHLD X
6461 EB         3770        XCHG
6462 21 A6 52   3780        LXI H,T1
6465 CD BA 57   3790        CALL ARRAY
6468 CD C6 57   3800        CALL CMD
646B 2A 20 54   3810        LHLD L1
646E 19         3820        DAD D
646F 4D         3830        MOV C,L
6470 2A 1A 54   3840        LHLD X
6473 EB         3850        XCHG
6474 21 0C 53   3860        LXI H,T2
6477 CD BA 57   3870        CALL ARRAY
647A CD 97 5D   3880        CALL FNG
647D 3A E3 53   3890        LDA SOST
6480 FE 2C      3900        CPI ','
6482 CA E6 63   3910        JZ L4050
6485 21 29 20   3920        LXI H,' )'
6488 22 D9 53   3930        SHLD FNE1ST
648B 21 1F 00   3940        LXI H,31
648E CD 3D 5D   3950        CALL FNE1
6491 C3 DC 5A   3960        JMP S1240
6494 21 5B 20   3970  L4190 LXI H,' ['
6497 22 D9 53   3980        SHLD FNE1ST
649A 21 21 00   3990        LXI H,33
649D CD 38 5D   4000        CALL FNE2
64A0 CD DC 5A   4010        CALL S1240
64A3 CD 0E 62   4020        CALL S3290
64A6 21 5D 20   4030        LXI H,' ]'
64A9 22 D9 53   4040        SHLD FNE1ST
64AC 21 22 00   4050        LXI H,34
64AF CD 3D 5D   4060        CALL FNE1
64B2 21 10 00   4070        LXI H,16
64B5 22 0C 54   4080        SHLD L0
64B8 C3 2B 64   4090        JMP L4100
64BB            4100  ASPC EQU $
>

64BB 21 28 20   0010  L4240 LXI H,' ('
64BE 22 D9 53   0020        SHLD FNE1ST
64C1 21 1F 00   0030        LXI H,31
64C4 CD 38 5D   0040        CALL FNE2
64C7 CD DC 5A   0050        CALL S1240
64CA CD 0E 62   0060        CALL S3290
64CD 21 29 20   0070        LXI H,' )'
64D0 22 D9 53   0080        SHLD FNE1ST
64D3 21 16 00   0090        LXI H,22
64D6 CD 3D 5D   0100        CALL FNE1
64D9 01 FF 04   0110        LXI B,4FFH
64DC 11 00 00   0120        LXI D,0
64DF CD 97 5D   0130        CALL FNG
64E2 C3 DC 5A   0140        JMP S1240
64E5 21 00 00   0150  L4290 LXI H,0
64E8 22 28 54   0160        SHLD K2
64EB 2A 14 54   0170        LHLD I
64EE 22 2A 54   0180        SHLD K3
64F1 EB         0190        XCHG
64F2 21 72 53   0200        LXI H,T3
64F5 CD BA 57   0210        CALL ARRAY
64F8 7B         0220        MOV A,E
64F9 B2         0230        ORA D
64FA CA 5E 65   0240        JZ L4400
64FD 21 28 20   0250        LXI H,' ('
6500 22 D9 53   0260        SHLD FNE1ST
6503 21 1F 00   0270        LXI H,31
6506 CD 38 5D   0280        CALL FNE2
6509 2A 28 54   0290  L4320 LHLD K2
650C 22 1A 54   0300        SHLD X
650F CD 77 5E   0310        CALL S6120
6512 2A 2A 54   0320        LHLD K3
```

```
6515 22 1A 54   0330        SHLD X
6518 CD 77 5E   0340        CALL S6120
651B CD DC 5A   0350        CALL S1240
651E CD 0E 62   0360        CALL S3290
6521 CD 8F 5E   0370        CALL S6150
6524 22 2A 54   0380        SHLD K3
6527 CD 8F 5E   0390        CALL S6150
652A 23         0400        INX H
652B 22 28 54   0410        SHLD K2
652E 3A E3 53   0420        LDA S0ST
6531 FE 2C      0430        CPI ','
6533 CA 09 65   0440        JZ L4320
6536 2A 2A 54   0450        LHLD K3
6539 11 72 53   0460        LXI D,T3
653C EB         0470        XCHG
653D CD BA 57   0480        CALL ARRAY
6540 CD C6 57   0490        CALL CMD
6543 2A 2A 54   0500        LHLD K3
6546 19         0510        DAD D
6547 7D         0520        MOV A,L
6548 B7         0530        ORA A
6549 C2 52 65   0540        JNZ L4390
654C 21 23 00   0550        LXI H,35
654F C3 57 5D   0560        JMP FNE
6552 21 29 20   0570 L4390  LXI H,' )'
6555 22 D9 53   0580        SHLD FNE1ST
6558 21 16 00   0590        LXI H,22
655B CD 3D 5D   0600        CALL FNE1
655E 06 04      0610 L4400  MVI B,4
6560 2A 2A 54   0620        LHLD K3
6563 11 A6 52   0630        LXI D,T1
6566 EB         0640        XCHG
6567 CD BA 57   0650        CALL ARRAY
656A CD C6 57   0660        CALL CMD
656D 2A 20 54   0670        LHLD L1
6570 19         0680        DAD D
6571 4D         0690        MOV C,L
6572 2A 2A 54   0700        LHLD K3
6575 11 0C 53   0710        LXI D,T2
6578 EB         0720        XCHG
6579 CD BA 57   0730        CALL ARRAY
657C CD 97 5D   0740        CALL FNG
657F 2A 28 54   0750        LHLD K2
6582 7C         0760        MOV A,H
6583 B5         0770        ORA L
6584 CA DC 5A   0780        JZ S1240
6587 EB         0790        XCHG
6588 CD C6 57   0800        CALL CMD
658B 01 00 05   0810        LXI B,500H
658E CD 97 5D   0820        CALL FNG
6591 C3 DC 5A   0830        JMP S1240
6594 CD DC 5A   0840 L4440  CALL S1240
6597 CD 0E 62   0850        CALL S3290
659A 21 B0 54   0860        LXI H,WOST+125
659D 11 D9 53   0870        LXI D,FNE1ST
65A0 01 FB FF   0880        LXI B,-5
65A3 CD 00 01   0890        CALL MOVE
65A6 21 10 00   0900        LXI H,16
65A9 CD 3D 5D   0910        CALL FNE1
65AC CD DC 5A   0920        CALL S1240
65AF 2A 0E 54   0930        LHLD C1
65B2 22 1A 54   0940        SHLD X
65B5 CD 77 5E   0950        CALL S6120
65B8 01 00 07   0960        LXI B,700H
65BB 11 00 00   0970        LXI D,0
65BE CD 97 5D   0980        CALL FNG
65C1 CD 03 4F   0990        CALL F3490
65C4 21 60 54   1000        LXI H,WOST+45
65C7 11 E3 53   1010        LXI D,S0ST
65CA CD 84 5A   1020        CALL STCMP
65CD C2 1C 5E   1030        JNZ S6520
65D0 CD 8F 5E   1040        CALL S6150
65D3 22 10 54   1050        SHLD K
65D6 2A 0E 54   1060        LHLD C1
65D9 22 1A 54   1070        SHLD X

65DC CD 77 5E   1080        CALL S6120
65DF 01 00 06   1090        LXI B,600H
65E2 11 00 00   1100        LXI D,0
65E5 CD 97 5D   1110        CALL FNG
65E8 2A 10 54   1120        LHLD K
65EB 22 1A 54   1130        SHLD X
65EE CD 1F 5E   1140        CALL L6540
65F1 CD DC 5A   1150        CALL S1240
65F4 CD 03 4F   1160        CALL F3490
65F7 C3 1C 5E   1170        JMP S6520
65FA CD DC 5A   1180 L4590  CALL S1240
65FD CD 03 4F   1190        CALL F3490
6600 3A E3 53   1200        LDA S0ST
6603 FE 3B      1210        CPI ';'
6605 CA FA 65   1220        JZ L4590
6608 21 65 54   1230        LXI H,WOST+50
660B 11 E3 53   1240        LXI D,S0ST
660E CD 84 5A   1250        CALL STCMP
6611 CA DC 5A   1260        JZ S1240
6614 21 11 00   1270        LXI H,17
6617 C3 57 5D   1280        JMP FNE
661A 21 5B 20   1290 L4650  LXI H,' ['
661D 22 D9 53   1300        SHLD FNE1ST
6620 21 21 00   1310        LXI H,33
6623 CD 38 5D   1320        CALL FNE2
6626 CD DC 5A   1330        CALL S1240
6629 CD 0E 62   1340        CALL S3290
662C 3A E3 53   1350        LDA S0ST
662F FE 5D      1360        CPI ']'
6631 CA 3A 66   1370        JZ L4680
6634 21 22 00   1380        LXI H,34
6637 C3 57 5D   1390        JMP FNE
663A 21 3A 3D   1400 L4680  LXI H,'=:'
663D 22 D9 53   1410        SHLD FNE1ST
6640 21 0D 00   1420        LXI H,13
6643 CD 38 5D   1430        CALL FNE2
6646 CD DC 5A   1440        CALL S1240
6649 CD 0E 62   1450        CALL S3290
664C 01 FF 03   1460        LXI B,3FFH
664F 11 00 00   1470        LXI D,0
6652 C3 97 5D   1480        JMP FNG
6655 2A 0E 54   1490 L4730  LHLD C1
6658 22 1A 54   1500        SHLD X
665B CD 77 5E   1510        CALL S6120
665E CD DC 5A   1520 L4740  CALL S1240
6661 CD 03 4F   1530        CALL F3490
6664 3A E3 53   1540        LDA S0ST
6667 FE 3B      1550        CPI ';'
6669 CA 5E 66   1560        JZ L4740
666C 21 BF 54   1570        LXI H,WOST+140
666F 11 D9 53   1580        LXI D,FNE1ST
6672 01 FB FF   1590        LXI B,-5
6675 CD 00 01   1600        CALL MOVE
6678 21 0A 00   1610        LXI H,10
667B CD 3D 5D   1620        CALL FNE1
667E CD DC 5A   1630        CALL S1240
6681 CD 0E 62   1640        CALL S3290
6684 CD 8F 5E   1650        CALL S6150
6687 EB         1660        XCHG
6688 01 00 07   1670        LXI B,700H
668B C3 97 5D   1680        JMP FNG
668E CD DC 5A   1690 L4800  CALL S1240
6691 2A 0E 54   1700        LHLD C1
6694 22 1A 54   1710        SHLD X
6697 CD 77 5E   1720        CALL S6120
669A CD 0E 62   1730        CALL S3290
669D 2A 0E 54   1740        LHLD C1
66A0 22 1A 54   1750        SHLD X
66A3 CD 77 5E   1760        CALL S6120
66A6 01 00 07   1770        LXI B,700H
66A9 11 00 00   1780        LXI D,0
66AC CD 97 5D   1790        CALL FNG
66AF 21 44 4F   1800        LXI H,'OD'
66B2 22 D9 53   1810        SHLD FNE1ST
66B5 21 12 00   1820        LXI H,18
```

Address	Bytes	Line	Instruction
66B8	CD 3D 5D	1830	CALL FNE1
66BB	CD DC 5A	1840	CALL S1240
66BE	CD 03 4F	1850	CALL F3490
66C1	CD 8F 5E	1860	CALL S6150
66C4	22 10 54	1870	SHLD K
66C7	CD 8F 5E	1880	CALL S6150
66CA	EB	1890	XCHG
66CB	01 00 06	1900	LXI B,600H
66CE	CD 97 5D	1910	CALL FNG
66D1	2A 10 54	1920	LHLD K
66D4	22 1A 54	1930	SHLD X
66D7	C3 1F 5E	1940	JMP L6540
66DA	CD DC 5A	1950	L4890 CALL S1240
66DD	CD 0E 62	1960	CALL S3290
66E0	21 4F 46	1970	LXI H,'FO'
66E3	22 D9 53	1980	SHLD FNE1ST
66E6	21 19 00	1990	LXI H,25
66E9	CD 3D 5D	2000	CALL FNE1
66EC	21 01 00	2010	LXI H,1
66EF	22 1E 54	2020	SHLD I2
66F2	21 00 00	2030	L4920 LXI H,0
66F5	22 1C 54	2040	SHLD I1
66F8	CD DC 5A	2050	L4930 CALL S1240
66FB	CD 35 5F	2060	CALL S2240
66FE	01 00 01	2070	LXI B,100H
6701	11 15 00	2080	LXI D,21
6704	CD 97 5D	2090	CALL FNG
6707	01 00 00	2100	LXI B,0
670A	2A 18 54	2110	LHLD N3
670D	EB	2120	XCHG
670E	CD 97 5D	2130	CALL FNG
6711	01 00 01	2140	LXI B,100H
6714	11 08 00	2150	LXI D,8
6717	CD 97 5D	2160	CALL FNG
671A	CD DC 5A	2170	CALL S1240
671D	3A E3 53	2180	LDA SOST
6720	FE 3A	2190	CPI ':'
6722	CA 4A 67	2200	JZ L4990
6725	21 2C 20	2210	LXI H,' ,'
6728	22 D9 53	2220	SHLD FNE1ST
672B	21 05 00	2230	LXI H,5
672E	CD 3D 5D	2240	CALL FNE1
6731	2A 0E 54	2250	LHLD C1
6734	22 1A 54	2260	SHLD X
6737	CD 77 5E	2270	CALL S6120
673A	01 01 07	2280	LXI B,701H
673D	11 00 00	2290	LXI D,0
6740	CD 97 5D	2300	CALL FNG
6743	2A 1C 54	2310	LHLD I1
6746	23	2320	INX H
6747	C3 F5 66	2330	JMP L4930-3
674A	2A 0E 54	2340	L4990 LHLD C1
674D	22 10 54	2350	SHLD K
6750	01 00 07	2360	LXI B,700H
6753	11 00 00	2370	LXI D,0
6756	CD 97 5D	2380	CALL FNG
6759	21 01 00	2390	LXI H,1
675C	22 14 54	2400	SHLD I
675F	EB	2410	L5000 XCHG
6760	2A 1C 54	2420	LHLD I1
6763	CD C6 57	2430	CALL CMD
6766	19	2440	DAD D
6767	7C	2450	MOV A,H
6768	B7	2460	ORA A
6769	FA 79 67	2470	JM $+13
676C	CD 1C 5E	2480	CALL S6520
676F	2A 14 54	2490	LHLD I
6772	23	2500	INX H
6773	22 14 54	2510	SHLD I
6776	C3 5F 67	2520	JMP L5000
6779	2A 10 54	2530	LHLD K
677C	22 1A 54	2540	SHLD X
677F	CD 77 5E	2550	CALL S6120
6782	CD DC 5A	2560	CALL S1240
6785	2A 1E 54	2570	LHLD I2
6788	22 1A 54	2580	SHLD X
678B	CD 77 5E	2590	CALL S6120
678E	CD 03 4F	2600	CALL F3490
6791	CD 8F 5E	2610	CALL S6150
6794	22 1E 54	2620	SHLD I2
6797	21 60 54	2630	LXI H,WOST+45
679A	11 E3 53	2640	LXI D,SOST
679D	CD 84 5A	2650	CALL STCMP
67A0	CA D0 67	2660	JZ L5090
67A3	3A E3 53	2670	LDA SOST
67A6	FE 3B	2680	CPI ';'
67A8	C2 00 68	2690	JNZ L5130
67AB	2A 0E 54	2700	LHLD C1
67AE	22 10 54	2710	SHLD K
67B1	01 00 06	2720	LXI B,600H
67B4	11 00 00	2730	LXI D,0
67B7	CD 97 5D	2740	CALL FNG
67BA	CD 1C 5E	2750	CALL S6520
67BD	2A 10 54	2760	LHLD K
67C0	22 1A 54	2770	SHLD X
67C3	CD 77 5E	2780	CALL S6120
67C6	2A 1E 54	2790	LHLD I2
67C9	23	2800	INX H
67CA	22 1E 54	2810	SHLD I2
67CD	C3 F2 66	2820	JMP L4920
67D0	2A 0E 54	2830	L5090 LHLD C1
67D3	22 10 54	2840	SHLD K
67D6	01 00 06	2850	LXI B,600H
67D9	11 00 00	2860	LXI D,0
67DC	CD 97 5D	2870	CALL FNG
67DF	CD 1C 5E	2880	CALL S6520
67E2	2A 10 54	2890	LHLD K
67E5	22 1A 54	2900	SHLD X
67E8	CD 77 5E	2910	CALL S6120
67EB	CD DC 5A	2920	CALL S1240
67EE	2A 1E 54	2930	LHLD I2
67F1	22 1A 54	2940	SHLD X
67F4	CD 77 5E	2950	CALL S6120
67F7	CD 03 4F	2960	CALL F3490
67FA	CD 8F 5E	2970	CALL S6150
67FD	22 1E 54	2980	SHLD I2
6800	21 65 54	2990	L5130 LXI H,WOST+50
6803	11 D9 53	3000	LXI D,FNE1ST
6806	01 FB FF	3010	LXI B,-5
6809	CD 00 01	3020	CALL MOVE
680C	21 11 00	3030	LXI H,17
680F	CD 3D 5D	3040	CALL FNE1
6812	21 01 00	3050	LXI H,1
6815	22 14 54	3060	SHLD I
6818	CD 1C 5E	3070	L5140 CALL S6520
681B	2A 14 54	3080	LHLD I
681E	23	3090	INX H
681F	22 14 54	3100	SHLD I
6822	EB	3110	XCHG
6823	2A 1E 54	3120	LHLD I2
6826	CD C6 57	3130	CALL CMD
6829	19	3140	DAD D
682A	7C	3150	MOV A,H
682B	B7	3160	ORA A
682C	F2 18 68	3170	JP L5140
682F	01 00 05	3180	LXI B,500H
6832	11 FF FF	3190	LXI D,-1
6835	CD 97 5D	3200	CALL FNG
6838	C3 DC 5A	3210	JMP S1240
683B	21 D3 54	3220	L5170 LXI H,IDENT
683E	11 D9 53	3230	LXI D,FNE1ST
6841	01 FB FF	3240	LXI B,-5
6844	CD 00 01	3250	CALL MOVE
6847	21 04 00	3260	LXI H,4
684A	CD 38 5D	3270	CALL FNE2
684D	CD 68 62	3280	CALL L3630
6850	CD 77 5E	3290	CALL S6120
6853	21 01 00	3300	LXI H,1
6856	22 22 54	3310	SHLD F9
6859	21 B5 54	3320	LXI H,WOST+130
685C	11 E3 53	3330	LXI D,SOST
685F	CD 84 5A	3340	CALL STCMP

```
6862 CA 7D 68    3350       JZ L5210              6925 CD 97 5D    0510       CALL FNG
6865 21 5B 54    3360       LXI H,WOST+40         6928 2A 1A 54    0520       LHLD X
6868 11 D9 53    3370       LXI D,FNE1ST          692B 22 10 54    0530       SHLD K
686B 01 FB FF    3380       LXI B,-5              692E CD 8F 5E    0540       CALL S6150
686E CD 00 01    3390       CALL MOVE             6931 EB          0550       XCHG
6871 21 1C 00    3400       LXI H,28              6932 CD C6 57    0560       CALL CMD
6874 CD 3D 5D    3410       CALL FNE1             6935 21 14 00    0570       LXI H,20
6877 21 00 00    3420       LXI H,0               6938 19          0580       DAD D
687A 22 22 54    3430       SHLD F9               6939 EB          0590       XCHG
687D CD DC 5A    3440 L5210 CALL S1240            693A 01 00 01    0600       LXI B,100H
6880 CD 0E 62    3450       CALL S3290            693D CD 97 5D    0610       CALL FNG
6883 CD 8F 5E    3460       CALL S6150            6940 D1          0620       POP D
6886 22 10 54    3470       SHLD K                6941 C1          0630       POP B
6889 2A 0E 54    3480       LHLD C1               6942 04          0640       INR B
688C 22 1A 54    3490       SHLD X                6943 CD 97 5D    0650       CALL FNG
688F CD 77 5E    3500       CALL S6120            6946 CD 8F 5E    0660       CALL S6150
6892 01 00 01    3510       LXI B,100H            6949 22 10 54    0670       SHLD K
6895 11 15 00    3520       LXI D,21              694C CD 8F 5E    0680       CALL S6150
6898 CD 97 5D    3530       CALL FNG              694F EB          0690       XCHG
689B 06 02       3540       MVI B,2               6950 01 00 06    0700       LXI B,600H
689D 2A 10 54    3550       LHLD K                6953 CD 97 5D    0710       CALL FNG
68A0 11 A6 52    3560       LXI D,T1              6956 2A 10 54    0720       LHLD K
68A3 EB          3570       XCHG                  6959 22 1A 54    0730       SHLD X
68A4 CD BA 57    3580       CALL ARRAY            695C CD 1F 5E    0740       CALL L6540
68A7 CD C6 57    3590       CALL CMD              695F 11 FF FF    0750       LXI D,-1
                                                  6962 01 00 05    0760       LXI B,500H
68AA 2A 20 54    0010       LHLD L1               6965 C3 97 5D    0770       JMP FNG
68AD 19          0020       DAD D                 6968 CD 59 5E    0780 S3490 CALL CKRES
68AE 4D          0030       MOV C,L               696B C0          0790       RNZ
68AF 2A 10 54    0040       LHLD K                696C 3E A0       0800       MVI A,160
68B2 11 0C 53    0050       LXI D,T2              696E 95          0810       SUB L
68B5 EB          0060       XCHG                  696F CA 68 62    0820       JZ L3630
68B6 CD BA 57    0070       CALL ARRAY            6972 D6 05       0830       SUI 5
68B9 CD 97 5D    0080       CALL FNG              6974 CA 25 63    0840       JZ L3870
68BC 2A 22 54    0090       LHLD F9               6977 D6 05       0850       SUI 5
68BF 11 0D 00    0100       LXI D,13              6979 CA 8E 66    0860       JZ L4800
68C2 EB          0110       XCHG                  697C D6 28       0870       SUI 40
68C3 CD C6 57    0120       CALL CMD              697E CA 55 66    0880       JZ L4730
68C6 19          0130       DAD D                 6981 D6 05       0890       SUI 5
68C7 19          0140       DAD D                 6983 CA DA 63    0900       JZ L4040
68C8 EB          0150       XCHG                  6986 D6 1E       0910       SUI 30
68C9 01 00 01    0160       LXI B,100H            6988 CA 1A 66    0920       JZ L4650
68CC CD 97 5D    0170       CALL FNG              698B D6 0A       0930       SUI 10
68CF 2A 0E 54    0180       LHLD C1               698D CA 94 65    0940       JZ L4440
68D2 22 1A 54    0190       SHLD X                6990 D6 0A       0950       SUI 10
68D5 CD 77 5E    0200       CALL S6120            6992 CA 3B 68    0960       JZ L5170
68D8 01 00 07    0210       LXI B,700H            6995 D6 23       0970       SUI 35
68DB 11 00 00    0220       LXI D,0               6997 CA DA 66    0980       JZ L4890
68DE CD 97 5D    0230       CALL FNG              699A D6 05       0990       SUI 5
68E1 2A 22 54    0240       LHLD F9               699C CA BB 64    1000       JZ L4240
68E4 22 1A 54    0250       SHLD X                699F D6 05       1010       SUI 5
68E7 CD 77 5E    0260       CALL S6120            69A1 CA FA 65    1020       JZ L4590
68EA 2A 10 54    0270       LHLD K                69A4 C9          1030       RET
68ED 22 1A 54    0280       SHLD X                69A5 21 D3 54    1040 L5730 LXI H,IDENT
68F0 CD 77 5E    0290       CALL S6120            69A8 11 D9 53    1050       LXI D,FNE1ST
68F3 21 44 4F    0300       LXI H,'OD'            69AB 01 FB FF    1060       LXI B,-5
68F6 22 D9 53    0310       SHLD FNE1ST           69AE CD 00 01    1070       CALL MOVE
68F9 21 12 00    0320       LXI H,18              69B1 21 04 00    1080       LXI H,4
68FC CD 3D 5D    0330       CALL FNE1             69B4 CD 38 5D    1090       CALL FNE2
68FF CD DC 5A    0340       CALL S1240            69B7 21 00 00    1100       LXI H,0
6902 CD 68 69    0350       CALL S3490            69BA 22 26 54    1110       SHLD K1
6905 CD 8F 5E    0360       CALL S6150            69BD 3E 50       1120       MVI A,'F'
6908 06 02       0370       MVI B,2               69BF 32 E8 53    1130       STA KST
690A 11 A6 52    0380       LXI D,T1              69C2 CD 16 5A    1140       CALL S1960
690D EB          0390       XCHG                  69C5 2A 20 54    1150       LHLD L1
690E CD BA 57    0400       CALL ARRAY            69C8 23          1160       INX H
6911 CD C6 57    0410       CALL CMD              69C9 22 20 54    1170       SHLD L1
6914 2A 20 54    0420       LHLD L1               69CC C3 FE 69    1180       JMP L5810
6917 19          0430       DAD D                 69CF 21 D3 54    1190 L5770 LXI H,IDENT
6918 4D          0440       MOV C,L               69D2 11 D9 53    1200       LXI D,FNE1ST
6919 C5          0450       PUSH B                69D5 01 FB FF    1210       LXI B,-5
691A 2A 1A 54    0460       LHLD X                69D8 CD 00 01    1220       CALL MOVE
691D EB          0470       XCHG                  69DB 21 04 00    1230       LXI H,4
691E 21 0C 53    0480       LXI H,T2              69DE CD 38 5D    1240       CALL FNE2
6921 CD BA 57    0490       CALL ARRAY            69E1 3E 46       1250       MVI A,'F'
6924 D5          0500       PUSH D                69E3 32 E8 53    1260       STA KST
```

```
69E6 CD 16 5A   1270       CALL  S1960
69E9 2A 20 54   1280       LHLD  L1
69EC 23         1290       INX   H
69ED 22 20 54   1300       SHLD  L1
69F0 21 01 00   1310       LXI   H,1
69F3 22 26 54   1320       SHLD  K1
69F6 3E 59      1330       MVI   A,'Y'
69F8 32 E8 53   1340       STA   KST
69FB CD 16 5A   1350       CALL  S1960
69FE 2A 26 54   1360 L5810 LHLD  K1
6A01 22 28 54   1370       SHLD  K2
6A04 CD DC 5A   1380       CALL  S1240
6A07 2A A6 52   1390       LHLD  T1
6A0A 22 1A 54   1400       SHLD  X
6A0D CD 77 5E   1410       CALL  S6120
6A10 2A 2C 54   1420       LHLD  D0
6A13 22 1A 54   1430       SHLD  X
6A16 CD 77 5E   1440       CALL  S6120
6A19 3A E3 53   1450       LDA   SOST
6A1C FE 28      1460       CPI   '('
6A1E C2 6E 6A   1470       JNZ   L5890
6A21 CD DC 5A   1480 L5850 CALL  S1240
6A24 21 00 00   1490       LXI   H,0
6A27 22 22 54   1500       SHLD  F9
6A2A CD 8E 5F   1510       CALL  S2340
6A2D 2A 26 54   1520       LHLD  K1
6A30 23         1530       INX   H
6A31 22 26 54   1540       SHLD  K1
6A34 3A E3 53   1550       LDA   SOST
6A37 FE 2C      1560       CPI   ','
6A39 CA 21 6A   1570       JZ    L5850
6A3C 21 29 20   1580       LXI   H,' )'
6A3F 22 D9 53   1590       SHLD  FNE1ST
6A42 21 16 00   1600       LXI   H,22
6A45 CD 3D 5D   1610       CALL  FNE1
6A48 CD DC 5A   1620       CALL  S1240
6A4B 2A 26 54   1630       LHLD  K1
6A4E EB         1640       XCHG
6A4F CD C6 57   1650       CALL  CMD
6A52 2A A6 52   1660       LHLD  T1
6A55 19         1670       DAD   D
6A56 EB         1680       XCHG
6A57 21 72 53   1690       LXI   H,T3
6A5A CD BA 57   1700       CALL  ARRAY
6A5D E5         1710       PUSH  H
6A5E 2A 28 54   1720       LHLD  K2
6A61 EB         1730       XCHG
6A62 CD C6 57   1740       CALL  CMD
6A65 2A 26 54   1750       LHLD  K1
6A68 19         1760       DAD   D
6A69 EB         1770       XCHG
6A6A E1         1780       POP   H
6A6B 73         1790       MOV   M,E
6A6C 23         1800       INX   H
6A6D 72         1810       MOV   M,D
6A6E 21 3B 20   1820 L5890 LXI   H,' ;'
6A71 22 D9 53   1830       SHLD  FNE1ST
6A74 21 05 00   1840       LXI   H,5
6A77 CD 3D 5D   1850       CALL  FNE1
6A7A 2A 26 54   1860       LHLD  K1
6A7D 4D         1870       MOV   C,L
6A7E 44         1880       MOV   B,H
6A7F 21 01 00   1890       LXI   H,1
6A82 22 14 54   1900       SHLD  I
6A85 2A A6 52   1910       LHLD  T1
6A88 EB         1920       XCHG
6A89 21 0C 53   1930       LXI   H,T2
6A8C CD BA 57   1940       CALL  ARRAY
6A8F EB         1950       XCHG
6A90 2A 14 54   1960       LHLD  I
6A93 EB         1970 L5910 XCHG
6A94 CD C6 57   1980       CALL  CMD
6A97 1B         1990       DCX   D
6A98 1B         2000       DCX   D
6A99 1B         2010       DCX   D
6A9A 73         2020       MOV   M,E
6A9B 23         2030       INX   H
6A9C 72         2040       MOV   M,D
6A9D 2B         2050       DCX   H
6A9E 2B         2060       DCX   H
6A9F 2B         2070       DCX   H
6AA0 EB         2080       XCHG
6AA1 2A 14 54   2090       LHLD  I
6AA4 23         2100       INX   H
6AA5 22 14 54   2110       SHLD  I
6AA8 CD D1 57   2120       CALL  BHCMP
6AAB D2 93 6A   2130       JNC   L5910
6AAE CD DC 5A   2140       CALL  S1240
6AB1 CD 09 4F   2150       CALL  F5340
6AB4 2A 20 54   2160       LHLD  L1
6AB7 2B         2170       DCX   H
6AB8 22 20 54   2180       SHLD  L1
6ABB CD 8F 5E   2190       CALL  S6150
6ABE 22 2C 54   2200       SHLD  D0
6AC1 CD 8F 5E   2210       CALL  S6150
6AC4 22 A6 52   2220       SHLD  T1
6AC7 21 3B 20   2230       LXI   H,' ;'
6ACA 22 D9 53   2240       SHLD  FNE1ST
6ACD 21 05 00   2250       LXI   H,5
6AD0 CD 3D 5D   2260       CALL  FNE1
6AD3 CD DC 5A   2270       CALL  S1240
6AD6 CD 59 5E   2280       CALL  CKRES
6AD9 3E 64      2290       MVI   A,100
6ADB 95         2300       SUB   L
6ADC CA A5 69   2310       JZ    L5730
6ADF D6 28      2320       SUI   40
6AE1 CA CF 69   2330       JZ    L5770
6AE4 D6 32      2340       SUI   50
6AE6 CA EF 6A   2350       JZ    L5980
6AE9 21 19 00   2360       LXI   H,25
6AEC C3 57 5D   2370       JMP   FNE
6AEF CD DC 5A   2380 L5980 CALL  S1240
6AF2 CD 8F 5E   2390       CALL  S6150
6AF5 22 10 54   2400       SHLD  K
6AF8 EB         2410       XCHG
6AF9 21 0C 53   2420       LXI   H,T2
6AFC CD BA 57   2430       CALL  ARRAY
6AFF EB         2440       XCHG
6B00 22 1A 54   2450       SHLD  X
6B03 D5         2460       PUSH  D
6B04 CD 1F 5E   2470       CALL  L6540
6B07 2A 0E 54   2480       LHLD  C1
6B0A EB         2490       XCHG
6B0B E1         2500       POP   H
6B0C 73         2510       MOV   M,E
6B0D 23         2520       INX   H
6B0E 72         2530       MOV   M,D
6B0F 2A 2C 54   2540       LHLD  D0
6B12 EB         2550       XCHG
6B13 01 00 05   2560       LXI   B,500H
6B16 CD 97 5D   2570       CALL  FNG
6B19 CD 68 69   2580 L6020 CALL  S3490
6B1C 3A E3 53   2590       LDA   SOST
6B1F FE 3B      2600       CPI   ';'
6B21 C2 2A 6B   2610       JNZ   L6050
6B24 CD DC 5A   2620       CALL  S1240
6B27 C3 19 6B   2630       JMP   L6020
6B2A 21 65 54   2640 L6050 LXI   H,WOST+50
6B2D 11 E3 53   2650       LXI   D,SOST
6B30 CD 8A 5A   2660       CALL  STCMP
6B33 CA 3C 6B   2670       JZ    L6060
6B36 21 11 00   2680       LXI   H,17
6B39 C3 57 5D   2690       JMP   FNE
6B3C CD DC 5A   2700 L6060 CALL  S1240
6B3F 01 00 01   2710       LXI   B,100H
6B42 11 00 00   2720       LXI   D,0
6B45 C3 97 5D   2730       JMP   FNG

6B48 21 00 00   0010 S5340 LXI   H,0
6B4B 22 2C 54   0020       SHLD  D0
6B4E 2A 26 54   0030       LHLD  K1
6B51 EB         0040       XCHG
```

```
6B52  2A A6 52    0050        LHLD T1
6B55  CD C6 57    0060        CALL CMD
6B58  19          0070        DAD D
6B59  22 1A 54    0080        SHLD X
6B5C  EB          0090        XCHG
6B5D  21 0C 53    0100        LXI H,T2
6B60  CD BA 57    0110        CALL ARRAY
6B63  EB          0120        XCHG
6B64  2A 0E 54    0130        LHLD C1
6B67  EB          0140        XCHG
6B68  73          0150        MOV M,E
6B69  23          0160        INX H
6B6A  72          0170        MOV M,D
6B6B  01 00 06    0180        LXI B,600H
6B6E  11 00 00    0190        LXI D,0
6B71  CD 97 5D    0200        CALL FNG
6B74  CD 77 5E    0210        CALL S6120
6B77  CD 59 5E    0220        CALL CKRES
6B7A  C2 97 6B    0230        JNZ L5440
6B7D  3E 91       0240        MVI A,145
6B7F  95          0250        SUB L
6B80  CA CD 6B    0260        JZ L5550,
6B83  D6 2D       0270        SUI 45
6B85  CA A5 69    0280        JZ L5730
6B88  D6 28       0290        SUI 40
6B8A  CA CF 69    0300        JZ L5770
6B8D  D6 23       0310        SUI 35
6B8F  CA 9D 6B    0320        JZ L5460
6B92  D6 0F       0330        SUI 15
6B94  CA EF 6A    0340        JZ L5980
6B97  21 19 00    0350        L5440 LXI H,25
6B9A  C3 57 5D    0360        JMP FNE
6B9D  CD DC 5A    0370        L5460 CALL S1240
6BA0  CD EE 5E    0380        CALL S2180
6BA3  21 3B 20    0390        LXI H,' ;'
6BA6  22 D9 53    0400        SHLD FNE1ST
6BA9  21 05 00    0410        LXI H,5
6BAC  CD 3D 5D    0420        CALL FNE1
6BAF  CD DC 5A    0430        CALL S1240
6BB2  CD 59 5E    0440        CALL CKRES
6BB5  3E 91       0450        MVI A,145
6BB7  95          0460        SUB L
6BB8  CA CD 6B    0470        JZ L5550
6BBB  D6 2D       0480        SUI 45
6BBD  CA A5 69    0490        JZ L5730
6BC0  D6 28       0500        SUI 40
6BC2  CA CF 69    0510        JZ L5770
6BC5  D6 32       0520        SUI 50
6BC7  CA EF 6A    0530        JZ L5980
6BCA  C3 A0 6B    0540        JMP L5460+3
6BCD  21 00 00    0550        L5550 LXI H,0
6BD0  22 0C 54    0560        SHLD L0
6BD3  2C          0570        INR L
6BD4  22 22 54    0580        SHLD F9
6BD7  CD DC 5A    0590        L5560 CALL S1240
6BDA  CD 8E 5F    0600        CALL S2340
6BDD  2A 0C 54    0610        L5570 LHLD L0
6BE0  23          0620        INX H
6BE1  22 0C 54    0630        SHLD L0
6BE4  3A E3 53    0640        LDA S0ST
6BE7  FE 2C       0650        CPI ','
6BE9  CA D7 6B    0660        JZ L5560
6BEC  21 3A 20    0670        LXI H,' :'
6BEF  22 D9 53    0680        SHLD FNE1ST
6BF2  21 05 00    0690        LXI H,5
6BF5  CD 3D 5D    0700        CALL FNE1
6BF8  CD DC 5A    0710        CALL S1240
6BFB  21 38 54    0720        LXI H,WOST+5
6BFE  11 E3 53    0730        LXI D,S0ST
6C01  CD 84 5A    0740        CALL STCMP
6C04  CA 1C 6C    0750        JZ L5610
6C07  21 79 54    0760        LXI H,WOST+70
6C0A  11 D9 53    0770        LXI D,FNE1ST
6C0D  01 FB FF    0780        LXI B,-5
6C10  CD 00 01    0790        CALL MOVE
6C13  21 24 00    0800        LXI H,36
6C16  CD 3D 5D    0810        CALL FNE1
6C19  C3 AE 6C    0820        JMP L5670
6C1C  21 5B 20    0830        L5610 LXI H,' ['
6C1F  22 D9 53    0840        SHLD FNE1ST
6C22  21 21 00    0850        LXI H,33
6C25  CD 38 5D    0860        CALL FNE2
6C28  CD DC 5A    0870        CALL S1240
6C2B  CD 35 5F    0880        CALL S2240
6C2E  21 5D 20    0890        LXI H,' ]'
6C31  22 D9 53    0900        SHLD FNE1ST
6C34  21 22 00    0910        LXI H,34
6C37  CD 38 5D    0920        CALL FNE2
6C3A  21 4F 46    0930        LXI H,'FO'
6C3D  22 D9 53    0940        SHLD FNE1ST
6C40  21 1A 00    0950        LXI H,26
6C43  CD 38 5D    0960        CALL FNE2
6C46  21 79 54    0970        LXI H,WOST+70
6C49  11 D9 53    0980        LXI D,FNE1ST
6C4C  01 FB FF    0990        LXI B,-5
6C4F  CD 00 01    1000        CALL MOVE
6C52  21 24 00    1010        LXI H,36
6C55  CD 38 5D    1020        CALL FNE2
6C58  2A 0C 54    1030        LHLD L0
6C5B  EB          1040        XCHG
6C5C  2A 2C 54    1050        LHLD D0
6C5F  CD C6 57    1060        CALL CMD
6C62  19          1070        DAD D
6C63  22 2C 54    1080        SHLD D0
6C66  2A A6 52    1090        LHLD T1
6C69  E5          1100        PUSH H
6C6A  19          1110        DAD D
6C6B  23          1120        INX H
6C6C  22 14 54    1130        SHLD I
6C6F  C1          1140        POP B
6C70  11 9C 50    1150        L5650 LXI D,T0ST
6C73  19          1160        DAD D
6C74  2B          1170        DCX H
6C75  36 41       1180        MVI M,'A'
6C77  2A 14 54    1190        LHLD I
6C7A  EB          1200        XCHG
6C7B  21 72 53    1210        LXI H,T3
6C7E  CD BA 57    1220        CALL ARRAY
6C81  EB          1230        XCHG
6C82  2A 18 54    1240        LHLD N3
6C85  23          1250        INX H
6C86  EB          1260        XCHG
6C87  73          1270        MOV M,E
6C88  23          1280        INX H
6C89  72          1290        MOV M,D
6C8A  2A 2C 54    1300        LHLD D0
6C8D  EB          1310        XCHG
6C8E  19          1320        DAD D
6C8F  22 2C 54    1330        SHLD D0
6C92  D5          1340        PUSH D
6C93  2A 14 54    1350        LHLD I
6C96  EB          1360        XCHG
6C97  21 0C 53    1370        LXI H,T2
6C9A  CD BA 57    1380        CALL ARRAY
6C9D  D1          1390        POP D
6C9E  73          1400        MOV M,E
6C9F  23          1410        INX H
6CA0  72          1420        MOV M,D
6CA1  2A 14 54    1430        LHLD I
6CA4  23          1440        INX H
6CA5  22 14 54    1450        SHLD I
6CA8  CD D1 57    1460        CALL BHCMP
6CAB  D2 70 6C    1470        JNC L5650
6CAE  21 3B 20    1480        L5670 LXI H,' ;'
6CB1  22 D9 53    1490        SHLD FNE1ST
6CB4  21 05 00    1500        LXI H,5
6CB7  CD 38 5D    1510        CALL FNE2
6CBA  CD DC 5A    1520        CALL S1240
6CBD  CD 59 5E    1530        CALL CKRES
6CC0  3E 64       1540        MVI A,100
6CC2  95          1550        SUB L
6CC3  CA A5 69    1560        JZ L5730
```

```
6CC6 D6 28        1570      SUI 40              6D86 47           2330      MOV B,A
6CC8 CA CF 69     1580      JZ L5770            6D87 CD F8 09     2340      CALL CRLF
6CCB D6 32        1590      SUI 50              6D8A 78           2350      MOV A,B
6CCD CA EF 6A     1600      JZ L5980            6D8B FE 49        2360      CPI 'I'
6CD0 21 00 00     1610      LXI H,0             6D8D CA 9E 6D     2370      JZ INTRP
6CD3 22 0C 54     1620      SHLD L0             6D90 FE 54        2380      CPI 'T'
6CD6 2C           1630      INR L               6D92 CA A4 6D     2390      JZ TRANS
6CD7 22 22 54     1640      SHLD F9             6D95 2A 0E 0C     2400      LHLD 0C0EH
6CDA CD 8E 5F     1650      CALL S2340          6D98 22 7F 72     2410      SHLD 727FH
6CDD C3 DD 6B     1660      JMP L5570           6D9B C3 90 73     2420      JMP 7390H
6CE0 AF           1670 RUN  XRA A               6D9E 11 56 55     2430 INTRP LXI D,L360
6CE1 D3 04        1680      OUT 4               6DA1 C3 A7 6D     2440      JMP $+3
6CE3 31 00 10     1690      LXI P,1000H         6DA4 11 63 55     2450 TRANS LXI D,L370
6CE6 CDFD 09      1700      CALL CLEAR          6DA7 2A BC 73     2460      LHLD MENTR+2CH
6CE9 21 33 54     1710      LXI H,WOST          6DAA EB           2470      XCHG
6CEC 11 F4 B0     1720      LXI D,-TST          6DAB 01 F3 FF     2480      LXI B,-13
6CEF 19           1730      DAD D               6DAE CD 00 01     2490      CALL MOVE
6CF0 11 0C 4F     1740      LXI D,TST           6DB1 3E 0D        2500      MVI A,0DH
6CF3 EB           1750      XCHG                6DB3 12           2510      STAX D
6CF4 36 00        1760 ZER  MVI M,0             6DB4 21 90 73     2520      LXI H,MENTR
6CF6 23           1770      INX H               6DB7 22 BA 73     2530      SHLD MENTR+2AH
6CF7 1B           1780      DCX D               6DBA 2A 0E 0C     2540      LHLD 0C0EH
6CF8 7B           1790      MOV A,E             6DBD 22 7F 72     2550      SHLD 727FH
6CF9 B2           1800      ORA D               6DC0 2A BC 73     2560      LHLD MENTR+2CH
6CFA C2 F4 6C     1810      JNZ ZER             6DC3 C3 C2 73     2570      JMP MENTR+32H
6CFD CD 4B 5D     1820      CALL BLST           6DC6              2580 LSTBYT EQU $-1
6D00 21 00 10     1830      LXI H,SRCFIL
6D03 22 F4 53     1840      SHLD BOFP
6D06 22 F6 53     1850      SHLD EOFP
6D09 22 F2 53     1860      SHLD FPTR
6D0C 36 01        1870      MVI M,1
6D0E 21 EA 51     1880      LXI H,SST
6D11 22 FA 53     1890      SHLD P8
6D14 21 00 2C     1900      LXI H,PCODES
6D17 22 FC 53     1910      SHLD P9
6D1A 22 F8 53     1920      SHLD P7
6D1D 21 FD 54     1930      LXI H,L250
6D20 CD AD 05     1940      CALL OSEQ
6D23 CD F8 09     1950      CALL CRLF
6D26 21 FF 4E     1960      LXI H,MEMLIM
6D29 22 FE 53     1970      SHLD Q9
6D2C 21 14 55     1980      LXI H,L280
6D2F CD AD 05     1990      CALL OSEQ
6D32 CD 20 0C     2000      CALL WH0
6D35 CD 24 0C     2010      CALL WH1
6D38 47           2020      MOV B,A
6D39 CD F8 09     2030      CALL CRLF
6D3C 78           2040      MOV A,B
6D3D FE 59        2050      CPI 'Y'
6D3F 21 00 00     2060      LXI H,0
6D42 CA 46 6D     2070      JZ $+1
6D45 2C           2080      INR L
6D46 22 04 54     2090      SHLD Y9
6D49 3E 20        2100      MVI A,' '
6D4B 32 D8 53     2110      STA XST
6D4E CD DC 5A     2120      CALL S1240
6D51 CD 48 6B     2130      CALL S5340
6D54 21 2E 20     2140      LXI H,' .'
6D57 22 D9 53     2150      SHLD FNE1ST
6D5A 21 09 00     2160      LXI H,9
6D5D CD 3D 5D     2170      CALL FNE1
6D60 2A FC 53     2180      LHLD P9
6D63 36 FF        2190      MVI M,0FFH
6D65 23           2200      INX H
6D66 36 FF        2210      MVI M,0FFH
6D68 11 28 55     2220      LXI D,L339
6D6B EB           2230      XCHG
6D6C CD AD 05     2240      CALL OSEQ
6D6F CD 0C 0A     2250      CALL DEOUT
6D72 3E 04        2260      MVI A,H
6D74 CD 24 0C     2270      CALL WH1
6D77 CD F8 09     2280      CALL CRLF
6D7A 21 36 55     2290      LXI H,L340
6D7D CD AD 05     2300      CALL OSEQ
6D80 CD 20 0C     2310      CALL WH0
6D83 CD 24 0C     2320      CALL WH1
```

Symbol Table for listing 5.

Symbol	Value	Symbol	Value	Symbol	Value
F3490	4F03	STR	54DD	L3910	6366
F4290	4F06	MST	54E2	L3920	636D
F5340	4F09	L250	54FD	L3930	6382
PCODES	2C00	L280	5514	L3940	6393
MEMLIM	4EFF	L339	5528	L3950	6399
SRCFIL	1000	L340	5536	L3980	63B0
N0	0020	L360	5556	L3990	63B9
T0	0032	L370	5563	L4000	63C3
N1	7FFF	L6570	5753	L4040	63DA
N2	0008	L1300	57AE	L4050	63E6
TST	4F0C	WH0	0C20	L4070	6406
T0ST	509C	WH1	0C24	L4090	6425
LST	50CE	MOVE	0100	L4100	642B
AST	510E	OSEQ	05AD	L4130	6442
BST	511A	CROUT	09F8	L4190	6494
S	5122	CRLF	09F8	ASPC	64BB
SST	51EA	CLEAR	09FD	L4240	64BB
CST	524E	BLK1	0A02	L4290	64E5
OST	529E	DEOUT	0A0C	L4320	6509
T1	52A6	ARRAY	57BA	L4390	6552
T2	530C	CMD	57C6	L4400	655E
T3	5372	BHCMP	57D1	L4440	6594
XST	53D8	READ	57DE	L4590	65FA
FNE1ST	53D9	DECOUT	589E	L4650	661A
YST	53DE	DECFMT	58A7	L4680	663A
S0ST	53E3	S1030	58D3	L4730	6655
KST	53E8	S1090	58F7	L4740	665E
ZST	53ED	MENTR	7390	L4800	668E
FPTR	53F2	READ0	599A	L4890	66DA
BOFP	53F4	S1960	5A16	L4920	66F2
EOFP	53F6	STCMP	5A84	L4930	66F8
P7	53F8	COMS	5A89	L4990	674A
P8	53FA	SEAR	5AA1	L5000	675F
P9	53FC	S2060	5AB7	L5090	67D0
Q9	53FE	S1240	5ADC	L5130	6800
S9	5400	FNE2	5D38	L5140	6818
F5	5402	FNE1	5D3D	L5170	683B
Y9	5404	BLST	5D4B	L5210	687D
Z	5406	FNE	5D57	S3490	6968
C0	5408	FNG	5D97	L5730	69A5
E9	540A	S6520	5E1C	L5770	69CF
L0	540C	L6540	5E1F	L5810	69FE
C1	540E	CKRES	5E59	L5850	6A21
K	5410	S6120	5E77	L5890	6A6E
T	5412	S6150	5E8F	L5910	6A93
I	5414	S6180	5EA2	L5980	6AEF
J	5416	S6240	5ECD	L6020	6B19
N3	5418	S2180	5EEE	L6050	6B2A
X	541A	S2240	5F35	L6060	6B3C
I1	541C	S2340	5F8E	S5340	6B48
I2	541E	S2380	5FAB	L5440	6B97
L1	5420	S2610	6031	L5460	6B9D
F9	5422	S2850	60B5	L5550	6BCD
L00	5424	S3290	620E	L5560	6BD7
K1	5426	BHCMPJ	6243	L5570	6BDD
K2	5428	L3630	6268	L5610	6C1C
K3	542A	L3650	6274	L5650	6C70
D0	542C	L3700	6294	L5670	6CAE
N	542E	L3760	62C7	RUN	6CE0
NCHR	5430	L3780	62D9	ZER	6CF4
ADDS	5431	L3810	62EE	INTRP	6D9E
W0ST	5433	L3870	6325	TRANS	6DA4
IDENT	54D3	L3880	6331	LSTBYT	6DC5
NUM	54D8				

Listing 6: Sample Code for DEOUT, OSEQ and MOVE Routines

```
0010 * SAMPLE SOURCE CODE FOR UTILITIES DEOUT, OSEQ AND
0020 *   MOVE REQUIRED BY THE TINY PASCAL PACKAGE
0030 DEOUT MOV A,D
0040   CALL BYTEO
0050   MOV A,E
0060 BYTEO PUSH P
0070   ANI OFOH
0080   RAR
0090   RAR
0100   RAR
0110   RAR
0120   CALL NYBO
0130   POP P
0140   ANI OFH
0150 NYBO ADI 30H
0160   CPI 3AH
0170   JC $+2
0180   ADI 7
0190   JMP WH1
0200 OSEQ MOV A,M
0210   CPI 13
0220   RZ
0230   INX H
0240   CALL WH1
0250   JMP OSEQ
0260 MOVE MOV A,M
0270   STAX D
0280   INX H
0290   INX D
0300   INX B
0310   MOV A,B
0320   ORA C
0330   JNZ MOVE
0340   RZ
0350 * WH1 IS THE ROUTINE THAT PUTS OUT THE ACCUMULATOR
0360 *        CONTENTS TO THE CONSOLE DEVICE.
```

Appendix C:

An APL Interpreter in Pascal

APL in CDC Pascal

PASCAL COMPILER - E.T.H. ZURICH, SWITZERLAND PASCAL CYBER V2.0   78/10/06. 11.48.26.
                                              UNIVERSITY OF MINNESOTA   (77/03/14)

```
00100 PROGRAM SCANNER(INPUT+, OUTPUT, APLFILE);
00110
00120    LABEL 100;
00130 CONST
00140 PREFIX1 = 60; PREFIX2 = 62; (* PREFIX FOR CDC ASCII 12-BIT CODES *)
00150 MAXVARNAMELENGTH = 10;
00160 MAXINPUTLINE = 132;
00170 INPUTARRAYSIZE = 134;
00180 NUMBEROFMESSAGES = 100; MESSAGELENGTH = 80;
00190
00200 TYPE
00210    PACKEDSTRING = PACKED ARRAY[1..MAXVARNAMELENGTH] OF 0..8191;
00220
00230    TOKENNOUN = (FORMRES,FORMARG,GLOBVAR,MONADOPER,
00240             REDUCTOPER,DYADOPER,SPECOPER,CONSTANT,
00250             STATEND);
00260
00270    VALUES = RECORD
00280        REALVAL: REAL;
00290        NEXTVALUE: +VALUES;
00300    END;
00310    VARTAB = RECORD
00320        VARNAME: PACKEDSTRING;                          (* V1 *)
00330        FUNCTABPTR: +FUNCTAB;                           (* V2 - FTAB *)
00340        VALTABPTR: +VALTAB;                             (* V3 - VTAB *)
00350        DEFEREDVALTABPTR:+FPARMTAB;
00360        NEXTVARTABPTR: +VARTAB;
00370    END;
00380
00390    VALTAB = RECORD
00400        INTERMEDRESULT: BOOLEAN;
00410        DIMENSIONS: INTEGER;
```

```
00420          FIRSTDIMEN: ↑DIMENINFO;
00430          FORWARDORDER: BOOLEAN;
00440          FIRSTVALUE: ↑VALUES;
00450          NEXTVALTABLINK:↑VALTAB
00460     END;
00470
00480     TOKENTABLE = RECORD
00490          NEXTOKEN: ↑TOKENTABLE;
00500          CASE NOUN      :   TOKENNOUN OF                      (* P *)
00510               FORMRES,FORMARG,GLOBVAR:                        (* VTAB *)
00520                              (VARTABPTR: ↑VARTAB);
00530               MONADOPER: (MONINDX:INTEGER);
00540               REDUCTOPER: (REDINDX:INTEGER);
00550               DYADOPER: (DOPINDX:INTEGER);
00560               SPECOPER: (CHARINDX:INTEGER);
00570               CONSTANT: (VALTABPTR: ↑VALTAB);
00580               STATEND: (ENDADJ:INTEGER);
00590     END;
00600     VFUNC = RECORD
00610          NEXTSTMNT:↑TOKENTABLE;
00620          NEXTVFUNCPTR:↑VFUNC;
00630          STATLABEL:PACKEDSTRING
00640     END;
00650
00660     FUNCTAB = RECORD
00670          FUNCNAME: PACKEDSTRING;                              (* F1 *)
00680          ARITY: (NILADIC,MONADIC,DYADIC);                     (* F2 *)
00690          RESULT : BOOLEAN; (* TRUE = EXPLICIT *)              (* F3 *)
00700          RESULTNAME: PACKEDSTRING;                            (* F4 *)
00710          LEFTARG: PACKEDSTRING;                               (* F5 *)
00720          RIGHTARG: PACKEDSTRING;                              (* F6 *)
00730          FIRSTATEMENT:↑VFUNC;
00740          NEXTFUNCTABPTR : ↑FUNCTAB;
00750          NUMOFSTATEMENTS: INTEGER;
00760     END;
00770
00780     FPARMTAB=RECORD
00790               PTRVAL:↑VALTAB;                      (* SD1 AND SD2 *)
00800               LASTPARM:↑FPARMTAB;                  (* LINK TO LAST *)
00810                                                        (* SD1 OR SD2 *)
00820                    END;
00830
00840     DIMENINFO = RECORD
00850          NEXTDIMEN: ↑DIMENINFO;
00860          DIMENLENGTH: INTEGER;
00870     END;
00880
00890     OPRECORD = RECORD
00900          OPINDEX: INTEGER;
00910          OPSYMBOL: INTEGER;
00920     END;
00930
00940     OPERANDTAB=RECORD
00950               OPERPTR:↑VALTAB;                         (* SVAL *)
00960               LASTOPER:↑OPERANDTAB;            (* LINK TO LAST SVAL *)
00970               END;
00980     SUBRTAB=RECORD                                 (* SF *)
00990          CALLEDSUBR:↑FUNCTAB;                          (* S1 *)
01000          TOKENCALLINGSUBR:↑TOKENTABLE;                 (* S2 *)
01010          STATEMCALLINGSUBR:↑VFUNC;                  (* S3 *)
01020          LASTSUBRPTR:↑SUBRTAB;               (* LINK 'O LAST SF *)
01030             END;
01040       OPTABLE = ARRAY[1..16] OF OPRECORD;
01050
01060     VARTABPTRTYPE = ↑VARTAB;
01070     TYPEVALTABPTR = ↑VALTAB;
01080     TOKENPTR=↑TOKENTABLE;
01090     PTRFUNCTAB=↑FUNCTAB;
01100     TYPEVALUESPTR=↑VALUES;
```

```
01110
01120 APLCHARSET=(ASYMBOL, BSYMBOL, CSYMBOL, DSYMBOL, ESYMBOL, FSYMBOL, GSYMBOL,
01130             HSYMBOL, ISYMBOL, JSYMBOL, KSYMBOL, LSYMBOL, MSYMBOL, NSYMBOL,
01140             OSYMBOL, PSYMBOL, QSYMBOL, RSYMBOL, SSYMBOL, TSYMBOL, USYMBOL,
01150             VSYMBOL, WSYMBOL, XSYMBOL, YSYMBOL, ZSYMBOL,
01160
01170             ONESYMBOL, TWOSYMBOL, THREESYMBOL, FOURSYMBOL, FIVESYMBOL,
01180             SIXSYMBOL, SEVENSYMBOL, EIGHTSYMBOL, NINESYMBOL, ZEROSYMBOL,
01190
01200             COLON, RIGHTARROW, LEFTARROW, SMALLCIRCLE, PERIOD, LEFTPAREN,
01210             RIGHTPAREN, LEFTBRACKET, RIGHTBRACKET, SEMICOLON, QUADRANGLE,
01220             SPACE,
01230
01240             PLUS, MINUS, TIMES, DIVIDE, ASTERISK, IOTA, RHO, COMMA, TILDE,
01250             EQUALS, NOTEQUAL, LESSTHAN, LESSOREQUAL, GREATEROREQUAL,
01260             GREATERTHAN, ANDSYMBOL, ORSYMBOL,
01270
01280             CEILING, FLOOR, LARGECIRCLE, FORWARDSLASH,
01290
01300             DOUBLEQUOTE, NEGATIVE, QUESTIONMARK, OMEGA, EPSILON,
01310             UPARROW, DOWNARROW, ALPHA, UNDERSCORE, DEL, DELTA,
01320             SINGLEQUOTE, EASTCAP, WESTCAP, SOUTHCAP, NORTHCAP,
01330             IBEAM, TBEAM, VERTICALSTROKE, BACKWARDSLASH);
01340
01350 VAR
01360 XCOLONSYM,XRIGHTARROW,XLEFTARROW,XLITTLECIRCLE,XPERIOD,
01370 XLEFTPAR,XRIGHTPAR,XLEFTBRACKET,XRIGHTBRACKET,XSEMICOLSYM,XQUADSYM:INTEGER;
01380 CHARACTER:ARRAY[APLCHARSET] OF INTEGER;
01390 APLSTATEMENT:ARRAY[1..INPUTARRAYSIZE] OF INTEGER;
01400 DIGITS:ARRAY[ONESYMBOL..ZEROSYMBOL] OF INTEGER;
01410 ERRORMSGS:PACKED ARRAY[1..NUMBEROFMESSAGES,1..MESSAGELENGTH] OF CHAR;
01420
01430 APLFILE:TEXT;
01440 MOPTAB, DOPTAB, REDTAB, CHARTAB, SPECTAB:OPTABLE;
01450 SAVELABEL:PACKEDSTRING;
01460 NAME: PACKEDSTRING;
01470
01480 NEWTOKENPTR, OLDTOKENPTR, HOLDTOKENPTR, SAVETOKENPTR: +TOKENTABLE;
01490 TESTFUNCPTR, NEWFUNCTABPTR, OLDFUNCTABPTR: +FUNCTAB;
01500 NEWVARTABPTR, OLDVARTABPTR: +VARTAB;
01510 LEFTVALPTR,RIGHTVALPTR,VALPTR:+VALUES;
01520 NEWVALUES, NEWVALPTR: +VALUES;
01530 NEWDIM: +DIMENINFO;
01540 DIMPTR,NEWPTR,LEFTDIMPTR,RIGHTDIMPTR:+DIMENINFO;
01550 VARPOINTER:+VARTAB;
01560 OLDVFUNCPTR, NEWVFUNCPTR:+VFUNC;
01570 NEWVALTABLINK, OLDVALTABLINK: +VALTAB;
01580
01590 POSITION:INTEGER;
01600 LINELENGTH:INTEGER;
01610 CODE,COLCNT:INTEGER;
01620 FUNCSTATEMENTS:INTEGER;
01630
01640 TOKENERROR, FIRSTFUNCTION:BOOLEAN;
01650 LINETOOLONG,HASLABEL:BOOLEAN;
01660 SWITCH, FUNCTIONMODE, TOKENSWITCH, ITSANIDENTIFIER:BOOLEAN;
01670
01680 OPERTABPTR:+OPERANDTAB;                              (* SV *)
01690 PTRLASTOPER:+OPERANDTAB;
01700 SUBRTABPTR:+SUBRTAB;
01710 RPARMPTR:+FPARMTAB;                          (* P1 *)
01720 LPARMPTR:+FPARMTAB;                          (* P2 *)
01730 VFUNCPTR:+VFUNC;                               (* NL *)
01740 HOLD:+TOKENTABLE;                       (* HOLDS LAST SYMBOL *)
01760
01790
01800 PROCEDURE INITPARSER;
01810 BEGIN
01830     OPERTABPTR:=NIL;
```

```
01840       SUBRTABPTR:=NIL;
01850       LPARMPTR:=NIL;
01860       RPARMPTR:=NIL;
01870       VFUNCPTR:=NIL;
01880       HOLD:=NIL;
01890       XCOLONSYM:=1;
01900       XRIGHTARROW:=2;
01910       XLEFTARROW:=3;
01920       XLITTLECIRCLE:=4;
01930       XPERIOD:=5;
01940       XLEFTPAR:=6;
01950       XRIGHTPAR:=7;
01960       XLEFTBRACKET:=8;
01970       XRIGHTBRACKET:=9;
01980       XSEMICOLSYM:=10;
01990       XQUADSYM:=11;
02000       NEW(OPERTABPTR);
02010       OPERTABPTR↑.LASTOPER:=NIL;
02020       PTRLASTOPER:=OPERTABPTR;
02030 END;
02040
02090
02100 PROCEDURE INITIALIZECHARACTERSET; (*READ INSTALLATION CHARACTER SET FROM FILE*)
02110 VAR
02120 TESTFORPREFIX:INTEGER;
02130 FILECHARACTER:CHAR;
02140 SYMBOLINDEX:APLCHARSET;
02150 BEGIN
02160 RESET(APLFILE);
02170 FOR SYMBOLINDEX:=ASYMBOL TO BACKWARDSLASH DO
02180   BEGIN
02190     READ(APLFILE,FILECHARACTER);
02200
02210     (* THE FOLLOWING CODE WOULD BE REMOVED FOR NON-CDC INSTALLATIONS *)
02220     TESTFORPREFIX:=ORD(FILECHARACTER);
02230     IF (TESTFORPREFIX = PREFIX1) OR (TESTFORPREFIX = PREFIX2)
02240       THEN
02250         BEGIN
02260           READ(APLFILE,FILECHARACTER);
02270           CHARACTER[SYMBOLINDEX]:=100*TESTFORPREFIX + ORD(FILECHARACTER);
02280           END
02290       ELSE
02300     (*                                                              *)
02310
02320           CHARACTER[SYMBOLINDEX]:=ORD(FILECHARACTER)
02330   END
02340 END; (* INITIALIZECHARACTERSET *)
02350
02370
02380 PROCEDURE READINERRORMSGS;
02390 VAR
02400 MSGROW,MSGCOL:INTEGER;
02410 BEGIN
02420 READLN(APLFILE);
02430 FOR MSGROW:=1 TO NUMBEROFMESSAGES DO
02440   FOR MSGCOL:=1 TO MESSAGELENGTH DO
02450     ERRORMSGS[MSGROW,MSGCOL]:=Ξ Ξ; (* BLANK OUT ERROR MESSAGES *)
02460 FOR MSGROW:=1 TO NUMBEROFMESSAGES DO
02470   BEGIN (* READ IN ERROR MESSAGES FROM FILE *)
02480     MSGCOL:=0;
02490     WHILE NOT EOLN(APLFILE) DO
02500       BEGIN
02510         MSGCOL:=MSGCOL + 1;
02520         READ(APLFILE,ERRORMSGS[MSGROW,MSGCOL]);
02530       END;
02540     READLN(APLFILE);
02550   END
02560 END; (* READINERRORMSGS *)
02570
```

294

```
02610
02620 PROCEDURE FILLUPTABLES;
02630 BEGIN
02640
02650 (*          MONADIC OPERATORS              *)
02660 MOPTAB[1].OPSYMBOL := CHARACTER[PLUS];     MOPTAB[1].OPINDEX := 2;
02670 MOPTAB[2].OPSYMBOL := CHARACTER[MINUS];    MOPTAB[2].OPINDEX := 3;
02680 MOPTAB[3].OPSYMBOL := CHARACTER[TIMES];    MOPTAB[3].OPINDEX := 4;
02690 MOPTAB[4].OPSYMBOL := CHARACTER[DIVIDE];   MOPTAB[4].OPINDEX := 5;
02700 MOPTAB[5].OPSYMBOL := CHARACTER[ASTERISK]; MOPTAB[5].OPINDEX := 6;
02710 MOPTAB[6].OPSYMBOL := CHARACTER[IOTA];     MOPTAB[6].OPINDEX := 21;
02720 MOPTAB[7].OPSYMBOL := CHARACTER[RHO];      MOPTAB[7].OPINDEX := 22;
02730 MOPTAB[8].OPSYMBOL := CHARACTER[COMMA];    MOPTAB[8].OPINDEX := 23;
02740 MOPTAB[9].OPSYMBOL := CHARACTER[TILDE];    MOPTAB[9].OPINDEX := 1;
02750
02760 (*          DYADIC OPERATORS               *)
02770 DOPTAB[1].OPSYMBOL := CHARACTER[PLUS];     DOPTAB[1].OPINDEX := 52;
02780 DOPTAB[2].OPSYMBOL := CHARACTER[MINUS];    DOPTAB[2].OPINDEX := 53;
02790 DOPTAB[3].OPSYMBOL := CHARACTER[TIMES];    DOPTAB[3].OPINDEX := 54;
02800 DOPTAB[4].OPSYMBOL := CHARACTER[DIVIDE];   DOPTAB[4].OPINDEX := 55;
02810 DOPTAB[5].OPSYMBOL := CHARACTER[ASTERISK]; DOPTAB[5].OPINDEX := 56;
02820 DOPTAB[6].OPSYMBOL := CHARACTER[IOTA];     DOPTAB[6].OPINDEX := 87;
02830 DOPTAB[7].OPSYMBOL := CHARACTER[RHO];      DOPTAB[7].OPINDEX := 88;
02840 DOPTAB[8].OPSYMBOL := CHARACTER[COMMA];    DOPTAB[8].OPINDEX := 89;
02850 DOPTAB[9].OPSYMBOL := CHARACTER[EQUALS];   DOPTAB[9].OPINDEX := 71;
02860 DOPTAB[10].OPSYMBOL := CHARACTER[NOTEQUAL];  DOPTAB[10].OPINDEX := 72;
02870 DOPTAB[11].OPSYMBOL := CHARACTER[LESSTHAN];  DOPTAB[11].OPINDEX := 73;
02880 DOPTAB[12].OPSYMBOL := CHARACTER[LESSOREQUAL];  DOPTAB[12].OPINDEX := 74;
02890 DOPTAB[13].OPSYMBOL := CHARACTER[GREATEROREQUAL];  DOPTAB[13].OPINDEX := 75;
02900 DOPTAB[14].OPSYMBOL := CHARACTER[GREATERTHAN];  DOPTAB[14].OPINDEX := 76;
02910 DOPTAB[15].OPSYMBOL := CHARACTER[ANDSYMBOL];  DOPTAB[15].OPINDEX := 77;
02920 DOPTAB[16].OPSYMBOL := CHARACTER[ORSYMBOL];   DOPTAB[16].OPINDEX := 78;
02930
02940 (*          SPECIAL CHARACTER              *)
02950 CHARTAB[1].OPSYMBOL := CHARACTER[COLON];
02960 CHARTAB[2].OPSYMBOL := CHARACTER[RIGHTARROW];
02970 CHARTAB[3].OPSYMBOL := CHARACTER[LEFTARROW];
02980 CHARTAB[4].OPSYMBOL := CHARACTER[SMALLCIRCLE];
02990 CHARTAB[5].OPSYMBOL := CHARACTER[PERIOD];
03000 CHARTAB[6].OPSYMBOL := CHARACTER[LEFTPAREN];
03010 CHARTAB[7].OPSYMBOL := CHARACTER[RIGHTPAREN];
03020 CHARTAB[8].OPSYMBOL := CHARACTER[LEFTBRACKET];
03030 CHARTAB[9].OPSYMBOL := CHARACTER[RIGHTBRACKET];
03040 CHARTAB[10].OPSYMBOL := CHARACTER[SEMICOLON];
03050 CHARTAB[11].OPSYMBOL := CHARACTER[QUADRANGLE];
03060 CHARTAB[12].OPSYMBOL := CHARACTER[SPACE];
03070
03080 SPECTAB[1].OPSYMBOL:=CHARACTER[COLON];
03090 SPECTAB[2].OPSYMBOL:=CHARACTER[RIGHTARROW];
03100 SPECTAB[3].OPSYMBOL:=CHARACTER[LEFTARROW];
03110 SPECTAB[4].OPSYMBOL:=CHARACTER[LEFTPAREN];
03120 SPECTAB[5].OPSYMBOL:=CHARACTER[SEMICOLON];
03130 SPECTAB[6].OPSYMBOL:=CHARACTER[LEFTBRACKET];
03140
03150 (*          REDUCTION OPERATOR             *)
03160 REDTAB[1].OPSYMBOL := CHARACTER[PLUS];     REDTAB[1].OPINDEX := 2;
03170 REDTAB[2].OPSYMBOL := CHARACTER[MINUS];    REDTAB[2].OPINDEX := 3;
03180 REDTAB[3].OPSYMBOL := CHARACTER[TIMES];    REDTAB[3].OPINDEX := 4;
03190 REDTAB[4].OPSYMBOL := CHARACTER[DIVIDE];   REDTAB[4].OPINDEX := 5;
03200 REDTAB[5].OPSYMBOL := CHARACTER[ASTERISK]; REDTAB[5].OPINDEX := 6;
03210 REDTAB[6].OPSYMBOL := CHARACTER[EQUALS];   REDTAB[6].OPINDEX := 21;
03220 REDTAB[7].OPSYMBOL := CHARACTER[NOTEQUAL]; REDTAB[7].OPINDEX := 22;
03230 REDTAB[8].OPSYMBOL := CHARACTER[LESSTHAN]; REDTAB[8].OPINDEX := 23;
03240 REDTAB[9].OPSYMBOL := CHARACTER[LESSOREQUAL]; REDTAB[9].OPINDEX := 24;
03250 REDTAB[10].OPSYMBOL := CHARACTER[GREATEROREQUAL]; REDTAB[10].OPINDEX := 25;
03260 REDTAB[11].OPSYMBOL := CHARACTER[GREATERTHAN]; REDTAB[11].OPINDEX := 26;
03270 REDTAB[12].OPSYMBOL := CHARACTER[ANDSYMBOL]; REDTAB[12].OPINDEX := 27;
03280 REDTAB[13].OPSYMBOL := CHARACTER[ORSYMBOL]; REDTAB[13].OPINDEX := 28;
03290 REDTAB[14].OPSYMBOL := CHARACTER[CEILING]; REDTAB[14].OPINDEX := 29;
```

```
03300 REDTAB[15].OPSYMBOL := CHARACTER[FLOOR];  REDTAB[15].OPINDEX := 30;
03310 REDTAB[16].OPSYMBOL := CHARACTER[LARGECIRCLE];  REDTAB[16].OPINDEX := 31;
03320
03330     DIGITS[ONESYMBOL]:=1; DIGITS[TWOSYMBOL]:=2; DIGITS[THREESYMBOL]:=3;
03340     DIGITS[FOURSYMBOL]:=4; DIGITS[FIVESYMBOL]:=5; DIGITS[SIXSYMBOL]:=6;
03350     DIGITS[SEVENSYMBOL]:=7; DIGITS[EIGHTSYMBOL]:=8;
03360     DIGITS[NINESYMBOL]:=9; DIGITS[ZEROSYMBOL]:=0;
03460
03470 END; (* FILLUPTABLES *)
03480
04610
04620 PROCEDURE PRINTAPLSTATEMENT;
04630 VAR
04640 PREFIX,NUM:INTEGER;
04650 INDEX:INTEGER;
04660 BEGIN
04670 FOR INDEX:=1 TO LINELENGTH DO
04680   BEGIN
04690     IF APLSTATEMENT[INDEX] > 6000
04700       THEN
04710         BEGIN
04720           PREFIX:=APLSTATEMENT[INDEX] DIV 100;
04730           WRITE(CHR(PREFIX));
04740           NUM:=APLSTATEMENT[INDEX] - 100*PREFIX;
04750           WRITE(CHR(NUM))
04760         END
04770       ELSE
04780         WRITE(CHR(APLSTATEMENT[INDEX]))
04790   END;
04800 WRITELN
04810 END; (* PRINTAPLSTATEMENT *)
04820
04880
04890 PROCEDURE SERROR(ERRORINDEX:INTEGER);
04900 VAR
04910 MSGCOL:INTEGER;
04920 BEGIN
04930 TOKENERROR:=TRUE;
04940 FOR MSGCOL:=1 TO MESSAGELENGTH DO
04950    WRITE(ERRORMSGS[ERRORINDEX,MSGCOL]);
04960 WRITELN;
04970 PRINTAPLSTATEMENT; (* ECHO STATEMENT TO USER *)
04980 FOR MSGCOL:=1 TO (POSITION - 1) DO
04990   WRITE(Ξ Ξ);
05000 WRITELN(CHR(CHARACTER[UPARROW])); (* PRINT POINTER TO USER ERROR *)
05010 END; (* ERROR *)
05020
05070
05080 PROCEDURE SKIPSPACES;
05090 BEGIN
05100 WHILE (APLSTATEMENT[POSITION] = CHARACTER[SPACE])
05110   AND (POSITION <= LINELENGTH) DO
05120   POSITION:=POSITION + 1
05130 END; (* SKIPSPACES *)
05140
05190
05200 PROCEDURE GETAPLSTATEMENT;
05210 VAR
05220 INPUTCHAR:CHAR;
05230 TESTFORPREFIX:INTEGER;
05240 FIRSTTRY:BOOLEAN;
05250 BEGIN
05260 FOR LINELENGTH:=1 TO MAXINPUTLINE DO
05270 APLSTATEMENT[LINELENGTH]:=CHARACTER[SPACE]; (* BLANK OUT LINE *)
05280 LINELENGTH:=0;
05290 FIRSTTRY:=TRUE;
05300 POSITION:=1;
05310 LINETOOLONG:=FALSE;
05320 APLSTATEMENT[INPUTARRAYSIZE]:=CHARACTER[OMEGA];
```

```
05330 APLSTATEMENT[INPUTARRAYSIZE - 1]:=CHARACTER[SPACE];   (* SET END-OF-LINE *)
05340 REPEAT
05350   BEGIN
05360     IF NOT FIRSTTRY THEN GETSEG(INPUT); (* TEST FOR *CR* ONLY *)
05370     FIRSTTRY:=FALSE;
05380 WHILE (NOT EOLN) AND (NOT LINETOOLONG) DO
05390     IF LINELENGTH < MAXINPUTLINE
05400       THEN
05410         BEGIN
05420           LINELENGTH:=LINELENGTH + 1;
05430           READ(INPUTCHAR);
05440
05450           (* THE FOLLOWING CODE WOULD BE REMOVED FOR NON-CDC INSTALLATIONS *)
05460           TESTFORPREFIX:=ORD(INPUTCHAR);
05470           IF (TESTFORPREFIX = PREFIX1) OR (TESTFORPREFIX = PREFIX2)
05480             THEN
05490               BEGIN
05500                 READ(INPUTCHAR);
05510                 APLSTATEMENT[LINELENGTH]:=100*TESTFORPREFIX + ORD(INPUTCHAR);
05520               END
05530             ELSE
05540           (*                                                                    *)
05550
05560                 APLSTATEMENT[LINELENGTH]:=ORD(INPUTCHAR)
05570         END
05580       ELSE LINETOOLONG:=TRUE
05590   END
05600 UNTIL LINELENGTH <> 0; (* REJECT NULL LINES *)
05610 IF LINETOOLONG THEN SERROR(71)
05620 END; (* GETAPLSTATEMENT *)
05630
05690
05700 FUNCTION ITSADIGIT(TESTCHAR:INTEGER):BOOLEAN;
05710 VAR
05720 DIGITINDEX:APLCHARSET;
05730 BEGIN (* TEST TO SEE IF INPUT CHARACTER IS A DIGIT *)
05740 ITSADIGIT:=FALSE;
05750 FOR DIGITINDEX:=ONESYMBOL TO ZEROSYMBOL DO
05760   IF TESTCHAR = CHARACTER[DIGITINDEX] THEN ITSADIGIT:=TRUE
05770 END; (* ITSADIGIT *)
05780
05800
05810 FUNCTION ITSALETTER(TESTCHAR:INTEGER):BOOLEAN;
05820 VAR
05830 LETTERINDEX:APLCHARSET;
05840 BEGIN (* TEST TO SEE IF INPUT CHARACTER IS A LETTER *)
05850 ITSALETTER:=FALSE;
05860 FOR LETTERINDEX:=ASYMBOL TO ZSYMBOL DO
05870   IF TESTCHAR = CHARACTER[LETTERINDEX] THEN ITSALETTER:=TRUE
05880 END; (* ITSALETTER *)
05890
05940
05950 FUNCTION CHARTONUM(TESTCHAR:INTEGER):INTEGER;
05960 VAR
05970 DIGITINDEX:APLCHARSET;
05980 BEGIN (* CHAGE A CHARACTER TO A NUMBER *)
05990 FOR DIGITINDEX:=ONESYMBOL TO ZEROSYMBOL DO
06000   IF TESTCHAR = CHARACTER[DIGITINDEX] THEN CHARTONUM:=DIGITS[DIGITINDEX]
06010 END; (* CHARTONUM *)
06020
06070
06080 FUNCTION NAMESMATCH(NAMEONE, NAMETWO:PACKEDSTRING):BOOLEAN;
06090 VAR
06100 INDEX:INTEGER;
06110 BEGIN (* SEE IF TWO NAMES (IDENTIFIERS) ARE THE SAME *)
06120 NAMESMATCH:=TRUE;
06130 FOR INDEX:=1 TO MAXVARNAMELENGTH DO
06140   IF NAMEONE[INDEX] <> NAMETWO[INDEX]
06150     THEN NAMESMATCH:=FALSE
```

```
06160 END; (* NAMESMATCH *)
06170
06240
06250 PROCEDURE TABLELOOKUP(TESTCHAR,TABLELENGTH:INTEGER;TABLE:OPTABLE;
06260                       VAR TABLEINDEX:INTEGER);
06270 VAR
06280 INDEX:INTEGER;
06290 BEGIN (* CHECK FOR MEMBERSHIP IN A GIVEN TABLE *)
06300 TABLEINDEX:=0;
06310 FOR INDEX:=1 TO TABLELENGTH DO
06320   IF TESTCHAR = TABLE(INDEX).OPSYMBOL
06330     THEN TABLEINDEX:=INDEX
06340 END; (* TABLELOOKUP *)
06350
06420
06430 PROCEDURE IDENTIFIER(VAR NAME:PACKEDSTRING; VAR ITSANIDENTIFIER:BOOLEAN);
06440 VAR
06450 NAMELENGTH:INTEGER;
06460 NAMETOOLONG:BOOLEAN;
06470 BEGIN
06480 ITSANIDENTIFIER:=FALSE;
06490 SKIPSPACES;
06500 IF ITSALETTER(APLSTATEMENT(POSITION))
06510   THEN
06520     BEGIN
06530       NAMETOOLONG:=FALSE;
06540       ITSANIDENTIFIER:=TRUE;
06550       FOR NAMELENGTH:=1 TO MAXVARNAMELENGTH DO (* BLANK OUT NAME *)
06560         NAME(NAMELENGTH):=CHARACTER(SPACE);
06570       NAMELENGTH:=0;
06580       WHILE (ITSALETTER(APLSTATEMENT(POSITION))) OR
06590             (ITSADIGIT(APLSTATEMENT(POSITION))) DO
06600         BEGIN (* BUILD IDENTIFIER *)
06610           NAMELENGTH:=NAMELENGTH + 1;
06620           IF NAMELENGTH <= MAXVARNAMELENGTH
06630             THEN
06640               NAME(NAMELENGTH):=APLSTATEMENT(POSITION)
06650             ELSE
06660               NAMETOOLONG:=TRUE;
06670           POSITION:=POSITION + 1
06680         END;
06690       IF NAMETOOLONG
06700         THEN
06710             SERROR(70)   (* NAME GREATER THAN MAXLENGTH *)
06720     END
06730 END; (* IDENTIFIER *)
06740
06790
06800 PROCEDURE MAKEANUMBER(VAR REALNUMBER:REAL; VAR ITSANUMBER:BOOLEAN);
06810 VAR
06820 SIGN,DIGITCOUNT:INTEGER;
06830 BEGIN (* CONVERT CHARACTER INPUT STRING TO NUMERICAL REPRESENTATION *)
06840 ITSANUMBER:=FALSE;
06850 SKIPSPACES;
06860 SIGN:=1;
06870 DIGITCOUNT:=0;
06880 REALNUMBER:=0.0;
06890 IF(APLSTATEMENT(POSITION) = CHARACTER(NEGATIVE)) OR
06900   (ITSADIGIT(APLSTATEMENT(POSITION)))
06910   THEN
06920     BEGIN
06930       ITSANUMBER:=TRUE;
06940       IF APLSTATEMENT(POSITION) = CHARACTER(NEGATIVE)
06950         THEN
06960           BEGIN
06970             SIGN:=-1;
06980             POSITION:=POSITION + 1
06990           END;
07000       IF NOT ITSADIGIT(APLSTATEMENT(POSITION))
```

```
07010           THEN
07020            BEGIN
07030             SERROR(1); (* DIGIT MUST FOLLOW A MINUS SIGN *)
07040             ITSANUMBER:=FALSE;
07050            END
07060             ELSE
07070               BEGIN (* FORM WHOLE NUMBER PORTION *)
07080                 WHILE ITSADIGIT(APLSTATEMENT[POSITION]) DO
07090                   BEGIN
07100                     REALNUMBER:=10.0*REALNUMBER+CHARTONUM(APLSTATEMENT[POSITION]);
07110                     POSITION:=POSITION + 1
07120                   END;
07130                 IF APLSTATEMENT[POSITION] = CHARACTER[PERIOD]
07140                   THEN
07150                     BEGIN
07160                       POSITION:=POSITION + 1;
07170                       WHILE ITSADIGIT(APLSTATEMENT[POSITION]) DO
07180                         BEGIN (* FORM FRACTIONAL PORTION *)
07190                           REALNUMBER:=REALNUMBER +
07200                                       CHARTONUM(APLSTATEMENT[POSITION]) *
07210                                       EXP( (-1.0 - DIGITCOUNT) * 2.3025851);
07220                           DIGITCOUNT:=DIGITCOUNT + 1;
07230                           POSITION:=POSITION + 1;
07240                         END;
07250                       IF DIGITCOUNT = 0
07260                         THEN BEGIN
07270                                 SERROR(2); (* DIGITS MUST FOLLOW A DECIMAL POINT *)
07280                                 ITSANUMBER:=FALSE;
07290                                 END
07300                     END;
07310                 REALNUMBER:=REALNUMBER*SIGN
07320               END
07330         END
07340 END; (* MAKEANUMBER *)
07350
07400
07410 FUNCTION MONADICREFERENCE:BOOLEAN;
07420 VAR
07430 SUBPOSITION, TABLEINDEX:INTEGER;
07440 BEGIN (* SEE IF OPERATOR IS MONADIC WITHIN CONTEXT OF INPUT LINE *)
07450 MONADICREFERENCE:=FALSE;
07460 IF NEWTOKENPTR↑.NEXTOKEN↑.NOUN = STATEND
07470  THEN MONADICREFERENCE:= TRUE
07480   ELSE
07490     BEGIN
07500       SUBPOSITION:=POSITION - 1;
07510       WHILE (SUBPOSITION > 0) AND
07520             (APLSTATEMENT[SUBPOSITION]=CHARACTER[SPACE]) DO
07530             SUBPOSITION:=SUBPOSITION - 1; (* GET LAST NON-BLANK *)
07540       IF SUBPOSITION  <> 0 THEN
07550         TABLELOOKUP(APLSTATEMENT[SUBPOSITION],6,SPECTAB,TABLEINDEX);
07560       IF (TABLEINDEX <> 0) OR (SUBPOSITION = 0)
07570       THEN MONADICREFERENCE:=TRUE
07580         ELSE
07590           IF  (NEWTOKENPTR↑.NEXTOKEN↑.NOUN <> FORMRES) AND
07600               (NEWTOKENPTR↑.NEXTOKEN↑.NOUN <> FORMARG) AND
07610               (NEWTOKENPTR↑.NEXTOKEN↑.NOUN <> GLOBVAR) AND
07620               (NEWTOKENPTR↑.NEXTOKEN↑.NOUN <> CONSTANT) AND
07630               (APLSTATEMENT[SUBPOSITION] <> CHARACTER[PERIOD]) AND
07640               (APLSTATEMENT[SUBPOSITION] <> CHARACTER[RIGHTPAREN]) AND
07650               (APLSTATEMENT[SUBPOSITION] <> CHARACTER[RIGHTBRACKET])
07660             THEN MONADICREFERENCE:=TRUE
07670     END
07680 END; (* MONADICREFERENCE *)
07690
07740
07750 PROCEDURE DYADICOPCHECK;
07760 VAR
07770 TABLEINDEX:INTEGER;
```

```
07780  BEGIN
07790  TABLELOOKUP(APLSTATEMENT[POSITION],16,DOPTAB,TABLEINDEX);
07800  IF TABLEINDEX = 0
07810    THEN
07820      BEGIN
07830        TABLELOOKUP(APLSTATEMENT[POSITION],12,CHARTAB,TABLEINDEX);
07840        IF TABLEINDEX = 0
07850          THEN
07860            IF APLSTATEMENT[POSITION] = CHARACTER[SOUTHCAP]
07870              THEN
07880                BEGIN
07890                  OLDTOKENPTR:=SAVETOKENPTR;
07900                  DISPOSE(NEWTOKENPTR);
07910                  NEWTOKENPTR:=SAVETOKENPTR;
07920                  POSITION:=LINELENGTH + 1;
07930                END (* THIS WAS A COMMENT - IGNORE REMAINDER OF LINE *)
07940              ELSE SERROR(4) (* INVALID CHARACTER ENCOUNTERED *)
07950          ELSE
07960            BEGIN (* SPECIAL CHARACTER ENCOUNTERED *)
07970              NEWTOKENPTR+.NOUN:=SPECOPER;
07980              NEWTOKENPTR+.CHARINDX:=TABLEINDEX
07990            END
08000      END
08010    ELSE
08020      IF MONADICREFERENCE
08030        THEN SERROR(74) (*MONADIC REFERENCE TO DYADIC OPERATOR*)
08040        ELSE
08050          BEGIN (* OPERATOR IS DYADIC *)
08060            NEWTOKENPTR+.NOUN:=DYADOPER;
08070            NEWTOKENPTR+.DOPINDX:=TABLEINDEX
08080          END
08090  END;(*DYADICOPCHECK*)
08100
08150
08160  PROCEDURE CHECKOTHERTABLES;
08170  VAR
08180  TABLEINDEX:INTEGER;
08181  CHKINDEX:INTEGER;
08182  FUNCTION NEXTNONBLANK:INTEGER;
08183  BEGIN
08184    CHKINDEX:=POSITION + 1;
08185    WHILE (CHKINDEX < LINELENGTH) AND
08186          (APLSTATEMENT[CHKINDEX] = CHARACTER[SPACE]) DO
08187            CHKINDEX:=CHKINDEX + 1;
08188    NEXTNONBLANK:=APLSTATEMENT[CHKINDEX];
08189  END; (* NEXTNONBLANK *)
08190  BEGIN
08200  IF NEXTNONBLANK = CHARACTER[FORWARDSLASH]
08210  THEN
08220    BEGIN
08230      TABLELOOKUP(APLSTATEMENT[POSITION],16,REDTAB,TABLEINDEX);
08240      IF TABLEINDEX = 0
08250        THEN SERROR(72) (* INVALID REDUCTION OPERATOR *)
08260        ELSE
08270          IF NOT MONADICREFERENCE
08280            THEN SERROR(73) (* DYADIC REDUCTION REFERENCE *)
08290            ELSE
08300              BEGIN (* OPERATOR IS VALID REDUCTION OPERATOR *)
08310                NEWTOKENPTR+.NOUN:=REDUCTOPER;
08320                NEWTOKENPTR+.REDINDX:=TABLEINDEX;
08330              END;
08340        POSITION:=CHKINDEX + 1;
08350    END
08360  ELSE
08370    BEGIN
08380      TABLELOOKUP(APLSTATEMENT[POSITION],9,MOPTAB,TABLEINDEX);
08390      IF TABLEINDEX = 0
08400        THEN DYADICOPCHECK
08410        ELSE
```

300

```
08420               IF NOT MONADICREFERENCE
08430                 THEN DYADICOPCHECK
08440                 ELSE
08450                   BEGIN (* OPERATOR IS MONADIC *)
08460                     NEWTOKENPTR↑.NOUN:=MONADOPER;
08470                     NEWTOKENPTR↑.MONINDX:=TABLEINDEX;
08480                   END;
08490         POSITION:=POSITION + 1;
08500     END
08510 END; (* CHECKOTHERTABLES *)
08520
08570
08580 PROCEDURE TRYTOGETANUMBER;
08590 VAR
08600 NUMBERCOUNT:INTEGER;
08610 REALNUMBER:REAL;
08620 ITSANUMBER:BOOLEAN;
08630 BEGIN
08640 NUMBERCOUNT:=0;
08650 MAKEANUMBER(REALNUMBER,ITSANUMBER);
08660 IF NOT ITSANUMBER
08670   THEN CHECKOTHERTABLES
08680   ELSE
08690     BEGIN (* STORE VALUES IN VALUE TABLE *)
08700        NEW(NEWVALTABLINK);
08710        NEWVALTABLINK↑.NEXTVALTABLINK:=OLDVALTABLINK;
08720        OLDVALTABLINK:=NEWVALTABLINK;
08730        NEWVALTABLINK↑.FORWARDORDER:=TRUE;
08740        IF FUNCTIONMODE
08750          THEN NEWVALTABLINK↑.INTERMEDRESULT:=FALSE
08760          ELSE NEWVALTABLINK↑.INTERMEDRESULT:=TRUE;
08770        SWITCH:=TRUE;
08780        WHILE ITSANUMBER DO
08790          BEGIN
08800            NUMBERCOUNT:=NUMBERCOUNT + 1;
08810            NEW(NEWVALUES);
08820            IF SWITCH = TRUE
08830              THEN
08840                BEGIN
08850                  SWITCH:=FALSE;
08860                  NEWVALTABLINK↑.FIRSTVALUE:=NEWVALUES
08870                END
08880              ELSE
08890                NEWVALPTR↑.NEXTVALUE:=NEWVALUES;
08900            NEWVALUES↑.REALVAL:=REALNUMBER;
08910            NEWVALPTR:=NEWVALUES;
08920            MAKEANUMBER(REALNUMBER,ITSANUMBER)
08930          END;
08940        NEWVALUES↑.NEXTVALUE:=NIL;
08950        IF NUMBERCOUNT > 1
08960          THEN
08970            BEGIN
08980              NEWVALTABLINK↑.DIMENSIONS:=1; (* NUMBER IS A VECTOR *)
08990              NEW(NEWDIM);
09000              NEWVALTABLINK↑.FIRSTDIMEN:=NEWDIM;
09010              NEWDIM↑.DIMENLENGTH:=NUMBERCOUNT;
09020              NEWDIM↑.NEXTDIMEN:=NIL
09030            END
09040          ELSE
09050            BEGIN
09060              NEWVALTABLINK↑.DIMENSIONS:=0; (* NUMBER IS A SCALAR *)
09070              NEWVALTABLINK↑.FIRSTDIMEN:=NIL
09080            END;
09090        NEWTOKENPTR↑.NOUN:=CONSTANT;
09100        NEWTOKENPTR↑.VALTABPTR:=NEWVALTABLINK;
09110     END
09120 END; (* TRYTOGETANUMBER *)
09130
09180
```

```
09190 FUNCTION NAMEINVARTABLE(NAME:PACKEDSTRING;VAR VARPOINTER:VARTABPTRTYPE;
09200                          TESTFUNCPTR:PTRFUNCTAB):BOOLEAN;
09210 VAR
09220 FOUND:BOOLEAN;
09230 BEGIN
09240 FOUND:=FALSE;
09250 VARPOINTER:=OLDVARTABPTR;
09260 WHILE (VARPOINTER <> NIL) AND (FOUND = FALSE) DO
09270   BEGIN
09280     IF (NAMESMATCH(NAME,VARPOINTER+.VARNAME)) AND
09290        (VARPOINTER+.FUNCTABPTR = TESTFUNCPTR) (* TEST FOR GLOBAL VAR *)
09300        THEN FOUND:=TRUE
09310        ELSE VARPOINTER:=VARPOINTER+.NEXTVARTABPTR
09320   END;
09330 NAMEINVARTABLE:=FOUND;
09340 END; (*NAMEINVARTABLE*)
09350
09400
09410 PROCEDURE ADDNAMETOVARTABLE(NAME:PACKEDSTRING);
09420 BEGIN (* NEW VARIABLE NAME ENCOUNTERED *)
09430 NEW(NEWVARTABPTR);
09440 NEWVARTABPTR+.NEXTVARTABPTR:=OLDVARTABPTR;
09450 OLDVARTABPTR:=NEWVARTABPTR;
09460 NEWVARTABPTR+.VARNAME:=NAME;
09470 NEWVARTABPTR+.VALTABPTR:=NIL;
09480 IF NEWTOKENPTR <> NIL THEN
09490 IF (NEWTOKENPTR+.NOUN = FORMRES) OR (NEWTOKENPTR+.NOUN = FORMARG)
09500   THEN NEWVARTABPTR+.FUNCTABPTR:=NEWFUNCTABPTR
09510   ELSE NEWVARTABPTR+.FUNCTABPTR:=NIL
09520 END; (* ADDNAMETOVARTABLE *)
09530
09580
09590 FUNCTION FUNCTIONALREADYDEFINED(VAR NEWFUNAME:PACKEDSTRING;VAR FUNCINDEX:
09600 PTRFUNCTAB):BOOLEAN;
09610 VAR
09620 FOUND:BOOLEAN;
09630 BEGIN
09640 FOUND:=FALSE;
09650 FUNCINDEX:=OLDFUNCTABPTR;
09660 WHILE (FUNCINDEX <> NIL) AND (FOUND = FALSE) AND
09670       (NEWFUNCTABPTR <> NIL) DO
09680   IF NAMESMATCH(FUNCINDEX+.FUNCNAME,NEWFUNAME)
09690     THEN FOUND:=TRUE
09700     ELSE FUNCINDEX:=FUNCINDEX+.NEXTFUNCTABPTR;
09710 FUNCTIONALREADYDEFINED:=FOUND
09720 END; (* FUNCTIONALREEADYDEFINED *)
09730
09780
09790 PROCEDURE MAKETOKENLINK;
09800 BEGIN
09810 NEW(NEWTOKENPTR);
09820 NEWTOKENPTR+.NEXTOKEN:=OLDTOKENPTR;
09830 SAVETOKENPTR:=OLDTOKENPTR;
09840 OLDTOKENPTR:=NEWTOKENPTR
09850 END; (* MAKETOKENLINK *)
09860
09910
09920 PROCEDURE PROCESSFUNCTIONHEADER;
09930 VAR
09940 DUMMYPTR:+FUNCTAB;
09950 NAME1,NAME2,NAME3:PACKEDSTRING;
09960 ITSANIDENTIFIER,FUNCHEADERROR:BOOLEAN;
09970 ARITYINDEX:INTEGER;
09980 BEGIN
09990 FUNCHEADERROR:=FALSE;
10000 FUNCTIONMODE:=TRUE;
10010 FUNCSTATEMENTS:=-1;
10020 IF FIRSTFUNCTION THEN BEGIN
10030                          FUNCSTATEMENTS:=0;
```

```
10040                              FIRSTFUNCTION:=FALSE;
10050                         END;
10060 ARITYINDEX:=1;
10070 POSITION:=POSITION + 1;
10080 IDENTIFIER(NAME1,ITSANIDENTIFIER);
10090 IF NOT ITSANIDENTIFIER
10100   THEN
10110     BEGIN
10120       SERROR(7); (* UNRECOGNIZABLE FUNCTION/ARGUMENT NAME *)
10130       FUNCTIONMODE:=FALSE; (* EXIT FUNCTION MODE *)
10140       FUNCHEADERROR:=TRUE
10150     END
10160   ELSE
10170     BEGIN
10180       NEW(NEWFUNCTABPTR);
10190       SKIPSPACES;
10200       IF APLSTATEMENT[POSITION] = CHARACTER[LEFTARROW]
10210         THEN
10220           BEGIN
10230             NEWFUNCTABPTR+.RESULT:=TRUE; (* EXPLICIT RESULT *)
10240             NEWFUNCTABPTR+.RESULTNAME:=NAME1;
10250             POSITION:=POSITION + 1;
10260             IDENTIFIER(NAME1,ITSANIDENTIFIER);
10270             IF NOT ITSANIDENTIFIER
10280               THEN
10290                 BEGIN
10300                   SERROR(6);(*UNRECOGNIZABLE NAME TO RIGHT OF EXPLICIT RES*)
10310                   FUNCHEADERROR:=TRUE
10320                 END
10330           END
10340         ELSE
10350           NEWFUNCTABPTR+.RESULT:=FALSE; (* NO EXPLICIT RESULT *)
10360       SKIPSPACES;
10370       IF (POSITION <= LINELENGTH) AND (NOT FUNCHEADERROR)
10380         THEN
10390           BEGIN
10400             IDENTIFIER(NAME2,ITSANIDENTIFIER);
10410             IF NOT ITSANIDENTIFIER
10420               THEN
10430                 BEGIN
10440                   SERROR(7);(* INVALID FUNCTION/ARGUMENT NAME *)
10450                   FUNCHEADERROR:=TRUE
10460                 END
10470               ELSE
10480                 ARITYINDEX:=2
10490           END;
10500       SKIPSPACES;
10510       IF (POSITION <= LINELENGTH) AND (NOT FUNCHEADERROR)
10520         THEN
10530           BEGIN
10540             IDENTIFIER(NAME3,ITSANIDENTIFIER);
10550             IF NOT ITSANIDENTIFIER
10560               THEN
10570                 BEGIN
10580                   SERROR(9); (* INVALID FUNCTION RIGHT ARGUMENT NAME *)
10590                   FUNCHEADERROR:=TRUE
10600                 END
10610               ELSE
10620                 ARITYINDEX:=3
10630           END;
10640       SKIPSPACES;
10650       IF (POSITION <= LINELENGTH) AND (NOT FUNCHEADERROR)
10660         THEN
10670           BEGIN
10680             SERROR(3); (* EXTRANEOUS CHARACTERS TO RIGHT OF FUNCTION HEADER *)
10690             FUNCHEADERROR:=TRUE
10700           END;
10710       CASE ARITYINDEX OF
10720         1: BEGIN
```

```
10730          NEWFUNCTABPTR↑.ARITY:=NILADIC;
10740          NEWFUNCTABPTR↑.FUNCNAME:=NAME1;
10750       END;
10760    2: BEGIN
10770          NEWFUNCTABPTR↑.ARITY:=MONADIC;
10780          NEWFUNCTABPTR↑.FUNCNAME:=NAME1;
10790          NEWFUNCTABPTR↑.RIGHTARG:=NAME2;
10800          ADDNAMETOVARTABLE(NAME2);
10810          NEWVARTABPTR↑.FUNCTABPTR:=NEWFUNCTABPTR;
10820       END;
10830    3: BEGIN
10840          NEWFUNCTABPTR↑.ARITY:=DYADIC;
10850          NEWFUNCTABPTR↑.LEFTARG:=NAME1;
10860          NEWFUNCTABPTR↑.FUNCNAME:=NAME2;
10870          NEWFUNCTABPTR↑.RIGHTARG:=NAME3;
10880          ADDNAMETOVARTABLE(NAME1);
10890          NEWVARTABPTR↑.FUNCTABPTR:=NEWFUNCTABPTR;
10900          ADDNAMETOVARTABLE(NAME3);
10910          NEWVARTABPTR↑.FUNCTABPTR:=NEWFUNCTABPTR;
10920       END
10930    END; (* CASE *)
10940    IF FUNCTIONALREADYDEFINED(NEWFUNCTABPTR↑.FUNCNAME,DUMMYPTR)
10950      THEN
10960        BEGIN
10970           SERROR(5); (* FUNCTION ALREADY DEFINED *)
10980           FUNCHEADERROR:=TRUE;
10990        END;
11000    IF FUNCHEADERROR
11010      THEN BEGIN
11020           DISPOSE(NEWFUNCTABPTR); (* HEADER NO GOOD *)
11030           FUNCTIONMODE:=FALSE; (* EXIT FUNCTION MODE *)
11040           NEWFUNCTABPTR:=OLDFUNCTABPTR;
11050           END
11060    END
11070 END; (* PROCESSFUNCHEADER *)
11080
11130
11140 PROCEDURE DESTROYSTATEMENT;
11150 VAR
11160 DUMTOKENPTR:↑TOKENTABLE;
11170 AUXSUBRTABPTR:↑SUBRTAB;
11180 BEGIN
11190    IF SUBRTABPTR <> NIL THEN
11200       BEGIN
11210         WHILE SUBRTABPTR↑.LASTSUBRPTR <> NIL DO
11220           BEGIN
11230             AUXSUBRTABPTR:=SUBRTABPTR;
11240             SUBRTABPTR:=SUBRTABPTR↑.LASTSUBRPTR;
11250             DISPOSE(AUXSUBRTABPTR);
11260           END;
11270         DISPOSE(SUBRTABPTR);
11280       END;
11290 DUMTOKENPTR:=OLDTOKENPTR;
11300 WHILE DUMTOKENPTR <> HOLDTOKENPTR DO
11310   BEGIN
11320     OLDTOKENPTR:=OLDTOKENPTR↑.NEXTOKEN;
11330     DISPOSE(DUMTOKENPTR);
11340     DUMTOKENPTR:=OLDTOKENPTR
11350   END;
11360 NEWTOKENPTR:=HOLDTOKENPTR;
11370 OLDTOKENPTR:=HOLDTOKENPTR   (* RETURN POINTER TO END OF LAST GOOD LINE *)
11380 END; (* DESTROYSTATEMENT *)
11390
11430
11440 PROCEDURE REVERSELINKLIST(VAR ARGPTR:TYPEVALTABPTR);
11450 VAR
11460 HOLD,TEMPTR:↑VALUES;
11470 BEGIN (* REVERSELINKLIST *)
11480 VALPTR:=ARGPTR↑.FIRSTVALUE;
```

```
11490 TEMPTR:=VALPTR+.NEXTVALUE;
11500 WHILE TEMPTR <> NIL DO
11510   BEGIN
11520     HOLD:=TEMPTR+.NEXTVALUE;
11530     TEMPTR+.NEXTVALUE:=VALPTR;
11540     VALPTR:=TEMPTR;
11550     TEMPTR:=HOLD
11560   END;
11570 ARGPTR+.FIRSTVALUE+.NEXTVALUE:=NIL;
11580 ARGPTR+.FIRSTVALUE:=VALPTR;
11590 IF ARGPTR+.FORWARDORDER = TRUE
11600   THEN ARGPTR+.FORWARDORDER:=FALSE
11610   ELSE ARGPTR+.FORWARDORDER:=TRUE (* TOGGLE LIST ORDER SWITCH *)
11620 END; (* REVERSELINKLIST *)
11630
11680
11690   PROCEDURE PARSER(VAR TOKENTABPTR:TOKENPTR;VAR PTRTODA:TYPEVALTABPTR);
11700     VAR
11710       VFUNCHOLD:+VFUNC;                              (* HOLD WHILE SEARCHING *)
11720       AUXOPERTABPTR:+OPERANDTAB;
11730       AUXSUBRTABPTR:+SUBRTAB;
11740       AUXRPARMPTR:+FPARMTAB;
11750       AUXLPARMPTR:+FPARMTAB;
11760       VALIDEXP:BOOLEAN;    (* TRUE IF VALID EXPRESSION *)
11770       CNT:INTEGER;
11780       NPV:INTEGER;    (* NUMBER OF INDICES *)
11790       ASSIGN,ASSIGN1:BOOLEAN;   (* ASSIGN.IN PROGRESS *)
11800       DONESUCCESSOR:BOOLEAN;
11810       DONEPARSE:BOOLEAN;
11820
11840
11850 PROCEDURE ERROR(ERRORINDEX:INTEGER);
11860 VAR
11870 MSGCOL:INTEGER;
11880 BEGIN
11890 WRITE(Ξ Ξ,ERRORINDEX,Ξ  Ξ);
11900 FOR MSGCOL:=1 TO MESSAGELENGTH DO
11910   WRITE(ERRORMSGS[ERRORINDEX,MSGCOL]);
11920 WRITELN;
11930 GOTO 100; (* RETURN TO SCANNER *)
11950 END; (* ERROR *)
11960
12020
12030         PROCEDURE RELEASE;
12040           BEGIN (* RELEASEOPERTAB *)
12060             OPERTABPTR:=PTRLASTOPER;
12070             WHILE OPERTABPTR+.LASTOPER<>NIL DO
12080               BEGIN
12090                 AUXOPERTABPTR:=OPERTABPTR;
12100                 OPERTABPTR:=OPERTABPTR+.LASTOPER;
12110                 DISPOSE(AUXOPERTABPTR);
12120               END;
12130           END; (* RELEASEOPERTAB *)
12140
12200
12210     PROCEDURE EXPRESSION(VAR VALIDEXP:BOOLEAN);FORWARD;
12220
12270
12280     PROCEDURE RETURNTOCALLINGSUBR;
12290       VAR
12300         NAMEPTR:+VARTAB;
12310       BEGIN (* RETURNTOCALLINGSUBR *)
12330         IF SUBRTABPTR+.CALLEDSUBR+.RESULT THEN
12340           BEGIN (* PLACE EXPLICIT RESULT IN OPERTAB *)
12350             IF NOT NAMEINVARTABLE(SUBRTABPTR+.CALLEDSUBR+.RESULTNAME,NAMEPTR,
12360                                   SUBRTABPTR+.CALLEDSUBR)
12370               THEN ERROR(11) (* +SYMBOL NOT FOUND+ *)
12380             ELSE
12390               BEGIN
```

```
12400              AUXOPERTABPTR:=OPERTABPTR;
12410              NEW(OPERTABPTR);
12420              OPERTABPTR+.LASTOPER:=AUXOPERTABPTR;
12430              PTRLASTOPER:=OPERTABPTR;
12440              OPERTABPTR+.OPERPTR:=NAMEPTR+.VALTABPTR;
12450            END;
12460          END;
12470      (* RETURN TO CALLING FUNCTION *)
12480        VFUNCPTR:=SUBRTABPTR+.STATEMCALLINGSUBR;
12490        TOKENTABPTR:=SUBRTABPTR+.TOKENCALLINGSUBR+.NEXTOKEN;
12500        IF SUBRTABPTR+.CALLEDSUBR+.ARITY<>NILADIC THEN
12510          BEGIN (* MONADIC OR DYADIC *)
12520            AUXRPARMPTR:=RPARMPTR;
12530            RPARMPTR:=RPARMPTR+.LASTPARM;
12540            DISPOSE(AUXRPARMPTR);
12550            IF SUBRTABPTR+.CALLEDSUBR+.ARITY=DYADIC THEN
12560              BEGIN (* DYADIC ONLY *)
12570                AUXLPARMPTR:=LPARMPTR;
12580                LPARMPTR:=LPARMPTR+.LASTPARM;
12590                DISPOSE(AUXLPARMPTR);
12600              END;
12610          END;
12620        AUXSUBRTABPTR:=SUBRTABPTR;
12630        SUBRTABPTR:=SUBRTABPTR+.LASTSUBRPTR;
12640        DISPOSE (AUXSUBRTABPTR);
12650      END; (* RETURNTOCALLINGSUBR *)
12660
12720
12730    FUNCTION SPECSYMBOL(SYM:INTEGER):BOOLEAN;
12740      VAR
12750        VALIDSYM:BOOLEAN;
12760      BEGIN (* SPECSYMBOL *)
12780        VALIDSYM:=FALSE;
12790        IF TOKENTABPTR+.NOUN=SPECOPER THEN
12800          IF TOKENTABPTR+.CHARINDX=SYM THEN
12810            BEGIN
12820              HOLD:=TOKENTABPTR;
12830              TOKENTABPTR:=TOKENTABPTR+.NEXTOKEN;
12840              VALIDSYM:=TRUE;
12850            END;
12860        SPECSYMBOL:=VALIDSYM;
12870      END; (* SPECSYMBOL *)
12880
12940
12950      PROCEDURE CALLSUBR;
12960        VAR
12970          PTRTOVARTAB:+VARTAB;
12980        BEGIN (* CALLSUBR *)
13000          IF SUBRTABPTR+.CALLEDSUBR+.ARITY<>NILADIC THEN
13010            BEGIN
13020          IF NOT NAMEINVARTABLE(SUBRTABPTR+.CALLEDSUBR+.RIGHTARG,PTRTOVARTAB,
13030                            SUBRTABPTR+.CALLEDSUBR)
13040              THEN ERROR(32);
13050            IF PTRTOVARTAB+.FUNCTABPTR<>SUBRTABPTR+.CALLEDSUBR THEN
13060              ERROR(32);(* PROGRAM LOGIC ERROR, VARIABLE NAME OF *)
13070                      (* FUNCTION ARGUMENT NOT FOUND IN SYMBOL TABLE *)
13080            AUXRPARMPTR:=RPARMPTR;
13090            NEW(RPARMPTR);
13100            RPARMPTR+.LASTPARM:=AUXRPARMPTR;
13110            PTRTOVARTAB+.DEFEREDVALTABPTR:=RPARMPTR;
13120            IF SUBRTABPTR+.CALLEDSUBR+.ARITY=DYADIC THEN
13130              BEGIN (* IF DYADIC *)
13140                IF NOT NAMEINVARTABLE(SUBRTABPTR+.CALLEDSUBR+.LEFTARG,
13150                PTRTOVARTAB,SUBRTABPTR+.CALLEDSUBR) THEN ERROR(33);
13160                IF PTRTOVARTAB+.FUNCTABPTR<>SUBRTABPTR+.CALLEDSUBR THEN
13170                  ERROR(33); (* SAME AS ERROR(32) *)
13180                AUXLPARMPTR:=LPARMPTR;
13190                NEW(LPARMPTR);
13200                LPARMPTR+.LASTPARM:=AUXLPARMPTR;
```

```
13210                         PTRTOVARTAB↑.DEFEREDVALTABPTR:=LPARMPTR;
13220                         LPARMPTR↑.PTRVAL:=OPERTABPTR↑.OPERPTR;
13230                         AUXOPERTABPTR:=OPERTABPTR;
13240                         OPERTABPTR:=OPERTABPTR↑.LASTOPER;
13250                         DISPOSE(AUXOPERTABPTR);
13260                         PTRLASTOPER:=OPERTABPTR;
13270                       END;
13280                   RPARMPTR↑.PTRVAL:=OPERTABPTR↑.OPERPTR;
13290                   AUXOPERTABPTR:=OPERTABPTR;
13300                   OPERTABPTR:=OPERTABPTR↑.LASTOPER;
13310                   DISPOSE(AUXOPERTABPTR);
13320                   PTRLASTOPER:=OPERTABPTR;
13330                 END;
13340             TOKENTABPTR:=SUBRTABPTR↑.CALLEDSUBR↑.FIRSTATEMENT↑.NEXTSTMNT;
13350             VFUNCPTR:=SUBRTABPTR↑.CALLEDSUBR↑.FIRSTATEMENT;
13360           END; (* CALLSUBR *)
13370
13430
13440         FUNCTION FUNCTCALL:BOOLEAN;
13450           VAR
13460             PTRTOFUNCTAB:↑FUNCTAB;
13470             NAMEOFFUNC:PACKEDSTRING;
13480             VALIDFN:BOOLEAN;
13490           BEGIN (* FUNCTCALL *)
13510             VALIDFN:=FALSE;
13520             IF TOKENTABPTR↑.NOUN=GLOBVAR THEN
13530               BEGIN
13540                 NAMEOFFUNC:=TOKENTABPTR↑.VARTABPTR↑.VARNAME;
13550                 IF FUNCTIONALREADYDEFINED(NAMEOFFUNC,PTRTOFUNCTAB) THEN
13560                   BEGIN
13570                     AUXSUBRTABPTR:=SUBRTABPTR;
13580                     NEW(SUBRTABPTR);
13590                     SUBRTABPTR↑.LASTSUBRPTR:=AUXSUBRTABPTR;
13600                     SUBRTABPTR↑.CALLEDSUBR:=PTRTOFUNCTAB;
13610                     SUBRTABPTR↑.TOKENCALLINGSUBR:=TOKENTABPTR;
13620                     SUBRTABPTR↑.STATEMCALLINGSUBR:=VFUNCPTR;
13630                     HOLD:=TOKENTABPTR;
13640                     TOKENTABPTR:=TOKENTABPTR↑.NEXTOKEN;
13650                     VALIDFN:=TRUE;
13660                   END;
13670               END;
13680             FUNCTCALL:=VALIDFN;
13690           END; (* FUNCTCALL *)
13700
13720
13730 PROCEDURE NUMWRITE(REALNO:REAL);
13740 VAR
13750     PREFIX,ROOT:INTEGER;
13760 SIGDIG,COLCNT:INTEGER;
13770 BEGIN (* OUTPUT A NUMBER *)
13780 IF REALNO >= 0.0
13790    THEN WRITE(Ξ Ξ, REALNO:12:2) (* OUTPUT POSITIVE NUMBER *)
13800    ELSE
13810      BEGIN (* OUTPUT NEGATIVE NUMBER *)
13820      REALNO:=-1.0*REALNO;
13830        SIGDIG:=TRUNC((LN(REALNO))/(LN(10.0)));
13840        FOR COLCNT:=1 TO (7 - SIGDIG) DO
13850          WRITE(Ξ Ξ);
13860        IF CHARACTER[NEGATIVE] < 6000
13870          THEN WRITE(CHR(CHARACTER[NEGATIVE]))
13880          ELSE
13890            BEGIN
13900              PREFIX:=CHARACTER[NEGATIVE] DIV 100;
13910              ROOT:=CHARACTER[NEGATIVE] - (100*PREFIX);
13920              WRITE(CHR(PREFIX), CHR(ROOT));
13930            END;
13940        SIGDIG:=SIGDIG + 5;
13950        WRITE(REALNO:SIGDIG:2);
13960      END
```

```
13970 END; (* NUMWRITE *)
13980
14010
14020          PROCEDURE OUTPUTVAL;
14030            VAR
14040              CNT:INTEGER;
14050              AUXVALUESPTR:+VALUES;
14060            DIMHOLD, DIMEN1,DIMEN2, DIMEN3:INTEGER;
14070            OUTCNT1,OUTCNT2,OUTCNT3:INTEGER;
14080            IDIMENS:INTEGER;
14090          BEGIN (* OUTPUTVAL *)
14110            CNT:=0;
14120            WRITELN;WRITELN;
14130            IF NOT OPERTABPTR+.OPERPTR+.FORWARDORDER THEN
14140              REVERSELINKLIST(OPERTABPTR+.OPERPTR);
14150            AUXVALUESPTR:=OPERTABPTR+.OPERPTR+.FIRSTVALUE;
14160            IDIMENS:=OPERTABPTR+.OPERPTR+.DIMENSIONS;
14170            IF NOT(IDIMENS IN [0..3] ) THEN
14180              BEGIN
14190                FOR COLCNT:=1 TO MESSAGELENGTH DO
14200                  WRITE(ERRORMSGS[60,COLCNT]);
14210                WRITELN;
14220              END
14230            ELSE
14240              IF AUXVALUESPTR=NIL THEN
14250              BEGIN
14260                FOR COLCNT:=1 TO MESSAGELENGTH DO
14270                  WRITE(ERRORMSGS[61,COLCNT]);
14280                WRITELN;
14290              END
14300              ELSE
14310                IF IDIMENS=0 THEN
14320                      BEGIN
14330                    NUMWRITE(AUXVALUESPTR+.REALVAL);
14340                    WRITELN;
14350                    END
14360                  ELSE
14370                    BEGIN
14380                      DIMEN1:=OPERTABPTR+.OPERPTR+.FIRSTDIMEN+.DIMENLENGTH;
14390                      IF IDIMENS>=2 THEN DIMEN2 :=
14400                      OPERTABPTR+.OPERPTR+.FIRSTDIMEN+.NEXTDIMEN+.DIMENLENGTH
14410                      ELSE DIMEN2:=1;
14420                      IF IDIMENS=3 THEN DIMEN3:=
14430                      OPERTABPTR+.OPERPTR+.FIRSTDIMEN+.NEXTDIMEN+.
14440                      NEXTDIMEN+.DIMENLENGTH
14450                      ELSE DIMEN3:=1;
14460                      IF IDIMENS=3 THEN BEGIN (* ROTATE DIMENSIONS *)
14470                                  DIMHOLD:=DIMEN1; DIMEN1:=DIMEN2;
14480                                  DIMEN2:=DIMEN3; DIMEN3:=DIMHOLD;
14490                                  END;
14500                  FOR OUTCNT3:=1 TO DIMEN3 DO
14510                    BEGIN
14520                  FOR OUTCNT2:=1 TO DIMEN1 DO
14530                    BEGIN
14540                      FOR OUTCNT1:=1 TO DIMEN2 DO
14550                        BEGIN
14560                            CNT:=CNT + 1;
14570                          IF(((CNT-1)MOD 5)=0) AND
14580                            (CNT<>1) THEN
14590                            BEGIN
14600                              WRITELN;
14610                              WRITE(≡   ≡);
14620                            END;
14630                          NUMWRITE(AUXVALUESPTR+.REALVAL);
14640                          AUXVALUESPTR:=AUXVALUESPTR+.NEXTVALUE;
14650                        END;
14660                      IF IDIMENS>=2 THEN
14670                        BEGIN
14680                          WRITELN;
```

```
14690                                  CNT:=0;
14700                               END;
14710                            END;
14720                       WRITELN; WRITELN;
14730                       END;
14740                    (*WRITELN;*)
14750                    END;
14760            END; (* OUTPUTVAL *)
14770

14830

14840        FUNCTION VARIABLE:BOOLEAN;
14850          VAR
14860             GLOBORDUMMY:BOOLEAN;                   (* GORD *)
14870             PASSEDADJ:↑VARTAB;                     (* K *)
14880             RARG:BOOLEAN;                          (* RD *)
14890             PARMPTR:↑VALTAB;                       (* PT *)
14900             VALIDVAR:BOOLEAN;
14910             VALIDINDEX:BOOLEAN;
14920

14980

14990        PROCEDURE INPUTVAL;
15000          VAR
15010             AUXPTRTODA:↑VALTAB;
15020             AUXVALUESPTR:↑VALUES;
15030             AUX2VALUESPTR:↑VALUES;
15040             REALV:REAL;
15050             BOOLV:BOOLEAN;
15060             CCNTR,CNT:INTEGER;
15070             AUXDIMENINFOPTR:↑DIMENINFO;
15080          BEGIN (* INPUTVAL *)
15100             CNT:=0;
15110             POSITION:=1;
15120             AUXPTRTODA:=PTRTODA;
15130             NEW(PTRTODA);
15140             AUXPTRTODA↑.NEXTVALTABLINK:=PTRTODA;
15150             AUXOPERTABPTR:=OPERTABPTR;
15160             NEW(OPERTABPTR);
15170             PTRLASTOPER:=OPERTABPTR;
15180             OPERTABPTR↑.LASTOPER:=AUXOPERTABPTR;
15190             OPERTABPTR↑.OPERPTR:=PTRTODA;
15200             NEW(AUX2VALUESPTR);
15210             PTRTODA↑.FIRSTVALUE:=AUX2VALUESPTR;
15220             FOR CCNTR:=1 TO MESSAGELENGTH DO
15230                WRITE(ERRORMSGS[63,CCNTR]);WRITELN;
15240             READLN;
15250             GETAPLSTATEMENT;
15260             REPEAT
15270                MAKEANUMBER(REALV,BOOLV);
15280                SKIPSPACES;
15290                IF NOT BOOLV THEN
15300                   BEGIN
15310                      FOR COLCNT:=1 TO MESSAGELENGTH DO
15320                         WRITE(ERRORMSGS[62,COLCNT]);
15330                      WRITELN;
15340                      POSITION:=1;
15350                      CNT:=0;
15360                      AUX2VALUESPTR:=OPERTABPTR↑.OPERPTR↑.FIRSTVALUE;
15370                      FOR CCNTR:=1 TO MESSAGELENGTH DO
15380                         WRITE(ERRORMSGS[63,CCNTR]);WRITELN;
15390                      READLN;
15400                      GETAPLSTATEMENT
15410                   END
15420                ELSE
15430                   BEGIN
15440                      CNT:=CNT+1;
15450                      AUXVALUESPTR:=AUX2VALUESPTR;
15460                      NEW(AUX2VALUESPTR);
15470                      AUXVALUESPTR↑.REALVAL:=REALV;
15480                      AUXVALUESPTR↑.NEXTVALUE:=AUX2VALUESPTR;
```

```
15490            END;
15500         UNTIL POSITION>LINELENGTH;
15510         DISPOSE(AUX2VALUESPTR);
15520         AUXVALUESPTR↑.NEXTVALUE:=NIL;
15530         PTRTODA↑.INTERMEDRESULT:=FALSE;
15540         PTRTODA↑.DIMENSIONS:=1;
15550         PTRTODA↑.FORWARDORDER:=TRUE;
15560         PTRTODA↑.NEXTVALTABLINK:=NIL;
15570         NEW(AUXDIMENINFOPTR);
15580         PTRTODA↑.FIRSTDIMEN:=AUXDIMENINFOPTR;
15590         AUXDIMENINFOPTR↑.DIMENLENGTH:=CNT;
15600         AUXDIMENINFOPTR↑.NEXTDIMEN:=NIL;
15610      END; (* INPUTVAL *)
15620
15670
15680      PROCEDURE GETARRAYPOSITION(VAR VALUESPTR:TYPEVALUESPTR);
15690         VAR
15700            INDICE:REAL;
15710            KCNT:INTEGER;
15720            SL:INTEGER;
15730            AUXDIMENINFOPTR:↑DIMENINFO;
15740         BEGIN (* GETARRAYPOSITION *)
15750            IF NPV<>PARMPTR↑.DIMENSIONS THEN ERROR(35);
15760                            (* ↑WRONG NUM. OF SUBSCRIPTS↑ *)
15770            SL:=0;
15780            AUXOPERTABPTR:=OPERTABPTR;
15790            AUXDIMENINFOPTR:=PARMPTR↑.FIRSTDIMEN;
15800            FOR KCNT:=1 TO NPV DO
15810               BEGIN
15820                  IF AUXOPERTABPTR↑.OPERPTR.DIMENSIONS<>0 THEN
15830                     ERROR(35); (* ↑NON-SCALER INDICES↑ *)
15840                  INDICE:=AUXOPERTABPTR↑.OPERPTR.FIRSTVALUE↑.REALVAL;
15850                  IF INDICE-1.0*TRUNC(INDICE)<>0.0 THEN
15860                     ERROR(37); (* ↑NON-INTEGER INDICES↑ *)
15870                  IF NOT(TRUNC(INDICE)
15880                  IN [1..AUXDIMENINFOPTR↑.DIMENLENGTH]) THEN
15890                     ERROR(38); (* ↑OUT OF RANGE INDEX↑ *)
15900                  SL:=(SL*AUXDIMENINFOPTR↑.DIMENLENGTH)+TRUNC(INDICE)-1;
15910                  AUXOPERTABPTR:=AUXOPERTABPTR↑.LASTOPER;
15920                  DISPOSE(OPERTABPTR);
15930                  OPERTABPTR:=AUXOPERTABPTR;
15940                  AUXDIMENINFOPTR:=AUXDIMENINFOPTR↑.NEXTDIMEN;
15950               END;
15960            VALUESPTR:=PARMPTR↑.FIRSTVALUE;
15970            WHILE SL<>0 DO(* DETERMINE WHICH VALUE IN  *)
15980                     (* PT[SVAL(SV)][SVAL(SV-1)]...[SVAL(SV-NPV+1)]*)
15990                     (*            := SVAL(SV-NPV)                 *)
16000               BEGIN
16010                  VALUESPTR:=VALUESPTR↑.NEXTVALUE;
16020                  SL:=SL-1;
16030               END;
16040         END; (* GETARRAYPOSITION *)
16050
16110
16120      PROCEDURE LINKRESULTS;
16130         VAR
16140            PTRTOVALUES:↑VALUES;
16150         BEGIN (* LINKRESULTS *)
16170            IF NPV=0 THEN
16180               BEGIN
16190                  IF NOT GLOBORDUMMY THEN
16200                     IF RARG THEN
16210                        RPARMPTR↑.PTRVAL:=OPERTABPTR↑.OPERPTR
16220                     ELSE
16230                        LPARMPTR↑.PTRVAL:=OPERTABPTR↑.OPERPTR
16240                  ELSE
16250                     PASSEDADJ↑.VALTABPTR:=OPERTABPTR↑.OPERPTR
16260               END
16270            ELSE
```

310

```
16280                    BEGIN
16290                       IF GLOBORDUMMY THEN PARMPTR:=PASSEDADJ+.VALTABPTR
16300                       ELSE PARMPTR:=PASSEDADJ+.DEFEREDVALTABPTR+.PTRVAL;
16310                       GETARRAYPOSITION(PTRTOVALUES);
16320                       IF OPERTABPTR+.OPERPTR+.DIMENSIONS<>0 THEN
16330                          ERROR(36); (* +ASSIGNED EXPRESSION NOT A SCALAR+ *)
16340                       PTRTOVALUES+.REALVAL:=
16350                       OPERTABPTR+.OPERPTR+.FIRSTVALUE+.REALVAL;
16360                    END;
16370                  AUXOPERTABPTR:=OPERTABPTR;
16380                  OPERTABPTR:=OPERTABPTR+.LASTOPER;
16390                  DISPOSE(AUXOPERTABPTR);
16400                  PTRLASTOPER:=OPERTABPTR;
16410              END; (* LINKRESULTS *)
16420
16480
16490              PROCEDURE STACKPOINTERS;
16500                VAR
16510                  AUXPTRTODA:+VALTAB;
16520                  PTRTOVALUES,AUXVALUESPTR:+VALUES;
16530                BEGIN (* STACKPOINTERS *);
16550                  IF NPV=0 THEN
16560                    BEGIN
16570                      AUXOPERTABPTR:=OPERTABPTR;
16580                      NEW(OPERTABPTR);
16590                      OPERTABPTR+.LASTOPER:=AUXOPERTABPTR;
16600                      OPERTABPTR+.OPERPTR:=PARMPTR;
16610                      PTRLASTOPER:=OPERTABPTR
16620                    END
16630                  ELSE
16640                    BEGIN
16650                      AUXPTRTODA:=PTRTODA;
16660                      NEW(PTRTODA);
16670                      PTRTODA+.NEXTVALTABLINK:=AUXPTRTODA;
16680                      PTRTODA+.INTERMEDRESULT:=TRUE;
16690                      PTRTODA+.DIMENSIONS:=0;
16700                      PTRTODA+.FIRSTDIMEN:=NIL;
16710                      PTRTODA+.FORWARDORDER:=TRUE;
16720                      NEW(AUXVALUESPTR);
16730                      PTRTODA+.FIRSTVALUE:=AUXVALUESPTR;
16740                      GETARRAYPOSITION(PTRTOVALUES);
16750                      PTRTODA+.FIRSTVALUE+.REALVAL:=PTRTOVALUES+.REALVAL;
16760                      PTRTODA+.FIRSTVALUE+.NEXTVALUE:=NIL;
16770                      AUXOPERTABPTR:=OPERTABPTR;
16780                      NEW(OPERTABPTR);
16790                      OPERTABPTR+.LASTOPER:=AUXOPERTABPTR;
16800                      OPERTABPTR+.OPERPTR:=PTRTODA;
16810                      PTRLASTOPER:=OPERTABPTR;
16820                    END;
16830                END; (* STACKPOINTERS *)
16840
16900
16910              FUNCTION SIMPLEVARIABLE:BOOLEAN;
16920                VAR
16930                  VALIDSV:BOOLEAN;
16940                BEGIN (* SIMPLEVARIABLE *)
16960                  VALIDSV:=FALSE;
16970                  RARG:=FALSE;
16980                  GLOBORDUMMY:=FALSE;
16990                  IF ASSIGN THEN
17000                    BEGIN
17010                      IF (TOKENTABPTR+.NOUN=FORMRES) OR
17020                         (TOKENTABPTR+.NOUN=GLOBVAR) THEN
17030                        BEGIN
17040                          GLOBORDUMMY:=TRUE;
17050                          PASSEDADJ:=TOKENTABPTR+.VARTABPTR;
17060                          HOLD:=TOKENTABPTR;
17070                          TOKENTABPTR:=TOKENTABPTR+.NEXTOKEN;
17080                          VALIDSV:=TRUE
```

```
17090                         END
17100                      ELSE
17110                      IF TOKENTABPTR+.NOUN=FORMARG THEN
17120                         BEGIN
17130                            IF NAMESMATCH
17140                            (TOKENTABPTR+.VARTABPTR+.FUNCTABPTR+.LEFTARG,
17150                            TOKENTABPTR+.VARTABPTR+.VARNAME ) THEN RARG:=TRUE;
17160                            PASSEDADJ:=TOKENTABPTR+.VARTABPTR
17170                         END
17180                   END
17190                ELSE
17200                   BEGIN
17210                   IF (TOKENTABPTR+.NOUN=FORMRES) OR
17220                      (TOKENTABPTR+.NOUN=GLOBVAR) THEN
17230                      BEGIN
17240                         PARMPTR:=TOKENTABPTR+.VARTABPTR+.VALTABPTR;
17250                         IF PARMPTR<>NIL THEN
17260                            BEGIN
17270                               HOLD:=TOKENTABPTR;
17280                               TOKENTABPTR:=TOKENTABPTR+.NEXTOKEN;
17290                               VALIDSV:=TRUE
17300                            END
17310                      END
17320                   ELSE
17330                      BEGIN
17340                         IF TOKENTABPTR+.NOUN=FORMARG THEN
17350                            BEGIN
17360                               IF NAMESMATCH
17370                               (TOKENTABPTR+.VARTABPTR+.FUNCTABPTR+.LEFTARG,
17380                               TOKENTABPTR+.VARTABPTR+.VARNAME) THEN
17390                                  PARMPTR:=LPARMPTR+.PTRVAL
17400                               ELSE
17410                                  PARMPTR:=RPARMPTR+.PTRVAL;
17420                               HOLD:=TOKENTABPTR;
17430                               TOKENTABPTR:=TOKENTABPTR+.NEXTOKEN;
17440                               VALIDSV:=TRUE;
17450                            END;
17460                      END;
17470                   END;
17480             SIMPLEVARIABLE:=VALIDSV;
17490          END; (* SIMPLE VARIABLE *)
17500
17560
17570          PROCEDURE INDEX(VAR VALIDI:BOOLEAN);
17580            VAR
17590             VALIDE1,VALIDE2:BOOLEAN;
17600          BEGIN (* INDEX *)
17620            VALIDI:=FALSE;
17630            EXPRESSION(VALIDE1);
17640            IF VALIDE1 THEN
17650               BEGIN
17660                  NPV:=1; (* NO. OF INDEX EXPRESSIONS *)
17670                  WHILE SPECSYMBOL(XSEMICOLSYM) DO
17680                     BEGIN
17690                        NPV:=NPV+1;
17700                        EXPRESSION(VALIDE2);
17710                        IF NOT VALIDE2 THEN ERROR(39);
17720                              (* +INVALID INDEX EXPRESSION+ *)
17730                     END;
17740                  VALIDI:=TRUE;
17750               END;
17760          END; (* INDEX *)
17770
17830
17840          BEGIN (* VARIABLE *)
17860            VALIDVAR:=FALSE; NPV:=0;
17870            IF NOT ASSIGN THEN
17880               IF SPECSYMBOL(XQUADSYM) THEN
17890                  BEGIN
```

```
17900              INPUTVAL$
17910              VALIDVAR:=TRUE
17920           END
17930         ELSE
17940           BEGIN
17950             IF SPECSYMBOL(XRIGHTBRACKET) THEN
17960               BEGIN
17970                 INDEX(VALIDINDEX)$
17980                 IF (NOT VALIDINDEX) OR (NOT SPECSYMBOL(XLEFTBRACKET))
17990                   THEN ERROR(34)$ (* INVALID INDEX EXPRESSION *)
18000               END$
18010             IF SIMPLEVARIABLE THEN
18020               BEGIN
18030                 STACKPOINTERS$
18040                 VALIDVAR:=TRUE
18050               END
18060           END
18070       ELSE
18080         IF SPECSYMBOL(XQUADSYM) THEN
18090           BEGIN
18100             OUTPUTVAL$
18110             VALIDVAR:=TRUE
18120           END
18130         ELSE
18140           BEGIN
18150             IF SPECSYMBOL(XRIGHTBRACKET) THEN
18160               BEGIN
18170                 INDEX(VALIDINDEX)$
18180                 IF (NOT VALIDINDEX) OR (NOT SPECSYMBOL(XLEFTBRACKET))
18190                   THEN ERROR(34)$ (* INVALID INDEX EXPRESSION *)
18200               END$
18210             IF SIMPLEVARIABLE THEN
18220               BEGIN
18230                 LINKRESULTS$
18240                 VALIDVAR:=TRUE$
18250               END$
18260           END$
18270       VARIABLE:=VALIDVAR$
18280     END$ (* VARIABLE *)
18290
18360
18370   PROCEDURE PRIMARY(VAR VALID:BOOLEAN)$   (* RECURSIVE ENTRY *)
18380     VAR
18390       VALIDX:BOOLEAN$
18400       ASSIGN:BOOLEAN$
18410
18470
18480     FUNCTION VECTOR:BOOLEAN$
18490       VAR
18500         VEC:BOOLEAN$
18510       BEGIN (* VECTOR *)
18530         VEC:=FALSE$
18540         IF TOKENTABPTR+.NOUN=CONSTANT THEN
18550           BEGIN
18560             AUXOPERTABPTR:=OPERTABPTR$
18570             NEW(OPERTABPTR)$
18580             PTRLASTOPER:=OPERTABPTR$
18590             OPERTABPTR+.LASTOPER:=AUXOPERTABPTR$
18600             OPERTABPTR+.OPERPTR:=TOKENTABPTR+.VALTABPTR$
18610             HOLD:=TOKENTABPTR$
18620             TOKENTABPTR:=TOKENTABPTR+.NEXTOKEN$
18630             VEC:=TRUE$
18640           END$
18650         VECTOR:=VEC$
18660       END$ (* VECTOR *)
18670
18680     BEGIN (* PRIMARY *)
18700       VALID:=TRUE$
18710       IF NOT VECTOR THEN
```

```
18720                    BEGIN
18730                      ASSIGN:=FALSE;
18740                      IF NOT VARIABLE THEN
18750                        IF SPECSYMBOL(XRIGHTPAR) THEN
18760                          BEGIN
18770                            EXPRESSION(VALIDX);
18780                            IF NOT VALIDX THEN ERROR(14)
18790                                  (* +NON-VALID EXP WITHIN PARENS+ *)
18800                            ELSE
18810                              IF NOT SPECSYMBOL(XLEFTPAR) THEN ERROR(15)
18820                                  (* +RIGHT PAREN NOT BALANCED WITH LEFT PAREN+ *)
18830                              ELSE
18840                                VALID:=TRUE
18850                          END
18860                        ELSE
18870                          IF NOT FUNCTCALL THEN VALID:=FALSE
18880                          ELSE
18890                            BEGIN
18900                              CALLSUBR;
18910                              PRIMARY(VALID);
18920                            END;
18930                    END;
18940          END; (* PRIMARY *)
18950

19010

19020      PROCEDURE EXPRESSION; (* RECURSIVE *)
19030        VAR
19040          DONEXP,VALIDPRI,VALIDFUNC,VALIDASSN:BOOLEAN;
19050          CODE:INTEGER;

19060
19110
19120          PROCEDURE ASSIGNMENT(VAR VALIDA:BOOLEAN);
19130            BEGIN (* ASSIGNMENT *)
19150              VALIDA:=FALSE;
19160              IF SPECSYMBOL(XLEFTARROW) THEN
19170                BEGIN
19180                  ASSIGN:=TRUE;ASSIGN1:=TRUE;
19190                  IF VARIABLE THEN VALIDA:=TRUE
19200                  ELSE ERROR(8); (* RESULT OF AN ASSN NOT A VALID VARIABLE *)
19210                  VALIDA:=TRUE;
19220                  ASSIGN:=FALSE;
19230                END;
19240            END; (* ASSIGNMENT *)
19250

19310
19320          FUNCTION MOP:BOOLEAN;
19330            VAR
19340              VALIDM:BOOLEAN;
19350            BEGIN (* MOP *)
19370              VALIDM:=FALSE;
19380              IF (TOKENTABPTR+.NOUN=MONADOPER) OR
19390                 (TOKENTABPTR+.NOUN=REDUCTOPER) THEN
19400                BEGIN
19410                  IF TOKENTABPTR+.NOUN=MONADOPER THEN
19420                    CODE:=MOPTAB[TOKENTABPTR+.MONINDX].OPINDEX
19430                  ELSE
19440                    CODE:=REDTAB[TOKENTABPTR+.REDINDX].OPINDEX;
19450                  HOLD:=TOKENTABPTR;
19460                  TOKENTABPTR:=TOKENTABPTR+.NEXTOKEN;
19470                  VALIDM:=TRUE;
19480                END;
19490              MOP:=VALIDM;
19500            END; (* MOP *)
19510

19570
19580          FUNCTION DOP:BOOLEAN;
19590            VAR
19600              VALIDD:BOOLEAN;
19610            BEGIN (* DOP *)
```

```
19630              VALIDD:=FALSE;
19640              IF TOKENTABPTR↑.NOUN=DYADOPER THEN
19650                BEGIN
19660                  CODE:=DOPTAB[TOKENTABPTR↑.DOPINDX].OPINDEX;
19670                  HOLD:=TOKENTABPTR;
19680                  TOKENTABPTR:=TOKENTABPTR↑.NEXTOKEN;
19690                  IF (CODE>80) THEN VALIDD:=TRUE
19700                  ELSE
19710                    IF TOKENTABPTR↑.NOUN=SPECOPER THEN
19720                      IF SPECSYMBOL(XPERIOD) THEN
19730                        BEGIN
19740                          IF TOKENTABPTR↑.NOUN=DYADOPER THEN
19750                            BEGIN
19760                              IF DOPTAB[TOKENTABPTR↑.DOPINDX].OPINDEX<=80
19770                                THEN BEGIN
19780                                  CODE:=CODE+(100*
19790                                  DOPTAB[TOKENTABPTR↑.DOPINDX].OPINDEX);
19800                                  HOLD:=TOKENTABPTR;
19810                                  TOKENTABPTR:=TOKENTABPTR↑.NEXTOKEN;
19820                                  VALIDD:=TRUE
19830                                END
19840                              ELSE
19850                                ERROR(27) (* *INVALID INNER PRODUCT EXP *)
19860                            END
19870                          ELSE
19880                            IF TOKENTABPTR↑.NOUN=SPECOPER THEN
19890                              BEGIN
19900                                IF SPECSYMBOL(XLITTLECIRCLE) THEN
19910                                  BEGIN
19920                                    CODE:=10*CODE;
19930                                    VALIDD:=TRUE
19940                                  END
19950                                ELSE
19960                                  ERROR(26) (* *INVAL OUTER PROD EXP* *)
19970                              END
19980                            ELSE ERROR(26) (* SAME AS ABOVE *)
19990                        END
20000                      ELSE
20010                        VALIDD:=TRUE
20020                    ELSE
20030                      VALIDD:=TRUE;
20040                END;
20050            DOP:=VALIDD;
20060          END; (* DOP *)
20070
20100
20110 FUNCTION ITSBOOLEAN(TEST:REAL):BOOLEAN;
20120 BEGIN
20130 IF (TEST = 1.0) OR (TEST = 0.0)
20140   THEN ITSBOOLEAN:=TRUE
20150   ELSE ITSBOOLEAN:=FALSE
20160 END; (* ITSBOOLEAN *)
20170
20210
20220 PROCEDURE DYADCOMP(VAR SFLOAT:REAL; VALUE:REAL; CODE:INTEGER);
20230         (* COMPUTE RESULT OF DYADIC OPERATION *)
20240 BEGIN
20250 CASE CODE OF (*LEFT CODES - REDUCTION OPS / RIGHT CODES - DYADIC OPS*)
20260    2,52: SFLOAT:=VALUE + SFLOAT; (*ADDITION*)
20270    3,53: SFLOAT:=VALUE - SFLOAT; (*SUBTRACTION*)
20280    4,54: SFLOAT:=VALUE * SFLOAT; (*MULTIPLICATION*)
20290    5,55: IF SFLOAT = 0.0
20300            THEN ERROR(20) (*ATTEMPTED DIVISION BY ZERO*)
20310            ELSE SFLOAT:=VALUE / SFLOAT; (*DIVISION*)
20320    6,56: IF VALUE > 0.0
20330            THEN SFLOAT:=EXP(SFLOAT*LN(VALUE)) (*NUMBER RAISED TO A POWER*)
20340            ELSE SFLOAT:=1.0 / (EXP(SFLOAT*LN(ABS(VALUE)))));
20350    21,71: IF VALUE = SFLOAT    (*EQUALITY*)
20360            THEN SFLOAT:=1.0
```

```
20370              ELSE SFLOAT:=0.0$
20380    22,72: IF VALUE <> SFLOAT      (*INEQUALITY*)
20390              THEN SFLOAT:=1.0
20400              ELSE SFLOAT:=0.0$
20410    23,73: IF VALUE < SFLOAT       (*LESS THAN*)
20420              THEN SFLOAT:=1.0
20430              ELSE SFLOAT:=0.0$
20440    24,74: IF VALUE <= SFLOAT      (*LESS THAN OR EQUAL TO*)
20450              THEN SFLOAT:=1.0
20460              ELSE SFLOAT:=0.0$
20470    25,75: IF VALUE >= SFLOAT      (*GREATER THAN OR EQUAL TO*)
20480              THEN SFLOAT:=1.0
20490              ELSE SFLOAT:=0.0$
20500    26,76: IF VALUE > SFLOAT       (*GREATER THAN*)
20510              THEN SFLOAT:=1.0
20520              ELSE SFLOAT:=0.0$
20530    27,77: IF (ITSBOOLEAN(VALUE)) AND (ITSBOOLEAN(SFLOAT)) THEN
20540           IF (VALUE = 1.0) AND (SFLOAT = 1.0)   (* AND *)
20550              THEN SFLOAT:=1.0
20560              ELSE SFLOAT:=0.0
20570           ELSE ERROR(19)$ (* VALUE NOT BOOLEAN *)
20580    28,78: IF (ITSBOOLEAN(VALUE)) AND (ITSBOOLEAN(SFLOAT)) THEN
20590           IF (VALUE = 1.0) OR (SFLOAT = 1.0)   (* OR *)
20600              THEN SFLOAT:=1.0
20610              ELSE SFLOAT:=0.0
20620           ELSE ERROR(19)$ (* VALUE NOT BOOLEAN *)
20630    29   : IF VALUE > SFLOAT        (*MAXIMUM OR CEILING*)
20640              THEN SFLOAT:=VALUE$
20650    30   : IF VALUE < SFLOAT        (*MINIMUM OR FLOOR*)
20660              THEN SFLOAT:=VALUE$
20670    31   : IF (VALUE*SFLOAT) < 0.0
20680              THEN ERROR(50) (*NUMBER AND BASE OF DIFFERENT SIGN*)
20690              ELSE SFLOAT:=(LN(ABS(SFLOAT))) / (LN(ABS(VALUE))) (*LOG TO A BASE*)
20700 END (*CASE*)
20710 END$ (* DYADCOMP *)
20720
20770
20780 PROCEDURE INDEXGENERATOR(ARG:TYPEVALTABPTR)$
20790        (* MONADIC IOTA OPERATOR *)
20800 VAR
20810 IOTAINDEX,TOPVALUE:INTEGER$
20820 BEGIN
20830 IF ARG↑.DIMENSIONS <> 0
20840  THEN ERROR(21) (*ARGUMENT NOT A SCALAR*)
20850  ELSE
20860     IF ARG↑.FIRSTVALUE↑.REALVAL < 0.0
20870        THEN ERROR(22) (* ARGUMENT IS NEGATIVE *)
20880        ELSE
20890           IF (ARG↑.FIRSTVALUE↑.REALVAL) - (1.0*TRUNC(ARG↑.FIRSTVALUE↑.REALVAL))
20900              <> 0.0
20910             THEN ERROR(23) (*ARGUMENT IS NOT AN INTEGER*)
20920             ELSE
20930               BEGIN
20940                  NEW(NEWVALTABLINK)$
20950                  OLDVALTABLINK↑.NEXTVALTABLINK:=NEWVALTABLINK$
20960                  NEWVALTABLINK↑.NEXTVALTABLINK:=NIL$
20970                  NEWVALTABLINK↑.FORWARDORDER:=TRUE$
20980                  NEWVALTABLINK↑.INTERMEDRESULT:=TRUE$
20990                  NEWVALTABLINK↑.DIMENSIONS:=1$ (*RESULT IS A VECTOR*)
21000                  NEW(NEWDIM)$
21010                  NEWVALTABLINK↑.FIRSTDIMEN:=NEWDIM$
21020                  TOPVALUE:=TRUNC(ARG↑.FIRSTVALUE↑.REALVAL)$ (*LAST INDEX GENERD*)
21030                  NEWDIM↑.DIMENLENGTH:=TOPVALUE$
21040                  NEWDIM↑.NEXTDIMEN:=NIL$
21050                  IOTAINDEX:=1$
21060                  SWITCH:=TRUE$
21070                  WHILE IOTAINDEX <= TOPVALUE DO
21080                     BEGIN
21090                        NEW(NEWVALUES)$
```

```
21100                     NEWVALUES+.REALVAL:=IOTAINDEX;
21110                     IF SWITCH = TRUE
21120                       THEN
21130                         BEGIN
21140                           SWITCH:=FALSE;
21150                           NEWVALTABLINK+.FIRSTVALUE:=NEWVALUES
21160                         END
21170                       ELSE
21180                         NEWVALPTR+.NEXTVALUE:=NEWVALUES;
21190                     NEWVALPTR:=NEWVALUES;
21200                     IOTAINDEX:=IOTAINDEX + 1
21210                   END;
21220                 IF SWITCH = TRUE
21230                   THEN NEWVALTABLINK+.FIRSTVALUE:=NIL
21240                     (*RESULT IS VECTOR OF LENGTH 0*)
21250                   ELSE NEWVALUES+.NEXTVALUE:=NIL
21260               END
21270 END; (* INDEXGENERATOR *)
21280
21330
21340 PROCEDURE RAVEL(ARG:TYPEVALTABPTR);
21350        (* MONADIC COMMA OPERATOR *)
21360 VAR
21370 ELEMENTS:INTEGER;
21380 BEGIN
21390 NEW(NEWVALTABLINK);
21400 OLDVALTABLINK+.NEXTVALTABLINK:=NEWVALTABLINK;
21410 NEWVALTABLINK+.NEXTVALTABLINK:=NIL;
21420 NEWVALTABLINK+.INTERMEDRESULT:=TRUE;
21430 NEWVALTABLINK+.FORWARDORDER:=ARG+.FORWARDORDER;
21440 NEWVALTABLINK+.DIMENSIONS:=1; (*RESULT IS A VECTOR*)
21450 NEW(NEWDIM);
21460 NEWVALTABLINK+.FIRSTDIMEN:=NEWDIM;
21470 NEWDIM+.NEXTDIMEN:=NIL;
21480 SWITCH:=TRUE;
21490 VALPTR:=ARG+.FIRSTVALUE;
21500 ELEMENTS:=0;
21510 WHILE VALPTR <> NIL DO
21520   BEGIN (*DUPLICATE VALUES INTO RESULT*)
21530     NEW(NEWVALUES);
21540     NEWVALUES+.REALVAL:=VALPTR+.REALVAL;
21550     ELEMENTS:=ELEMENTS + 1;
21560     IF SWITCH = TRUE
21570       THEN
21580         BEGIN
21590           SWITCH:=FALSE;
21600           NEWVALTABLINK+.FIRSTVALUE:=NEWVALUES
21610         END
21620       ELSE
21630         NEWVALPTR+.NEXTVALUE:=NEWVALUES;
21640     NEWVALPTR:=NEWVALUES;
21650     VALPTR:=VALPTR+.NEXTVALUE
21660   END;
21670 NEWDIM+.DIMENLENGTH:=ELEMENTS;
21680 IF SWITCH = TRUE
21690   THEN NEWVALTABLINK+.FIRSTVALUE:=NIL
21700   ELSE NEWVALUES+.NEXTVALUE:=NIL
21710 END; (* RAVEL *)
21720
21770
21780 PROCEDURE SHAPEOF(ARG:TYPEVALTABPTR);
21790        (* MONADIC RHO OPERATOR *)
21800 BEGIN
21810 NEW(NEWVALTABLINK);
21820 OLDVALTABLINK+.NEXTVALTABLINK:=NEWVALTABLINK;
21830 NEWVALTABLINK+.NEXTVALTABLINK:=NIL;
21840 NEWVALTABLINK+.INTERMEDRESULT:=TRUE;
21850 NEWVALTABLINK+.FORWARDORDER:=TRUE;
21860 NEWVALTABLINK+.DIMENSIONS:=1; (*RESULT IS A VECTOR*)
```

317

```
21870 NEW(NEWDIM);
21880 NEWDIM+.DIMENLENGTH:=ARG+.DIMENSIONS;
21890 NEWVALTABLINK+.FIRSTDIMEN:=NEWDIM;
21900 NEWDIM+.NEXTDIMEN:=NIL;
21910 SWITCH:=TRUE;
21920 DIMPTR:=ARG+.FIRSTDIMEN;
21930 WHILE DIMPTR <> NIL DO
21940  BEGIN (*ARGUMENT DIMENSIONS BECOME RESULT VALUES*)
21950     NEW(NEWVALUES);
21960     NEWVALUES+.REALVAL:=DIMPTR+.DIMENLENGTH;
21970     IF SWITCH = TRUE
21980       THEN
21990         BEGIN
22000            SWITCH:=FALSE;
22010            NEWVALTABLINK+.FIRSTVALUE:=NEWVALUES
22020         END
22030       ELSE
22040         NEWVALPTR+.NEXTVALUE:=NEWVALUES;
22050     NEWVALPTR:=NEWVALUES;
22060     DIMPTR:=DIMPTR+.NEXTDIMEN
22070  END;
22080 IF SWITCH = TRUE
22090  THEN NEWVALTABLINK+.FIRSTVALUE:=NIL (*RESULT IS A VECTOR OF LENGTH 0*)
22100  ELSE NEWVALUES+.NEXTVALUE:=NIL
22110 END; (* SHAPEOF *)
22120
22170
22180 PROCEDURE REDUCTION(ARG:TYPEVALTABPTR);
22190 VAR
22200 COUNTER,ROWLENGTH:INTEGER;
22210 SFLOAT:REAL;
22220 BEGIN
22230 IF (ARG+.DIMENSIONS = 0) OR (ARG+.FIRSTVALUE = NIL)
22240  THEN ERROR(24) (*ARGUMENT IS A SCALAR OR VECTOR OF LENGTH ZERO*)
22250  ELSE
22260    IF (ARG+.DIMENSIONS = 1) AND (ARG+.FIRSTDIMEN+.DIMENLENGTH = 1)
22270      THEN ERROR(51) (*ARGUMENT IS A VECTOR OF LENGTH ONE*)
22280      ELSE
22290        BEGIN
22300           NEW(NEWVALTABLINK);
22310           OLDVALTABLINK+.NEXTVALTABLINK:=NEWVALTABLINK;
22320           NEWVALTABLINK+.NEXTVALTABLINK:=NIL;
22330           NEWVALTABLINK+.INTERMEDRESULT:=TRUE;
22340           IF ARG+.FORWARDORDER = TRUE
22350             THEN REVERSELINKLIST(ARG);
22360           NEWVALTABLINK+.FORWARDORDER:=FALSE;
22370           NEWVALTABLINK+.DIMENSIONS:=ARG+.DIMENSIONS - 1;
22380           DIMPTR:=ARG+.FIRSTDIMEN;
22390           SWITCH:=TRUE;
22400           WHILE DIMPTR+.NEXTDIMEN <> NIL DO
22410             BEGIN (*BUILD DIMENSIONS OF RESULT*)
22420                NEW(NEWDIM);
22430                IF SWITCH = TRUE
22440                  THEN
22450                    BEGIN
22460                       SWITCH:=FALSE;
22470                       NEWVALTABLINK+.FIRSTDIMEN:=NEWDIM
22480                    END
22490                  ELSE
22500                    NEWPTR+.NEXTDIMEN:=NEWDIM;
22510                NEWDIM+.DIMENLENGTH:=DIMPTR+.DIMENLENGTH;
22520                NEWPTR:=NEWDIM;
22530                DIMPTR:=DIMPTR+.NEXTDIMEN
22540             END;
22550           IF SWITCH = TRUE
22560             THEN NEWVALTABLINK+.FIRSTDIMEN:=NIL
22570                (*ARG IS VECTOR,RESULT IS SCALAR*)
22580             ELSE NEWDIM+.NEXTDIMEN:=NIL;
```

318

```
22590              ROWLENGTH:=DIMPTR+.DIMENLENGTH;
22600              VALPTR:=ARG+.FIRSTVALUE;
22610              SWITCH:=TRUE;
22620              WHILE VALPTR <> NIL DO
22630                BEGIN (*PERFORM REDUCTION*)
22640                  SFLOAT:=VALPTR+.REALVAL; (*SFLOAT GETS LAST VALUE IN ROW*)
22650                  VALPTR:=VALPTR+.NEXTVALUE;
22660                  FOR COUNTER:=2 TO ROWLENGTH DO
22670                    BEGIN
22680                      DYADCOMP(SFLOAT,VALPTR+.REALVAL,CODE);
22690                      VALPTR:=VALPTR+.NEXTVALUE
22700                    END;
22710                  NEW(NEWVALUES);
22720                  NEWVALUES+.REALVAL:=SFLOAT;
22730                  IF SWITCH = TRUE
22740                    THEN
22750                      BEGIN
22760                        SWITCH:=FALSE;
22770                        NEWVALTABLINK+.FIRSTVALUE:=NEWVALUES
22780                      END
22790                    ELSE
22800                      NEWVALPTR+.NEXTVALUE:=NEWVALUES;
22810                  NEWVALPTR:=NEWVALUES
22820                END;
22830              NEWVALUES+.NEXTVALUE:=NIL
22840            END;
22850 END; (*REDUCTION*)
22860
22910
22920 PROCEDURE MONADIC(ARG:TYPEVALTABPTR; TOKEN:TOKENPTR);
22930          (* OPERATIONS WITH CODES BETWEEN 1 AND 31 *)
22940 BEGIN
22960 IF TOKEN+.NOUN = REDUCTOPER
22970  THEN REDUCTION(ARG)
22980  ELSE
22990     IF CODE > 20
23000        THEN
23010          CASE CODE OF
23020            21: INDEXGENERATOR(ARG);
23030            22: SHAPEOF(ARG);
23040            23: RAVEL(ARG)
23050          END (*CASE*)
23060        ELSE
23070          BEGIN
23080            NEW(NEWVALTABLINK);
23090            OLDVALTABLINK+.NEXTVALTABLINK:=NEWVALTABLINK;
23100            NEWVALTABLINK+.NEXTVALTABLINK:=NIL;
23110            NEWVALTABLINK+.INTERMEDRESULT:=TRUE;
23120            NEWVALTABLINK+.FORWARDORDER:=ARG+.FORWARDORDER;
23130            NEWVALTABLINK+.DIMENSIONS:=ARG+.DIMENSIONS;
23140            SWITCH:=TRUE;
23150            DIMPTR:=ARG+.FIRSTDIMEN;
23160            WHILE DIMPTR <> NIL DO
23170              BEGIN (*DUPLICATE DIMENSIONS OF ARG INTO RESULT*)
23180                NEW(NEWDIM);
23190                NEWDIM+.DIMENLENGTH:=DIMPTR+.DIMENLENGTH;
23200                IF SWITCH = TRUE
23210                  THEN
23220                    BEGIN
23230                      SWITCH:=FALSE;
23240                      NEWVALTABLINK+.FIRSTDIMEN:=NEWDIM
23250                    END
23260                  ELSE
23270                    NEWPTR+.NEXTDIMEN:=NEWDIM;
23280                NEWPTR:=NEWDIM;
23290                DIMPTR:=DIMPTR+.NEXTDIMEN
23300              END;
23310            IF SWITCH = TRUE
23320              THEN NEWVALTABLINK+.FIRSTDIMEN:=NIL (*RESULT IS A SCALAR*)
```

```
23330              ELSE NEWDIM+.NEXTDIMEN:=NIL;
23340          SWITCH:=TRUE;
23350          VALPTR:=ARG+.FIRSTVALUE;
23360          WHILE VALPTR <> NIL DO,
23370            BEGIN
23380              NEW(NEWVALUES);
23390              IF SWITCH = TRUE
23400                THEN
23410                  BEGIN
23420                    SWITCH:=FALSE;
23430                    NEWVALTABLINK+.FIRSTVALUE:=NEWVALUES
23440                  END
23450                ELSE
23460                  NEWVALPTR+.NEXTVALUE:=NEWVALUES;
23470              NEWVALPTR:=NEWVALUES;
23480              CASE CODE OF
23490                1: IF ITSBOOLEAN(VALPTR+.REALVAL)  (* LOGICAL NEGATION *)
23500                     THEN NEWVALUES+.REALVAL:=1.0 - VALPTR+.REALVAL
23510                     ELSE ERROR(19); (*VALUE NOT BOOLEAN *)
23520                2: NEWVALUES+.REALVAL:=VALPTR+.REALVAL; (* NO-OP *)
23530                3: NEWVALUES+.REALVAL:=0.0 - VALPTR+.REALVAL; (* NEGATION *)
23540                4: IF VALPTR+.REALVAL > 0.0  (* SIGNUM *)
23550                     THEN NEWVALUES+.REALVAL:=1.0
23560                     ELSE
23570                       IF VALPTR+.REALVAL < 0.0
23580                         THEN NEWVALUES+.REALVAL:=-1.0;
23590                5: IF VALPTR+.REALVAL = 0.0  (* RECIPROCAL *)
23600                     THEN ERROR(54) (*ATTEMPTED INVERSE OF ZERO*)
23610                     ELSE NEWVALUES+.REALVAL:=1.0 / VALPTR+.REALVAL;
23620                6: NEWVALUES+.REALVAL:=EXP(VALPTR+.REALVAL)
23630              END; (*CASE*)
23640              VALPTR:=VALPTR+.NEXTVALUE
23650            END;
23660          IF SWITCH = TRUE
23670            THEN NEWVALTABLINK+.FIRSTVALUE:=NIL
23680            ELSE NEWVALUES+.NEXTVALUE:=NIL
23690        END
23700 END; (* MONADIC *)
23710
23760
23770 PROCEDURE CATENATE(LEFTARG,RIGHTARG:TYPEVALTABPTR);
23780        (* DYADIC COMMA OPERATOR - JOINS 2 ARGUMENTS *)
23790 VAR
23800 RESULTLENGTH:INTEGER;
23810 BEGIN (*CATENATE*)
23820 IF (RIGHTARG+.DIMENSIONS > 1) OR (LEFTARG+.DIMENSIONS > 1)
23830   THEN ERROR(53) (*ARGUMENT(S) WITH RANK GREATER THAN 1*)
23840   ELSE
23850     BEGIN
23860       NEW(NEWVALTABLINK);
23870       OLDVALTABLINK+.NEXTVALTABLINK:=NEWVALTABLINK;
23880       NEWVALTABLINK+.NEXTVALTABLINK:=NIL;
23890       NEWVALTABLINK+.INTERMEDRESULT:=TRUE;
23900       IF LEFTARG+.FORWARDORDER = FALSE
23910         THEN REVERSELINKLIST(LEFTARG);
23920       IF RIGHTARG+.FORWARDORDER = FALSE
23930         THEN REVERSELINKLIST(RIGHTARG);
23940       NEWVALTABLINK+.FORWARDORDER:=TRUE;
23950       NEWVALTABLINK+.DIMENSIONS:=1; (*RESULT IS A VECTOR*)
23960       NEW(NEWDIM);
23970       NEWVALTABLINK+.FIRSTDIMEN:=NEWDIM;
23980       NEWDIM+.NEXTDIMEN:=NIL;
23990       RESULTLENGTH:=0;
24000       IF LEFTARG+.DIMENSIONS = 0
24010         THEN RESULTLENGTH:=RESULTLENGTH + 1 (*LEFT ARG IS A SCALAR*)
24020         ELSE RESULTLENGTH:=RESULTLENGTH + LEFTARG+.FIRSTDIMEN+.DIMENLENGTH;
24030       IF RIGHTARG+.DIMENSIONS = 0
24040         THEN RESULTLENGTH:=RESULTLENGTH + 1 (*RIGHT ARG IS A SCALAR*)
24050         ELSE RESULTLENGTH:=RESULTLENGTH + RIGHTARG+.FIRSTDIMEN+.DIMENLENGTH;
```

```
24060          NEWDIM↑.DIMENLENGTH:=RESULTLENGTH;
24070          SWITCH:=TRUE;
24080          IF RESULTLENGTH = 0
24090            THEN NEWVALTABLINK↑.FIRSTVALUE:=NIL (*RESULT IS VECTOR OF LENGTH 0*)
24100            ELSE
24110              BEGIN (*TRANSFER VALUES TO RESULT*)
24120                LEFTVALPTR:=LEFTARG↑.FIRSTVALUE;
24130                WHILE LEFTVALPTR <> NIL DO
24140                  BEGIN (*TRANSFER LEFT ARG VALUES (IF ANY) *)
24150                    NEW(NEWVALUES);
24160                    IF SWITCH = TRUE
24170                      THEN
24180                        BEGIN
24190                          SWITCH:=FALSE;
24200                          NEWVALTABLINK↑.FIRSTVALUE:=NEWVALUES
24210                        END
24220                      ELSE
24230                        NEWVALPTR↑.NEXTVALUE:=NEWVALUES;
24240                    NEWVALUES↑.REALVAL:=LEFTVALPTR↑.REALVAL;
24250                    NEWVALPTR:=NEWVALUES;
24260                    LEFTVALPTR:=LEFTVALPTR↑.NEXTVALUE
24270                  END;
24280                RIGHTVALPTR:=RIGHTARG↑.FIRSTVALUE;
24290                WHILE RIGHTVALPTR <> NIL DO
24300                  BEGIN (*TRANSFER RIGHT ARG VALUES (IF ANY) *)
24310                    NEW(NEWVALUES);
24320                    IF SWITCH = TRUE
24330                      THEN
24340                        BEGIN
24350                          SWITCH:=FALSE;
24360                          NEWVALTABLINK↑.FIRSTVALUE:=NEWVALUES
24370                        END
24380                      ELSE
24390                        NEWVALPTR↑.NEXTVALUE:=NEWVALUES;
24400                    NEWVALUES↑.REALVAL:=RIGHTVALPTR↑.REALVAL;
24410                    NEWVALPTR:=NEWVALUES;
24420                    RIGHTVALPTR:=RIGHTVALPTR↑.NEXTVALUE
24430                  END;
24440                NEWVALUES↑.NEXTVALUE:=NIL
24450              END (*TRANSFER OF VALUES*)
24460      END
24470 END; (* CATENATE *)
24480
24530
24540 PROCEDURE INDEXOF(LEFTARG,RIGHTARG:TYPEVALTABPTR);
24550          (* DYADIC IOTA OPERATOR *)
24560 VAR
24570 MAPINDEX,ICOUNT,TESTLENGTH,ONEMORE:INTEGER;
24580 BEGIN (* INDEXOF *)
24590 IF LEFTARG↑.DIMENSIONS <> 1
24600   THEN ERROR(29) (* LEFT ARGUMENT IS NOT A VECTOR *)
24610   ELSE
24620     BEGIN
24630       NEW(NEWVALTABLINK);
24640       OLDVALTABLINK↑.NEXTVALTABLINK:=NEWVALTABLINK;
24650       NEWVALTABLINK↑.NEXTVALTABLINK:=NIL;
24660       NEWVALTABLINK↑.INTERMEDRESULT:=TRUE;
24670       IF LEFTARG↑.FORWARDORDER = FALSE
24680         THEN REVERSELINKLIST(LEFTARG);
24690       NEWVALTABLINK↑.FORWARDORDER:=RIGHTARG↑.FORWARDORDER;
24700       NEWVALTABLINK↑.DIMENSIONS:=RIGHTARG↑.DIMENSIONS;
24710       IF RIGHTARG↑.DIMENSIONS = 0
24720         THEN NEWVALTABLINK↑.FIRSTDIMEN:=NIL (*RIGHT ARGUMENT IS A SCALAR*)
24730         ELSE
24740           BEGIN (*BUILD DIMENSIONS OF RESULT*)
24750             SWITCH:=TRUE;
24760             DIMPTR:=RIGHTARG↑.FIRSTDIMEN;
24770             WHILE DIMPTR <> NIL DO
24780               BEGIN
```

```
24790                     NEW(NEWDIM)$
24800                     IF SWITCH = TRUE
24810                       THEN
24820                         BEGIN
24830                            SWITCH:=FALSE$
24840                            NEWVALTABLINK+.FIRSTDIMEN:=NEWDIM
24850                         END
24860                       ELSE
24870                         NEWPTR+.NEXTDIMEN:=NEWDIM$
24880                     NEWDIM+.DIMENLENGTH:=DIMPTR+.DIMENLENGTH$
24890                     NEWPTR:=NEWDIM$
24900                     DIMPTR:=DIMPTR+.NEXTDIMEN
24910                   END$
24920                   NEWDIM+.NEXTDIMEN:=NIL
24930                 END$
24940           SWITCH:=TRUE$
24950           RIGHTVALPTR:=RIGHTARG+.FIRSTVALUE$
24960           WHILE RIGHTVALPTR <> NIL DO
24970             BEGIN
24980               NEW(NEWVALUES)$
24990               IF SWITCH = TRUE
25000                 THEN
25010                   BEGIN
25020                      SWITCH:=FALSE$
25030                      NEWVALTABLINK+.FIRSTVALUE:=NEWVALUES
25040                   END
25050                 ELSE
25060                   NEWVALPTR+.NEXTVALUE:=NEWVALUES$
25070               ICOUNT:=1$
25080               LEFTVALPTR:=LEFTARG+.FIRSTVALUE$
25090               TESTLENGTH:=LEFTARG+.FIRSTDIMEN+.DIMENLENGTH$ (*LENGTH OF LEFT ARG*)
25100               ONEMORE:=TESTLENGTH + 1$   (*LENGTH OF LEFT ARG PLUS ONE*)
25110               MAPINDEX:=ONEMORE$
25120               WHILE (ICOUNT <= TESTLENGTH) AND (MAPINDEX = ONEMORE) DO
25130                 BEGIN (*TRY TO MATCH VALUE IN RIGHT ARG WITH ONE IN LEFT ARG*)
25140                    IF LEFTVALPTR+.REALVAL = RIGHTVALPTR+.REALVAL
25150                      THEN MAPINDEX:=ICOUNT$ (*VALUE MATCH*)
25160                    ICOUNT:=ICOUNT + 1$
25170                    LEFTVALPTR:=LEFTVALPTR+.NEXTVALUE
25180                 END$
25190               NEWVALUES+.REALVAL:=MAPINDEX$
25200               NEWVALPTR:=NEWVALUES$
25210               RIGHTVALPTR:=RIGHTVALPTR+.NEXTVALUE
25220             END$ (*IF NO MATCH, INDEX BECOMES ONE MORE THAN LENGTH OF LEFT ARG*)
25230           NEWVALUES+.NEXTVALUE:=NIL
25240       END
25250 END$ (* INDEXOF *)
25260
25310
25320 PROCEDURE RESHAPE(LEFTARG,RIGHTARG:TYPEVALTABPTR)$
25330          (* DYADIC RHO OPERATOR - CHANGE DIMENSIONS OF *)
25340 VAR
25350 RESULTLENGTH,ELEMENTS:INTEGER$
25360 DIMPTR:+DIMENINFO$ NEWPTR:+VALUES$
25370 BEGIN (* RESHAPE *)
25380 IF LEFTARG+.DIMENSIONS  > 1
25390   THEN ERROR(56) (* LEFT ARGUMENT NOT A VECTOR OR A SCALAR *)
25400   ELSE
25410     BEGIN
25420       NEW(NEWVALTABLINK)$
25430       OLDVALTABLINK+.NEXTVALTABLINK:=NEWVALTABLINK$
25440       NEWVALTABLINK+.NEXTVALTABLINK:=NIL$
25450       NEWVALTABLINK+.INTERMEDRESULT:=TRUE$
25460       IF LEFTARG+.FORWARDORDER = FALSE
25470         THEN REVERSELINKLIST(LEFTARG)$
25480       IF RIGHTARG+.FORWARDORDER = FALSE
25490         THEN REVERSELINKLIST(RIGHTARG)$
25500       NEWVALTABLINK+.FORWARDORDER:=TRUE$
25510       IF LEFTARG+.FIRSTDIMEN=NIL
```

```
25520          THEN NEWVALTABLINK↑.DIMENSIONS:=1 ELSE
25530       NEWVALTABLINK↑.DIMENSIONS:=LEFTARG↑.FIRSTDIMEN↑.DIMENLENGTH;
25540       RESULTLENGTH:=1;
25550       LEFTVALPTR:=LEFTARG↑.FIRSTVALUE;
25560       SWITCH:=TRUE;
25570       WHILE LEFTVALPTR <> NIL DO (*LEFT ARG VALUES ARE DIMENSIONS OF RESULT*)
25580         BEGIN (*BUILD RESULT DIMENSIONS*)
25590           RESULTLENGTH:=RESULTLENGTH*TRUNC(LEFTVALPTR↑.REALVAL);
25600           NEW(NEWDIM);
25610           NEWDIM↑.DIMENLENGTH:=TRUNC(LEFTVALPTR↑.REALVAL);
25620           LEFTVALPTR:=LEFTVALPTR↑.NEXTVALUE;
25630           IF SWITCH = TRUE
25640             THEN
25650               BEGIN
25660                 SWITCH:=FALSE;
25670                 NEWVALTABLINK↑.FIRSTDIMEN:=NEWDIM
25680               END
25690             ELSE
25700               DIMPTR↑.NEXTDIMEN:=NEWDIM;
25710           DIMPTR:=NEWDIM
25720         END;
25730       NEWDIM↑.NEXTDIMEN:=NIL;
25740       RIGHTVALPTR:=RIGHTARG↑.FIRSTVALUE;
25750       ELEMENTS:=0; SWITCH:=TRUE;
25760       WHILE ELEMENTS < RESULTLENGTH DO
25770         BEGIN (*DUPLICATE RIGHT ARG VALUES INTO RESULT VALUES*)
25780           ELEMENTS:=ELEMENTS + 1;
25790           NEW(NEWVALUES);
25800           IF RIGHTVALPTR = NIL (*EXTEND RIGHT ARGUMENT IF NECESSARY*)
25810             THEN RIGHTVALPTR:=RIGHTARG↑.FIRSTVALUE;
25820           NEWVALUES↑.REALVAL:=RIGHTVALPTR↑.REALVAL;
25830           IF SWITCH = TRUE
25840             THEN
25850               BEGIN
25860                 SWITCH:=FALSE;
25870                 NEWVALTABLINK↑.FIRSTVALUE:=NEWVALUES
25880               END
25890             ELSE
25900               NEWPTR↑.NEXTVALUE:=NEWVALUES;
25910           NEWPTR:=NEWVALUES;
25920           RIGHTVALPTR:=RIGHTVALPTR↑.NEXTVALUE
25930         END;
25940       NEWVALUES↑.NEXTVALUE:=NIL;
25950     END
25960 END; (* RESHAPE *)
25970
26020
26030 PROCEDURE INNERPRODUCT(LEFTARG,RIGHTARG:TYPEVALTABPTR);
26040 VAR
26050 INPRO1CODE,INPRO2CODE,LEFTSKIP,RIGHTSKIP:INTEGER;
26060 ICOUNT,JCOUNT,KCOUNT,LCOUNT,MCOUNT:INTEGER;
26070 LASTLEFTDIM,FIRSTRIGHTDIM,COMMONLENGTH:INTEGER;
26080 LPTR:↑VALUES;
26090 HOLD:REAL;
26100 SFLOAT,VALUE:REAL;
26110 BEGIN   (*INNER PRODUCT IS MATRIX MULTIPLICATION*)
26120 DIMPTR:=LEFTARG↑.FIRSTDIMEN;
26130 IF LEFTARG↑.FIRSTDIMEN <> NIL
26140   THEN
26150     WHILE DIMPTR↑.NEXTDIMEN <> NIL DO
26160       DIMPTR:=DIMPTR↑.NEXTDIMEN;   (*GET LAST DIMEN OF LEFT ARG(IF ANY)*)
26170 IF (DIMPTR <> NIL) AND (RIGHTARG↑.FIRSTDIMEN <> NIL)
26180   THEN
26190     IF DIMPTR↑.DIMENLENGTH <> RIGHTARG↑.FIRSTDIMEN↑.DIMENLENGTH
26200       THEN ERROR(52) (*LAST DIM OF LEFT ARG NOT = TO FIRST DIM OF RIGHT ARG*)
26210       ELSE
26220         BEGIN
26230           INPRO1CODE:=CODE DIV 100;    (*SEPARATE OPERATORS*)
26240           INPRO2CODE:=CODE -   100*INPRO1CODE;
```

```
26250          NEW(NEWVALTABLINK);
26260          OLDVALTABLINK+.NEXTVALTABLINK:=NEWVALTABLINK;
26270          NEWVALTABLINK+.NEXTVALTABLINK:=NIL;
26280          NEWVALTABLINK+.INTERMEDRESULT:=TRUE;
26290          IF LEFTARG+.FORWARDORDER = FALSE
26300            THEN REVERSELINKLIST(LEFTARG);
26310          IF RIGHTARG+.FORWARDORDER = FALSE
26320            THEN REVERSELINKLIST(RIGHTARG);
26330          NEWVALTABLINK+.FORWARDORDER:=TRUE;
26340          NEWVALTABLINK+.DIMENSIONS:=LEFTARG+.DIMENSIONS + RIGHTARG+.DIMENSIONS
26350          -2;
26360          IF NEWVALTABLINK+.DIMENSIONS < 0
26370            THEN NEWVALTABLINK+.DIMENSIONS:=0;
26380          SWITCH:=TRUE;
26390          LASTLEFTDIM:=0;
26400          IF LEFTARG+.FIRSTDIMEN <> NIL
26410            THEN
26420              BEGIN (*COPY ALL BUT LAST OF LEFT ARG DIMS INTO RESULT*)
26430                LEFTSKIP:=1;
26440                DIMPTR:=LEFTARG+.FIRSTDIMEN;
26450                WHILE DIMPTR+.NEXTDIMEN <> NIL DO
26460                  BEGIN (*COPY LEFT ARG DIMENSIONS*)
26470                    NEW(NEWDIM);
26480                    NEWDIM+.DIMENLENGTH:=DIMPTR+.DIMENLENGTH;
26490                    LEFTSKIP:=LEFTSKIP*DIMPTR+.DIMENLENGTH;
26500                    IF SWITCH = TRUE
26510                      THEN
26520                        BEGIN
26530                          SWITCH:=FALSE;
26540                          NEWVALTABLINK+.FIRSTDIMEN:=NEWDIM
26550                        END
26560                      ELSE
26570                        NEWPTR+.NEXTDIMEN:=NEWDIM;
26580                    NEWPTR:=NEWDIM;
26590                    DIMPTR:=DIMPTR+.NEXTDIMEN
26600                  END;
26610                LASTLEFTDIM:=DIMPTR+.DIMENLENGTH
26620              END;
26630          IF RIGHTARG+.FIRSTDIMEN <> NIL
26640            THEN
26650              BEGIN (*COPY ALL BUT FIRST OF RIGHT ARG DIMS INTO RESULT*)
26660                RIGHTSKIP:=1;
26670                DIMPTR:=RIGHTARG+.FIRSTDIMEN+.NEXTDIMEN;
26680                WHILE DIMPTR <> NIL DO
26690                  BEGIN (*COPY RIGHT ARG DIMENSIONS*)
26700                    NEW(NEWDIM);
26710                    NEWDIM+.DIMENLENGTH:=DIMPTR+.DIMENLENGTH;
26720                    RIGHTSKIP:=RIGHTSKIP*DIMPTR+.DIMENLENGTH;
26730                    IF SWITCH = TRUE
26740                      THEN
26750                        BEGIN
26760                          SWITCH:=FALSE;
26770                          NEWVALTABLINK+.FIRSTDIMEN:=NEWDIM
26780                        END
26790                      ELSE
26800                        NEWPTR+.NEXTDIMEN:=NEWDIM;
26810                    NEWPTR:=NEWDIM;
26820                    DIMPTR:=DIMPTR+.NEXTDIMEN
26830                  END
26840              END;
26850          IF SWITCH = TRUE
26860            THEN NEWVALTABLINK+.FIRSTDIMEN:=NIL
26870            ELSE NEWDIM+.NEXTDIMEN:=NIL;
26880          IF LEFTARG+.FIRSTVALUE = NIL
26890            THEN LEFTSKIP:=0;
26900          IF RIGHTARG+.FIRSTVALUE = NIL
26910            THEN RIGHTSKIP:=0;
26920          SWITCH:=TRUE;
26930          IF RIGHTARG+.FIRSTDIMEN <> NIL
```

```
26940            THEN FIRSTRIGHTDIM:=RIGHTARG↑.FIRSTDIMEN↑.DIMENLENGTH
26950            ELSE FIRSTRIGHTDIM:=0;
26960         IF FIRSTRIGHTDIM > LASTLEFTDIM
26970            THEN COMMONLENGTH:=FIRSTRIGHTDIM
26980            ELSE COMMONLENGTH:=LASTLEFTDIM;
26990         ICOUNT:=0;
27000         LEFTVALPTR:=LEFTARG↑.FIRSTVALUE;
27010         WHILE ICOUNT < LEFTSKIP DO
27020           BEGIN (*LOOP FOR EACH ROW IN LEFT ARG*)
27030             LPTR:=LEFTVALPTR; (*HOLD START OF ROW POSITION*)
27040             JCOUNT:=0;
27050             WHILE JCOUNT < RIGHTSKIP DO
27060               BEGIN (*LOOP FOR EACH COLUMN IN RIGHT ARG*)
27070                 LEFTVALPTR:=LPTR;
27080                 RIGHTVALPTR:=RIGHTARG↑.FIRSTVALUE;
27090                 LCOUNT:=0;
27100                 WHILE LCOUNT < JCOUNT DO
27110                   BEGIN (*SKIP TO STARTING VALUE IN RIGHT ARG*)
27120                     RIGHTVALPTR:=RIGHTVALPTR↑.NEXTVALUE;
27130                     IF RIGHTVALPTR = NIL
27140                        THEN RIGHTVALPTR:=RIGHTARG↑.FIRSTVALUE; (*EXTEND ARG*)
27150                     LCOUNT:=LCOUNT + 1
27160                   END;
27170                 KCOUNT:=0;
27180                 WHILE KCOUNT < COMMONLENGTH DO
27190                   BEGIN (*LOOP FOR EACH ELEMENT IN ROW/COLUMN*)
27200                     SFLOAT:=RIGHTVALPTR↑.REALVAL;
27210                     DYADCOMP(SFLOAT,LEFTVALPTR↑.REALVAL,INPRO2CODE);
27220                     VALUE:=SFLOAT;
27230                     IF KCOUNT = 0
27240                        THEN (*SET IDENTITY VALUE FOR FIRST TIME THROUGH*)
27250                          CASE INPRO1CODE OF
27260                            52,53,78: SFLOAT:=0.0;
27270                            54,55,56,77: SFLOAT:=1.0;
27280                            71,72,73,74,75,76:     (*NULL CASE*)
27290                          END (*CASE*)
27300                        ELSE
27310                          SFLOAT:=HOLD;
27320                     DYADCOMP(SFLOAT,VALUE,INPRO1CODE);
27330                     HOLD:=SFLOAT; (*SAVE SUMMER RESULT*)
27340                     LEFTVALPTR:=LEFTVALPTR↑.NEXTVALUE;
27350                     IF LEFTVALPTR = NIL
27360                        THEN LEFTVALPTR:=LEFTARG↑.FIRSTVALUE; (*EXTEND ARG*)
27370                     MCOUNT:=0;
27380                     WHILE MCOUNT < RIGHTSKIP DO
27390                       BEGIN (*SKIP TO NEXT VALUE IN RIGHT ARG*)
27400                         MCOUNT:=MCOUNT + 1;
27410                         RIGHTVALPTR:=RIGHTVALPTR↑.NEXTVALUE;
27420                         IF RIGHTVALPTR = NIL
27430                            THEN RIGHTVALPTR:=RIGHTARG↑.FIRSTVALUE;
27440                       END;
27450                     KCOUNT:=KCOUNT + 1
27460                   END;
27470                 NEW(NEWVALUES);
27480                 NEWVALUES↑.REALVAL:=SFLOAT;
27490                 IF SWITCH = TRUE
27500                    THEN
27510                      BEGIN
27520                        SWITCH:=FALSE;
27530                        NEWVALTABLINK↑.FIRSTVALUE:=NEWVALUES
27540                      END
27550                    ELSE
27560                      NEWVALPTR↑.NEXTVALUE:=NEWVALUES;
27570                 NEWVALPTR:=NEWVALUES;
27580                 JCOUNT:=JCOUNT + 1;
27590               END;
27600             ICOUNT:=ICOUNT + 1
27610           END;
27620         IF SWITCH = TRUE
```

```
27630            THEN NEWVALTABLINK↑.FIRSTVALUE:=NIL
27640            ELSE NEWVALUES↑.NEXTVALUE:=NIL
27650         END
27660 END; (* INNERPRODUCT *)
27670
27720
27730 PROCEDURE OUTERPRODUCT(LEFTARG,RIGHTARG:TYPEVALTABPTR);
27740 VAR
27750 OUTPROCODE:INTEGER;
27760 SFLOAT:REAL;
27770 BEGIN
27780 OUTPROCODE:=CODE DIV 10;
27790 NEW(NEWVALTABLINK);
27800 OLDVALTABLINK↑.NEXTVALTABLINK:=NEWVALTABLINK;
27810 NEWVALTABLINK↑.NEXTVALTABLINK:=NIL;
27820 NEWVALTABLINK↑.INTERMEDRESULT:=TRUE;
27830 IF LEFTARG↑.FORWARDORDER = FALSE
27840   THEN REVERSELINKLIST(LEFTARG);
27850 IF RIGHTARG↑.FORWARDORDER = FALSE
27860   THEN REVERSELINKLIST(RIGHTARG);
27870 NEWVALTABLINK↑.FORWARDORDER:=TRUE;
27880 NEWVALTABLINK↑.DIMENSIONS:=LEFTARG↑.DIMENSIONS + RIGHTARG↑.DIMENSIONS;
27890 SWITCH:=TRUE;
27900 DIMPTR:=LEFTARG↑.FIRSTDIMEN;
27910 WHILE DIMPTR <> NIL DO
27920   BEGIN (*COPY LEFT ARG DIMENSIONS TO RESULT*)
27930     NEW(NEWDIM);
27940     NEWDIM↑.DIMENLENGTH:=DIMPTR↑.DIMENLENGTH;
27950     IF SWITCH = TRUE
27960       THEN
27970         BEGIN
27980           SWITCH:=FALSE;
27990           NEWVALTABLINK↑.FIRSTDIMEN:=NEWDIM
28000         END
28010       ELSE
28020         NEWPTR↑.NEXTDIMEN:=NEWDIM;
28030     NEWPTR:=NEWDIM;
28040     DIMPTR:=DIMPTR↑.NEXTDIMEN
28050   END;
28060 DIMPTR:=RIGHTARG↑.FIRSTDIMEN;
28070 WHILE DIMPTR <> NIL DO
28080   BEGIN   (*COPY DIMENSIONS OF RIGHT ARG TO RESULT*)
28090     NEW(NEWDIM);
28100     NEWDIM↑.DIMENLENGTH:=DIMPTR↑.DIMENLENGTH;
28110     IF SWITCH = TRUE
28120       THEN
28130         BEGIN
28140           SWITCH:=FALSE;
28150           NEWVALTABLINK↑.FIRSTDIMEN:=NEWDIM
28160         END
28170       ELSE
28180         NEWPTR↑.NEXTDIMEN:=NEWDIM;
28190     NEWPTR:=NEWDIM;
28200     DIMPTR:=DIMPTR↑.NEXTDIMEN
28210   END;
28220 IF SWITCH = TRUE
28230   THEN NEWVALTABLINK↑.FIRSTDIMEN:=NIL
28240   ELSE NEWDIM↑.NEXTDIMEN:=NIL;
28250 SWITCH:=TRUE;
28260 LEFTVALPTR:=LEFTARG↑.FIRSTVALUE;
28270 WHILE LEFTVALPTR <> NIL DO
28280   BEGIN
28290     RIGHTVALPTR:=RIGHTARG↑.FIRSTVALUE;
28300     WHILE RIGHTVALPTR <> NIL DO
28310       BEGIN
28320         SFLOAT:=RIGHTVALPTR↑.REALVAL;
28330         DYADCOMP(SFLOAT,LEFTVALPTR↑.REALVAL,OUTPROCODE);
28340         NEW(NEWVALUES);
28350         IF SWITCH = TRUE
```

```
28360            THEN
28370              BEGIN
28380                SWITCH:=FALSE;
28390                NEWVALTABLINK↑.FIRSTVALUE:=NEWVALUES
28400              END
28410            ELSE
28420              NEWVALPTR↑.NEXTVALUE:=NEWVALUES;
28430        NEWVALUES↑.REALVAL:=SFLOAT;
28440        NEWVALPTR:=NEWVALUES;
28450        RIGHTVALPTR:=RIGHTVALPTR↑.NEXTVALUE
28460      END;
28470    LEFTVALPTR:=LEFTVALPTR↑.NEXTVALUE
28480  END;
28490 IF SWITCH = TRUE
28500   THEN NEWVALTABLINK↑.FIRSTVALUE:=NIL
28510   ELSE NEWVALUES↑.NEXTVALUE:=NIL
28520 END; (* OUTERPRODUCT *)
28530
28580
28590 PROCEDURE DYADIC(LEFTARG,RIGHTARG:TYPEVALTABPTR);
28600          (* OPERATORS WITH CODES OF 52 AND HIGHER *)
28610 VAR
28620 COMPATIBLE:BOOLEAN;
28630 ARG:TYPEVALTABPTR;
28640 SFLOAT:REAL;
28650 BEGIN
28670 IF CODE > 1000
28680   THEN INNERPRODUCT(LEFTARG,RIGHTARG)
28690   ELSE
28700      IF CODE > 100
28710        THEN OUTERPRODUCT(LEFTARG,RIGHTARG)
28720        ELSE
28730          IF CODE > 80
28740            THEN
28750              CASE CODE OF
28760                87: INDEXOF(LEFTARG,RIGHTARG);
28770                88: RESHAPE(LEFTARG,RIGHTARG);
28780                89: CATENATE(LEFTARG,RIGHTARG);
28790              END (*CASE*)
28800            ELSE
28810              BEGIN (*SIMPLE DYADICS*)
28820                COMPATIBLE:=TRUE;
28830                IF (LEFTARG↑.DIMENSIONS >= 1) AND (RIGHTARG↑.DIMENSIONS >= 1)
28840                  THEN
28850                    IF LEFTARG↑.DIMENSIONS <> RIGHTARG↑.DIMENSIONS
28860                      THEN COMPATIBLE:=FALSE (*DIFFERENT RANKS/NEITHER SCALAR*)
28870                      ELSE
28880                        BEGIN (*RANKS MATCH - CHECK LENGTHS*)
28890                          LEFTDIMPTR:=LEFTARG↑.FIRSTDIMEN;
28900                          RIGHTDIMPTR:=RIGHTARG↑.FIRSTDIMEN;
28910                          WHILE LEFTDIMPTR <> NIL DO
28920                            BEGIN
28930                              IF LEFTDIMPTR↑.DIMENLENGTH <>
28940                                              RIGHTDIMPTR↑.DIMENLENGTH
28950                                THEN COMPATIBLE:=FALSE; (*DIFFERENT LENGTH(S)*)
28960                              LEFTDIMPTR:=LEFTDIMPTR↑.NEXTDIMEN;
28970                              RIGHTDIMPTR:=RIGHTDIMPTR↑.NEXTDIMEN
28980                            END
28990                        END;
29000                IF COMPATIBLE = TRUE (*ARGUMENTS SUITIBLE FOR DYADIC OPERATION*)
29010                  THEN
29020                    BEGIN (*BUILD DIMENSIONS OF RESULT*)
29030                      IF RIGHTARG↑.DIMENSIONS > LEFTARG↑.DIMENSIONS
29040                        THEN ARG:=RIGHTARG
29050                        ELSE ARG:=LEFTARG; (*RESULT HAS SHAPE OF LARGER ARG*)
29060                      NEW(NEWVALTABLINK);
29070                      OLDVALTABLINK↑.NEXTVALTABLINK:=NEWVALTABLINK;
29080                      NEWVALTABLINK↑.NEXTVALTABLINK:=NIL;
29090                      NEWVALTABLINK↑.INTERMEDRESULT:=TRUE;
```

```
29100                    IF LEFTARG↑.FORWARDORDER <> RIGHTARG↑.FORWARDORDER
29110                      THEN REVERSELINKLIST(LEFTARG)$
29120                    NEWVALTABLINK↑.FORWARDORDER:=ARG↑.FORWARDORDER$
29130                    NEWVALTABLINK↑.DIMENSIONS:=ARG↑.DIMENSIONS$
29140                    SWITCH:=TRUE$
29150                    DIMPTR:=ARG↑.FIRSTDIMEN$
29160                    WHILE DIMPTR <> NIL DO
29170                      BEGIN (*COPY DIMENSIONS TO RESULT*)
29180                        NEW(NEWDIM)$
29190                        NEWDIM↑.DIMENLENGTH:=DIMPTR↑.DIMENLENGTH$
29200                        IF SWITCH = TRUE
29210                          THEN
29220                            BEGIN
29230                              SWITCH:=FALSE$
29240                              NEWVALTABLINK↑.FIRSTDIMEN:=NEWDIM
29250                            END
29260                          ELSE
29270                            NEWPTR↑.NEXTDIMEN:=NEWDIM$
29280                        NEWPTR:=NEWDIM$
29290                        DIMPTR:=DIMPTR↑.NEXTDIMEN
29300                      END$
29310                    IF SWITCH = TRUE
29320                      THEN NEWVALTABLINK↑.FIRSTDIMEN:=NIL (*RESULT IS A SCAL*)
29330                      ELSE NEWDIM↑.NEXTDIMEN:=NIL$
29340                    SWITCH:=TRUE$
29350                    RIGHTVALPTR:=RIGHTARG↑.FIRSTVALUE$
29360                    LEFTVALPTR:=LEFTARG↑.FIRSTVALUE$
29370                    VALPTR:=ARG↑.FIRSTVALUE$
29380                    WHILE VALPTR <> NIL DO
29390                      BEGIN (*PERFORM OPERATION*)
29400                        NEW(NEWVALUES)$
29410                        SFLOAT:=RIGHTVALPTR↑.REALVAL$
29420                        DYADCOMP(SFLOAT,LEFTVALPTR↑.REALVAL,CODE)$
29430                        NEWVALUES↑.REALVAL:=SFLOAT$
29440                        IF SWITCH = TRUE
29450                          THEN
29460                            BEGIN
29470                              SWITCH:=FALSE$
29480                              NEWVALTABLINK↑.FIRSTVALUE:=NEWVALUES
29490                            END
29500                          ELSE
29510                            NEWVALPTR↑.NEXTVALUE:=NEWVALUES$
29520                        NEWVALPTR:=NEWVALUES$
29530                        VALPTR:=VALPTR↑.NEXTVALUE$
29540                        LEFTVALPTR:=LEFTVALPTR↑.NEXTVALUE$
29550                        RIGHTVALPTR:=RIGHTVALPTR↑.NEXTVALUE$
29560                        IF LEFTVALPTR = NIL
29570                          THEN LEFTVALPTR:=LEFTARG↑.FIRSTVALUE$ (*EXTEND ARG*)
29580                        IF RIGHTVALPTR = NIL
29590                          THEN RIGHTVALPTR:=RIGHTARG↑.FIRSTVALUE   (*EXTEND *)
29600                      END$
29610                    IF SWITCH = TRUE
29620                      THEN NEWVALTABLINK↑.FIRSTVALUE:=NIL (*VECTOR OF LEN 0*)
29630                      ELSE NEWVALUES↑.NEXTVALUE:=NIL
29640                  END
29650                ELSE ERROR(55) (*ARGUMENTS IMCOMPATIBLE FOR DYADIC OPERATION*)
29660              END
29670 END$ (* DYADIC *)
29680
29700
29710        PROCEDURE FUNCALL(VAR VALIDFUNK:BOOLEAN)$
29720          VAR
29730            VALIDPM:BOOLEAN$
29740          BEGIN (* FUNCALL *)
29760            VALIDFUNK:=FALSE$
29770            IF FUNCTCALL THEN
29780              BEGIN
29790                IF TOKENTABPTR↑.NOUN<>STATEND THEN
29800                  BEGIN
```

```
29810                    SUBRTABPTR+.TOKENCALLINGSUBR:=TOKENTABPTR;
29820                    PRIMARY(VALIDPM);
29830                    IF NOT VALIDPM THEN ERROR(17);
29840                            (* +LEFTARG OF DYADIC FUNC CALL NOT A PRIMARY+ *)
29850                 END;
29860              CALLSUBR;
29870              VALIDFUNK:=TRUE;
29880           END;
29890      END; (* FUNCALL *)
29900
29960
29970      BEGIN (* EXPRESSION *)
29990        PRIMARY(VALIDPRI);
30000        IF NOT VALIDPRI THEN
30010          BEGIN
30020            IF TOKENTABPTR+.NOUN=STATEND THEN
30030          BEGIN
30040            VALIDEXP:=TRUE;
30050            ASSIGN1:=TRUE
30060          END
30070            ELSE VALIDEXP:=FALSE
30080          END
30090        ELSE BEGIN
30100          DONEXP:=FALSE;
30110          WHILE NOT DONEXP DO
30120            BEGIN
30130              FUNCALL(VALIDFUNC);
30140              IF VALIDFUNC THEN
30150                BEGIN
30160                  EXPRESSION(VALIDEXP);
30170                  DONEXP:=TRUE
30180                END
30190              ELSE
30200                BEGIN
30210                  ASSIGNMENT(VALIDASSN);
30220                  IF VALIDASSN AND (TOKENTABPTR+.NOUN=STATEND) THEN
30230                    BEGIN
30240                      DONEXP:=TRUE;
30250                      VALIDEXP:=TRUE;
30260                    END;
30270                  IF NOT VALIDASSN THEN
30280                    IF MOP THEN
30290                    BEGIN
30300                      MONADIC(OPERTABPTR+.OPERPTR,HOLD);
30310                      OPERTABPTR+.OPERPTR:=NEWVALTABLINK
30320                    END
30330                    ELSE
30340                      IF NOT DOP THEN
30350                        BEGIN
30360                          VALIDEXP:=TRUE;
30370                          DONEXP:=TRUE
30380                        END
30390                      ELSE
30400                        BEGIN
30410                          PRIMARY(VALIDPRI);
30420                          IF NOT VALIDPRI THEN
30430                            ERROR(13) (* DYAD OPER NOT PRECEDED BY A PRI *)
30440                            ELSE
30450                              BEGIN
30460                                DYADIC(OPERTABPTR+.OPERPTR,
30470                                OPERTABPTR+.LASTOPER+.OPERPTR);
30480                                AUXOPERTABPTR:=OPERTABPTR;
30490                                OPERTABPTR:=OPERTABPTR+.LASTOPER;
30500                                PTRLASTOPER:=OPERTABPTR;
30510                                DISPOSE(AUXOPERTABPTR);
30520                                OPERTABPTR+.OPERPTR:=NEWVALTABLINK;
30530                              END;
30540                    END;
30550              END;
```

```
30560              END;
30570           END;
30580        END; (* EXPRESSION *)
30590

30650

30660     BEGIN (* PARSER *)
30670        ASSIGN:=FALSE; ASSIGN1:=FALSE;
30680
30690        DONEPARSE:=FALSE;
30700        REPEAT
30710           EXPRESSION(VALIDEXP); (* CHECKS FOR VALID EXPRESSION *)
30720           IF NOT VALIDEXP THEN ERROR(10) (* ↑INVALID EXPRESSION↑ *)
30730           ELSE
30740            IF SPECSYMBOL(XRIGHTARROW) THEN IF NOT((OPERTABPTR↑.OPERPTR↑.FIRSTVALUE
30750            =NIL) AND (OPERTABPTR↑.OPERPTR↑.DIMENSIONS>0))THEN
30760                                                             (* BRANCH *)
30770                    (* RESULT OF EXPRESSION IS AT OPERTABPTR *)
30780               IF OPERTABPTR↑.OPERPTR↑.FIRSTVALUE↑.REALVAL
30790                  -1.0*TRUNC(OPERTABPTR↑.OPERPTR↑.FIRSTVALUE↑.REALVAL)<>0.0 THEN
30800                   ERROR(12) (* STMT.NUM.TO BRANCH TO NOT AN INTEGER *)
30810               ELSE
30820               IF SUBRTABPTR = NIL THEN
30830                BEGIN (* FUNCTION MODE *)
30840                   TOKENTABPTR:=HOLD;
30850                   DONEPARSE:=TRUE
30860                END
30870               ELSE
30880                 IF TRUNC(OPERTABPTR↑.OPERPTR↑.FIRSTVALUE↑.REALVAL) IN
30890                    [1..      (SUBRTABPTR↑.CALLEDSUBR↑.NUMOFSTATEMENTS)] THEN
30900                    BEGIN
30910                      VFUNCHOLD:=SUBRTABPTR↑.CALLEDSUBR↑.FIRSTATEMENT;
30920                      FOR CNT:=1 TO TRUNC(OPERTABPTR↑.OPERPTR↑.FIRSTVALUE↑.
30930                        REALVAL) DO BEGIN
30940                          VFUNCPTR:=VFUNCHOLD;
30950                          TOKENTABPTR:=VFUNCPTR↑.NEXTSTMNT;
30960                          VFUNCHOLD:=VFUNCPTR↑.NEXTVFUNCPTR
30970                        END;
30980                      AUXOPERTABPTR:=OPERTABPTR;
30990                      OPERTABPTR:=OPERTABPTR↑.LASTOPER;
31000                      DISPOSE(AUXOPERTABPTR);
31010                      PTRLASTOPER:=OPERTABPTR;
31020                      TOKENTABPTR:=VFUNCPTR↑.NEXTSTMNT
31030                    END

31050          ELSE (* SUCCESSOR *)
31060          ELSE (* SUCCESSOR *)
31070            BEGIN
31080              IF NOT ASSIGN1 THEN
31090              OUTPUTVAL;
31100              ASSIGN1:=FALSE;
31110              IF SUBRTABPTR=NIL THEN
31120                BEGIN(* INTERPRETIVE *)
31130                  HOLD:=TOKENTABPTR;
31140                  TOKENTABPTR:=TOKENTABPTR↑.NEXTOKEN;
31150                  DONEPARSE:=TRUE
31160                END
31170              ELSE (* FUNCTION *)
31180                BEGIN
31190                  VFUNCPTR:=VFUNCPTR↑.NEXTVFUNCPTR;
31200                  DONESUCCESSOR:=FALSE;
31210                  REPEAT
31220                    IF VFUNCPTR<>NIL THEN
31230                      BEGIN
31240                        TOKENTABPTR:=VFUNCPTR↑.NEXTSTMNT;
31250                        DONESUCCESSOR:=TRUE
31260                      END
31270                    ELSE
31280                      BEGIN
31290                        RETURNTOCALLINGSUBR;
31300                        IF TOKENTABPTR↑.NOUN=STATEND THEN
31310                        DONESUCCESSOR:=TRUE;
```

```
31320                    END;
31330                 UNTIL DONESUCCESSOR;
31340              END;
31350           END
31360       UNTIL DONEPARSE;
31370       RELEASE;                   (* RELEASE MEMORY *)
31380    END; (* PARSER *)
31390
31440
31450 BEGIN (* SCANNER *)
31460 INITIALIZECHARACTERSET;
31470 READINERRORMSGS;
31480 INITPARSER; (* INITIALIZE TABLES ETC. *)
31490 FILLUPTABLES;
31500 FUNCTIONMODE:=FALSE;
31510 FIRSTFUNCTION:=TRUE;
31520 OLDVALTABLINK:=NIL;
31530 OLDFUNCTABPTR:=NIL;
31540 OLDVARTABPTR:=NIL;
31550 OLDTOKENPTR:=NIL; NEWTOKENPTR:=NIL;
31560 NEWFUNCTABPTR:=NIL; NEWVFUNCPTR:=NIL;
31570 HOLDTOKENPTR:=NIL; TOKENERROR:=FALSE;
31580 NEWVALTABLINK:=NIL; NEWVARTABPTR:=NIL;
31590 GETAPLSTATEMENT;
31600 WHILE (APLSTATEMENT[1] <> CHARACTER[FORWARDSLASH]) OR
31610    (APLSTATEMENT[2] <> CHARACTER[ASTERISK]) DO (*  /* ENDS PROGRAM *)
31620   BEGIN
31630     SKIPSPACES;
31640     TOKENSWITCH:=TRUE;
31650     WHILE (POSITION <= LINELENGTH) AND (NOT TOKENERROR)
31660            AND (NOT LINETOOLONG) DO
31670       BEGIN (* SCANNING *)
31680         IF APLSTATEMENT[POSITION] = CHARACTER[DEL]  (* FUNCTION DELIMITER *)
31690           THEN (* DEL ENCOUNTERED *)
31700              IF FUNCTIONMODE
31710                THEN
31720                   BEGIN  (* END OF CURRENT FUNCTION *)
31730                      IF NEWFUNCTABPTR <> NIL THEN
31740                     NEWFUNCTABPTR↑.NUMOFSTATEMENTS:=FUNCSTATEMENTS;
31750                      IF FUNCSTATEMENTS > 0
31760                        THEN
31770                        BEGIN
31780                           NEWFUNCTABPTR↑.NEXTFUNCTABPTR:=OLDFUNCTABPTR;
31790                           OLDFUNCTABPTR:=NEWFUNCTABPTR;
31800                           NEWVFUNCPTR↑.NEXTVFUNCPTR:=NIL
31810                        END
31820                      ELSE SERROR(75); (* FUNCTION DEFINED WITH NO STATEMENTS*)
31830                      FUNCTIONMODE:=FALSE;
31840                      POSITION:=POSITION + 1
31850                   END
31860                ELSE PROCESSFUNCTIONHEADER (* START OF A NEW FUNCTION *)
31870           ELSE (* NOT A DEL ENCOUNTERED *)
31880             BEGIN
31890               IF TOKENSWITCH = TRUE
31900                 THEN
31910                   BEGIN (* THIS IS START OF A NEW STATEMENT *)
31920                      TOKENSWITCH:=FALSE;
31930                      HOLDTOKENPTR:=OLDTOKENPTR; (*SAVE STARTING POSITION*)
31940                      MAKETOKENLINK;
31950                      NEWTOKENPTR↑.NOUN:=STATEND;
31960                      NEWTOKENPTR↑.ENDADJ:=0;
31970                      HASLABEL:=FALSE
31980                   END;
31990                 MAKETOKENLINK;
32000                 IDENTIFIER(NAME,ITSANIDENTIFIER);
32010                 IF NOT ITSANIDENTIFIER
32020                   THEN TRYTOGETANUMBER
32030                   ELSE
32040                      BEGIN (* PROCESS IDENTIFIER *)
```

331

```
32050                        SKIPSPACES#
32060                        IF (APLSTATEMENT[POSITION] = CHARACTER[COLON]) AND
32070                           (NEWTOKENPTR↑.NEXTOKEN↑.NOUN = STATEND)
32080                           THEN
32090                             BEGIN (* PROCESS STATEMENT LABEL *)
32100                                SAVELABEL#=NAME#
32110                                HASLABEL#=TRUE#
32120                                POSITION#=POSITION + 1
32130                             END
32140                           ELSE
32150                             BEGIN (* PROCESS VARIABLE NAME *)
32160                                IF NOT FUNCTIONMODE
32170                                  THEN NEWTOKENPTR↑.NOUN#=GLOBVAR
32180                                  ELSE
32190                                    IF NAMESMATCH(NAME,NEWFUNCTABPTR↑.RESULTNAME)
32200                                      THEN NEWTOKENPTR↑.NOUN#=FORMRES
32210                                      ELSE
32220                                        IF (NAMESMATCH(NAME,NEWFUNCTABPTR↑.LEFTARG))
32230                                        OR (NAMESMATCH(NAME,NEWFUNCTABPTR↑.RIGHTARG))
32240                                          THEN NEWTOKENPTR↑.NOUN#=FORMARG
32250                                          ELSE NEWTOKENPTR↑.NOUN#=GLOBVAR#
32260                                IF NEWTOKENPTR↑.NOUN <> GLOBVAR
32270                                  THEN TESTFUNCPTR#=NEWFUNCTABPTR
32280                                  ELSE TESTFUNCPTR#=NIL#
32290                                IF NOT NAMEINVARTABLE(NAME,VARPOINTER,TESTFUNCPTR)
32300                                  THEN
32310                                    BEGIN
32320                                       ADDNAMETOVARTABLE(NAME)#
32330                                       NEWTOKENPTR↑.VARTABPTR#=NEWVARTABPTR
32340                                    END
32350                                  ELSE NEWTOKENPTR↑.VARTABPTR#=VARPOINTER
32360                             END
32370                        END#
32380                   END#
32390              SKIPSPACES#
32400            END#
32410       IF NEWTOKENPTR <> NIL THEN
32420       IF (TOKENERROR) OR (NEWTOKENPTR↑.NOUN = STATEND)
32430         THEN DESTROYSTATEMENT
32440         ELSE
32450           IF FUNCTIONMODE
32460             THEN
32470               BEGIN
32480                  FUNCSTATEMENTS#=FUNCSTATEMENTS + 1#
32490                  IF FUNCSTATEMENTS > 0
32500                    THEN
32510                      BEGIN (* CATALOG FUNCTION STATEMENT *)
32520                         NEW(NEWVFUNCPTR)#
32530                         IF FUNCSTATEMENTS = 1
32540                           THEN NEWFUNCTABPTR↑.FIRSTATEMENT#=NEWVFUNCPTR
32550                           ELSE OLDVFUNCPTR↑.NEXTVFUNCPTR#=NEWVFUNCPTR#
32560                         OLDVFUNCPTR#=NEWVFUNCPTR#
32570                         IF HASLABEL
32580                           THEN NEWVFUNCPTR↑.STATLABEL#=SAVELABEL#
32590                         NEWVFUNCPTR↑.NEXTSTMNT#=NEWTOKENPTR
32600                      END
32610               END
32620             ELSE
32630               IF APLSTATEMENT[1] <> CHARACTER[DEL]
32640                 THEN
32650                   BEGIN
32660                      PARSER(NEWTOKENPTR,NEWVALTABLINK)#
32680          100: DESTROYSTATEMENT
32690                   END#
32700       READLN#
32710        TOKENERROR#=FALSE#
32720       GETAPLSTATEMENT#
32730     END#
32740 END.
```

Authors Directory

Stephen R Alpert
Worcester Polytechnic Institute
Worcester MA 01609

Larry R Atkin
Health Information Services
542 Michigan Av
Evanston IL 60202

Kenneth L Bowles
Professor, Director
Institute for Information Systems
University of California San Diego
La Jolla CA 92093

Kin-Man Chung
124 Scottswood Dr
Urbana IL 61801

Vincent DiChristofaro
1327 McKinley St
Philadelphia PA 19111

Gary A Ford, Assistant Professor
Dept of Mathematics
Arizona State University
Tempe AZ 85281

Charles H Forsyth
Computer Communications Networks Group
University of Waterloo
Waterloo Ontario
CANADA N2L 3G1

Peter W Frey
Dept of Psychology
Northwestern University
Evanston IL 60201

Carl Helmers
Editorial Director, BYTE Publications Inc.
70 Main St
Peterborough NH 03458

Randall J Howard
Computer Communications Networks Group
University of Waterloo
Waterloo Ontario
CANADA N2L 3G1

Alan Kaniss
1327 McKinley St
Philadelphia PA 19111

Larry Kheriaty
Computer Center
Western Washington University
Bellingham WA 98225

Dr B Gregory Louis
OB/GYN Dept
St Michael's Hospital
30 Bond Street
Toronto CANADA M5B 1W8

David A Mundie
104B Oakhurst Cir
Charlottesville VA 22903

John Santini
1327 McKinley St
Philadelphia PA 19111

Allan M Schwartz
114-2 Nimitz Dr
West Lafayette IN 47906

Stephen P Smith
POB 841
Parksley VA 23421

Herbert Yuen
POB 2591 Station A
Champaign IL 61820

BYTE Books

Blaise W Liffick, technical editor
Lynn Woodbury, designer-production manager
Patricia Curran, production editor
Richard Farley, production art
Holly LaBossiere, production art
Wai Chiu Li, production art
Deborah Porter, production art
George Banta Company, printing

BYTE Magazine

Christopher P Morgan, executive editor
Raymond G A Cote, editor in chief

The BYTE Books Library

For a complete catalog of our publications, write:

BYTE Books
70 Main Street
Peterborough, NH 03458